MISSED 2 SESSIONS   8 ATTENDED
@ 3 m. ea

CORPORATE FINANCIAL REPORTING
Text and Cases

The Willard J. Graham Series in Accounting

Consulting Editor   ROBERT N. ANTHONY   *Harvard University*

Corporate Financial Reporting

TEXT AND CASES

David F. Hawkins

Professor of Business Administration
Graduate School of Business Administration
Harvard University

1977
Revised Edition

RICHARD D. IRWIN, INC.   Homewood, Illinois   60430
Irwin-Dorsey Limited   Georgetown, Ontario   L7G 4B3

Revised Edition

7 8 9 0 MP 5 4 3 2 1

Case material of the Harvard Graduate School of
Business Administration is made possible by the
cooperation of business firms who may wish to remain
anonymous by having names, quantities, and other
identifying details disguised while basic relationships
are maintained. Cases are prepared as the basis for
class discussion rather than to illustrate either effective
or ineffective handling of administrative situations.

ISBN 0-256-01643-7
Library of Congress Catalog Card No. 76–57330

Printed in the United States of America

To Barbara

PREFACE

Published corporate profit figures can represent genuine managerial operating performance, or they can represent the illusion of performance. Investors who can tell the difference have a considerable advantage in making their investment decisions. Similarly, the corporate manager who understands the relationship between corporate reporting and business policy as well as how other managers can influence profits through the judicious use of alternative accounting practices is more likely to succeed than his less knowledgeable competitors. Ignorance of the options, uncertainties, and ambiguities of the practices underlying the construction of corporate financial statements can lead creditors to make poor credit decisions. On the other hand, unless those practicing public accountancy know how investors use financial data, how to identify and interpret the motives of managers issuing financial reports, and the relationship between business-operating and financial-reporting decisions, they can not satisfactorily fulfill their third-party responsibility to the issuers and users of corporate financial statements. In short, an intimate understanding of the practices and subtleties of financial accounting can be critical to the success of many of those who participate in our business system.

Today corporations have considerable leeway in the reporting of their financial condition and results of operations. Despite recent progress in eliminating undesirable reporting practices, there are many areas in which equally acceptable alternative practices exist for reporting essentially identical business situations. The profits of the reporting company will vary depending on which alternative is selected. Some of these alternatives are:

1. The investment in a capital asset can be written off against revenues by either a "fast" or "slow" depreciation method.
2. Certain expenditures can be charged to income in the period in which they are incurred or carried as an asset and written off as expenses over several reporting periods.

3. Inventory can be valued at current costs or at some other cost that may reflect 20-year-old price levels.
4. Investment tax-type credits can be recognized as income either in the year they are granted or over the life of the asset giving rise to the tax credit.

This book provides the reader with an understanding of the current state of these and many other financial reporting practices; the ways in which the corporate financial statements published in annual reports, prospectuses, and proxy statements influence our economic system; and the significant consequences of these data for the people who depend on their credibility. It is not a book on accounting methodology.

The subject matter is approached from a variety of points of view. First, and foremost, are the interests of those closest to the corporation, namely, the management publishing the financial statements; the existing and potential stockholders; financial analysts using the statements for investment recommendations; the grantors of trade and commercial credit; and the independent certified public accountant responsible for expressing an opinion on the fairness of the statements issued by the management. Also covered are the interests of others in a number of different business negotiations and transactions where the use and interpretation of financial statements has assumed major proportions, such as the determination of rates in regulated industries; the purchase and sale of businesses; government investigation of prices and other practices of particular industries and individual enterprises; and the determination by unions as to what to demand through collective bargaining.

Changing Accounting Principles

The accounting principles and disclosure rules upon which corporate financial reports are based on continually being revised by the Financial Accounting Standards Board and the Securities and Exchange Commission. One way to keep abreast of these changes is to read either *The Wall Street Journal* or the *New York Times*. Both of these newspapers cover proposed and actual changes in accounting principles. More complete, but less timely, coverage can be found in either *The Journal of Accountancy,* published by the American Institute of Certified Public Accountants, or the *Financial Executive,* published by the Financial Executives' Institute.

At the time this book went to press the Financial Accounting Standards Board had either released proposed changes for public comment or was considering drafts of a number of future accounting principles

changes. Since each of these decisions will have important implications for the future, the reader is urged to follow the newspaper reports
of the board's deliberations on a current basis. To help the reader put
these proposed changes in their proper perspective, each one of them
is discussed in later chapters.

Textual Material

The first two chapters of this book do not include cases. They are
presented as background material. The purpose of Chapter 1 is to
familiarize the reader with (1) some of the fundamental issues in corporate reporting and (2) some of the key institutions that influence
corporate reporting standards and practices. Chapter 2 provides a historical background for putting into perspective these issues and the
roles of the key institutions.

Each of the other chapters consists of text and selected case studies.
The split of pages between cases and text is about even. Thus, unlike a
number of other casebooks, there should be sufficient textual material
in this book to satisfy the noncollege user seeking to gain a better
understanding of fundamentals and current practices in the area of
corporate financial reporting. Such readers might include corporate
executives, bankers, financial analysts, and individual investors.

A Clinical Approach

The case studies have been prepared as a basis for discussion of the
topics covered in the related text. They have not been selected to
present illustrations of either appropriate or inappropriate handling of
financial reporting problems. To decide what is appropriate action is
the purpose of the case discussion.

Most of the cases require a decision on the part of the student.
Typically, the student is asked to assume the role with a real sense of
the professional and personal involvement of top management responsible for issuing financial data to the public in a particular situation. To
make this decision realistically, the student must identify the administrative burdens of the decision maker, the opportunities for creative
action, and the manager's responsibilities. In particular, the student
must be concerned with the relationship between financial reporting
and the other areas of top management concern, such as stockholder
relations, the market price of the company's stock, dividend policy,
capital structure, union wage demands, product pricing, and antitrust
actions. The student must think through the implications for the company of the actions that investors, the company's independent auditor,
the regulatory authorities, and others might take as a result of the

company's decision. Seldom will there be a simple, easy answer to the problem posed.

Discussion of the case studies within a decision-making framework should give students an appreciation of:

1. The "real world" difficulties in resolving financial reporting issues.
2. The role of judgment in the selection of appropriate accounting practices.
3. The evolutionary state of accounting principles.
4. The significance and limitations of financial accounting data for corporate decision-making purposes and security valuations.
5. The need for managers to involve themselves in the financial reporting process.
6. The vital communication function financial reports play in our economic system.
7. The difficulties encountered in trying to develop an integrated statement of a basic theory of accounting that is acceptable to accounting theoreticians and at the same time is responsive to the subtleties of our complex economic system.
8. The relationship between the accounting systems and reports management uses for management control and financial reporting purposes.
9. The urgent need for the business and accounting professions to develop a set of accounting principles that eliminate the differences in accounting practices not justified by different circumstances.

Uses of Financial Data

Part IV of this book deals with the uses of financial data. Some may argue that this material rightly belongs in a statement analysis text, not an accounting book. It is included, however, since an understanding of this material is vital to anyone concerned with the task of making accounting data more responsive to the needs of statement users. Also, if a financial statement issuer hopes to use his statements to influence the actions of statement users, the issuer had better understand how statement users view corporate financial reports.

Reading Plan

The cases and chapters included in this book have been used in many undergraduate and graduate courses at both the introductory and advanced level. In each of these courses the order and manner in which the materials were used varied according to the student's prior background in the field and the instructor's course objectives. Consequently, it is unlikely that the materials included in this book could be put together in an order that would meet the needs of all readers and courses.

It is suggested that each reader skim the table of contents before reading the text and determine where to begin and in what order the chapters should be covered. For example, readers with limited or no prior understanding of financial accounting probably should read the chapters in the order presented. On the other hand a reader with considerable exposure at the introductory level might just skim the first eight chapters and begin reading seriously at Chapter 9.

The Revised Edition

Those familiar with the first edition will find a number of differences in the revised edition. The section on the uses of financial data has been expanded considerably. New chapters have been added on three accounting topics and a number of the old chapters have been completely rewritten to reflect the comments of those who used the first edition. New cases have also been added.

This edition covers all of the *Opinions* published by the Accounting Principles Board and, up to the time of publication, all of the statements of the Financial Accounting Standards Board and The Accounting Series Releases of the Securities and Exchange Commission.

Acknowledgments

A number of people have helped in the preparation of this book and the financial accounting course at the Harvard Business School from which the book draws heavily. Walter Frese provided the pedagogical and corporate-reporting-philosophy foundation for both the book and the financial accounting course. Two of my colleagues—Robert Madera and Mary Wehle—were responsible for many of the original course materials that were subsequently incorporated into the book. The difficult and frustrating task of typing and controlling the manuscript in its many drafts was ably accomplished by Gertrude Nierman and Ms. Janet Vehr. My family provided both the inspiration needed and the continuing support that was required for me to squeeze out of a busy family and professional life the time needed to complete the manuscript. Professor Robert Anthony provided helpful editorial advice. I am grateful to all of these people and hope they will share with me a feeling of accomplishment and pride in this most recent outgrowth of the Harvard Business School's very successful financial accounting course. In addition, I wish to thank the President and Fellows of Harvard College for their permission to reproduce the case and textual materials copyrighted in their name, as well as Robert Sprouse, Richard Vancil, Walter Frese, Robert Anthony, Brandt Allen, Russell Nelson, John Yeager, Andrew McCosh, John Shank, Ross Walker, T. F. Bradshaw, C. A. Bliss, and Derek Newton for allowing me to use or adapt cases originally prepared by them. Others who have been associated with the development of the cases in the book include Len Savoie, Ed Jepson, David Macey, Arnie Ludwick, Don Bryant, David Koenig, Bob McInnis, Jerry Brougher, Neil Churchill, Keith Butters, Warren McFarlan, Dennis Frolin and William J. Bruns, Jr. Finally, I would like to thank Hugo Nurnberg, William L. Felix and Carl Nelson for their detailed review of the first edition. Their comments were very helpful in preparing this revised edition.

The cases in Chapter 11 are based on examples included in J. T. Ball's *Computing Earnings per Share*. The Holden case is based on an illustration presented in *Accounting Research Study No. 6*, "Reporting the Financial Effects of Price-Level Changes." Another case, Southerland, is based on an article by Professor Briloff.

April 1977   DAVID F. HAWKINS

CONTENTS

XV

Dual Aspect. Reliability of Evidence. Disclosure. Conservatism. Materiality. Substance over Form. Application.

Cases

4. Basic Financial Statements 69

Objectives. General Requirements. Statement of Financial Position. Assets: *Current Assets. Investments. Property. Other Assets.* Liabilities: *Current Liabilities. Long-Term Liabilities.* Owners' Equity. Income Statement: *Statement No. 4. Basic Conventions. Expenditures and Expenses. Statement Format. Interrelationship. Changes in Owners' Equity.* Other Considerations: *Notes to Financial Statements. Auditor's Report. Interim Statements. Forecasts. Summary of Financial Results. Text.* Proposed Changes in Statements. Basic Accounting Mechanics: *Accounts. Debit-Credit Mechanism. An Example.*

Cases

5. Consolidated Financial Statements 106

Single Economic Unit. Consolidation Policy. Disclosure. Accounting Concepts Peculiar to Consolidated Statements. Investment in Subsidiary. Consolidation Procedures.

Cases

6. Statement of Changes in Financial Position 124

Nature of the Statement of Changes in Financial Position: *Current Practice. Definition of "Funds." Statement of Balance Sheet Charges.* Working Papers for Changes in Financial Position Statements: *Format and Content. Cash Flow per Share.*

Case

PART III
ROLE OF CERTIFIED PUBLIC ACCOUNTANTS

The Auditor's Profession. The Auditor's Report: *Forms of the Audit Report.* The Auditor's Work: *The Audit Program. Evaluation of Internal Controls. Auditing Procedures. Audit Committee. Summary.*

Cases

PART IV
ANALYSIS OF CORPORATE FINANCIAL REPORTS

Financial Analysis: *Liquidity Ratios. Solvency Ratios. Funds Management Ratios. Profitability Ratios. Basis of Comparison. A Warning.* Security Valuation: *Asset Valuation. Business Valuation. Fair Market Value. Range of Values. Financial Analysis and Decision Models. Accounting Alternatives, Statement Analysis, and Efficient Equity Markets. Red Flags.* Financial Analysis.

Cases

PART V
INCOME DETERMINATION

The Critical Event. Revenue Recognition Methods. Services. Nonmonetary Transactions. Inappropriate Interest Rates. Accounting for Bad Debts: *Direct Write-Off Method. Bad Debt Estimation Method. Accounting Entries for Bad Debt Estimation Method. Financial Statement Presentation.* Warranties and Service Guarantees. Realization Controversy.

**10. Extraordinary Items, Discontinued Operations, and
      Accounting Changes** **243**

Two Points of View. Extraordinary Items, Unusual Events, and Prior
Period Adjustments: *Unusual Events and Transactions. Prior Period Ad-
justments. APB Appraisal. No Solution.* Discontinuance or Disposal of a
Business Segment. Accounting Principle, Estimates, and Entity
Changes: *Changes in Accounting Principles. Changes in Accounting
Estimates. Changes in the Entity.* Correction of an Error: *Disclosure.
Requirements. Different Viewpoints.*

11. Earnings per Share **283**

Dual Presentation: Summary: *Legal Considerations. Opinion No. 15:
Simple Capital Structures. Complex Capital Structures. At Issue. In-
vestment Value Test Rejected. Fully Diluted Earnings per Share. Earn-
ings Data Adjustments: Convertible Securities. Computation Examples.
Two-Class Method. Earnings Data Adjustments: Options and Warrants.
Computation Example.* Paragraph 38: *Twenty Percent Test. Contingent
Issues. Securities of Subsidiaries. Further Requirements. Weighted Av-
erage Computations. Effective Date.* Conflicting Viewpoints.

**PART VI
ASSET VALUATION AND EXPENSE DETERMINATION**

12. Accounting for Income Taxes **315**

Origins of the Problem: *Permanent and Timing Differences.* Three Approaches. Example: *First-Year Taxes. Second-Year Taxes. Opinion No.*

11. The Controversy: *Flow-Through Method. Comprehensive Allocation. Partial Allocation. Deferred Taxes: A Liability? Measurable Funds Effect. Extending the Argument. Income Measurement. Present Value Approach. Rate Changes. Effective Tax Rate Reduction?* Public Utilities: *Tax Reform Act.* Loss Carry-Back—Carry-Forward Credits. Statement Presentation: *Income Statement.* Special Areas: *Undistributed Earnings of Subsidiary Companies. Joint Ventures. Other Equity Method Investments. Domestic International Sales Corporation (DISC). Savings and Loan and Stock Life Insurance Companies. Oil and Gas Producing Companies. Disclosure. Continuing Controversy.*

Cases

Capitalization Criteria. Cost Basis. Expenditures Subsequent to Acquisition and Use: *Repairs and Maintenance. Betterments, Improvements, and Additions.* Land. Wasting Assets. Historical Costs and Accountability. Alternative Proposals. Investment Tax Credit.

Cases

Computing Depreciation: *Estimating the Useful Life of Fixed Assets.* Depreciation Methods: *Straight-Line Depreciation. Accelerated Depreciation. Units-of-Production Depreciation.* Accounting for Depreciation: *Group Depreciation. Depreciation and Federal Income Tax. Depreciation Schedule Revisions. Depreciation Method Changes. Additions. Donated Assets. Asset Write-Downs. Written-Up Assets. Accounting for Retirements. Capital Investment Decisions. Depletion. Replacement Depreciation. Depreciation Decisions.*

Cases

Measures of Inflation. Business Considerations. Accounting Requirements: *General Purchasing Power Restatement: APB and FASB Ap-*

proach. An Example: The Cruzeiro Corporation: *Degree of Restatement.*
APB *Statement No. 3: Replacement Cost: SEC Approach.*

16. Intangible Assets 460

Authoritative Sources: Opinion No. 17. Statement No. 2. Income Tax
Treatment. Specific Intangible Assets: *Patents. Copyrights. Franchises.
Trademarks and Trade Names. Leasehold Improvements. Organization
Costs. Intangible Development Costs.* Role of Judgment: *Profit Impact
of Shift. Inappropriate Practices.*

17. Inventory Pricing 485

Periodic and Perpetual Inventory Systems. Pricing Bases. Cost Methods.
Inventory Methods: *Specific Identification. Last Invoice Price. Simple
Average. Weighted Average. Moving Average. First-In, First-Out. Last-
In, First-Out. Lifo versus Fifo. Disclosure. Lifo Methodology. Specific
Identification Method. Dollar Value Method. Base Stock.* Cost or Market,
Whichever Is Lower: *Retail Method.* Selling Price. Statement Presenta-
tion. Summary.

18. Intercorporate Investments and Business Combinations 523

Equity Investments: *Ownership Interests of Less than 20 Percent.
Ownership Interests of More than 20 Percent.* Business Combinations:
Two Approaches: *Purchase Method. Pooling of Interest Method.* Opin-
ion No. 16, "Business Combinations": *Conditions Requiring Pooling
Treatment. The 90 Percent Test. Accounting Mechanics. Reporting Re-
quirements. Disclosure of Poolings. Purchase Accounting.* Goodwill:
*The Nature of Goodwill. "Negative Goodwill." Goodwill Tax Considera-
tion.* Research Efforts of the APB: ARS No. 10. ARS No. 5. *Criticisms.*

PART VII
LONG-TERM COMMITMENTS

Characteristics of Long-Term Debt: *Bond Prices. Registration. Financial Consideration.* Accounting Practices: *Issuance of Bonds. Amortization of Bond Premium and Discount. Extinguishment before Maturity. Refunding. Conversion. Debt Issued with Stock Warrants. Debt Issued with Conversion Privileges. Classification of Short-Term Debt Expected to Be Refinanced. Inappropriate Interest Rates.* Accounting Practices: The Buyer: *Purchase of Bonds. Interest Payments Received.* Restructured Debt. Value of Real Estate and Related Receivables.

Leasing Practices. Lessee's Statements: *Accounting Entries. Disclosure.* Lessor's Statements: *APB Lessor Accounting. FASB Proposed Lessor Accounting.* Related Parties. Leases Involving Real Estate. Sale and Leaseback. Transition. The Controversy.

Pension Plans: *Valuation. Assumptions. Funding Instruments and Agencies. Funding Methods. Income Tax Considerations in Plan Selection. Summary.* Accounting Considerations. *Opinion No. 8: An Overview. Pension Costs: Maximum and Minimum Limits. Vested Benefits. Illustration. Income Taxes. Other Considerations. Employee Retirement Income Security Act of 1974. Continuing Controversy.*

PART I

Corporate Reporting Environment

Chapter 1

INSTITUTIONS AND ISSUES

The function of accounting is to provide information, primarily financial in nature, about economic entities that is intended to be useful in making economic decisions. Accounting includes several branches, for example, financial or corporate accounting, managerial accounting, and government accounting. This book is concerned with financial accounting, which is the branch of accounting used by business enterprises when reporting to parties outside of the business. It provides, within limitations, a continual history expressed in money terms of the economic resources and obligations of a business enterprise and of the economic activities that change those resources and activities. These items and the changes in them are identified and measured in conformity with those financial accounting principles that are generally accepted at the time the statements are prepared. The typical outputs of this process are the statement of financial position, income statement, and the changes in financial position statement.

The management of the company publishing financial statements is responsible for their content. Many people mistakenly believe that the statements are the responsibility of the public accountant who audited them. A careful reading of the statement accompanying audited financial statements issued by the independent certified public accountant shows he or she is only expressing a personal opinion as to (1) the fairness of statements, (2) their degree of conformity with the recognized generally accepted accounting principles, and (3) the consistency of the accounting practices used to prepare the statements with those followed in the previous accounting period.

The adequacy of financial statements is judged in terms of the fairness and usefulness of the data provided to all of the interested parties. These are difficult standards to define, and there is considerable disagreement as to their definition. Nevertheless, a great number of financial accounting conventions, concepts, principles, and standards of disclosure have evolved and been supported by recognized account-

3

ing authorities. These authorities include the recently created Financial Accounting Standards Board (FASB), the American Institute of Certified Public Accountants (AICPA), the Securities and Exchange Commission (SEC), and the predecessor of the Financial Accounting Standards Board, the now defunct Accounting Principles Board (APB).

One of the early actions of the Securities and Exchange Commission was to rule that companies under its jurisdiction be audited by independent public accountants. Although the SEC was given the power to establish accounting rules by the Securities Exchange Acts of 1933–34, very early in its existence the Commission made it known that it expected the private sector through the accounting profession to assume the main part of this activity. With few exceptions the accounting profession carried out this responsibility through the AICPA's APB and its predecessor the Committee on Accounting Procedure (CAP). However, in 1973 the accounting profession voluntarily gave up its central role in developing generally accepted accounting principles to a newly created independent private body called the Financial Accounting Standards Board. At that time, the SEC indicated that it would continue its policy of leaving the determination of accounting rules to a responsible private body and that it would support the FASB in a manner similar to the way it had worked with the AICPA's earlier rule-making bodies.

ACCOUNTING PRINCIPLES AUTHORITIES

The AICPA's activities in the development of a formal statement of accounting principles began in 1938 when it formed a Committee on Accounting Procedure (CAP) to "narrow the areas of difference in corporate reporting" by gradually eliminating less desirable practices. Over a period of 20 years, 51 *Accounting Research Bulletins* (ARBs) were issued, indicating preferred treatments of various items and transactions. Although these bulletins were advisory rather than binding, they became highly influential. They were supported by the SEC and the stock exchanges and were observed by the profession generally. (The SEC and the stock exchanges ordinarily will not accept a company's financial statements if the auditor's opinion contains an exception to the accounting principles used.)

Despite this progress, a feeling persisted, both within and without the profession, that there were still too many alternative accounting principles applicable in similar circumstances regarded as "generally accepted." It was also recognized that changed business conditions—new forms of financing, new tax laws, and the evolution of more complex corporate structures—required the development of some new accounting principles, and at a pace faster than had been previously considered necessary.

The AICPA in 1959 therefore created a new body, the APB, to succeed the Committee on Accounting Procedure and to carry on its work in a broader and more intensive way.

Between 1959 and 1973 the leading authority on accounting principles for business was the 18-member Accounting Principles Board of the AICPA. Periodically, it issued *Opinions* to be used as guidelines by business executives and independent certified public accountants in determining the general acceptability of specific corporate financial reporting practices. The FASB, which became the leading authority in 1973 after the APB was disbanned, supports the *Opinions*. So, until some specific action is taken by the FASB, the *APB Opinions* still dictate what constitutes acceptable corporate reporting practices.

Financial Accounting Standards Board

During the late 1960s a number of leading authorities on corporate reporting became critical of the APB and increasingly proposals were made which recommended an alternative approach to the development of generally accepted accounting principles be explored. In the spring of 1971, the AICPA in response to these concerns set up two study groups, each comprising of members from industry, the financial community, the accounting, academic, and legal professions. One group headed by former Commissioner Wheat of the SEC studied the establishment of accounting principles and made recommendations on improving that process. The other group under the leadership of Robert Trueblood, an outstanding accounting practitioner, studied the objectives of financial statements and issued a report suggesting guidelines and criteria for improving accounting and financial reporting.

In 1972 the Wheat study group issued its report, *Establishing Financial Accounting Standards*. It recommended that a new, independent full-time board replace the APB and a more direct responsibility for establishing accounting standards be given to the principal groups with a substantial interest in corporate reporting—namely, auditors, preparers of financial statements, users of financial statements, and accounting academicians. The report was acceptable to the AICPA, SEC, and all of the major institutions and associations interested in corporate reporting. Subsequently, the FASB was incorporated and it took over the formulation of corporate reporting standards from the APB in June 1973.

The FASB consists of seven full-time members with specific terms of appointment drawn from the fields of public accounting, industry, government, and education. They are selected by the trustees of the FASB. Assisting the board members is a full-time research staff, knowledgeable individuals who are invited to join ad hoc task forces to resolve specific issues, and an appointed Financial Accounting Standards Advisory Council. This broadly representative Advisory Council meets periodically and advises the FASB on agenda topics and priorities, members for task forces, and numerous other technical and administrative matters.

The standard-setting process of the FASB begins with the placing of an accounting problem on the board's technical agenda. Next, a board member is assigned to prepare, with staff assistance, a preliminary definition of the problem and a bibliography of the significant litera-ture on the subject. Once this step is completed, the problem is re-viewed by the FASB and a task force is appointed to continue work on the project. The task force, which consists of at least one member of the board, who serves as chairperson, as well as members of the Advisory Council and other persons with expertise in some aspect of the prob-lem, is responsible for preparing a neutral and comprehensive discus-sion memorandum on the agenda item. This document outlines alter-native solutions to the problem and the arguments and implications relative to each alternative solution.

Upon completion of the required research and the discussion memorandum, the FASB initiates a procedure to establish financial accounting standards that seeks to ensure that the interests and points of view of all concerned parties are considered. This process begins with the issuance of a 60-day notice of a public hearing on the problem and the simultaneous publication of the discussion memorandum. At the public hearings oral reports and written papers are solicited and presented. After the public hearing, a proposed Statement of Financial Accounting Standards is prepared. An affirmative vote of at least five of the seven members is required before the draft statement will be re-leased to the public. Next, after a public comment exposure period of at least 60 days, the FASB reviews the exposure comments, and if the required five out of seven votes needed for approval are obtained, it issues a final draft of its statement. Normally, the effective date of application of a Statement of Financial Accounting Standards will not be earlier than the beginning of the reporting entities' fiscal years commencing 90 days or more after the statement is issued.

The initial technical agenda of the FASB included a consideration of the Trueblood Committee report, which was published in October 1973. After examining the report the FASB decided to expand on the work of the committee and issue a statement of its own that would encompass the entire conceptual framework of financial accounting and reporting. Hopefully, this statement would be a useful guide to the FASB in its deliberations. Other items on the FASB's initial agenda included financial reporting for research and development, leases, fu-ture losses, foreign currency translation, and diversified companies.

The issue of materiality was also listed. In 1974 the FASB decided to issue periodically interpretations of existing accounting standards.

Securities and Exchange Commission

The Securities and Exchange Commission is responsible for administrating the Securities Acts of 1933 and 1934. These acts give the SEC the power to set accounting standards and to require specific kinds of financial disclosure by corporations covered by the acts. The commissioners are appointed by the President of the United States. The Commission's budget is approved by Congress.[1]

The Securities Act of 1933 deals primarily with the registration of securities in public offerings. Under this act the Commission is concerned with the adequacy and validity of the information disclosed to investors in the registration statements filed with the Commission by corporations and the prospectus furnished to investors by the seller of securities. The Commission does not pass on the merits of the securities offered.

The Securities Exchange Act of 1934 regulates the trading in securities. This act requires among other things that corporations registered with the Commission under this act periodically file reports on their operations and conditions. The most important of these SEC corporate reports are the—

. *10-K.* This annual report is filed by most publicly held corporations. It must be filed within 90 days following the close of the company's fiscal year. 10-Ks contain extensive, certified financial data, descriptions of various company activities, and detailed schedules of changes in specific accounts.
. *10-Q.* The quarterly financial report filed by most companies. It is the quarterly update to 10-K financial information. It is not certified. This report must be filed within 45 days of the close of the fiscal quarter.
. *8-K.* A report of unscheduled material events or corporate changes of interest to shareholders or to the SEC. Among the events reported by the 8-K are changes in securities, business, financial, or corporate positions or assets.

The SEC's pronouncements on accounting matters are usually issued in the form of an Accounting Series Release. These releases, which registered companies must adopt may set new disclosure re-

---

[1] The SEC is also charged with administering four additional pieces of legislation: the Public Utilities Holding Act of 1935, the Trust Indenture Act of 1939, the Investment Company Act of 1940, and the Investment Advisors Act of 1940.

quirements, state the SEC's interpretation of a specific accounting standard or describe the SEC's response to a common accounting problem encountered during the review of filings by corporations. Typically, the releases are concerned with disclosure problems, rather than the setting of accounting principles. The Commission through its office of Chief Accountant maintains a close liaison with the FASB. The SEC is very influential in the FASB's decisions, since the SEC in effect holds a veto power over its decisions due to the fact that if the SEC does not require corporations filing with it to follow a FASB proposal, the FASB is powerless to enforce its decision.

FASB's INDIRECT POWER

Cost Accounting Standards Board

Another influence on corporate reporting standards is the Cost Accounting Standards Board (CASB). This body, which was established in 1970, is an appointed board responsible to the legislative branch of the federal government. By law the CASB was empowered to issue cost accounting standards to be followed by defense contractors and subcontractors in accounting on a contract basis for government contract costs and profits. Subsequently, the General Services Administration extended the applicability of CASB standards to many nondefense federal government contracts. To insure that the CASB and FASB pronouncements are not in conflict, the two groups maintain a close liaison with each other.

American Institute of Certified Public Accountants

The AICPA's Accounting Standards Executive Committee (AcSec) is the senior technical committee authorized to speak for the Institute in the area of financial and cost accounting. The Institute's Auditing Standards Committee (AuSec) performs a similar function in the field of auditing.

AcSec consists of 15 CPAs in public practice. Periodically it publishes Statements of Position ("SOPs") on accounting matters. These pronouncements are advisory to the Institute's members rather than authoritative. However, in areas not covered by FASB pronouncements, the FASB and SEC have indicated that the SOPs are useful guides and should be followed as long as they are not in conflict with other existing official FASB pronouncements.

BASIC ISSUES

Underlying much of the contemporary controversy over corporate financial reporting practices covered in this book are these basic issues:

1. What should be the objective of the corporate reporting process?
2. Should corporate reports be reports prepared by management or reports on management prepared by some nonmanagement related party?
3. Should the accounting principles on which corporate reports are based be derived from business practice, their validity resting upon their general acceptance; or should they be developed conceptually, in a manner analogous to the principles of Euclidean geometry?
4. Should accounting principles be *uniform* in their application or should they permit *flexibility* on the part of the person responsible for the financial reports to choose from equally acceptable alternatives for reporting essentially identical transactions?
5. To what extent should corporate income, resources, and obligations reflect their current value and the changes in their value?

How each of these questions is ultimately decided will have an important impact on the means by which we measure and communicate managerial performance to investors.

Financial Accounting's Objective

The basic purpose of financial accounting and financial statements is to provide timely, reliable quantitative financial information about a business enterprise that is useful to statement users. There is little argument about this general objective. However, the implementation of the objective in practice involves considerable controversy.

For example, such issues as the following arise: Should the corporate statements be prepared for a particular class of users, such as investors, or should the statements be more general in their purpose? Should the reader be assumed to be naive or knowledgeable in accounting? What data is useful for users? Should the burden of the financial communication be carried by footnote disclosure or the values shown on the face of the statements?

There have been a number of attempts, such as *Statement No. 4* of the APB and the *Trueblood Committee Report*, to propose solutions to these issues over the last 15 years, but to date no authoritative body such as the FASB or SEC has settled on a clear-cut statement of objectives.

Management's Statements

Today, management has the responsibility for measuring and reporting its own performance. A number of critics of the present corporate reporting system believe it is unreasonable to expect management to fulfill this public reporting responsibility objectively. In their opinion, the pressures upon management from stockholders to show a pattern of increasing annual earnings per share are so enormous that managers of companies in trouble find it hard to avoid puffing up their earnings through accounting policy decisions. Or, conversely, in periods of when the public is critical of unusually high corporate profits, some believe management is tempted to use accounting decisions to understate its otherwise excessive profits. Therefore, in order to ensure that stockholders obtain an objective measure of managerial performance, the critics believe it is necessary to shift the responsibility for the reports to a disinterested third party, such as the independent public accountant.

Others believe that the application of responsible management judgment is most likely to lead to the selection of the most meaningful accounting principles in particular situations. This point of view attaches importance to the need for each company to select accounting policies which best communicate its management's unique policies, objectives, and the factors which guided their decisions. Since few public accountants are trained to bring this perspective and understanding to the financial reporting process, it is argued that it can be accomplished best through the exercise of responsible management judgment.

Different Approaches

Most managers, public accountants, and others involved in the corporate financial reporting process are uneasy about the present differences and inconsistencies in the preparation and presentation of financial information to stockholders. There is little agreement on how best to proceed to resolve these problems, however. The two principal alternative approaches implemented in practice are the case-by-case process and the conceptual method.

The advocates of the conceptual approach believe that if a consistent theory of financial accounting could be developed, many of the current controversies would be resolved. Those supporting this approach view current accounting practices as a collection of mutually inconsistent principles and practices which no systematic theory can describe. Therefore, they believe it is necessary to look elsewhere for a set of concepts which can be used to measure and communicate the results of business operations. There is little agreement on the methodology to be followed, however. The most popular approach has been to identify some accounting axioms and then use logic to construct a theory of accounting. Few of the recommendations resulting from this process have been adopted, principally because they have seemed impractical to most practicing accountants.

The case-by-case approach, with its heavy reliance on acceptance, is directed to identifying from the accounting practices that have evolved from actual business experience those principles that are generally accepted. Those advocating this approach also believe that restraint should be followed in trying to impose unilaterally any set of standards on the business community. Thus, the role of the standard setting body is viewed as being more that of a catalyst than a prescriber of standards. This approach is based on the belief that fairness in financial reporting cannot be fully realized unless it has a high degree of acceptance and is consistent with the modes of thought and customs of all major segments of the business community.

Uniformity versus Flexibility

The broad accounting issue commonly known as "uniformity versus flexibility" arose when an increasing number of thoughtful business executives, accountants, and members of the financial community became concerned over the difficulties involved in making meaningful comparisons of the financial reports of different companies. These problems arose because business executives could (and still can) choose between several equally authoritative accounting treatments to report to investors on such items as inventories, pensions, depreciation, and long-term contracts. The results? Profits vary greatly depending on the alternative chosen.

Some claimed that uniformity in the application of accounting principles to similar transactions would be the solution to these inadequacies of accounting practice. Greater uniformity is needed to produce financial statements that are fair to all those who rely upon financial data. If such statements are not forthcoming, the supporters of uniformity predict a general lack of confidence in financial statements and an inevitable increase in governmental control over the accounting practices followed by industry.

The supporters of a more flexible approach also recognized that generally accepted accounting principles needed a thorough overhaul. However, they cautioned against seeking uniformity solely for its own sake. Some flexibility must be retained, they argued, for management to choose between accounting principles, for only in this way can the variations in basic business policies and management attitudes toward risk which exist in actual business practice be reflected. The proponents of flexibility charge that to give these variations the appearance of comparability through uniform accounting, when in fact they are not uniform, would be misleading. The answer to this issue is not a simple one. Specifically, if generally accepted accounting principles become too inflexibile, it is possible that business practice may be unduly constricted. At the other extreme, if generally accepted accounting principles become too flexible, business practice may degenerate into confusion and mistrust. Both are undesirable situations. Where to draw the line is the critical issue.

In the future, as the FASB's statements on accounting matters are made known, the issue of uniformity versus flexibility will be faced again and again by business executives. Management's decisions will have to be made on each statement as it is offered, since there is no general, simple, ready-made solution to this broad issue. One fact is clear however. Some reform is needed if financial reports between different companies are to become more comparable. The character of these reforms will depend greatly on how the issue of uniformity versus flexibility in accounting principles is resolved.

Current Values

A fundamental controversy that underlies much of the ferment over accounting practices is the question of whether or not accounting measurement should reflect the historical cost of an item or some measure of its current value. Much more will be said on this issue in Chapter 3.

MANAGER'S ROLE

The controversy over the basic issues discussed above raises another basic question: What is management's role in the development and statement of generally accepted accounting principles?

Despite the obvious reasons why accounting principles are of vital interest to management, management has played only a small part in the development and statement of generally accepted accounting principles. In the absence of management participation, the problems of financial reporting, which have a broad social impact, have had to be dealt with by the accounting profession. The unfortunate result is that the crucial need for management's recognition of its far-reaching public responsibilities in financial reporting has been deemphasized among management people.

The outcome has been inevitable. A number of the less responsible individual managements, feeling no public responsibility, have been inclined to take advantage of the alternatives and gray areas of generally accepted accounting principles to report profits which best serve their individual purposes. Unhappily, these laggard managements all too often have set the reporting standards of their industry. For, in the face of competitive pressures, it takes courage to report, say, lower profits just for the sake of supporting a more desirable accounting principle, when others regard it as only one of several equally authoritative alternatives.

This observation should not be interpreted as a general indictment of all business managers for lack of responsibility or for low morality. It is made solely to indicate that the unsatisfactory state of accounting principles and the acts of a few irresponsible business executives have made it more difficult for business as a whole to fulfill its public responsibility in the area of corporate financial reporting.

If managements wish to lessen the probability of government control over financial reporting, they must support and participate in the accounting reform movement. Many are convinced that without responsible management participation, the FASB will be unsuccessful in its current efforts to narrow the areas of inconsistency in financial reporting practices. The FASB has recognized the necessity of joint effort with industry, appointing representatives from industry to the FASB and its advisory groups.

The controversy over accounting practices has alerted management to the fact that it shares a responsibility in setting realistic and workable ground rules for financial reporting. Whether or not uniformity or flexibility in accounting principles is fundamental to progress in formulating improved principles is yet to be decided. In deciding this and the other fundamental issues, however, the FASB must have the assistance and support of the business community. For, in the end, the success or failure of the FASB will rest largely with business executives.

MANAGEMENT ACCOUNTING

This book focuses on *financial* accounting—accounting that has the goal of providing stockholders and other external parties to the company with useful financial information. Nearly all businesses have another closely related system of accounting which provides management with useful financial information for running the business. This internally oriented system is concerned with *management* accounting.

A company's management accounting need not conform to the generally accepted accounting principles that govern its financial accounting. However, in practice a close relationship between these two accounting systems usually exists. One of the principal functions of management accounting is to measure the performance of the various units of a company against a set of measurement standards. These measures of performance are selected on the basis that if the unit managers can be motivated to achieve these standards their actions will collectively move the company toward the realization of its overall corporate objectives. Since generally accepted accounting principles will be used to measure the total corporate progress, there must be a link between the two systems. It is not sensible to motivate unit managers to achieve results that look good according to internal accounting but poor when the same results are translated into external accounting terms. Also, if a company's rules for maintaining the internal and external systems are very different, the company must maintain two sets of books to record its business transactions. This can be very expensive. Therefore, to reduce their accounting costs, most companies collect and record their basic management accounting data according to financial accounting rules.

While most companies use essentially the same accounting principles for management and financial accounting purposes, a number of companies have explicitly decided not to adopt this practice. In their opinion some of the company's external reporting practices cannot be used internally because they might introduce an undesirable behavioral bias in the decisions of unit managers. This practice raises a disturbing question: How can a company justify for external reporting the use of a generally accepted principle that does not lead to a useful measure of performance for internal purposes, because it either motivates managers to follow operating policies not desired by the company, provides top management with misleading measures of performance, or fails to reflect the company's real prospect?

BEHAVIORAL IMPLICATIONS

Research into the behavioral implications of management accounting and measurement systems has led some financial accounting authorities to conclude that generally accepted accounting principles can condition the decisions of managers as well as measure their performance for external reporting purposes. Unfortunately, in the opinion of these researchers, this has not always led to desirable results.

A number of these external reporting principles have a built-in bias which motivates managers under certain circumstances to adopt them in preference to alternative principles that may better reflect the operating results and financial condition of their company. In addition, other generally accepted accounting principles may induce managers to adopt specific operating policies to justify the use of these principles, even though these operating policies may not necessarily be the most appropriate.

The APB reduced the number of behaviorally undesirable accounting principles, but some still persist. A number of people believe that the goal of the accounting and management professions should be to eliminate these remaining objectionable practices and to create a set of generally accepted principles that will motivate managers to make sound economic and factual reporting decisions. If this is not possible, our corporate reporting system should at least not encourage managers to act against what appear to be the best interests of their stockholders and society.

Those who hold this view believe the FASB and others who now influence the definition of what constitutes acceptable corporate financial accounting practices must ask themselves when considering the appropriateness of an accounting principle:

1. What might this accounting principle or practice motivate managers to do in their own selfish interest?
2. Could this possible action obscure actual managerial performance, give the illusion of performance where none exists, or lead to unsound economic actions?

If the answer to any part of the second question is yes, and the probability that it will occur is reasonably high in even a few cases, then the use of the accounting practice should not be encouraged, even though it may be sound from the technical viewpoint of accounting theory.

National Economic Interests

One of the events that hastened the demise of the ABP was the congressional rejection of the APB's recommendation that one method be used to account for the investment tax credit. In the opinion of some congressional leaders the method proposed by the APB was at variance with the national economic goals and the government's programs to achieve these goals.

Briefly, the incident was as follows: The APB proposed that the profit gain from the investment tax credit be spread over the life of the assets giving rise to the credit. Congress favored the alternative approach that would have allowed corporations to record the full credit in the year in which it was granted. Congress felt this approach, which the APB had specifically rejected, would be a more positive incentive for business executives to invest in capital assets, which was the goal of the investment tax credit incentive. Accordingly, Congress wrote into the investment tax credit legislation the requirement that nobody could restrict the manner in which corporations accounted for the tax credit. Faced with this situation, the APB withdrew its recommendations.

This clash between the APB and Congress led to a debate as to whether or not private groups responsible for setting accounting standards should be responsive to the economic programs of the national government, even though this concern might favor the adoption of an accounting principle alternative that is not thought to represent the best accounting standard. Those favoring the view that accounting standards should not be at variance with national economic program goals believe that private regulatory bodies like the FASB must gain acceptance of their point of view from all interested parties, which includes the government, before issuing recommendations. Those who reject this argument believe that the role of the FASB is to set accounting standards which in the FASB's opinion represent the best accounting practice among the alternatives available. Only in this way it is claimed that the level of corporate reporting can be raised.

Marketing Efficiency and Accounting Data

Some of those involved in examining the behavior of security prices with respect to accounting data believe the acrimony that arose out of the investment tax credit incident described above was a needless controversy, because those involved in the dispute were ignorant of much of the so-called efficient markets research.

This research suggests to some that the stock market, as reflected in price behavior, acts as if it looks through the reported accounting numbers and takes into account when reaching market values the fact that earnings are being generated by different methods. If this is so, it doesn't matter if companies use different accounting methods. The market understands this fact and adjusts the earnings of the companies to reflect the economic reality of the company.

Furthermore, this research indicates that the market is efficient. That is, security prices act as if they fully reflect all of the publically available information, including financial statement data, and no investor can expect to use published information in such a way as to earn abnormal returns on his or her security portfolio. As a consequence knowing that different companies use different accounting practices is of little value in trying to outperform the market, since this fact is already reflected in the relative values of securities.

As a consequence of these findings, some researchers have suggested that the APB should have had different objectives. It should have been more concerned with full disclosure of information, rather than the measurement of transactions and accounting principles. There in turn would have led to very different behavior by the APB with respect to the investment tax accounting controversy, for example. In their opinion, the APB should have sought to achieve full and comprehensive disclosure of how corporations accounted for the investment tax credit and either left the decision on how to account for the tax credit to each company or to approve only the approach favored by Congress. Irrespective of the accounting principle decision, the goal should have been to give statement users adequate data to recompute the reporting company's profit according to the user's preferred method of investment tax credit accounting.

Four major implications of these research findings have been suggested for the FASB and other accounting standard setting bodies. The recommendations placed more emphasis on a goal of adequate disclosure than on a goal which seeks to refine the profit calculation.

First, some reporting issues, like the investment tax credit, are trivial and can be resolved by adequate disclosures. In these cases the difference in the accounting accord keeping cost difference of using one alternative method over another are not significant to the issuer of statements. Similarly, the cost of the statement user of adjusting profit data from one method to another is nominal. The solution to these accounting issues is simple: Report by one method, with sufficient footnote disclosure to convert to other methods. Then let the statement user decide for himself (or herself) the relevance of these data.

Second, the publication of financial data should prevent abnormal returns from accruing to individuals using inside information. Therefore, in deciding disclosure issues, if there are no additional costs to the issues, the presumption should be that the data in question should be disclosed. This would reduce any advantage that might accrue to insiders.

Third, the FASB, SEC, and Congress should become less concerned in their accounting reforms with protecting the naive or ignorant investor and its associated objective of attempting to reduce the complexities of modern corporations to the level of understanding of these individuals. Rather, the goal should be to educate investors to the fact that accounting data cannot be used to detect overvalued or undervalued securities and that the naive investor is best protected if there is full disclosure.

Fourth, accountants must stop acting as if they are the only supplier of information about the firm, since in an efficient market the value of a security may be the same under a variety of different accounting methods because the market is using alternative nonaccounting sources of information, for example, security analysts reports and the data presented in trade magazines. Thus, the FASB should seek as its objective to provide information to investors by the most economical means and to encourage the development of nonaccounting sources if these sources can convey the data more cheaply than the accounting statements.

The acceptance of the theory promoted by the efficient market researchers that accounting alternatives do not make a difference to *equity* market values is not shared by all accounting authorities. In the opinion of some the research findings are very inconclusive. Also, this research does not consider the impact of accounting alternatives on trade creditors, bank loan officers, and other nonstock market users of accounting data.

TAX ACCOUNTING

The objective of corporate tax planning is to minimize the current tax liability and then to defer the payment of this liability to the government as long as possible. A firm's taxable income is established by two sets of accounting rules and conventions that impinge upon each other. One set is established by the Internal Revenue Service. The other set is generally accepted accounting principles.

In general, a firm's taxable income is determined by the accounting system based on generally accepted accounting principles that it uses in the normal course of its business. However, with one major exception involving inventory accounting, the tax code allows companies to deviate from this practice in specific areas when calculating taxable income without having to change the corporate financial reports issued to stockholders. As a result, in such areas as fixed asset accounting, a company can maintain two sets of accounting data: one for determining the current tax payments to the government, another for preparing the statements for public reporting purposes. This is legal. However, it does create financial accounting problems related to how to account for the current corporate income tax expenses in financial reports to stockholders. These will be discussed at considerable length in Chapter 12.

From time to time somebody advocates that greater harmony, if not complete agreement, should exist between the income figures determined for income tax and financial reporting purposes. This position fails to recognize that the objectives of financial and tax accounting are different. The objective of financial accounting is to present fairly the results of operations and the financial condition of a company to its stockholders and other interested parties external to the firm, such as employees and creditors. Tax accounting's objective is to raise tax revenues and to help carry out the government's economic, political, and social policies. For example, tax surcharges and investment credits are adopted to manipulate the growth of the economy. The tax provision permitting 60-month amortization of certain pollution control facilities is an example of congressional concern over the ecological problem of pollution. In addition, some tax accounting practices are based on administrative practicalities. For example, a basic tax concept is that the timing of a tax liability should be influenced by when the taxpayer can most readily pay and the government can most readily collect. Clearly, this concept is at odds with the accrual concept of financial accounting, which says income should be recognized when it is earned.

In general, business has been unwilling to accept an accounting principle for financial reporting purposes that reduces financial income unless it produces a tax reduction. For example, many business executives oppose the amortization of goodwill (i.e., excess cost of assets acquired in acquisitions over their fair market value) for financial reporting purposes because it is not a deductible expense for determining income tax payments. Similarly, many believe it is the inability to claim a tax deduction for employee stock options that justifies the similar treatment for financial accounting purposes, despite the fact that many accounting authorities believe that stock options represent a form of compensation that should be charged to earnings. Thus, while we often argue that because of their different objectives, tax and financial accounting should be kept separate, in practice tax accounting does influence financial accounting.

Social Cost and Human Resource Accounting

In recent years, some accountants have been exploring the possibility of extending the traditional role of accounting to include the measurement and disclosure of a corporation's social contribution. Other accountants have been experimenting with accounting systems and concepts that would communicate to management and interested outsiders better data on a corporation's investment in and utilization of human resources. These two activities have generated considerable controversy as to the appropriateness of accountants undertaking these responsibilities, the relevance of the data produced, the methods used to measure costs and benefits, and the interest of management and the public in the data generated.

The supporters of social cost accounting believe society is a system in which business is only one part. Increasingly, it is argued, the public is accepting this view of society; and as a consequence, each unit of society, such as a business, is being viewed by the public in terms of its contribution to the whole society. As a result, the public needs to have access to data that permits an evaluation of a corporation in terms of both its income responsibility to shareholders and its social contribution to society as a whole. It is logical and reasonable for social accounting proponents to argue that accounting, because of its existing measurement and disclosure interests in the firm, should assume a role in informing the public of the social-responsibility activities of corporations.

Accordingly, it is proposed, accounting presentations of corporate results needs to be expanded to incorporate the measurement of the social costs and benefits of business activities. Such social costs and benefits might include the degree to which a company's operations add or reduce the pollution of the environment; enhance or destroy public properties; or, utilize or contribute to society's resources. To the extent possible, these costs and benefits should be measured. At a minimum, however, they need to be identified, disclosed, and discussed in corporate reports and presented along with traditional accounting data so that the public can evaluate the net social contribution of corporations.

Those opposed to a social welfare accountability role for accounting reports believe that other vehicles are more appropriate for conveying these social welfare data. Others believe that since reliable social data cannot be obtained, any attempt to measure social costs and benefits is futile and potentially misleading. Another view expressed by those opposing a social reporting role for accounting is that the profits of a firm that operates within the legal framework provide the all inclusive criterion for evaluating its social performance.

Human resource accounting advocates believe that accounting communications currently do not deal adequately with one of a corporations most important resources; namely, its human resources. These resources are developed at a considerable cost to corporations, and the success a corporation has in developing and acquiring its employees may be vital to its success. Traditional accounting, however, treats expenditures to acquire, develop, and hold human resources as expenses rather than as assets; rarely identifies and discloses the extent of these expenditures; and makes no effort to evaluate the effectiveness or value of a corporation's human resources. Those interested in human resource accounting are experimenting with different financial and nonfinancial measurements and disclosures of corporate human resources with the goal of incorporating human resource data in accounting communications.

The work of the social cost and human resource accountants should be followed closely, since it may lead to a significant expansion in the concept of what is considered to be the role of corporate reporting.

AN APPROACH TO FINANCIAL REPORTING DECISIONS

The process of analyzing and resolving financial reporting problems is similar to that followed in other business decision-making situations, except that the decision maker must usually work within the constraints of generally accepted accounting principles. Typically, the business executive is faced with a problem to which there is more than one possible solution. His (or her) task is to choose what he believes to be the best possible course of action. He can do this intuitively or through careful, systematic consideration and weighting of the anticipated consequences; or some combination of these two approaches. Whatever the approach used, he must eventually make a decision.

The evaluation of the alternative courses of action can be facilitated if "yardsticks" or criteria, weighted by their relative importance, are first developed. Then, for any particular problem these criteria can be used as guides to distinguish between acceptable and unacceptable solutions. The criteria can also be used to rank the acceptable solutions in their relative order of attractiveness.

In the case of financial reporting problems, the decision criteria are usually developed from an analysis of the company's overall objectives and the operating strategy to achieve those objectives. This is done by answering these questions: Given the company's objectives and operating plan, what characteristics must the financial reporting policy satisfy if it is to significantly contribute to the realization of these plans? What are the implications for the company's financial reporting policies of the characteristics of the company's particular operations, relations with external groups, competitors' policies and plans, industry, financial structure, and management? Answers to these questions require a detailed analysis of such areas as the company's operations and plans, the stock market's evaluation of such companies, the company's business environment, and the public interest and regulatory requirements that may be present.

The identification and correct definition of the problem to be solved is a critical stage in the decision-making process. Unless this is done well, the decision maker may solve the wrong issue or only part of the problem, which may leave him (or her) with a more unsatisfactory situation than before he took action. In most of the cases presented, at least part of the problem is fairly evident. How well one is able to clearly and fully state the problem will depend in large part on the quality of the operating and environmental analysis described above.

Financial reporting problems usually involve the selection of the appropriate generally accepted accounting principles to handle a specific item. These problems involve at least five interrelated considerations:

1. Which principles are the most appropriate?
2. How should the decision on this accounting policy application be communicated to the public?
3. As a result of this decision what other adjustments, if any, must be made in the particular mix of generally accepted accounting principles that collectively constitute the company's financial reporting policy?
4. What operating or financial bias will this decision have on management's future business decisions or policies?
5. How will this decision contribute to the real or apparent achievement of management's objectives?

The third question recognizes that a company's earnings per share and financial image is the net result of applying accounting policy decisions to a variety of individual transactions. Therefore, a change in one part of this mix may necessitate changes in other parts to achieve the overall effect management is seeking.

The alternative solutions to financial reporting problems usually involve a choice between alternative generally accepted accounting principles. Therefore, in order for the decision maker in any particular situation to fully appraise and consider the full range of solutions open to him, he must be familiar with generally accepted accounting principles, the conditions justifying the usage of particular principles, and the principal theoretical arguments for and against each principle.

Once the criteria, the problem, and the possible solutions are identified the decision maker must sift through the facts available to him to extract those that are relevant to the problem.

These facts, of which some are measurable and others are not, must be related to the solutions so that the advantages and disadvantages of each solution can be identified. The decision maker must then use judgment to decide which solution has the greatest net advantage.

There is seldom a right answer to financial reporting problems, or even an answer to which everyone will agree. The decision maker must make the best decision he can with the facts available to him, knowing that two people may interpret or weigh the same facts differently and reach quite different conclusions. Decision making under these circumstances is a complicated and difficult task, fraught with uncertainty.

THE CHALLENGE

The challenge to those who define generally accepted accounting principles is to develop a set of principles that are both behaviorally and technically sound. They should be behaviorally sound in that they:

1. Inhibit managers from taking undesirable operating actions to justify the adoption of an accounting alternative.
2. Inhibit the adoption of accounting practices by corporations which create the illusion of performance.

The traditional approach to defining generally accepted accounting principles has focused principally on technical considerations. Typically, this has been done well. The time has come, however, to pay greater attention to the possible impact of accounting practices on people's actions. If this is also done well, financial accounting will do a better job of communicating the financial facts of a business situation, rather than being a convenient vehicle for unscrupulous managers to mislead unwitting investors.

SUGGESTED FURTHER READING

AMERICAN INSTITUTE OF CERTIFIED PUBLIC ACCOUNTANTS. *Establishing Financial Accounting Standards.* New York, 1972.
——. *Objectives of Financial Statements.* New York, 1973.
BURTON, JOHN C., ed. *Corporate Financial Reporting: Conflicts and Challenges.* New York: American Institute of Certified Public Accountants, 1969.
FINANCIAL ACCOUNTING STANDARDS BOARD. *Conceptual Framework for Accounting and Reporting: Elements of Financial Statements and Their Measurement.* Stamford, Conn., December 2, 1976.

Chapter 2

THE DEVELOPMENT OF CORPORATE REPORTING PRACTICES

From 19th-century traditions of corporate secrecy, American corporations have moved slowly toward more public and credible financial disclosure practices. This chapter examines the variety of political, technical, social, and economic pressures from the business community, the accounting profession, the government, and the public which have impelled this movement and governed its direction and tempo. An appreciation of this process is necessary to put our contemporary practices and problems into proper perspective. People with such a sense of history seem to be more closely in touch with reality and able to deal with change more creatively. The study of corporate reporting history also sharpens one's sense of when to introduce change and how long it may take.

As late as 1900, the amount of financial information presented to stockholders by the managers of most publicly owned American manufacturing corporations was meager. After 1900, the level and frequency of corporate financial disclosure by industrial management began to rise slowly and the credibility of its representations began to improve. These changes in the quality of the financial reporting practices of American manufacturing concerns have four principal causes: (1) gradual recognition by some managers of their public responsibility; (2) increasing criticism of corporate reporting practices by a number of influential groups and individuals outside of the management class; (3) direct federal government regulation, such as the Securities Acts of 1933 and 1934; and (4) the recognition by the American accounting profession, and acceptance by the business community, of some common accounting and reporting standards. Underlying and contributing to these forces for change have been a number of social, political, and economic factors such as the emergence of a large number of small investors, the evolution of big business, and the increasing willingness of the public to seek government action to reform undesirable commercial practices.

NINETEENTH CENTURY

The modern reviewer of management financial reporting practices during the 19th century is immediately struck by the limited amount of information made public by manufacturing firms—even the larger ones with widespread public ownership. Not only was there inadequate financial disclosure, but some companies were irregular in the frequency with which they issued reports. For example, between 1897 and 1905, the Westinghouse Electric and Manufacturing Company neither published an annual financial report to its stockholders nor held an annual meeting.

This lack of financial information pertaining to manufacturing concerns was in contrast to the reporting practices of public utilities, insurance companies, banks, and railroads, whose activities (being more in the public service) were more closely regulated and more fully reported. Even here, however, practice varied in accordance with state requirements, and there were some notable nonreporters. For instance, in 1866, the treasurer of the Delaware, Lackawanna, and Western Rail Road Company, in response to a request for information from the New York Stock Exchange replied simply: "The Delaware Lackawanna R.R. Co. make no reports and publish no statements and have done nothing of the sort for the last five years."

Before 1900, for the few publicly held manufacturing corporations in existence, it was possible for investors to obtain some information pertaining to the companies' capitalization, if not from management, from the standard financial sources such as *Hunt's Merchant's Magazine,* and later, the *Commercial and Financial Chronicle.* Less frequently was a simple balance sheet available and seldom were sales and profit figures released—an income statement showing sales less the major expense items was rare. In addition, few of these published financial facts were accompanied by either a company or independent auditors' certificate, since neither the theory nor practice of these procedures was common in America. The public had to rely upon management's integrity in determining if published financial information was reliable.

After 1890, a few of the newly created industrial combinations sometimes published more detailed financial statements. By modern standards, even in these cases, the amount of data released was sketchy. Companies, such as American Tobacco, which issued the more detailed financial reports usually did so because of enlightened managers or because of their heavy dependence on outside sources for capital.

Generally, as might be expected, the small and the closely held manufacturing corporations were the more secretive. Yet as late as 1900 there were some notoriously secretive managements among the large publicly traded corporations. This group included such companies as the American Tin Plate Company, a large publicly owned company, which controlled 95 percent of the tin-plate production in the United States and whose stock was traded on the New York and Chicago stock exchanges. It published in 1900 a balance sheet containing only four asset and five liability accounts.

FACTORS CONTRIBUTING TO FINANCIAL SECRECY

The principal reasons why corporate managers were so secretive with regard to their companies' financial affairs during most of the 19th century were four in number: (1) there was no tradition of publicity, for no one would have thought of asking individual proprietors, partners, or early family owners to divulge such information; (2) management believed the public had no right to information on these matters; (3) managers feared that by revealing financial information they would unwittingly assist their competitors; and (4) to many, the doctrine of *caveat emptor* seemed as applicable to buyers of securities as to purchasers of horses. For instance, during the testimony heard before the Industrial Commission in 1899, Henry O. Havemeyer, the president of American Sugar Refining Company, and commission member Thomas Phillips had the following exchange:

Phillips: You think, then, that when a corporation is chartered by the State, offers stock to the public, and is one in which the public is interested, that the public has no right to know what its earning power is or to subject them to any inspection whatever, that the people may not buy stock blindly?

Havemeyer: Yes; that is my theory. Let the buyer beware; that covers the whole business. You cannot wet-nurse people from the time they are born until the day they die. They have got to wade in and get stuck and that is the way men are educated and cultivated.

The testimony of another witness before the commission, Charles W. King, secretary and general manager of the New Jersey Corporation Agency,[1] illustrates another of the reasons for secrecy:

---

[1] The New Jersey Corporations Agency was formed in 1895 for the purpose of furnishing corporations chartered in New Jersey but operating out of state with the necessary facilities for complying with the state's liberal incorporation laws. Mr. King's office represented several hundred such corporations, including the Amalgamated Copper Company, the American Car and Foundry Company, the American Thread Company, the Pressed Steel Car Company, and the American Soda Fountain Company.

Livingston (commission member): Now, then, when the people ask for information, why not just give it? You say because it would be giving away your private business. Well, you did not think of that when you went to the public for your franchise, did you?

King: The public may not be your competitors, but you may have competitors, and in giving it to the public you would have to give it to your competitors.

These comments of Havemeyer and King represented in part an inheritance by late 19th-century management of a number of the attitudes of the owner-managers of the century's earlier industrial ventures. Ownership and management, if not the same persons, were closely related; and the owners were in continual personal touch with the affairs of the enterprise. Because there were few or no outside investors, there was little need for management to think about the problems of financial disclosure. Under these conditions a company's financial statements were considered private, just as were the financial affairs of any private citizen.

State corporation laws reflected this antipublicity sentiment of managers and their agents. By 1900, reports of some kind were required in 27 states. The remainder of the states required no report whatsoever.

About half the states provided for reports to stockholders. In general, these statutes merely specified that an "annual report" be provided the stockholders. Seldom were the contents of the report specified or a provision included to require the mailing of annual reports to those stockholders who were unable to attend the stockholders' meeting. To have imposed the burden of detailed public reports upon management would not have improved a state's chances of attracting incorporations—a lucrative business few states wished to discourage.

The accepted method of marketing new industrial securities also placed little pressure upon management for greater financial disclosure. During the 19th century, investors bought securities primarily on the basis of their confidence in the promoter or the investment banker offering the issue. In particular, investment bankers, it was widely believed, undertook searching investigations of all securities before they were offered to the public, only offered securities of investment quality, and practically guaranteed the security. Consequently, prospectuses offering new industrial securities seldom ran more than two pages and contained sketchy financial data. The first test of a security was the reliability of the investment bankers involved, not the financial conditions of the issuing company. Under these conditions, as long as companies paid their dividends, investors rarely needed, or demanded, financial statements.

Finally, the absence of a strong accounting profession and an established body of accounting theory in America contributed to the inadequacy of management's financial reports. Not only was there nondisclosure, but when information was released it was of dubious value, since different companies used different accounting concepts to measure and report similar transactions. For instance, the concept of depreciation was little understood. A number of firms made no provisions for depreciation. Some related depreciation expense to changes in appraised asset values. There were also several other areas where accounting practice was far from standardized and the use of different accounting practices created confusion—including the treatment of unusual charges and credits, the valuation of assets, and the consolidation of subsidiaries.

These accounting vagaries existed partly because little attention had been given in the United States to the logic of accounting. Prior to 1900, nearly all of the American textbooks pertaining to the subject were concerned principally with the rules of bookkeeping.

In addition, the function of public accountants and their reports was misunderstood. For a company to call in independent auditors to examine its books was often taken by the public as an indication of suspected fraud, irregularity, losses, and doubt regarding the reporting company's financial strength. Some managers regarded such action as a reflection on their integrity. Even as late as 1900, many business executives were still reluctant to call in an accountant, and many investigations by public accountants were made secretly, often at night and on Sundays. Consequently, it is not surprising that an English chartered accountant wrote of American practice before 1905: "the profession of accounting has hitherto been little understood in America." The accountant in the United States was little known, little recognized, little wanted; most accountants neither could nor desired to modify management's desire for corporate secrecy.

TOWARD THE SECURITIES ACTS AND IMPROVED DISCLOSURE, 1900–1933

Almost as soon as business became big, a number of people became disturbed by its growth in power and critical of its practices. It was argued by many, for instance, that the large combinations should be dissolved, since the very existence of these new and powerful industrial groups threatened the fundamental civil liberties and morality of American society.

One of the most popular remedies suggested to rectify this imbalance of power and to end the predatory methods of large corporations was improved corporate financial publicity. For example, in 1900, the Industrial Commission recommended to Congress:

The larger corporations—the so-called trusts—should be required to publish annually a properly audited report, showing in reasonable detail their assets and liabilities, with profit or loss; such report and audit under oath to be subject to Government inspection. The purpose of such publicity is to encourage competition when profits become excessive, thus protecting consumers against too high prices and to guard the interests of employees by a knowledge of the financial condition of the business in which they are employed.

The increasing number of investors, it was thought, would also be protected by improved corporate publicity. While little correlation between the issuance of informative reports and willingness on the part of investors to buy stock was noted, public opinion nevertheless was appalled by the stock market manipulations of many managements and promoters who sought to enrich themselves at the expense of their stockholders. According to one contemporary observer:

The suppression and misstatement of facts by corporations have in recent years misled investors as well as speculators to buy shares in concerns financially unsound and on the verge of bankruptcy. To prevent the "watering" of stock or to find some method of furnishing investors a basis of judging the condition of companies has absorbed the attention of the "public mind" for some time. "Secrecy" was said to be the evil; nor is it to be wondered at that "publicity" was the remedy suggested. No one word has been more frequently upon the lips of the American public in the last three years [1900 1903] than "publicity."

These pre-World War I demands for fuller financial disclosure, both by the critics of big business and the public, were generally ignored by management. Few companies, for instance, followed United States Steel Corporation's declared policy of presenting full and definite financial information, which first found expression in the 35 pages of financial data contained in the company's annual report of 1902. In contrast, most managements did not seem to care about public opinion. They disregarded it. In fact, some companies which had previously published financial statements quit issuing financial reports altogether. For instance, in 1901, George Westinghouse, president of Westinghouse Electric and Manufacturing, said:

. . . if some should be surprised that more complete statements have not been previously submitted to them, it can only be said that the Directors as well as the stockholders who own the largest amounts of stock, have believed that in view of the existing keen competition and the general attitude toward industrial enterprises, the interests of all would be served by avoiding, to as great an extent as possible, giving undue publicity to the affairs of the Company.

While the pioneer critics of big business had little direct impact on management, they greatly influenced, nevertheless, those who later played important roles in increasing the federal government's control over business affairs. For instance, before World War I, among early advocates of greater publicity of corporate affairs, few became more widely read and respected than the future associate justice of the Supreme Court, Louis D. Brandeis. In 1913, Brandeis said: "Publicity is justly commended as a remedy for social and industrial diseases. Sunlight is said to be the best of disinfectants; electric light the most efficient policemen." Later in 1933, it was Mr. Frankfurter—surrogate for Justice Brandeis—in his visits with President Roosevelt who argued for this approach to business regulation.

Following World War I, and until the economic and stock market disasters of 1929, there was a shift in the American political, social, economic, and ethical climate. The nation became more prosperous, and the public grew weary and disillusioned with the crusades of the preceding progressive era. Business executives were regarded with a new respect. The public, instead of disapproving, now looked upon the large-scale efforts to rig the securities market by such market operators as Harry F. Sinclair, Percy A. Rockefeller, and Bernard E. Smith with breathless admiration.

Consequently, during the period 1918–29, the public appeal of the critics of business waned but did not disappear. In 1926, for instance, Professor William Z. Ripley of Harvard University created "quite a flutter in financial centers" when he proclaimed: "let the word go forth that the Federal Trade Commission is henceforth to address itself vigorously to the matter of adequate and intelligent corporate publicity, and taken in conjunction with the helpful agencies at work the thing is as good as done." Ripley was particularly disturbed by the "enigmatic" accounting practices which made possible financial "obfuscation" and "malfeasance." Another who spoke in the same vein was the young Adolph Berle, Jr., who, as part of his notion of the "social corporation," demanded as an expression of the public responsibility of management fuller disclosure of corporate affairs, particularly to investors.

As with that of their predecessors, the immediate impact of such critics as Ripley was almost nil; but after 1930, when the nation lay in economic disorder, business executives were more easily discredited. The public once again became sympathetic to the opinions of those critical of business and finance, and it was the critics' standards—not those of management—by which managers were finally judged.

Between 1900 and 1933, others more closely allied with management sought to raise the level of financial reporting, including the New York Stock Exchange, the Investment Bankers Association of America, and the public accounting profession. Of these private groups, the New York Stock Exchange was perhaps the leading influence in the promotion of adequate corporate disclosure. The exchange's direct influence, however, was limited to companies listed on the exchange. The influence of the Investment Bankers Association and the public accounting profession was severely curtailed by the unwillingness of much of their membership to act independently of management.

The New York Stock Exchange

As early as 1869, the New York Stock Exchange's Committee on Stock List adopted a policy that companies should agree that once listed on the exchange they would publish some form of an annual financial report. Few companies, however, agreed to observe this stipulation. In fact, it was not until the Kansas City (Missouri) Gas Company listing agreement of 1897 that the exchange extracted from a listed company a substantive promise to observe some minimum reporting requirements. Nevertheless, from 1910 onward, the exchange influenced improvements in financial reporting practices of listed companies.

Before 1900, so reluctant was the exchange to enforce its reporting requirements upon industrial management that in 1885 it created the so-called Unlisted Department. This department sought to grasp business then going to outside street markets where fewer restrictions were placed upon issuers. The companies whose stocks were traded by the Unlisted Department (mainly industrials) were not required to furnish the exchange with financial information relevant to the issue. Nevertheless, these shares were traded with regularly listed securities, unlisted stocks being distinguished on quotation sheets only by an asterisk. In this manner, such active stocks as those of Amalgamated Copper and the American Sugar Refining Companies were dealt in on the exchange for many years without the public having any information regarding their affairs. They were in effect conducted and maintained as "blind pools." Those in control were then enabled to use their information for speculative purposes.

In 1910, under growing threats of government regulation, the New York Stock Exchange abolished its Unlisted Department. Thereafter, over the next 20 years, the exchange's Committee on Stock List actively sought to improve the reporting practices of listed companies, particularly with respect to the frequency with which they published financial statements. For example, in 1916, General Motors Company agreed to publish semi-annually a consolidated income statement and balance sheet. In 1924, Inland Steel Company modified its original listing agreement and agreed to issue a public statement of quarterly earnings.

In 1926, the NYSE officially recommended the publication of quarterly reports by all listed companies. Also, by this time, nearly all listed manufacturing companies had adopted the practice of issuing annual reports covered by an independent auditor's opinion certificate, a practice made mandatory by the exchange in 1933. Such progress was not easy, however, since as late as 1931 many an executive of a listed company held the exchange's suggested publicity requirements to be arbitrary and unreasonable.

The exchange's control, of course, was restricted only to those corporations which sought to list securities. The securities handled on the over-the-counter markets and the securities listed on the regional exchanges—Chicago, Boston, Pittsburgh—were not only beyond the New York Stock Exchange's control but were also subject to less rigorous requirements so as to attract local lesser corporations, more closely controlled and less susceptible to educational appeal. Yet, these were the very corporations where the most need for improved financial reporting existed.

The Investment Bankers Association of America

Between 1920 and 1927, the Investment Bankers Association of America on several occasions sought, through voluntary action of its membership, to standardize the information regarding industrial securities presented to the public, particularly that in prospectuses. The initial impetus for these reform efforts grew out of a desire on the part of some association members to protect investors, to protect legitimate investment bankers from the growing public resentment against the sellers of fraudulent securities, and to forestall federal and state governmental regulation of securities. Already, by 1920, some 20 states, alarmed by the prevalence of fraudulent stock promotions, had passed so-called blue-sky laws; and on the federal level, security bills had been placed before Congress in 1918, 1919, and 1921, respectively.

On at least six occasions between 1920 and 1928 the Investment Bankers Association issued reports setting forth recommended minimum standards for financial disclosure in prospectuses. In general, these reports, three of which were related to industrial companies, called for an "adequate" and "understandable" balance sheet with some comments on such items as inventory, working capital, and depreciation policy, as well as a presentation of earnings by years. In the case of holding companies, it was suggested that investors be provided with a consolidated balance sheet, a consolidated statement of earnings, and an income statement for the holding company.

Few of these recommendations were ever followed in practice by investment bankers or their corporate clients. The reasons for the failure of the association's voluntary reform program were many. A number of members of the association were indifferent with respect to these recommendations. Also, among those companies that issued securities, some of the bigger and better known companies objected to allowing financial information to go beyond the eyes of their investment bankers.

In addition, a number of investment bankers still preferred to follow the 19th-century practice of selling securities on the basis of the investment banker's reputation alone, rather than on the merits of the issue and issuer. As late as 1923, "confidence," one investment banker said, "was the bulwark in the relationship between the dealer and the client." Earlier, in 1918, another investment banker had stated, "The questions of brick and mortar and turnover and rate of profit and all the other fine points are secondary considerations." Other investment bankers relied upon the 19th-century custom of nondisclosure to justify the hiding of weakness in the dubious securities they offered.

Clearly, such attitudes as these were hardly likely to lead to universal voluntary acceptance among investment bankers of the association's suggestions regarding financial disclosure. Some investment bankers, it would seem, were just as desirous as their corporate clients of fostering financial secrecy.

The Accounting Profession

During the years 1900 to 1933, with the growing dependence of business on outside sources of capital, with the introduction of the income tax law in 1913, and with the passage of the excess profits tax in 1917, the accounting profession became an essential part of American business life. Credit granters came to depend upon financial statements as the basis for credit decisions, and complete and accurate accounting records became necessary for income tax purposes.

Throughout most of this 33-year period the primary force among accountants for improved corporate financial disclosure came from three sources: educators, individual practitioners, and the American Institute of Accountants. Around 1900, because of a growing recognition of the importance of business in American life, universities added to their curricula business courses which included accounting as a primary subject. University professors began to probe behind accounting practice and explore its logic, and the first university department of accounting, as such, was established by New York University in 1900. For the first time in the United States, accounting education was rising above the level of bookkeeping, and an ideology for accounting technology was slowly developed.

Among business executives, perhaps a more influential group were the leading practitioners of the accounting profession. Such men as George O. May and A. Lowes Dickinson of Price Waterhouse & Company, and Robert H. Montgomery of Lybrand, Ross Brothers & Montgomery, through their day-to-day contracts—literary and personal—with other accountants and business executives, sought to raise the level of industrial financial disclosure and hasten the adoption of sounder accounting practices. In general, these men, whose early training had been in England, believed that the disclosure standards included in the English Companies Acts should be adopted by American business executives. Later, the framers of the securities acts exhibited a similar belief when they based the disclosure philosophy underlying the Securities Act of 1933 on the existing English Company Law.

The genesis of the modern American Institute of Certified Public Accountants (American Institute of Accountants) and its work to raise the standards of the American accounting profession can be traced back to similar earlier attempts in Great Britain before 1880. In Great Britain, a vital and influential accounting profession had existed since about 1850. Beginning in the 1880s, a number of these British chartered accountants came to the United States, principally to audit the various British investments there. To these transplanted Britishers the first steps necessary to improve the stature of accounting in the United States appeared to be the establishment of a nationwide society of accountants, along the lines of the Institute of Chartered Accountants in England and Wales.

The first organized body of professional accountants in the United States was formed in New York in 1886. Soon after, other state and national accounting bodies were founded. In 1905, the contending national organizations were united to form one principal organization: the American Association of Public Accountants. In 1916, the association was reorganized as the American Institute of Accountants.

The first attempt of the Institute to set some auditing and reporting standards came in 1917 when it joined with the Federal Trade Commission and the Federal Reserve Board in publishing *Uniform Accounting*, the most comprehensive and authoritative document related to corporate financial disclosure and balance sheet audits yet published in the United States. Over the years, the Federal Trade Commission, in the course of its investigation of business conditions, had become disturbed over the lack of uniformity in balance sheet audits and financial reports. As the very first step toward standardization of practices relating to the compiling and verifying of corporate reports, the Commission requested the Institute to prepare a memorandum on balance sheet audits.

The Institute's memorandum was eventually prepared by a committee under George O. May's direction, approved by the Federal Trade Commission, and given tentative endorsement by the Federal

Reserve Board. This tentative document was then submitted to bankers throughout the country for their consideration and criticism. Later in 1917, the final draft of *Uniform Accounting* was published by the Federal Reserve Board. In 1918, it was reissued under the name, *Approved Methods for the Preparation of Balance Sheet Statements.* Subsequently, in 1929, it was revised by the Institute for the Federal Reserve Board, republished, and renamed *Verification of Financial Statements.*

Uniform Accounting and its later versions were widely distributed. The bulk of this document related to balance sheet audits. Its last three pages, however, presented suggested forms for comparative income statements and balance sheets. The model income statement provided for some 29 revenue and expense items. The asset side of the proposed balance sheet called for details under the following headings: cash, notes and accounts receivable (less provision for bad debts), inventories, other quick assets, securities, fixed assets (less reserves for depreciation), deferred charges, and other assets. The liability side of the balance sheet indicated detailed information should be presented under these headings: unsecured bills and notes, unsecured accounts, secured liabilities, other current liabilities, fixed liabilities, and net worth.

Despite their prestigious backers, the recommendations outlined in *Uniform Accounting* were not quickly adopted by corporations, bankers, or the accounting profession—chiefly because bankers, out of fear of driving away customers, refrained from insisting upon audited statements from their clients. Nevertheless some progress was made.

Except for the recommendations pertaining to inventories and disclosure of asset values, few of the improvements ever found their way into public reports. Business executives in general believed that the standard form of financial statements outlined in the Federal Reserve Board's publication called for too much information and would be used to their detriment by competitors.

Encouraged by the publication of *Uniform Accounting,* the Institute directed its main educational efforts for the next nine years toward encouraging business executives to use balance sheet audits for credit purposes. By 1926, George O. May declared to the accounting profession that, among prominent industrial companies, the practice of having audits "had become almost universal." Now, he said, the time had come for the Institute to assume a larger responsibility and "render a higher service to the community." The new goal he proposed for the profession was the adoption by industrial corporations of the financial disclosure standards embodied in the English Companies Act. To achieve this end, he suggested that the Institute cooperate with "such bodies as the leading stock exchange, the investment bankers and the commercial banks which grant credit." It was impractical, May believed, to consider bringing about improved corporate disclosure in the United States through direct legislation, as had happened in England.

During the next four years, the Institute undertook two cooperative efforts along the lines suggested by May. The first undertaking with the Investment Bankers Association of America in 1928 produced little. The second was much more fruitful. In 1930, with the long-standing urging of J. M. B. Hoxsey, the executive assistant on stock list of the New York Stock Exchange, and May, reinforced by the effects of the market crash of 1929, the Institute appointed a committee to cooperate with the exchange "in consideration of all problems which are of common interest to investors, exchanges, and accountants."

Hoxsey's concern was principally for the protection of investors, of whom there were some ten million in 1930. "Accounting," Hoxsey told the Institute, "is a matter of convention but it is questionable whether these conventions have kept pace with the changes in modern business conditions."

At Hoxsey's suggestion, the American Institute appointed a Special Committee on Cooperation with Stock Exchanges, with George O. May as chairman, to work with the New York Stock Exchange to explore the issues raised by Hoxsey. This undertaking was a significant development as it represented a change in outlook by the accounting profession. *Uniform Accounting* had been prepared with an institution concerned with the quality of credit and the recommendations contained therein made with the credit granter in mind; the new undertaking was with the New York Stock Exchange and the accounting problems were to be considered from the standpoint of those who traded in securities—that is, investors.

On September 22, 1932, the Institute's special committee submitted its report to the exchange's Committee Stock List. The report, which was published in 1933 under the title *Audits of Corporate Accounts*, listed four principal objectives the committee thought the exchange should "keep constantly in mind and do its best to gradually achieve." These goals were to bring about a better recognition by the public that balance sheets did not show present values of the assets and liabilities of corporations, to encourage the adoption of balance sheets which more clearly showed on what basis assets were valued, to emphasize the cardinal importance of the income account, and to make universal the usage by listed corporations of certain broad principles of accounting which had won fairly general acceptance. On this last point the report warned the exchange against attempting "to restrict the right of corporations to select detailed methods of accounting deemed by them to be best adapted to the requirements of their business." In addition, the report suggested each listed corporation should submit to the exchange a clear and detailed statement of the accounting principles it observed when compiling financial statements.

This document, which was the most specific statement yet formulated on just how financial reports could be made more informative and reliable, was given warm approval by the Controllers Institute and the Investment Bankers Association. Taking a lead from the report's recommendations, on January 6, 1933, the exchange announced that henceforth corporations seeking listing must submit financial statements audited by independent public accountants and agree to have all future reports to stockholders similarly inspected. In addition, the scope of the audit was to be no less than that indicated in *Verification of Financial Statements*.

The accountants read Whitney's announcement with "a feeling of hearty gratification" according to Richardson, the editor of the *Journal of Accountancy*. Richardson had campaigned long and hard for such a listing requirement and hailed the announcement as probably the "most important forward step in the history of accounting within recent years."

Such joy was short-lived. Within six months the envisioned role of the Committee on Stock List and that of the Institute's special committee in effect passed to a federal agency—first to the Federal Trade Commission and then to the Securities and Exchange Commission. In 1934, many accountants, including George O. May, believed that the profession might in the future "all too easily, find itself merely the ciphering agency for vitally unreviewable bureaucrats." To date, such has not been the case.

Management and Financial Disclosure

Between 1900 and 1933, the financial disclosure practices of industrial corporations improved somewhat. Nevertheless, despite such exceptions as United States Steel Corporation, Bethlehem Steel Corporation, and General Motors Company, the financial reporting practices lagged far behind the recommendations for greater and more useful corporate financial disclosure made by the New York Stock Exchange. Also, the numerous alternative accounting principles which had caused so much confusion during the late 19th century were still observed in practice.

As time passed, however, the statements of industrial corporations became more uniform as to the degree and form of disclosure. By 1933, most publicly owned manufacturing corporations were publishing annual reports containing fairly detailed balance sheets. Furthermore, in line with the shift of emphasis in common stock evaluation techniques from the balance sheet to the income statement, a sketchy income statement showing sales, several major expense items, and current profits was now usually included. Auditing by outside accountants was also becoming more common.

Yet some of the larger companies still refused to provide stockholders with written financial statements. For instance, the Singer Sewing Machine Company did not issue annual reports, information regarding the company's affairs being given orally at the annual stockholders' meetings. As late as 1927 the Royal Baking Powder Company had issued no financial statement whatsoever. In addition to the nonreporting companies, a number of large companies rendered their reports to the public well after the close of their fiscal year.

There were two basic reasons for management's slow progress in improving corporate financial reporting. First, managers did not consider public reports a matter of prime importance. Second, and more important, business executives were still inclined toward financial secrecy, principally because of their fear of assisting competitors.

Financial chicanery and business custom were also responsible for corporate secrecy. Unfortunately, there were still a few industrial directors and officers who practiced financial secrecy so as to profit in their stock market activities through the use of corporate information not available to others. While the motivation of management in such cases was clearly to deceive or mislead, in most instances of nondisclosure, it should be noted, corporate financial secrecy resulted primarily because it was simply a custom that had been handed down from generation to generation to tell as little as possible.

In addition, there were still few external restraints upon management's financial reporting practices. State corporation laws relating to corporate financial reports had not advanced much beyond the 19th-century stage. Federal law was still silent on industrial financial publicity, as it was assumed this was a state matter. Also, after 1914, public opinion was indifferent to the attempts to improve the financial reports of industrial companies. In particular, investors, the very group the reformers sought to protect, were usually satisfied with generalities and did not request detailed financial statistics.

Similarly, accounting practice placed few restrictions on industrial management. There was an inviting variety of alternatives approved by accountants and employed by business executives. For example, there still were many different theories of depreciation. No consensus yet existed as to the degree of ownership which warranted consolidation. Frequently, no distinction was made between operating income and other income. And a variety of methods pertaining to the recording of asset values persisted. Such accounting freedom unfortunately tempted a number of managements to inflate reported profits through questionable adjustments to surplus and profits. These adjustments were seldom revealed to the public.

Finally, the reformers were powerless to force their proposed financial reporting standards upon industrial management. Business executives, in the absence of regulatory restraints, held the balance of power vis-à-vis the would-be reformers. The efforts of the Investment Bankers Association were thwarted by its own membership, and the accounting profession was not yet willing to be truly independent. Even the New York Stock Exchange was unable to enforce its authority upon the recalcitrant listed companies.

Thus, as late as the 1920s, industrial management could ignore with impunity the demands for improved financial disclosure. The economic depression of 1930, the subsequent shift in the public's attitude toward business, the election of Franklin D. Roosevelt as President in 1932, and the passage of the Securities Acts of 1933 and 1934 brought this situation to an end. Henceforth, for most publicly owned industrial companies, the Securities and Exchange Commission became the final arbiter in matters of financial disclosure, not management.

THE SECURITIES ACT AND ITS AFTERMATH

On May 29, 1933, President Roosevelt requested Congress to enact a federal securities bill which would add "to the ancient rule of *caveat emptor,* the further doctrine, 'let the seller also beware.' " The President's bill proposed to put the burden of telling the whole truth on those connected with the sale of securities—corporate officers, investment bankers, and accountants. Congress responded to the President's request, and on May 27, 1933, Roosevelt signed into law the Securities Act—"an act to provide full and fair disclosure of the character of the securities sold in interstate and foreign commerce. . . ."

The Securities Act was originally administered by the Federal Trade Commission, but in 1934, the act was amended to provide for the creation of a special body—the Securities and Exchange Commission—to assume its administration. Specifically, the Securities and Exchange Commission's task was to regulate the degree of disclosure, financial and nonfinancial, associated with new public security offerings as well as to require reports from those companies whose securities were already traded on the public security markets. Furthermore, the Commission was given broad statutory authority to state accounting rules for registered companies and to enforce them.

In line with its power to prescribe accounting practices, the SEC quickly standardized the format of required financial statements it received. More important, the Commission issued, from time to time, a number of opinions on accounting principles to encourage the development of uniform standards and practices in major accounting questions.

These opinions, however, cover but a small number of accounting practices. In those cases where no opinion has been expressed by the Commission, its policy is to accept a registrant's accounting practice "if the points involved are such that there is a substantial authoritative support," which in most instances has meant acceptance by the accounting profession. So far, these opinions of the SEC, it should be noted, apply only to those publicly available, prescribed statements which registrants are required to file with the Commission. The management representations contained in periodic reports to stockholders have not yet been placed under the direct control of the Commission. However, the Commission will not permit registered companies to disclose information in their reports to stockholders which is different from that filed with the SEC.

Next, beginning in 1939 and continuing through 1958, the Committee on Accounting Procedure of the American Institute issued a series of 51 *Accounting Research Bulletins,* touching upon a number of accounting problems and procedures. The principal objective of the bulletins was "to narrow areas of difference and inconsistency in accounting practices, and to further the development and recognition of generally accepted accounting principles." Each bulletin's opinions and recommendations "would serve as criteria for determining the suitability of accounting practices reflected in financial statements and representations of commercial and industrial companies." The authority of the opinions set forth in these bulletins rested "upon their general acceptability" among accountants and business executives. In practice, however, the bulletins' authority has been greatly strengthened by the reliance placed upon them by the New York Stock Exchange and the Securities and Exchange Commission in determining the acceptability of any questionable accounting practice.

Today, the reports filed by corporations with the Securities and Exchange Commission and the national stock exchanges are perhaps the most comprehensive, reliable, and detailed financial statements available publicly anywhere in the world. The financial statements published in periodic reports to stockholders are almost as detailed.

In 1959, faced with the growing discontent over current financial, reporting practices and the increasing demand for more uniformity in accounting principles, the American Institute of Certified Public Accountants[2] dissolved its Committee on Accounting Procedure, the group that had issued the *Accounting Research Bulletins,* and created the Accounting Principles Board. This substitution was intended to

---

[2] The American Institute of Accountants was renamed the American Institute of Certified Public Accountants in 1957.

intensify efforts toward defining accounting "principles." The APB was provided with both an administrative director and the services of a research staff (the Accounting Research Division).

During its existence, the APB issued 31 *Opinions* and a number of research studies. However, in the early 1970s the APB came under increasing criticism for its slow progress in resolving the many outstanding accounting controversies. As noted in Chapter 1, in June 1973 the APB was dissolved and the Financial Accounting Standards Board took over the task of defining what constitutes generally accepted accounting principles.

Some predict that if the FASB cannot succeed in its task, it is quite possible that the government will promulgate accounting principles, as has been done in several European countries.

SUMMARY: EVOLVING STANDARDS AND LAGGING PRACTICE

The financial disclosure practices of modern American industrial management have nearly all developed since 1933. Yet modern standards have sprung from an earlier reaction to the secrecy which surrounded the financial affairs of most 19th-century manufacturing firms. This reaction, which began around 1900, is the historical base upon which recent developments rest. Improvements in reporting practices came principally as the result of continuing pressure from individuals outside the managerial group for improved corporate publicity. This nonmanagement group included such diverse characters as the so-called critics of big business and leaders of the public accounting profession, and set the evolving standards by which the public evaluated corporate financial disclosures. The tempo of these critics' activities varied directly with the public attitude toward business, increasing markedly during those periods when management had fallen from popular favor.

Persistently, management's financial reporting practices lagged far behind the externally set standards, since management favored corporate secrecy and the would-be reformers were powerless to force their recommendations upon managers. Eventually, because management generally had not voluntarily adjusted its financial reporting practices to society's evolving financial informational needs (as perceived by management's critics), amid the business disorder following the 1929 stock market collapse the federal government intervened in the field of corporate financial disclosure, in 1933.

Thereafter, some authoritative, but nevertheless permissive, accounting standards were developed by the SEC, CAP, and APB. To comply with these new standards, industrial management rapidly improved its financial reporting practices in a number of areas. Yet, in the meantime, the demand for fuller, more reliable, and more comparable financial data has again outstripped management practice and the expressed standards of the accounting profession.

Once more, the possibility of further government intervention in industrial reporting matters is imminent, principally because of the difficulty the accounting profession has had in its efforts to narrow the areas of difference in accounting principles and the resistance of some managements to the critics' demands for improved corporate financial disclosure. Whether or not it will be necessary to expand government authority in the area of industrial accounting practice will probably depend upon the acceptance by both management and its critics of the authority and contents of the pronouncements of the FASB, as well as the FASB's willingness and ability to resolve quickly the issues confronting it. In any case, the historical evaluation of acceptable standards of financial disclosure among American industrial firms is far from complete.

SUGGESTED FURTHER READING

CHATFIELD, MICHAEL. *Contemporary Studies in the Evolution of Accounting Thought.* Belmont, Calif.: Dickenson Publishing Co., 1968.
CHATFIELD, MICHAEL. *A History of Accounting Thought.* Hinsdale, Ill.: Dryden Press, 1974.
LITTLETON, A. C., and ZIMMERMAN, V. K. *Accounting Theory: Continuity and Change.* Englewood Cliffs, N.J.: Prentice-Hall, Inc., 1962.

PART II

Corporate Reporting Fundamentals

Chapter 3

BASIC CONCEPTS AND ACCOUNTING PRINCIPLES

Corporate reporting does not rest on one generally accepted theory of accounting. Rather, financial accounting decisions reflect a number of basic conventions which are more or less commonly accepted as useful guides to selecting appropriate accounting policies. These conventions have grown out of the experiences of accountants and business executives in trying to measure and communicate the results of operations and the financial condition of corporations as well as the theoretical works of accounting scholars. In practice, accounting conventions seem to be utilitarian. Their degree of acceptance stems from their usefulness to those making decisions involving accounting data. This usefulness is determined in turn by the convention's congruence with the social and economic conditions, needs, and concepts of the time. Clearly, as these factors change over time, so must accounting conventions.

This chapter briefly describes a number of basic conventions. Not everyone will agree with this list. Some may argue certain conventions should be combined or dropped. Others might try to break the list into categories which distinguish between postulates and principles. Many of these proposals have merit. The purpose of our list, however, is simply to cover the basic conventions that seem to be accepted to some degree that are included in a number of the outstanding books on this subject and statements on accounting's basic concepts issued by such groups as the APB and the American Accounting Association, which is the principal professional organization for academic accountants.

Each of these conventions will be discussed in greater detail in later chapters when the accounting principle most relevant to the convention is discussed. For example, the accounting for fixed asset chapter will include an expanded discussion of the historical cost convention and some of the alternative approaches proposed by accounting theorists.

Business Entity

what

why

The business entity convention is that financial statements are for a business entity which is separate and distinct from its owners. What happens to its owners affairs is irrelevant. The principal reason for this convention is that it defines the area of interest of the accountant and sets the limits on the possible objectives and contents of financial reports. Consequently, the analysis of business transactions involving costs and revenue is expressed in terms of the changes in a firm's financial condition. Similarly, the assets and liabilities devoted to business activities are entity assets and liabilities. Also, since business activity is carried on between particular firms, financial statements must clearly identify the specific companies involved. This separation of ownership and management also recognizes the fiduciary responsibility to the stockholders of those who manage the business.

The boundaries of the business entity are sometimes difficult to establish. Typically the accountant defines these boundaries in terms of the firm's economic activities and administrative control, rather than legal relationships. For example, consolidated financial statements often present the financial condition and results of operations of different entities with common ownership in a single set of statements, thus treating the various entities as a single economic unit, even though they consist of several legal entities. Here the accountant is trying to present useful statements which look beyond the legal relationships to the underlying economic and managerial relationships. The legal considerations are relevant only insofar as they define or influence economic activities and managerial control.

An alternative approach proposed to defining the boundaries of the accounting entity is to define it in terms of the conomic interests of the statement users, rather than the economic activities of the unit. In practice accounting reports may reflect to some degree this concept of the entity.

The entity concept applies equally to incorporated, unincorporated, small, and big businesses. In the case of incorporated, widely held, publicly owned companies, such as General Motors, it is not difficult to keep separate the affairs of the business and its owners. However, in the case of small unincorporated businesses where the owners exert day-to-day control over the affairs of the business and personal and business assets are intermingled, the definition of the business entity is more difficult for financial—as well as managerial—accounting purposes.

The entity concept recognizes the long-standing belief that management has a stewardship responsibility to owners. Owners entrust funds to management, and management is expected to use these funds wisely. Periodically, management must report to the owners the results of management's actions. Financial statements are one of the principal means whereby management fulfills this reporting responsibility. In the case of owner-manager businesses, the stewardship responsibility is assumed to exist principally because of the analytical value of separating how well the owner-managers did as investors in contrast to managers.

Going Concern

Unless evidence suggests otherwise, those preparing accounting statements for a business entity assume it will continue operations into the foreseeable future. This convention reflects the normal expectation of management and investors. So that readers of financial statements will not be misled, the statements of business entities with limited lives must clearly indicate the terminal data and type of liquidation involved (i.e., receiver's statements, etc.). Otherwise, the reader will assume that the accounts are based on the presumption that the enterprise has an indefinitely long life.

Accounting emphasizes and reflects the continuing nature of business activity. For example, the accountant expects that the company in the normal course of business will receive the full value of most of its accounts receivable. Accordingly, the accountant records these items at their face value, less some deductions for anticipated bad debts, rather than at current liquidation value. Similarly, the expenditures made to create finished goods inventories are recorded as assets, since the accountant assumes the inventories will be disposed of later in the normal course of operations. However, the continuity assumption does not imply that the future will be the same as the past.

The going-concern convention leads to the corollary that individual financial statements are part of a continuous, interrelated series of statements. This further implies that data communicated are tentative.

Not all accounting theorists support the common interpretation of the continuity convention. For example, one author claims that the continuity assumption underlying accounting is misleading since rather than being an assumption it is a prediction. Another views the firm as being in a continual state of orderly liquidation.

Monetary

Accounting is a measurement process dealing only with those events which can be measured in monetary terms. This convention reflects the fact that money is the common denominator used in business to measure the exchangeability of goods, services, and capital. Obviously, financial statements should indicate the money unit used.

The monetary convention leads to one of the limitations of accounting. Accounting, for example, does not record or communicate the state of the president's health, the attitude of the labor force, or the relative advantage of competitive products. Consequently, the most important aspects of a business may not be reflected in the financial statements.

Another potential limitation of the monetary convention is that it does not distinguish between the purchasing power of monetary units in different periods. This can become a significant problem when trying to issue financial statements in times of inflation. For example, the expenses of the current period may include dollars that are spent currently and dollars spent in earlier periods when the dollar purchased more goods and services.

Accounting Period

For decision-making purposes, management and investors need periodic "test readings" of the progress of their business. Accounting recognizes this need and breaks the flow of business activity into a series of reporting or fiscal periods. These periods are usually 12 months in length. Most companies also issue quarterly or semiannual statements to stockholders. These are considered to be *interim,* and essentially different from annual statements. For management use, statements covering shorter periods such as a month or week may be prepared. Irrespective of the length of the period, the statements must indicate the period covered.

The success of a business can only be determined accurately upon liquidation. Consequently, the periodic financial statements are at best estimates which are subject to change as future events develop.

Breaking business activity into a series of discrete segments creates a number of accounting problems. For example, given the uncertainties surrounding the life of an asset and its scrap value, how should the cost of the asset be allocated to specific periods? How should the income and costs associated with long-term contracts covering several accounting periods be treated? Such questions must be resolved in the light of the particular circumstances. There is no easy, general solution. The accountant and business executive must rely upon their experience, knowledge, and judgment to come to the appropriate answer.

The timing of the accounting period will depend upon the nature of the business. For most companies the accounting period runs from January 1 to December 31. Some companies use a different period, principally because their yearly business cycle does not conform to the calendar year. For example, typically the annual statements of department stores are more meaningful if their fiscal period ends January 31. This is a time when inventories are low and the Christmas selling peak is over.

Consistency

The consistency convention requires that similar transactions be reported in a consistent fashion from period to period. Clearly, for example, comparison of interperiod results would be difficult if a company changed its depreciation policy each year. The consistency concept is not inflexible, however. Changes in accounting policies are appropriate when justified by changing circumstances.

Accountants place considerable emphasis on consistency. When expressing an audit opinion the accountant notes whether or not the statements were prepared "on a basis consistent with that of the preceding year." If changes were made, he notes these in his opinion and insists that the nature and impact of these changes be fully disclosed.

The consistency concept does not necessarily mean uniformity exists among the accounting practices of affiliated business units or even within a single company. For example, one unit may value inventory on the so-called Lifo basis whereas another may use the Fifo basis. Similarly, a single unit might use both methods to value different parts of its inventory. In either case the policy should be disclosed and consistently followed.

The consistency concept does not imply uniformity in the treatment of particular items among different independent companies. One of the characteristics of American accounting practice is the accounting diversity among different companies, all of which meets the criterion of "generally accepted accounting principles."

Historical Cost

For accounting purposes, business transactions are normally measured in terms of the actual prices or costs at the time the transaction was consummated. This convention applies to both the initial recording and subsequent reporting of transactions. While agreeing with the need to record historical costs initially, some influential accountants argue accounting would be "more useful" if estimates of current and future values were substituted for historical costs under certain conditions. The extent to which cost and value should be reflected in the accounts is central to much of the current accounting controversy.

The market value of assets may change with time. Typically, accounting does not recognize these changes in value. Thus, the cost of assets shown on financial statements seldom reflects their current market value. Some believe that the historical cost convention flows from the going-concern concept, which implies that since the business is not going to sell its fixed assets as such there is little point in revaluing assets to reflect current values. In addition, for practical reasons, the accountant prefers the reporting of actual costs to less certain estimates which are difficult to verify. By using historical costs, the accountant's already difficult task is not further complicated by the need to keep additional records of changing market values.

There is little disagreement among theorists that accounting should record the original cost value of a transaction initially. However, not all believe that this value should be used to measure expenses, to determine income, or asset values over time. For example, one proposal is that fixed assets be reported at their replacement cost and that the related expense arising from their use be based on this value. Another suggestion is that appraisals of current market values ought to be the basis for recording asset values. A third alternative suggestion is that the current cash equivalent value be used. The proponents of these recommendations argue that the going-concern assumption does not necessarily require that historical costs be the basis for accounting measurement; appraisal or replacement costs may be determined in a more objective fashion than historical costs; and the data communicated to statement users is more useful for such purposes as appraising management's use of the firm's resources or valuing securities.

While accounting is still based on historical costs, these proposals are slowly beginning to influence corporate reporting. For example, the SEC required in 1976 that replacement cost data be included in the footnotes accompanying financial statements in 10-K filings.

In practice, there are a number of modifications to the historical cost concept. For example, under special conditions, inventory may be reported at market values if this value is less than the historical cost. Assets acquired for stock are recorded at the estimated market value of the stock exchanged. Mutual funds and some pension funds whose assets consist almost entirely of securities report the market value of their investments, taking the gain or loss into income at the end of each reporting period. Similarly, donated assets may be carried at their appraised value at the time of acquisition.

The definition of the content of cost, irrespective of whether the historical cost convention or one of the alternative proposals is used, poses problems. For example, issues arise as to what cost elements should be included in the cost of assets created by the company, rather than bought from outsiders. Or, if an asset is acquired through a swap of assets other than cash, the value to be placed on the asset given up or received may be unclear.

Realization

For accounting purposes, revenue is realized during the period either when services or goods are exchanged for a valuable considera- /when tion or when the amount of the revenue can be verified with a reasonable degree of objectivity. In practice, no one test, such as sale or delivery, has proven satisfactory, given the diversity of industry's production, sale, and credit practices. Consequently, the timing of revenue realization ranges from the act of production, in the case of gold mining operations, to the receipt of cash, in the case of some installment sales contracts. Clearly, the application of the realization concept depends upon the circumstances of each case.

Some authorities claim revenue is earned during the process of operations, rather than, say, entirely at the time of sale. All activities related to production and sales contribute to the final product and, hence, to revenue, they argue. Accordingly, they state that accounting should recognize revenue in proportion to the costs accumulated to date of such activities. In practice, one method of accounting for long-term construction contracts covering several accounting periods does recognize revenue as it is earned by permitting revenues to be recognized in the proportion the estimated progress bears to the total job, provided it is anticipated that the contract can be completed and the originally estimated profit obtained. In the absence of firm contracts or reasonable certainty as to the course of future events, accounting practice does not normally recognize revenue during production.

Some accountant theorists advocate that revenue should be recognized when asset values change due to accretion, such as occurs when timber grows or whiskey ages. This is a similar view to that proposed by the production supporters, but it does not require a transaction to occur before revenue is recognized. In contrast, accretion revenue would be recognized through the process of comparing inventory values at different points in time. This view of revenue may be acceptable in economic theory, but it is generally rejected in accounting practice because of the difficulty in determining asset values prior to sale and the tentativeness of the figures so derived.

Matching of Costs and Revenues

Accounting income or profit is the net result of the accountant's trying to match the related costs and revenues of the period. This process can be described as matching "effort and accomplishments," where costs measure effort, and revenue the related accomplishments. Often this ideal cannot be achieved, since costs cannot be easily identified with specific current or anticipated revenues.

The matching of costs and revenues may require deferring recognition of expenses and revenues to future periods. For example, cash may be spent today for new equipment which is expected to generate revenues for the next five years. In this case, the accountant will defer recognizing the cash outlay as an expense until the expected revenues materialize. At this time the costs and the revenues would be matched. In the meantime, however, the unexpired cost would be reported as an asset (i.e., capitalized). Whether or not costs should be deferred and, if deferred, over what time period are difficult questions to resolve in practice.

The matching process is usually achieved through application of the accrual method of accounting rather than the cash method. The cash method of accounting records cash receipts and disbursements and focuses on the changes in the Cash account. The accrual method seeks to measure changes in the owner's equity during the accounting period. Revenues are realized noncapital transactions that result in an increase in owner's equity. In contrast, expenses are expired costs that decrease owner's equity which are associated with the period or the period's revenues. The difference between revenues and expenses is net income for the period. These changes in owner's equity may not necessarily result in changes in the Cash account. For example, a $100 sale on credit will increase accounts receivable and owner's equity. The accrual method recognizes the fact that the service has been performed and a valuable asset received. If a cash method was being used, no record of the event would be made until the customer's $100 cash was received.

The accrual method also leads to the accounting practice of recognizing costs as expenses when they expire (i.e., lose their future benefit generation value), rather than when they are incurred. In addition, the accrual method requires that costs be recognized as incurred when the firm receives goods and services, even though the actual billing or payment date is sometime in the future.

Dual Aspect

The dual aspect convention recognizes that someone has a claim on all the resources owned by the business. These resources are called "assets." The creditor's claims against these assets are usually referred to as "liabilities." The owners' claims are called either "stockholders' equity," "owners' equity," or "proprietorship." Consequently, since the total assets of the business are claimed by somebody, it follows that:

$$\text{Assets} = \text{Liabilities} + \text{Stockholders' Equity}$$

Assets represent expected future economic benefits to which the reporting entity holds the right and which have been acquired through a current or past transaction. An asset can represent an expected future economic benefit for several reasons:

1. The asset may be used to acquire other assets. Cash is the principal example of an asset that derives its value from its purchasing power.
2. The asset represents a claim upon another entity for money—for example, accounts receivable, which are amounts owed to the company for credit sales.
3. The asset can be converted to cash or a money claim. Finished goods inventories that will be sold in the normal course of business are an example.
4. The asset has potential benefits, rights, or services which will result in the entity earning something from its use in some future accounting period. Such assets include items like buildings and raw materials.

The term liabilities may be defined as the entity's obligations to convey assets or perform services to a person, firm, or other organization outside of the entity at some time in the future. These obligations require future settlement and represent claims on the entity's assets by nonownership interests. Accounts payable to trade creditors, bonds payable, and taxes payable are examples of liabilities.

Liabilities also include so-called deferred credits. These do not represent clear-cut claims on the entity. They result from the need to recognize some expenses currently in order to get a "proper" matching of costs and revenues. The offsetting entity to the expense item is a reserve balance that is reported as a liability. Examples of deferred credits are reserves set up for tax expenses currently that may or may not be paid in the future, but which accounting standards require to be recognized now.

Stockholders' equity is thought to represent ownership interest in the entity. It is a residual item. It is the excess of the entity's total assets over its liabilities.

Clearly, the measurement of owner's equity in the accounting equation represents no problem once liabilities and assets have been defined and measured. The problem arises in describing the nature of this residual amount. Certainly, it is not the market value of the firm to the owners. Some of the principal theories as to the nature of ownership equity are discussed below.

The *proprietary theory* regards the proprietor as the focus of interest in the accounting equation. Assets are owned by the proprietor, and liabilities are his (or her) obligations. The basic accounting equation is: Assets − Liabilities = Proprietorship Interest. The proprietorship interest implies that liabilities are negative assets, since the proprietor is thought to own all of the assets and the goal of accounting is to determine the net value of these assets to the proprietor.

The *entity theory* regards the business entity as being separate from the wealth and personalities of its owners. The assets of the entity are the entity's assets, and against these assets are equity claims by creditors and owners, who are regarded as the principal beneficiaries of the business' activities. This view of the entity is probably a better description of the typical corporate-investor relationship than the proprietorship theory. The entity theory's basic accounting equation is:

$$Assets = Equities$$

The *enterprise theory* regards the business-owner relationship in a similar fashion to the *entity theory*, but it does not hold that beneficiaries of business activity are limited to the creditors and owners. It regards the entity as being operated for the benefit of society as a whole. As a result, the capital contributed and earnings retained in a business are thought of as benefiting more than just the stockholders, since the capital may produce benefits for society. So, society has an interest in the so-called net worth of a company.

A few accounting authors argue that the traditional accounting equation should be changed to reflect current thinking in finance and business.

One such aproach suggests that contemporary financial accounting practice is becoming increasingly concerned with maintaining a continuing record of capital invested in an enterprise from a two-sided point of view: the *sources* and *uses* of funds, with funds broadly defined as all financial resources. This concern, it is argued, is in line with modern financial theory and practice, which tends to view assets as funds invested within the business, and liabilities and net worth as financial resources obtained from sources external to the firm. As a result, the balance sheet can be regarded as a report, at an instant of time, of the status of funds obtained from sources external to the business and the items in which these funds (and those generated by drawing down other assets) are invested.

Those who support this point of view express the dual aspect of transactions in terms of sources and uses of funds. Since for each use of funds there must be a matching source and for each source a use, the basic accounting equation suggested is:

$$Items \text{ in Which Capital Is Invested (assets) } =$$
$$External \text{ Sources of Capital (equities)}$$

Accounting systems are designed so that events are recorded in terms of their influence on assets, liabilities, or owners' equity. Every event has a dual aspect. For example, assume John Smith invested $5,000 in a new business; the accounting entry would recognize the $5,000 asset of the business and John Smith's claim upon this asset:

$$\text{Assets, \$5,000} = \text{Stockholders' Equity, \$5,000}$$

Now, if the company borrowed $1,000 from the bank, the firm's accounting statement would be:

Assets		Liabilities and Stockholders' Equity	
Cash	$6,000	Bank loan payable	$1,000
		Stockholders' equity	5,000
Total	$6,000	Total	$6,000

Next assume the business used $2,000 of its cash to acquire some inventory, the new statement would be:

Assets		Liabilities and Stockholders' Equity	
Cash	$4,000	Bank loan payable	$1,000
Inventory	2,000	Stockholders' equity	5,000
Total	$6,000	Total	$6,000

Thus, the *double-entry* system requires two entries for each event. Other systems are possible, such as a single-entry system, but the double-entry system is the most widely used.

Reliability of Evidence

Accountants recording events rely as much as is possible upon objective, verifiable documentary evidence, in contrast to the subjective judgments of a person who may be biased. Acceptable evidence includes such items as approved sales or purchase invoices. This desire to base decisions on objective evidence is one of the principal supports of the historical cost convention, although as noted earlier some of the proponents of alternative approaches believe these approaches can be objective also.

In practice, accountants do not apply the absolute standard of objective, verifiable evidence. Many major decisions, such as the allocation of costs between periods, must be based on reasonable estimates after considering all of the relevant facts. In many instances it is not feasible for an auditor to verify the recording of every event. As a result, he bases his opinion in large part upon his assessment of management's internal controls, which are the measures adopted by management to safeguard assets, check the reliability and accuracy of data, and encourage adherence to operating policies and programs.

The definition of what constitutes an objective measurement is not a settled matter. At least four different approaches have been identified among accounting writers. One author defines objective measurements as being impersonal and outside of the mind of the person making the measurement. Another thinks of it as being based on the consensus of qualified experts. A third considers a measurement to be objective if it is based on verifiable evidence. The fourth approach rates objectiveness in terms of the narrowness of the statistical dispersion around the mean measurement after results are obtained by different measurers. The narrower the dispersion, the less subjective is the mean considered to be.

A convention closely related to the reliability convention proposed by some is the standard that accounting statements should be free from bias, which means that the facts have been impartially determined and reported and they contain no built-in bias.

Disclosure

The disclosure convention requires that accounting reports disclose enough information so that they are not misleading to those readers who are careful and reasonably well informed in financial matters. Special disclosure is made of unusual items, changes in expectations, significant contractual relations, and new activities. The disclosure can be in the body of the financial statements, the auditor's opinion, or the notes to the statements.

The disclosure convention has received increasing attention in recent years. For example, financial analysts have been pressing for fuller disclosure of sales and profits by divisions and major product lines. It is anticipated that the pressure for fuller disclosure will continue. In general, while management has cooperated with these demands, it has refused to disclose information of a "competitive" nature. The question of what constitutes "competitive" information has yet to be settled, however.

Conservatism

The conservatism convention prescribes that when choosing between two permissible accounting alternatives, some added weight be given to the alternative that leads to the lower current income and assets or highest liability figures. If not carefully applied, this convention can lead to abuses which result in unnecessary or dishonest understatement. Also, by understating income in one period, income in another period will be overstated. Thus, the application of this convention requires considerable judgment, especially since an accountant may be sued if he (or she) condones grossly misleading statements.

A number of accounting theorists reject conservatism as a legitimate accounting convention. In their opinion it leads to a deliberate misstatement, which can be misleading to statement users and as such has no place in accounting. Also, they believe that statement issuers should provide unbiased data so that statement users can evaluate the risks of, say, investing in the issuer company. If conservatism is applied, the issuer substitutes his (or her) evaluation of risk for the user's evaluation, which might have been different to that of the issuers if the user had had unbiased data. Finally, they argue the convention of conservatism in practice is capricious. There are no uniform approaches to its application.

Materiality

Accounting conventions apply only to material and significant items. Inconsequential items can be dealt with expediently. However, in applying this convention, care must be taken to see that the cumulative effect of treating a series of immaterial items does not materially alter the total statements. Whether or not an item is immaterial depends on judgment and the particular circumstances. One common test of materiality is: Would the investment decision of a reasonably well-informed user of the statements be altered if the item was treated differently? If the decision would change, the item is material.

Substance over Form

In order to reflect economic activities, accounting emphasizes the economic substance of events even though the legal form may differ from the economic substance and suggest a different treatment.

Application

The application of these conventions in specific instances is left to the judgment of management and the accountants. The relative importance of these conventions changes from decision to decision. Also, in any one instance, two or more conventions may be in conflict. The problem facing the accountant or business executive is to select those conventions most relevant to the facts of his or her situation and the particular needs of the dominant user of the statements. Whether or not a convention leads to a feasible solution will also determine its relevance.

SUGGESTED FURTHER READING

ACCOUNTING PRINCIPLES BOARD. "Basic Concepts and Accounting Principles Underlying Financial Statements of Business Enterprises." *Statement of the Accounting Principles Board No. 4.* New York, 1970.

AMERICAN ACCOUNTING ASSOCIATION. *A Statement of Basic Accounting Theory.* Evanston, Ill., 1966.

CHAMBERS, R. J. *Accounting, Evaluation and Economic Behavior.* Englewood Cliffs, N.J.: Prentice-Hall, Inc., 1966.

EDWARDS, E. O., and BELL, P. W. *The Theory and Measurement of Business Income.* Berkeley and Los Angeles: University of California Press, 1961.

GRADY, PAUL. "Inventory of Generally Accepted Accounting Principles for Business Enterprises." *Accounting Research Study No. 7.* New York: American Institute of Certified Public Accountants, 1965.

HENDRIKSEN, ELDON S. *Accounting Theory.* 3d ed. Homewood, Ill.: Richard D. Irwin, Inc., 1977.

MOONITZ, MAURICE. "The Basic Postulates of Accounting." *Accounting Research Study No. 1.* New York: American Institute of Certified Public Accountants, 1961.

PATON, W. A., and LITTLETON, A. C. *An Introduction to Corporate Accounting Standards.* Evanston, Ill.: American Accounting Association, 1962.

SPROUSE, ROBERT T., and MOONITZ, MAURICE. "A Tentative Set of Broad Accounting Principles for Business Enterprises." *Accounting Research Study No. 3.* New York: American Institute of Certified Public Accountants, 1962.

CASES

CASE 3–1. OMEGA NOVELTY SHOP
Economic versus Accounting Concepts

Paul Stone submitted to the Research Division of an eastern business school the most recent annual profit and loss statement for his retail novelty shop shown in Exhibit 1.

EXHIBIT 1

OMEGA NOVELTY SHOP
Profit and Loss Statement

Gross sales	$104,850.48	
Less: Returns and allowances to customers	4,500.00	
Net sales		$100,350.48
Net inventory of merchandise at beginning of year	$ 50,258.79	
Plus: Purchases of merchandise at billed cost	74,762.67	
Inward freight, express, and parcel postage	428.61	
Gross cost of merchandise handled	$125,450.07	
Less: Cash discounts taken	1,276.95	
Net cost of merchandise handled	$124,173.12	
Less: Net inventory of merchandise at end of year	55,245.84	
Net cost of merchandise sold		68,927.28
Gross margin		$ 31,423.20
Expenses:		
Total salaries and wages	$ 9,480.39	
Advertising	1,702.56	
Boxes and wrappings	556.41	
Office supplies and postage	1,220.73	
Taxes, insurance, repairs, and depreciation of real estate	2,616.30	
Heat, light, and power	515.79	
Taxes	342.00	
Insurance	863.31	
Depreciation of store equipment	660.00	
Interest on borrowed capital	178.80	
Miscellaneous expense	1,533.63	
Income taxes	1,125.30	
Total Expenses		20,795.22
Net Profit		$ 10,627.98

On writing to Mr. Stone for supplementary information, the division learned that of the net profit of $10,627.98 shown on his statement, Mr. Stone had withdrawn $4,500. He did not make a charge for his own services as manager, but up to a few years ago he had been employed in a similar capacity in another store at a salary of $5,400 a year. Mr. Stone stated that he owned his store building, which had a rental value of $3,900 a year. From the balance sheets submitted for this firm, the division computed the net worth of the business exclusive of real estate to be $98,677.98. Interest on this sum at 6 percent, which Mr. Stone stated to be the local rate on reasonably secure long-time investments, amounted to $5,920.68.

On the basis of these additional data, the division adjusted the profit and loss statement for the Stone store and sent it back as shown in Exhibit 2.

EXHIBIT 2

OMEGA NOVELTY SHOP

Profit and Loss Statement

Merchandise Statement

Gross sales	$104,850.48		
Less: Returns and allowances to customers	4,500.00		
Net sales		$100,350.48	100.00%
Net inventory of merchandise at beginning of year	$ 50,258.79		
Plus: Purchases of merchandise at billed cost	74,762.67		
Inward freight, express, and parcel postage	428.61		
Gross cost of merchandise handled	$125,450.07		
Less: Cash discounts taken	1,276.95		
Net cost of merchandise handled	$124,173.12		
Less: Net inventory of merchandise at end of year.............................	55,245.84		
Net cost of merchandise sold		68,927.28	68.69
Gross margin		$ 31,423.20	31.31%

Expense Statement

Proprietor's salary	$ 5,400.00		5.38%
All other salaries and wages	9,480.39		9.45
Total Salaries and Wages	$ 14,880.39		14.83%
Advertising	1,702.56		1.70
Boxes and wrappings	556.41		0.55
Office supplies and postage	1,220.73		1.21
Rent	3,900.00		3.89
Heat, light, and power	515.79		0.51
Taxes	342.00		0.34
Insurance	863.31		0.86
Depreciation of store equipment	660.00		0.66

EXHIBIT 2 (continued)

Interest on borrowed capital	$ 178.80		
Interest on owned capital invested in the business	5,920.68		
Total Interest	6,099.48		6.08
Miscellaneous expense	1,533.63		1.53
Total Expenses		$ 32,274.30	32.16%

Net Gain Statement

Net loss		$ 851.10	0.85%
Interest and rentals earned:			
Interest on owned capital invested in the business		$ 5,920.68	
Rent of owned store building	$3,900.00		
Less: Expense on owned store building (taxes, insurance, repairs, depreciation, interest on mortgages)	2,616.30	1,283.70	
Total Interest and Rentals		7,204.38	
Net gain		$ 6,353.28	
Provision for federal and state income taxes	$ 1,125.30		
Withdrawals	4,500.00	5,625.30	
Surplus for the Year		$ 727.98	

After receiving this adjusted profit and loss statement, Mr. Stone wrote the following letter to the division:

Dear Sirs·

I have received a copy of my most recent profit and loss statement as adjusted by you, and I am at a loss to understand some of the changes you have made.

For instance, the statement which I sent you showed a net profit of $10,627.98 but the copy which you have returned to me shows a net loss of $851.10. I notice that you have charged $5,400 as my salary. I do not draw any regular salary from the business, and since I am in business for myself I consider that I am not working for a salary but for profits. Also you have shown a rental expense of $3,900. Since I own the building, I consider that the item of rent is adequately taken care of by the expenses incurred in connection with the building, such as taxes, insurance, and so on. Furthermore, you have shown an expense of $5,920.68 for interest on owned capital. I have worked hard to put this business in a position where I would not have to borrow money, but if I have to charge interest on my own capital, I do not see where I am any better off, according to your version of affairs, than if I were continually in debt to banks and wholesalers.

In short, it seems to me that your adjustment of my statement amounts merely to shifting money from one pocket to another and calling it salary, rent, or interest, as the case may be; whereas what I am really interested in is the profit that I make by being in business for myself rather than working for somebody else.

An explanation from you will be appreciated.

Yours very truly,

PAUL STONE

Questions

1. Did Mr. Stone make a profit from his novelty business during the current year? How much, if any? How may the difference between Mr. Stone's computation of profits and that of the Research Division be explained?
2. Was Mr. Stone a successful business executive?
3. Should Mr. Stone have sold his novelty business?
4. What were the incentives which motivated Mr. Stone?

CASE 3–2. THE GETTY FORMULA
Different Concepts of Value

On June 16, 1960, George F. Getty II, president of Tidewater Oil Company, addressed a regular luncheon meeting of the New York Society of Security Analysts. According to Mr. Getty, the appraised value of Tidewater Oil Company can be estimated by using the following generally accepted method:

1. Proven and developed crude oil and liquids reserves are valued at $1 per barrel.
2. Proven and developed natural gas reserves are valued at $0.05 per MCF (thousand cubic feet).
3. Probable reserves of liquids and natural gas are appraised at one fourth of the unit values above.
4. Refining, marketing, transportation, and other miscellaneous assets, including investments and advances, are assessed at net book value.
5. Add net working capital.
6. Deduct long-term debt and preferred stock.

The appraised value of Tidewater's common stock at December 31, 1959, determined by this method is about $80 per share. This appraised value of $80 per share is four times the current market value.[1]

---

[1] The price of Tidewater common was $24 on December 31, 1959; on June 16, 1960, it was $17.50.

This case uses Mr. Getty's formula (1) to explore the meaning and significance of "value" to majority and minority owners, potential owners, managers, security analysts, and accountants; and (2) to establish the usefulness of accounting information in measuring "value." To emphasize the importance of "value," information about a proposed merger between Tidewater and the Skelly Oil Company is included.

Tidewater Oil Company

Tidewater Oil Company, a medium-sized, domestic, integrated firm operated in all phases of the oil business. The company was engaged in exploration, development, and production of crude oil and natural gas. It operated an extensive transportation system consisting of pipelines and a fleet of tankers. Tidewater's refinery capacity placed it 11th in a list of top United States refiners. The eastern refinery, located in Delaware, was generally regarded as the most advanced in the world. Tidewater also engaged in retail distribution, selling its products through retail outlets principally on the east and west coasts of the United States.

Instead of cash dividends Tidewater had followed the practice, since 1955, of declaring a 5 percent stock dividend each year.

After 1952, Tidewater was especially active in finding new oil and gas reserves. From 1953 to 1959 its proven reserves of petroleum liquids (crude oil and natural gas liquids) increased 30 percent, to 693.3 million barrels, from 533.3 million barrels, or more than twice the rate of increase for the industry. Proven natural gas reserves increased even more dramatically, to 3,510 billion cubic feet from 1,674 billion cubic feet, nearly four times the rate of increase in the industry. In addition, the company owned probable reserves of 134 million barrels of crude and 424 billion cubic feet of natural gas.

During 1959, Tidewater earned $34 million from sales of $600 million. Tidewater's 1959 balance sheet is shown in Exhibit 1. Information concerning the earnings, dividends, and market price of Tidewater and other selected oil companies during several recent years is presented in Exhibit 2.

Proposed Merger with Skelly Oil Company

The merger negotiations between Tidewater and Skelly Oil Company which began during April 1959 gave rise to considerable discussion regarding the value of Tidewater stock. Skelly, one of the smaller integrated domestic companies, was engaged in the production, refining, pipeline transportation, and marketing of petroleum products. With crude production about 50 percent greater than its refinery capacity, it seemed a natural complement to Tidewater, which had excess refinery capacity and whose operations were hampered by import quotas on foreign oil. The Tidewater and Skelly marketing organizations were also complementary, since Skelly's outlets were concentrated in the middle, southwest, and southern states. Combining the two firms would help to balance their refining operations and lead to national distribution.

In contrast to Tidewater, Skelly had paid a cash dividend of $1.80 in each of the last five years.

EXHIBIT 1

TIDEWATER OIL COMPANY
Consolidated Balance Sheet
As of December 31, 1959
(in thousands)

Assets

Cash	$ 36,183	
U.S. government securities	390	
Accounts receivable	74,560	
Inventories*	61,618	
Deferred charges	9,955	
Total Current Assets		$182,706
Investments and advances		15,476
Plant, property, and equipment, net†		658,231
Total Assets		$856,413

Equities

Accounts payable	$ 50,553	
Accrued taxes payable	15,734	
Dividends payable	739	
Current portion of long-term debt	25,973	
Total Current Equities		$ 92,999
Long-term debt		284,751
Preferred stock	$ 62,393	
Less: Preferred stock in treasury	697	61,696
Common stock	$139,594	
Less: Common stock in treasury	2,901	$136,693
Paid-in capital	69,298	
Retained earnings	210,976	416,967
Total Equities		$856,413

* Crude oil and products, $42,409; materials and supplies, $19,209.
† These items include:

	Gross	Depreciation	Net
Production	$ 545,878	$324,542	$221,336
Transportation	141,943	42,654	99,289
Manufacturing	331,250	101,347	229,903
Marketing	142,930	46,831	96,099
Miscellaneous	12,648	1,044	11,604
Totals	$1,174,649	$516,418	$658,231

Source: Adapted from Tidewater *Annual Report*, 1959.

EXHIBIT 2

Tidewater and Other Selected Oil Companies (earnings, dividends, and market price, 1955–1959)

IS ON PAR VALUE

	1959	1958	1957	1956	1955
Tidewater:					
Earnings per share	$2.23	−$0.03	$2.31	$2.58	$2.53
Cash flow per share	6.67	3.94	7.08	5.89	6.19
Dividends per share	5% stock	5% stock	5% stock	5% stock	5% stock
Price range:					
High	28⅛	27⅛	38⅜	41⅜	38¾
Low	20	18⅛	17⅝	28⅝	20
Continental:					
Earnings per share	$2.85	$2.40	$2.38	$2.65	$2.38
Cash flow per share	4.34	3.99	3.82	3.97	3.71
Dividends per share	1.70	1.60	1.60	1.52½	1.42½
Price range:					
High	69¾	64	70¼	69	52½
Low	45⅛	38⅝	41½	27	35
Phillips:					
Earnings per share	$3.05	$2.45	$2.80	$2.77	$2.78
Cash flow per share	6.61	6.14	6.40	6.03	5.47
Dividends per share	1.70	1.70	1.70	1.60	1.50
Price range:					
High	52¾	49¼	53¼	56¾	41⅞
Low	41	36⅜	35⅜	39⅜	34¾
Pure:					
Earnings per share	$3.32	$3.35	$4.13	$4.26	$4.05
Cash flow per share	6.56	6.40	7.14	7.14	6.93
Dividends per share	1.60	1.60	1.60	1.60	1.51¼
Price range:					
High	48⅛	45	48⅞	51¾	41½
Low	34⅛	29	29¾	37¾	32
Skelly:					
Earnings per share	$4.87	$4.82	$6.40	$5.93	$5.61
Cash flow per share	9.74	10.35	11.87	11.29	10.63
Dividends per share	1.80	1.80	1.80	1.80	1.80
Price range:					
High	74¼	72⅜	80¾	73	57½
Low	50¼	48	49	52⅞	46¼
Sun:					
Earnings per share	$3.48	$2.60	$3.86	$4.56	$3.89
Cash flow per share	7.76	7.54	8.88	9.16	8.90
Dividends per share	0.95	0.92½	0.87½	0.82½	0.76
Price range:					
High	62⅝	63⅞	71½	71½	62½
Low	52⅞	54½	61⅛	57¾	52¼
Mean P/E ratio for the industry	11.16	17.1	11.8	14.0	13.7

Sources: *Moody's Industrial Manual;* Standard & Poor's *Industry Surveys.*

As the merger talks progressed, joint committees representing the two companies were established. These committees, together with technical experts and appraisers, examined all phases of the two firms' operations. Earnings were recalculated on comparable bases for several past years and forecasts of operations and earnings were prepared. Reserves were valued and stock prices were compared. Nevertheless, D. H. Miller, the president of Skelly, stated that:

After several months of studying and comparing asset values of the companies . . . it became apparent that there was a wide difference between the companies in their estimates of the relative value of the common stocks.[2]

During October, negotiations were terminated. In commenting on the failure of the companies to agree on merger terms, George Getty noted that the indicated exchange ratio of Tidewater to Skelly stock, when based on appraised value, was three for two, while market prices suggested a ratio closer to three for one. According to Getty, this "created a gulf between us that appraisals and so forth could not bridge."[3]

Excerpts from George Getty's Speech to the Security Analysts

During the postwar years prior to 1953, the principal objective of Tidewater's management was the retirement of the large debt accumulated by the company during the late 1920s and early 1930s. This philosophy was reflected in the company's aging plant and equipment, in its static organization, and in its timid attitude toward postwar expansion opportunities. When new management entered Tidewater Oil Company in May 1953, it was faced immediately with the necessity of rebuilding and revitalizing the company. Promptly, plans were laid for strengthening the company's organization, for rebuilding its physical facilities and for expanding the scope and magnitude of its operations.

This program got under way in 1954 and required a vast amount of money, demanding a reversal of the company's long-standing, ultraconservative financial policy. Long-term financing was arranged at attractive rates; cash dividends on the common stock were eliminated to conserve internally generated funds. Since 1954, the company has paid no cash dividend on its common stock, but has, instead, paid an annual 5 percent stock dividend. I do not anticipate a resumption of cash dividends in the near future.

During the years 1954 through 1959, Tidewater's capital expenditures for rebuilding, modernization, and expansion amounted to $775 million, of which

---

[2] "President's Letter," *Annual Report*, Skelly Oil Company, 1959.

[3] "J. Paul Getty's Well-Heeled Woe," *Forbes*, October 15, 1959, p. 43.

60 percent was internally generated. Sources of funds for this capital program were:

      Long-term borrowing .... $310 million
      Depreciation, depletion, and amortization 300
      Retained earnings 165

These expenditures again placed Tidewater in a leading competitive position in the oil industry.

Our shareholders are benefiting from this more aggressive financial policy and from the fact Tidewater has avoided the pitfall of borrowing money to pay dividends. Since 1953, the common shareholder's equity has increased by more than 50 percent—from $19.32 a share to $30.49 per share at March 31, 1960. This, of course, does not reflect the real value of oil and gas reserves, which are carried on our books at cost. . . .

Tidewater's common stock is traded on the New York and Pacific Coast Stock Exchanges. Also, Tidewater can be purchased at a discount through Mission Development Company which owns 1.41 shares of Tidewater per each Mission Development share, yet currently sells around 17 compared to around 19 for Tidewater. Mission Development Company's sole holding is 6,942,955 shares or 47.48 percent of the outstanding common shares of Tidewater. . . .

Turning now to Tidewater's operations, in 1953 we recognized that while markets for our products would continue to grow, competition for those markets would increase in intensity. We felt the only way we would be able to compete successfully for future markets would be on the basis of efficiency and quality. The four refineries we had in 1953 met neither of these requirements. Therefore, we have since closed down three of our refineries, built the new Delaware refinery from the ground up and modernized our large refinery in California. Thus, we have two, large, modern, manufacturing centers, with capacity of 275,000 barrels per calendar day, capable of supplying us with the quantity and quality of products demanded by our customers.

For many years Tidewater has been a large purchaser of raw materials. On a net basis, we purchase half the raw materials processed in our refineries. One of our objectives in 1953—as it is today—was to increase our self sufficiency in crude oil production. . . . Our efforts to become increasingly self-sufficient have been enhanced by the excellent results of our exploratory drilling. More than one third of Tidewater's exploratory wells drilled in the United States in the past five years have produced oil or gas, compared with only one sixth for the domestic industry as a whole.

As a result of this success, Tidewater's proved reserves reached new highs in 1959—693 million barrels of petroleum liquids and 3.5 trillion cubic feet of natural gas. As a measure for your consideration, this represents the equivalent per common share of stock of 50 barrels of petroleum liquids and 250,000 cubic feet of natural gas. At current valuations, these oil and gas reserves are worth $62.50 per share. . . .

Tidewater's picture will not be complete for you as analysts, I know, unless we take a look at the immediate future.

Our forecast is for a modest percentage rise in domestic oil consumption in 1960. Actually, this small percentage gain tends to obscure the fact that domestic oil consumption has been growing at an average rate of a thousand barrels every day for the last 15 years. This means that some 365,000 barrels of new oil a day are required each year to satisfy the constantly growing demand for petroleum products in the United States. I expect oil demand in the United States to grow at the rate of a thousand barrels or more a day for the foreseeable future.

We expect that Tidewater will share in the increase in business in 1960 as it did in 1959. While we cannot safely predict our 1960 earnings at this time, because so much depends upon the level of product prices, I anticipate they will be about the same as those of 1959. Our capital expenditures for the year are budgeted at $100 million, about the same as last year.

In summary, then, since 1953 Tidewater has changed its financial policies, built up the quality and effectiveness of its organization, modernized or rebuilt its principal operating plants, added significant new facilities, and expanded the scope and magnitude of its operations.

We stand now on the threshold of the sixties with an aggressive management, a strong and efficient organization, and the finest facilities in our entire history. Our achievements during this decade should be outstanding.

Reactions to the Getty Speech

According to *Forbes* magazine: "There is just one big drawback to Getty's formula: oilmen use it, but very few security analysts do."[4] Another view was expressed by Professor Donald A. Corbin of the University of California, Riverside:

It appears that oil company balance sheet figures for assets deviate materially from their current values. . . . Income was earned (but not reported because it was not "realized") when oil and gas reserves were discovered. . . . If the assets in the company's balance sheets are undervalued, then income statement figures are understated also.[5]

Questions

1. Identify the different concepts of value in this case. How do they differ from each other? Why?
2. How should the management of Tidewater Oil Company reflect in the company's financial statements the "value" of the oil and gas reserves discovered as a result of the exploration program?
3. Why do Tidewater and Skelly Oil value the Tidewater stock differently?

---

[4] "The Getty Formula," *Forbes*, July 1, 1960, p. 22.

[5] Donald A. Corbin, "Current Reading," *Journal of Accountancy*, October 1960, pp. 91–92.

Chapter 4

BASIC FINANCIAL STATEMENTS

The typical corporate annual report to stockholders contains three basic statements: a statement of financial position or balance sheet, a statement of net income, and changes in financial position statement. Occasionally, a fourth statement showing the changes in owners' equity is also presented. In practice there are many variations in the titles, form, content, and coverage of these statements. For example, they may be for a parent company alone or for a consolidated entity representing the parent and its subsidiaries. Annual statements, in contrast to interim statements, are nearly always covered by a certified public accountant's opinion. They are presented on a comparative basis with the previous year. Irrespective of their title or whether they are annual or interim statements, the function of these basic statements is to communicate useful quantitative information of a financial nature about a business to stockholders, creditors, and others interested in the reporting company's financial condition, results of operations, and uses and sources of funds.

This chapter describes the purpose and contents of the typical balance sheet and income statement and the basic accounting mechanics used to record the transactions summarized by these statements. The statement of changes in owners' equity is discussed also. Chapter 4 also expands upon some of the definitions and concepts discussed in the previous chapter. The change in financial position statement is covered in Chapter 6.

Objectives

The general objectives of financial statements are:

1. To provide reliable financial information about the economic resources and obligations of a business enterprise and the changes in these items.

69

2. To provide reliable information about changes in the net resources of an enterprise that result from its profit-directed activities.
3. To provide financial information that assists in estimating the earnings potential of the enterprise.
4. To disclose to the extent possible other information related to the financial statements, such as the company's accounting policies, that is relevant to the statement user's needs.

General Requirements

All financial statements must carry the name of the reporting company, the dates of the period covered, and an indication of whether or not the statements and accompanying footnotes are audited. Unless otherwise indicated, it is presumed that the statements are for a going concern. However, in practice this assumption should not be accepted literally in all cases, since the future prospects of reporting companies for survival over the long run varies greatly. In addition, companies under the jurisdiction of the Securities and Exchange Commission should not publish statements that differ materially from those required to be filed with the Commission on an annual and interim basis.

Financial statements should present data that can be understood by users of the statements and in a form and with terminology compatible with the user's range of understanding. In practice, this requirement assumes the users have some basic familiarity with the business activities of the reporting entity, the financial accounting process, and the technical language used in financial statements.

Another basic requirement is that the comparative statements issued by a company be comparable. This requires that (1) the format of the statements be identical, (2) the same items from the underlying accounting records are classified under the same captions, (3) the accounting principles followed in preparing the statements are not changed (or if they are changed the changes and their effects are disclosed), (4) changes in the circumstances of the enterprise are disclosed, and (5) the comparative reporting periods are of equal length.

Other requirements include: the statements must be complete for the periods covered; the data must be communicated soon enough after the close of the accounting period to be useful to the statement users; the disclosure of all data relevant to the users' needs must be adequate; and a summary of the accounting principles must be presented.

STATEMENT OF FINANCIAL POSITION

The statement of financial position or balance sheet purports to present data related to a company's financial condition as of a specific time, based on the conventions and generally accepted principles of accounting. The amounts shown on this statement are the balances at the date of the statement in the various balance sheet accounts. Typically these amounts, except for monetary items, such as cash, accounts receivable, and accounts payable balances, may have little financial significance. For example, inventory may be stated at a cost that does not come close to approximating the actual investment in inventory. Similarly, the net asset value reported for plant and equipment may be only a small fraction of the cash value of the asset. This situation occurs because of the historical cost convention and the preoccupation of accounting with the measurement of income. As a result, in practice the statement of financial position has become increasingly thought of as a step between two income statements that shows the residual balances that remain in the accounts after current income has been determined. Increasingly, concern is being expressed by some statement users about the fact that much of the statement of financial position data may be of little significance to investors seeking to analyze the financial status of a company.

All balance sheets do not follow the same precise format or use the same account titles. However, within reasonable limits of flexibility the items on a balance sheet are typically grouped in the following general categories:

Assets		*Liabilities and Owners' Equity*	
Current assets	xxx	Liabilities:	
Long-term investment	xxx	Current liabilities	xxx
Fixed assets	xxx	Long-term liabilities	xxx
Other assets (sometimes divided into noncurrent, prepaid and deferred charges, and		Other liabilities (sometimes divided into deferred credits and accumulated	
intangible assets)	xxx	provisions)	xxx
		Total Liabilities	xxx
		Owners' Equity:	
		Capital stock	xxx
		Other paid-in capital	xxx
		Retained earnings	xxx
		Total Owners' Equity	xxx
		Total Liabilities and	
Total Assets	xxx	Owners' Equity	xxx

The totals of the amounts listed in each of three major categories of the statement of financial position conform to the basic accounting equation.

$$\text{Assets} = \text{Liabilities} + \text{Owners' Equity}$$

ASSETS

As noted in Chapter 3, assets represent expected future economic benefits to which the business holds the right and which have been acquired through a current or past transaction. These resources may be considered to have future economic benefits for a variety of different reasons. For example, some expenditures, such as capitalized[1] franchise acquisition expenditures, are called assets because it is thought that they will contribute to the generation of income in future accounting periods. Some assets represent resources that can readily be converted into cash, such as accounts receivable. Other resources are called assets because they represent valuable property rights, such as

ILLUSTRATION 4–1

Asset Section of a Major Corporation's Consolidated Balance Sheet
December 31, 1976
(in thousands)

Current Assets:

Cash	$ 39,274
U.S. government and other marketable securities, at lower of cost or market (quoted market value: 1976, $3,726,000)	3,722
Notes and accounts receivable (less estimated losses, 1976, $4,251,000)	165,288
Inventories	193,795
Prepayments and other current assets	9,979
Total Current Assets	$ 412,058

Investments:

Investments in jointly owned companies, at equity	$ 36,068
Investments in subsidiaries not consolidated, at cost or less	9,690
Other, at cost or less	9,739
Total Investments	$ 55,497

Property:

Land, buildings, machinery, and equipment, etc. (at cost)	$1,199,489
Less: Accumulated depreciation and depletion	594,085
Net Property	$ 605,404

Other Assets:

Excess of cost of investments in consolidated subsidiaries over equities in net assets	$ 11,165
Deferred charges	10,629
Total Other Assets	$ 21,794
Total Assets	$1,094,753

---

[1] An expenditure is said to be capitalized when it is recorded as an asset rather than an expense.

the land owned by the business. Irrespective of the principal criterion used to determine if an item is an asset or not, assets are typically not carried at a value which is more than the lower of either their original cost or their net realizable value through direct sale or use in future operations. Monetary assets such as cash, accounts receivable, and marketable securities are carried at the equivalent of their cash value that is expected to be realized in the normal course of business.

Illustration 4–1 presents the asset section of a major corporation's consolidated balance sheet. The assets are divided into four categories that are common to many other statements—current assets, investments, property, and other assets. Although they are not shown, the notes to the statements provided additional information relevant to understanding the data in the asset section of the statement. For example, the method used to determine inventory values and the company's depreciation accounting policy were disclosed. This illustration will be used to explain briefly the nature of the asset accounts found on most balance sheets. A fuller explanation of these items is presented in subsequent chapters.

Current Assets

Current assets include cash and other assets that are reasonably expected to be realized in cash or sold or consumed during the normal operating cycle of the business or within one year if the operating cycle is shorter than one year. The operating cycle can be represented as that period during which the series of events described in Illustration 4–2 occur in sequence.

For most companies the operating cycle is less than 12 months. However, there are some notable exceptions. For example, one large bowling equipment manufacturer sold bowling alley equipment in

ILLUSTRATION 4–2

Normal Operating Cycle Illustrated

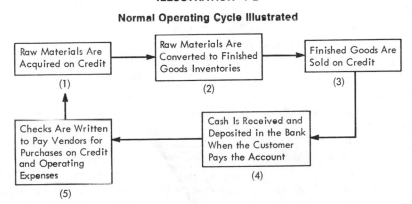

return for long-term notes with payment schedules ranging up to seven years. These notes receivable from customers were classified as a current asset on the grounds that the company's "normal operating cycle" was seven years, since it took that long to complete all of the events related to each sale. Other more common examples of industries with operating cycles longer than one year are the distilling and tobacco industries. Their inventories must age for a long period of time before being offered for sale. In other cases, such as land development companies, no distinction is made between current and noncurrent assets, since the period during which land must be held for sale can be very long and the period over which the purchase price is paid by the buyer of the land even longer.

Current assets include cash, accounts receivable, marketable securities, and inventories. Cash is shown at its face value and includes cash on hand, undeposited checks at the date of the balance sheet, cash in banks, and checks in transit to banks. Checks written by the company but not yet deposited and charged to the company's bank account are treated as if they had been deposited.

Sometimes corporations invest surplus cash on a temporary basis in securities that can be readily sold under normal conditions. These marketable securities are held for investment purposes rather than to control the operations of the entity issuing the securities. Typically these securities, as in Illustration 4–1, are short-term obligations of the United States government. Marketable securities are presented at the lower of their cost or current market. In addition, their current market value is shown parenthetically (i.e., in brackets next to the account).

Notes and accounts receivable represent the claims against customers generated by credit sales for amounts still due to the company. The balance of such an account only includes billings for services performed on or before the balance sheet date. The amount presented in the balance sheet is net of the company's estimated losses from uncollectible accounts. The procedures used to estimate these amounts is described in Chapter 9.

Inventories include tangible items that will be either sold directly or included in the production of items that will be sold in the normal course of operations. The inventory account shown in Illustration 4–1 probably includes three types of inventory: a finished goods inventory, consisting of products ready for sale; a work in process inventory, consisting of products in various stages of production; and a raw materials and supplies inventory, consisting of items that will enter directly or indirectly into the production of finished goods.

Inventories are carried at cost, unless their utility is no longer as great as their cost. The so-called lower-of-cost-or-market rule to determine if the carrying value of inventories should be written down below cost is covered in Chapter 17. This same chapter discusses also the alternative methods for determining the cost value of inventories shown on the balance sheet. These methods include the first-in, first-out method, which values the inventory on the balance sheet date at the most recent cost; and the last-in, first-out method, which uses the oldest cost of goods in inventory to value the asset inventory.

The current assets category may include other accounts which will be realized during the normal operating cycle. Examples are unbilled costs on construction contracts performed by contractors for customers, prepaid insurance and expenses where the benefits to be derived from the prepayment extend beyond the current accounting period, and tax refunds receivable. Even though they do not result in a conversion into cash, prepaid expenses are listed among current assets. This practice is followed because these expenditures are expected to be recovered in cash through sales during the operating cycle or the benefits from the expenditure are to be received during the operating cycle.

It is customary to list current assets in their descending order of liquidity. For example, in Illustration 4–1 cash is listed first, marketable securities next, and then accounts receivable. Marketable securities precede accounts receivable because, of the two items, marketable securities can more easily be turned into cash by management. For a similar reason, inventories are listed after accounts receivable but before prepayments.

Investments

Investments made in other companies are carried on the consolidated balance sheet as noncurrent items when the investing company's objective is one of control, affiliation, or some continuing business relationship with the company and the circumstances of the investment do not require the subsidiary to be consolidated. These investments may be common stock, debt securities, or long-term advances. It is not customary to state the market value of such noncurrent investments, since it is assumed that there is no present intention to sell the securities. Depending on the circumstances, these securities may be carried at their original cost or at an amount equal to the investing company's original cost plus its proportional share of the subsidiary's retained earnings. This latter approach is called the equity method. Chapters 5 and 18, "Consolidated Financial Statements" and "Intercorporate Investments and Business Combinations," explain the cost and equity methods in greater detail.

Illustration 4–1 shows three types of long-term investments and their valuation basis: investments in joint ventures, valued according to the equity method; investments in unconsolidated subsidiaries, valued by the cost method at their original cost or less (these subsidiaries could be overseas subsidiaries in countries with unusual economic or political problems that limit the parent company's ability to influence their operations); and other miscellaneous long-term investments, shown at cost or less. Investments are shown at less than their original cost when there has been a loss in their value.

Property

Long-lived tangible assets, such as equipment acquired to produce goods for sale, are referred to as "fixed assets." Assets in this category are land, buildings, machinery, equipment, and any other long-lived tangible items used in the company's operations. These assets are stated at their original cost less depreciation, rather than at their replacement value or current market value. The one exception is land, which is always stated at its original cost.

Depreciation represents the allocation of the cost of fixed assets to the income statement due to use and obsolescence. An annual charge for depreciation is included in the expenses of current operations. The amount of this depreciation expense is related to the anticipated useful life of the asset, which may be computed on the basis of either expected years of service or actual use (i.e., hours of operation, units produced, etc.). The accumulated amount of depreciation expense related to the fixed assets still carried on the books of the company is presented on the balance sheet in an account called "accumulated depreciation." Sometimes the term "reserve for depreciation" is used. However, it is gradually being abandoned in favor of "allowance for depreciation" or "accumulated depreciation."

Chapter 14, "Depreciation Accounting," discusses the various depreciation methods. The two principal approaches to depreciation are the straight-line and accelerated methods. Straight-line depreciation allocates the cost of a fixed asset, less any estimated salvage value, equally to operations over the life of the asset. Accelerated depreciation methods charge a greater proportion of an asset's total depreciation to operations during the early years of its life than during the latter years.

It is customary, as presented in Illustration 4–1 under the caption "property," to show both the original cost and the depreciated book value of the fixed assets available for use in operations. The difference between these two amounts, accumulated depreciation, is shown as a deduction from the total original cost of the fixed assets to arrive at the net book value of the assets. This net book value, called "net property" in Illustration 4–1, seldom reflects the current market value of the asset. It is simply the balance left in the property accounts of the company's accounting records after deducting the related accumulated depreciation charges.

Illustration 4–1 refers to "accumulated depreciation and depletion." The term *depletion* relates to investments in natural resources, whereas the term *depreciation* is associated with plant and equipment investments. Depletion is the amount of a company's investment in natural resources that is charged to operations over the period during which these resources are extracted or exhausted. Accumulated depletion is the cumulative total of these charges related to the natural resource investments still available to the company for the generation of future revenues. Depletion is often charged on a units-of-production basis.

Other Assets

Items included in the "other assets" category include intangible assets and deferred charges. Intangible assets are assets that are not of a tangible nature. Assets that fall into this category are patents, trademarks, copyrights, and franchises. To be recorded, these assets must be created or acquired through a business transaction. Intangible assets are carried at cost initially and then charged to operations in a systematic manner over their useful life. Chapter 16 covers the topic of intangible assets in greater detail.

Illustration 4–1 lists an intangible asset labeled "excess of cost of investments in consolidated subsidiaries over equities in net assets." The popular name for this item is "goodwill." It arises when a company purchases another company for a price in excess of the net fair market value of its assets. Goodwill, which is the difference between the purchase price and the net asset values acquired, must be charged to operations over a period of not more than 40 years. However, the actual period used varies greatly from company to company. The accounting for business acquisitions and goodwill is covered in Chapter 18, "Intercorporate Investments and Business Combinations."

Deferred charges are very similar in nature to prepaid expenses, since both are payments or accruals recognized before the balance sheet date that properly should be charged to operations subsequent to that date. However, it is important to distinguish between them, since prepaid expenses are a current asset and deferred charges are assigned to the other-asset category. Prepaid expenses relate to amounts paid for services yet to be received from the seller and which are properly related to future revenues. In contrast, deferred charges represent amounts paid for services already received by the business but not yet charged to operations. For example, the prepayment of the premiums on a three-year insurance policy is a prepaid expense, since the insurance protection has yet to be received. In addition, since the benefit of the insurance is to be received over the next three years, it should be charged against income over this period. In contrast, preoperating expenditures for opening a new store that are expected to produce benefits beyond the current period may be considered a deferred charge, since the company has already received the preopening service. However, in order to determine income in accordance with the accrual convention, the company has elected to hold off expensing this item until the income benefits are received.

LIABILITIES

In Chapter 3 liabilities were defined as the entity's obligations to convey assets or perform services to a person, firm, or other organization outside of the entity at some time in the future, plus deferred credits.

Liabilities include all of those claims of a nonownership type against the business by outsiders. Stated another way, they represent the amounts owed to creditors. These obligations include such items as amounts due to vendors, bank loans payable, and debentures outstanding.

Liabilities are claims against all assets. Typically where liabilities relate to specific assets, it is not acceptable to show the liability as a deduction from the asset. For example, the mortgage on a building is shown on the right-hand or liability side of the balance sheet and the asset "building" is listed on the left-hand side.

The accounting concept of liabilities is broader than liabilities in the popular sense of legal debts and obligations. The accounting concept includes certain deferred credits that do not involve a debtor-creditor relationship. For example, for accounting purposes, the seller's profit on a sale and leaseback transaction is not recognized in the income statement as a gain at the time of the sale. The preferred treatment is to list the profit as a deferred credit on the right-hand side of the balance sheet and allocate this amount to the income statement as a reduction to lease rentals over the life of the lease. This practice leads to a better matching of costs and revenues.

Illustration 4–3 (on page 80) presents an example of the right-hand side of a major corporation's consolidated balance sheet, the liabilities and owner's equity section. Taken together, Illustrations 4–1 and 4–3 comprise this company's entire balance sheet with the exception of the related notes.

Current Liabilities

Current liabilities are defined as: (1) those liabilities that the company expects to satisfy with either assets classified as current in the same balance sheet or the creation of other current liabilities; (2) all obligations arising from operations directly related to the company's operating cycle; or (3) those liabilities expected to be satisfied during the following year. The one-year rule is widely considered to be the cutoff between current and noncurrent liabilities. However, if the enterprise's operating cycle is longer than 12 months, an exception is made to this rule and the operating cycle period issued.

Current liabilities include the current portion (i.e., due within 12 months) of notes payable to banks, amounts owed to trade creditors, wages earned by employees but not paid to them, and funds received in advance for services not yet rendered. The order of presentation followed in the current liability section of Illustration 4–3 is typical of most balance sheets.

The captions of the various current liabilities listed in Illustration 4–3 are almost self-explanatory. Notes payable to banks represent the company's obligations to banks arising from short-term borrowing arrangements. The amount shown as the current maturities on long-term debt is a portion of the long-term debt's principal that must be repaid during the next 12 months. Accounts payable represent the claims of trade creditors for goods and services provided on an open account basis. If these trade obligations were evidenced by a note or similar written promise to pay, they would be included with notes payable. The sundry accruals combined with the accounts payable in Illustration 4–3 are most probably items such as wages owed to employees or deposits owed to customers on returnable containers not yet returned. The taxes owed as of the balance sheet date to various taxing authorities that will be paid during the next 12 months are included in the obligation listed as "domestic and foreign taxes on income."

Long-Term Liabilities

Long-term liabilities are all of an enterprise's noncurrent liabilities. They are often subdivided on the balance sheet into several different categories. For example, the long-term liabilities shown in Illustration 4–3 are presented in three groups; Long-term debt, deferred credits, and accumulated provisions.

Long-term debt represents those debt obligations of a company that will mature beyond one year's time. These obligations are recorded at their principal value. However, in the case of long-term debt, such as bonds and debentures issued at a discount or premium, the discount or

ILLUSTRATION 4–3

Liability and Owners' Equity Section of a Major Corporation's
Consolidated Balance Sheet
December 31, 1976
(in thousands)

Liabilities and Owners' Equity

Current Liabilities:

Notes payable—banks	$ 59,504
Current maturities of long-term debt	7,953
Accounts payable and sundry accruals	113,953
Domestic and foreign taxes on income	19,700
Total Current Liabilities	$ 201,110

Long-Term Debt:

5⅝% sinking fund debentures	$ 125,000
4½% term loan	42,088
Other	26,666
Total Long-Term Debt	$ 193,754

Deferred Credits:

Deferred income tax	$ 36,186
Investment credit—unamortized balance	17,959
Other	1,793
Total Deferred Credits	$ 55,938

Accumulated Provisions:

Maintenance and repairs	$ 6,623
Product warranties	3,733
Foreign operations	543
Total Accumulated Provisions	$ 10,899
Total Liabilities	$ 461,701

Capital and Retained Earnings:

Cumulative preferred stock—authorized 5,000,000 shares, without par value; no shares issued	—
Common stock—authorized, 50,000,000 shares, par value $2.50 each; issued, 1976, 21,721,988 shares	$ 212,850
Earnings retained for use in the business	462,972
Less common stock in treasury, 1976, 1,245,420 shares at cost	(42,770)
Total Capital and Retained Earnings	$ 633,052
Total Liabilities and Owners' Equity	$1,094,753

premium is shown as an adjustment to the principal amount. In the case of bank loans, the principal value is the amount owed the banks. The current interest on these obligations is charged to operating income as the interest obligation is incurred. Chapter 19 discusses the accounting for long-term debt in greater detail.

Deferred credits are the opposite of deferred charges. They are unearned revenues, such as subscriptions collected in advance of providing the service; or deferred profits, such as the deferral of profit on a sale-and-leaseback transaction. Another important class of deferred credits results from charges required by generally accepted accounting principles to current or past income in advance of the actual expenditure or obligation being incurred, such as the deferred credit resulting from income tax allocation requirements (see below). Some deferred credits, such as subscriptions received in advance, are obligations; whereas others, such as deferred sale-and-leaseback profits, are not.

Illustration 4–3 shows two significant deferred credits: namely, the deferred income tax and the unamortized investment tax credit items. Both of these accounts and the controversy surrounding them are covered in Chapter 12.

Deferred income tax represents the amount of the company's potential income tax obligation that the company has deferred from past periods to future periods by following different accounting practices for book and tax purposes. For example, deferred income tax arises in situations where a company uses straight-line depreciation for book purposes and accelerated depreciation for its tax returns. If the company's depreciable assets are new, this can result in a lower income for tax purposes than that reported to stockholders, since the depreciation charge for tax reporting purposes is bigger than the book depreciation expense. In such situations, the Accounting Principles Board decided that the tax expense calculation for book purposes should be based on the profits before tax reported to stockholders, rather than the taxable income actually used to determine the company's current income tax payments. Thus, in the example, the company's current book tax expense will be greater than actual payments due to the government. The difference between the tax actually due and the book tax expense recognized is the addition to the deferred tax account. This amount is not a legal obligation like long-term debt. It simply results from the accounting requirement to reconcile book tax expenses recognized and actual taxes paid. Double-entry bookkeeping forces the recognition of this deferred tax item on the liability side of the balance sheet when the cumulative tax payments actually made or due to the government lag behind the cumulative tax expenses recognized for book purposes.

Beginning in the early 1960s the federal government has from time to time granted an investment tax credit for certain qualified investments in tangible property. This amount was deducted from the company's current tax bill. Some companies, for book purposes, recognized the full benefit of this reduction of taxes during the period in which the credit was granted. Other companies spread the tax expense reduction benefit over the life of the asset giving rise to the credit. This is the method adopted by the company in Illustration 4–3. In 1974 the investment tax credit was once again effective. In 1975 the tax credit was raised to 10 percent for certain classes of property and 7 percent for others.

Accumulated provisions are estimates of future expenditures, asset impairments, or liabilities that have been accrued by a change to income. Illustration 4–3 presents three examples of accumulated provisions.

In some companies, the need for maintenance and repairs is level and the annual charges are constant. In other companies, the need fluctuates from year to year in a predictable manner. Some companies in these circumstances charge to operations a fixed amount each year for maintenance and repairs. These charges to income are accumulated in the liability account "accumulated provision for maintenance and repairs." Actual expenditures for maintenance and repairs are then charged directly to this liability account.

The remaining two examples of accumulated provisions shown in Illustration 4–3 are contingencies for future losses. In both cases, the estimated loss from the future contingencies has been already charged to income in anticipation of the event. The offsetting accounting entry was made to the related liability account. When the actual loss occurs, it will be charged to this liability account. Loss contingencies are discussed further in Chapter 26.

Product warranties are obligations incurred in connection with the sale of goods or services that may require further performance by the seller after the sale has taken place. In order to record the correct profit from a sale, it is necessary to recognize as a current expense all of the past, current, and future costs associated with each sale at the same time as the sale revenue is recorded. Warranty obligations are future costs of current sales. Because of the uncertainty surrounding claims that may be made under warranties, warranty obligations fall within the definition of a contingency. The amount shown in Illustration 4–3 for this item should be a reasonable estimate of the probable future warranty costs associated with recorded sales.

The provision for foreign operations represents the recognition by management that they will probably sustain some identifiable losses overseas. The provision was set up by a charge to income. When the actual extent of the losses is known, they will be charged to the liability account. Any actual losses in excess of the amount set aside in the liability account will be charged to income directly.

OWNERS' EQUITY

Owners' equity represents the interest of the owners in an enterprise. It is the balance that remains after deducting the total liabilities of the enterprise from its total assets. For most companies the residual owners' interest determined in this fashion bears little relationship to the actual market value of that interest. Two companies identical in all respects except their accounting policy could show in the balance sheets very different values for their owners' equity. The company with the more conservative accounting practices would report the lower book value for owners' equity. Yet the market value of the two companies could be the same.

Illustration 4–3 presents the owners' equity for our example company under the caption "capital and retained earnings." Other terms used to describe the owners' equity are "net worth," "net assets," and "stockholders' equity." Chapter 22 covers equity capital transactions.

The *capital* section of the balance sheet lists (1) the amount and type of capital stock authorized, (2) the number of shares issued, (3) the net amount received by the company for the issued stock, and (4) the number of shares and acquisition costs of the company's own stock held by the company. Illustration 4–3 shows that the company's stockholders have authorized five million shares of no-par-value preferred stock, but none have been issued. The authorized number of shares represents the maximum number of shares the company may sell under the terms of its charter. Thus, the principal source of the company's capital from stock issues was the 21.7 million shares of $2.50 par-value common stock sold at various times to the public for a total consideration of $212 million.

Rather than showing, as in Illustration 4–3, the value of the total consideration received from the issuance of common stock, a preferred approach is to value the common stock account at the par value of the securities issued. Then, if the company sells any of this stock for more than its par value, this excess is shown in an account labeled "Capital Received in Excess of Par Value of Stock Issued." This account appears immediately below the common stock account.

The *Earnings Retained in the Business* (or simply, Retained Earnings) account represents the balance of net income of the enterprise from the date of incorporation, after deducting distributions of dividends to shareholders. In addition, under some circumstances transfers may be made from Retained Earnings to the capital stock accounts. As indicated in Illustration 4–3, this account presents the value of the resources earned by the business through profit-directed activities that are retained for use in the business. Another common but less acceptable term used to describe this item is "earned surplus."

Data related to issued stock reacquired by the issuing company are presented in the *Treasury Stock* account. This stock is carried at its acquisition cost and is always presented as a deduction from the owners' equity. Accounting regards only the stock actually in the hands of the stockholders as outstanding stock for computing earnings per share. This is different from the legal position that considers all stock not formally retired to be outstanding.

INCOME STATEMENT

The results of operations of a business for a period of time are presented in the income statement.[2] From the accounting systems point of view, the income statement is subordinate to the balance sheet, since the income statement simply presents the details of the changes in the Retained Earnings balance sheet account due to profit directed activities. In contrast to this limited perspective, however, for most users of financial statements the income statement is a more important source of information than the balance sheet because changes in net income influence equity stock prices and dividend payments.

Statement No. 4

The elements of a business's profit-directed operations and their net results can be represented by the equation:

$$\text{Revenues} - \text{Expenses} = \text{Net Income (net loss)}$$

The income statement presents the details of this expression in a commonly agreed upon format according to generally accepted accounting principles.

Revenue (as sales) is defined in *Statement No. 4* as

Gross increases in assets or gross decreases in liabilities recognized and measured in conformity with generally accepted accounting principles that result from those types of profit-directed activities of an enterprise that can change owners' equity.

Not all increases in assets or decreases in liabilities are included in revenue. For example, the receipt of cash from a bank loan is not a sale. This transaction does not change owners' equity. It increases an asset (cash) and a liability (bank loans payable). In contrast, a cash sale of inventory in the normal course of business is revenue. It increases the asset cash and changes the owners' equity account, Retained Earnings. If the goods are sold at a profit, Retained Earnings will increase by the after tax amount of the profit.

Different concepts of revenue can be found in accounting theory. This diversity reflects the lack of common agreement as to the nature of revenue. One approach regards revenues as an inflow of assets

---

[2] Common alternative titles are: statement of profit and loss, statement of earnings, and statement of operations.

derived from the sale of goods and rendering of services. An opposite concept of this inflow theory is the so-called outflow approach which considers revenue to be the goods and services created by a business that are transferred to customers. Some accounting theorists are not very pleased with *Statement No. 4*'s definition of revenue, which focuses on the effect of profit-directed activities on stockholder's equity. In their opinion this definition derives the concept of revenue from the double-entry bookkeeping convention rather than from the basic nature of revenue.

Expenses are the goods and services of a business that are used in the process of creating revenues. In this process the expenditures incurred for this business's goods and services are said to have expired. Some of these expenditures, like administrative costs, may be incurred and expire in the same accounting period. Others like inventory may be incurred in one period; held as unexpired costs on the balance sheet; and then expensed as expired costs in a later period when the inventory transfers to the customer.

Statement No. 4 defines expenses as:

> Gross decreases in assets or gross increases in liabilities recognized and measured in conformity with generally accepted accounting principles that result from those types of profit-directed activities of an enterprise that can change owners' equity.

Like revenues, expenses can only result from profit-directed activities that change owners' equity. The reduction of inventory as the result of a sale is an expense, since the net result of this transaction is a change in the owners' equity account, Retained Earnings. The purchase of an inventory on credit is not an expense, since this does not change owners' equity. The purchase increases the asset inventory and the liability trade payables.

Although the payment of dividends reduces owners' equity, it is not an expense. This transaction reduces cash and the owners' equity Retained Earnings account, but it is not a profit-directed activity. It is a distribution of capital.

Given these definitions of revenues and expenses, *Statement No. 4* concludes that net income (net loss) is:

> The excess (deficit) of revenue over expenses for an accounting period, which is the net increase (net decrease) in owners' equity (assets minus liabilities) of an enterprise for an accounting period from profit-directed activities that is recognized and measured in conformity with generally accepted accounting principles.

Chapter 9 discusses the many problems associated with income recognition. Particular aspects of expense measurement are discussed in a number of different chapters.

Basic Conventions

Four basic conventions discussed in the last chapter influence the preparation of the income statement. These are the accrual concept, the accounting period concept, the realization concept, and the matching concept. Each will be reviewed here briefly.

The *accrual concept* relates revenues and expenses to changes in owners' equity, not cash. Statements prepared on this basis recognize and report the effects of transactions and other events on the assets and liabilities of a business in the time period to which they relate, rather than only when cash is received or paid. Accordingly, for example, wage expense is recognized when labor services are performed, not when the workers are paid.

The *accounting period* is the segment of time covered by the income statement. All events affecting income determination occurring during this period should be measured and recorded in the company's accounting records and assigned to this period for income determination purposes. The accounting period is bounded by a beginning and ending balance sheet. The income statement relates to the changes in owners' equity from one balance sheet date to another due to profit-directed activities.

The *realization concept,* according to *Statement No. 4,* holds that "revenue is generally recognized when both of the following conditions are met: (1) the earnings process is complete or virtually complete and (2) an exchange has taken place." For example, interest revenue from loans to others is recognized as time passes, since that, assuming the borrower is solvent, is the critical event dictating the timing and amount of interest receivable.

The *matching concept* recognizes that some costs have a presumed direct association with specific revenues or time periods. This is a process of associating cause and effect. It is through this matching process that income is determined.

Expenditures and Expenses

A troublesome accounting problem is the determination whether a purchase results in an asset or an expense. An expenditure occurs whenever an asset or service is purchased. At the moment of the transaction, all expenditures for purchases can be thought to result in assets. These assets will then become expenses if they *(a)* are directly or indirectly related or associated with the revenue of the period, or *(b)* suffer a loss during the period in their future revenue-generating capacity, such as in the case of assets destroyed by fire or patents carried as assets in prior periods that now become worthless due to the development of a new technology.

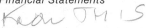

Statement Format

A common order of items in the income statement is:

1. Revenues (the sales for the period).
2. Cost of sales (the manufacturing or acquisition costs of the goods sold during the period).
3. Gross profit or margin (the difference between revenues and cost of sales; item 1 less item 2).
4. Operating expenses (the selling, administration, and general expenses associated with operating the company's principal business activity during the period).
5. Operating income (item 3 less item 4).
6. Nonoperating revenues (revenues derived from sources other than operations during the period, such as interest on the temporary investment of excess cash).
7. Nonoperating expenses (expenses not directly related to the principal business activity and the financial cost of borrowed money).
8. Provision for taxes (the income tax expense, based on item 5 plus item 6 less item 7).
9. Income before extraordinary items (item 5 plus item 6 less item 7 and item 8).
10. Extraordinary items.[3] (These are infrequent, abnormal gains or losses that are clearly not related to the company's normal operations or business activities. These items are shown net of their tax effect.)
11. Net income (item 9 plus or minus item 10).[4]

An alternative form of income statement is shown in Illustration 4–4. This statement omits the gross and operating profit calculations. It is known as single-step statement. Each of the items on this statement will be discussed briefly.

The *net sales* figure represents the company's net sales during the calendar year 1975. It is derived by deducting from gross sales any sales returns, allowances, and discounts. The gross sales amount is the invoice price of the goods and services sold. Sales returns and allowances result from the credit given to customers for sales returns or defective goods. Sales discounts are discounts granted to customers for prompt payment of amounts owed to the seller. Sometimes this

---

[3] Chapter 10, "Extraordinary Items, Discontinued Operations, and Accounting Changes," discusses extraordinary items.

[4] A more complicated statement is presented when a company makes a change in an accounting principle or discontinues a part of its operations. These more complicated statements are presented in Chapter 10.

ILLUSTRATION 4–4

EXAMPLE: A MAJOR CORPORATION'S SINGLE-STEP INCOME STATEMENT

Statement of Earnings
For the Year Ended December 31, 1975

Net sales	$1,962,487,755
Costs and Expenses:	
Cost of products sold	$1,445,785,281
Selling, advertising, general, and administrative expenses	182,507,421
Interest and debt expense	7,581,223
	$1,635,873,925
Earnings before provision for taxes	$ 326,613,830
Provision for federal and state taxes on income	176,569,000
Net Income	$ 150,044,830

item is shown as a sales expense rather than as a reduction of gross sales. Discounts from list price granted to members of the seller's trade do not enter into the accounting records. These sales are recorded at the actual invoice price.

Cost of products sold is the manufactured cost or, in the case of merchandising companies, the purchase price of the goods sold during the period. The manufactured cost includes the cost of direct labor, raw materials, and manufacturing overhead. The amount of cost of goods sold expense matched with current revenues will depend in large part on the company's inventory valuation practices, since any current expenditures for products not included in cost of products sold must be assigned to the inventory account.

Selling, general, and administrative expenses are all of the expenses incurred for these activities during the accounting period. Generally these expenditures are not assumed to have a lasting value beyond the current period. Therefore they are related directly to the current accounting period for income determination purposes.

Interest and debt expenses are financial charges. It is customary to segregate these items from operating expenses. This approach assumes that users of the statements wish (1) to identify and evaluate the cost of financing operations and (2) to determine whether or not management's return from operations is adequate, given the financing costs.

Earnings before provision for taxes are the basis for determining the company's tax expense. It should be remembered that this amount most likely will be different from the taxable income shown on the company's tax return. Two common reasons for this difference are that some cost items included in the income statement are not recognized for tax purposes, and that some revenue items recognized currently to determine book income are deferred to future periods for tax purposes.

Provisions for federal and state taxes on income will, for most companies, consist of two parts: the taxes actually payable based on the income shown in the current tax return and the taxes recognized for book purposes for which there is no current tax liability. This latter type of accounting expense is the source of the changes in deferred tax liability discussed earlier.

Net income is the final figure on the statement. It represents the net impact of profit-directed activities on owners' equity after considering all items of profit and loss recognized during the period.

Interrelationship

The items on the income statement and the balance sheet are interrelated. For example, when a credit sale is made, revenues and accounts receivable both increase. In addition, the sale causes finished goods inventory to decline and cost of goods sold to increase, and the increased tax expense related to the profit on the sale causes taxes payable to increase. Therefore, in order to gain a full appreciation of any item on one statement, it is necessary to examine also the related items on the other.

Changes in Owners' Equity

The income statement alone does not present all of the changes in owners' equity during an accounting period since it relates only to profit-directed activities. Therefore, to describe the changes due to capital additions and distributions, an additional statement or disclosure is sometimes required of the changes in owners' equity, which presents both changes in the Retained Earnings and the Capital Stock accounts.

The Retained Earnings account is the link between the net income figure and the owners equity. The retained earnings balance at the end of the period is derived as follows:

1. Beginning retained earnings (the balance at the beginning of the accounting period).
2. Net income (shown in the income statement for the period—add to 1).
3. Dividends paid to common stockholders. (Subtract from sum of 1 and 2.)
4. Ending retained earnings (the amount appearing in the balance sheet at the end of the period—equal to item 1 plus item 2 less item 3).

OTHER CONSIDERATIONS

Notes to Financial Statements

Financial statements are inevitably accompanied by notes. These are an integral part of the statements and should be read before relying on the accounting figures. The functions of notes are:

1. To amplify the numerical data and descriptive captions presented on the face of the statements by giving such details as the requirements of bond indentures and the terms of lease agreements.
2. To present additional information on events that may subsequently affect the data reported, such as contingencies that may arise from outstanding legal suits or the future audit of current tax returns by the tax authorities.
3. To disclose events that have occurred subsequent to the balance sheet date that may materially affect the statement users' evaluation of the data presented but not require adjustment to the statements, such as an issue of debentures after the balance sheet date.
4. To identify the particular accounting methods used to prepare the statements and the impact on key financial statistics of any changes in these methods.
5. To disclose commitments of an unusual nature, such as a major plant expansion program.

Auditor's Report

The auditor's report accompanying financial statements should always be read in conjunction with the statements. It is important for anyone using the statements to know the auditor's appraisal of the statements.

Financial statements are the direct responsibility of the management and directors of the reporting company. Although the company's public auditor may assist and advise management in its preparation of the statements, management alone is responsible for their contents. Management is not compelled to follow the auditor's advice. However, the auditor does have a responsibility in his report accompanying the statements to state whether or not he agrees with the fairness of the financial presentation. In practice, it is this duty of the auditor to state exceptions in his report that brings reluctant managements to accept the auditor's recommendation in those cases where differences of opinion exist between management and auditors. Chapter 7 discusses in greater detail the nature of the auditor's opinion and his basis for reaching this opinion.

Interim Statements

All SEC corporations publish at least quarterly condensed income statements for the quarter and the year to date on a comparative basis with the same periods during the previous year. Companies also present in their quarterly reports a condensed balance sheet as of the end of the quarter.

Considerable caution should be exercised when using quarterly statements, since:

1. Although the SEC is encouraging companies to involve their auditors in the preparation of quarterly statements, quarterly statements are usually unaudited. Some managements in trouble take advantage of this to hide their problems from stockholders during the year in the hope that all can be made right by year-end.
2. Adjustments to data reported in earlier interim statements and decisions to change accounting methods are made usually during the fourth quarter. This results from the fact more data are available as year-end approaches; management has a better feel of whether or not it can reach its earnings goals as a result of operations; and lax accounting practices are revealed by the auditor, who during this period is spending an increasing amount of time with the company conducting his audit related to the annual statements.
3. Comparisons of the current interim results with those of the same period during the period year may not be entirely valid, because the structure of the business may be constantly expanding and changing.
4. Annual predictions based on interim results may be misleading due to the seasonality of the business.
5. APB *Opinion No. 28* on interim statements may be interpreted differently by different managers as they apply it to their business.

   Despite these limitations, a number of authorities on stock price determinants believe interim results influence stock market price movements more than the information in annual statements.

Forecasts

A few companies include forecasts of net income for future periods in their public reports.

Some accounting authorities advocate that annual reports should disclose in summary form the reporting companies' budgeted results for the next annual period. It is argued that these data would provide stockholders with a better basis for evaluating management's planning capabilities and how well management achieved its objectives for the reporting period. In addition, it would put the current results into better perspective.

The accounting profession has not encouraged this type of reporting because of the problems associated with objectively auditing these reports. Also managements have been reluctant to publish these data, since they often consider budget data to be competitive data that should not be revealed publicly.

However, under certain circumstances, the SEC encourages the publication of forecasts. The AICPA has published proposed guidelines for preparing these forecasts.

Summary of Financial Results

In addition to the financial statements covered by the auditor's opinion, annual reports typically include two sets of summary financial statistics. First, inside the front cover, and opposite the chief executive officer's letter to the stockholders that inevitably begins the text of the report, selected statistical data on a two-year comparative basis are shown related to such items as current earnings per share, sales volume, dividends per share, return on investment, net income as a percentage of sales, and the ratio of current assets to current liabilities. Second, usually following the notes to the financial statements, a five- or ten-year statistical summary is presented. The basic data included in this summary are similar to that covered in the two-year statistical presentation at the beginning of the report. Additional statistics presented may include such data as the number of employees, the number of common shares outstanding, and the preferred dividends paid per share.

These statistical summaries are not covered by the auditor's opinion. However, for companies under the jurisdiction of the SEC these disclosures should not be materially different from tne data presented in the audited statements. The SEC also requires management to include an analysis of the current and past few years' results along with the summary of financial results.

Text

Most annual reports include textual material describing, primarily in qualitative terms, the companies' activities, plans, and problems. A thorough reading of this material is essential for anyone trying to determine the significance of the communication contained in the financial statements.

PROPOSED CHANGES IN STATEMENTS

The Trueblood Committee proposed a number of statement changes. These proposals flowed from the committee's belief that financial statements are used by their readers to predict, compare, and evaluate the cash consequences of their economic decisions.

The study assumed that data about the cash consequences of decisions made by the enterprise, adjusted for either deflation or inflation, was useful for such users. In addition, the committee concluded that financial statements are more useful if they distinguish between information that is primarily factual, and therefore can be measured objectively, from information that is primarily interpretive.

These conclusions led the committee to suggest that several new forms of financial statement format and disclosure should be considered. Some of these are discussed below.

The financial position statement, in the committee's view, should provide specific information concerning the business transactions and other events that are part of an incomplete earnings cycle. Current values should also be reported when they differ significantly from historical costs. Account should be taken also in the statements that the purchasing power of the dollar may have changed. Assets and liabilities, the committee believed, should be grouped or segregated by the relative uncertainty of the amount and timing of prospective realization and liquidation. The report also implied that a different classification scheme was needed to distinguish between factual and interpretive information. Since it may be difficult to include all of these data in one financial position statement, supplemental statements might have to be used.

The income statement needed to be modified in the committee's view to disclose and distinguish between the net results of completed earnings cycles (typically the receipt of cash) and the business activities that resulted in recognizable progress toward the completion of incomplete cycles. In addition, the committee believed changes in the values reflected in successive statements of financial position should be reported, but separately, since these value changes differ in terms of the certainty of realization from completed earnings cycles. Another possible statement the committee suggested was a statement that would report mainly on the factual aspects of an enterprise's transactions that were expected to have significant cash consequences. This statement would report data that required the minimal judgment and interpretation by the preparer.

The committee suggested that a financial forecast statement be included in corporate reports. In addition, the committee believed financial statements should include some data on those activities of business that affected society which can be determined and described or measured and which are important to the role of the enterprise in its social environment.

These recommendations gain their significance from the fact that they evolved from the deliberation of a special study group of the AICPA. They indicate that perhaps the idea that some major revisions to the traditional statements need to be made may be gaining greater acceptance in the accounting profession.[5]

BASIC ACCOUNTING MECHANICS

So far, we have discussed the effect of individual transactions in terms of their impact on the balance sheet and income statement with little concern for accounting mechanics. This section of Chapter 4 will present a summary of the systematic procedure used by accountants to record and summarize transactions. These procedures are called bookkeeping. The objective of this material is to help the reader without prior accounting training learn how to reduce, in an efficient manner, a complex set of business facts to the comprehensible set of relationships expressed in financial statements.

Accounts

Accountants use a series of accounts to record transactions. These accounts correspond to the items shown on the financial statements. The simplest form of account, and the one we will use, is a T-account. The Cash account of a company might look like this:

Cash

(Increases)		(Decreases)
Beginning balance at beginning of accounting period	100,000	3,000
	5,000	8,000
	20,000	40,000
	10,000	
	135,000	51,000
New beginning balance at end of accounting period	84,000	

All of the increases in cash are shown on one side. All of the decreases are recorded on the other. The new balance is determined by (1) add-

---

[5] At the time of publication the FASB was reviewing the Trueblood Committee report as part of the FASB's program to develop a statement of the conceptual framework of financial accounting and reporting.

ing all of the amounts listed on the increases and decreases side and (2) subtracting these totals from each other.

Debit-Credit Mechanism

Each accounting transaction has two parts. This is the dual aspect convention discussed in Chapter 3. It is reflected in the statement "the payment of an accounts receivable increases cash and reduces accounts receivable." This statement uses laymen's language to describe what occurred. The accountant would describe this transaction in terms of the debit-credit mechanism.

The accountant uses the term *debit* (dr.) to describe that part of a transaction that—

1. Increases an asset account.
2. Decreases a liability account.
3. Decreases an owners' equity account.
4. Decreases a revenue account.
5. Increases an expense account.

The term *credit* (cr.) is used to describe that part of the transaction that—

1. Decreases an asset account.
2. Increases a liability account.
3. Increases an owners' equity account.
4. Increases a revenue account.
5. Decreases an expense account.

The reader is encouraged to memorize these debit-credit rules rather than to try and determine their algebraic relationship to the basic accounting equation: Assets = Liabilities + Owners' Equity.

Here are some examples of the debit-credit terminology used to describe transactions:

1. A company borrows $10,000 cash from the bank. The accounting effect of the transaction is:

    Dr. Cash 10,000
    Cr.   Bank Notes Payable   10,000

2. The company repays the loan. The accountant would describe the transaction as:

    Dr. Bank Notes Payable 10,000
    Cr.   Cash   10,000

The words debit and credit have no meaning in accounting other than the following: debit means the amount is entered on the left-hand side of the T-account; credit means the amount is entered on the right-hand side of the T-account. The words carry no moral judgment. Depending on the account involved, they can be "desirable" or "undesirable" from the company's point of view. These are neutral terms.

Illustration 4–5 shows the relationship between T-accounts and the

ILLUSTRATION 4–5

Debit-Credit Rules

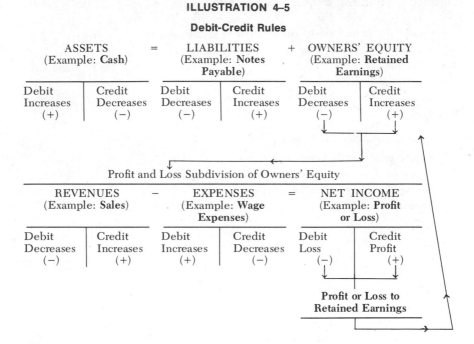

debit-credit mechanism. The reader should note that because debit and credit are used to signify the left and right sides of the T-account, the side used to record an increase or a decrease depends on the account. For example, increases in assets are recorded on the left or debit side, whereas increases in liabilities are listed on the right or credit side.

An Example

The following problem will be used to illustrate the steps in the process that you can use to prepare the financial statements required in your case problems.

Climax Industries, Inc., a new company started on January 1, 1975, sold at the beginning of the year 10,000 of common stock for $50,000. The company bought for cash $20,000 worth of raw materials and processing equipment worth $10,000. During the year the company had sales of $45,000, of which $5,000 was still owed by customers at year-end; consumed $15,000 worth of raw materials; spent $10,000 cash on wages; and paid $5,000 cash for administration, rent, and selling activities. During the year the company also bought $15,000 of raw materials for which it still owed $5,000 at the end of the year. Dividends of $2,000 were declared and paid at year-end. The company anticipates it will have no bad debts. Your assignment is to prepare an income statement for the period and a balance sheet as of the end of the year. (Disregard taxes.)

The first step is to *analyze* the transactions and record them in the debit-credit form. This is called *journalizing original entries.* It is purely mechanical. Here are the journal entries. To help you understand the debit-credit decisions better, each account will be labeled *A* if it is an asset account, *L* if it is a liability account, and *OE* if it is an owners' equity account.

1. To record the sale of capital stock for cash:

   Dr. Cash *(A)* 50,000
   Cr.   Capital Stock *(OE)*   50,000

2. To record the initial purchase of raw materials for cash:

   Dr. Raw Materials Inventory *(A)* 20,000
   Cr.   Cash *(A)*   20,000

3. To record the purchase of processing equipment for cash:

   Dr. Processing Equipment *(A)* 10,000
   Cr.   Cash *(A)*   10,000

4. To record the sales during the period:

   Dr. Cash *(A)* 40,000
       Accounts Receivable *(A)* 5,000
   Cr.   Sales *(OE)*   45,000

5. To record the period's wage expense:

   Dr. Wage Expense *(OE)* 10,000
   Cr.   Cash *(A)*   10,000

6. To record the period's administration, rent, and selling expense:

   Dr. Administration, Rent, and Selling Expense *(OE)* 5,000
   Cr.   Cash *(A)*   5,000

7. To record the purchase of raw materials during the year:

   Dr. Raw Materials Inventory *(A)* 15,000
   Cr.   Cash *(A)*   10,000
            Accounts Payable *(L)*   5,000

8. To record dividend declaration and payment:

   Dr. Retained Earnings *(OE)* 2,000
   Cr.   Cash *(A)*   2,000

9. To record the Raw Materials Inventory withdrawals during the year:[6]

    Dr. Raw Materials Expenses *(OE)* 15,000
    Cr.   Raw Materials Inventory *(A)*   15,000

10. To record the processing equipment's depreciation expense (see below for the debit-credit treatment of the "contra asset" account accumulated depreciation):

    Dr. Depreciation Expense *(OE)* 1,000
    Cr.   Accumulated Depreciation *(L)*   1,000

This last journal entry is called an adjusting entry. There is no transaction with parties outside the entity to prompt the recording of the event or to determine the amounts. These entries are made at the end of the period. They are the adjustments to assets or liabilities previously recorded that are required to achieve a periodic matching of costs and revenues. These entries require considerable judgment to determine the amounts involved.

Using the scheme of T-accounts similar to those in Illustration 4–5, the next step is to *post* the journal entries to the appropriate T-accounts. The results of this process are shown in Illustration 4–6. The numbers beside each amount refer to the journal entries describing the transaction.

Illustration 4–6 shows the accumulated depreciation account under the "liabilities" caption. The debit-credit mechanism treats this account as a liability. However, for statement purposes it is shown as a deduction, or a contra account, to the asset "processing equipment."

The next step is to calculate the *ending balances* in the asset and liability accounts, *close out* the expense and revenue accounts to the net income account, and then close the balance in this account to retained earnings. Here are the required journal entries to reduce the revenue, expense and net income accounts to zero:

11. To close the revenue account:

    Dr. Revenues 45,000
    Cr.   Net Income   45,000

12. To close the expense account:

    Dr. Net Income 31,000
    Cr.   Expenses   31,000

13. To close the net income account:

    Dr. Net Income 14,000
    Cr.   Retained Earnings   14,000

---

[6] Beginning inventory $20,000
    Plus: Purchases   15,000
    Less: Withdrawals   15,000
    Ending inventory $20,000

ILLUSTRATION 4-6

T-Accounts for Climax Industries, Inc., Example

ASSETS

Cash

+		−	
50,000(1)		20,000(2)	
40,000(4)		10,000(3)	
		10,000(5)	
		5,000(6)	
		10,000(7)	
		2,000(8)	
90,000		57,000	
33,000			

Raw Materials

+		−	
20,000(2)		15,000(9)	
15,000(7)			
35,000		15,000	
20,000			

Processing Equipment

+		−	
10,000(3)		0	
10,000			

Accounts Receivable

+		−	
5,000(4)		0	
5,000			

*Contra asset account.

LIABILITIES

Accounts Payable

−		+	
0		5,000(7)	
		5,000	

Accumulated Depreciation*

−		+	
0		1,000(10)	
		1,000	

OWNERS' EQUITY

Capital Stock

−		+	
0		50,000(1)	
		50,000	

Retained Earnings

−		+	
2,000(8)		14,000(13)	
2,000		14,000	
		12,000	

Retained Earnings Subdivisions

REVENUES

−		+	
		45,000(4)	
45,000(11)		45,000	

EXPENSES

+		−	
10,000 (5)		31,000(12)	
5,000 (6)			
15,000 (9)			
1,000(10)			
31,000		31,000	

= NET INCOME

−		+	
31,000(12)		45,000(11)	
14,000(13)			
45,000		45,000	

Now the statements can be prepared. Illustration 4–7 presents the company's income statement combined with a statement of changes in retained earnings. Illustration 4–8 presents the balance sheet of Climax Industries, Inc.

ILLUSTRATION 4–7

CLIMAX INDUSTRIES, INC.
Statement of Earnings and Changes in Retained Earnings
For the Year Ended December 31, 1975

Sales		$45,000
Cost of goods sold:		
Raw materials	$15,000	
Direct labor	10,000	
Manufacturing depreciation	1,000	26,000
Gross profit....................................		$19,000
Selling, rent, and administration		5,000
Net income.....................................		$14,000
Less: Common stock dividends declared		2,000
Additions to Income Retained in the Business		$12,000

ILLUSTRATION 4–8

CLIMAX INDUSTRIES, INC.
Statement of Financial Condition
December 31, 1975

Assets		Liabilities and Owners' Equity	
Current Assets:		Current Liabilities:	
Cash	$33,000	Accounts payable	$ 5,000
Accounts receivable	5,000	Long-term liabilities	—
Raw materials inventory	20,000	Total Liabilities	$ 5,000
Total Current Assets	$58,000		
Property (at cost):		Owners' Equity:	
Processing equipment	$10,000	Capital stock	$50,000
Less: Accumulated		Retained earnings	12,000
depreciation	1,000	Total Owners' Equity ...	$62,000
Net property	$ 9,000	Total Liabilities and	
Total Assets	$67,000	Owners' Equity ..	$67,000

SUGGESTED FURTHER READING

MAY, ROBERT G.; MUELLER, GERHARD G.; and WILLIAMS, THOMAS H. *A New Introduction to Financial Accounting.* Englewood Cliffs, N.J.: Prentice-Hall, Inc., 1975.

MEIGS, WALTER B.; JOHNSON, CHARLES E.; and MOSICH, A. N. *Financial Accounting.* New York: McGraw-Hill Book Co., 1970.

NISWONGER, ROLLIN C., and FESS, PHILIP E. *Accounting Principles.* Cincinnati, Ohio: South-Western Publishing Co., 1973.

CASES

CASE 4–1. OTTOMAN CAR COMPANY
Preparation of Journal Entries, Balance Sheet, and Income Statement

Fred Ottoman was a fire truck salesman for many years, while Bill, his brother, worked as a book salesman for a major publishing house. Although they had done fairly well financially, they wanted to "be their own bosses," so they decided to go into business together.

They agreed that selling cars would be a good line for them to go into as both had been interested in sports cars for many years. Also the small town in Ohio where they lived did not have any automobile dealerships. The nearest dealer, a Ford dealer, was some 30 miles away.

After some searching, they chose a suitable site for their proposed operation. It was situated on a popular shopping street. A dilapidated apartment building which had been condemned by the local authorities stood on the site.

At this point in time, the brothers decided to incorporate the business. The services of a lawyer were obtained to draw up the legal papers and to handle all aspects of the execution of the incorporation. The fee for this service was $200, and each of the brothers paid half of it.

Fred purchased 1,800 shares of the company's stock for $18,000, and Bill purchased 500 shares for $5,000. The above-mentioned payments for legal services were considered part of these investments; so, the actual cash received was $22,800. Further purchases of the company's shares could be made only at the prevailing book value per share at the time of the purchase and only if both parties agreed to the transaction. If either brother wished at any time to sell his shares back to the company, this transaction would also be conducted at the prevailing book value of the shares. The brothers also agreed that they should each receive salaries of $6,000 per year at all times during which they were engaged on the company's business on a full-time basis.

On November 1, 1969, with the aid of a $10,000 bank loan and

$8,000 of the company's money, Fred purchased the property which had been selected. The same day, he left his job to devote his full attention to the new enterprise.

First, Fred arranged to have the old building demolished. A cursory examination revealed there was nothing of any significance that could be salvaged, except for some building stone. Mr. Mahoney, the wrecker, agreed to clear the site for $3,500, provided he could have the stone. Otherwise, he would want $4,500. Fred was convinced he could get a better price for the stone, so he instructed Mr. Mahoney to clear the site and store the stone in a corner of it. This work was started immediately, and completed before Christmas. Mr. Mahoney agreed to defer collection of payment until May 31, 1970.

In the meantime, Fred got in touch with a large automobile manufacturer, National Cars, Inc., who had previously indicated interest in the projected dealership. Fred asked National for financial help to construct the buildings needed to carry on business. National agreed to provide all the finances needed for the building through a loan repayable in ten equal annual installments, provided Ottoman Cars sold only National models. The loan earned an interest rate of 4 percent per year, payable from April 1, 1970. The first repayment, including interest, would fall due on March 31, 1971.

On December 31, National Cars sent a check for $10,000 to get Ottoman Cars started. Fred deposited the check in the business's bank account. The remainder of the loan would be forthcoming when the building was completed.

Next Fred arranged through a consulting architect for several construction companies to bid for the job. The lowest bidder was the Birkett and Snell Company. They agreed to construct the specified building for $31,500. On the advice of his architect, however, Fred Ottoman decided to accept the Holmes Bros. Construction Company bid of $35,000; the architect knew Birkett and Snell Company was less reliable than Holmes in meeting promised completion dates.

The construction was started immediately, Holmes promising completion by the end of March 1970. Progress payments on certificates from the architects were to be made at the end of January, the end of February, and the date of completion in amounts of $10,000, $10,000, and $15,000.

During the winter period, Fred tried to obtain some orders for the 1970 model cars, which he planned to deliver directly to customers from National's warehouse in Cleveland. Fred had some success with the model he had recently bought for himself. Between January 1 and March 30, Fred sold 17 of this model at an average cash cost to Ottoman Cars of $2,250. Nothing was paid to National for these cars during the period. These 17 sales realized $45,900, whereof $14,500 represented trade-in allowances, $28,000 was in cash, and the rest was outstanding at March 30. Fred sold all the trade-in cars for $13,700 cash before March 30. Bill and Fred agreed that the latter should receive $10 for every new car sale as compensation for using his private car as a display model.

At the end of March, the building was completed. However, there was an additional charge of $600 for materials, which Ottoman had to pay according to the provisions of the building contract. At the same time, the architect's bill for $650 arrived.

Fred sent the progress payments to the builder as previously arranged, making the January payment with $10,000 of the company's money and the February payment with the National loan. On March 31 the last $15,000 progress payment and the $600 materials surcharge were paid. The $10,000 bank loan plus interest of $300 was repaid by check on March 30.

On March 30, Bill quit his job with the publishing house and joined Ottoman Cars on a full-time basis. At Bill's request, it was agreed that financial statements would be prepared, to allow the two brothers to see where they stood as at the end of March. National Cars, Inc., asked that a portion of the amount the dealership owed the manufacturers for cars be regarded as the payment due to the dealership under the building contract, and Fred accepted this arrangement on behalf of Ottoman Cars. The two brothers agreed that they would invite Mr. William Hurley, an accountant who was a mutual friend of theirs to prepare the accounts.

Questions

1. As Mr. Hurley, prepare journal entries to record the events that have taken place in the business up to March 31, 1970.
2. From these journal entries, prepare a balance sheet as of March 31, 1970, and an income statement for the period to that date.
3. Based on your financial statements, what is the value of each brother's equity in the company?
4. Prepare a statement showing the sources and uses of cash from the formation of the business until March 31, 1970.

CASE 4–2. PETER FULLER
Determining Financial Reporting Policy and Preparation of Projected Financial Statements

Peter Fuller was the inventor of a metal hoseclamp for automobile hose connections. Having confidence in its commercial value, but owning no surplus funds of his own, he sought among his friends and acquaintances for the necessary capital to put it on the market. The proposition which he placed before possible associates was that a corporation should be formed with capital stock of $30,000, that he be given $16,000 par value of stock for his patent, and that the remaining $14,000 be sold for a sum as near par as possible.

The project looked attractive to a number of the individuals to whom the inventor presented it, but the most promising among them—a retired manufacturer—said he would be unwilling to invest his capital without knowing what uses were intended for the cash to be received from the proposed sale of stock. He suggested that the inventor determine the probable costs of experimentation and of special machinery, and prepare for him a statement of the estimated assets and liabilities of the proposed company when ready to begin actual operations. He also asked for a statement of the estimated transactions for the first year of production and sales operations, together with an analysis of the operating results indicated by those expectations. This information would be based on the studies the inventor had made of probable markets and costs of labor and materials. It would include a listing of resulting assets and liabilities; and analysis of expected sales, expenses, and profits; and an explanation of expected flow of cash over the course of the year.

After consulting the engineer who had aided him in constructing his patent models, Fuller drew up the following list of data relating to the transactions of the proposed corporation during its period of organization and development.

1. Probable selling price of $14,000 par value of stock, $18,000.
2. Probable cost of incorporation and organization, $825, which includes estimated officers' salaries during developmental period.
3. Probable cost of developing special machinery, $13,000. This sum includes the cost of expert services, materials, rent of a small shop, and the cost of power, light, and miscellaneous expenditures.
4. Probable cost of raw material, $500, of which $300 is to be used in experimental production.

Fuller drew up the first of the statements desired by his prospective associate in the following manner:

Probable Assets and Liabilities of the Proposed Company
When Ready to Begin Actual Operations

Assets		Liabilities and Proprietorship	
Patent	$16,000	Capital stock at par	$30,000
Machinery	13,000	Plus premium on stock	4,000
Organization costs	825	Capital paid in	$34,000
Experimental costs	300		
Raw materials and supplies	200		
Cash	3,675		
Total Assets	$34,000	Total Liabilities	$34,000

With this initial part of his assignment completed, the inventor set down the following estimates as a beginning step in furnishing the rest of the information desired.

1. Expected sales, $28,000, all to be received in cash by the end of the first year following completion of organization and initial experimentation.
2. Expected additional purchases of raw materials and supplies during the course of this operating year, all for cash, paid by end of year, $9,000.
3. Expected help from the banks during year—but loans, including $50 interest, to be repaid before close of year—$2,000.
4. Expected payroll and other cash expenses and manufacturing costs for the operating year, $14,000 (of which $3,000 is to be for selling and administrative expenses).
5. Expected inventory of raw materials and supplies at close of period, at cost, $1,800.
6. No inventory of unsold process or finished stock expected as of the end of the period. All goods to be sold "on special order"; none to be produced "for stock."
7. All experimental and organization costs, previously capitalized as essentially going-concern assets or "valuations," to be charged against income of the operating year.
8. Estimated depreciation of machinery, $1,300, based on a ten-year life. (However, Fuller was aware of a plastic hoseclamp being developed by a major corporation that might make his product and the equipment used to produce it obsolete in about four years' time. If this occurred, Fuller thought that it might be possible to convert special machinery into general-purpose equipment at a cost of several thousand dollars.)
9. Machinery maintenance, cash, $75.
10. New machinery and equipment to be purchased for cash, $1,000.
11. Profit distributions of net cash proceeds of sales, $3,000.

The above transaction data were for the most part cumulative totals, and should not be interpreted to mean that the events described were to take place in the precise order or sequence indicated.

Questions

1. Prepare the information wanted by the retired manufacturer.
2. What kind of a financial image do you think Fuller should present to the retired manufacturer? Do statements prepared according to Fuller's proposed accounting rules create this image? What changes would you make?

Chapter 5

CONSOLIDATED FINANCIAL STATEMENTS

Business executives and accountants generally recognize: "Where there is a parent company and one or more subsidiaries, there is a presumption that consolidated statements are more meaningful than separate statements."[1] Consolidated financial statements present the financial position and the results of operation for a parent company and its subsidiaries as if the group were a single company. The corporation owning a major portion (more than 50 percent) of the outstanding capital stock of another corporation is the parent, while the controlled corporation is the subsidiary. The parent and its subsidiaries are sometimes called affiliated companies, although the term "affiliate" is typically reserved for companies in which the parent's ownership interest is less than 50 percent.

The subject of accounting for intercorporate investments is covered in greater detail in Chapter 18. In that chapter accounting for nonconsolidated subsidiaries, joint ventures, equity interests between 20 and 50 percent, and marketable securities are discussed. In addition, the accounting for business acquisitions is presented. This chapter focuses on the nature of the consolidated statement and the process followed in preparing it. It comes early in the book since most of the statements that the reader will use will probably be consolidated statements.

Single Economic Unit

Consolidated statements treat parent and subsidiary corporations as though they were a single economic unit, even though the parent and subsidiary companies are legally separate entities. Financial information is combined as if the corporations involved were merely depart-

---

[1] Principle E–2 in Paul Grady, "Inventory of Generally Accepted Accounting Principles for Business Enterprises," *Accounting Research Study No. 7* (New York: American Institute of Certified Public Accountants, 1965), p. 67.

ments or divisions of a larger corporation. The consolidating procedure cancels out on work sheets all offsetting reciprocal pairs of assets and liabilities, revenues and costs, and investment and equity accounts which appear on the statements of the affiliated corporations. For example, a parent may lend its subsidiary $100,000. This will appear as a loan receivable on the parent's statements. It will be carried as a loan payable on the subsidiary's books. When the statements of the two companies are consolidated, these items will be eliminated. Similarly all such transactions involving intercompany investments and gains and losses on intercompany transactions are reversed on the work sheets so that only events involving the economic unit and outside parties will show on the consolidated statements.

Consolidation Policy

At least two conditions should be present to justify consolidation: control and homogeneity of operations.

Control.   In general, the parent must have presently, and expect to continue, ownership and management control over the subsidiary. For full consolidation the parent company must have a minimum ownership in the subsidiary of "more than 50 percent."

Irrespective of the degree of ownership control, however, managerial control is a prerequisite for consolidation. Adequate control is not considered to be present if the parent-subsidiary relationship is hampered or threatened by currency, dividend, legal, or political restrictions. Principally for these reasons, foreign subsidiaries may be excluded from consolidation when there are significant limitations or threats to the economic flexibility or the continuity of these operations. Also, these conditions justify the nonconsolidation of bankrupt or insolvent subsidiaries.

Homogeneity.   In earlier periods, it was believed that statements for a parent and its consolidated subsidiaries should represent a homogeneous economic unit. However, increasing corporate diversification and the increase in "conglomerates" has resulted in substantial relaxation of this requirement. So long as the parent retains control, nonhomogeneous subsidiaries may be and often are consolidated. Typically, however, manufacturing entities do not consolidate their financial subsidiaries, such as finance or insurance companies. These interests are reported on an equity basis.

The equity method is also used to report on parent-company-only statements investments in companies that represent between 20 and 100 percent of the investee's common stock. Another use of the equity method is to report on consolidated statements investments of between 20 and 50 percent in the equity of affiliated companies.

The equity method limits effect of the investment in the subsidiary to one line of the parent company or consolidated balance sheet and income statement. When the equity method is used, the reporting entity includes its share of the subsidiary's net income, after removing the effect of intercompany transactions, as a single line on the reporting entity's income statement. None of the subsidiary's revenue and expense amounts are combined with the reporting entity's revenue and expense items. Similarly, none of the subsidiary's balance sheet accounts are combined with the reporting entity's balance sheet amounts. The only effect of the equity method on the reporting entity's balance sheet is an entry to the investment in unconsolidated subsidiary asset account. This account reflects the cost of the investment in the subsidiary plus the reporting entity's share of the subsidiary's retained earnings since acquisition, again after all intercompany transactions have been eliminated. The equity method is discussed in greater detail later in this chapter.

Disclosure

The parent company policy regarding consolidation policy is disclosed in notes to the financial statements, as in the following example:

Consolidation Principles: The consolidated financial statements cover the accounts of all significant majority-owned subsidiaries, after including Somerset Fire Insurance Company and other financial subsidiaries on an equity basis. Consolidated financial statements for Somerset and combined financial statements for the other financial subsidiaries are included in support of the consolidated financial statements of the Corporation. The financial statements include retroactively the accounts of and shares issued in exchange for companies added through poolings of interests in 1976, the effect of which was insignificant on the prior year's financial statements.

Other investments are carried at cost, except investments in 20–50% owned companies ($52,482,000 and $45,045,000 at December 31, 1976 and 1975, respectively) which are included on an equity basis.

Intercompany transactions are eliminated in the consolidated financial statements except for intercompany sales to telecommunication subsidiaries, which are made at prices equivalent to generally available commercial prices, and intercompany profits in certain manufacturing inventories. These transactions are not deemed to have a material effect on consolidated sales, inventories, fixed assets, or net income.

Accounting Concepts Peculiar to
Consolidated Statements

Most items appearing on consolidated financial statements are comparable to those found on statements of the individual corporations. There are four items which are peculiar to consolidated statements: minority interest, goodwill, consolidated net income, and consolidated retained earnings.

Minority Interest. Financial statements prepared for single corporations do not distinguish between the individuals or groups owning a single class of capital stock. In the case of consolidated statements, if the parent does not own 100 percent of the capital stock of a subsidiary, that part of ownership equity not owned by the parent is presented separately on the consolidated balance sheet and identified as minority interest. This practice conforms to the concept of preparing consolidated financial statements from the point of view of the parent company which exercises controlling ownership over its subsidiaries.

After total net income for the affiliated group is determined, a deduction is made for that part of the subsidiary's earnings applicable to the minority ownership.

Thus, the minority interest shown on the consolidated balance sheet consists of a pro rata share of net worth based on capital contribution plus accumulated earnings less any dividends paid.

From the parent's point of view, some accountants argue that the minority interest has characteristics of a liability. Others claim it represents a separate class of equity. As a result, in practice "minority interest" is usually recorded between liabilities and ownership rather than being included in either category.

Goodwill. The intangible asset goodwill is recognized only when a going business is acquired through a purchase transaction at a price greater than the value of the acquired company's net assets.[2] When a parent acquires an interest in a subsidiary under these circumstances, this excess of investment over the market value of the net assets acquired is not separated on the parent's statements. It remains as an unidentified part of parent's total investment in the subsidiary, which is listed as an asset. On the parent's statements the portion of the investment account representing goodwill is amortized against the parent's share of the subsidiary's net income recognized on the equality basis over a period not to exceed 40 years.

When the subsidiary and the parent are combined in consolidated statements, the parent's investment in the subsidiary is eliminated along with the parent's interest in the equity of the subsidiary. If the original purchase transaction created goodwill on the parent's accounts, the investment and equity amounts eliminated in consolidation will differ by the amount of the original goodwill less any goodwill amortized since the acquisition date. This goodwill balance is recorded on the consolidated statements as an asset. In addition, the

---

[2] The nature and handling of goodwill will be treated in greater detail in Chapter 18.

current amount of goodwill amortized is included as a current expense of the consolidated entity.

Consolidated Net Income.   Consolidated income statements present the total net income during the period for the affiliated group as if it were operating as a single corporation. To achieve this, all intercompany transactions giving rise to gains or losses are eliminated. Also, those earnings applicable to minority ownership are deducted from consolidated net income and included as part of minority interest. The resulting consolidated net income consists of parent company earnings plus the parent's share of subsidiary earnings for the period arising from external transactions, less goodwill amortized during the period.

Consolidated Retained Earnings.   Consolidated retained earnings include all of the retained earnings of the parent plus the parent's share of the subsidiary's retained earnings from the date of acquisition less any goodwill amortized and intercompany transaction effects. Of course, earnings applicable to the minority interest have been removed. Also, dividends paid by subsidiary companies to the parent have been eliminated, since they are merely transfers of cash within the consolidated entity.

Investment in Subsidiary

There are two methods for recording in a parent company's accounts its ownership interest in a subsidiary corporation. These are the cost and equity methods. APB *Opinion No. 18* requires that the equity method be used if the investor company has "the ability to exercise significant influence over the operating and financial policies of the investee company." There is a presumption that ownership of 20 percent or more of the voting stock gives the investor this control. Typically, the equity method is used to account for subsidiary investments that are not fully consolidated.

Cost Method.   Under the cost method, the original price paid for the subsidiary is recorded on the parent's records as the "investment in subsidiary." This original investment figure remains unchanged by the subsequent activities of the subsidiary. Neither subsequent profits nor losses of the subsidiary are given any recognition in the parent's accounts. However, any cash dividends received from the subsidiary are recorded as income at the time of receipt.

Equity Method.   Under the equity method, or as it sometimes is called one-line consolidation, initially the acquisition price is recorded on the parent's books as "Investment in Subsidiary," as under the cost method. Subsequently, this investment account is increased by the parent's pro rata share of the subsidiary's additions to stockholders equity (or decreased by reduction in stockholders' equity). The parent's share of the subsidiary's profits (or losses) are shown on the parent's books as being the parent's equity in the subsidiary's earnings and included in the "other income" (or "other expense") category at the close of each accounting period. The offsetting debit entry is to the investment account. Cash dividends received by the parent from the subsidiary are recorded as reductions to the investment account and increases in the Cash account. Thus, the account labeled "Investment in Subsidiary (equity method)" reflects the original investment cost plus (or minus) the parent's share of changes in the subsidiary's retained earnings from the date of acquisition. (i.e., profits − dividends).

As noted above, when the equity method is used any goodwill created must be amortized and the effect of intercompany transactions eliminated.

The equity method is not a valid substitute for full consolidation and should not be used to justify exclusion of a subsidiary when full consolidation is otherwise appropriate.

Opinion No. 10.   In *Opinion No. 10,* "Omnibus Opinion—1966," the Accounting Principles Board expressed the opinion that if a domestic subsidiary controlled by the parent is not consolidated, the equity method should be used to report investment in the subsidiary. Later, in *Opinion No. 18* the APB extended this requirement to foreign subsidiaries. The one exception was in the case of foreign subsidiaries operating under conditions of exchange restrictions, controls, or other uncertainties of a type that would lead to a decision not to consolidate. In these cases the cost method is permissible.

Consolidation Procedures

A number of alternative methods involving work sheets are used to accomplish consolidation. The act of consolidation occurs only on the work sheet used for assembling the consolidated data, not in the accounts or records of the parent or subsidiary corporations. Each parent and subsidiary's accounting records and financial statements are based upon the principle that each company is a separate legal entity.

None of the alternative work sheet procedures, or methods of recording ownership of subsidiaries prior to consolidation, have any distinguishing effect upon the final consolidated financial statements. The reader of the consolidated statements cannot determine which alternative was used.

Confusion in consolidating procedures is minimized if one is mindful constantly that (1) consolidating adjusting and eliminating entries are never recorded in the accounts of the affiliated group and (2) each periodic or annual consolidation is made as if it were the initial consolidation.

A common procedure for preparing consolidated financial statements involves the following steps:

1. Arrange vertically in parallel columns on a work sheet the unconsolidated statements of the parent and of the subsidiaries to be consolidated, as shown in Illustration 5-1.

2. Make any preconsolidating adjustments necessary to bring consistency into the statements. For example, a work sheet adjustment

ILLUSTRATION 5-1
Consolidation Working Papers

	Parent	Sub-sidiary	Adjustments Debits	Adjustments Credits	Con-solidated Statement
Assets					
Cash	$ 400	$ 20	(1) 10		$ 430
Accounts receivable	700	125		(1) 10	815
Inventory	1,200	275			1,475
Investment in subsidiary	400			(5) 400	
Note due from subsidiary	175	—		(2) 175	—
Plant and equipment (net)	300	200			500
Goodwill			(5) 240		240
Other assets	25	10			35
Total Assets	$3,200	$630			$3,495
Liabilities					
Accounts payable	$ 200	$100			$ 300
Notes payable	400	30			430
Loans payable—bank	1,000	25			1,025
Loans payable—parent		175	(2) 175		—
Common stock	1,000	200	(4) 40 (5) 160		1,000
Retained earnings	600	100	(4) 20 (5) 0		680
Minority interest				(4) 60	60
Total Liabilities	$3,200	$630			$3,495
Income Statement					
Sales	$1,200	$475	(3) 150		$1,525
Cost of goods sold	800	125		(3) 150	775
Gross margin	$ 400	$350			$ 750
Selling expense	$ 50	$ 75			$ 125
Operating expense	75	125			200
Total Expense	$ 125	$200			$ 325
Net Income	$ 275	$150			$ 425

would be required if an affiliate had forwarded cash to another affiliate in payment of a debt but the other affiliate had not yet received the cash as of the closing date. In this case the statement of the affiliate to whom the cash was sent would be adjusted as if the cash had been actually received. All intercompany relationships such as these must be reconciled and brought into agreement before eliminations can be made. (The receipt of cash such as $10,000 for payment of accounts receivable by the parent from the subsidiary is shown as adjustment 1 in the illustration.)

3. Eliminate intercompany assets and liabilities. All debtor-creditor relationships between affiliates to be consolidated are offset on the work sheet. This is achieved by making work sheet entries which cancel the asset of one affiliate against the liability of another affiliate. The effect of these eliminations is reversal of transactions which created the intercompany assets and liabilities in the accounts of affiliates. For example, if a subsidiary borrowed $175,000 from its parent, the subsidiary would enter the transaction on its books by debiting Cash $175,000 and crediting Loans Payable $175,000. The parent's records will reflect an entry debiting Loans Receivable and crediting Cash $175,000. On the consolidating work sheet the eliminating entry will debit Loans Payable and credit Loans Receivable for $175,000. (See adjustment number 2.) This entry involves accounts which are in the statements of different corporations. The effect of this entry is to reverse the entries made on the books of the affiliates, but no entries to Cash are necessary because assets and liabilities of all affiliates will be combined. As noted earlier, all eliminating entries are made only on the consolidating work sheets and are not entered in the accounts of the individual corporations.

4. Eliminate (or cancel out) any intercompany revenue against the appropriate costs or expenses. Adjustment number 3 shows the entries reversing $150,000 of intercompany sales. This entry assumes none of the goods sold to the subsidiary are still in its inventory account.

5. Eliminate the effect of dividends declared by a corporation to another member of the affiliated group. (None shown in the example.)

6. Eliminate from the accounts all intercompany profits or losses which may be cumulatively included in asset accounts of the purchaser and in equity accounts of the seller. The gains or losses of prior periods of affiliation as well as those of the current period must be canceled.

Illustration 5–1 does not include an example of this kind of adjustment. If such an adjustment were required, however, it might be handled as follows: Assume the parent had sold three years earlier to its subsidiary a machine for $20,000, including the parent's $2,000 profit, and the subsidiary was depreciating this machine over ten years, the adjustments would be:

a. To eliminate the profit on the intercompany sale from the gross
    carrying value of the assets of the subsidiary and the retained
    earnings of the parent:

    Retained Earnings (parent) 2,000
        Plant and Equipment (sub)   2,000

b. To eliminate the depreciation expense based on the intercompany
    profit of $2,000 included in the subsidiary's fixed asset account.
    This requires $200 (or $2,000/10 years) to be deducted from this
    year's depreciation expense and an elimination from the sub-
    sidiary's retained earnings of $400 representing the last two year's
    depreciation charged by the subsidiary on the intercompany pro-
    fits included in its asset base.

    Accumulated Depreciation (sub) 600
        Depreciation Expense (sub)   200
        Retained Earnings (sub)   400

7. Eliminate the investment account of the parent in those subsidiaries being consolidated and adjust those subsidiaries' equity accounts for any minority interests that may be present. The minority
interest is equal to the minority stockholders' proportional share of the
subsidiaries *current* net worth.

The computation of the minority interest is:

    Minority Interest (in subsidiary):
        Capital stock ....   20% × $200 = $40
        Retained earnings ....   20% × $100 =   20
            Minority Interest $60

The adjusting entries in Illustration 5–1 (number 4) are:

    Capital Stock (sub)   40
    Retained Earnings (sub)   20
        Minority Interest   60

If the parent's investment in the subsidiary exceeded its proportional share of the subsidiary's equity capital and Retained Earnings
accounts at the *acquisition date,* an adjustment will also be required to
determine the goodwill amount on the consolidated statements. To
illustrate, assume the $400 "investment in subsidiary" balance shown
in Illustration 5–1 represents an 80 percent interest in the subsidiary's
equity and the subsidiary's retained earnings were zero at the time the
investment was made because prior to this time it had been the practice of the investee to pay out all of its profits in dividends. (The
retained earnings is now $100.) Also assume that the long-term asset
values on the subsidiaries books approximate their market values.

The goodwill calculation is:

Goodwill:
Investment (parent) $400
Common Stock (sub), 80% × 200 .... $160
Retained Earnings (sub), 80% × $0   0   160
    Goodwill $240

The adjusting entries in illustration 5–1 (number 5) are:

Common Stock (sub)   160
Retained Earnings (sub)   0
Goodwill   240
    Investment in Subsidiary (parent)   400

The goodwill amount, if positive, is usually labeled descriptively as "excess of cost over book value" and presented as an asset on the consolidated balance sheet. A negative balance is identified as "excess of book value over cost." The amount of positive or negative goodwill is amortized as a charge against income over a period not to exceed 40 years.

In the case of Illustration 5–1, the amortization of the goodwill in the consolidated statement would involve (1) a write-down of the goodwill asset by an amount equal to the sum of the annual charges to date, (2) an increase in the operating expense by the annual charge (and a decrease in profits by the amount of this charge), and (3) a decrease in retained earnings by the cumulative effect of the goodwill charges to profits. Thus, assume a 24-year write-off period, the goodwill balance shown of Illustration 5–1 would be decreased by 30[(240/24) × 3]; retained earnings would decline by 30 (prior two-year charges plus current year charge); operating profits would decrease by 10 (current years charge); and operating expenses would increase by 10. If goodwill is being amortized these adjustments should be made to the consolidated statement figures in Illustration 5–1. Goodwill acquired before November 1970 need not be amortized.

8. Combine all remaining statement amounts for all affiliates being considered. The balances can then be arranged in the traditional financial statement form, modified for the four concepts peculiar to consolidation described previously.

Consolidated Federal Income Tax Returns. The choice of filing consolidated federal income tax returns by an affiliated group is completely independent of financial reporting practices. In general, domestic industrial corporations which are related by a minimum of 80 percent control (or have this degree of common ownership) may elect to report on a consolidated basis. The complex regulations governing the filing of consolidated returns provide for elimination of intercompany gains and losses and for offsetting profits of one affiliate against losses of another member of the group.

Limitations of Consolidated Financial Statements.   The underlying assumption that consolidated financial statements are more meaningful than separate statements for affiliated companies needs to be qualified. Since consolidated financial statements ignore the separate legal character of affiliated corporations, information concerning any of the individual companies included in the consolidated statements cannot be obtained from the statements. For example, creditors and investors cannot evaluate the profitability or financial condition of any single corporation within the group on the basis of the consolidated statements. The analyst is unable to identify the assets and liabilities of the consolidated group with any of the individual corporations. Similarly, the statements are of limited value to the minority stockholder interested in a subsidiary company.

SUGGESTED FURTHER READING

COPELAND, RONALD; CRUMBLEY, LARRY D.; and WOJDAK, JOSEPH F.   *Advanced Accounting.* New York: Holt, Rinehart and Winston, Inc., 1971.

GRIFFIN, CHARLES H.; WILLIAMS, THOMAS H.; and LARSON, KERMIT D.   *Advanced Accounting.* 3d ed. Homewood, Ill.: Richard D. Irwin, Inc., 1977.

MOONITZ, MAURICE. *The Entity Theory of Consolidated Statements.* Bloomington, Ind.: American Accounting Association, 1944.

CASES

CASE 5–1. COMPANY P AND SUBSIDIARY COMPANY S
Preparation of Consolidated Statements

Company P purchased 80 percent of the outstanding capital stock of Company S from individual stockholders for $290,000 cash on January 1, 1972. On this date the retained earnings of Company S were $30,000.

Company S was primarily, but not exclusively, engaged in marketing goods purchased from Company P. Though purchases from Company P during the year 1976 were $1,200,000, the inventory held by Company S at the beginning or the close of the year did not include any merchandise acquired from Company P. On December 31, 1976, the balance due to Company P for these intercompany purchases was $280,000.

All plant and equipment owned by Company S was acquired for cash from Company P on January 1, 1974, and has been depreciated on the basis of its estimated life of ten years, using the straight-line method without salvage value. In 1974, Company P recorded a $50,000 profit on the sale of these fixed assets to its subsidiary.

A 10 percent cash dividend was declared and paid by Company S on its outstanding capital stock on July 1, 1976.

Financial statements of Company P and of Company S are presented in vertical form on the accompanying work sheet (Exhibit 1) to facilitate assembly of information for consolidated statements.

Questions

1. Complete the work sheet provided (or use any method you prefer) to assemble the information necessary for—
   a. A consolidated income statement.
   b. A consolidated retained earnings statement.
   c. A consolidated balance sheet.
2. Compare the financial condition of Company P on an unconsolidated basis with that presented by the consolidated statements. Your comparison should include computations of—

EXHIBIT 1

COMPANY P AND SUBSIDIARY COMPANY S
Working Papers for Consolidated Statements
For the Year Ended December 31, 1976
(in thousands; parentheses indicate deductions)

	Company P	Company S	Adjustments and Eliminations Dr.	Adjustments and Eliminations Cr.	Consolidated Statements
Income Statement					
Sales	$1,500	$1,800			
Cost of sales	(900)	(1,400)			
	$ 600	$ 400			
Depreciation	(40)	(20)			
Operating expenses...........	(440)	(290)			
Net income from operations	$ 120	$ 90			
Dividend income..............	24				
Minority net income					
Net Income	$ 144	$ 90			
Retained Earnings Statement					
Retained earnings, Jan. 1, 1976:					
Company P	$ 248				
Company S		$ 70			
Net income (as above)	144	90			
Dividends:					
Company P	(72)				
Company S		(30)			
Retained earnings,					
Dec. 31, 1976	$ 320	$ 130			
Balance Sheet					
Cash	$ 110	$ 150			
Accounts receivable (net)	375	410			
Inventories	310	75			
Plant and equipment	885	200			
Accumulated depreciation ...	(265)	(60)			
Investment in Company S (at cost)	290				
Goodwill					
Total Assets	$1,705	$ 775			
Accounts payable	$ 385	$ 345			
Minority interest					
Capital stock:					
Company P	1,000				
Company S		300			
Retained earnings (as above) ...	320	130			
Total Liabilities	$1,705	$ 775			

    a. Working capital (current assets − current liabilities).
    b. Total assets.
    c. Long-term capital.
    d. Any ratios or relationships you think significant.
3. Compare the profitability of Company P on an unconsolidated basis with that shown by the consolidated statements.
4. How meaningful are consolidated statements to you as—
    a. A stockholder of Company P?
    b. A minority stockholder of Company S?

CASE 5–2. MOHAWK PRODUCTS, INCORPORATED
Determination of the Consolidated Entity

In 1933, Edwin Franklin, following the inheritance of a large fortune, established Mohawk Products, Inc., in Greensville, Quebec, Canada, to manufacture textile products. Between 1933 and 1970 the company prospered and expanded to the point where it was one of the largest privately held companies in the nation. In 1970 its operations included two foreign and one domestic textile subsidiaries, a real estate subsidiary, a finance subsidiary, an electronics subsidiary, a bank, and a farm equipment company. Mohawk Products or one of its subsidiaries established each of these companies and owned 100 percent of their outstanding common stock.

In early 1970, James Franklin, president and principal stockholder of Mohawk Products, was considering the possibility of making a small private offering to a limited number of investors of some of his Mohawk Products common stock. Several members of the Franklin family thought a wider market holding of their stock would simplify the valuation of their holdings in the company for estate tax purposes. In 1970 Mohawk had outstanding, and in the hands of the Franklin family, one million shares of common stock.

To date, Mohawk had carried its subsidiaries on Mohawk's financial statement as an "investment in unconsolidated subsidiaries." The investment was valued according to the cost method.

Mr. Franklin was considering whether it would be better for the purposes of the stock offering to present the company's financial statements on a consolidated basis. In addition, if he decided to change the parent company's consolidation policy, he was not sure which subsidiaries he should consolidate. He was determined, however, to continue using the cost method to value all unconsolidated subsidiaries.

Mr. Edwin Franklin, Mohawk's founder, believed "every tub should stand on its own bottom." In line with this policy, it had been Mohawk's practice to reinvest the earnings of its subsidiaries in the subsidiary creating the earnings; to minimize intercompany investment and operating transactions; and to satisfy the needs of the Mohawk stockholders for dividends from the current earnings of the parent. To date, the parent had never received dividends from its subsidiaries. For income tax purposes, the company submitted unconsolidated returns.

Textile Companies. Mohawk Products owned three subsidiaries in the textile area: Iroquois Woolens, Inc.; Bull Dog Linens Proprietary, Ltd.; and Mohawk Products (Australia) Ltd. Iroquois Woolens was formed in 1939 to manufacture blankets in Madison, Quebec. Bull Dog Linens, the company's British subsidiary, was created in 1953 to produce fine linen goods for the British and European markets. Bull Dog's two plants were located in Manchester and Liverpool. During recent years, repeated labor troubles had plagued Bull Dog Linens. The Australian subsidiary, Mohawk Products (Australia) was formed in 1963 to operate a small textile mill near Sydney, Australia.

Banking   Company. In   1939,   following   the   collapse   of Greensville's two banks, Mr. Edwin Franklin created the Franklin Trust Company in Greensville. Since the Mohawk mill was the major company in Greensville, Mr. Franklin saw an opportunity for Mohawk Products to make a profit by becoming its own banker and the banker for its employees, their relatives, and the many local tradespeople who relied upon the mill and its employees for their livelihood. Over the years new companies moved into the town and its population increased considerably. Throughout this period, the Franklin Trust was the town's only bank and its business expanded.

Since it had been founded, the Franklin Trust had held all of Mohawk's cash balances. However, it had never loaned money to its parent or its subsidiaries. This "no loan" practice followed Mr. Edwin Franklin's promise to the townspeople and the province's banking commission that the bank would avoid conflict-of-interest situations, such as lending money to its parent or any of its parent's subsidiaries. As a result, whenever Mohawk or its subsidiaries needed financing they obtained it from Franklin's correspondent bank in Montreal.

Farm Equipment Company. In 1937, Mr. Edwin Franklin's youngest daughter married John Atkins, the sales vice president for one of the largest farm equipment manufacturers in the country. As a wedding present, Mr. Franklin used Mohawk Products' cash to buy at a distress price the Eastern Canadian franchise to distribute and sell the well-known Walpole farm equipment line and made Mr. Atkins the president of the new company, Consolidated Farm Equipment,

Inc. Mr. Atkins quickly developed an effective system of subdistributors, and the company made progress, despite the unfavorable state of the farm economy.

In early 1939 the franchise became worthless when the Walpole Farm Equipment Company of Canada went bankrupt. Mr. Atkins, aware of the growing threat of war in Europe, bought the assets of Walpole at book value, with the expectation that in the event of war Consolidated Farm Equipment could use the Walpole plants to profitably manufacture tanks and small arms. Mohawk guaranteed the loans Consolidated Farm Equipment used to finance this acquisition. Accordingly, during World War II, Consolidated Farm Equipment manufactured farm equipment, tanks, and small arms. The company's wartime profits were used to extinguish the loans obtained to buy Walpole.

With the advent of peace, the company turned its attention to developing the Walpole farm equipment line on a national basis. Since World War II, Consolidated Farm Equipment had been profitable, except during 1964 and 1965, when the company introduced a new line of farm equipment at the same time as the level of farm equipment purchases fell drastically.

Finance Company.   In early 1966, for tax, financial, and administrative reasons, Consolidated Farm Equipment created a wholly owned finance subsidiary, Consolidated Finance Corporation, to finance the company's credit sales to dealers. Beginning in 1966, Consolidated Farm Equipment began a major program to increase both the number of its dealers and the levels of their inventories. As part of this program, Consolidated Farm Equipment sold equipment to its dealers on extremely favorable credit terms. In turn, Consolidated Farm Equipment sold at a discount its dealers' accounts receivable to Consolidated Finance. As part of this arrangement, the banks lending to Consolidated Finance forced Consolidated Farm Equipment to agree to take back any dealer receivables falling in default.

Electronics Company.   In 1968, Mohawk bought a patent covering a new technique for manufacturing transistors. In order to exploit this patent, Mohawk established a new company called Transiton, Inc. Within six months, the company was in business and rapidly developed a market for its transistors. Unlike the other Mohawk subsidiaries, Transiton had yet to earn a profit.

Real Estate Company.   For tax reasons, Transiton leased its buildings from Equity Real Estate Company, a wholly owned subsidiary of Mohawk. In 1970 the Equity Real Estate Company did not have any other business. Sometime in the future, however, Mr. James Franklin planned to extend Equity's activities in the real estate area to include some form of non-Mohawk business.

Exhibit 1 presents the profits after taxes of Mohawk Products and its subsidiaries for the period 1960–69, inclusive. Exhibit 2 shows condensed balance sheets for Mohawk Products and its subsidiaries as of December 31, 1968, and 1969, respectively.

Questions

1. Assuming that you are not constrained by any generally accepted accounting principles, what subsidiaries do you think ought to be included in the consolidated statements for prospectus purposes?

2. Given your answer to Question 1, what will Mohawk's annual earning per share be for the last seven years (assume one million shares outstanding in each of the seven years)?

3. Under the existing generally accepted accounting principles followed in the United States of America, what consolidation policy would Mr. Franklin have to adopt?

EXHIBIT 1

MOHAWK PRODUCTS, INC.

Mohawk Products and Subsidiaries, Profits after Taxes, 1960–1969
(millions of dollars; 0 = less than $100,000)

	1969	1968	1967	1966	1965	1964	1963	1962	1961	1960
Mohawk Products	4.2	4.5	4.1	4.5	3.2	3.1	5.1	4.7	4.8	4.2
Iroquois Woolens	2.9	3.2	3.1	2.9	1.9	1.4	2.9	2.8	2.7	2.6
Franklin Trust	0.5	0.4	0.3	0.2	0.1	0.1	0.2	0.1	0.2	0.1
Consolidated Farm	2.8	2.9	3.9	1.9	(0.4)	(1.0)	3.4	3.7	3.6	2.4
Bull Dog Linens	(0.4)	(0.6)	0.4	0.7	0.6	0.4	0.5	0.4	0.1	0.1
Mohawk (Australia)	2.5	1.9	1.3	(0.6)	0.8	0.9	(0.4)			
Consolidated Finance	0.2	0.2	0.2	0.1						
Transiton	(0.6)	(1.5)								
Equity Real Estate	0.0	0.0								

MOHAWK PRODUCTS AND SUBSIDIARIES

Condensed Balance Sheets

(millions of dollars; 0 = less than $100,000)

	Mohawk Products	Iroquois Woolens	Franklin Trust	Consolidated Farm	Bull Dog Linens	Mohawk (Australia)	Consolidated Finance	Transition	Equity Real Estate
				December 31, 1968					
Assets									
Cash	3.8	2.3	4.9	1.7	0.9	1.2	0.7	0.8	0.1
Accounts (loans) receivable	8.7	5.4	77.0	-0-	1.4	4.0	30.7	2.3	-0-
Investment in subsidiaries (at cost)	36.5	-0-	-0-	2.5	-0-	-0-	-0-	-0-	-0-
Other assets	81.3	69.2	10.2	48.4	7.1	12.5	2.3	6.8	3.2
Total Assets	130.3	76.9	92.1	52.6	9.4	17.7	33.7	9.9	3.3
Equities									
Accounts payable (deposits)	5.7	5.8	81.2	3.1	1.3	2.0	-0-	2.1	-0-
Other current liabilities	8.7	2.7	2.3	3.6	0.7	1.8	0.7	4.3	0.3
Long-term debt	-0-	-0-	-0-	-0-	-0-	5.0	30.0	-0-	2.5
Capital stock*	50.0	10.0	3.5	8.5	4.0	5.0	2.5	5.0	0.5
Retained earnings	65.9	58.4	5.1	37.4	3.4	3.9	0.5	(1.5)	0.0
Total Equities	130.3	76.9	92.1	52.6	9.4	17.7	33.7	9.9	3.3
				December 31, 1969					
Assets									
Cash	4.2	2.1	5.2	1.4	0.7	1.3	0.6	0.7	0.1
Accounts (loans) receivable	9.2	5.2	76.9	-0-	1.5	4.3	32.3	2.4	-0-
Investment in subsidiaries (at cost)	36.5	-0-	-0-	2.5	-0-	-0-	-0-	-0-	-0-
Other assets	80.7	72.7	12.7	51.3	6.7	15.0	2.2	6.5	3.1
Total Assets	130.6	80.0	94.8	55.2	8.9	20.6	35.1	9.6	3.2
Equities									
Accounts payable (deposits)	4.9	6.2	83.3	2.7	1.4	2.3	-0-	3.7	-0-
Other current liabilities	7.7	2.5	2.4	3.8	0.5	1.9	0.7	3.0	0.2
Long-term debt	-0-	-0-	-0-	-0-	-0-	5.0	31.2	-0-	2.4
Capital stock*	50.0	10.0	3.5	8.5	4.0	5.0	2.5	5.0	0.5
Retained earnings	68.0	61.3	5.6	40.2	3.0	6.4	0.7	(2.1)	0.1
Total Equities	130.6	80.0	94.8	55.2	8.9	20.6	35.1	9.6	3.2

* Original investment.

Chapter 6

STATEMENT OF CHANGES IN FINANCIAL POSITION

The statement of changes in financial position presents a company's sources and uses of financial resources during an accounting period. In March 1971, the APB concluded that information concerning the financing and investing activities of a business and the changes in its financial position was essential for financial statement users. Accordingly, in *Opinion No. 19* the APB required that whenever a balance sheet and income statement are presented, a statement of the changes in financial position must also be included. Earlier, in 1963, in *Opinion No. 3* the APB had encouraged companies to publish funds flow statements. *Opinion No. 19* made this practice mandatory and changed the name of the statement from the sources and application of funds statement to the statement of changes in financial position.[1] In addition, this *Opinion* made it mandatory that the auditor's opinion cover the changes in financial position statement.

NATURE OF THE STATEMENT OF CHANGES IN FINANCIAL POSITION

Funds flow reporting can be distinguished from the other concepts of financial reporting. The funds flow statement shows changes in the firm's assets, liabilities, and equity accounts during a specified period of time. In contrast, the balance sheet presents the company's financial position at an instant of time. The income statement shows revenues, expenses, and profit for a period of time.

Causes for changes in the firm's financial position can be readily observed in a well-prepared funds flow statement. Funds flowing from operations, borrowing, sale of properties, and equity contributions are

---

[1] In conversation the term "funds flow statement" is used frequently. Both descriptive titles will be used interchangeably in this chapter.

related to outflows for property acquisitions, dividends, and debt retirement. Answers are provided to such questions as: What happened to profits generated by operations? How was it possible for the firm to distribute dividends? What happened to money borrowed during the period? What caused the change in the working capital position?

Current Practice

Opinion No. 19 defined the concept of funds and the statement format that is used currently in public corporate reports. Previously, many different fund concepts and formats had been employed in practice. *Opinion No. 19* stated:

. . . the statement summarizing changes in financial position should be based on a broad concept embracing all changes in financial position . . . . The Statement of each reporting entity should disclose all important aspects of its financing and investing activities regardless of whether cash or other elements of working capital are directly affected.

Using the APB's definition of funds, sources and uses of financial resources or funds may be defined as:

Sources of Funds	*Uses of Funds*
Increases in liabilities	Decreases in liabilities
Increases in owners' equity	Decreases in owners' equity
Decreases in assets	Increases in assets

The above table of sources and uses of funds can be related to the debit-credit accounting process as follows: All of the sources of funds are credit entries, and all of the uses of funds are debit entries. If the above table was expanded to show revenues as a source of funds and expenses as a use of funds, this relationship of funds flow to the dual entry convention remains.

Illustration 6–1 presents a typical statement of changes in financial position.

Definition of "Funds"

For analytical purposes the term "funds flow analysis" can be defined in at least five different ways. These definitions, beginning with the narrowest and moving to the broadest, define funds flows as changes in (1) cash, (2) the sum of cash and marketable securities, (3) net monetary assets, (4) working capital, and (5) all financial resources. (*Opinion No. 19* requires this latter approach for public reporting purposes.) Each of these definitions leads to emphasis being placed on a different aspect of funds flow. The appropriateness of any definition

ILLUSTRATION 6–1

GENERAL ELECTRIC COMPANY AND CONSOLIDATED AFFILIATES
Statement of Changes in Financial Position
For the Years 1973 and 1974
(in millions)

	1974	1973
Source of Funds:		
From operations:		
Net earnings	$ 608.1	$ 585.1
Less earnings retained by the Credit Corporation	(8.7)	(10.7)
Depreciation	376.2	334.0
Income tax timing differences	26.0	—
	$1,001.6	$ 908.4
Major domestic long-term borrowings	300.0	—
Overseas Capital Corporation long-term borrowings	8.1	17.1
Increases in other long-term borrowings—net	13.9	2.0
Newly-issued common stock	24.6	11.7
Total Source of Funds	$1,348.2	$ 939.2
Application of Funds:		
Plant and equipment additions	$ 671.8	$ 598.6
Dividends declared	291.2	272.9
Investments	135.1	114.8
Reduction in major domestic long-term borrowings	17.0	31.5
Reduction in Overseas Capital Corporation long-term borrowings	27.0	17.7
Other—net	(144.0)	20.3
Total Application of Funds	$ 998.1	$1,055.8
Net Increase (decrease) in Working Capital	$ 350.1	$ (116.6)
Analysis of Changes in Working Capital:		
Cash and marketable securities	$ 49.7	$ 27.8
Current receivables	416.7	251.1
Inventories	270.8	227.2
Short-term borrowings	20.3	(225.8)
Other payables	(407.4)	(396.9)
Net Increase (decrease) in Working Capital	$ 350.1	$ (116.6)

will depend upon the particular circumstances of the firm and the purpose of the user of the statement.

Whether or not a particular accounting transaction is defined as a funds flow will depend on the definition of funds used. For example, the *declaration* of dividends changes a company's net monetary assets, net working capital, and "all financial resources." Thus, in a company that used a funds definition based on changes in any one of these items this transaction would be regarded as a funds flow for accounting purposes. If the company used a funds definition related to changes in cash or cash and marketable securities, this transaction would not be recorded as a funds flow, since it does not change either of these two asset accounts (only the liability and net worth accounts are changed). On the other hand, the *payment* of the dividends previously declared (and recorded on the company's books as "dividends payable") would be regarded as a funds flow in companies defining funds as changes in either cash, cash and marketable securities, or all financial resources. This transaction changes these items. However, since the transaction did not change the company's net monetary assets or working capital, it would not be regarded as a funds flow if these balance sheet categories were the basis for the funds definition.

These five definitions of funds are demonstrated below. The changes in financial position statements resulting from each definition will be based upon the simplified balance sheets and statement of retained earnings for the Carter Company shown in Illustration 6–2. As the various changes in financial position statements are developed,

ILLUSTRATION 6–2

CARTER COMPANY

Balance Sheets at December 31, 1977, and 1978

Assets

	1977	1978	*Difference*
Cash	$ 28	$ 30	$ 2
Marketable securities	10	15	5
Receivables	32	40	8
Inventories	40	35	(5)
Fixed assets (net)	130	140	10
Total Assets	$240	$260	$20

Liabilities

	1977	1978	*Difference*
Current payables	$ 54	$ 47	$ (7)
Long-term debt	46	53	7
Capital stock	100	105	5
Retained earnings	40	55	15
Total Liabilities	$240	$260	$20

Statement of Retained Earnings
For the Year Ended December 31, 1978

Balance, December 31, 1977	$40
Net income for the year	20
	$60
Less: Dividends paid on December 31, 1978	5
Balance, December 31, 1978	$55

Additional data: Depreciation of $8 was charged against operations in 1978. Long-term debt of $10 was issued for fixed assets in the same amount.

it must be remembered that each is entirely based upon the balance
sheet and statement of retained earnings. That is, each statement must
be considered independently, rather than as part of a continuing
illustration.

1. Funds Defined as Cash.   When funds are defined as cash, the
increase in the Cash account of $2 in Illustration 6–2 can be explained
by a rearrangement of differences in the balance sheet accounts other
than cash.

The handling of the investment in fixed assets is tricky in this case.
The amount shown in the cash flow statement (Illustration 6–3) for

ILLUSTRATION 6–3

CARTER COMPANY
Cash Flow Statement
For the Year Ended December 31, 1978

Funds Provided:

From operations:

Net income	$20	
Depreciation	8	$28
From decrease in inventories		5
From increase in capital stock		5
Total		$38

Funds Applied:

To increase in marketable securities	$ 5	
To increase in receivables	8	
To increase in fixed assets	8	
To decrease in current payables	7	
To decrease in long-term debt	3	
To payment of dividends	5	
Total		36
Net Increase in Funds (cash)		$ 2

"increase in fixed assets" is $8, not the $10 indicated in Illustration
6–2. The issuance of $10 of long-term debt for fixed assets is ignored in
changes in cash statement, using the cash definition of funds in its
most restricted sense, since it did not result in a change in cash. (See
"additional data" note to Illustration 6–2.) If the $10 is deducted
from both fixed assets and long-term debt in the 1978 balance sheet,
fixed assets for 1977 and 1978 are $130. Since depreciation of $8 was
charged in 1978, fixed assets must have been increased by $8 in 1978
(i.e., 1977 balance – 1978 depreciation + 1978 additions = 1978
ending balance).

Depreciation is added to net income to determine total funds provided from operations as depreciation charges requiring no expenditure of funds were subtracted in the determination of net income.

It should be noted that in the Carter Company example dividends were paid out on December 31, 1978. As a result, the Cash account was reduced by 5 and the payment of dividends is a use of cash. If on the other hand, the company had simply declared a dividend of 5, but not paid it yet, the declaration of the dividend would not be a cash flow since the declaration of a dividend does not change the Cash account's balance.

Cash flow statements can be very helpful in analyzing the liquidity of a firm; its ability to generate cash from operations; its debt coverage and capacity; and its dividend paying ability. Typically, in analyzing cash flows it is useful to distinguish among those cash flows that are (1) recurring and one time, (2) do not relate directly to operations, (3) occur spasmodically, and (4) are variable at management's discretion. Such distinctions are particularly useful when trying to predict future dividends. For example, a company that cannot create enough cash flow from operations to finance its growth may resort to borrowing from banks to pay its dividends. However, in some years the company may not borrow cash because it pays dividends with the cash receipts from the sale of fixed assets. An analysis which distinguishes among the nature of a firm's cash flows would highlight these practices and raise questions in the analyst's mind as to the continuing ability of the company to maintain or raise dividends.

2. Funds Defined as Cash and Marketable Securities. Under this definition of funds, arrangement of balance sheet accounts other than Cash and marketable securities will result in the funds flow statement shown in Illustration 6–4. This statement differs from the preceding illustration only in that marketable securities are considered as funds in addition to cash. The comments made previously about the difference between the declaration and payment of dividends on the cash flow statement shown in Illustration 6–3 apply also in this example.

Since marketable securities are for all practical purposes the equivalent of cash, the definition of funds as cash and marketable securities may be superior to the more limited cash definition for most analytical purposes that involve an analysis of cash.

3. Funds Defined as Net Monetary Assets. Under this alternative, funds are identified as net quick assets: that is, monetary assets less those short-term obligations that require cash to extinguish them. For the Carter Company the total of cash, marketable securities, and receivables reduced by current payables is $16 and $38 at the close of 1977 and 1978 respectively. This net increase in funds of $22 can be explained by the statement shown in Illustration 6–5.

Using the funds definition in Illustration 6–5, both the declaration and payment of a dividend would be a funds flow.

ILLUSTRATION 6–4

CARTER COMPANY

Changes in Cash and Marketable Securities
For the Year Ended December 31, 1978

Funds Provided:

From operations:

Net income	$20	
Depreciation	8	$28
From decrease in inventories		5
From increase in capital stock		5
Total		$38

Funds Applied:

To increase in receivables	$ 8	
To increase in fixed assets	8	
To decrease in current payables	7	
To decrease in long-term debt	3	
To payment of dividends	5	
Total		31
Net Increase in Funds (cash and marketable securities)		$ 7

ILLUSTRATION 6–5

CARTER COMPANY

Changes in Net Monetary Assets
For the Year Ended December 31, 1978

Funds Provided:

From operations:

Net income	$20	
Depreciation	8	$28
From decrease in inventories		5
From increase in capital stock		5
Total		$38

Funds Applied:

To increase in fixed assets	$ 8	
To decrease in long-term debt	3	
To payment of dividends	5	
Total		16
Net Increase in Funds (quick assets)		$22

The net monetary asset definition of funds is considered by some to be superior to the cash flow definitions. These people believe that accounts receivable and accounts payable can be considered to represent in essence constructive receipts and payments of cash. As a result, they believe the broader net monetary asset definition to be more useful since it includes all of the cash-type fund movements.

4. Funds Defined as Working Capital. This definition of funds treats current assets less current liabilities as a single body of funds. The working capital of the Carter Company can be summarized as shown in Illustration 6–6.

ILLUSTRATION 6–6

	December 31 1977	December 31 1978	Difference
Current Assets:			
Cash	$ 28	$ 30	$ 2
Marketable securities	10	15	5
Receivables	32	40	8
Inventories	40	35	(5)
	$110	$120	$10
Less: Current liabilities:			
Current payables	54	47	7
Working Capital	$ 56	$ 73	$17

The changes in financial position statement is prepared by analyzing all noncurrent balance sheet accounts to explain the increase in working capital of $17, as shown in Illustration 6–7.

The working capital funds definition was the most popular definition used prior to *Opinion No. 3*. This definition was thought to have the advantages of presenting a clear picture of a company's general liquidity and of concentrating on the funds flow that resulted from long-term major transactions, rather than those that arose from the day-to-day operating cycle. The principal disadvantage of this defini-

ILLUSTRATION 6–7

CARTER COMPANY

Changes in Working Capital
For the Year Ended December 31, 1978

Funds Provided:
From operations:

Net income ....:......	$20	
Depreciation	8	$28
From increase in capital stock		5
Total		$33

Funds Applied:

To increase fixed assets	$ 8	
To decrease long-term debt	3	
To payment of dividends	5	
Total		16
Net Increase in Funds (working capital)		$17

tion is that it treats nonmonetary items, like inventory and payments in advance, as being the same as cash, which they are not. In addition this definition if literally interpreted may obscure major movements within the working capital accounts since only the net change in working capital is shown. In practice this is not a major problem since the details of the changes in working capital items is required to be shown as an explanation of the changes in working capital balance.

5. *Funds Defined as All Financial Resources.* This concept of funds is required for general usage. When funds are defined in this broad manner, the preceding working capital concept of funds flow is extended to include all transactions involving financial resources even though working capital is not directly affected. For example, the Carter Company issued $10 long-term debt directly for fixed assets; current asset and liability accounts were not changed in any way. Statements of changes in financial position prepared under previous narrower definitions of funds deliberately excluded the effect of this transaction. Such omissions obscure an important event in Carter's financial affairs. Therefore the transaction should be recognized in the changes in financial position statement. In addition, the details of the working capital changes are shown if the all financial resources definition is used. The statement resulting from application of this broadest concept of funds is shown in Illustration 6–8. Also, if the broad definition

ILLUSTRATION 6–8

CARTER COMPANY
Changes in Financial Position
For the Year Ended December 31, 1978

Funds Provided:		
From operations:		
Net income	$20	
Depreciation	8	$28
From increase in capital stock		5
From increase in long-term debt		10
Total		$43
Funds Applied:		
To increase in fixed assets		$18
To decrease long-term debt		3
To payment of dividends		5
To Increase in Working Capital		17
Increases (decreases) in Working Capital:		
Increase in cash		2
Increase in market securities		5
Increase in receivables		8
Decrease in inventory		⟨5⟩
Decrease in current payables		7
Increase in Working Capital		17

of funds is used, it is permissible to show the net differences between the uses and sources of funds as a change in cash.

Balance sheet changes that increase or decrease the working capital balance (current assets − current liabilities) are:

Increases	*Decreases*
Additions to current assets	Decreases in current assets
Decreases in current liabilities	Increases in current liabilities
(both debit entries)	(both credit entries)

The $10 increase in long-term debt is listed as a source of funds and the $3 retirement of long-term debt is included as an application of funds. As an alternative, these items might be netted and the resulting $7 increase would be included as a source of funds. Since the underlying objective of the funds flow statement is to provide useful information to the reader, the APB requires that all material information be presented in gross terms.

The increase in fixed assets is shown as $18. This is the $8 previously calculated using more restrictive funds definitions plus the $10 purchased using long-term debt.

Statements of changes in financial position are provided in many forms. Often the details of the changes in working capital are not shown separately but are presented as in Illustration 6–9.

In each of the example statements funds from operations was derived by adding the nonfund expense item (depreciation) back to net

ILLUSTRATION 6–9

CARTER COMPANY

Changes in Financial Position Statement
For the Year Ended December 31, 1978

Funds Provided:

From operations:

Net income	$20	
Depreciation	8	$28
From increase in capital stock		5
From increase in long-term debt		10
From decrease in inventories		5
Total		$48

Funds Applied:

To increase in fixed assets	$18
To decrease in long-term debt	3
To payment of dividends	5
To increase in receivables	8
To decrease in current payables	7
To increase in cash and marketable securities	7
Total	$48

income. An acceptable alternative to this add-back presentation is to show funds from operations as being revenues generating funds less those expenses requiring the use of funds.

Other nonfund expenses besides depreciation include such charges as the amortization of goodwill, the write-off of other capitalized intangibles, and the deferred tax portion of the current book tax expense. Some nonfund credit items may be excluded from net income to derive the funds from operations figure. A common example of a nonfund credit is the equity in the earnings of unconsolidated subsidiaries or investee companies that is included in net income. In this case only the dividends received from these companies is shown as a source of funds. The difference between the equity method income figure and these dividends is backed out of net income as a nonfund credit. (See Illustration 6–1 for an example of this nonfund credit arising from General Electric's use of the equity method to account for its credit corporation.)

Statement of Balance Sheet Charges

For a number of analytical purposes, a rough approach to funds flow analysis can be accomplished by summarizing increases and decreases in comparative balance sheet accounts without adjustments. Such a statement for the Carter Company might appear as shown in Illustration 6–10.

ILLUSTRATION 6–10

CARTER COMPANY

Changes in Financial Position Statement
For the Year Ended December 31, 1978

Sources:

Decreases in assets:

Inventories	$ 5

Increases in liabilities and owners' equity:

Long-term debt	7
Capital stock	5
Retained earnings	15
Total	$32

Applied:

Increases in assets:

Cash	$ 2
Marketable securities	5
Receivables	8
Fixed assets	10

Decreases in liabilities and owners' equity:

Current payables	7
Total	$32

WORKING PAPERS FOR CHANGES IN FINANCIAL POSITION STATEMENTS

It was noted earlier that the statements of changes in financial position could be prepared directly from an analysis of the differences between balance sheet accounts at the beginning and close of the accounting period. Minimum analysis of account balances is ordinarily required to obtain the needed information. When the number of accounts is unusually great or when transactions are complex, it may be desirable to prepare working papers to assemble the information for the changes in financial position statement in an orderly manner.

The working paper for the changes in financial position statement of the Dexter Company is presented in Illustration 6–11 as an example of the procedure which might be used to eliminate inaccuracy and confusion. The broad definition of funds as all financial resources is used. The following additional information is offered to make the illustration more comprehensive. During the year Dexter issued $12,000 in long-term notes payable for fixed assets, charged $5,000 of goodwill and $35,000 of depreciation to earnings, and received $10,000 for its capital stock with a par value of $8,000. Operations resulted in net income after taxes of $20,000, and dividends of $5,000 were declared and paid during 1978.

The working paper consists of five pairs of columns in which net changes in the balance sheet accounts are computed, adjusted if necessary, and classified to assemble information needed for preparation of the funds flow statement. In the first pair of columns, the balance sheet accounts at the beginning and close of the period are listed and net changes during the year are extended into the second pair of columns. In the Adjustments columns, certain of the net changes are eliminated, combined, or separated into component items after considering the effect upon funds flow. New accounts are created in the lower part of the work sheet to handle reclassification or labeling of items for the funds flow statement. The noncurrent items explaining funds flow are extended into the Funds Applied and Funds Provided columns, while current assets and liabilities are extended into the final pair of Working Capital columns. The computation of the balance "increase in working capital" in the fourth and fifth pairs of columns aids in proving mathematical accuracy of the work sheet.

The eight keyed adjustments of the working paper are explained briefly:

1. Net income of $20,000 for the year is entered as the explanation for increased retained earnings.
2. Dividends of $5,000 required the expenditure of funds and caused a corresponding decrease in retained earnings.

ILLUSTRATION 6-11

Dexter Company
Working Paper - Changes in Financial Position Statement
For the year ended December 31, 1978 (in thousands of dollars)

Accounts	Balances 1977	Dec. 31 1978	Net Changes Dr	Net Changes Cr	Adjustments Dr	Adjustments Cr	Funds Applied Dr	Funds Provided Cr	Working Capital Increase Dr	Working Capital Decrease Cr
Debits										
Cash	50	60	10						10	
Marketable securities	20	25	5						5	
Inventories	71	65		6						6
Investments	74	82	8						8	
Fund assets	320	373	53			(6) 53				
Goodwill	5	–		5	(3) 5					
	540	605								
Credits										
Accumulated depreciation	65	100		35	(4) 35					
Current payables	105	100	5						5	
Long-term notes payable	80	90		10	(5) 12	(7) 2				
Capital stock - at par	180	188		8	(8) 8					
Other paid-in capital	20	22		2	(8) 2					
Retained earnings	90	105		15	(1) 20	(2) 5				
	540	605	81	81						
Funds provided by operations										
Net income per income statement					(1)	20		60		
Add: depreciation					(4)	35				
Add: amortization of goodwill					(3)	5				
Funds applied to dividends					(2) 5		5			
Funds provided by long-term notes					(5)	12		12		
Funds applied to purchase fixed assets					(6) 53		53			
Funds applied to retirement of long-term notes					(7) 2		2			
Funds provided by sale of capital stock					(8)	10		10		
					142	142	60	82	28	6
Increase in working capital							22			22
							82	82	28	28

3. Amortization of goodwill is recorded as a nonfund addition to income, as the charge did not result in a funds outflow.
4. Depreciation charged for the year of $35,000 (the amount of the increase in accumulated depreciation) is recorded as an addition to net income to compute total funds derived from operations.
5. The $12,000 issue of long-term notes payable for fixed assets is recognized. In the strictest sense, working capital was not affected by this transaction. However, in order to present funds flow in a broader manner, the event is treated as though notes payable had been issued for cash which was immediately paid for fixed assets.
6. The acquisition of fixed assets for $53,000 is entered. (This amount includes $12,000 acquired by issuing long-term notes payable. See 5 above.)
7. Payment of long-term notes payable of $2,000 can be inferred from the net increase of $10,000 during the year and the effect of adjustment 5 above. The notes payable account increased by $10,000. However, we know that $12,000 of notes payable were issued. Therefore, $2,000 of notes payable were retired.
8. Proceeds from the sale of capital stock is identified on the working paper as a single item by bringing together the net increases in the capital stock and other paid-in capital accounts.

ILLUSTRATION 6–12

DEXTER COMPANY

Changes in Financial Position

For the Year Ended December 31, 1978

Funds Sources:

From operations:

Net income for the year	$20	
Depreciation and amortization of goodwill	40	$60
Increase in long-term debt		12
Sales of capital stock		10
Total		$82

Funds Applications:

Dividends paid	$ 5
Purchase of capital equipment	53
Repayment of long-term debt	2
Increase in working capital	22

Increases (decreases) in Working Capital:

Increase in cash	10
Increase in marketable securities	5
Decrease in receivables	(6)
Increase in inventories	8
Decrease in payables	5
Increase in Working Capital	22

The working paper should not be considered a substitute for the changes in financial position statement. It merely provides a means for assembling the information for the statement. The formal changes in financial position statement can be easily prepared from the amounts extended into the Funds Applied and Provided columns, as shown in Illustration 6–12.

A number of alternative forms of the funds flow working paper might be used instead of the particular columnar headings and procedures illustrated. For example, the entire working paper could be simplified significantly by omitting the first and last pairs of columns and using only net changes in the noncurrent accounts along with the single balancing amount of the net increase (or decrease) in working capital. Simplifications of this type emphasize that changes in financial position statements may ordinarily be prepared directly from comparative balance sheets with a minimum analysis of accounts.

Format and Content

Opinion No. 19 set forth the following guides that should be applied in preparing and presenting the changes in financial position statement:

The ability of an enterprise to provide working capital or cash from operations is an important factor in considering its financing and investing activities. Accordingly, the Statement should prominently disclose working capital or cash provided from or used in operations for the period, and the Board believes that the disclosure is most informative if the effects of extraordinary items are reported separately from the effects of normal items. The Statement for the period should begin with income or loss before extraordinary items, if any, and add back (or deduct) items recognized in determining that income or loss which did not use (or provide) working capital or cash during the period. Items added and deducted in accordance with this procedure are not sources or uses of working capital or cash, and the related captions should make this clear, e.g., "Add—Expenses not requiring outlay of working capital in the current period." An acceptable alternative procedure, which gives the same result, is to begin with total revenue that provided working capital or cash during the period and deduct operating costs and expenses that required the outlay of working capital or cash during the period. In either case the resulting amount of working capital or cash should be appropriately described, e.g., "Working capital provided from [used in] operations for the period, exclusive of extraordinary items." This total should be immediately followed by working capital or cash provided or used by income or loss from extraordinary items, if any; extraordinary income or loss should be similarly adjusted for items recognized that did not provide or use working capital or cash during the period.

Provided that these guides are met, the Statement may take whatever form gives the most useful portrayal of the financing and investing activities and the changes in financial position of the reporting entity. The Statement may be in balanced form or in a form expressing the changes in financial position in terms of cash, of cash and temporary investments combined, of all quick assets, or of working capital. The Statement should disclose all important changes in financial position for the period covered; accordingly, types of transactions reported may vary substantially in relative importance from one period to another.

Whether or not working capital flow is presented in the Statement, net changes in each element of working capital (as customarily defined) should be appropriately disclosed for at least the current period, either in the Statement or in a related tabulation.

a. If the format shows the flow of cash, changes in other elements of working capital (e.g., in receivables, inventories, and payables) constitute sources and uses of cash and should accordingly be disclosed in appropriate detail in the body of the Statement.
b. If the format shows the flow of working capital and two-year comparative balance sheets are presented, the changes in each element of working capital for the current period (but not for earlier periods) can be computed by the user of the statements. Nevertheless, the Board believes that the objectives of the Statement usually require that the net change in working capital be analyzed in appropriate detail in a tabulation accompanying the Statement, and accordingly this detail should be furnished.

The effects of other financing and investing activities should be individually disclosed. For example, both outlays for acquisitions and proceeds from retirements of property should be reported; both long-term borrowings and repayments of long-term debt should be reported; and outlays for purchases of consolidated subsidiaries should be summarized in the consolidated Statement by major categories of assets obtained and obligations assumed. Related items should be shown in proximity when the result contributes to the clarity of the Statement. Individual immaterial items may be combined.

In addition to working capital or cash provided from operations and changes in elements of working capital, the Statement should clearly disclose:

a. Outlays for purchase of long-term assets (identifying separately such items as investments, property, and intangibles).
b. Proceeds from sale (or working capital or cash provided by sale) of long-term assets (identifying separately such items as investments, property, and intangibles) not in the normal course of business, less related expenses involving the current use of working capital or cash.
c. Conversion of long-term debt or preferred stock to common stock.
d. Issuance, assumption, redemption, and repayment of long-term debt.
e. Issuance, redemption, or purchase of capital stock for cash or for assets other than cash.
f. Dividends in cash or in kind or other distributions to shareholders (except stock dividends and stock split-ups).

Cash Flow per Share

In recent years, as part of the growing use of funds flow analysis, security analysts and financial reporting services have given greater weight to a figure commonly called cash flow per share, which is usually defined as net profit after taxes plus noncash expenses such as depreciation. Often, the impression is given that cash flow per share is a superior measurement to net income as a measure of management performance. In response to this development, the Accounting Principles Board in *Opinion No. 3* stated:

The amount of funds derived from operations cannot be considered as a substitute for or an improvement upon properly determined net income as a measure of results of operations and the consequent effect on financial position. Misleading implications can result from isolated statistics in annual reports of "cash flow" which are not placed in proper perspective to net income figures and to a complete analysis of source and application of funds. "Cash flow" and related terms should not be used in annual reports in such a way that the significance of net income is impaired, and "cash earnings" or other terms with a similar connotation should be avoided. The Board regards computations of "cash flow per share" as misleading since they ignore the impact of cash expenditures for renewal and replacement of facilities and tend to downgrade the significant economic statistic of "earnings per share."

Cash flow per share computed by adding nonfund expenses back to net income is not cash flow, since it does not recognize that the revenues may be tied up in accounts receivable and expenses not yet paid. It is a funds concept, not a cash flow value.

Later, in 1974 the SEC discouraged the use of cash flow per share presentations.

SUGGESTED FURTHER READING

MASON, PERRY. "Cash Flow" Analysis and the Funds Statement." *Accounting Research Study No. 2.* New York: American Institute of Certified Public Accountants, 1961.

CASE

CASE 6–1. LAKELAND AIRLINES, INCORPORATED
Determination of Funds Flow Disclosure Policy

On January 15, 1970, the board of directors of Lakeland Airlines, Inc., was considering what the content and format of the statement of changes in financial position should be that the company intended to include in its 1969 annual report to stockholders. The directors believed the addition of a funds flow statement would greatly enhance the ability of stockholders to analyze the company's activities as well as provide management with a useful means of communication with stockholders.

The Company

Lakeland Airlines, Inc., was founded in 1952 by Mr. John Drew, a former military air transport pilot. Originally the airline's only aircraft, a Korean war surplus Douglas DC–3, operated between Philadelphia and a number of small towns in upper Pennsylvania. During the following years, as more and more cities built airports and existing feeder lines went out of business, the company acquired CAB approval to fly additional routes throughout the mid-Atlantic states, Ohio, West Virginia, Kentucky, and upper New York state.

Initially, Mr. Drew financed this expansion through the sale of common stock and convertible debentures to a number of the major industrial companies within the area serviced by his company. These companies bought Lakeland stock so that the cities where their plants were located would have reliable air service. In 1960, in order to finance the acquisition of a number of turbo-prop Viscount aircraft, Lakeland offered some common shares to the public. This offering was well received and the securities were traded actively on the New York over-the-counter market. Subsequently, in 1965, a larger common stock offering was made in order to finance the purchase of several Caravelle jet aircraft. As of December 31, 1969, Lakeland had over

2,500 stockholders, of which 25 were corporations in towns serviced by Lakeland.

Through its 17-year history, Lakeland had almost constantly been short of cash, principally because of its policy of using the most modern aircraft available for its type of business and the increasing investments required to service its expanding route system. Consequently, small dividends had been declared only twice, and the company had entered into a number of bank loans. While no stockholder had ever questioned the "no dividend–heavy bank loan" policy, Mr. Drew believed many of the stockholders did not really understand the company's financial policy.

In early 1969, Lakeland acquired the Pioneer Airlines, a major feeder line servicing parts of West Virginia, Ohio, and Kentucky. Lakeland exchanged shares with a market value of $2.5 million for the Pioneer plant, equipment, and routes. These assets were carried on Pioneer's books at $2 million. The excess of investment over these values was added to the Lakeland Goodwill account. The board intended to write this goodwill off as a special charge against income over a five-year period, beginning in 1969.

To bring the Pioneer service up to Lakeland's high standards of quality, two secondhand Convair 440's were added to the Pioneer fleet at a cost of $1.7 million. In order to finance this purchase, $1 million was borrowed from the Marine Merchants Bank, New York, and $0.7 million of stock was sold to several insurance companies. In the near future, Mr. Drew planned to replace these aircraft with British Aircraft Corporation 1–11 fan-jets.

John Drew's ambition was to build Lakeland into a major airline before he retired in 1980. Therefore, he anticipated there would be more stock issues, more route acquisitions, more bank loans and more equipment investments during the remaining ten years of his presidency.

Exhibits 1 and 2 present the financial statements management planned to include in the 1969 annual report to stockholders.

Questions

1. Why should companies like Lakeland include a statement of changes in financial position in their annual report to stockholders?
2. Which definition of "funds" do you think Lakeland should adopt?
3. Construct the statement of changes in financial position that you believe Lakeland should present to its stockholders.
4. Prepare a one-paragraph interpretive comment explaining the significant flows indicated by your statement.

EXHIBIT 1

LAKELAND AIRLINES, INC.

Income Statement
For the Year Ended December 31, 1969
(millions of dollars)

Operating Revenue:

Commercial revenue	25.6
Federal subsidy	4.2
Total Operating Revenue	29.8

Operating Expense:

Flying operations	7.3
Direct maintenance, flight equipment	4.5
Depreciation, flight equipment*	1.0
Total Direct Expense	12.8
Direct maintenance, ground equipment	0.3
Maintenance burden	1.9
Passenger servicing	1.1
Aircraft servicing	2.9
Traffic servicing	3.4
Reservation and sales	2.9
General and administrative	1.5
Depreciation, ground equipment*	0.3
Development and preoperating costs	0.1
Total Indirect Expense	14.4
Total Operating Expense	27.2
Operating profit	2.6

Nonoperating Expense:

Interest and amortization of debt expense	0.3
All other expense (income)	(0.1)
Total Nonoperating Expense	0.2
Net income before taxes and special item	2.4

Provision for Federal Income Taxes:*

Current	1.0
Deferred	0.1
Total Income Taxes	1.1
Net earnings before special item	1.3

Special Item:

Amortization of goodwill	0.1
Net Earnings Retained for the Year	1.2

* See Note D to Exhibit 2.

EXHIBIT 2

LAKELAND AIRLINES, INC.

Balance Sheets at December 31, 1969 and 1968

(millions of dollars)

Resources	1969	1968
Current Assets:		
Cash	2.1	0.8
Accounts receivable:		
U.S. government agencies	0.7	0.9
Airline traffic, less reserve	2.2	2.0
Other, less reserve	0.3	0.3
Inventories (Note A)	1.9	1.7
Prepaid expenses	0.3	0.2
Total Current Assets	7.5	5.9
Assets Applied to Aircraft Order (Note B):		
Cash deposits, restricted	0.0	3.6
Deposits on aircraft and engines	4.3	0.5
Aircraft acquisition costs	0.4	0.3
Total	4.7	4.4
Operating Property and Equipment (at cost):		
Flight equipment (Notes B, C)	13.5	12.4
Ground property and equipment	2.0	1.7
Construction in progress	0.0	0.1
	15.5	14.2
Less: Amortization and depreciation provisions (Note D)	6.9	6.0
Net Operating Property and Equipment	8.6	8.2

Liabilities and Shareholders' Equity	1969	1968
Current Liabilities:		
Equipment obligations (Note B)	0.5	0.3
Accounts payable and accrued expenses	3.6	4.0
Accrued taxes on income (Note D)	1.0	0.2
Unearned transportation revenue	0.2	0.1
Total Current Liabilities	5.3	4.6
Long-Term Debt (Note C):		
Equipment obligations	0.7	0.4
Subordinated notes and debentures	6.4	9.2
Total Long-Term Debt	7.1	9.6
Future Liabilities:		
Deferred income taxes (Note D)	0.4	0.3
Lease and purchase commitments (Notes B, E)	0.0	0.0
Total Future Liabilities	0.4	0.3
Shareholders' Equity:		
Capital stock, common, $1 par, authorized shares, 3,000,000; outstanding shares:		
1,770,142, less 57,220 in treasury	1.7	
1,143,906, less 57,220 in treasury		1.1
Additional paid-in capital	5.8	3.2
Retained earnings	1.6	0.4
Total Shareholders' Equity	9.1	4.7

Deferred Charges:

Development and preoperating costs	0.3	0.2
Discount and expense on debt	0.1	0.2
Total Deferred Charges	0.4	0.4

Other Assets:

Investments and advances	0.1	0.1
Notes receivable:		
Officers, secured by capital stock	0.0	0.1
Goodwill	0.4	0.0
Capital stock expense	0.2	0.1
Total Other Assets	0.7	0.3
Total Resources	21.9	19.2

Total Liabilities and Shareholders' Equity	21.9	19.2

A *Inventories.* The company's inventories consist of operating supplies and aircraft expendable parts. These inventories are carried at cost less valuation reserves established to provide for estimated losses from obsolescence and deterioration.

B *Replacement of Flight Equipment.* The company has signed contracts and letters of intent under which it will during 1970–73 sell or trade most of its present aircraft and will purchase BAC 1–11 fan-jet and FH 227 turbo prop aircraft. Net cost of the 25 new aircraft is estimated at $49 million. Under contractual agreements the company has made payments aggregating $4.3 million in advance of delivery on its purchase of BAC 1–11 aircraft and Rolls-Royce fan-jet engines. Preacuisition costs, including financing expense, incurred for purpose of acquiring these aircraft have been capitalized.

C *Notes Payable and Long-Term Debt.* Equipment obligations and subordinated notes and debentures mature in various amounts over a 14-year period ending 1983. Six of the company's aircraft are pledged to secure equipment notes. The company has a bank loan commitment for $6 million and an informal agreement to obtain loans aggregating as much as $34 million in connection with its acquisition of new aircraft.

D *Income Taxes.* Current income taxes are shown net after deducting allowable investment credits. Adjustments of relatively immaterial amounts have been made in deferred income taxes to reflect changes caused by the Revenue Act of 1954. Deferred income tax liability results primarily from use of straight-line depreciation and amortization rates suggested by the Civil Aeronautics Board for statement purposes, while accelerated methods are used in computing deductions for current income taxes.

E *Lease Commitments.* The company's headquarters and primary maintenance plant, as well as facilities in communities served by Lakeland, are entirely leased. Terms of these leases and contracts vary from 30 days to 25 years. It is estimated that present commitments will require anual net payments of approximately $1.3 million.

PART III

Role of Certified Public Accountants

Chapter 7

THE AUDITOR'S OPINION

The financial statements published by management in corporate reports are usually accompanied by a signed auditor's report. This report means that a member of a licensed profession, who is morally bound to exercise his competent independent judgment, has examined management's financial statements to the extent he thinks necessary and stakes his professional reputation upon his opinion that the financial statements present fairly the financial position and results of operations of the company. The criteria upon which he bases this opinion are "generally accepted auditing standards" and "generally accepted accounting principles."

It is important to note that the auditor in his report expresses his professional *opinion* as to the *fairness* of financial statements prepared and presented by management. For many years, until the early 1930s, it was customary for auditors to use the phrase "we hereby certify" in their reports on financial statements. Even today the term "auditor's certificate" is used interchangeably with "auditor's report." This unfortunate terminology may be partly responsible for the confusion as to the nature of the auditor's work. The professional auditor may well be certified by a state licensing board, but he does not certify financial statements.

Almost all publicly owned businesses offer audited statements, because they are required by stock exchange regulations or federal or state laws or because management recognizes a responsibility to include auditor's opinions in its report to stockholders.

THE AUDITOR'S PROFESSION

The professional auditor has two characteristics which make his opinion on published financial statements useful: namely, independence and competence. The role of the auditor will continue to be significant only to the extent that the public generally continues to attribute these two qualities to the profession of public accountancy.

From the public's point of view, independence is perhaps the more important of the auditor's characteristics; certainly it is the more difficult for the auditor to achieve. A basic conflict arises because the client whose financial statements are examined pays for the services of the auditor. To be independent, the professional auditor must be prepared to place his responsibilities to third-party readers of financial reports higher than a desire to continue offering his services to a particular client. This attitude of public responsibility and service is an essential element which characterizes a profession and distinguishes it from commercial enterprise. Because public accountants have been able to achieve this sense of public responsibility, they have earned the right to call auditing a "profession."

Competence is the second characteristic which the auditor must achieve and maintain. The professional accountant offering his services to the public must comply with the licensing restrictions of the states in which he practices. Public accountancy boards are appointed by the state governors to administer each state's public accounting regulations. All those wishing to become certified public accountants must pass a two-and-one-half day examination prepared and graded by the American Institute of Certified Public Accountants. This exam is given simultaneously by each state board in May and November. Typically, candidates must meet qualifying requirements of citizenship, education, experience, and personal character. These licensing requirements have developed over a period of some 70 years to protect the public interest by restricting the practice of public accountancy to those who have a demonstrated proficiency in accounting and its applications.

The American Institute of Certified Public Accountants is a national organization with more than 120,000 members, all of whom are certified public accountants and have met certain experience requirements. All of the Institute's extensive programs are directed toward enhancing the level of the profession. Its members are subject to a code of professional ethics adopted voluntarily and enforced by the group. Training and professional development programs are sponsored continuously. The Institute has, as the voice of the accounting profession, assumed the position of leadership in the development of auditing standards. Its publications include the monthly *Journal of Accountancy,* Statements on Auditing Standards, and many technical and professional books and pamphlets.

The auditor, as a member of a profession, has a legal responsibility to his client and to third parties who might be injured by shortcomings in his audit opinions. As a general rule, the client may recover dam-

ages from an auditor who has been negligent in the performance of his
examination, and third parties may claim damages in case of the auditor's fraud, negligence, or failure to adhere to professional standards.

The professional accountant offers his services to the public in a number of areas related to financial reporting and management. Traditionally he is best known as an auditor reviewing the accounting statements and records of business firms so that his opinion can be given. The work of the professional accountant includes preparation of tax returns and counseling in related matters, installation of accounting systems, and the newer field of management consulting services. The following comments are concerned only with auditing.

ILLUSTRATION 7–1

Report of Independent Certified Public Accountants

To the Share Owners and Board of Directors of General Electric Company

We have examined the statement of financial position of General Electric Company and consolidated affiliates as of December 31, 1974 and 1973, and the related statements of current and retained earnings and changes in financial position for the years then ended. Our examination was made in accordance with generally accepted auditing standards, and accordingly included such tests of the accounting records and such other auditing procedures as we considered necessary in the circumstances.

In our opinion, the aforementioned financial statements present fairly the financial position of General Electric Company and consolidated affiliates at December 31, 1974 and 1973, and the results of their operations and the changes in their financial position for the years then ended, in conformity with generally accepted accounting principles applied on a consistent basis.

Peat, Marwick, Mitchell & Co.

Peat, Marwick, Mitchell & Co.
345 Park Avenue, New York, N.Y. 10022
February 14, 1975

THE AUDITOR'S REPORT

The auditor's report is addressed to the directors and stockholders of the client corporation. It usually follows closely a standard form and language. A typical short-form report is presented in Illustration 7–1. Each word and phrase in this report has been carefully chosen to describe concisely the examination and to state the opinion to which the examination has led.

The first paragraph of the standard short-form report is called the "scope paragraph" and emphasizes that the auditor's examination has conformed to "generally accepted auditing standards." Auditing standards are the criteria for measuring the quality of the auditor's performance in his engagements. The auditing standards generally accepted by the profession have been described by the American Institute of Certified Public Accountants Auditing Standards Executive Committee. They are:[1]

General Standards

1. The examination is to be performed by a person or persons having adequate technical training and proficiency as an auditor.
2. In all matters relating to the assignment an independence in mental attitude is to be maintained by the auditor or auditors.
3. Due professional care is to be exercised in the performance of the examination and the preparation of the report.

Standards of Field Work

1. The work is to be adequately planned and assistants, if any, are to be properly supervised.
2. There is to be a proper study and evaluation of the existing internal control as a basis for reliance thereon and for the determination of the resultant extent of the tests to which auditing procedures are to be restricted.
3. Sufficient competent evidential matter is to be obtained through inspection, observation, inquiries, and confirmations to afford a reasonable basis for an opinion regarding the financial statements under examination.

Standards of Reporting

1. The report shall state whether the financial statements are presented in accordance with generally accepted principles of accounting.

---

[1] These standards are explained in greater detail in Statements on Auditing Standards published by the American Institute of Certified Public Accountants in 1975.

2. The report shall state whether such principles have been consistently observed in the current period in relation to the preceding period.
3. Informative disclosures in the financial statements are to be regarded as reasonably adequate unless otherwise stated in the report.
4. The report shall either contain an expression of opinion regarding the financial statements, taken as a whole, or an assertion to the effect that an opinion cannot be expressed. When an overall opinion cannot be expressed, the reasons therefor should be stated. In all cases where an auditor's name is associated with financial statements, the report should contain a clear-cut indication of the character of the auditor's examination, if any, and the degree of responsibility he is taking.

The second paragraph of the standard short-form report is called the "opinion paragraph." In a single sentence the auditor attests that the financial statements:

1. Present fairly the financial position and the results of operations.
2. Are in conformity with generally accepted accounting principles.
3. Are on a basis consistent with that of the prior year.

The phrase "present fairly" means that the opinion applies to the statements taken as a whole. The auditor does not imply that any single item on the statements is exact or precisely correct. Instead he professes that the statements as a whole are a complete disclosure and free from any material bias or misstatement.

"Generally accepted accounting principles" is perhaps the most debated phrase in the area of financial accounting. Though the term has been commonly used for at least a quarter of a century, there has been no single definition or listing of principles which has been universally accepted by accounting theorists and practitioners.

The most authoritative enumeration of accounting principles has been published by the Financial Accounting Standards Board. Members of the AICPA are required to disclose departures from these principles in financial statements for fiscal years beginning after December 31, 1965. Another authoritative source is the publications of the Securities and Exchange Commission.

The auditor's reference to "consistency" assures the reader that alternative accounting procedures and statement presentation methods used for the current period do not vary from those of the previous year. This uniformity allows useful comparisons of financial position and operating results for successive periods.

In 1976 the SEC required the auditors of companies registered with the SEC in accounting principle change situations to comment on the preferability of the new accounting principle adopted by their client company.

Forms of the Audit Report

There are four different forms in which the auditor's opinion might be expressed. They are (1) an unqualified opinion, (2) a qualified opinion, (3) an adverse opinion, and (4) a disclaimer of opinion. The choice of the form of opinion and the language used in departures from the recommended short-form opinion are a part of the auditor's responsibility for the application of informed judgment in all matters concerning the audit.

The auditor's standard short-form report presented earlier illustrated an unqualified opinion. The auditor made no reservations and stated no conditions precedent to his opinion about the fairness of management's financial statements. Typically, in most audit engagements, conditions which might lead to a restricted opinion can be eliminated by agreement between the auditor and the client to extend the auditing procedure or revise the financial statements.

The qualified opinion includes a statement indicating that the auditor is unable to express a full unqualified opinion. There are a number of reasons why this style of opinion might be appropriate. The client's unwillingness to permit some essential auditing procedure, such as confirming accounts receivable or observation of the taking of inventories, would require qualification of the auditor's opinion. Failure of the auditor to agree with the propriety of an accounting method or a presentation on the financial statements would also result in a qualification. Phrases including "except" or "exception" are usually inserted in either or both paragraphs of the short-form opinion together with necessary explanation why the auditor used a qualified opinion. Occasionally an opinion notes another type of qualification; the phrase "subject to" followed by an explanation of uncertainties about valuation or realization of assets or prediction of contingent liabilities is used when the auditor has reservation regarding these items as represented by management, but the auditor can neither reject or accept the accounting decision of management.

An adverse opinion is a completely negative expression by the auditor about the fairness of the financial statements. If exceptions concerning fairness of presentation are so material that a qualified opinion would not be justified, the auditor must state that in his opinion the statements "do *not* present fairly" the financial position and results of operations. A separate paragraph inserted between the scope and opinion paragraphs of the short-form report presents the reasons for the adverse opinion. This type of report is rarely published. Indeed, the engagement leading to an adverse opinion would probably be terminated prior to its completion.

The disclaimer of opinion is a pronouncement by the auditor that he is unable to express any of the preceding three types of opinion on the financial statements. A disclaimer is used when the auditor has not obtained "sufficient competent evidential matter" to form an opinion on the fairness of the financial statements. The reasons for the use of the disclaimer, which must be fully disclosed, might include a serious limitation on the scope of the examination or the existence of unusual uncertainties concerning the amounts reported in the statements.

Frequently the auditor's examination results in a so-called long-form report. This report contains all of the essential elements of the more familiar short-form but includes supplementary information about the business entity and its financial position and operations. Comments about the history of the business, comparative analyses, ratios, and a statement of application of funds might be presented. Management and creditors may find this type of report more useful for their purposes. The examining procedures used and the responsibility of the auditor are the same for both the short-form and long-form reports.

Typically, the auditor's short-form report presented in annual reports to stockholders covers the comparative balance sheet, income statement, statement of retained earnings, and funds flow statement. Other financial and nonfinancial information included elsewhere in the annual report is not usually covered by the auditor's opinion.

THE AUDITOR'S WORK

Auditors use a variety of techniques to examine the financial statements of a company. The techniques applied in carrying out an "audit program" can be grouped into four categories: internal analysis, inspection, external communication, and analytical review. The specific auditing procedures used in any engagement will be determined by the relevance of the "Standards of Field Work" to the particular situation. As noted earlier, these standards relate to planning and supervision, evaluation of the internal control system, and evidential matter.

The Audit Program

The auditor prepares his audit program early in his examination after appraisal of the company's situation. The audit program is a schedule of audit procedures and the extent to which they will be applied during the course of the audit. This formalized plan of audit procedures prepared by the auditor in charge of the engagement serves several vital needs. First, it enables him to anticipate time and manpower requirements. Second, it permits effective assignments to assistants and aids coordination of their efforts. Third, the audit program serves as a master list of the audit procedures facilitating indexing of working papers prepared during the examination. Some audit forms have developed standard "checklist" programs which are used on all engagements to insure that no essential procedure is omitted. Other firms insist that the auditor in charge prepare a program specifically for each engagement. In any event, each audit will require program modifications to fit the requirements of the investigation. The audit program is subject to constant revision as the audit progresses and new circumstances are revealed by the examination. In this sense, the audit program is not in final form until the entire audit is completed and the auditor's report has been drafted.

Since the audit is essentially an examination of the financial statements, it is logical that investigations of the financial accounts are, in general, accomplished in the order of their appearance on the balance sheet and on the income statement. However, the interrelationship of the accounts makes it impractical to audit any single segment of the client's operations without recognizing the effect upon other accounts. For example, the examination of accounts receivable will directly relate to cash receipts, income recognition, and finished goods shipments. Therefore, the audit proceeds by investigation of various areas of functional activity rather than of individual account balances.

Evaluation of Internal Controls

Early in the examination, the auditor must make a study of the internal controls existing in the organization. The system of internal controls includes all measures instituted by management: (1) to insure accuracy and dependability of financial data, (2) to protect assets from improper or inefficient use, and (3) to control and evaluate operations. The present-day concept of internal control is much broader than that of a generation ago, when internal controls were almost limited to prevention of fraud and clerical inaccuracy.

The modern auditor is concerned with all administrative aspects of the business entity he examines, as well as its financial records and properties. The extent of the auditing procedures to be required by the auditor will depend almost entirely upon the adequacy of the system of internal controls he observes. The evaluation of internal controls continues throughout the entire course of the audit. Financial and administrative procedures are investigated by inquiry and observation. Usually the results of this essential part of the examination are summarized in a separate report to management, together with recommendations for improved internal controls. The auditor's evaluation of internal controls is the basis for determining the degree of reliability of the resulting financial statements. Obviously, there is an inverse relationship between reliability of financial data and the amount of evidential matter the auditor requires to reach his opinion on the financial statements.

Auditing Procedures

A comprehensive view of auditing procedures would require detailed consideration of the many groups of accounts which make up the financial statements. Auditing procedures might be classified by the types of investigative activities employed by the auditor: (1) internal analysis, (2) inspection, (3) external communication, and (4) analytical review. Each of these groups is considered briefly to describe the varied techniques used by the auditor to help form his opinion of management's financial statements.

The principles of testing and sampling must be extensively employed throughout the audit procedure. It would be impractical (and probably impossible) for the auditor to examine and review all records and activities of a business entity. The auditor's judgment, supplemented to an increasing extent by scientific sampling methods, is the basis for determining testing procedures.

1. Internal Analysis. A major part of the auditor's time is devoted to an analysis of the company's internal financial records. The extent of his internal analysis to verify mathematical accuracy is minimized by the presence of internal controls. Many of the accounts are analyzed so that the auditor may independently verify changes and balances. For example, receivable and payable accounts may be analyzed and listed for subsequent investigation. Plant asset and security investment accounts are analyzed to show necessary details of balances. Supporting business documents such as purchase invoices, checks issued, and cash remittance receipts are traced and compared to the accounting entries. The client's employees may assist with clerical work, but the auditor's independence must be maintained by close supervision and verification.

2. Inspection. Auditors make extensive visual inspections of their client's properties in order to independently satisfy themselves that assets are properly presented. Cash on hand is counted, and securities are inspected for reconciliation with records. Physical inventories taken by the client's employees are observed by the auditor. Plant assets may be inspected in at least a limited manner. These inspections and observations must of necessity be coordinated with the client's business operations and with preparation of appropriate analyses of the financial accounts.

3. *External Communication.* The auditor should communicate directly with individuals, businesses, and institutions having dealings with his audit client. These external communications or confirmations aid the auditor in verifying relationships independently of the client's records. In all instances, information is requested from outsiders only with the client's approval and cooperation. Confirmations might be obtained (1) from banks, to verify balances of cash on deposit and amounts of indebtedness; (2) from trade creditors; (3) from customers; (4) from corporate transfer agents and registrars; (5) from sinking fund trustees; (6) from public warehouses; and (7) from others, such as appraisers and attorneys. Typically, these direct communications with third parties produce evidence that is considered highly credible by the auditor in forming his independent opinion.

4. *Analytical Review.* An analytical review of the relationships between data shown by the financial records and revealed during the audit examination add significantly to the auditor's satisfaction with resulting financial statements. It is in this general area that the ingenuity and imagination of the auditor become especially important. For example, comparisons of the client's current bad debt losses with those of prior periods and with those for other businesses in the industry provide insights into the adequacy of the client's bad debt provisions. Analysis of changes in departmental gross profit rates and inventory turnover may help substantiate the recorded income and inventory levels. Comparison of income from securities with records of security ownership adds assurance that financial statements present consistent data. Property tax payments will corroborate property ownership.

Audit Committee

At the urging of the SEC and the New York Stock Exchange, corporations are appointing audit committees of their board of directors. These committees usually consist of outside directors. Their function is to monitor the corporations corporate reporting practices, review the work of the company's CPA as to his audit scope and results, and watch over the quality and appropriateness of the company's internal controls. The widespread appointment of such committees has been viewed with favor as it is believed that the involvement of outside board members in the corporate reporting process should lessen the frequency of some of the shortcomings of corporate reports prepared and published by management without board review.

SUMMARY

Auditing procedures include an almost unlimited variety of investigations designed by the auditor so that he can form his independent professional opinion of management's financial statements. This opinion is expressed in his audit report. In an unqualified report the auditor states to management and owners that: (1) he has completed his examination of the business in a manner required by the application of generally accepted auditing standards, and (2) he offers his opinion, backed by his competence and independence, that management's financial statements present fairly the entity's financial position and the results of its operation in accordance with "generally accepted accounting practices."

SUGGESTED FURTHER READING

AMERICAN INSTITUTE OF CERTIFIED PUBLIC ACCOUNTANTS. *Audit Guides* (various dates and subjects). New York.

HOLMES, ARTHUR W. *Auditing, Principles and Procedure.* 7th ed. Homewood, Ill.: Richard D. Irwin, Inc., 1970.

CASES

CASE 7–1. COMET SERVICE, INCORPORATED
Testing Internal Controls for Cash Receipts and Disbursements

Comet Service, Inc., was engaged in servicing and repairing elevator equipment. Maintenance service contracts were the major source of revenue. Substantial repair jobs furnished the remainder of the company's revenue. Annual sales were approximately $10 million, and there were about 150 men engaged in service and repair work.

The company had not been previously audited. Your public accounting firm has been engaged to make annual examinations. You have been assigned to review and test the cash receipts and disbursements procedures and to make suggestions for improvements where the internal accounting controls appear to be deficient.

The company's accounting staff consists of—

1. Cashier.
2. Assistant cashier, who also posted the detail accounts receivable ledger.
3. Bookkeeper.
4. Assistant bookkeeper.
5. Billing and job cost clerk.
6. Two general clerks—filing, general office work, incoming and outgoing mail.
7. Secretary.
8. Messenger.

The vice president, who is engaged mostly in the technical end of the business, is also the treasurer. You are favorably impressed with the caliber of the staff, who appear to carry out their duties efficiently. The accounting records are kept on a manual basis.

The following is a brief summary of the procedures as you have recorded them in your notes:

Cash Receipts

a. All incoming remittances were received by check.

b. Incoming mail was opened by one of the general clerks.

c. Clerk prepared two adding machine tapes of checks as a means of control, one tape of checks accompanied by remittance advices and another of checks for which remittance advices were not received. On the latter tape, the clerk noted against each item the name of the customer for the information of the accounts receivable ledger clerk in posting collections. Tapes were delivered to the ledger clerk, who was also the assistant cashier.

d. Clerk delivered checks to the cashier, who endorsed them, prepared bank deposit, agreed amount with tapes, and wrote up cash receipts entry, which was supported by the adding machine tapes and remittance advices received from customers.

e. Bank deposit was taken to the bank by the assistant cashier.

Cash Disbursements

a. Invoices were processed for payment by assistant bookkeeper; invoices were matched up with receiving reports (received directly from receiving department) and with copies of purchase orders as to quantity, description, and price; invoices were matched with freight and trucking charges (if any); mathematical accuracy of invoices was checked; work done was not initialed for by the assistant bookkeeper.

b. On the 10th and 25th of the month (or on discount date), invoices were assembled by vendor and vouchered for payment by the assistant bookkeeper, who also kept the accounts payable ledger. Amounts vouchered were entered in the accounts payable ledger.

c. The vouchers with documents attached were sent to the cashier, who prepared the checks and entered them in the cash disbursements book.

d. Checks and vouchers with attached documents were sent by the cashier to the vice president–treasurer; he reviewed the vouchers and supports, initialed the vouchers, signed the checks (one signature only on checks), and sent them back to the cashier. The vouchers and supporting documents were not canceled with a dated paid stamp or by machine.

e. As the recording of checks was time-consuming, the cashier abbreviated somewhat by using initials only instead of full names for some companies (e.g., TCSI for Technical Control Systems, Inc.). Apparently, some of the larger suppliers emphasized initials on their invoices and letterheads, and they had no difficulty cashing checks prepared in this manner.

f. Upon occasion, a representative of the company was required to visit certain suppliers to expedite shipments of sorely needed material for jobs. For psychological reasons, it was decided that the request for early shipments would be aided by the presentation of a check in payment of past orders, and therefore certain checks were secured from the mail clerk before mailing.

g. No examination of endorsements on paid checks was made at any time by the cashier in making the monthly bank reconciliation.

Questions

1. On the basis of the foregoing information, what recommendations would you make for improvement in internal accounting controls over cash receipts and disbursements?

2. Based on your appraisal of the company's internal controls, what audit steps would you undertake to examine cash receipts and disbursements and related areas?

CASE 7–2. EAGLE BRANDS, INCORPORATED
Audit Tests of Year-End Inventories when Physical Inventory Is Taken at an Interim Date

Eagle Brands, Inc., manufactured a line of small hand tools and machines. Your public accounting firm audited the company's books, and you have been assigned responsibility for the inventory items.

Eagle's perpetual inventory records were maintained for raw materials and finished goods, showing quantities and dollar amounts; general ledger control accounts were maintained for raw materials and finished goods. No work in process records were maintained, since the production time of each of the company's lines was generally one day. The cost of raw materials put into process and productive labor was charged directly to the finished goods account.

Charges to the raw material perpetual records were made from vendors' invoices and receiving reports. Credits for materials put into production were based on material requisitions, priced at weighted average cost.

A lot (or production) order was issued for the manufacture of quantities to be produced of each type of tool or machine, and a requisition was prepared for the required amount of raw materials to produce the quantity of finished product ordered. Labor tickets prepared by shop workers showed lot order number, hours worked, and units processed. These time tickets were extended for labor charges by the cost clerk; the hours were agreed with time-clock cards. Daily production line inspection counts were made by the timekeeper of finished products, and the quantities were agreed by the cost clerk with the production reported by the shop workers. A summary by lot orders was made by the cost clerk of materials, labor charges, and quantities produced, and the totals were charged to the perpetual records of finished products. A new weighted average was computed each time a production order was completed, and this new average was used by the cost clerk to calculate the cost of the sales made under shipping reports.

Requisitions for additional raw materials to replace items spoiled in manufacture, and an estimate of labor spent on the spoiled materials, were charged to shop overhead (spoilage account), with an offsetting credit to finished goods.

Monthly trial balances of the perpetual stock records of raw materials and finished products were reconciled monthly by the bookkeeper with the general ledger control accounts. Overhead was apportioned to inventory at year-end only (December 31), based on the relation of overhead for the year to direct labor costs for the year.

Because Eagle experienced heavy production demands during the month of December and business was relatively slow in late summer, a complete physical inventory was taken at September 30, after shutting down production and clearing all in-process work. Your accounting firm had generally found the inventory to be carefully taken and the perpetual records to be reasonably accurate. Shipping and receiving cutoffs were properly recorded. The physical inventory at the interim date was priced as follows:

1. Raw materials at the latest weighted average cost of purchases.
2. Finished goods at the latest weighted average cost per unit (material and labor only).

Question

Your audit tests have satisfactorily established the reasonableness of the company's inventory as at the interim date. What audit tests do you suggest to determine that the inventories in the company's financial statements at the year-end are reasonably stated?

CASE 7–3. WILEY INTERNATIONAL OIL
Confirmation of Accounts Receivable

Wiley International Oil Company, a medium-sized integrated oil company, maintained three large sales divisions in the United States and three small sales divisions outside the United States. In addition, a separate sales division in the head office handled all large special sales and direct refinery shipments.

Divisions in the United States sold both at retail and wholesale. Retail accounts receivable arose through sales on credit cards. There were some 115,000 active credit card accounts. There were about 30,000 wholesale accounts and 200 general sales (special and refinery shipment) accounts. The accounts receivable and annual sales by divisions are summarized below (all *dollar* amounts are in thousands):

| | Accounts Receivable | | | | Annual Sales | |
| | Retail | | Wholesale | | | |
	No. of Accounts	Amount	No. of Accounts	Amount	Retail	Wholesale
Divisions in U.S.:						
No. 1	50,000	$ 700	10,000	$2,500	$10,000	$20,000
No. 2	35,000	500	10,000	2,000	7,000	18,000
No. 3	30,000	450	8,000	1,500	5,000	15,000
Divisions outside U.S.:						
No. 4			800	250		3,000
No. 5			1,000	400		4,000
No. 6			200	100		1,000
Special division			200	3,000		35,000
Total	115,000	$1,650	30,200	$9,750	$22,000	$96,000

The company's system of internal accounting control at the three U.S. divisions was satisfactory, the accounting staff at each of the sales divisions being sufficiently large to permit adequate segregation of duties. The company maintained a staff of internal auditors at each of the U.S. divisions.

The number of employees at each of the sales divisions outside the United States was small, and a certain amount of overlapping of duties existed. The company auditors did not regularly visit these divisions, their last visit having been about five years ago.

The company used the cycle method of billing retail accounts; that is, the accounts were divided into five groups or cycles, the billings of which were staggered throughout the month, one cycle being billed every five days. Trial balances of past-due accounts only were run for each cycle immediately before the cycle billing, and current billings were entered on these trial balances in one amount to balance to the controls maintained for each cycle. The cycle controls were balanced monthly with the divisional ledger.

Wholesale accounts were kept on bookkeeping machines, from four to six machines being used at each U.S. division. The accounts were segregated by area, and separate controls were maintained for each marketing area, of which there were between 60 and 100 in each division.

The number of transactions in the special sales division was relatively small, and the internal accounting control was considered adequate. The company auditors did not examine the records of this division.

The company maintained a credit section at each of the sales divisions, and the head office credit department controlled and supervised the divisional credit sections and received for review copies of all divisional trial balances.

Early in the year the chief internal auditor submitted his proposed program of circularization (confirmation) of accounts receivable as of an interim date and told you that it was similar to those of the past five years:

1. No work would be undertaken at any of the divisions outside the United States or at the special sales division.
2. Retail accounts: 100 accounts at each U.S. division would be circularized by use of the positive form of confirmation (i.e., the customer would be requested to confirm his balance shown in the confirmation letter, regardless of whether or not the balance was correct). The chief auditor explained that only a token number of retail accounts would be circularized because (1) the credit risk was well spread, (2) it was his experience that most replies were unsatisfactory because of cycle billing, and (3) he considered a test of a significant portion of the accounts to be impracticable.
3. Wholesale accounts: 5 percent of the wholesale accounts at each U.S. division would be circularized by use of the positive form. The chief auditor maintained records of the ledgers circularized each year, so that over a period of years all ledgers would be circularized. The ledgers which he selected each year included some from each of the bookkeepers.
4. Accounts written off: Twenty-five percent of the accounts written off in the preceding two years would be circularized. This work would include examination of the credit files on accounts circularized.
5. Second requests would be mailed to all regular wholesale accounts failing to reply at the end of one month if such accounts had not then been paid in full. Second requests would not be mailed on accounts written off. Confirmation requests returned unclaimed would be remailed if another address could be determined.
6. All incoming mail for a period of ten days would be opened and remittances received noted for subsequent tracing to individual accounts.

7. All postings to wholesale accounts for a two-day period would be checked.
8. A report summarizing the results of the circularization would be prepared and furnished to you for review. The internal auditors' working papers would also be made available to you.

Questions

1. The work of the internal auditors is considered satisfactory by the external auditor. On that basis, to what extent should the independent certified public accountant circularize accounts receivable in his examination for the year ending December 31?
2. In reviewing the work of the internal auditors, what points would you keep in mind?
3. Do you recognize any situations in the facts stated that might call for recommendations to Wiley? What might customers' replies disclose that could prove helpful to management?

CASE 7–4. FAIRMUIR INSTRUMENT CORPORATION
The Audit Opinion

Fairmuir Instrument Corporation sold a line of high-temperature measuring instruments (pyrometers). The principal users of the equipment were steel mills and various metal extraction companies, and Fairmuir's small sales force had concentrated almost exclusively on establishing good relations with these customers. Occasional inquiries and orders came from other sources, such as scientific laboratories, but the company had never actively solicited these markets.

The device in its present form had been developed and put into production in the early 1960s. Essentially it utilized principles which had been known for almost a hundred years, but until recently the accuracy attainable had fallen short of the requirements of modern industry. The company had introduced no new products until the last quarter of 1974. Effectively the company had not faced any serious competition in its market area until 1970 and had maintained a stable sales level of around $3 million until that time.

During 1970 a competing product had been introduced to the market. Operating on completely different principles, this device performed substantially the same job as Fairmuir's product and gave similar levels of accuracy. The only major differences were in its useful life (five years) and its purchase price, each of which were about half of those of the Fairmuir product. The lower purchase price was a telling sales advantage, and Fairmuir's sales had suffered accordingly. Exhibit 1 gives some of the financial data of Fairmuir Instrument Corporation from 1970 through 1974.

EXHIBIT 1

FAIRMUIR INSTRUMENT CORPORATION

Financial Data as of December 31

(dollar figures in thousands)

	Audited Results				Unaudited
	1970	1971	1972	1973	1974
Inventories related to pyrometers	791	806	909	805	627
Working capital	933	1,021	1,165	1,155	819
Net assets	1,889	1,965	1,995	1,926	1,549
Net sales of pyrometers	2,881	2,475	2,025	996	583
Other sales (net)	—	—	—	—	115
Net income (loss)	108	77	67	(91)	(376)

By 1971 the management of Fairmuir realized that without a new product to bolster its faltering sales volume, the company was facing a serious predicament. They, therefore, began a search for an additional product which would be suited to the competences of the company. In 1972 they approached an inventor, who held patents for just such a product, with a view to buying the patents. After some negotiation a mutually satisfactory price was reached, and, as part of the agreement, the inventor agreed to join the company and lead the additional development work which was required before a commercial product was ready for marketing.

On top of the cost of the patents and the development expenses, the company was faced with substantial start-up costs and investment in inventories. The company's financial resources, already adversely affected by the lagging sales of pyrometers, were inadequate without an injection of fresh capital. The company's capital stock was closely held by members of top management and a few of their friends and family members. None of these people was willing to contribute any further capital.

Management believed that the recent poor operating results made it unwise to seek fresh equity capital at that time and they, therefore, decided that a bank loan was the only feasible recourse. It did not prove an easy matter to find a bank willing to make the required loan, but eventually the capital was obtained from a bank. In extending the loan the bank imposed several restrictions upon the management of Fairmuir, one of these being that a minimum working capital level of $800,000 should be maintained. By the end of 1974, with the sales of pyrometers still falling and the new product only just introduced to the market, the company was close to defaulting on the requirements of the working capital covenant.

In the 1974 audit, the public accountant was satisfied with all the accounts except for the valuation of the inventories related to pyrometers. Most of this inventory was in good condition, and had been carefully handled and stored. A few items of purchased parts had become obsolete, and management had written them down. This represented an insignificant adjustment, however, and the bulk of the inventory was still reported on the company's books at cost. The auditor was not concerned about the physical condition of the inventory, but he had serious reservations as to the marketability of the product, and therefore the realization of the investment through profitable sales. In approaching management on this matter the auditor was aware that a large adjustment would throw the company into default on its loan covenant concerning working capital.

The auditor, Mr. Bill Adams, arranged a meeting with the president of Fairmuir Instrument Corporation, Mr. Tom Fairmuir, in order to discuss the 1974 financial statements, part of the meeting is recorded below.

Mr. Adams: Everything seems to be in fine order except for your valuation of inventories relating to pyrometers, Tom. Now we discussed this matter briefly a few days ago and you expressed the opinion that there would be no material loss of value in the inventories and that you would in fact be able to sell it all in the normal course of business. Since then I have examined your record of sales orders, and at present you have only $58,000 worth of open orders on your books, compared with $65,000 worth at the beginning of the year. Your billings by quarters for the past year were fairly stable: $149,000 first quarter, $136,000 second quarter, $141,000 third quarter, and $157,000 in the final quarter.

I have also read several articles in trade publications, such as this one in *Steel Monthly,* which seem to indicate that your type of pyrometer is at a technical as well as an economic (in terms of purchase price), disadvantage.

Frankly, it appears to me that you are going to be left with a lot of inventory which will have to be marked down very significantly to sell it.

Mr. Fairmuir: Now hold it, Bill, things are not so bleak as that. In fact, we have plans for our pyrometers which will return the sales volume to its previous level, or close to it. Look at these letters, Bill. These are inquiries concerning substantial orders, and we have been receiving such inquiries at a greatly increased rate recently. If this continues, and I have no doubt that it will, and even half of them become firm orders, we shall be selling pyrometers in 1975 at twice the 1974 level.

You know we hired a new sales manager this year? Well, he has reorganized our sales force and is beginning to get results. At the same time we have gone over our production process and reduced the manufacturing cost of our lines by some 10 percent. No doubt you noticed that our cost of goods figures, which have been stable at about 60 percent of selling price for several years, were lower for the past two or three months. We expect to improve on that further in 1975. Of course this gives us some price flexibility when we are faced with a competitive situation. So you see, I have good reason to predict better results in the future.

Mr. Adams: What exactly has the new sales manager done?

Mr. Fairmuir: He reorganized the sales territories and reassigned the salesmen so that we should get greater market penetration. He released a couple of the men who have clearly not been pulling their weight and hired a couple of bright young men to replace them. The main thing is that he has done wonders for the morale of the sales force.

In addition he has identified new markets and is helping the men to break into these markets.

Mr. Adams: Why don't we look at the prospects market by market, Tom? You had sales of only $62,000 to steel mills in 1974. It seems as if the steel mills market is almost defunct, wouldn't you agree?

Mr. Fairmuir: It has certainly declined. However, some of our men have built up a good relationship with their customers in the steel industry and we expect this to produce a certain loyalty. We should keep a small part of the business, say, billings of about $50,000 a year.

Then in the other metal extraction industries we know that our product has some distinct competitive advantages, such as its ruggedness and lower maintenance costs. With the new emphasis on selling we expect that our customers will be well aware of these advantages, and the downward sales trend should be reversed this year. On this basis we expect 1975's sales to this market to be at least $400,000 and to increase further in the future.

Mr. Adams: But look, Tom, that means an increase over this year's sales, bucking a strong downward trend. I can't base my opinion on your optimism, you know.

Mr. Fairmuir: Well, look at this market which we think has great potential—scientific laboratories. We are going to place advertisements in some of the engineering journals and pay direct sales calls to many of the labs in our market areas, those which do a lot of high-temperature work. We anticipate a yearly volume of $200,000 to $300,000 in this market.

And, finally, we have set up a contract with a representative in Washington to handle our line in government sales. He has already got some orders for us, and he seems certain that we can build up a stable volume of some $300,000 a year. Several government agencies are testing our product at the moment, including the Atomic Energy Commission. If we get our equipment specified for installation into government nuclear plants, we shall have a large continuing market.

Mr. Adams: So you expect sales of about $1 million this year, twice 1974's sales?

Mr. Fairmuir: No, not right away. But we are confident of substantially reversing the trend of recent years and eventually, say, in two years or so,
building our sales up to at least $1.5 million for pyrometers. For 1975 we
predict sales of about $800,000.

Mr. Adams: Well, look at this from my point of view. I have a professional
responsibility to give an opinion on your company's financial statements
and I cannot base my opinion on your predictions. I have to go on historic
facts and reasonable expectations. The historic facts are that sales of
pyrometers have been falling and you have only a small volume of open
orders on your books.

You have a substantial inventory, the value of which can only be
realized through the sale of pyrometers. Any other representation of these
facts would mislead the reader of the statements.

Mr. Fairmuir: I agree with you on that, and in my opinion, we *will* realize
the value of our inventory through normal sales. I could not contemplate a
write-down in the value of the inventory. For one thing, it would not be
right to do so since it would be misleading in valuing our assets. And for
another, it could easily lead to a difficult situation with the bank and, at
worst, lead to liquidation of the company. True, we have experienced a
few bad years. But we are fighting back, and I am confident we shall save
our pyrometer line. And also our new line will start to contribute to profits
this coming year.

The discussion continued for some time and became fairly heated.
Finally, Mr. Adams terminated the discussion in order to consider the
question further. He arranged a meeting with Mr. Fairmuir for three
days later, at which time the two men agreed they would come to a
decision as to whether or not the value of the inventory should be
written down. Mr. Adams was concerned as to what opinion he should
issue on Fairmuir's financial statements of 1974.

Questions

1. What further steps should Mr. Adams take in preparing for the coming
   meeting with Mr. Fairmuir?
2. Putting yourself in Mr. Fairmuir's position, what steps would you take in
   preparing for the meeting? If Mr. Adams insists that the value of the
   inventory be written down, what would you do?
3. Do you think that the value of the inventory should be written down? If so,
   how should the adjustment be made?
4. If it were not written down, how would you, as auditor, phrase your
   opinion?

PART IV

Analysis of Corporate Financial Reports

Chapter 8

FINANCIAL STATEMENT ANALYSIS

The analysis of financial statements provides an important basis for valuing securities and appraising managerial performance. Consequently, one measure of the usefulness of financial statements is how well they help investors to appraise the financial condition of the issuing company and the effectiveness of its management in earning a return on its invested capital. This chapter introduces some of the basic concepts of financial ratio analysis and common stock valuation. The valuation of debt securities is discussed in Chapter 19. A knowledge of these techniques is essential to appreciate fully the communications aspect of financial reports.

FINANCIAL ANALYSIS

Financial analysis is a tool for interpreting financial statements. It can provide insight into two important areas of management: the return on investment earned and the soundness of the company's financial position. This technique compares certain related items in the statements to each other in a meaningful manner. The analyst evaluates these results against the particular characteristics of the company and its industry. The astute analyst seldom expects answers from this process. Rather, he hopes it will provide him with clues as to where he should focus his subsequent analysis.

Financial ratios fall into four classes: ratios appraising liquidity, ratios measuring solvency, ratios evaluating funds management, and ratios measuring profitability. The categories indicate that different ratios may be more helpful than others for particular purposes. Therefore, rather than calculating ratios indiscriminately, the experienced analyst precedes his ratio computation with some consideration of the kinds of insights he believes will be helpful in understanding the problem he faces. He then calculates those ratios that best serve his purpose. To get the most meaningful results, the analysis compares these ratios over a period of several years against some standard; examines in depth major variations from this standard; and cross-checks the various ratios against each other.

The 1975 balance sheet and income statement of the Ampex Corporation, a retailing business, will be used to illustrate some of the more common ratios (see Illustrations 8–1 and 8–2).

Liquidity Ratios

Liquidity ratios appraise a company's ability to meet its current obligations. These ratios compare current liabilities, which are the

ILLUSTRATION 8–1

AMPEX CORPORATION
Comparative Balance Sheets, December 31, 1974, and 1975
(in thousands of dollars)

Assets

	1974	1975
Current Assets:		
Cash	$ 30	$ 20
Accounts receivable (net)	95	95
Inventory	110	130
Total Current Assets	$235	$245
Fixed Assets:		
Land	$ 10	$ 10
Building and equipment (net)	100	120
Total Fixed Assets	$110	$130
Other Assets:		
Goodwill and organization costs	$ 10	$ 10
Total Assets	$355	$385

Liabilities and Stockholders' Equity

	1974	1975
Current Liabilities:		
Accounts payable	$ 40	$ 50
Estimated income taxes payable	10	10
Total Current Liabilities	$ 50	$ 60
Fixed Liabilities:		
Mortgage bonds, 4 percent	$ 50	$ 50
Total Liabilities	$100	$110
Stockholders' Equity:		
Preferred stock, 5 percent	$ 20	$ 20
Common stock (10,000 shares outstanding)	50	50
Retained earnings	185	205
Total Stockholders' Equity	$255	$275
Total Liabilities and Stockholders' Equity	$355	$385

ILLUSTRATION 8–2

AMPEX CORPORATION
Condensed Income Statement, 1975
(in thousands of dollars)

Gross sales	$1,516	100.66%
Less: Returns and allowances	10	0.66
Net sales	$1,506	100.00%
Less: Cost of goods sold	1,004	66.67
Gross profit	$ 502	33.33%
Operating expenses*	400	26.56
Operating profit	$ 102	6.77%
Interest	2	0.13
Profit before taxes	$ 100	6.64%
Income tax expense	50	3.32
Net income	$ 50	3.32%
Less: Preferred dividends	1	0.07
Common dividends	29	1.93
Change in Retained Earnings	$ 20	1.32%

* Includes lease rental costs of $30,000 and depreciation of $10,000.

obligations falling due in the next 12 months, and current assets, which typically provide the funds to extinguish these obligations. The difference between current assets and current liabilities is called "net working capital."

Current Ratio

$$\frac{\text{Current Assets}}{\text{Current Liabilities}} = \frac{\$245,000}{\$60,000} = 4.1 \text{ Times, or } 4.1 \text{ to } 1$$

The meaningfulness of the current ratio as a measure of liquidity varies from company to company. Typically, it is assumed that the higher the ratio, the more protection the company has against liquidity problems. However, the ratio may be distorted by seasonal influences, slow-moving inventories built up out of proportion to market opportunities, or abnormal payment of accounts payable just prior to the balance sheet date. Also, the nature of some businesses is such that they have a steady, predictable cash inflow and outflow, and a low current ratio is appropriate for such a business.

Acid-Test or Quick Ratio

$$\frac{\text{Quick Assets}}{\text{Current Liabilities}} = \frac{\$115,000}{\$60,000} = 1.9 \text{ Times, or } 1.9 \text{ to } 1$$

The acid-test or quick ratio measures the ability of a company to use its current assets to immediately extinguish its current liabilities.

Quick assets include those working capital items that presumably can be quickly converted to cash at close to their book value. Such items are cash, stock investments, and accounts receivable. Like the working capital ratio, this ratio implicitly implies a liquidation approach and does not recognize the revolving nature of current assets and liabilities.

Solvency Ratios

Solvency ratios describe a company's ability to meet long-term debt payment schedules. There are a number of ratios which compare stockholders' equity to funds provided by creditors. All of these ratios are designed to give some measure of the extent to which ownership funds provide protection to creditors should a company incur losses.

Times Interest Earned

$$\frac{\text{Operating Profit}}{\text{Long-Term Debt Interest}} = \frac{\$102,000}{\$2,000} = 51 \text{ Times}$$

This coverage ratio is calculated on a pretax basis, since bond interest is a tax deductible expense. The ratio in the example implies that operating profits cover interest payments 51 times. This indicates the extent to which income can decline without impairing the company's ability to pay the interest on its long-term debt.

Some analysts prefer to use operating profit plus noncash charges as the numerator of this ratio. This modification indicates the ability to the company to cover its cash outflow for interest from its funds from operations. For example, the only so-called noncash charge in the Ampex income statement is depreciation; that is, no cash outflow results from incurring this expense. Adding the company's $10,000 depreciation expense to operating profit changes the numerator to $112,000 and increases the coverage to 56 times.

Coverage ratios can be computed for preferred stock dividends and other fixed charges, such as lease rentals. The preferred-stock-dividend-coverage ratio is calculated on an aftertax basis, since preferred stock dividends are not considered a tax deductible expense. For example, the Ampex *preferred-stock-dividend-coverage* ratio is:

$$\frac{\text{Profits after Taxes}}{\text{Preferred Stock Dividends}} = \frac{\$50,000}{\$1,000} = 50 \text{ Times}$$

A coverage ratio for all of a company's fixed charges is called the times-fixed-charges-earned ratio. The denominator of this ratio includes such items as lease rentals, interest, and preferred dividends converted to a pretax basis. The numerator is operating profit before these charges. The *times-fixed-charges-earned* ratio for Ampex is:

$$\frac{\text{Operating Profit before Fixed Charges}}{\text{Lease Rentals, Interest, Preferred Dividends}} = \frac{\$132,000}{\$34,000} = 3.9 \text{ Times}$$

Debt-to-Equity Ratios. The relationship of borrowed funds to ownership funds is an important solvency ratio. Capital from debt and other creditor sources is more risky for a company than equity capital. Debt capital requires fixed interest payments on specific dates and eventual repayment. If payments to a company's creditors become overdue, the creditors can take legal action which may lead to the company being declared bankrupt. Ownership capital is less risky. Dividends are paid at the discretion of the directors, and there is no provision for repayment of capital to stockholders. It is generally assumed that the more ownership capital relative to debt a company has in its capital structure, the more likely it is that the company will be able to meet its fixed obligations. An excessive amount of ownership capital relative to debt capital may not necessarily indicate sound management practices, however. Equity capital is typically more costly than debt capital. Also, the company may be forgoing opportunities "to trade on its equity," that is, borrow debt at relatively low interest rates and hope to earn greater rates of returns on these funds. The difference between these two rates can increase earnings per share without having to increase the number of common shares outstanding.

There are a number of debt-to-equity ratios. Three of the most common are:

$$\frac{\text{Total Liabilities}}{\text{Total Assets}} = \frac{\$110,000}{\$385,000} = 28.6\%, \text{ or } 0.286 \text{ to } 1$$

This ratio indicates the proportion of a company's total assets financed by short-term and long-term credit sources.

$$\frac{\text{Long-Term Debt}}{\text{Capitalization}} = \frac{\$50,000}{\$325,000} = 15.4\%, \text{ or } 0.154 \text{ to } 1$$

This measure, which excludes current liabilities, reflects management's policy on the mix of long-term funds obtained from ownership and non-ownership sources.

$$\frac{\text{Total Liabilities}}{\text{Stockholders' Equity}} = \frac{\$110,000}{\$275,000} = 40\%, \text{ or } 0.4 \text{ to } 1$$

This ratio is another way of measuring the relative mix of funds provided by owners and creditors. Ampex appears to have an adequate cushion of ownership funds against losses from operations, decreases in the book value of assets, and poor estimates of future cash flows.

Funds Management Ratios

The financial situation of a company turns in large measure on how its investment in accounts receivable, inventories, and fixed assets is managed. As a business expands its sales, it is not uncommon to find that the associated expansion of these three items is so great that despite profitable operations the company is short of cash. In such situations the management of trade credit becomes critical. It is a source of capital which should expand along with the increased sales.

Receivables to Sales

$$\frac{\text{Receivables (net)}}{\text{Net Sales}} = \frac{\$95,000}{\$1,506,000} = 6.3\%$$

In the absence of an aging of accounts receivable (classification of receivables by days since billing) or other detailed credit information, the receivables-to-sales ratio, computed over a number of years, can give a crude indication of the trend in a company's credit policy. In those cases where a company sells for cash and credit, only net credit sales should be used in the denominator. Receivables include accounts receivables, trade receivables, and trade notes receivable. The rather low receivables-to-sales percentage for Ampex is indicative that this retailer's sales most probably include a high proportion of cash sales.

Average Collection Period

$$\left(\frac{\text{Receivables}}{\text{Sales}}\right) \times \text{Days in the Period} = \text{Collection Period}$$

$$6.3\% \quad \times \quad 365 \quad = 23 \text{ Days}$$

A two-step method to get the same result is:

1. Calculate the average daily sales:

$$\frac{\text{Sales}}{\text{Days}} = \frac{\$1,506,000}{365} = \$4,126 \text{ per Day}$$

2. Calculate the days' sales represented by receivables:

$$\frac{\text{Receivables}}{\text{Sales per Day}} = \frac{\$95,000}{\$4,126} = 23 \text{ Days}$$

To appraise the quality of accounts receivable, the average collection period can be related to the typical credit terms of the company. A collection period substantially longer than this standard might indicate poor credit management, resulting in an increasing amount of funds being tied up in this asset. On the other hand, a significantly shorter collection period than is typical in the industry might mean profitable sales to slower paying customers were being missed. This may well be the case at Ampex, since 23 days seems very short for a retail business.

Average Accounts Payable Period. Similar tests can be made of accounts payable to see how well they are managed. In this case the accounts payable are compared to the purchases for the period (costs of goods sold plus inventory changes). The calculation of the average day's payables is made as follows:

1. Calculate the average daily purchases:

$$\frac{\text{Purchases}}{\text{Days}} = \frac{\$1,024,000}{365} = \$2,805 \text{ per Day}$$

2. Calculate the day's purchases represented by payables:

$$\frac{\text{Accounts Payable}}{\text{Purchase per Day}} = \frac{\$50,000}{\$2,805} - 18 \text{ Days}$$

The day's-payables ratio becomes meaningful when compared to the credit terms given by the suppliers of the industry. If a company's average day's payables is growing larger, it may mean trade credit is being used increasingly as a source of funds. If the period is less than the average for the industry, it may indicate that management has not used this source of funds as much as is possible. If it is longer, it may mean the company is overdue on its payables and is using this source of funds beyond the normal trade limits.

Rarely is the purchase figure available to people outside of the company. Consequently, the analyst has to approximate this figure. One way is to take the cost of goods sold figure, adjust it for inventory changes, and then try to estimate how much of the resulting figure represents outside purchases. In merchandising situations, like the Ampex illustration, this is less difficult. The merchandiser's cost of goods sold is the price he paid his suppliers for the goods sold. In manufacturing situations, this is not such an easy task. The cost of goods sold expense includes direct labor, raw materials, and some manufacturing overheads. If the raw materials portion of the cost of goods sold and inventories figures are available, they can be used to calculate an approximation of the raw materials purchases, which in most cases represents the minimum level of purchases.

Another difficulty is that the accounts payable figure may include payables incurred for other than items included in cost of goods sold. As a result of this problem and the other measurement problems, this ratio is usually not regarded as being a particularly reliable indication of the quality of the accounts payable.

Inventory Turnover

$$\frac{\text{Cost of Sales}}{\text{Average Inventory}} = \frac{\$1,004,000}{\$120,000} = 8.4 \text{ Times}$$

The inventory turnover ratio shows how fast the inventory items move through the business. It is an indication of how well the funds invested in inventory are being managed. The analyst is interested in two items: the absolute size of the inventory in relationship to the other fund needs of the company, and the relationship of the inventory to the sales volume it supports. A decrease in the turnover rate indicates that the absolute size of the inventory relative to sales is increasing. This can be a warning signal, since funds may be tied up in this inventory beyond the level required by the sales volume, which may be rising or falling.

Average inventory is used in the denominator because the sales volume is generated over a 12-month period. The average inventory is obtained by adding the opening inventory and closing inventory balances and dividing the sum by two.

If the cost of goods sold figure is not available, an approximation of the inventory turnover rate can be obtained by using the sales figure in the numerator. If profit margins have remained fairly steady, then this sales-to-average-inventory ratio can provide, over a period of years, an indication of inventory management trends.

By dividing the turnover rate into 365 days, the analyst can estimate the average length of time items spent in inventory:

$$\frac{365 \text{ Days}}{\text{Inventory Turnover}} = \frac{365}{8.4} = 43 \text{ Days}$$

Fixed Asset Turnover.   A similar turnover ratio can also be calculated for fixed assets. It provides a crude measure of how well the investment in plant and equipment is being managed relative to the sales volume it supports. The usefulness of this measure is reduced considerably because book values seldom approximate market values or are comparable from company to company due to different depreciation policies.

$$\frac{\text{Net Sales}}{\text{Average Fixed Assets}} = \frac{\$1,506,000}{\$120,000} = 12.6 \text{ Times}$$

Profitability Ratios

The analysts look at profits in two ways: first, as a percentage of sales; second, as a return on the funds invested in the business.

Profit Margin. Profit margins relative to sales can be evaluated in a number of different ways.

a. Net income as a percentage of sales measures the total operating and financial quality of management, since net profit after taxes includes all of the costs of doing business:

$$\frac{\text{Net Income}}{\text{Sales}} = \frac{\$50,000}{\$1,506,000} = 3.32\%$$

b. Net profit before taxes and interest is indicative of management's operating ability. Interest is excluded because it relates to financing policy rather than operating efficiency:

$$\frac{\text{Earnings before Interest and Taxes}}{\text{Sales}} = \frac{\$102,000}{\$1,506,000} = 6.77\%$$

c. Gross profit (sales minus cost of sales) as a percentage of sales is an indication of the ability of the management to mark up its products over their costs:

$$\frac{\text{Gross Profit}}{\text{Sales}} = \frac{\$502,000}{\$1,506,000} = 33.3\%$$

In addition to these ratios, it is often informative to express as a percentage of net sales all of those expense items relevant to the area being explored (see Illustration 8–2). This is called a common size statement.

Return on Investment. The relationship between profitability and investment is considered the key ratio by many analysts. It provides a broad measure of management's operating and financial success. Several different return-on-investment ratios are commonly used.

a. *Return on Total Assets*

$$\frac{\text{Profit before Taxes and Interest}}{\text{Average Total Assets}} = \frac{\$102,000}{\$370,000} = 27.6\%$$

This ratio gauges how well management has managed the total resources at its command, before consideration of taxes and credit costs. It focuses on the earning power of the assets and is not influenced by how they are financed. Average total assets is used as the denominator since profit is earned over a 12-month period.

b. *Return on Total Assets*

$$\frac{\text{Net Income after Taxes and Interest}}{\text{Average Total Assets}} = \frac{\$50,000}{\$370,000} = 13.5\%$$

This variation of *(a)* measures the return on total assets from the point of view of the profits accruing to the stockholders.

c. *Return on Total Capital*

$$\frac{\text{Net Income}}{\text{Average Total Capital}} = \frac{\$50,000}{\$315,000} = 15.9\%$$

Another ratio measuring return on investment equates investment with total long-term capital (equity capital plus long-term liabilities). This ratio indicates how well management has invested the permanent funds at its disposal. The ratio can be computed on a before- or aftertax basis. If interest is paid on long-term liabilities, then this amount is sometimes added to the net income figure, since it relates to the financial management of those items.

d. *Return on Net Worth*

$$\frac{\text{Net Income}}{\text{Average Stockholders' Equity (net assets)}} = \frac{\$50,000}{\$265,000} = 18.9\%$$

This method measures the return on ownership capital after all taxes and interest payments. It is perhaps the most common return-on-investment figure published by financial services.

e. *Return on Tangible Net Worth*

$$\frac{\text{Net Income}}{\text{(average net worth} - \text{average intangible assets)}} = \frac{\$50,000}{(\$265,000 - 10,000)}$$
$$= \quad 19.6\%$$

This modification of *(d)* measures the return on net worth less the intangible assets, such as goodwill and capitalized organization costs. The principal use of this ratio is to present a more conservative measure of the investment base than *(d)*.

Investment Turnover.   A ratio similar to the inventory and asset turnover ratios can also be calculated for investment:

$$\frac{\text{Sales}}{\text{Average Total Capital}} = \frac{\$1,506,000}{\$315,000} = 4.78 \text{ Times}$$

This ratio, when combined with the net-profit-to-sales ratio, produces the return-on-total-capital rate:

Investment Turnover × Net Profit Ratio = Return on Total Capital
      4.78 Times   ×   3.32%   =   15.9%

This formula indicates that a business return on investment can be improved by increasing the sales volume per dollar of investment; by generating more profit per dollar of sales; or some mix of these two factors. Thus, a store earning 2 percent on sales with an inventory turnover of 10 can be doing just as good a job as another company with a profit margin of 10 percent and an inventory turnover of two times. Both have the same return on investment, 20 percent.

A number of other ratios are closely related. The analyst often uses these relationships to learn more about a particular area of interest. For example, a greater appreciation of the relationship between asset turnover and profit rates can be obtained as follows:

$$\frac{\text{Net Income}}{\text{Sales}} = 3.32\%$$

$$\text{Asset Turnover} = \frac{\text{Net Sales}}{\text{Average Total Assets}} = 4.07 \text{ Times}$$

$$\frac{\text{Net Income}}{\text{Net Sales}} \times \frac{\text{Net Sales}}{\text{Average Total Assets}} = \frac{\text{Net Profit}}{\text{Average Total Assets}}$$
$$\quad 3.32\% \quad \times \quad 4.07 \text{ Times} \quad = \quad 13.5\%$$

A similar set of ratios which have more meaning when examined together are the components of the current ratio. For example, an examination of the relationship between inventory turnover and the receivables and payables periods demonstrates how changes in these working capital items influence funds flow.

Return on Stockholders' Equity Analysis. An analysis of the causes of changes in the level and quality of the company's return on stockholders' equity can be facilitated by the use of the equation presented in Illustration 8–3, which incorporates the 1975 Ampex Corporation data and ratios. Average asset and net worth values are used in all of the ratios incorporating these accounts.

The only new ratio introduced Illustration 8–3 is the so-called tax retention ratio, which measures the percentage of pretax profits retained by the company after payment of income taxes. This ratio is expressed as one minus the book tax rate, which is the ratio of the book tax expense to the pretax profits stated as a percentage.

Implied Growth Rate. A corporation's implied growth rate is set by (1) its capability to finance growth through internally generated capital, new equity issues and financial leverage, and (2) its ability to use its capital. A corporation's actual growth rate may be smaller than this figure because its potential market opportunities may be such that

ILLUSTRATION 8–3

Analysis of Ampex Corporation's Return on Stockholders' Equity

$$\frac{\text{Pretax Profits}}{\text{Sales}} \times \frac{\text{Sales}}{\text{Assets}} = \frac{\text{Pretax Profits}}{\text{Assets}} \times \frac{\text{Assets}}{\text{Net Worth}} = \frac{\text{Pretax Profits}}{\text{Net Worth}} \times (1 - \text{Tax Rate}) = \frac{\text{Net Income}}{\text{Net Worth}}$$

$$6.64\% \times 4.07 = 27.0\% \times 1.40 = 37.7\% \times .5 = 18.9\%$$

Pretax Profit Margin × Asset Turnover Ratio = Pretax Return on Assets × Total Leverage Ratio = Pretax Return on Stockholders' Equity × Tax Retention Rate = Return on Stockholders' Equity

ILLUSTRATION 8–4

Implied Growth Rate

$$\frac{\text{Pretax Profits}}{\text{Sales}} \times \frac{\text{Sales}}{\text{Assets}} = \frac{\text{Pretax Profits}}{\text{Assets}} \times (1 - \text{Tax Rate}) \times (1 - \text{Dividend Payout}) \times \frac{\text{Assets}}{\text{Net Worth}} = \frac{\text{Change in Retained Earnings}}{\text{Net Worth}}$$

$$6.64\% \times 4.07 = 27.0\% \times .5 \times .4 \times 1.40 = 7.56\%$$

Pretax Profit Margin × Asset Turnover Ratio = Pretax Return on Assets × Tax Retention Rate × Profit Retention Rate × Total Leverage Ratio = Implied Growth Rate

Operating Constraints Financial Policy Constraints

the company cannot use its capital and operating potential to its full advantage.

The implied growth rate of a corporation using internally generated funds and leverage to finance growth is set by the corporation's return on assets and financial policies. For such corporations the implied growth rate can be computed by using the equation presented in Illustration 8–4.

The equation in Illustration 8–4 breaks down into two parts: the operating constraints, which can be summarized by the pretax percentage return on assets; and the financial policy constraints, which are management's tax, dividend, and leverage policies. A corporation can increase its implied growth rate by improving any of the pretax and aftertax operating ratios that contribute to a higher return on capital; deciding to lower its dividend payout ratio; or electing to increase its total leverage ratio.

For example, using a contracted form of the equation in Illustration 8–4, a company with the characteristics described in equation 1 below has an implied growth rate of 10 percent. (See equation 1.)

$$1. \quad \frac{\text{Sales}}{\text{Assets}} \times \frac{\text{Profit}}{\text{Sales}} \times 1 - \frac{\text{Dividend}}{\text{Payout}} \times \frac{\text{Assets}}{\text{Net Worth}} = \frac{\text{Implied}}{\text{Growth Rate}}$$
$$2.0 \quad \times \quad .05 \quad \times \quad (1 - .5) \quad \times \quad 2.0 \quad = \quad \underline{\underline{10\%}}$$

According to equation 1, every dollar of retained earnings creates $2 of assets. The equation in turn assumes that these assets will produce sales at the rate indicated by the asset turnover ratio. Using equation 1, the $2 of assets would create $4 of sales. These sales in turn produce profits at the rate indicated by the profit margin percentage, which would be 20 cents for each $4 of sales. Next, part of the profits are paid out in dividends, 20 cents times 50 percent or 10 cents, and the remainder is reinvested in the business. This reinvested 10 cents is leveraged, and the process is repeated—the new retained earnings produces new growth at 10 percent per year.

If a corporation with the characteristics described in equation 1 finds a way to improve the returns it obtains on its incremental capital, its growth rate will improve.

For example, assume the corporation described in equation 1 is able to obtain an asset turnover ratio of 3.0. The new implied growth rate of the company is 15 percent (see equation 2).

$$2. \quad \frac{\text{Sales}}{\text{Assets}} \times \frac{\text{Profit}}{\text{Sales}} \times 1 - \frac{\text{Dividend}}{\text{Payout}} \times \frac{\text{Assets}}{\text{Net Worth}} = \frac{\text{Implied}}{\text{Growth Rate}}$$
$$3.0 \quad \times \quad .05 \quad \times \quad (1 - .5) \quad \times \quad 2.0 \quad = \quad \underline{\underline{15\%}}$$

Statement users find it enlightening to apply the growth rate equation to the companies they follow. This analysis can provide insights into the company's growth potential, what it must do to achieve or change this potential, and how it has achieved growth in the past.

One important point should be noted before using the growth note equation: A company can have a higher rate of growth in any period than indicated by the equation at the beginning of the period. This occurs when a company's incremental characteristics during the period are different from those assumed in the equation; the company raises equity capital from external sources; makes replacement asset investments that return less than the existing rate of return; or repays the debt that existed at the beginning of the period with the incremental profits.

Common Stock Ratios. Buyers and sellers of common stocks use a number of ratios relating market values to earnings and dividends. The significance of these ratios is discussed in the "Security Valuation" section of this chapter.

Earnings per Share. the most straightforward computation of earnings per share is for companies with simple capital structures. In these situations the calculation is:

$$\frac{\text{Net Income}}{\text{Common Shares Outstanding}} = \frac{\$49,000}{10,000} = \$4.90 \text{ per Share}$$

Preferred stock dividends, if any, are deducted from net income before calculating earnings per share. The divisor is the weighted average number of shares determined by relating *(a)* the portion of time within a reporting period that a number of shares of a certain security has been outstanding, to *(b)* the total time in that period.

The number of earnings-per-share figures a company may report will vary with the complexity of its capital structures and whether or not its net income calculations involve extraordinary items.

Since the adoption of *Opinion No. 9*, "Results of Operations[1]," by the Accounting Principles Board, the profit figure used by most analysts in this computation is the net profit before extraordinary items, since this figure is thought to be more representative of the company's continuing income stream.

The term net income per share should be used only in those cases where the capital structure of the company is such that there are no potentially dilutive convertible securities, options, warrants, or other agreements providing for contingency issuances of common stock out-

---

[1] *Opinion No. 9* and its successor *Opinion No. 30* are discussed in detail in Chapter 10.

standing. *Opinion No. 15, Earnings per Share,*[2] requires that companies with complex capital structures present with equal prominence two types of earnings-per-share amounts on the face of the income statement: one, primary earnings per share; the other, fully diluted earnings per share. Primary earnings per share is the amount of earnings attributable to each share of common stock outstanding, including securities that are equivalent to common stock—such as convertible preferred stock with a relatively low dividend rate at issue. Fully diluted earnings per share is the amount of current earnings per share reflecting the maximum dilution that would have resulted from conversions, exercises, and other contingent issues that individually in the future may decrease earnings per share and in the aggregate might have a dilutive effect. Because of the variety of earnings-per-share data which is possible in some situations, it is always dangerous to use these figures without insisting first on knowing which definition is being used.

Typically, financial analysts eliminate nonrecurrent items from a single-year analysis of companies but include them in long-term analysis. In single-year analysis, financial analysts tend to want to know whether or not the current earnings are in line with the "normal" earnings of the company. Consequently, unusual items such as material refunds of over-paid taxes are excluded from these analyses.

In long run analyses of historical data, financial analysts tend to include in income every profit and loss item, unless it is quite unrelated to normal operations. This practice recognizes that many of these so-called unusual items are elements of profit and loss that would have been included in income if the accounting period had been longer than, say, one year. In this latter case, the tax refund excluded from the single-year analysis would be included. Examples of items typically excluded from long-term analyses are gains and losses from property sales and voluntary markdown of capital items, such as plant.

Price-Earnings Ratio. Assuming the average price for the Ampex stock is $40, the price-earnings ratio is:

$$\frac{\text{Market Price per Share}}{\text{Earnings per Share}} = \frac{\$40.00}{\$4.90} = 8.2 \text{ to } 1$$

Since the stock market is responsive to anticipated earnings-per-share estimates, the price-earnings ratio is often quoted using the projected next year's earnings-per-share figure of the company. Typically, the net income figure before extraordinary items is used to compute this ratio. Also, all potential dilutive capital is included in the earnings-per-share calculation.

---

[2] *Opinion No. 15* is discussed in detail in Chapter 11.

The reciprocal of the price-earnings ratio gives the *capitalization rate:*

$$\frac{\text{Earnings per Share}}{\text{Market Price per Share}} = \frac{\$4.90}{\$40.00} = 12.2\%$$

Dividend Yield.   In situations where cash dividends have been increased at the last payment date, the current dividend rate converted to a yearly basis is often used for the numerator:

$$\frac{\text{Cash Dividends per Share}}{\text{Price per Share}} = \frac{\$2.90}{\$40.00} = 7.3\%$$

Stock dividends are not included in this calculation. The *payout ratio* is the percentage cash dividends paid on common stock are of earnings per share:

$$\frac{\text{Cash Dividends per Share}}{\text{Earnings per Share}} = \frac{\$2.90}{\$4.90} = 59\%$$

"Quality of Earnings."   Investors rate earnings-per-share figures on a scale of low to high according to their "quality." Those companies with the highest quality earnings per share within their industry are usually given a higher price earnings ratios than those companies in the same industry category with the lowest quality earnings.

In assessing the "quality" of a company's earnings per share, the six factors shown in Illustration 8–5 and their relationship to the absolute and change in earnings per share seem to be relevant. This assessment is a qualitative judgment.

ILLUSTRATION 8–5

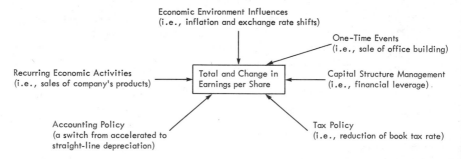

High-quality earnings companies have these characteristics:

1. A consistent conservative accounting policy that results in a prudent measurement of the company's financial condition and net income.

2. A pretax income stream that is derived from recurring, rather than one-time, transactions related to the basic business of the company.
3. Sales that quickly convert to cash after being recorded for accounting purposes.
4. A net income level and growth rate that is not dependent on a lowering of the tax rate through means which may be vulnerable to future tax code changes or place detrimental constraints on the company's use of the tax savings or deferrals.
5. A debt level that is appropriate for the business.
6. A capital structure that has not been manipulated to produce earnings-per-share effects.
7. Earnings that are not materially inflated by unrealizable inflation or currency gains.

Low-quality earnings-per-share companies have the opposite characteristics.

When using the framework presented in Illustration 8–5 it is important to realize that there is no agreed-upon way that the various elements listed affect stock values. Also, there are no commonly agreed-upon standards to follow in rating the relative importance individually or collectively that the six elements bear on the quality assessment. Finally, the significance of the elements can change as the economy's prospects change; a company's growth prospects change; and the individual investors preferences for risk shift.

The factors that enter into the quality of earnings assessment are similar to those used by analysts to quantify and classify the sources of the year-to-year changes in a company's earnings per share.

Basis of Comparison

The results of financial ratio analysis take on real meaning when compared to a standard appropriate to the company's stage of development, seasonal pattern, and industry and management plans. The selection of a relevant standard is always difficult.

The management of a company can use its budgets as a basis of comparison. These are rarely available to the outside analyst. Therefore, he must seek other sources. By comparing a company's current results as shown in its financial reports to similar data in past reports, the analyst can get some indication of how much "better" or "worse" things are compared to the past.

Important sources of average ratios for a particular industry are Dun & Bradstreet's *Modern Industry*, Moody's *Manual of Investment*, and Standard & Poor's *Corporation Records*. Another source of comparison bases are the publications of the various trade associations. Often, these publications report selected financial ratios for industries broken down by sales volume categories. These ratios can be used to highlight variations from the average company situation.

Another source of standards can be ratios computed from the data in the annual reports of individual companies in the same industry. This type of external comparison when used with good judgment can indicate the relative quality of the company's operating performance and funds management compared to its competitors.

The experienced analyst rarely relies on any one standard. He uses several standards. He also looks at a variety of related ratios and knows from experience that he must have a good appreciation of the particular company's business before he should take action based upon his analysis.

A Warning

Financial ratio analysis can be a useful analytical tool if used wisely. It has many limitations which the unsophisticated analyst must remember.

First, it deals only with numerical items. It does not look at non-measurable factors such as management's ethical values or the quality of the management. These are important considerations which should be taken into account when evaluating a company.

Second, management can take certain short-run actions prior to the statement dates to influence the ratios. For example, a company with a better than 1 : 1 current ratio can improve this ratio by paying off as many of its current liabilities as possible just prior to the balance sheet date.

Third, comparison of ratios between companies can be misleading due to differences in accounting practices in such areas as depreciation, income recognition, and intangible assets. For this reason analysts often put companies on a comparable accounting basis before making a comparison.

Fourth, different definitions of common ratios are used by different analysts. Often, two analysts' reports may include the same ratios for a particular company but give very different results.

Fifth, because accounting records are maintained in historical dollars, a change in the value of the dollar can distort the comparability of ratios computed for different time periods.

Sixth, in periods of inflation the ratios comparing sales and net income to assets and equity may be biased upwards.

Finally, ratios show relationships as they existed in the past at a particular balance sheet date. The analyst interested in the future should not be misled into believing that the past data necessarily reflects the current or future situation.

SECURITY VALUATION

Valuation of securities problems arise in such situations as the pricing of new issues, the purchase or sale of securities, and the exchange of stock in mergers or reorganizations. There are a variety of ways to determine value. The approach to valuation used in any particular situation depends on the particular circumstances of the buyer and seller.

Asset Valuation

There are three basic asset valuation approaches: book value, reproduction value, and liquidation value.

The *book value* of a company's common stock is the difference between the accounting value assigned to its assets and the sum of the liabilities and preferred stock, if any. This amount divided by the number of shares outstanding gives the book value per share. A more conservative approach also eliminates the intangible assets, such as organization expense and bond discounts, from the total asset values shown on the books. The resulting amount is labeled "tangible book value."

The principal weakness of the book value approach is its dependence on the accounting policies of the company. Comparing the book value of different companies is therefore difficult. Some analysts try to overcome this problem by readjusting the accounting statements to some comparable basis. This is a difficult and potentially dangerous task, since putting all companies on the same accounting basis may obscure important differences between the companies.

Book value rarely approximates the market value of the owner's equity in a company or its assets, principally due to the accountant's use of the historical cost convention. Consequently, book values are usually appropriate only in appraising companies, such as mutual funds, whose assets are mostly liquid and reflect current market values.

Reproduction value is the cost of reproducing at current prices the physical assets of a going concern. The principal deficiency of this approach is that the value of a going business is typically more than the sum of its individual physical asset values, which individually can be appraised reasonably accurately. What value to assign to the company's reputation and other intangible assets is much more difficult. This approach is sometimes used by governmental agencies as a basis for setting public utility rates and in valuation situations where physical assets are the principal asset of the company, such as in real estate businesses, where reproduction of the buildings would be the principal cost of going into business.

Liquidation value focuses on the resale value of assets, principally their scrap value. It usually sets the lower valuation limit.

Sometimes the liquidation value approach is used in conjunction with the earnings approach. In cases where a company is bought for its income potential, but has excess assets, the excess assets can be valued without reference to the company's value based on earning power and then properly added to the earning power value of the company. This approach is called the "redundant asset method." Similarly, if the potential purchaser must acquire additional assets to maintain a company's earning power, the value of these additional assets can be subtracted from the value derived from the earnings approach.

Business Valuation

The current value of a business is determined in many cases by the estimated future earnings it can produce, adjusted for the degree of risk the investor associates with realizing his earnings projections. In these situations the stockholder values the income flow rather than the physical and intangible assets themselves which give rise to this income. This concept is widely accepted, but it is not easy to apply.

There are two steps in the capitalization of earnings valuation method: first, future earnings available to stockholders must be estimated; and second, a capitalization rate must be selected to apply to this estimate.

Typically the analyst bases his estimate of a company's future earnings on its average earnings for the last few years plus or minus some adjustment to reflect his feelings about the company's prospects over the next five or so years. Rather than trying to predict earnings for each of these future years, he simply settles on an average earnings figure for this period or projects a smooth trend line. His adjustments to the historical pattern of earnings may reflect anticipated changes in the national economy, new product introductions, potential mergers, conversion to common stock of convertible senior securities, and other similar factors which influence earnings per share.

The *capitalization rate* is the price-earnings ratio upside down. It reflects the rate at which the market is capitalizing the value of current earnings. For example, multiplying an average earnings figure by a capitalization rate of 10 percent (or 10 times) is equivalent to calculating the present value of a stream of equal annual earnings over a long period of time discounted at 10 percent. Similarly, a capitalization rate of 20 percent is equivalent to a price-earnings ratio of five times, which when multiplied by the average projected earnings gives a value which is the present value of an equal earnings stream discounted at 20 percent. Clearly, earnings streams are not constant over time.

However, because of the high degree of uncertainty as to what the actual earnings will be in any particular year, the analyst feels more comfortable simplifying the problem by using an average projected earnings estimate.

In most situations, the more certain the analyst is that his projected earnings will be realized, the lower the capitalization rate he is willing to apply to those earnings. For example, in the case of a business with very stable earnings historically and the prospect of continued stable earnings, the analyst might use a capitalization rate of 7 percent. Assuming projected earnings were $5 per share, this rate would imply a market value of about $70 ($5/0.07 = $71.43). Similarly, the analyst valuing high-risk businesses can use either a conservative earnings forecast or a high capitalization rate. In the case of companies with outstanding growth potential, a very low capitalization rate is sometimes applied to the current earnings. In these cases the rate can approach 1 percent.

The selection of the appropriate capitalization rate is very subjective. It is a function of the estimated risk associated with realizing the projected earnings stream and the willingness of the investor to bear this risk given his financial condition and attitude toward risk bearing. For example, based upon earnings estimates, an analyst may decide a 15 percent capitalization rate is appropriate. However, an investor may decide this is too low, given the fact that if the company fails to reach its projected earnings his stock losses will eliminate most of his life savings. Consequently, the investor may demand a capitalization rate of 30 percent before undertaking this type of investment. One guide to appropriate capitalization rates is the price-earnings ratios range assigned by the market to the current earnings of particular industries.

Considerable controversy surrounds the role of cash dividends in security valuation. The capitalization of earnings approach assumes that a dollar of earnings is equally valuable to an investor whether it is paid out in dividends or retained for reinvestment in the company. Eventually, how the individual investor incorporates the dividend factor in his formula for stock valuation will depend on his financial needs and resources and the company's earnings prospects relative to the investor's potential rate of return on dividends.

The capitalization rate also reflects other considerations. For example, the interest rate obtainable on alternative investments, such as government and corporate bonds and the capitalization rates of other stocks; the projected state of the economy; and, as indicated earlier, the relative quality of the company's earnings. Typically, high capitalization rates are experienced in periods when interest rates on prime quality debt securities are high and the economy's prospects are dismal and uncertain. Low capitalization rates are often associated with the opposite circumstances.

Fair Market Value

If a stock is publicly traded, its current market price may not necessarily reflect a reasonable valuation. There are a number of reasons for this conclusion.

First, the markets for many listed and unlisted stocks is "thin." That is, there are few prospective buyers or sellers. In these cases, the price of the stock can fluctuate significantly with the addition of a small number of buy or sell orders.

Second, some stock prices are maintained at an artificial level by deliberate attempts to manipulate the price. A legal illustration of this practice is the price stabilization support often given initially to new issues by their underwriters.

Third, the marketplace tends to exaggerate upward and downward stock price movements. Consequently, at the peaks and troughs of price swings the market may not necessarily reflect reasonable values.

Finally, the market price of most stocks reflects transactions involving relatively small numbers of shares. Often it is not appropriate to use these prices as a basis for valuing large blocks of shares. The price of a large block of shares may be at a discount from the current market, since if they were dumped on the open market they might depress the price of the stock. However, if the sale gives the purchaser control of the company, the buyer may have to pay a premium for the stock.

These objections to current stock prices as a measure of value have led to the development of the "fair market value" or "intrinsic value" method. This method tries to establish the price at which a security would trade in a free market between fully informed, rational buyers and sellers. As a result, the intrinsic value method looks at the valuation problem from the point of view of the buyer and seller, using some of the asset and capitalized earnings valuation techniques described earlier.

Range of Values

The three principal security valuation methods help set the range of possible values for a company's common stock. In the case of the capitalization of earnings and intrinsic value methods, ratio analysis techniques can be helpful in getting a feel for a company's risk characteristics and the appropriateness of different capitalization rates. In any particular situation, the actual stock value settled upon will probably be based on an approach involving several of these methods, modified by the negotiating skills of the buyer and seller.

Financial Analysis and Decision Models

In recent years there has been considerable research into the role of the data generated through financial analysis in the decision-making process of statement users. This development, which is still in an embryonic stage, has focused on such topics as the usefulness of financial data in predicting bankruptcy, earnings growth rates, and bond ratings.

To date, the research into *rating prospective bond issues* has been aimed at simulating the rating system used by such rating agencies as Moody's and Standard and Poors. The models that seem to predict best the rating of a bond incorporate these variables: earnings variability, reliability in meeting financial obligations, the degree of financial leverage, the bond's marketability as measured by the size of issue, and the bond's subordination status.

High-quality bond ratings are typically associated with low earnings variability, a history of meeting of obligations, good market acceptance, a preferred claim on assets, and a prudent leverage rate, which in turn implies a high fixed charges coverage ratio.

Anticipated earnings and earnings growth rates are the major explanation of security prices in most *stock valuation* models. Therefore, it is not surprising that considerable research has been directed to the development of models that predict these variables using past accounting data. The research conducted so far indicates that interim report data are useful for improving the prediction of annual results. However, the research using annual data to predict future annual earnings has shown that overtime earnings have a random character. As a result, simple extrapolation of past earnings is not a useful earnings predictor. If better prediction models are to be developed, there is a concensus that they would probably have to include both accounting and nonaccounting data, such as the expected state of the economy and the economic characteristics of the firm and its industry.

Models that use financial data to predict *corporate insolvency or bankruptcy* due to severe financial and/or operational difficulties fall into two broad classes: univariate models that use a single variable to predict failure and multivariate models where several variables are used simultaneously in the prediction process.

The univariate approach research indicates that the financial ratios of failed firms differ from those of nonfailed firms. Also, the nonliquid asset ratios are better predictors of failure than the liquid asset ratios. Furthermore, the nonliquid asset ratios that seem to be the best predictors of failure are the cash flow to total debt, net income to total assets, and total debt to total assets ratios. Cash flow is defined as net income plus depreciation, depletion, and amortization. In addition, the "mixed ratios," which are those with income or cash flow in the numerator and assets and liabilities in the denominator, are better predictors of failure than the short-term solvency ratios. A list of the nonliquid and liquid ratios commonly used in this research are presented below:

List of Ratios Tested in Research

I. Nonliquid asset ratios	II. Liquid asset ratios (continued)
1. Cash flow to total debt*	B. Current department group
2. Net income to total assets	1. Current assets to current debt
3. Total debt to total assets	(current ratio)
II. Liquid asset ratios	2. Quick assets to current debt
A. Total asset group	(quick ratio)
1. Current assets to total assets	3. Cash to current debt
	C. Net sales or turnover group
2. Quick assets to total assets	1. Current assets to sales
3. Net working capital to total assets	2. Quick assets to sales
	3. Net working capital to sales
4. Cash to total assets	4. Cash to sales

* Total debt includes all liabilities plus preferred stock.

The multivariate approach research predicts a quantitative measure of solvency status. Scores below a critical level indicate a firm is very likely to slip from the nonfailed to failed firm category. The score is derived from a linear combination of some of the characteristics developed through mathematical techniques that best discriminate between failed and nonfailed firms.

For example, one researcher that used this approach developed the following discriminant function for small manufacturing firms:

$$Z = 0.012X_1 + 0.014X_2 + 0.033X_3 + 0.006X_4 + 0.010X_5$$

where:

X_1 = working capital/total assets (a liquidity measure).

X_2 = retained earnings/total assets (a measure for reinvested earnings).

X_3 = earnings before interest and taxes/total assets (a profitability measure).

X_4 = market value of equity/book value of total liabilities (a measure for the firm's financial structure or leverage).

X_5 = sales/total assets (a measure for the sales-generating ability of the firm's assets).

The ratios are expressed in absolute terms, for example, a working capital to asset ratio of 10 percent is noted at 10.0, and a sales to total asset ratio of 2.0 or 200 percent is noted as 200.0.

A Z score below 1.81 indicated potential bankruptcy. A score above 2.99 placed the company in the nonfailed category. And, scores between 1.81 and 2.99 indicate a gray area where a firm may or may not be approaching bankruptcy.

The variables that comprise a successful prediction equation may not be the most significant variables for predicting bankruptcy when measured independently (as in the univariate research). For instance, the equation above was derived by testing 22 potential variables. Among these variables X_5 was the least significant when measured individually. However, the multivariate approach derives the most successful prediction equation which takes into account the *interactions* among the variables. This is the principal difference between the multivariate and univariate models.

Accounting Alternatives, Statement Analysis, and Efficient Equity Markets

The efficient markets research referred to in Chapter 1 has reached these tentative conclusions that may be relevant to financial analysis and equity valuation: The major equity markets are efficient in that security prices typically reflect all of the publically available accounting and nonaccounting data. Inside information gives the holder of it an advantage over other investors until it is used. Financial statement data are used in investment decisions. The market is able to "look through" most accounting differences to distinguish real economic changes from the apparent changes reported by using different accounting alternatives. Finally, in the long run the market reflects economic reality.

Efficient market researchers believe these preliminary findings may have a number of implications for the field of financial analysis. Since traditional analysis and its results are widely known, the value of known analytical tools must already be impounded in security prices. Therefore, if security analysis is to be beneficial, it must be helpful in predicting future results or be of a novel nature. However, once these techniques become public, the advantages of the predictor and innovator will be quickly lost. Thus, the goal of the financial analyst is to convert publically available information to "inside" information by the use of new and different analytical tools and to keep secret the findings. However, once the analyst acts on the insight, it becomes impounded in the market price of the relevant security.

Another finding suggested by the research into the role of accounting data in equity markets is that companies that use the more liberal accounting practices tend to have the higher market risk, as measured by the relative volatility of a stock's price relative to some index of the volatility of the market as a whole.[3] Since companies that have liberal accounting often have weak operating and financial characteristics, some believe this market activity reflects the underlying corporate economics rather than the accounting practices. This belief is consistent with the efficient market theories.

Finally, it should be noted that the research to date has not been able to show satisfactorily the relationship between accounting information, stock prices, and investment returns.

Red Flags

Sometimes the stock market seems to anticipate the deterioration of a corporate earnings capacity and financial position before its actual publication by the company. One way investors are able to anticipate such situations is by detecting "red flags" in a company's financial statements. These are accounting signals that may suggest a worsening situation before it actually impacts the net income figure. Here is a brief discussion of some of the more popular "red flags." Remember that these are signals that suggest further analysis should be undertaken. They do not necessarily mean that things are deteriorating, management is trying to fool statement users, or the accounting is inappropriate.

Audit Reports.   Because of the many lawsuits against CPAs, CPAs are getting more independent and cautious in the expression of their opinions. Look for unusual wording in an audit opinion, an unusually long report, mention of material uncertainties, a date on the report that is later than the date on the prior years' opinions, an opinion that is dated long after the close of the fiscal year, and a change in auditors. Any one of these could be an indicator of a troubled company.

Managed Costs.   Managed costs are costs that management can increase or decrease by management decisions. They include research and development expenditures, maintenance, advertising, and promotion expenditures. Managements are reluctant to reduce expenditures in these areas, since these expenditures are often vital to the company's success in future years. However, when companies get into trouble and management wants to keep up their profits, management may cut their level of managed costs. So, decreases in the level of

---

[3] The most popular way of expressing this relationship is the so-called "beta" of a stock. A beta of 1.0 indicates that a stock's price fluctuates with the market index perfectly. A beta above 1.0 indicates that a stock is more volatile than the market index. A beta of less than 1.0 suggests that the stock is less volatile. That is, if the market index drops, the stock's price will decline at a slower rate. Or, if the market index rises, its price will rise slower.

managed costs may be an indicator of a company with problems. Look in the 10-K for these data and compute the trend in absolute dollars and as a percentage of some measure of business activity, such as sales.

Changes in Accounting Policies Methods or Estimates. Managements prefer to reach their profit objectives without changing their accounting practices. Consequently, any company that has to resort to a change in accounting principles, a change in the way it applies its accounting principles, or a change in accounting estimates to improve its profits or balance sheet ratios is perhaps signaling that it cannot reach the desired goal without resorting to accounting fictions.

Opinion No. 20 limits changes in accounting principles to situations where the new method is preferable to the old. The problem is that in accounting it is often difficult to tell which alternative principle is preferable. So, managements have little trouble justifying to their auditors accounting principle changes. As a result, it is often wise to ignore the explanation as to why the change was made and concentrate on the current and next year potential earnings impact of the change. These numbers will usually be the key to understanding why the change was made.

Increases in Accounts Receivables. When capital is expensive, business executives do not like to increase accounts receivable balances or let them get out of line with past experience any more than is absolutely necessary. So, increased accounts receivable balances, or a higher balance relative to sales, can many times be interpreted as a sign of trouble. For example, when year-to-date sales lag behind the company's budgeted annual sales and a company needs a quick year end sales increase to improve profits, a favorite response is to load customers up with unneeded products by granting generous credit terms. This transfer of goods is accounted for as a sale, but all that has happened is a shift of inventory from the seller's inventory to the customers inventory. Sales created this way are made at the expense of future sales.

Receivables that are out of line with past experience may also indicate the company is selling to more marginal credit risks.

Intangible Asset Increases. In many cases intangible assets end up on balance sheets because the company's profits are not sufficient to permit the expensing of these costs as incurred. Given a choice, most managements would prefer to expense as incurred—rather than defer—these kinds of costs. However, if current profits are not high enough to absorb these costs, some management may defer these costs in order to meet their current profit goals. The best assumption to make about any company that stretches to make its income more attractive by capitalizing intangibles is that it did so because it had no choice but to do otherwise. Look at the relationship of the change in capitalized intangibles (interest on construction, patents, etc.) to the changes in net income. If a material portion of the change in income came from capitalization rather than expensing, this should be regarded as a red flag.

Nonrecurring Sources of Income.   Most managements prefer not to use up their discretionary one-time profit generation opportunities, such as the sale of an office building with a cost basis substantially below market price. It gives them a sense of security to know that if profits need a sudden boost, the means are close at hand to do it. On the other hand, they are often reluctant to use this profit source since they know that if the market discovers that one-time gains were used to get earnings gains, their earnings quality may be rated lower. So, in many cases those managements that puff up profits with one-time gains usually do it because they have no other option. Also, as companies have a tougher time making earnings through operations, the frequency of one-time profit gains increases. Consequently, one-time gains may be a clue that all is not well with a company.

Declines in Gross Margin Percentages.   One key indicator of trouble is a decline in the gross margin as a percentage of sales. It may indicate an inability to raise prices, a cost price-squeeze, or a weakness in the market for the company's products.

Reserve Manipulations.   Corporations tend to establish reserves in high profit years. Then, when it becomes difficult to show profits, they draw on these reserves to help reach their profit forecasts. Watch out for companies that do the following with their reserves. Each may be a red flag.

A company that in the past regularly added to its reserves, fails to do so. This may have occurred because profit levels before reserve additions are lower than in the past. The management would probably have liked to continue to add to reserves, but it could not afford to do so.

A reserve set up in a prior period is reduced or reversed by a debit to the reserve and a credit to income. This is fictitious bookkeeping income. It is typically taken only when real profits are in trouble, which of course is usually the worst time to start eliminating reserves since these are the periods when the adverse event that a reserve anticipates is often most likely to occur. This kind of accounting can be interpreted as a desperate move.

A reserve is charged, and cash or some asset credited. This indicates the problem anticipated by the reserve has arrived. Fortunately, since the management had prudently set up the reserve earlier, the costs of the problem are kept out of the current income statement. This helps current profits, but it doesn't solve the problem.

Finally, some companies may well have a bad year. Also, as their management look ahead they see nothing but future problems. The management of such companies may well decide that since things are so bad currently, it will not hurt to write off a number of these future income losses to income currently. This will make it easier to report profits in the future. The management that reaches this decision will charge current income with provisions for future losses. In addition, they will probably try to leave the reader of the report with the impression that the setting up of reserves solves their problems. Be cautious of such companies. The creation of the reserve is nothing more than an accounting entry. The fundamental business problems still exist.

Liberal Accounting Policies. Given a choice, most managements would prefer to use conservative accounting practices. A principal reason why many companies use more liberal approaches is that the company cannot reach its profit goals with conservative accounting. So, management has to resort to liberal accounting practices. As it becomes tougher to do business, become more wary of any liberalization of accounting. It is a strong sign that the company may be struggling.

Using Other People's Money. There has been a long-term trend for U.S. corporations to use increasingly debt fund sources to finance growth and to maintain their return on stockholders' equity. However, increasing overreliance on financial leverage is not thought to be prudent when business becomes more difficult and uncertain. A deterioration in such ratios as the liabilities to assets ratio, all debt-to-equity ratio, and days payables suggest that financial leverage is being used to pump up earnings per share and to compensate for the fact that the company is not self-financing. If a company has to utilize this approach more than its competitors or the industry leaders, it probably did so because it was unable to make its profit goals through operations. Thus, as its operations weaken, the company is increasing its financial risk. This is not what managements prefer to do. So, if they are doing it, they may have operating problems.

Increased Tax Deferrals. An increase in the deferred tax element of the book tax expense provision is often an indicator that a company is changing (1) its way of doing business or (2) its revenue recognition, expense recognition, or asset amortization practices. For example, if a company shifts to more installment selling or capitalizing more of its costs of construction than it did in the past, its deferred tax provision will probably increase. These are subtle kinds of shifts which are hard to pick up since no change in accounting policy is involved. Unexplained increases in the deferred tax expense should be followed up to identify their causes.

FINANCIAL ANALYSIS

An understanding of financial analysis is essential to those who use and issue corporate financial statements. Issuers who hope to use financial statements to influence others will be more likely to succeed if they know how statement users analyze their data. On the other hand, financial statement users will be less likely to respond naively to financial data if they know how to analyze it correctly. Through research we are learning more each day about how statement users analyze financial statements and how the results of these analyses are used. Anyone interested in corporate financial reporting should follow these research efforts on a current basis as today's knowledge in this area is fast being made obsolete.

SUGGESTED FURTHER READING

BERNSTEIN, LEOPOLD A. *Financial Statement Analysis.* Homewood, Ill.: Richard D. Irwin, Inc., 1974.

FOULKE, ROY A. *Practical Financial Statement Analysis.* 6th ed. New York: McGraw-Hill Book Co., 1966.

HELFERT, ERICH A. *Techniques of Financial Analysis.* 4th ed. Homewood, Ill.: Richard D. Irwin, Inc., 1977.

KENNEDY, RALPH DALE, and MCMULLEN, STEWART YARWOOD. *Financial Statements: Form, Analysis, and Interpretation.* 6th ed. Homewood, Ill.: Richard D. Irwin, Inc., 1973.

LEV, BARUCH. *Financial Statement Analysis.* Englewood Cliffs, N.J.: Prentice-Hall, Inc., 1974.

CASES

CASE 8–1. THE CASE OF THE UNIDENTIFIED U.S. INDUSTRIES

Industry Ratio Characteristics

Despite variations in operational and financial policies and practices and in operating results between firms in the same industry, the nature of the industry has an important impact on the general patterns of the need for funds (asset allocation), the methods of meeting these needs, and the financial results of most firms in the industry. Presented in Exhibit 1 are balance sheets, in percentage form, and selected ratios drawn from the balance sheets and operating statements of 12 different firms in 12 different industries. Recognizing the fact of certain differences between firms in the same industry, each firm whose figures are summarized is broadly typical of those in its industry.

Question

See if you can identify the industry represented. Then, be prepared as best you can to explain the distinctive asset structures and ratios of each industry. The 12 firms are:

1. Basic chemical company.
2. Electric and gas utility.
3. Supermarket chain.
4. Maker of name-brand, quality men's apparel.
5. Meat-packer.
6. Retail jewelry chain (which leased its store properties).
7. Coal carrying railroad.
8. Automobile manufacturer.
9. Large department store (which owns most of its store properties).
10. Advertising agency.
11. A major airline.
12. Commercial bank (fitted into the most nearly comparable balance sheet and ratio categories of the nonfinancial companies).

EXHIBIT 1

The Case of the Unidentified U.S. Industries

	A	B	C	D	E	F	G	H	I	J	K	L
Balance sheet percentages:												
Cash and marketable securities	4.0	7.6	5.1	15.7	4.1	0.5	8.5	4.3	3.2	5.4	17.0	38.6
Receivables	3.9	8.6	16.4	26.8	21.5	3.8	13.7	5.4	27.6	13.0	72.1	59.2
Inventories	—	24.9	11.0	23.2	61.0	2.2	22.7	39.3	49.2	—	—	—
Other current assets	0.9	3.5	—	1.2	0.2	2.6	1.6	2.4	1.6	2.5	0.8	—
Plant and equipment (net)	78.7	44.6	49.5	33.4	10.9	90.0	45.4	44.1	17.1	73.9	7.4	1.1
Other assets	12.5[a]	10.8[b]	18.0[c]	0.7	2.3	0.9	8.1[d]	4.5	1.3	5.2	2.7	1.1
Total Assets	100.0	100.0	100.0	100.0	100.0	100.0	100.0	100.0	100.0	100.0	100.0	100.0
Notes payable	—	—	12.8	—	5.1	3.1	0.8	5.2	2.0	8.3	—	—
Accounts payable	2.9	23.9	5.3	29.3	12.6	2.6	10.0	25.3	10.5	—	50.3	84.4
Accrued taxes	2.6	3.6	1.9	1.4	6.6	1.4	2.7	2.4	3.1	7.7	—	—
Other current liabilities	0.6	4.9	5.7	1.7	1.2	2.6	12.0	10.4	5.8	45.6	2.6	1.6
Long-term debt	35.2	3.4	30.4	1.6	5.8	43.3	25.6	3.8	20.6	10.9	3.3	—
Other liabilities	3.8	6.4	—	1.6	1.0	1.8	7.5	8.2	—	—	1.0	5.9
Preferred stock	—	—	—	—	2.2	9.4	4.9	—	0.1	—	—	—
Capital stock and capital surplus	16.7	6.8	27.8	9.4	31.0	25.3	11.9	12.0	17.4	8.4	6.8	5.1
Retained earnings and surplus reserves	38.2	50.0	16.1	56.6	34.5	10.5	24.6	32.7	40.5	19.1	36.0	3.0
Total Liabilities and Stockholder Equity	100.0	100.0	100.0	100.0	100.0	100.0	100.0	100.0	100.0	100.0	100.0	100.0
Selected ratios:												
Current assets/current liabilities	1.45	1.38	1.25	2.06	3.41	0.92	1.85	1.19	3.81	1.29	1.44	—
Cash, marketable securities, and receivables/current liabilities	0.96	0.50	1.20	1.32	1.62	0.44	0.33	0.22	1.44	1.13	1.24	—
Inventory turnover(X)	—	6.4X	6X	23X	2.1X	—	8.8X	12.8X	3.1X	—	—	—
Receivables collection period (days)	20	19	64	18	64	44	30	4	66	69	42	—
Total debt/total assets	0.412	0.356	0.565	0.339	0.313	0.530	0.510	0.471	0.420	0.619	0.663	0.918
Long-term debt/capitalization	0.403	0.055	0.425	0.025	0.078	0.490	0.382	0.078	0.262	0.628	0.090	0.191
Net sales/total assets	0.32	1.61	0.69	5.40	1.30	0.32	1.65	5.03	1.51	0.69	5.33	0.06
Net profits/total assets	0.052	0.059	0.057	0.080	0.085	0.048	0.077	0.056	0.065	0.026	0.081	0.008
Net profits/total net worth	0.102	0.105	0.137	0.121	0.124	0.107	0.211	0.125	0.112	0.095	0.240	0.112
Net profits/net sales	0.167	0.037	0.083	0.015	0.065	0.153	0.047	0.011	0.043	0.037	0.015	0.131

[a] Includes 10.1 percent of investments in affiliated companies.
[b] Includes 9.2 percent of investments in affiliated companies.
[c] Includes 14.4 percent of investments in affiliated companies.
[d] Includes 5.9 percent of investments in affiliated companies.

CASE 8–2. UNION INVESTMENTS, INC.
Analysis of Financial Statements

In March 1975 Fred Aldrich, a summer trainee with the Union Investments, Inc., was called into the office of the head of the investment analysis section of the trust department. The following conversation took place:

Fred, here are the 1974, 1973, and 1965 General Electric financials (Exhibit 1) and a ten-year summary (Exhibit 2). Our trust department has owned this stock since the early 1960s. As you know our portfolio people place a lot of emphasis on the quality of a company's earnings and the return on owners' equity in making stock selections. Well, they are worried. The 1974 General Electric annual report shows a decline in the return on owners' equity. Now, they want us to comment on the way that the company has achieved its return on equity over the last ten years, starting with 1965. I would like you to prepare this analysis. I suggest you forget the strike years of 1969 and 1970. Also, concentrate on what happened in the 1973–74 period. I hope the analysis will include a direct comparison of the quality of the 1965 and 1974 returns on stockholders' equity and the other key financial ratios for these two years. In addition, see if the quality of earnings has declined in recent years. Finally, you should know that General Electric has not changed its accounting policies and practices materially over the last decade.

Here is a summary of General Electric's major accounting policies:

Consolidated financial statements include a consolidation of the accounts of the parent—General Electric Company—and those of all majority-owned affiliates (except finance affiliates since their operations are not similar to those of the consolidated group). All significant items relating to transactions between parent and affiliated companies are eliminated from consolidated statements.

Except for plant and equipment and accumulated depreciation, assets and liabilities of foreign affiliates are translated into U.S. dollars at year-end exchange rates, and income and expense items are translated at average rates prevailing during the year. Plant and equipment and accumulated depreciation are translated at rates in effect at dates of acquisition of the assets. The net effect of translation gains and losses is included as other costs in current year operations.

Net earnings include the net income of finance affiliates and the consolidated group's share of earnings of associated companies which are not consolidated but in which the group owns 20 percent or more of the voting stock.

Sales of products and services to customers are reported in operating results only as title to products passes to the customer and as services are performed as contracted.

Operating costs are classified in the statement of current earnings according to the principal types of costs incurred.

Current pension service costs and amortization of past-service costs over a period of 20 years are being charged to operations currently.

An accelerated depreciation method, based principally on a sum-of-the-years'-digits formula, is used to depreciate plant and equipment in the United States purchased in 1961 and subsequently. Assets purchased prior to 1961, and most assets outside the United States, are depreciated on a straight-line basis. Special depreciation is provided where equipment may be subject to abnormal conditions or obsolescence.

Provision has been made for federal income taxes to be paid on that portion of the undistributed earnings of affiliates and associated companies expected to be remitted to the parent.

The company follows the practice of amortizing the investment credit to income over the life of the underlying facilities rather than in the year in which facilities are placed in service.

Marketable securities are carried at the lower of amortized cost or market value.

Inventories in the United States are substantially all valued on a last-in, first-out (Lifo) basis. Substantially all of those outside the United States are valued on a first-in, first-out (Fifo) basis. Such valuations are not in excess of market and are based on cost, exclusive of certain indirect manufacturing expenses and profits on sales between the parent and affiliated companies.

Investments in nonconsolidated finance affiliates are carried at equity plus advances.

Investments in the common stock of Honeywell, Inc., and Honeywell Information Systems, Inc. (HIS), a subsidiary of Honeywell, are recorded at appraised fair value as of date of acquisition.

Investments in associated companies which are not consolidated but in which the company owns 20 percent or more of the voting stock are valued by the equity method.

Miscellaneous investments are valued at cost.

Plant and equipment represents the original cost of land, buildings, and equipment less estimated cost consumed by wear and obsolescence.

Expenditures for maintenance and repairs are charged to operations as incurred.

Research and development expenditures, except those specified as recoverable engineering costs on government contracts, are charged to operations as incurred.

Licenses and other intangibles acquired after October 1970 are being amortized over appropriate periods of time.

Question

Complete the assignment given to Fred Aldrich.

EXHIBIT 1

GENERAL ELECTRIC COMPANY AND CONSOLIDATED AFFILIATES
Statement of Current and Retained Earnings (as reported)
For the Years 1965, 1973, and 1974
(in millions)

	1974	1973	1965
Sales of products and services to customers ...	$13,413.1	$11,575.3	$6,213.6
Operating Costs:			
Employee compensation, including benefits	$ 5,223.0	$ 4,709.7	$2,440.8
Materials, supplies, services, and other costs	6,966.7	5,690.5	3,063.4
Depreciation	376.2	334.0	188.4
Taxes, except those on income	123.0	113.5	51.6
Increase in inventories during the year	(270.8)	(227.2)	(176.1)
	$12,418.1	$10,620.5	$5,568.1
Operating margin	$ 995.0	$ 954.8	$ 645.5
Other income	185.8	183.7	72.1
Interest and other financial charges	(180.1)	(126.9)	(27.4)
Earnings before income taxes and minority interest	$ 1,000.7	$ 1,011.6	$ 690.2
Provision for income taxes	(382.4)	(418.7)	(352.2)
Minority interest in earnings of consolidated affiliates	(10.2)	(7.8)	17.1
Net earnings applicable to common stock	$ 608.1	$ 585.1	$ 355.1
Dividends declared	(291.2)	(272.9)	(216.7)
Amount added to retained earnings	$ 316.9	$ 312.2	$ 138.4
Retained earnings at January 1	2,683.6	2,371.4	1,246.0
Retained Earnings at December 31	$ 3,000.5	$ 2,683.6	$1,384.4

EXHIBIT 1 *(continued)*

GENERAL ELECTRIC COMPANY AND CONSOLIDATED AFFILIATES
Statement of Financial Position (as reported)
December 31, 1965, 1973, 1974
(in millions)

Assets

	1974	1973	1965
Cash	$ 314.5	$ 296.8	$ 289.8
Marketable securities	57.3	25.3	353.3
Current receivables	2,593.8	2,177.1	1,062.5
Inventories	2,257.0	1,986.2	1,136.9
Current Assets	$5,222.6	$4,485.4	$2,842.5
Investments	1,004.8	869.7	241.0
Plant and equipment	2,615.6	2,360.5	1,037.0
Other assets	526.1	608.6	180.0
Total Assets	$9,369.1	$8,324.2	$4,300.0

Liabilities and Equity

	1974	1973	1965
Short-term borrowings	$ 644.9	$ 665.2	$ 120.6
Accounts payable	696.0	673.5	376.2
Progress collections and price adjustments accrued	1,000.5	718.4	300.5
Dividends payable	72.8	72.7	58.7
Taxes accrued	337.2	310.0	318.3
Other costs and expenses accrued	1,128.1	1,052.6	392.6
Current Liabilities	$3,879.5	$3,492.4	$1,566.9
Long-term borrowings	1,195.2	917.2	364.1
Other liabilities	518.9	492.1	221.0
Total Liabilities	$5,593.6	$4,901.7	$2,152.0
Minority interest in equity of consolidated affiliates	$ 71.2	$ 50.1	$ 41.4
Preferred stock	—	—	—
Common stock	$ 465.2	$ 463.8	$ 455.8
Amounts received for stock in excess of par value	414.5	409.5	266.8
Retained earnings	3,000.5	2,683.6	1,384.4
	$3,880.2	$3,556.9	$2,107.0
Deduct common stock held in treasury	(175.9)	(184.5)	—
Total Share Owners' Equity	$3,704.3	$3,372.4	$2,107.0
Total Liabilities and Equity	$9,369.1	$8,324.2	$4,300.4

EXHIBIT 2

Ten-Year Financial Highlights (as reported in 1974; dollar amounts in millions; per-share amounts in dollars)*

	1974	1973	1972	1971	1970	1969	1968	1967	1966	1965
Summary of operations:										
Sales of products and services	$13,413.1	$11,575.3	$10,239.5	$9,425.3	$8,726.7	$8,448.0	$8,381.6	$7,741.2	$7,177.3	$6,213.6
Materials, engineering, and production costs	10,137.6	8,515.2	7,509.6	6,962.1	6,423.6	6,346.1	6,251.7	5,779.4	5,311.0	4,449.2
Selling, general, and administrative expenses	2,280.5	2,105.3	1,915.2	1,726.2	1,754.2	1,615.3	1,482.1	1,320.9	1,234.3	1,118.9
Operating costs	$12,418.1	$10,620.5	$9,424.8	$8,688.3	$8,177.8	$7,961.4	$7,733.8	$7,100.3	$6,545.3	$5,568.1
Operating margin	$ 995.0	$ 954.8	$ 814.7	$ 737.0	$ 548.9	$ 486.6	$ 647.8	$ 640.9	$ 632.0	$ 645.5
Other income	185.8	183.7	189.2	152.0	106.8	98.7	86.3	91.4	72.4	72.1
Interest and other financial charges	(180.1)	(126.9)	(106.7)	(96.9)	(101.4)	(78.1)	(70.5)	(62.9)	(39.9)	(27.4)
Earnings before income taxes and minority interest	$ 1,000.7	$ 1,011.6	$ 897.2	$ 792.1	$ 554.3	$ 507.2	$ 663.6	$ 669.4	$ 664.5	$ 690.2
Provision for income taxes	(382.4)	(418.7)	(364.1)	(317.1)	(220.6)	(231.5)	(312.3)	(320.5)	(347.4)	(352.2)
Minority interest	(10.2)	(7.8)	(3.1)	(3.2)	(5.2)	2.3	5.8	12.5	21.8	17.1
Net earnings	$ 608.1	$ 585.1	$ 530.0	$ 471.8	$ 328.5	$ 278.0	$ 357.1	$ 361.4	$ 333.9	$ 355.1
Earnings per common share†	$ 3.34	$ 3.21	$ 2.91	$ 2.60	$ 1.81	$ 1.54	$ 1.98	$ 2.00	$ 1.88	$ 1.97
Dividends declared per common share†	$ 1.60	$ 1.50	$ 1.40	$ 1.38	$ 1.30	$ 1.30	$ 1.30	$ 1.30	$ 1.30	$ 1.20
Earnings as a percentage of sales	4.5%	5.1%	5.2%	5.0%	3.8%	3.3%	4.3%	4.7%	4.7%	5.7%
Earned on share owners' equity	17.2%	18.1%	18.0%	17.6%	13.2%	11.5%	15.4%	16.5%	16.2%	18.0%
Cash dividends declared†	$ 291.2	$ 272.9	$ 254.8	$ 249.7	$ 235.4	$ 235.2	$ 234.8	$ 234.2	$ 234.6	$ 216.7
Shares outstanding—average (in thousands)†	182,120	182,051	182,112	181,684	181,114	180,965	180,651	180,266	180,609	180,634
Share owner accounts—average	547,000	537,000	536,000	523,000	529,000	520,000	530,000	529,000	530,000	521,000
Market price range per share†‡	65–30	75¾–55	73–58¾	66½–46½	47¼–30%	49¾–37	50¾–40%	58–41¼	60–40	60%–45½
Price-earnings ratio range	19–9	24–17	25–20	26–18	26–17	32–24	25–20	29–21	32–21	31–23
Current assets	$ 5,222.6	$ 4,485.4	$ 3,978.3	$3,639.0	$3,334.8	$3,287.8	$3,311.1	$3,207.6	$3,013.0	$2,842.4
Current liabilities	2,879.5	3,492.4	2,869.7	2,840.4	2,650.3	2,366.7	2,104.3	1,977.4	1,883.2	1,566.8
Total assets	5,369.1	8,324.2	7,401.8	6,887.8	6,198.5	5,894.0	5,652.5	5,250.3	4,768.1	4,241.5
Share owners' equity	5,704.3	3,372.4	3,084.6	2,801.8	2,553.6	2,426.5	2,402.1	2,245.3	2,128.1	2,048.1
Plant and equipment additions	$ 671.8	$ 598.6	$ 435.9	$ 553.1	$ 581.4	$ 530.6	$ 514.7	$ 561.7	$ 484.9	$ 332.9
Depreciation	376.2	334.0	314.3	273.6	334.7	351.3	300.1	280.4	253.6	188.4
Employees—average worldwide	404,000	388,000	369,000	363,000	397,000	410,000	396,000	385,000	376,000	333,000
—average U.S.	307,000	304,000	292,000	291,000	310,000	318,000	305,000	296,000	291,000	258,000

* 1965 figures may differ slightly from amounts presented in 1965 financial statements due to changes in company's business which required retroactive restatement of prior years.

† Amounts have been adjusted for the two-for-one stock split in April 1971.

‡ Represents high and low market price on New York Stock Exchange for each year.

PART V

Income Determination

Chapter 9

INCOME RECOGNITION

The matching of costs and revenues to determine periodic net income is a principal purpose of accounting practice. This is a difficult task, since it requires allocating the various activities of a continuing business into arbitrary time periods which rarely coincide with the periods during which each of the various activities comprising the total business is started and completed. Nevertheless, managers try to accomplish this matching by associating as best they can their companies' accomplishments of the period (revenues) with the efforts expended to achieve these accomplishments (expenses). The result of this matching process is net income or profit.

The APB's *Statement No. 4*, "Basic Concepts and Accounting Principles Underlying Financial Statements of Business Enterprises," defined net income (net loss) as follows:

The excess of revenue over expenses for an accounting period, which is the net increase (net decrease) in owners' equity (assets minus liabilities) of an enterprise for an accounting period from profit-directed activities that is recognized and measured in conformity with generally accepted accounting principles.

Statement No. 4 also indicated that revenue should be recognized as follows:

Revenue is conventionally recognized at a specific point in the earnings process of a business enterprise, usually when assets are sold or services are rendered. This conventional recognition is the basis of the pervasive measurement principle known as realization.

Statement No. 4 in turn defined realization as follows:

Revenue is generally recognized when both the following conditions are met: (1) the earnings process is complete or virtually complete, and (2) an exchange has taken place.

213

The Critical Event

The recognition of income is generally considered to be determined in large part by the timing of revenue recognition, since the sale of goods and services is typically a necessary prerequisite to earning income. Starting from this position, management must still determine what the critical event is in the chain of business events from production through receiving an order to the receipt of the payment of an account receivable. In many cases, this determination requires the application of considerable management judgment in the light of a thorough and objective analysis of the particular circumstances.

No one accounting rule or practice covers all revenue recognition situations. Nevertheless, an analysis of revenue recognition practices seems to indicate that revenue is typically recognized when the event which reduces the risk of ultimately receiving the revenue is reduced to a minimum level which is considered to be prudent by those issuing and using financial statements. However, in a number of cases, there can be disagreement as to the nature of the critical event and what is prudent.

While income recognition seems to turn on the timing of revenue recognition, the final measurement of income must also include a consideration of the past, current, and estimated future costs related to the revenue recognized. In practice, management appears to tolerate slightly more uncertainty in the recognition of costs than it does in the case of revenues. However, if the total amount of revenue from a transaction is certain and the eventual costs of obtaining the revenue are fairly uncertain, the revenue should be deferred and held back from the income statement until the costs are more certain. To do otherwise might be misleading and imprudent. Again, the decision is a management one, involving a responsible and careful consideration of the particular facts.

Revenue Recognition Methods

The recognition of income varies from the time of production, in the case of certain mining operations, to the actual receipt of cash, in some installment sale situations. These variations fall into four revenue recognition categories:

a. Recognition at the time of sale (i.e., sales method).
b. Recognition at the time the sale price is collected (i.e., installment sales method).
c. Recognition at the time the product is completed (i.e., production method).

d. Recognition proportionally over the performance of a contract (i.e., percentage-of-completion method).

Sales. The time of sale is the most common revenue recognition method. *ARB No. 43* states:

> Profit is deemed to be realized when a sale in the ordinary course of business is effected, unless the circumstances are such that the collection of the sale price is not reasonably assured.

Typically, the act of invoicing, accompanied by delivery or consignment to a common carrier, is considered to constitute a sale for accounting purposes, rather than the legal criterion of title passing. In recognition of the fact that the cash eventually received from sales will fall short of the invoiced sales, a number of estimated deductions are made directly from the sales. These include: allowances for returns, warranty or service guarantees, and cash discounts. Allowances for bad debts are usually reported as an expense rather than a revenue deduction. Also, sometimes cash discounts are deducted from a customer's account at the time of sale and then any discounts not taken are reported as a separate revenue item.

Installment Sales. An installment sale involves a down payment and a specified series of payments over time. Depending on the circumstances, the gross profit from such sales can be recognized in one of two ways: at the time of sale, or proportionally as the cash payments are received. This latter approach is known as the installment method. Many retailers use the installment method for calculating tax payments while recognizing the income at the time of sale for accounting purposes. This practice is consistent with *Opinion No. 10*, which says that installment sales should ordinarily be accounted for by the sale method, with appropriate provision for uncollectable accounts. The *Opinion* is very emphatic that "unless the circumstances are such that the collection of the sale price is not reasonably assured," the installment method of recognizing income is not acceptable.

A third approach—the cost-recovery method—is seldom used. This method does not recognize any gross profit from the sale until the cumulative total of the payments received equals the cost of the item sold. It is only used in exceptional cases where receivables are collectible over an extended period of time and, because of the terms of the transaction or other conditions, there is no reasonable basis for estimating the degree of collectibility. Under these conditions it may also be permissible to use the installment method.

Production. There are some industries where the sale or the collection of cash is not the critical event in the recognition of income. For example, in the case of a number of extractive industries, there is a market that stands ready to take their product at the going price. The company has merely to make the decision as to when and where it will convert its inventory of products into a sale. For such companies, production is the critical event in the recognition of income. *ARB No. 43* discussed the recognition of income at the time the product is completed as follows:

It is generally recognized that income accrues only at the time of sale, and that gains may not be anticipated by reflecting assets at their current sales prices. For certain articles, however, exceptions are permissible. Inventories of gold and silver, when there is an effective government-controlled market at a fixed monetary value, are ordinarily reflected at selling prices. A similar treatment is not uncommon for inventories representing agricultural, mineral, and other products, units of which are interchangeable and have an immediate marketability at quoted prices and for which appropriate costs may be difficult to obtain. Where such inventories are stated at sales prices, they should of course be reduced by expenditures to be incurred in disposal, and the use of such basis should be fully disclosed in the financial statements.

Long-Term Contracts.   There are two methods for recognizing income from contracts covering a long period of time: the completed contract method and the percentage-of-completion method. Both of these methods are acceptable for federal income tax purposes, and it is possible to use one method for calculating income tax payments and the other for measuring accounting profit.

The percentage-of-completion method recognizes income as the work on the contract progresses. *ARB No. 45,* "Long-Term Construction-Type Contracts, discussed this method and its application:

The percentage-of-completion method recognizes income as work on a contract progresses. The committee recommends that the recognized income be that percentage of estimated total income either:
(a)   that incurred costs to date bear to estimated total costs after giving effect to costs to complete based upon most recent information, or
(b)   that may be indicated by such other measures of progress toward completion as may be appropriate having due regard to work performed.

Under this method current assets may include costs and recognized income not yet billed, with respect to certain contracts; and liabilities, in most cases current liabilities, may include billings in excess of costs and recognized income with respect to other contracts.

When the current estimate of total contract costs indicates a loss, in most circumstances provision should be made for the loss on the entire contract. If there is a close relationship between profitable and unprofitable contracts, such as in the case of contracts which are parts of the same project, the group may be treated as a unit in determining the necessity for a provision for loss.

There are two principal advantages of the percentage-of-completion method. First, periodic income is recognized currently rather than irregularly as contracts are completed. Second, the status of the uncompleted contracts is provided through the current estimates of costs to complete or of progress toward completion.

The principal disadvantage of the percentage-of-completion method is that it is necessarily dependent upon estimates of ultimate costs and consequently of currently accruing income. Typically, these are subject to the uncertainties frequently inherent in long-term contracts.

In discussing the completed-contract method, *ARB No. 45* stated:

The completed-contract method recognizes income only when the contract is completed or substantially so. Accordingly, costs of contracts in process and current billings are accumulated but there are no interim charges or credits to income other than provisions for losses. A contract may be regarded as substantially completed, if remaining costs are not significant in amount.

When the completed-contract method is used, it may be appropriate to allocate general and administrative expenses to contract costs rather than to periodic income. This may result in a better matching of costs and revenues than would result from treating such expenses as period costs, particularly in years when no contracts were completed. It is not so important, however, when the contractor is engaged in numerous projects and in such circumstances it may be preferable to charge those expenses as incurred to periodic income. In any case there should be no excessive deferring of overhead costs, such as might occur if total overhead were assigned to abnormally few or abnormally small contracts in process.

Although the completed-contract method does not permit the recording of any income prior to completion, provision should be made for expected losses in accordance with the well-established practice of making provision for foreseeable losses. If there is a close relationship between profitable and unprofitable contracts, such as in the case of contracts which are parts of the same project, the group may be treated as a unit in determining the necessity for a provision for losses.

When the completed-contract method is used, an excess of accumulated costs over related billings should be shown in the balance sheet as a current asset, and an excess of accumulated billings over related costs should be shown among the liabilities, in most cases as a current liability. If costs exceed billings on some contracts, and billings exceed costs on others, the contracts should ordinarily be segregated so that the figures on the asset side include only those contracts on which costs exceed billings, and those on the liability side include only those on which billings exceed costs. It is suggested that the asset item be described as "costs of uncompleted contracts in excess of related billings" rather than as "inventory" or "work in process," and that the item on the liability side be described as "billings on uncompleted contracts in excess of related costs."

The principal advantage of the completed-contract method is that it is based on final results, rather than on estimates for unperformed work which may involve unforeseen costs and possible losses.

The principal disadvantage of this method is that it does not reflect current performance when the period of any contract extends into more than one accounting period. Under these circumstances, it may result in irregular recognition of income.

The Committee on Accounting Procedure believed the use of the percentage-of-completion method was preferable in those situations where the estimates of costs to complete and the extent of progress toward completion are reasonably dependable. The committee also indicated interim billings should not be used as a basis for recognizing income, since considerations other than those acceptable as a basis for the recognition of income frequently enter into the determination of the timing and the amounts of interim billings.

Magazine publishers recognize profit on subscription sales proportionally as the magazines are delivered. This accounting practice is analogous to the percentage-of-completion-contract method. When the subscription is sold, the full subscription price is usually received in cash. The accounting entries increase cash and an accompanying liability account, such as deferred subscription liability. As the magazine subscription is fulfilled, the liability account is reduced and income recognized.

Services

Income from services is recognized during the period in which the service is rendered. For example, in the case of services such as the use of money or facilities, the interest or rent income is accrued and included in income as the services are used over time.

Because services cannot be stored, they must be marketed before they are provided. If these activities involve substantial outlays, some portion of the revenue from the sale of services may be attributed to the marketing costs. For instance, leasing companies spend a considerable sum on selling and negotiating leasing contracts before any receipts are received from lease agreements. For a number of years, in order to cover these costs, many leasing companies at the time the lease agreement was signed recognized for income determination purposes some portion of the lease rental receipts before they were received. Currently, the preferred practice is to spread these costs over the life of the lease.

Nonmonetary Transactions

Typically, business sale transactions involve the exchange of cash or other monetary[1] assets or liabilities for nonmonetary assets or ser-

---

[1] Monetary assets and liabilities are assets and liabilities whose amounts are fixed in terms of units of currency by contract or otherwise. Examples are cash and notes payable in cash.

vices. The monetary element of such exchanges generally provides an objective basis for measuring the cost of the goods and services received by an enterprise as well as the gain or loss on the business.

However, some business transactions do not involve monetary items, such as when a company exchanges inventory for equipment. Since there is no monetary element in the transaction, the determination of the value to assign to the nonmonetary asset transferred or the amount of gain or loss on the transaction is not clear. *Opinion No. 29* sets forth the accounting for such reciprocal nonmonetary exchanges as well as for nonreciprocal transfers of nonmonetary assets by a company for which no assets are received in exchange, such as in the case of a payment of dividends in kind rather than cash. Transactions of these kind are called nonmonetary transactions.

Prior to *Opinion No. 29* the accounting for nonmonetary transactions varied. Some nonmonetary transactions were accounted for at the estimated value of the assets transferred, and others at the amounts at which the assets transferred were previously recorded in the books of the company.

In *Opinion No. 29* the APB concluded that in general the accounting for nonmonetary transactions should be based on the fair values of the assets or services involved, which is the same basis as that used in transactions that involve monetary elements. The *Opinion* stated:

> . . . the cost of a nonmonetary asset acquired in exchange for another nonmonetary asset is the fair value of the asset surrendered to obtain it, and a gain of loss should be recognized on the exchange. The fair value of the asset received should be used to measure the cost if it is more clearly evident than the value of the asset surrendered. Similarly, a nonmonetary asset received in a nonreciprocal transfer should be recorded at the fair value of the asset received. A transfer of a nonmonetary asset to a stockholder or to another entity in a nonreciprocal transfer should be recorded at the fair value of the asset transferred, and a gain or loss should be recognized on the disposition of the asset. The fair value of an entity's own stock reacquired may be a more clearly evident measure of the fair value of the asset distributed in a nonreciprocal transfer if the transaction involves distribution of a nonmonetary asset to eliminate a disproportionate part of owners' interests (that is, to acquire stock for the treasury or for retirement).

According to the *Opinion* the fair value of a nonmonetary asset transferred to or from a business in a nonmonetary transaction could be determined in a number of ways. These included (1) reference to the estimated realizable values in cash transactions involving the same or similar assets; (2) quoted market prices for the same or similar assets; (3) independent appraisals; and (4) management estimates, if adequate evidence to support the estimate was available. If one of the parties to the nonmonetary transaction could have elected to receive cash rather than a nonmonetary asset, then the amount of cash that might have been received could be considered as evidence of the fair value of the nonmonetary asset.

There are certain modifications to the general principle laid out in *Opinion No. 29*. For example, if the fair value of the nonmonetary assets transferred cannot be determined within reasonable limits, then the transaction should be recorded at the book value of the assets transferred. Another exception occurs when the exchange is not essentially the culmination of an earnings process. In this case the accounting for its transaction should be based on the book value (after reduction, if appropriate, for any impairment of value) of the nonmonetary asset relinquished.

The APB defined two types of nonmonetary exchange transactions that do not culminate an earnings process:

a.   An exchange of a product or property held for sale in the ordinary course of business for a product or property to be sold in the same line of business to facilitate sales to customers other than the parties to the exchange and
b.   An exchange of a productive asset not held for sale in the ordinary course of business for a similar productive asset or an equivalent interest in the same or similar productive asset.[2]

An exchange of nonmonetary assets that qualified for being recorded at the asset's book value may sometimes include a monetary consideration. *Opinion No. 29* described the appropriate accounting for such transactions:

The recipient of the monetary consideration has realized gain on the exchange to the extent that the amount of the monetary receipt exceeds a proportionate share of the recorded amount of the asset surrendered. The portion of the cost applicable to the realized amount should be based on the ratio of the monetary consideration to the total consideration received (monetary consideration plus the estimated fair value of the nonmonetary asset received); or, if more clearly evident, the fair value of the nonmonetary asset transferred. The Board further believes that the entity paying the monetary consideration should not recognize any gain on a transaction that is not the culmination of an earnings process but should record the asset received at the amount of the monetary consideration paid plus the recorded amount of the nonmonetary asset surrendered. If a loss is indicated by the terms of a transaction described in this paragraph or is not the culmination of an earnings process, the entire indicated loss on the exchange should be recognized.

Sometimes corporations distribute nonmonetary assets to owners in a spin-off or some other form of reorganization or liquidation. The

---

[2] The *Opinion* defines a productive asset as an asset held for or used in the production of goods or services by the enterprise. Productive assets include an investment in another entity if the investment is accounted for by the equity method but exclude an investment not accounted for by that method. Similar productive assets are productive assets that are of the same general type, that perform the same function, or that are employed in the same line of business.

accounting for nonreciprocal transfers of this kind should be based on the recorded amount of the asset distributed. Other nonreciprocal transfers of nonmonetary assets to owners should be accounted for at fair value if the distributing entity could have realized this value in an outright sale at or near the time of distribution. If this circumstance cannot be met, book values must be used to value the transaction.

Inappropriate Interest Rates

Sometimes the seller of property, goods, or services may receive in exchange a note with a face value that does not reasonably represent the present value of the consideration given or received in the exchange. This situation may arise if the note is noninterest bearing or has a stated interest rate which is different from the rate of interest appropriate for the debt at the date of the transaction. Unless in these circumstances the note is recorded at its present value,[3] rather than the stated amount, the sales price and profit to the seller and cost to the buyer are misstated, and interest income and interest expense in subsequent periods are also misstated.

Opinion No. 21, "Interest on Receivables and Payables," sets forth the appropriate accounting in these cases.

It requires that the receivable or payable be recorded on the balance sheet at its face value less the amount required to arrive at its discounted value. Then, the interest income or expense is the market rate, which is the interest actually received or paid plus a portion of the discount amount shown on the balance sheet as a deduction from the note's face value.

ACCOUNTING FOR BAD DEBTS

Revenues are ordinarily accounted for at the time a transaction is completed, with appropriate provision for uncollectible amounts. This section presents alternative procedures used by businesses in recognizing and reporting losses from uncollectible receivables.

Every enterprise extending credit to customers sustains some losses from bad debts. An account receivable becomes a bad debt when all reasonable expectation of collection is exhausted. The amounts of bad debt loss to the business firm will depend upon such factors as the type of customer served, policies regarding investigative procedures prior to granting credit, and policies employed in the collection of receivables. In spite of efforts to minimize these losses, uncollectible accounts will result from the inability to predict the certainty of pay-

---

[3] The present value amount is the future cash payments required by the note discounted at the appropriate market interest rate.

ments by customers. Bad debt losses can be avoided only if a firm receives payment in cash at the time of sale.

There are two basic reasons for recognizing bad debt losses in the financial records. First, the determination of net income based upon the proper matching of revenue and expense must include these unavoidable losses. Second, the valuation of receivables in the balance sheet requires consideration of these losses to present a realistic estimate of the anticipated funds that will flow from the collection of receivables.

Accounting for bad debt losses can be accomplished by either of two methods: (1) the direct write-off method or (2) the bad debt estimation method. For federal income tax purposes, the deduction for bad debt expense can be determined by either of these two methods. In fact, one method can be used for financial reporting purposes while the other method is used for income tax purposes. However, for practical reasons, the method adopted by a business for tax or book purposes is usually used for both purposes.

Direct Write-Off Method

The direct write-off method of accounting for bad debt expense ignores the possibility of any bad debt loss until individual accounts receivable prove to be uncollectible. No advance provision is made for doubtful accounts. Under this method, the bad debt expense represents the amount of receivables which have actually become uncollectible during the operating period.

When an account receivable is considered uncollectible, the following entry is made:

Bad Debt Expense 000
    Accounts Receivable (customer A)   000

This entry has the effect of charging an asset account (Accounts Receivable) directly to an expense account (Bad Debt Expense) and gives this method its descriptive name.

If subsequent events prove that an account previously written off can be collected, the entry required to reinstate the receivable is:

Accounts Receivable (customer A) 000
    Bad Debts Recovered (or Bad Debt Expense)   000

At the close of the accounting period, Bad Debts Recovered must be recognized as revenue while Bad Debts Expense is deducted in the determination of net income. Alternatively, recoveries and expenses might be netted.

The direct write-off method has two severe limitations. First, the bad debt expense may be deducted from the revenue of an accounting period subsequent to the original sale. Hence, it fails to properly match income and expense of a particular operating period. Second, current assets in the balance sheet may be overstated, since no recognition is given to the probable uncollectibility of some part of the receivables. For these reasons, the direct write-off method is not widely used by businesses of significant size. However, its simplicity makes it a popular method among very small businesses.

Also, in those cases where a reasonable estimate of the anticipated bad debts cannot be made, FASB *Statement No. 5* requires that the direct write-off method be used.

Bad Debt Estimation Method

Matching of revenue and expense and a realistic valuation of accounts receivables is achieved by including an estimate of bad debt expense in the financial statements.[4] The estimated amount of bad debt losses which will eventually result from sales of an accounting period is treated as an expense of the period. That part of the estimated loss which cannot be identified with particular receivables is deducted from total receivables on the balance sheet to show the expected amount to be collected eventually.

The special feature of the bad debt estimation method is the creation of the asset valuation account deducted from receivables. This contra-asset account, called Allowance for Doubtful (or Uncollectible) Accounts, is increased as estimated bad debt expense is recorded and decreased by recognition of actual bad debt losses.

There are several different approaches to the estimation of bad debt expense. The estimated bad debt losses for a business enterprise can usually be estimated with a high degree of accuracy based upon its own experience of actual bad debt losses over a period of time or upon the experience of similar businesses. For estimating purposes, this experience can be related on a percentage basis to: (1) sales for a period of operations or (2) to the amount of receivables at the close of the operating period. Either of these approaches will, over a period of time, theoretically result in proper charges to income and proper valuation of receivables.

Percentage of Sales. The estimate for bad debt losses may be expressed as a percentage of sales. For example, historical experience might indicate that actual bad debt losses averaged 2 percent of sales.

---

[4] This method is sometimes called the "reserve" method. However, preferred modern terminology disapproves of the reserve label previously given to the accumulated estimate of uncollectibility.

This rate for estimating bad debt losses might be applied in successive operating periods until actual experience suggests that the rate be adjusted upward or downward to achieve greater accuracy. Frequently the rate is determined on the basis of a sales figure adjusted by eliminating cash sales and sales returns, in recognition that bad debts result only from net credit sales to customers.

Percentage of Receivables. The estimate for bad debt losses may be expressed as a percentage of receivables at the close of an accounting period. For example, prior experience might indicate that on the average 5 percent of the balance of receivables subsequently proves uncollectible. In each operating period sufficient bad debt expense might be charged to maintain the Allowance for Doubtful Accounts at 5 percent of receivables until actual experience requires revision of this rate.

To obtain greater accuracy in estimating uncollectibility, an analysis grouping accounts receivable by "age" from date of sale may be prepared. Since older accounts are more likely to be uncollectible, separate consideration of each group of accounts might suggest that the provision for uncollectibility should be equal, for example, to 1 percent of receivables 0 to 30 days old, 3 percent of receivables 31 to 60 days old, and 25 percent of receivables over 60 days old.

Accounting Entries for Bad Debt Estimation Method

The following accounting entries are typically required to handle estimated and actual bad debt losses under the estimation method.

1. To record estimated bad debt expense:

Dr. Bad Debt Expense... 000
Cr.   Allowance for Doubtful Accounts   000

This entry is usually made only at the close of the accounting period immediately before financial statements are prepared. The amount of the entry will be either (1) the amount of bad debt expense computed as a percentage of sales or (2) the amount necessary to bring the Allowance for Doubtful Accounts to a computed percentage of receivables.

2. To write off an account determined to be uncollectible:

Dr. Allowance for Doubtful Accounts......................... 000
Cr.   Accounts Receivable (customer A).....................   000

In this entry, specific uncollectible receivables are identified with the bad debt expense previously recognized on an estimated basis.

3. To recognize collectibility of a receivable previously written off:

Dr. Accounts Receivable (customer A)......................... 000
Cr.   Allowance for Doubtful Accounts   000

This entry will reflect the amount expected to be collected from the customer. Reinstatement of the receivable previously written off is accomplished so that a complete history of dealings with customers is maintained in the accounts receivable records. The actual collections on the reinstated account will then be recorded as though the account had never been written off.

Financial Statement Presentation

Bad debt expense recorded on the basis of an estimate is reported as an expense on the income statement. Usually this expense is classified as selling expense or as administrative expense, depending upon responsibility within the firm for the granting of credit.

The allowance for doubtful accounts is subtracted from the total of the related receivables in the current asset section of the balance sheet. This net amount presents the expected cash proceeds from subsequent collection of the receivables.

FASB *Statement No. 5* requires that the bad debt estimation method be used when the amount of the anticipated bad debts can be reasonably estimated.

WARRANTIES AND SERVICE GUARANTEES

Some merchandise is sold with a warranty against defects or a service guarantee, which when fulfilled is usually paid in labor and materials rather than cash. These items are similar to bad debts in that the future expense and accompanying liability are unknown at the time of sale. Therefore, initially, they must be estimated. If the amount of the future warranty cost can be reasonably estimated, FASB *Statement No. 5* requires that future warranty costs be recorded at the time a sale is made. If a reasonable estimate cannot be made, the warranty costs must be recognized as they are actually incurred in future accounting periods.

The accounting for warranty or service guarantees is analogous to bad debt accounting. The estimated expense is recognized at the time of the sale and an offsetting liability is established. This liability is then reduced when the cost of the guarantee or warranty is paid. Sometimes the estimated costs are shown as a revenue offset instead of an expense.

REALIZATION CONTROVERSY

Accounting practice has relied heavily on the realization principle as a guide to recognizing income. With the exceptions discussed earlier, this principle states that income arises at the point of sale. A number of accounting authors do not accept this concept and its related practices as an essential feature of accounting. They claim it lacks analytical precision. Also, it is in more or less continual conflict with the going-concern convention, which places emphasis on the continuity and whole process of business activity. In contrast, the realization principle places undue emphasis on the act of selling, which is only one point in a company's total economic activity.

The critics of the realization concept believe the proper function of accounting is the measurement of the resources of specific entities and of changes in these resources. These changes are attributable to the whole process of business activity. Accordingly, the principles of accounting should be directed at the fulfillment of this function. In their opinion changes in resources (income) should be classified among the amounts attributable to:

a.   Price level changes which lead to restatement of capital, but not to revenues and expenses.
b.   Changes in the current value of assets beyond the effect of price level changes.
c.   The recognition through sales and other operating related transfers of net realizable value which leads to revenue or gain.
d.   Other causes, such as the accretion or discovery of previously unknown natural resources.

This approach requires the use of price level accounting and current values of assets rather than the presently more accepted historical cost principle.

The supporters of the realization principle argue that it is difficult to determine the fairness and reasonableness of appraisals which seek to restate plant and equipment in terms of current values. They cite as evidence the disillusionment of investors from the experiences of the 1920s, when companies wrote up asset values only to have to write them down again during the 1930s. Those who argue for the realization concept do so principally on its demonstrated practical utility. In addition, they believe it is not prudent to recognize gains before they are realized.

Relaxation of the realization principle to reflect price level gains or losses on monetary items has been approved in countries with severe inflation. In the United States, APB *Statement No. 3* in June 1969 approved the issuance of supplemental statements showing gains or losses due to inflation. In 1976 the SEC required the larger companies under its jurisdiction to publish in their notes the replacement of cost of their inventories and productive assets. In addition, the FASB was considering the possibility of moving to a current value oriented accounting model.

SUGGESTED FURTHER READING

BEDFORD, NORTON M. *Income Determination Theory: An Accounting Framework.* Reading, Mass.: Addison-Wesley Publishing Co., Inc., 1965.

HANSEN, PALLE. *The Accounting Concept of Profit: An Analysis and Evaluation in the Light of the Economic Theory of Income and Capital.* Amsterdam: North-Holland Publishing Co., 1972.

THOMAS, ARTHUR L. *Revenue Recognition.* Michigan Business Report No. 49. Ann Arbor: Bureau of Business Research, Graduate School of Business Administration, University of Michigan, 1966.

WINDAL, FLOYD. *The Accounting Concept of Realization.* Occasional Paper No. 5. East Lansing: Bureau of Business and Economic Research, Michigan State University, 1961.

CASES

CASE 9-1. GOLDFINGER INCORPORATED
Alternative Realization Criteria

Early in 1970, Goldfinger Incorporated was formed to acquire and operate a Nevada mining property using newly developed extraction methods capable of processing profitably low-grade ores containing small quantities of gold.

Operations began promptly in 1970. Engineers' reports based upon extensive geological surveys indicated that 1.6 million ounces of gold would be recovered over the life of the mining properties. The mining properties were located in an arid mountainous area and would have no residual value after the gold deposits were exhausted. The existing equipment and property improvements were expected to be used during the period of production and abandoned thereafter. All production and operating expenses were paid during the year. Goldfinger's cash receipts and disbursements for the year are summarized in Exhibit 1.

EXHIBIT 1

GOLDFINGER INCORPORATED
Schedule of Cash Receipts and Disbursements for the Year 1970
(in thousands)

Cash Receipts:		
Sales of capital stock at par value		$10,000
Collections from sales (30,000 ounces at $35 per ounce)		1,050
Total Receipts		$11,050
Cash Disbursements:		
Cost of mining properties*	$8,000	
Production costs	2,250	
Delivery expenses	25	
Administrative expenses	150	
Total Disbursements		10,425
Cash on Hand, Balance at December 31, 1970		$ 625

* Including all mineral rights, engineers' surveys, roads, mine shafts, and equipment.

228

The Gold Reserve Act of January 1934 defined the United States dollar as 15 and 5/21 grains of gold 9/10 fine. Since there are 480 grains of pure gold to the ounce, the mint price for 9/10 fine gold became $35. The United States Treasury stands ready to buy gold from miners or importers at the $35 mint price, and to sell to industrial users, dentists, foreign governments, or central banks at the same price. Thus, gold is readily marketable at the fixed price of $35 and this price is subject to change only by the federal government.

Goldfinger's production records for 1970 show the following information (amounts are ounces of 9/10 fine):

Sold, delivered, and proceeds collected	30,000 *ounces*
Sold and delivered, but proceeds not collected	20,000
Produced but not sold or delivered	40,000
Total Production	90,000

Questions

1. Prepare a balance sheet at December 31, 1970, and an income statement for the year based on each of the following:
   a. Revenues are recognized upon the receipt of cash.
   b. Revenues are recognized at time of sale and delivery.
   c. Revenues are recognized upon the basis of production.
   (Ignore any income tax considerations.)
2. Evaluate the three sets of statements which you prepared in terms of the criteria of—
   a. Usefulness.
   b. Feasibility.
   c. Conformity to accepted definitions of income.

CASE 9–2. RAVENWOOD OIL CORPORATION
Carved-Out Oil and Gas Production Contracts

The Ravenwood Oil Corporation was formed in 1967 by a group of Denver business executives to engage in oil exploration in the western part of the United States. Its operations included exploration, development, and production activities in scattered areas from Texas to Canada and west to California. More than one half of the four million shares of common stock authorized by its Delaware charter were issued to the incorporators and about 750 investors through public offerings.

This case deals with the accounting methods used by the corporation to report *profits* from the sales of carved-out oil and gas production payments in 1974, 1975, and 1976.

To obtain funds for exploration or other purposes, the owner of a producing oil property may sell carved-out oil production payments. In exchange for an immediate payment in cash, the purchaser of the carved-out oil production payment receives the right to a certain amount of money to be paid from a specified percentage of the oil produced from an existing producing property. For example, Ravenwood, as an owner of oil properties, might sell to an investor for $100,000 cash the right to receive up to $125,000 from the proceeds of 20 percent of the oil produced from one of its producing properties. Ravenwood would continue to operate the property and bear all costs of producing the oil. The transaction is considered a sale of the oil under the ground; no liability for repayment is created by such sale. As the owner of the oil, the purchaser of the oil payment will receive the proceeds from the sale of the oil directly from the buyer of the crude

EXHIBIT 1

RAVENWOOD OIL CORPORATION
Balance Sheets at December 31
(in thousands)

Assets

	1975	1974
Cash	$ 262	$ 178
Receivables (net)	1,852	1,838
Materials and supplies (at cost)	158	162
Other current assets	98	44
Total Current Assets	$ 2,370	$ 2,222
Net property	6,846	6,640
Undeveloped leases	1,644	1,214
Other assets	137	114
Total Assets	$10,997	$10,190

Liabilities and Stockholders' Equity

	1975	1974
Accounts payable	$ 306	$ 496
Notes payable	520	2,468
Accrued expenses	430	88
Total Current Liabilities	$ 1,256	$ 3,052
Long-term notes payable	2,980	1,886
Total Liabilities	$ 4,236	$ 4,938
Stockholders' Equity:		
Common stock (par value $1)	$ 2,428	$ 2,396
Paid-in surplus	2,748	2,274
Retained earnings	1,585	582
Total Stockholders' Equity	$ 6,761	$ 5,252
Total Liabilities and Stockholders' Equity	$10,997	$10,190

oil. The excess of the oil payment over the cash paid by the investor indicates the risk assumed by the investor regarding the certainty that production will be sufficient to satisfy the payment. Typically, the level of risk assumed by the buyer of this carved-out oil payment is low.

Initially, Ravenwood's operations had been a disappointment to the incorporators. Between 1967 and 1973 irregular profits and losses had been reported, and at the close of 1973 retained earnings were $90,000.

Operations in 1974 and 1975 resulted in profits of $492,000 and $1,003,000, respectively, however (see Exhibits 1 and 2). Profits from

EXHIBIT 2

RAVENWOOD OIL CORPORATION
Income Statements for the Year Ended December 31
(in thousands)

	1975	1974
Income:		
Sales of oil and gas	$4,775	$4,228
Operating Costs and Expenses:		
Lease operations	$ 752	$ 864
Production and ad valorem taxes	234	216
Administrative and general	470	464
Interest on long-term debt	126	144
Other interest	26	14
Miscellaneous	4	2
	$1,612	$1,704
Other Costs:		
Intangible development costs	$ 728	$ 716
Dry holes and abandonments	102	166
Depreciation and depletion	1,012	1,034
Released or expired interests	318	116
	$2,160	$2,032
Total Costs and Expenses	$3,772	$3,736
Net Income	$1,003	$ 492

carved-out oil payments sold but not satisfied by production before year-end were $116,000 in 1974 and $1,360,000 in 1975. These amounts had been recognized as income at the time of sale and were included in the sales of oil and gas reported in those years, after making adequate provision for estimated future production costs. All oil payments were satisfied by production within 12 months following the sale of the oil payment.

On April 10, 1976, after the 1975 annual statements were issued to stockholders but before interim statements for the first quarter of 1976 were prepared, the company changed its method of accounting for the profits from the sale of carved-out oil production payments. Effective January 1, 1976, all such profits were to be deferred until the oil and gas was produced. So that the 1975 statements would be comparable to the 1976 statements prepared using the newly adopted accounting method, it was necessary to recast the 1975 financial statements applying this new policy.

Operations for the year 1976 resulted in a net loss of $275,000 exclusive of any consideration of profits from sales of oil production payments. By December 31, 1976, all oil payments sold in previous years had been satisfied by oil production. The single carved-out oil production payment sold in 1976 resulted in a profit of $255,000, but no oil was produced from this property in 1976.

To date, the company had not declared any dividends.

Questions

(NOTE: Ignore income tax considerations in your answers.)

1. What net income would Ravenwood report in 1976 if the accounting method used previously had been continued?
2. What is the net income for each of the years 1974, 1975, and 1976 under the newly adopted method of deferring profits from sales of carved-out oil production payments until production takes place?
3. What are the earnings per share in each of the three years under:
    a. The accounting method originally used?
    b. The newly adopted accounting method?
4. What reasons can you suggest for adoption of the new accounting method?
5. How do you think Ravenwood should report its profits from sales of carved-out oil production payments? Why?

CASE 9–3. LECTRO-MAGIC COMPANY
Accounting for Bad Debt and Warranty Service Costs

The Lectro-Magic Company was incorporated in Ohio, in April 1969, to produce and sell a new line of small electrical appliances. Organizational leadership for Lectro-Magic was provided by Roger Wiswell, who left his position as district sales manager for a national electrical appliance firm. Reluctant to accept a promotion requiring transfer to the West Coast, Wiswell had for more than a year been alert to an opportunity to use his abilities in a smaller firm in the Cleveland area.

In mid-1968, Wiswell was introduced to a young electrical engineer who had developed a miniature power unit around which he designed a number of unusual and effective small appliances. After a six-month investigation of product marketability and anticipated costs, the two decided to pool their resources to produce and market the line.

The limited financial resources of the promoters were supplemented by investments of four mutual friends. These investors were not interested in direct participation in the management of the enterprise. However, all six planned to serve as the firm's board of directors. After the corporate charter was granted by the State of Ohio, 100,000 of the 500,000 authorized $1 par value shares of capital stock were issued to the six incorporators at $3 per share. Roger Wiswell was elected president of the new corporation.

Several tentative agreements made prior to incorporation were now formalized by contracts. The corporation agreed to pay a 5 percent royalty, based on the selling price of appliances, to the engineer-inventor in return for exclusive rights to the use of his patents. Two small electrical and metal stamping firms agreed to manufacture and assemble the applicances at prices subject to periodic revision based upon negotiation.

Early in the planning stages of the venture, the principal promoters agreed that the mechanical nature of the products would require extensive servicing after sale in order to gain customer acceptability. Therefore, from the outset, all appliances were sold with a two-year warranty. Lectro-Magic was to provide unlimited service and repairs for this period without charge to the ultimate purchaser. Only transportation costs were paid by appliance owners under this liberal service policy. The manufacturer who contracted to produce the electrical components agreed to provide the required service and repairs for Lectro-Magic under a cost-plus arrangement.

By October 1969, Lectro-Magic's operations were well under way. Sizable expenditures for promotion and introduction of the product line resulted in almost immediate customer acceptance. During the balance of the year, efforts were concentrated upon marketing activities in a selected six-state area.

From the beginning, the firm's accounting and related clerical activities were supervised by a competent but inexperienced young accountant. His attention had been entirely directed toward establishing procedures and records for control of cash, inventories, accounts receivable, and accounts payable. Since Wiswell's time was taken by more pressing matters, accounting and reporting practices were given little consideration by him beyond the selection of a calendar-year closing date.

Early in January 1970, the company accountant prepared a balance sheet at December 31, 1969, and an income statement covering 1969 operations. These statements are shown in the first columns of Exhibits 1 and 2. All accounts payable and accruals of monetary liabilities had been recorded. Cash, receivables, and inventories had been carefully reconciled. A net loss from operations had been expected during this initial period, and no income tax liability was anticipated.

EXHIBIT 1

LECTRO-MAGIC COMPANY
Balance Sheets at December 31
(in thousands)

Assets

	1969 *(actual)*	1970 *(estimated)*
Current Assets:		
Cash	$125	$201
Accounts receivable	70	125
Inventories	30	151
Total Current Assets	$225	$477
Plant and equipment	$213	$213
Less: Accumulated depreciation	4	12
Net book value	$209	$201
Total Assets	$434	$678

Liabilities and Equity

	1969 *(actual)*	1970 *(estimated)*
Current Liabilities:		
Accounts payable	$137	$235
Taxes payable	—	45
Other accruals	13	35
Total Current Liabilities	$150	$315
Stockholders' Equity:		
Capital stock	$100	$100
Other paid-in capital	200	200
Retained earnings	(16)	63
Total Stockholders' Equity	$284	$363
Total Liabilities and Equity	$434	$678

Several events in January 1970 brought President Wiswell's attention directly to accounting matters. These related to bad debts and warranty service costs.

During the year 1969, bad debt losses had not been anticipated. Shipments had been made to retailer customers after cursory reference to a publication of a credit reporting service. In January, however, Lectro-Magic was notified that a customer owing $4,000 had been

EXHIBIT 2

LECTRO-MAGIC COMPANY
Income Statements for the Years 1969 and 1970
(in thousands)

	1969 (actual)	1970 (estimated)
Sales	$200	$600
Cost of Sales:		
Production costs	$100	$300
Royalties	10	30
Total	$110	$330
Gross profit...........................	$ 90	$270
Expenses:		
Warranty service costs	$ 6	$ 24
Selling expenses	16	48
General and administration	24	50
Bad debts	—	4
Promotional expenses	60	20
Total	$106	$146
Net income before taxes	$ (16)	$124
Provision for income taxes*	—	52
Net Income after Taxes	$ (16)	$ 72

* Federal income tax rates on corporations for 1969 and 1970 were: the normal tax rate of 22 percent on all taxable income, plus a surtax of 26 percent on taxable income over $25,000. (This does not include a special surtax imposed in 1969–70, which should not be considered in computation.)

declared bankrupt. There was little prospect of even a partial recovery of the unpaid balance.

In a review of the warranty service contract, Wiswell noted that costs to the end of 1969 had exceeded earlier projections. The costs taken into account in pricing the company's line were estimated to be 12 percent of the total sales price. These service costs were expected to be incurred as follows: 2 percent in the year of sale, 6 percent in the succeeding year, and 4 percent in the second year following sale. Wiswell noted, however, that a number of minor changes made in product design late in 1969 were expected to reduce the need for repairs and service from these projected levels.

While conferring with the company's legal counsel late in January, Wiswell was reminded that Lectro-Magic's federal income tax return would be due on March 15, 1970. The attorney suggested that it might be wise to retain a certified public accountant to make an audit of the firm's operations and prepare the income tax returns. He noted that accounting methods used by Taxpayers in initial periods must generally be continued in subsequent periods unless prior permission for change is obtained within 90 days after the beginning of the taxable year.[1] In addition, borrowing or security offerings to finance possible expansion would probably require financial statements with an independent accountant's opinion.

Immediately after returning to his office, Wiswell asked the company's accountant to prepare estimated statements for the year 1970 based upon projections of sales, costs, and expenses. These estimated statements appear in the second columns of Exhibits 1 and 2.

Mr. Wiswell planned to spend the evening studying the financial statements for 1969 and 1970.

Questions

1. How, if at all, should the company's financial statements reflect—
   a. Warranty service costs?
   b. Bad debt expense?
2. What other areas of financial reporting should be considered by management?
3. Using available information and any assumptions you choose to make, recast 1969 statements and 1970 estimates to reflect fairly the financial position and the results of operations.

CASE 9–4. GUIDO ANTONINI (A)
Accounting for Franchises

In May 1968, Guido (Guy) Antonini surveyed with pride his new business the "Easy Day Car Wash of Providence, Inc.," completed, ready to operate, and only several months behind schedule.

Mr. Antonini had been a very successful produce dealer in Philadelphia, finally employing six men and five trucks. He was then in his early 50s, and with two children educated and married, he decided that he and his wife Anna could retire and enjoy life. Anna had long wished to move back to Providence, where her family lived, and Guy had agreed. The decision was made in early 1966; by March the business and their home had been sold.

Guy found life moving very slowly once he and Anna had settled in

---

[1] As a general rule, estimated expenses cannot be deducted for federal income tax purposes. Expenses may be deducted only in the period in which they actually occur. Special statutory provisions do, however, permit deduction of reasonable additions to a "reserve" for bad debts instead of a deduction for specific bad debt items.

Providence. After a month of retirement, he started looking for something to do. The produce market in Providence was too small and tightly controlled. After 30 years of being his own boss, Guy had no desire to look for a regular job—even if he could find one where they would consider working experience more important than the fact that he had quit high school in the tenth grade.

Guy seriously considered opening a pizza parlor—his brother-in-law Rocco was doing very well with his—but Rocco was willing to work every night until midnight, and Guy was not interested in those hours. He searched for a location for a fruit and flower shop, but found none to his satisfaction.

In mid-July, another brother-in-law, Tony Cabrese, the service manager for a large Providence auto dealer, told him that the ARS Automotive Company was looking for a man to run a pilot car wash for them in the Providence area. Guy had been suggested by Tony as a "savvy businessman"; several days later, the local ARS representative called him and Guy indicated interest in the enterprise.

ARS was a leading manufacturer of automotive finishes, making paints, polishing compounds, and a line of liquid and solid automotive waxes. ARS had spent about $100,000 on consulting contracts, looking for diversification opportunities, and had determined that a car-wash operation presented potential for both sales of company products and for financial growth.

ARS had formed a subsidiary corporation, the Easy Day Car Wash Franchises, Inc. It assigned its $100,000 investment in research and development to EDCWF, Inc., and paid $40,000 cash in exchange for 140,000 shares of no-par common stock out of the total of 500,000 shares authorized. Mr. Stanley White was appointed president of EDCWF, Inc.; he had previously been vice president, sales, for ARS. Although Mr. White had no experience with franchising, he had extensive experience in the sale of ARS products, especially waxes and polishes.

Under Mr. White's leadership, the Easy Day Car Wash Franchises, Inc., set as its goal the installation of 200 car-washing facilities in the northeastern and central Atlantic areas within the next five years. To be able to finance the predicted expansion, the board of directors of EDCWF planned to offer 40 percent of its authorized common stock to the public as soon as possible. Based on the experience of other franchisors, the board felt that a public offering price of $15 to $20 a share would be possible.

EDCWF entered into a development agreement with the Drexsler Machine Company. Drexsler would design and build a self-contained unit for the proposed car wash at its own expense, if EDCWF would agree to use Drexsler equipment exclusively and would contract to purchase 30 machines, including the prototype, for $55,000 each over a period of two years. A penalty of $5,000 would be assessed for each of the 30 machines not ordered at the end of the two-year period. Drexsler developed the specialized equipment suitable for handling ARS detergents and waxes by early 1966. In addition, an architectural firm was retained to design a distinctive shell for a fee of $10,000.

Easy Day Car Wash Franchises, Inc., agreed to purchase all its washing and wax compounds from ARS for a per-drum price equivalent to $0.05 a car for each wash and $0.05 for each wax. This pricing agreement would be reviewed annually.

Guy Antonini was selected as the first franchisee; the Providence location was sufficiently close to company headquarters to permit close supervision of the pilot operation. The terms of EDCWF's agreement with Guy were relatively straightforward. The fee for the perpetual franchise was to be $15,000, payable $5,000 immediately and $1,000 a year for the next ten years. Four percent interest was to be charged on any unpaid balance. In addition, Antonini would pay the franchiser $200 a month, or 2 percent of gross receipts, whichever was the greater in any month. EDCWF would supply bookkeeping supervision and technical consultation.

Guy purchased the equipment from EDCWF for $60,000; $10,000 at once and the remainder payable over the next five years, at $10,000 each year, plus 5 percent interest on the unpaid balance. The equipment had an expected life of ten years.

The franchise agreement was signed December 10, 1967, and the initial fee paid. Construction and installation of equipment was scheduled to begin January 30, 1968.

EDCWF purchased the property on which the car wash was to be located from a local trust for $20,000 on January 1, 1968, and arranged for the construction of a shell building for $25,000 to house the equipment. The construction was to be supervised by EDCWF, Inc.; a rental of $3,000 a year and locally assessed taxes were to be paid by the franchisee. The initial lease period was five years, with provision for renewal for five years. The agreement was between Easy Day Car Wash Franchises, Inc., and Easy Day Car Wash of Providence, a Rhode Island corporation in which Guido and Anna were the sole stockholders. The Antoninis had paid $16,000 cash for 1,000 shares of common stock.

EDCWF supervised the construction of the shell and Drexsler the machinery installation, which allowed a double line of traffic to move through. The opening was delayed for two months by the unanticipated demand of the Providence Public Works Department that the Easy Day Car Wash of Providence install special sewage lines connecting with a main city line one-half mile distant. The cost of the sewer connection was $7,000, paid by the franchiser.

Easy Day of Providence opened June 1, 1968, with Guido as manager and Anna as bookkeeper-cashier. For the month of June, the special car wash and wax price was $2.50 instead of the regular price of $3 for washing and $1.50 additional for the wax. The Easy Day of Providence had a $15,000 line of credit at a local bank, guaranteed by EDCWF, Inc.

Questions

1. As the treasurer of EDCWF, Inc., how would you prepare a—
   a. Balance sheet on December 31, 1967?
   b. Balance sheet and income statement June 30, 1968?
2. Prepare a financial statement for Easy Day of Providence, Inc., on June 30, 1968. Sales were $3,600; cash wages, $925; electricity and water, $275; supplies, $72; annual salaries, Guido, $10,000, and Anna, $5,000. Ignore supplies inventory.

CASE 9–5. GUIDO ANTONINI (B)
Accounting For Franchises

In early December 1969, Stanley White, president of the Easy Day Car Wash Franchises, Inc., received the following letter forwarded from his sales manager, Frederic Behr:

Dear Mr. Behr:
I've decided to get out of the car-wash business. I've been shorthanded since last August when those college kids left. Anna and I have decided to go back to Philadelphia for Christmas, and we want to be out of this mess by then.
GUIDO ANTONINI

Since 1966, Easy Day Car Wash Franchises, Inc., had opened eight car-wash franchises in the New England and middle-Atlantic areas. Guido Antonini's franchise had been the first to be granted. The next six wash operations would be opened July 1, 1970.

After two days of discussion with Guido, Mr. Behr determined that he was serious. It was decided that EDCWF, Inc., would buy Guido's stock of Easy Day of Providence, Inc., after distribution of the cash, for $45,000, and would pay $5,000 for an agreement that Guido would stay out of the car-wash business within 50 miles of Providence for two years. Guido would pay the debts of Easy Day of Providence before making the stock transfer. EDCWF, Inc., was uncertain as to whether or not they would operate the franchise or would attempt to sell it to another franchise.

Questions

1. If you were EDCWF, Inc., with a fiscal year ending December 31, how would you account for the stock purchase? (Include the A case facts where relevant.) Do you think this is "fair"?
2. What are the alternative methods? Under what criteria would they be more appropriate?

CASE 9–6. SOUTHERN LAND COMPANY
Cash Flow and Income Recognition

In late 1972 the three members of the audit committee of the Southern Land Company was considering whether or not they should approve the proposal presented by management for the recognition of a substantial gain that would arise from the sale of the company's thematic recreation park in Miami. The management wished to recognize all of the profit at the time of the sale as ordinary income. However, at least one member of the audit committee believed that income should be recognized in some appropriate way over the buyer's payment period. Another member of the committee thought that possibly the gain should be shown as an extraordinary item.

The company's CPA firm backed management's position.

Southern Company

Southern Company owned large real estate holdings in the Southwest, California, and Hawaii. The company also operated two thematic recreation parks in Louisville and Miami. The Louisville park, which was operated under a management contract, had been sold by Southern in the previous year to a group of private investors. The sale of the Miami park was to be a similar deal.

Southern Company was controlled by the Cleveland Corporation, a widely diversified conglomerate. Cleveland owned 90 percent of the Southern equity. The other 10 percent was publically held.

Although it was not generally realized by the public, at the time of the Southern sale of its Miami property the Cleveland Corporation was close to bankruptcy. For 1972 the company's management expected Cleveland to report an operating loss of some $25 million, before the profits of the Miami park sale were included in Cleveland's consolidated income statement. In addition, the company's consolidated tax return would show a substantial loss.

In 1971 the Southern company reported sales of $117 million and a net income of $27.4 million.

The Miami Sale

In late 1972 a limited partnership of 152 individuals (Partnership No. 1) was formed to acquire Southern's Miami park. These partners contributed $5.95 million to the limited partnership. These funds were used to acquire the Miami park. Immediately after the purchase the limited partnership transferred the property to another partnership (Partnership No. 2) in which a new Southern subsidiary became the general partner for a contribution of $1,000. Partnership No. 1 was a limited partner in Partnership No. 2. Thereafter, the new Southern subsidiary became the sole and exclusive manager of the business of Partnership No. 2.

The $5.95 million of Partnership No. 1 was distributed as follows: $1.5 million as a downpayment for the Miami park; $3.93 million for the prepayment of interest; $416,000 to the underwriter for his commission; and the remainder to the partnership for working capital.

The selling price for the Miami park and a ten-year agreement by Southern not to compete was set at $40 million. This price was established through negotiations between Southern and Realty Appraisers, a Texan realty firm. Partnership No. 1 did not participate in these negotiations.

At the time of the proposed sale the gross book value of the Miami park as reported on Southern's balance sheet was $14.2 million. The related accumulated depreciation reserve was $4.9 million, and the net book value was $9.3 million.

The $40 million purchase price was allocated by the buyer as follows: land, $5 million; buildings and improvements and personal property, $25 million; the covenant not to compete, $8 million; and goodwill, $2 million.

Partnership No. 1 was to pay for the park as follows: $1.5 million cash and a 6.5 percent note for $38.5 million. (At the time the prime borrowing rate was over 8 percent.) The agreement did not require any principal payments for the first three years. Thereafter, for the next 32 years equal principal and interest payments of about $2.3 million annually were required to liquidate the note. In addition, should Partnership No. 1 default on the note, Southern's sole recourse was to recover the park. Neither of the partnerships nor any of the partners individually was liable for the payment of the note or for any deficiency if the property was foreclosed.

In the future all of the park's depreciation losses, tax credits, and amortization charges were to be allocated to the partners of Partnership No. 1.

For its part in the negotiations to set the selling price of the park, Realty Appraisers was paid $1.2 million in cash plus a $750,000 promissory note. In addition, Realty Appraisers was the sole owner of the Realty Interstate, the underwriters of Partnership No. 1. An underwriting commission of $416,000 was paid to Realty Interstate.

The Louisville Sale

On December 31, 1971, Southern had sold to a group of wealthy individuals all of the property and equipment of its Louisville park for $23 million. This sale resulted in a gain of $4.8 million. Upon completion of the sale the purchaser contributed the park to a limited partnership in which a Southern subsidiary was the General Partner and operater. As partial consideration of the sale, Southern received a 7 percent $21 million mortgage note secured by the park. The note was payable in annual principal installments of $700,000 beginning in March 1978.

The 1971 financial statements of Southern reported the $4.8 million gain as an extraordinary income item.

Subsequently, the company changed its policy toward amusement parks from one of constructing and operating parks to one of constructing, developing, selling, and operating parks. Management believed this change in company policy would require that the 1971 sale be reclassified in the comparative 1971 statement included in the 1972 annual report as an ordinary item rather than as an extraordinary item.

Question

What is the appropriate accounting for the gain on the Miami sale?

Chapter 10

EXTRAORDINARY ITEMS, DISCONTINUED OPERATIONS, AND ACCOUNTING CHANGES

One of accountings oldest controversies is how unusual gains or losses, the effects of an accounting change, and a decision to discontinue part of a company's operations should enter into the determination of periodic net income.

Unusual gains or losses include such diverse events as the sale of a plant, the loss of property due to a hurricane, a one-time payment as a result of successful litigation, and the settlement of a prior year's tax liability for an unexpected higher or lower amount than anticipated. The *discontinuance of a segment* of a business accounting problem arises when, for example, a company sells a division or closes down a segment of its business. *Accounting changes* include decisions to switch from one accounting principle to another, such as a change from accelerated to straight-line depreciation, and revisions of accounting estimates, such as the extension of depreciation lives from 10 to 12 years.

Currently, APB *Opinion No. 30* is the most authoritative guide to the accounting for extraordinary, unusual, or infrequent occurring events and transactions. It also covers the accounting for discontinued operations. APB *Opinion No. 20* is the principal source of accounting authority on accounting changes. In addition, there are a number of other APB *Opinions* and FASB *Statements* that touch on these accounting issues.

TWO POINTS OF VIEW

Despite these various APB and FASB decisions, the controversy over what constitutes net income persists. For a number of years, this controversy has revolved around two dominant concepts of income—

243

the so-called all-inclusive and current operating performance concepts. The all-inclusive supporters claim that the most useful concept of income includes all items affecting the net increase in shareholders' equity, except dividend distributions and capital transactions. The current operating performance advocates place considerable emphasis on the usefulness of an income figure that reflects the earnings from normal operations under the operating conditions of the period. Consequently, this concept excludes from the measurement of current income all items which are not clearly related to operations. Under this approach items excluded from income would be treated as direct adjustments to retained earnings.

Chapter 8 of *ARB No. 43* in its discussion of extraordinary items summarized the major arguments for and against the all-inclusive and current operating performance concepts thus:

Proponents of the *all-inclusive* type of income statement insist that annual income statements taken for the life of an enterprise should, when added together, represent total net income. They emphasize the dangers of possible manipulation of the annual earnings figure if material extraordinary items may be omitted in the determination of income. They also assert that, over a period of years, charges resulting from extraordinary events tend to exceed the credits, and the omission of such items has the effect of indicating a greater earnings performance than the corporation actually has exhibited. They insist that an income statement which includes all income charges or credits arising during the year is simple to prepare, is easy to understand, and is not subject to variations resulting from the different judgments that may be applied in the treatment of individual items. They argue that when judgment is allowed to enter the picture with respect to the inclusion or exclusion of special items, material differences in the treatment of borderline cases develop and that there is a danger that the use of *distortion* as a criterion may be a means of accomplishing the equalization of income. With full disclosure of the nature of any special or extraordinary items, this group believes the user of the financial statements can make his own additions or deductions more effectively than can the management or the independent accountant.

Those who favor the *all-inclusive* income statement largely assume that those supporting the *current operating performance* concept are mainly concerned with establishing a figure of net income for the year which will carry an implication as to future earning capacity. Having made this assumption, they contend that income statements should not be prepared on the *current operating performance* basis because income statements of the past are of only limited help in the forecasting of the earning power of an enterprise. This group also argues that items reflecting the results of unusual or extraordinary events are part of the earnings history of the company, and accordingly should be given weight in any effort to make financial judgments with respect to the company. Since a judgment as to the financial affairs of an enterprise should involve a study of the results of a period of prior years, rather than of a single year, this group believes that the omission of material extraordinary items from annual income statements is undesirable since there would be a greater tendency for those items to be overlooked in such a study.

On the other hand, those who advocate the *current operating performance* type of income statement generally do so because they are mindful of the particular business significance which a substantial number of the users of financial reports attach to the income statement. They point out that, while some users of financial reports are able to analyze a statement and eliminate from it those unusual and extraordinary items that tend to distort it for their purposes, many users are not trained to do so. Furthermore, they contend, it is difficult at best to report in any financial statement sufficient data to afford a sound basis upon which the reader who does not have an intimate knowledge of the facts can make a well-considered classification. They consider it self-evident that management and the independent auditors are in a better position than outsiders to determine whether there are usual and extrordinary items which, if included in the determination of net income, may give rise to misleading inferences as to current operating performance. Relying on the proper exercise of professional judgment, they discount the contention that neither managements nor the independent auditors, because of the absence of objective standards to guide them, have been able to decide consistently which extraordinary charges and credits should be excluded in determining earning performance. They agree it is hazardous to place too great a reliance on the net income as shown in a single annual statement and insist that a realistic presentation of current performance must be taken for what it is and should not be construed as conveying an implication as to future accomplishments. The net income of a single year is only one of scores of factors involved in analyzing the future earnings prospects or potentialities of a business. It is well recognized that future earnings are dependent to a large extent upon such factors as market trends, product developments, political events, labor relationships, and numerous other factors not ascertainable from the financial statements. However, this group insists that the net income for the year should show as clearly as possible what happened in that year under that year's conditions, in order that sound comparisons may be made with prior years and with the performance of other companies.

The advocates of this *current operating performance* type of statement join fully with the so-called *all-inclusive* group in asserting that there should be full disclosure of all material charges or credits of an unusual character, including those attributable to a prior year, but they insist that disclosure should be made in such manner as not to distort the figure which represents what the company was able to earn from its usual or typical business operations under the conditions existing during the year. They point out that many companies, in order to give more useful information concerning their earning performance, make a practice of restating the earnings of a number of prior years after adjusting them to reflect the proper allocation of items not related to the years in which they were first reported. They believe that material extraordinary charges or credits may often best be disclosed as direct adjustments of surplus. They point out that a charge or credit in a material amount representing an unusual item not likely to recur, if included in the computation of annual net income, may be so distorting in its results as to lead to unsound judgments with respect to the current earning performance of the company.

The controversy between these two points of view of income has acquired added significance in recent years as *(a)* the income statement emerged as the most popular statement of investors and *(b)* greater emphasis was placed on earnings per share as the most important statistic in the income statement. During this period of greater interest in earnings per share the concept of net income has shifted from an initial interest in income as a measure of management performance to a concern over the usefulness of current earnings figures and disclosures as a indicator of future earnings per share. As a result, statement users have become very interested in that portion of current earnings that relate to the ongoing, continuing operations of the company that will generate future earnings. This predictive use of current earnings has added a new dimension to the all-inclusive, current operating performance controversy.

To date, the FASB, SEC, and APB recommendations primarily reflect the all-inclusive point of view. The current operating performance concept has also been accepted in part, since the recommendations of these three bodies have provided for an identification of the nonrecurring and unusual items in the income statement.

EXTRAORDINARY ITEMS, UNUSUAL EVENTS, AND PRIOR PERIOD ADJUSTMENTS

APB *Opinion No. 30*[1] concluded that all items of profit and loss should be included in the determination of net income, with the exception of items which are essentially adjustments to the results reported in prior periods. In addition, the APB recommended extraordinary items, net of their related tax effect, should be segregated from the operating-related results in the income statement.

Opinion No. 30 adopted the point of view that an event or transaction should be presumed to be a usual and ordinary activity or event of the reporting entity, unless the evidence clearly justifies its classification as an extraordinary item. *Opinion No. 30* defines an extraordinary

---

[1] APB *Opinion No. 30* is the most authoritative guide to the accounting for extraordinary and unusual nonextraordinary events and transactions. However, since this *Opinion* was effective only from October 1973 and statement users often refer back to corporate reports of earlier periods, it is important that the statement user understand that the accounting for extraordinary items prior to this date was covered by APB *Opinion No. 9*. *Opinion No. 30* introduced radical changes in the accounting for these items. Accordingly, if the need arises to refer to financial statements prior to 1973, the now defunct *Opinion No. 9* should be read.

item as an event or transaction that is *both* unusual and infrequent. *Opinion No. 30* defines these qualities as follows:

(a) Unusual nature—the underlying event or transaction should possess a high degree of abnormality and be of a type clearly unrelated to, or only incidentally related to, the ordinary and typical activities of the entity, taking into account the environment in which the entity operates.

(b) Infrequency of occurrence—the underlying event or transaction should be of a type that would not reasonably be expected to recur in the foreseeable future, taking into account the environment in which the entity operates.

Since the environment in which the reporting company operates must be taken into account, judgment is required to determine whether or not an item is extraordinary. For example, an event or transaction may be unusual in nature for one entity but not for another because of differences in their respective industries, locations, or extent of government regulation. Similarly, because of different probabilities of occurrence arising out of differences in their environment, a specific transaction of one company may not meet the *Opinion*'s definition of infrequency of occurrence whereas a similar transaction of another company might. The fact that an unusual or infrequent event is beyond the control of management or significant financially does not automatically make it extraordinary.

The APB anticipated that extraordinary items would be rare. Gains or losses directly resulting from a major casualty or an expropriation are examples of extraordinary items cited in the *Opinion*.[2]

The *Opinion* specifically noted that the following gains and losses should *not* be reported as extraordinary items because they are usual in nature and may be expected to recur as a consequence of customary continuing business activities:

a. Write-down or write-off of receivables, inventories, equipment leased to others, deferred costs, or other intangible assets.

b. Gains or losses from exchange or translation of foreign currencies, including those relating to major devaluations and revaluations.

c. Gains or losses on disposal of a segment of a business.

d. Other gains or losses from sale or abandonment of property, plant, or equipment used in the business.

e. Effects of a strike, including those against competitors and major suppliers.

f. Adjustment of accruals on long-term contracts.

---

[2] Any portion of the losses from such events which would have resulted from a proper valuation of assets on a going-concern basis should be excluded from the extraordinary item.

Extraordinary items and prior year adjustments are reported in comparative statements, as shown in Illustration 10–1. It is important to note in Illustration 10–1 that *(a)* the earnings-per-share calculation is made for both the "income before extraordinary items" and "net income" amounts; *(b)* the earnings-per-share data are shown on the face of the income statement; and *(c)* the earnings-per-share amount for the extraordinary items and prior period adjustments are disclosed.

ILLUSTRATION 10–1

Illustrative Comparative Statement Presentation*
(amounts, except per-share figures, in thousands)

	1975	1974
Income before extraordinary items......................	$10,130	$ 7,990
Extraordinary items, net of applicable income tax of $1,880,000, in 1975 (Note 1)	(2,040)	(1,280)
Net income	$ 8,090	$ 6,710
Retained earnings at beginning of year:		
As previously reported...............................	$28,840	$25,110
Adjustments (Note 2)	(3,160)	(1,760)
As restated...	$25,680	$23,350
	$33,770	$30,060
Cash dividends on common stock, $0.75 per share	4,380	4,380
Retained Earnings at End of Year	$29,390	$25,680
Per share of common stock:		
Income from ordinary operations	$1.73	$1.37
Extraordinary items, net of tax	(0.34)	(0.22)
Net Income	$1.39	$1.15

Note 1. During 1975 one of the company's plants was destroyed by an earthquake at a net loss of $2,040,000 ($0.35 per share), after applicable income tax reduction of $1,880,000 ($0.32 per share). During 1974, one of the Company's South American plants was expropriated at a loss of $1,280,000 ($0.22 per share), with no income tax effect.

Note 2. The balance of retained earnings at December 31, 1974, has been restated from amounts previously reported to reflect a retroactive charge of $3,160,000 for additional income taxes settled in 1975. Of this amount, $1,400,000 ($0.24 per share) is applicable to 1974 and has been reflected as an increase in tax expense for that year, the balance (applicable to years prior to 1974) being charged to retained earnings at January 1, 1974.

* If there are no extraordinary items, then the caption "income before extraordinary items" becomes "net income."

In the case of, say, five-year summaries, the comparative income statement should disclose the data shown in Illustration 10–2.

Immaterial extraordinary items may be included in the income before extraordinary items category. *Opinion No. 30* discussed materiality as it related to extraordinary items as follows:

The effect of an extraordinary event or transaction should be classified separately in the income statement if it is material in relation to income before extraordinary items or to the trend of annual earnings before extraordinary

ILLUSTRATION 10–2

Illustrative Five-Year Historical Summary (000 omitted)

	1971	1972	1973	1974	1975
Income before extraordinary items	$7,340	$7,400	$7,480	$7,990	$10,130
Extraordinary items, net of applicable income tax (Note A)......	—	380	—	(1,280)	(2,040)
Net Income (Note B)	$7,340	$7,780	$7,480	$6,710	$ 8,090
Per share of common stock:					
Income before extraordinary items	$1.26	$1.27	$1.28	$ 1.37	$ 1.73
Extraordinary items, net of income tax.........................	—	$0.06	—	$(0.22)	$(0.34)
Net Income...........................	$1.26	$1.33	$1.28	$ 1.15	$ 1.39

Note A. The extraordinary items consist of the following: 1972 gain as a result of condemnation of idle land, less applicable income tax of $127,000; 1974, loss on expropriation of South American plant, with no income tax effect; 1975, loss on earthquake damage, less applicable income tax deduction of 1,880,000.*

Note B. The amounts of net income for 1971, 1972, and 1974 have been restated from amounts previously reported to reflect additional income taxes for such years settled in 1975. These retroactive adjustments reduced net income for such years by $860 ($0.15 per share), $900 ($0.15 per share), and $1,400 ($0.24 per share), respectively, as follows:

	1971	1972	1974
Previously reported	$8,200	$8,680	$8,110
Adjustments	860	900	1,400
As adjusted...............................	$7,340	$7,780	$6,710

* The 1972 extraordinary items was typical of the kind of item considered to be an extraordinary item prior to the adoption of *Opinion No. 30.* Since *Opinion No. 30* was not retroactive, historical summaries will show items as extraordinary in prior years that are not considered now to fall into that category.

items, or is material by other appropriate criteria. Items should be considered individually and not in the aggregate in determining whether an extraordinary event or transaction is material. However, the effects of a series of related transactions arising from a single specific and identifiable event or plan of action that otherwise meets the two (extraordinary item) criteria should be aggregated to determine materiality.

Unusual Events and Transactions

One of the potential major criticisms of *Opinion No. 30* is that many material transactions or events of an unusual nature or infrequent occurrence, *but not both,* may be included in the determination of income before extraordinary items. In the opinion of some statement users this requirement may obscure the profits from the continuing underlying business operations of the business, which is a figure many believe is very relevant to appraising the future prospects of a company. To counter this criticism, *Opinion No. 30* requires that such transactions or events should be reported as a separate component of income from continuing operations on the face of the statement, or, alternatively, disclosed in the notes to the statement. These items should not be reported net of taxes.

Prior Period Adjustments

The APB believed prior period adjustments were rare in modern business. The opinion defined prior period adjustments as those material adjustments related to transactions or events which occurred in a prior period, the accounting effect of which could not be determined with reasonable assurance at the time, usually because of some major uncertainty then existing. More specifically, the APB recommended originally in *Opinion No. 9* and reconfirmed in *Opinion No. 30* the following criteria for identifying prior period adjustments:

Adjustments related to prior periods—and thus excluded in the determination of net income for the current period—are limited to those material adjustments which *(a)* can be specifically identified with and directly related to the business activities of particular prior periods, and *(b)* are not attributable to economic events occurring subsequent to the date of the financial statements for the prior period, and *(c)* depend primarily on determinations by persons other than management, and *(d)* were not susceptible of reasonable estimation prior to such determination. . . . Evidence of such an uncertainty would be disclosure thereof in the financial statements of the applicable period, or of an intervening period in those cases in which the uncertainty became apparent during a subsequent period. Further, it would be expected that, in most cases, the opinion of the reporting independent auditor on such prior period would have contained a qualification because of the uncertainty. Examples are material, non-recurring adjustments or settlements of income taxes, of renegotiation proceedings, or of utility revenue under rate processes. Settlements of significant amounts resulting from litigation of similar claims may also constitute prior period adjustments.

In June 1976 the SEC in *Staff Accounting Bulletin No. 8* essentially eliminated the prior period adjustment treatment for out-of-court settlements of litigation.

This decision led the FASB to issue a proposed Statement revising *Opinion No. 9* and *No. 30*'s prior period adjustment recommendations. The proposed Statement, if adopted, would with two exceptions, require that all items of profit and loss recognized during a period, including accruals of estimated losses from loss contingencies, be included in the determination of net income of the period. The two prior period adjustments permitted would be corrections of errors in the financial statements of a prior period discovered subsequent to their issuance and adjustments that result from realization of income tax benefits of preacquisition operating loss carry-forwards of purchased subsidiaries.

APB Appraisal

The APB believed its approach to reporting net income had the following advantages and disadvantages:

The principal advantages are: (a) inclusion of all operating items related to the current period, with segregation and disclosure of the extraordinary items; (b) a reporting of current income from operations free from distortions resulting from material items directly related to prior periods; and (c) proper retroactive reflection in comparative financial statements of material adjustments relating directly to prior periods. . . . [The principal disadvantages are] (a) occasional revision of previously reported net income for prior periods to reflect subsequently recorded material items directly related thereto, (b) difficulty in segregating extraordinary items and items related to prior periods and (c) the possibility that disclosures regarding adjustments of opening balances in retained earnings or of net income of prior periods will be overlooked by the reader.

No Solution

Opinion No. 30 is regarded by a number of accounting authorities as not being an appropriate or useful solution to the extraordinary item accounting problem. Some believe the whole idea of trying to label some items as extraordinary and others as ordinary is unworkable and of secondary importance. What is needed these critics claim is a separate identification of abnormal, unusual, or infrequent items. Others believe the extraordinary item criteria was subjective and arbitrary. And, as indicated earlier, some believe the *Opinion* blurs the presentation of operating income. This, it is claimed, will confuse statement readers, particularly as the statement format implies that only ordinary events and transactions are included in income before extraordinary items. Still others feel that an event or transaction takes on the character of being extraordinary if it is a combination of infrequency of occurrence and abnormality of size.

As this debate on the proper way to measure business income continues, one fact becomes clearer every day: namely, the determinations of periodic income will always be an imprecise measure of performance involving human judgment. Also, those who seek to refine its computations, as well as those who rely on net income figures, would be well advised to reflect upon the words of the late Robert Frost: "No figure has ever caught the whole thing."

DISCONTINUANCE OR DISPOSAL OF A BUSINESS SEGMENT

Opinion No. 30 set forth accounting rules for discontinued business operations, whether by sale or abandonment. For the purposes of the *Opinion* a discontinued operation was defined as the operations of a segment of a business that has been sold, abandoned, spun off, or otherwise disposed of or, although still operating, is the subject of a formal plan for disposal. A segment of a business is a component of an entity whose activities represent a separate major line of business or class of customer. A segment may be in the form of a subsidiary, a division, or a department. It may also be a joint venture or nonsubsidiary investee, provided the entities are clearly distinguishable operationally and physically from the investor entity.

Opinion No. 30 concluded that the results of continuing operations should be reported separately from discontinued operations and that any gain or loss from disposal of a segment of a business should be reported in conjunction with the related results of discontinued operations and not as an extraordinary item. Accordingly, operations of a segment that has been or will be discontinued should be reported separately on a net of tax basis as a component of income before extraordinary items and the cumulative effect of accounting changes (if applicable) in the following manner:

Income for continuing operations			
before income taxes	$XXXX		
Provision for income taxes	XXX		
Income from continuing			
operations		$XXXX	
Discontinued operations (Note 6):			
Income (loss) from operations of			
discontinued Division A (less			
applicable income taxes of $XX)	$XXXX		
Loss on disposal of Division A			
including provision of $XX			
for operating losses during phase-			
out period (less applicable income			
taxes of $XX)	XXXX	$XXXX	
		$XXXX	

In addition, the statements of prior periods should be restated to disclose the results of operations of the disposed segment, less applicable income taxes, as a separate component of income before extraordinary items.

The measurement date of the gain or loss from a disposal of a business segment is the date when the management with the authority to approve the action commits itself to a formal plan to dispose of the segment. If a loss is anticipated on the disposal, the anticipated loss should be provided for in the accounting period that includes the measurement date. If a gain is expected, it should be recognized when it is realized, which ordinarily is at the time of disposal. Should the plan of disposal be expected to be carried out over several accounting periods, any estimated income or losses from the projected operations of the segment during these periods should be considered at the measurement date in determining the anticipated gain or loss.

All expected losses from future operations between the measurement and disposal date should be included in the gain or loss computation. If income is projected during this period, it should be included in the computation up to the amount of any projected losses. Income in excess of the projected losses should be recognized when realized. In addition to any projected income or losses from operating the segment, the gain or loss from disposal should include only those costs and expenses subsequent to the measurement date that are directly associated with the decision to dispose of the segment, such as severance pay and employee relocation expenses. Finally, should the estimate of the disposal loss included in the measurement date period later prove faulty, the revised estimates of the loss should be included in the determination of income in the period of the revised estimate.

ACCOUNTING PRINCIPLE, ESTIMATES, AND ENTITY CHANGES

The net income and financial condition of a company may change from one period to another due to accounting changes. This will affect the usefulness of historical data for trend analysis. It may also obscure poor managerial performance. Therefore, users of financial statements must be aware of (1) how changes in accounting are reflected in financial statements and (2) when and how to adjust accounting data to make the presentation comparable from one period to another.

The treatment of accounting changes is determined primarily by *Opinion No. 20*, "Accounting Changes," issued in July 1971. The *Opinion* covers: (1) changes in accounting principles, (2) changes in accounting estimates, and (3) reporting a change in the definition of the entity issuing the financial statements. These are considered to be accounting changes. In addition, the *Opinion* deals with the reporting of a correction of an error in previously issued financial statements. This is not considered to be an accounting change, however.

In general, *Opinion No. 20* requires that:

1. The cumulative effect of an accounting principle change is reported in the period of the change.

2. Changes in accounting estimates are accounted for prospectively.
3. Changes in the reporting entity requires the restatement of all prior period statements presented to conform to the new reporting entity.
4. A correction of an error in a previously issued financial statement is reported as a prior period adjustment.

Opinion No. 20 and several subsequent FASB *Statements* contain exceptions to the general rule for accounting principle changes. These exceptions will be discussed after the review of the general rules.

Changes in Accounting Principles

A change in accounting principle results from the adoption of a generally accepted accounting principle that is different from the one used previously to report a particular kind of transaction. The *Opinion* notes that an accounting principle change includes not only changes in accounting principles and practices but also changes in the method of applying them.

Common examples of an accounting change include: a shift from accelerated to straight-line depreciation and a change from reporting income on an installment basis to the sale method.

A characteristic of each of these changes is that it involves a choice between two or more generally accepted accounting principles.

A change in accounting principle does not occur when:

a. An accounting principle is adopted initially in recognition of events or transactions occurring for the first time or which were previously immaterial.
b. An adoption or modification of an accounting principle is required by a change that is clearly different in the substance of events or transactions from those previously occurring.

Whenever an accounting principle is changed, the statements of the period in which the change is made must include *(a)* the current annual charge or credit for the item according to the new principle as an element of operating income and *(b)* an adjustment to the current period's net income equal to the cumulative effect on the period's beginning retained earnings of applying the new accounting principle retroactively. This cumulative amount, which is the difference between the recomputed amount and the amount originally recorded, is shown after extraordinary items. In addition, pro forma net income figures based upon a retroactive adjustment of the prior periods' statements to reflect the new principle should be included for each period presented in the statements. Thus, the current comparative statement presents both actual and pro forma results.

Reporting the Cumulative Effect.   The cumulative effect of changing to a new accounting principle is shown in the income statement between the captions "extraordinary items" and "net income," but it should not be considered as an extraordinary item. This item is shown net of its related tax effect.

In addition, both the gross amount and the per-share amount of the effect of an accounting principle change must be disclosed. The per-share data on the face of the statement should also include the per-share amount of the cumulative effect of the accounting change.

The data for prior periods included in the comparative statements are not adjusted for the accounting change. It is the same as stated previously in the prior years' annual reports.

Presenting the Pro Forma Effects.   In addition to the current period's actual net income (including the cumulative effect) shown on the face of the statements, income before extraordinary items and net income on a pro forma basis computed as if the newly adopted accounting principle had been applied to all periods presented should be disclosed. These data should be also on a per-share basis.

In addition to the direct effect of the change, the pro forma income figures should include adjustments for any nondiscretionary items that are based on either income before taxes or net income. Such nondiscretionary items may be profit sharing expenses or royalties based on income. In these cases, if the accounting principle change would have resulted in a different income figure than reported previously, automatically these income-based expense items would have been different. Of course, in computing the pro forma data all related tax effects should be recognized.

Disclosure is required of the adjustments made to prior years' income before extraordinary items and net income to determine the pro forma amounts. In addition, if only an income statement for the current period is presented, the actual and pro forma amounts for the current and immediately preceding period should be disclosed.

Which Income Number?   Users of financial statements should base their evaluation of a company on both the net income and pro forma net income figures. Of the two, however, the pro forma figures are usually the better indicator of future earnings, since the current years' net income figure includes the one-time cumulative debit or credit and the prior years' net income was determined using the old accounting method. The footnote related to these presentations should always be examined since it will explain (1) the nature and effect of the accounting principle change and (2) the computation of the pro forma figures. There is no requirement that this footnote disclosure be repeated in subsequent periods.

Accounting Principle Change: An Illustration.   Illustration 10–3 presents the recommended way to report a change in accounting prin-

ILLUSTRATION 10–3

Reporting an Accounting Principle Change

	1971	1970
Income before extraordinary item and cumulative effect of a change in accounting principle	$1,200,000	$1,100,000
Extraordinary item (description)	(35,000)	100,000
Cumulative effect on prior years (to December 31, 1970) of changing to a different depreciation method (Note A)	125,000	
Net Income	$1,290,000	$1,200,000

Per share amounts—		
Earnings per common share—assuming no dilution:		
Income before extraordinary item and cumulative effect of a change in accounting principle	$1.20	$1.10
Extraordinary item.............................	(0.04)	0.10
Cumulative effect on prior years (to December 31, 1970) of changing to a different depreciation method	0.13	
Net income	$1.29	$1.20
Earnings per common share—assuming full dilution:		
Income before extraordinary item and cumulative effect of a change in accounting principle	$1.11	$1.02
Extraordinary item.............................	(0.03)	0.09
Cumulative effect on prior years (to December 31, 1970) of changing to a different depreciation method	0.11	
Net income	$1.19	$1.11

Pro forma amounts assuming the new depreciation method is applied retroactively—		
Income before extraordinary item	$1,200,000	$1,113,500
Earnings per common share—assuming no dilution	$1.20	$1.11
Earnings per common share—assuming full dilution	$1.11	$1.04
Net income	$1,165,000	$1,213,500
Earnings per common share—assuming no dilution	$1.17	$1.21
Earnings per common share—assuming full dilution	$1.08	$1.13

(See accompanying note to the financial statements)

Note A: Change in Depreciation Method for Plant Equipment. Depreciation of plant equipment has been computed by the straight line method in 1971. Depreciation of plant equipment in prior years, beginning in 1954, was computed by the sum-of-the-years'-digits method. The new method of depreciation was adopted to recognize . . . (state justification for change of depreciation method) . . . and has been applied retroactively to equipment acquisitions of prior years. The effect of the change in 1971 was to increase income before extraordinary item by approximately $10,000 (or one cent per share). The adjustment of $125,000 (after reduction for income taxes of $125,000) to apply retroactively the new method is included in income of 1971. The pro forma amounts shown on the income statement have been adjusted for the effect of retroactive application on depreciation, the change in provisions for incentive compensation which would have been made had the new method been in effect, and related income taxes.

ciples in a two-year comparative statement. If statements for more than two years are presented, the same format is used.

The situation assumed in Illustration 10–3 is: The ABC Company decided in 1971 to adopt the straight-line method of depreciation for plant equipment. The straight-line method will be used for new acquisitions as well as for previously acquired plant equipment for which depreciation has been provided on the accelerated method.

This illustration further assumes that the direct effects are limited to the effect on depreciation and related income tax provisions and that the direct effect on inventories is not material. The pro forma amounts have been adjusted for the hypothetical effects of the change in the provisions for incentive compensation. The per share amounts are computed assuming that 1,000,000 shares of common stock are issued and outstanding, that 100,000 additional shares would be issued if all outstanding bonds (which are not common stock equivalents) are converted, and that the annual interest expense, less taxes, for the convertible bonds is $25,000. Other data assumed for this illustration are—

Year	Excess of Accelerated Depreciation Over Straight-Line Depreciation	Effects of Change	
		Direct, Less Tax Effect	Pro Forma (after adjustment for incentive compensation)
Prior to 1967	$ 20,000	$ 10,000	$ 9,000
1967	80,000	40,000	36,000
1968	70,000	35,000	31,500
1969	50,000	25,000	22,500
1970	30,000	15,000	13,500
Total at beginning of 1971	$250,000	$125,000	$112,500

Amortization Method Changes. Long-lived assets are charged to income through a process which, depending on the type of asset involved, is called depreciation, depletion, or amortization (all of which are referred to as amortization in this chapter). Sometimes changes are made in the amortization method for classes of similar identifiable assets. In these cases, if the new method is adopted for all newly acquired assets of a particular class (and the old method is used for the previously recorded assets in that class), there is no need to adjust income figures shown on the face of the statements. That is, no cumulative effect is included and no pro forma data presented. Such data are presented only if the new method of amortization is applied to the previously recorded assets.

When an amortization method change is not applied to previously recorded assets, the nature of the change and its effects on income and related per-share data should be disclosed.

Amounts Not Determinable.   If it is impossible to compute the cumulative effect on beginning retained earnings, the effect of the change on the current period's results should be disclosed. In addition, an explanation should be given for omitting the cumulative effect and the pro forma amounts.

Should the pro forma amounts not be determinable for individual prior periods, the cumulative effect should nevertheless be computed and included as an adjustment to current income: The reason for not showing the pro forma amounts should be explained.

Special Retroactive Restatements.   Restatement of all prior periods presented to reflect the retroactive application of a newly adopted accounting principle is required by *Opinion No. 20* in three special cases. These are:

a.   A change from the Lifo method of inventory pricing to another method.
b.   A change in the method of accounting for long-term construction-type contracts, and
c.   A change to or from the "full cost" method of accounting, which is used in the extractive industries.[3]

The APB gave no reason for these special cases beyond saying:

Certain changes in accounting principles are such that the advantages of retroactive treatment in prior period reports outweigh the disadvantages.

Restatement is achieved by:

a.   Including in each statement for the periods presented an amount based upon the new principle. This replaces the amount determined by the old method in all periods preceding the current period.
b.   Adjusting each period's beginning retained earnings for the cumulative effect of the change up to that point in time.

Subsequently, the FASB added some more special cases to the APB's list of accounting principle changes that must be reported on a retroactive restatement basis. These are situations where a company must change its accounting principles to conform to:

. *Statement No. 2*'s requirement that research and development costs be expensed as incurred.

---

[3] This method writes off the cost of unsuccessful development drilling and exploration activities over the life of all of a company's successful wells. The alternative method is to write off the cost of unsuccessful activities over the life of the successful wells in the same field.

. *Statement No. 5*'s new accounting for contingency rules.
. *Statement No. 8*'s recommended foreign currency translation accounting practices.
. *Statement No. 9*'s requirement that oil and gas producing company's adopt interperiod tax allocation when accounting for intangible drilling and development cost.

The FASB permitted these exceptions to the "cumulative effect" accounting method because it believed that "the prior period adjustment method will provide the most useful information." In several of these special cases added by the FASB the cumulative effect method could be used if it was impractical to restate prior periods. In *Statement No. 9* the FASB also gave companies the option to adopt the new requirement prospectively.

Reporting Accounting Principle Changes in Interim Statements.
If an accounting principle change is made in the first interim period of a fiscal year, the cumulative effect of the change should be included in the first period's statement. In 1974 the FASB presented in *Statement No. 3* an interpretation of APB *Opinion No. 20* which said that cumulative effect-type accounting changes made during the accounting year should be presented as if the change had been made in the first interim period of the year. That is, the current period should not include the cumulative effect. However, the year-to-date figures and first interim period should be restated to include the cumulative effect of the change. All interim periods subsequent to the first period of the fiscal year should be restated to conform to this restatement.

Statement No. 3 also included a special section on the interim reporting of a change to the Lifo method of inventory pricing where the cumulative effect and the pro forma effects of the change could not be determined. If such a change is made in any other than the first interim period of the fiscal year, the pre-change interim periods of that fiscal year should be restated to conform to the new Lifo accounting.

Justification for a Change. Financial reporting presumes that once an accounting principle is selected, it will be applied consistently from one period to another to account for similar events and transactions. This makes statements comparable and enhances their usefulness and understandability.

If an accounting principle change is made, it must be justified on the grounds that the new principle is preferable. The issuance of an AICPA industry audit guide or an APB *Opinion* that creates a new accounting principle, or expresses preference for an accounting principle, is sufficient support for a change in accounting principles. The burden of justifying other changes rests with the entity proposing the change.

The nature, effect on income, and justification for an accounting change should be disclosed in the footnotes to the statements of the period in which the change is made. In addition, similar data related to accounting changes must be filed with the SEC along with a letter from the company's auditor stating that the new principle is preferable to the old one.

Changes in Accounting Estimates

The preparation of financial statements requires estimating the effects of future events, such as the life of a piece of equipment or the amount of future warranty expenses related to current sales. Since the future cannot be predicted accurately, it is desirable that accounting estimates be revised as more experience is acquired or additional information obtained.

Sometimes it is difficult to distinguish between a change in an accounting principle and a change in an accounting estimate. For example, a company may decide all of its deferred plant pre-operating costs should be written off immediately, because it is now considered unlikely that the related plant will become a profitable commercial venture. Thus, the new accounting method is adopted in part because of a change in the estimate of the investments future benefits. The principle and estimate changes are inseparable. Changes of this type are considered to be changes in estimates for the purposes of applying *Opinion No. 20.*

Prospective Treatment.   *Opinion No. 20* requires that the effect of a change in accounting estimate be recorded prospectively in financial statements. That is, the estimate change should be accounted for in *(a)* the period of change if the change affects that period only, or *(b)* the period of change and future periods if the change affects both. The statements of prior periods must not be restated on a direct or pro forma basis to reflect accounting estimate changes.[4]

Disclosure.   The effect on income before extraordinary items, net income, and related share amounts of an estimate change that affects future periods should be disclosed. Unless it's material, disclosure is not necessary of those estimates made each period in the ordinary course of accounting for such items as uncollectible accounts or inventory obsolescence.

Changes in the Entity

A change in the reporting entity occurs when the definition of the reporting entity and the resulting group of companies represented by the current period's statement is different from the entity represented

---

[4] The only exception occurs when the change meets all of the conditions for a prior period adjustment.

by the immediately prior period's statements. This situation results from (a) presenting consolidated or combined statements in place of individual company statements and (b) changing the specific subsidiaries comprising the group of companies for which consolidated or combined financial statements are presented.

Changes in the reporting entity should be reported by restating the financial statements of all prior periods presented in order to show the financial information for the new reporting entity for all periods.

Chapter 18 describes the accounting for a change in the method of reporting investments in subsidiaries and a change in the reporting entity due to a business combination.

Disclosure. The nature, the effect on income figures and related share amounts, and the reasons for a change in the reporting entity should be disclosed for all periods presented. Subsequent statements need not repeat this disclosure.

CORRECTION OF AN ERROR

Errors in financial statements result from mathematical mistakes, mistakes in the application of an accounting principle, or oversight or misuse of facts that existed at the time the statements were prepared. (In contrast, a change in estimate results from new information or subsequent developments which proved better insight or improved judgment.) A change to generally accepted accounting principle from one that is not generally accepted is considered to be a correction of an error.

An error in the statement of a prior period discovered subsequent to its issue should be reported as a prior period adjustment. That is, the beginning retained earnings of each period presented should be adjusted for the error. If the error relates to any of the income figures presented, these should be adjusted for the related amount of the error.

Disclosure

The nature of the error and its effect on the statements should be disclosed in the period in which the error was discovered and corrected. Future statements need not repeat this disclosure.

Requirements

Materiality is defined for the purposes of *Opinion No. 20* as being any effect of each change, or the combined effect of all changes, that (a) has a material effect on income before extraordinary items and net income or *(b)* the trend of earnings.[5] A change that does not materially affect the current status but is reasonably certain to affect later periods materially, should be disclosed in the period of change.

Historical summaries of financial information, such as the selected five-year balance sheet and income statement items included in annual reports, should be prepared in the same manner as prescribed by the *Opinion* for the primary financial statements and their related pro forma data. In particular, the cumulative effect included in the income of the period of a change should be shown separately along with any net income and related share amounts for that period. It should not be disclosed by a note or parenthetical notation.

Accounting changes made in anticipation of an *initial public distribution of stock* are exempt from the requirements of *Opinion No. 20*. Typically, closely held private companies follow accounting practices which they would not use if they were publicly held. Since it is anticipated these old practices will not be followed once the initial public distribution is made, the APB believes it would be more useful to investors if such companies adopted retroactively their new accounting principles and estimates in connection with their initial public stock offering.

This exemption is available only once. It is also available only when a company first issues its financial statements for any one of the following purposes: *(a)* obtaining additional equity capital from investors, *(b)* affecting a business combination, or *(c)* registering securities.

When a company uses this exemption, full disclosure of the nature of the changes and their justification is required.

The provisions of *Opinion No. 20* are effective for fiscal years beginning after July 31, 1971. Care must be exercised when examining 1970 and 1971 trend data for companies with 1971 fiscal years beginning prior to this effective date. Some companies made accounting changes in anticipation of the *Opinion* which were not reported according to the *Opinion*'s recommendations.

Different Viewpoints

The proper reporting of accounting changes was a very difficult issue for the APB to resolve. The principal differing viewpoints they considered were:

a.   The same accounting principle should be used for the current and past periods. The use of different principles in different periods

---

[5] This latter basis for determining materiality is a shift from past practices. It conforms closer to the security analyst's interest in statements. Analysts focus on both net income *and* the change in income from one period to another. Items that are immaterial relative to total income may be very relevant when compared to the amount of the change in income from the prior period.

may result in misinterpretation of earnings trends and other analytical data that are based on comparisons. Accordingly, restatement of prior period data should be required.

b.   The financial statements of prior periods were prepared under the conditions prevailing at the time. To restate these statements might suggest either (1) the conditions were different, which they were not, or (2) the accountant made a mistake, which he did not. Therefore, restating the financial results of prior periods may dilute the public confidence in corporate reports and confuse the users of these statements.

c.   It is sometimes impossible or very difficult to restate past statements since adequate information may not be available. This can occur when a company shifts from a completed contract method to a percentage of completion method. Consequently, restatement as a general requirement may not be feasible in all cases.

d.   Restatement may be required in some cases because the assumptions made about the data might be erroneous if restatement was not required. For example, if a company switched from the Lifo method to the Fifo method, without restatement, the statement user might assume the ending Lifo inventory of the prior period was the beginning inventory of the current Fifo inventory. To avoid this kind of problem, restatement of earlier periods is required in some cases.

e.   Unless the cumulative effect of the change is charged to current income, an accounting change could result in material revenue and expense amounts never being charged to income.

Six out of eighteen members of the APB dissented to *Opinion No. 20*. Some of the objections voiced by these dissenters included:

a.   The APB in most of its opinions had urged retroactive application of its recommendations. This opinion should have been consistent with these earlier recommendations.

b.   The cumulative effects applicable to earlier periods should not be included in the determination of current income as it is not related to current revenues or events.

c.   Because retroactive restatement is generally prohibited by the *Opinion,* it precludes the adoption of preferable accounting in prior periods and impairs the compatability of statements.

d.   Income and expense items should be included in financial statements once and neither more nor less than once. This can be done only if newly adopted principles are applied prospectively.

e.   The pro forma presentation of past years cannot properly report the results of those years. The operating results themselves have an influence on nonaccounting operating decisions, such as pricing. Therefore, arithmetically reconstructing prior years to reflect accounting principle changes cannot reflect how things might have been given these results.

f. The APB's solution (i.e., cumulative effect, pro forma data, special retroactive restatements, and prospective treatment of estimate changes) is an arbitrary compromise that lacks logical coherence and any supportable rationale. As a result, it will contribute to the confusion of statements users.

In contrast to these views, some believe that the inclusion of the cumulative effect in the current income statement is a clear signal to statement users that an accounting principle change has occurred. They also believe the *Opinion* is consistent with the objective of giving statement users a more realistic perspective regarding the judgments which underlie annual income determination.

SUGGESTED FURTHER READING

GOODMAN, HORTENSE, and RAE, THOMAS W.   *Illustrations of Reporting Accounting Changes.* New York: American Institute of Certified Public Accountants, 1974.

————, and LORENSEN, LEONARD.   *Illustrations of Reporting the Results of Operations.* New York: American Institute of Certified Public Accountants, 1974.

CASES

CASE 10–1. DEERFIELD EQUIPMENT COMPANY
Reporting the Results of Operations

In July 1971 the president of Deerfield Equipment Company, Walter B. Conant, opened the Executive Committee meeting of the company, with this statement:

As you all know, when I took the president's post last December the company was faced with severe problems in managing the results of the aggressive acquisition policy which had been followed for the previous five years. We had 26 different operating companies, primarily manufacturers, whose products ranged from portable generators to car wash equipment. These plants were located in 40 different cities, 3 of them outside the United States.

I hope you all remember the internal memorandum which I addressed to the key executives of this company shortly after my election, in which I defined the direction which this management should pursue:

Our objectives for the short term will be to build a solid foundation from which to thrust forward. We will be defining the mainstream of Deerfield and disengage from peripheral and marginal businesses in which we do not have a meaningful marketing or technological position, or which will tend to dilute management and financial resources disproportionately.

Our acquisitions will be internally growth motivated—stimulated by desires to strengthen management, marketing, or engineering capability.

Our objectives will be to—

1. Structure a management organization and participate in the dynamics of planning and control.
2. Put the primary emphasis on stimulating internal growth opportunities by supporting and encouraging that which makes sense, and remedying that which is weak or inadequate.

Following these guidelines, we have redefined the company's operations and have established seven "building blocks" which constitute the future of Deerfield Equipment. Our objective was to identify markets with meaningful growth potential where we can establish a position of uniqueness, outstanding capability, and leadership.

This restructuring of our business is shown in the analysis of sales by product lines:

FY1971 Sales Volume by Product Line

	Sales (millions of dollars)	Percent of Total Deerfield Sales
Diagnostic and Service Equipment (including car-wash systems)	19.3	18
Vehicular Heat Transfer Products	15.8	14
Automotive Accessories	25.7	23
Truck Cabs and Van Interiors	13.7	12
Automation and Material Handling	15.3	14
Mobile Communications	7.5	7
Other Products	13.2	12
	110.5	100

In those areas in which we intend to concentrate our activities, we have increased our commitment.

Further, in the definition of future directions for Deerfield, we concluded that a number of peripheral businesses not in the mainstream of Deerfield's future should be divested. This judgment led to the sale of the Zeus Portable Generator business, the proposed sale of the majority interest in the Flo-Tork Division of Crown, the closing of the steel frame plant in Drew, Mississippi, the phasing out of a prefabricated building business, and the consolidation and integration of a small electronics division, California Systems Components, into our Testproducts Division. We are currently in active negotiation for the sale of two other businesses.

To support the commitment to revised company goals, we arranged a long-term financing through a private placement. In addition, we organized Orion Industries by transferring to it the net assets, business, and stock of certain divisions and subsidiaries. In March we sold a 17 percent ownership in Orion in a public offering. Of course the gain on the sale will be included in the fiscal year ending June 30, 1971, income as an extraordinary item. As a result at year-end, the company had over $7 million in cash and marketable securities, an approximately 3 to 1 current ratio, a working capital position of $32.8 million, and no significant short-term bank debt.

It is my firm conviction that the constructive changes which were effected during FY 1971 will result in a significant improvement in the profitability of the company. I believe we can look forward to rapid improvement during FY 1972 and steady growth in the years beyond. However, in the near term we have a problem in communicating these substantial gains to our stockholders.

In FY 1971 we made only two changes in accounting policy.

We changed our Conveyor Engineering and Wilson Engineering divisions from a completed contract basis to a percentage of completion basis. Since the equipment manufactured by these companies typically requires very long production cycles, the completed contract method can result in distortions of earnings from period to period. The percentage of completion method will record income in proportion to work performed and will allow more meaningful management controls. This change reduces FY 1971 profits by $9,000, which is not a material amount.

We also changed our accounting policies relating to research and development costs. This change was made at the time of our six-month report. It is my belief that R&D costs, rather than being capitalized, should be charged against operations as incurred. This latter method of accounting is more conservative and more appropriate to a company of Deerfield's size. It is the method I have always followed in companies with which I have been associated.

As you know, my current thinking is that when such an accounting change is made, it should be given retroactive effect so as to maintain comparability of current results with those of prior years. Our interim reports in FY 1971 with the concurrence of our auditors, and the American Stock Exchange, reflected this treatment. However, representatives of the Securities and Exchange Commission have informed us that they believe that the previously deferred research and development costs should be written off as a one-time charge against current earnings. This would result in a net loss of $0.28 per share in 1971, compared with earnings of $0.75 per share, if the research and development were given retroactive treatment.

Each of the members of the Executive Committee has before him a summary of the Deerfield company's 1071 and 1970 financial statements, as prepared with our auditors, which treats the change in research and development cost retroactively (Exhibit 1). In addition, you have income statements for these two years using the method which the SEC may require (Exhibit 2).

Now, the whole issue has become more complicated. This month the APB has issued *Opinion No. 20*. It is effective for fiscal years beginning after July 31, 1971. However, the APB encourages application of this *Opinion* in reporting fiscal years beginning before August 1, 1971, but not yet reported in financial statements issued for the year of change.

Clearly, during fiscal 1971 as I made my various decisions I knew that the APB was contemplating issuing this *Opinion*. However, since I did not know what its recommendations would be, I did not let the accounting proposed in the exposure draft influence my decisions. I did what I thought was best for the company.

I hope we can resolve our 1971 reporting problems at this meeting as I would like to publish our statements as soon as possible.

Questions

1. How should Deerfield Equipment account in fiscal year 1971 for the accounting changes, unusual items, and discontinued businesses discussed by Mr. Conant?
2. What 1971 profit figure would be the most useful to someone interested in using the 1971 statements as a basis for predicting the company's 1972 net income? For example, would it be the net income number, the income before extraordinary items, or some other figure?

EXHIBIT 1

DEERFIELD EQUIPMENT COMPANY

Consolidated Statements of Income as Developed by the Company
For the Years Ended June 30, 1971, and 1970
(amounts in thousands)

	1971		1970	
	Amount	Per Share	Amount	Per Share
Net sales	$110,542		$100,373	
Cost of sales	81,446		73,328	
Gross profit	$ 29,096		$ 27,045	
Operating expenses	21,940		20,043	
Income from operations (before write-offs below)	$ 7,156		$ 7,002	
Other deductions principally interest—net	1,244		648	
	$ 5,912		$ 6,354	
Provision for taxes on income:				
Currently payable	$ 3,026		$ 1,854	
Deferred	—		1,378	
	$ 3,026		$ 3,232	
Income before charges below	$ 2,886	$1.15	$ 3,122	$1.36
Minority interest	55	0.03	—	—
Write-offs related to operational charges—net of tax effect (Note 1)	715	0.28	—	—
Income before extraordinary charges—net	$ 2,116	0.84	$ 3,122	1.36
Extraordinary charges—net (Note 2)	215	0.09	—	—
Net Income (loss)	$ 1,901	$0.75	$ 3,122	$1.36

Depreciation (straight-line method) amounted to $1,919,000 in 1971 and $1,703,000 in 1970.

EXHIBIT 1 *(continued)*

DEERFIELD EQUIPMENT COMPANY
Consolidated Balance Sheets as Developed by the Company
June 30, 1971, and 1970
(amounts in thousands)

Assets

	1971	1970
Current Assets:		
Cash and short-term investments	$ 7,135	$ 4,624
Accounts receivable, less allowance for doubtful accounts—		
1971, $562,000; 1970, $460,000	17,177	16,839
Inventories, at lower of cost (principally first-in, first-out)		
or market	25,067	20,939
Prepaid expenses	721	531
Total Current Assets	$50,100	$42,933
Property, plant, and equipment, at cost:		
Land and land improvements	1,754	1,685
Buildings	5,504	4,291
Machinery and equipment	16,282	14,824
Leasehold improvements	1,193	880
	$24,733	$21,680
Less: Accumulated depreciation and amortization	8,322	7,350
	$16,411	$14,330
Excess of purchase price over carrying value of		
assets acquired	6,739	6,586
Other assets and deferred charges (Note 4)	4,435	1,927
Deferred research and development costs (Note 5)	—	—
	$77,685	$65,776

EXHIBIT 1 *(continued)*

DEERFIELD EQUIPMENT COMPANY

Consolidated Balance Sheet as Developed by the Company

Liabilities and Shareholders' Equity	1971	1970
Current Liabilities:		
Notes payable, including current maturities of long-term debt	$ 2,217	$ 1,808
Accounts payable and accrued liabilities	14,703	9,588
Income taxes	341	1,541
Total Current Liabilities	$17,261	$12,937
Deferred federal income taxes	457	500
Long-term debt, less current maturities	20,021	18,011
Minority interest	1,459	—
Shareholders' Equity:		
$1 cumulative convertible preferred stock, series A, no-par value; authorized, 365,990 shares; issued and outstanding, 213,229 shares	135	135
Common stock, par value $1; authorized, 10,000,000 shares; issued and outstanding—1971, 2,258,505 shares; 1970, 2,087,746 shares	2,259	2,088
Additional paid-in capital	22,344	18,649
Retained earnings	13,749	13,456
	$38,487	$34,328
	$77,685	$65,776

EXHIBIT 1 *(continued)*

DEERFIELD EQUIPMENT COMPANY

Selected Notes to the Financial Statements

Principles of Consolidation

The consolidated financial statements include the accounts of the company, all wholly owned subsidiaries and an 81 percent owned subsidiary (Orion Industries, Inc.). The investment in a 60 percent owned subsidiary (not significant) is carried at equity in net assets. Foreign currencies (Canadian) have been converted into U.S. dollars at appropriate exchange rates.

In January 1971 the company organized Orion Industries, Inc., to which it transferred the net assets, business, and stock of certain divisions and subsidiaries. In March 1971 the company sold 17 percent of its ownership in Orion pursuant to a public offering. The resultant gain on the sale has been included in 1971 income as an extraordinary item.

Note 1—Operational Change Write-offs

Major changes in the company's management took place in fiscal year 1971. Redirection of marketing efforts and other operating policies resulted, among other things, in write-offs, principally of inventory and receivable items, of $715,000, net of $800,000 income tax effect. Since it is not anticipated that similar type write-offs will be made in the future, separate disclosure is made in order not to distort comparability with future periods.

Note 2—Extraordinary Charges

Extraordinary charges—net to 1971 income consist of the following:

Provision for estimated costs to be incurred upon disposition of marginal operations	$ 1,000,000
Losses on sale or abandonment of certain plant facilities and product lines	1,802,000
Terminated employment contracts	290,000
Gain on sale of partial interest in subsidiary	(1,607,000)
	$ 1,485,000
Less income tax effect	1,270,000
	$ 215,000

Note 3—Accounting Change: Percentage of Completion

Effective July 1, 1970, for financial reporting purposes, the company changed from the completed contract method to the percentage of completion method of accounting for long-term contracts. The 1970 consolidated financial statements have been retroactively restated to reflect current practice, resulting in a decrease in 1970 net income of approximately $150,000. Had the Company used the completed contract method for 1971, the net income for the year would have been increased by approximately $9,000.

Note 4—Other Assets and Deferred Charges

At June 30, 1971, other assets and deferred charges consisted of the following:

Unamortized discount applicable to sales of restricted stock	$ 932,000
Unamortized debt expense	1,272,000
Other deferred charges	882,000
Miscellaneous assets	1,349,000
	$4,435,000

During 1971 the company sold 34,500 shares of its common stock to certain executives for $34,500, representing the aggregate par value thereof. The shares are subject to various restrictions which limit disposition to a partial number of the shares each year for a period of years. The excess of fair market value of the shares issued over the purchase price is being amortized by charges to operations over the earn-out periods. Unamortized debt expense is being amortized by charges to operations over the life of the related debt.

Note 5—Accounting Change: Research and Development Costs

The company has followed the practice of deferring research and development costs, amortizing such costs over varying periods based upon sales of related products. Effective July 1, 1970, the company adopted the policy of expensing all research and development costs as incurred. In connection therewith, the unamortized balance of deferred research and development expense at June 30, 1970, $2,595,000, net of related deferred federal income taxes of $2,818,000 has been charged retroactively to 1970 and prior years.

EXHIBIT 1 *(concluded)*

DEERFIELD EQUIPMENT COMPANY
Five-Year Summary—As Developed by the Company
Five Years Ended June 30
(as adjusted for poolings of interest)
(amounts in thousands)

	1971	*1970*	*1969*	*1968*	*1967*
Operating Results:					
Net sales	$110,542	$100,373	$82,665	$55,477	$48,836
Pretax income before operational change write-offs and extraordinary charges	5,912	6,354	4,375	3,253	2,949
Income before operational change write-offs and extraordinary charges	2,886	3,122	2,656	1,670	1,611
Income before extraordinary charges	2,116	3,122	2,656	1,670	1,611
Net income	1,901	3,122	2,656	1,549	1,611
Per Share:					
Income before operational change write-offs and extraordinary charges	$1.15	$1.36	$1.22	$1.08	$1.13
Income before extraordinary charges	0.84	1.36	1.22	1.08	1.13
Net income	0.75	1.36	1.22	1.00	1.13
Year-End Financial Position:					
Working capital	$ 32,839	$ 29,996	$25,907	$14,575	$ 9,179
Shareholders' equity	38,487	34,328	28,360	15,575	11,919

EXHIBIT 2

DEERFIELD EQUIPMENT COMPANY

Consolidated Statements of Income—Recommended by the SEC
For the Years Ended June 30, 1971, and 1970
(amounts in thousands)

	1971		1970 (restated)	
	Amount	Per Share	Amount	Per Share
Net sales	$110,542		$100,373	
Cost of sales	81,446		73,328	
Gross profit...........................	$ 29,096		$ 27,045	
Operating expenses	21,940		17,714	
Income from operations (before write-offs below)	$ 7,156		$ 9,331	
Other deductions, principally interest—net	1,244		648	
	$ 5,912		$ 8,683	
Provision for taxes on income: Currently payable	$ 3,026		$ 1,854	
Deferred	—		2,477	
	$ 3,026		$ 4,331	
Income before charges below	$ 2,886	$ 1.15	4,352	$1.90
Minority interest	55	0.03	—	—
Write-offs related to operational charges—net of tax effect	715	0.28	—	—
Income before extraordinary charges—net	$ 2,116	0.84	$ 4,352	$1.00
Extraordinary charges—net	2,810	1.12	—	—
Net Income (loss)	$ (694)	$(0.28)	$ 4,352	$1.90

Depreciation (straight-line method) amounted to $1,919,000 in 1971 and $1,703,000 in 1970.

EXHIBIT 2 *(continued)*

DEERFIELD EQUIPMENT COMPANY

Five-Year Summary—Recommended by the SEC

	1971	*1970*	*1969*	*1968*	*1967*
Operating Results:					
Net sales	$110,542	$100,373	$82,665	$55,477	$48,836
Pretax income before operational change write-offs and extraordinary charges	5,912	8,683	6,563	4,186	3,191
Income before operational charges write-offs and extraordinary charges	2,886	4,352	3,637	2,262	1,207
Income before extraordinary charges	2,116	4,352	3,637	2,262	1,207
Net income (loss)	(694)	4,352	3,637	2,141	1,207
Per Share:					
Income before operational change write-offs and extraordinary charges	$1.15	$1.90	$1.68	$1.47	$1.28
Income before extraordinary charges	0.84	1.90	1.68	1.47	1.28
Net income (loss)	(0.28)	1.90	1.68	1.39	1.28
Year-End Financial Position:					
Working capital	$ 32,839	$ 29,996	$25,907	$14,575	$ 9,179
Shareholders' equity	38,487	36,923	29,301	16,035	12,046

CASE 10–2. QUALITY PRODUCTS, INCORPORATED
Accounting for Discontinued Operations and Unusual and Infrequent Events

In April 1975, David Strange, president, Quality Products, Inc. (QPI), said: "We believe it is clearly in the best interests of stockholders to discontinue QPI's feed business, to sell the assets of the Feed Division, and release capital funds for operations that offer greater opportunities for profit and growth." In late May the company's audit committee met to review the accounting issues facing the QPI top management as a result of the decision to discontinue the Feed Division.

In addition, the audit committee planned to review at this meeting the accounting for several other major events that had occurred during the last quarter of the company's fiscal year. These were: the write-off of a foreign subsidiary's inventories as a result of a new government regulation banning the use of a certain food preservative; the decision of management to extend the depreciation life of some domestic depreciable assets; the out-of-court settlement of a claim against the company; an uninsured loss arising from the destruction by a tornado of a major QPI grain storage facility in Kansas; and the gain on the sale of land acquired in the late 1950s for possible future plant sites.

The Company

In 1975, QPI was a large convenience foods manufacturer with diversified interests in specialty chemicals, electronics, materials testing equipment, and related fields. Sales for the fiscal year ended May 31, 1974, exceeded $575 million and net earnings after taxes were almost $13 million for the same period. (See Exhibits 1 and 2 for

EXHIBIT 1

QUALITY PRODUCTS, INC.
Consolidated Balance Sheet at May 31
(in thousands)

Assets

	1974	1973
Cash	$ 12,541	$ 15,211
Accounts receivable (net)	44,825	42,515
Inventories	69,513	55,879
Total Current Assets	$126,879	$113,605
Sundry costs chargeable to future periods	8,767	7,268
Land, buildings, and equipment (net)	124,780	121,048
Miscellaneous assets	2,816	2,790
Goodwill, patents, trade names, and other intangibles	4,646	3,970
Total Assets	$267,888	$248,681

Liabilities and Equity

	1974	1973
Notes payable	$ 7,250	—
Accounts payable and accrued expenses	29,611	$ 22,597
Accrued taxes	12,833	12,513
Thrift accounts of officers and employees	3,665	3,539
Dividends payable	277	277
Total Current Liabilities	$ 53,636	$ 38,926
Long-term debt	45,444	45,200
Reserves for self-insurance, price declines, and other purposes	4,837	4,959
Total Liabilities	$103,917	$ 89,085
Stockholders' Equity:		
Preferred stock, 5% cumulative	$ 22,147	$ 22,147
Common stock	46,276	45,123
Retained earnings	95,787	92,658
Treasury stock (deduct)	(239)	(332)
Total Stockholders' Equity	$163,971	$159,596
Total Liabilities and Equity	$267,888	$248,681

EXHIBIT 2

QUALITY PRODUCTS, INC.

Consolidated Income Statement for the Fiscal Year Ended May 31
(in thousands)

	1974	1973
Sales of products and services	$575,512	$537,818
Costs:		
Costs of products and services sold, exclusive of items shown below	$431,060	$405,256
Depreciation	8,427	7,681
Interest	2,989	2,502
Contribution to employees' retirement plans	2,779	2,435
Selling, general, and administrative expenses	105,966	97,582
Federal taxes on income	11,459	10,847
Total Costs	$562,680	$526,303
Earnings for the Year	$ 12,832	$ 11,515

financial statements.) The company's operations included more than
50 flour mills, terminal elevators, flour and food packaging plants, and
chemical and electronic installations throughout the United States and
in a number of foreign countries.

QPI was incorporated in 1936 to acquire several grain-handling and
milling firms in the midwest. Numerous acquisitions in related areas
were made in the years following. During its early years, the company
was essentially a holding company; but in 1945, most of the subsidiary
corporations were dissolved and the firm became an operating company. Rapid expansion followed as the company integrated vertically
and developed brand-name consumer goods including breakfast cereals, cake mixes, and similar products based upon its basic milling
activities. Livestock feed products were an integral part of operations
throughout most of the company's history.

Increased competition and declining profit margins for food manufacturers caused QPI to seek more rapid growth by diversification into
chemicals, electronics, oil-seed processing, and for a short time into
small household appliances. Sales increased only modestly in the
1960s and profits moved erratically. QPI found itself competing for
sales in industries that were dominated by large companies and
where, again, margins were very low or even nonexistent. This was the
case for a number of years in the company's Feed Division.

The company also sought to reach wider markets on an international scale. In 1962, productive and marketing facilities were constructed in Canada for several food products. In the early 1960s, acquisitions were made in Central and South America, in Pakistan, and
in Europe. Most of these international ventures were wholly owned

subsidiaries, but a few were joint enterprises with firms in foreign nations. The nature of these foreign operations varied from food product marketing and raw material processing to electronic activities.

The company's 1974 sales volume was distributed among the major segments of the company as follows: consumer foods, $260 million; flour, $161 million; feed, $78 million; specialty products, $28 million; chemicals, $15 million; and electronics, $33 million.

Change in Management and Company Policy

In December 1974, several important changes were made in the QPI top management. David Strange, who had come to the company from a top management position in the food industry, was named president. Several new vice presidents and divisional managers were also announced about this time.

The change in management was followed by a change in corporate policy directed toward improved profitability and growth through concentration in the areas of convenience foods and specialty chemicals. Early in 1975, in response to a stockholder's question, "Where is the company's profit potential?" management published its succinct answer in QPI *News*, a quarterly publication directed to stockholders: "Our combined chemical and electronics business was still less than 10 percent of total sales in the last fiscal year. We expect growth in these areas, but our greatest profit potential is in packaged convenience food products." A large consumer foods research facility was completed, and expenditures for research and development and for advertising were increased markedly. Management believed that development and marketing of new convenience food products would bring the desired higher sales and wider profit margins.

All areas of the company's activities were reorganized to conform to this new policy. For example, several further changes were made in the organization and personnel of the company's Electronic Group, which had been created a year earlier to combine all electronic, mechanical, aerospace, and related operations into a single unit. In line with these changes, management was considering the discontinuance of several of its electronic operations at a later date.

Decision to Liquidate the Feed Division

For several years the entire operation of the Feed Division of QPI had been under study. Management could not see any means of changing operations to make a satisfactory return on investment in the future, despite efforts to build needed volume in the highly competitive, low-margin feed industry through extensive expansion into poultry, broiler, and turkey growing operations. Prices of broilers and turkeys during most of the 1975 fiscal year were below the costs of production. In addition, many direct feed customers, suffering from the same depressed prices, were unable to buy in normal volumes and some could not meet their financial obligations. Increasing bad debt losses from uncollectible receivables added to the company's operating losses in this area.

Feed Division operating losses had been substantial for several prior years, and losses for the fiscal year to end May 31, 1975, were expected to be $5 million before tax credits of $2.3 million.[1] Total company sales and profits were expected to be significantly lower than those reported in the 1974 fiscal year.

The decision to begin liquidation of the Feed Division was made and announced in April 1975. An orderly withdrawal extending over a two- or three-year period was planned. During this period, all plant facilities of the division were to be sold. Operations were to be continued into the 1976 fiscal accounting period, but only to honor existing firm contracts which were to require several months for completion. The 900 or more employees were to be transferred and absorbed into other QPI operations or to be terminated with benefits in line with existing company policies.

Reporting the Feed Division Liquidation to Stockholders

The controller was asked by the audit committee to prepare a projection of the amounts involved in the Feed Division liquidation. This report did not include the 1975 $5 million pretax operating loss of the division. His report was submitted to the QPI audit committee in late May. The controller's projections were made to May 31, 1975, and gave recognition to the operations and partial liquidation transactions that were expected to occur both prior to and after that date. A summary of his detailed report is shown in Exhibit 3.

The analysis pointed out that neither the timing nor the method of reporting the liquidation in the annual report to stockholders would have any effect upon income tax reporting. The estimated total book loss of more than $15 million was significantly reduced by computed tax benefits, to a projected net loss of $4,438,838.

The loss on liquidation was significant in amount in comparison to both net income and financial size.

Over a period of several years, QPI had accumulated "reserves for self-insurance, price declines, and other purposes" by charges to re-

---

[1] The estimated operating losses of the division between the measurement date April 1975 and May 31, 1975, included in this amount were $1 million before a tax credit of nearly $500,000.

EXHIBIT 3

QUALITY PRODUCTS, INC.

Projection of Estimated Costs and Losses Arising from
Feed Division Liquidation as of May 31, 1975

Accounts receivable charged off between measurement date (April 1975) and end of fiscal year	$5,110,461	
Less: Bad debt allowance provided from operations to date	3,644,536	
	$1,465,925	
Estimated future additional uncollectible receivables	570,000	$ 2,035,925
Losses and write-down of land, building, and equipment: Recorded between measurement date and end of fiscal year	$1,465,425	
Estimated additional losses in future dispositions	6,867,608	8,333,033
Costs and expenses related to discontinuance of operations: Incurred between measurement date and end of fiscal year	$2,294,559	
Estimated future liquidation costs, including fiscal year 1976 operation to satisfy existing contracts	2,803,073	5,097,632
Total		$15,466,590
Less income tax credits*		11,027,752
Total after Income Tax Credits		$ 4,438,838

* Income tax credits will be claimed against actual tax liability when expenses are incurred or when properties are sold. Loss carry-over provisions in the tax law will provide full benefit of losses not used currently. Tax credits include benefit of write-off of feed division goodwill not carried on books as an asset. This goodwill resulting from acquisitions of feed companies in earlier years was written off the books, but a deduction for income taxes was not allowable until liquidation of feed operations.

tained earnings. These reserves totaled $4,836,654 on the consolidated balance sheet at May 31, 1974, of which $2,855,786 applied to the Feed Division. This amount would no longer be required after liquidation of the division. The controller's analysis of estimated losses in Exhibit 3 was before possible credits from these reserves.

Other Agenda Items

In addition to the Feed Division liquidation accounting issue, the audit committee had to consider five other accounting items on its agenda.

In early March 1975, after several years of litigation, the French courts upheld a government ban on the use in food products of certain preservatives that were thought to cause cancer. This ruling required the company to destroy all of its existing inventories containing the banned preservatives and recall all of the affected products from the marketplace. The estimated cost of this action was $500,000 after tax credits. It was expected that the recall program would be completed by May 31, 1975. In addition, it was anticipated that in the near future other Common Market governments might follow the lead of the French government. To avoid any possible trouble in these other Common Market countries, QPI had stopped using the banned preservative in all of the other Common Market countries. The estimated after tax cost of reformulation and testing associated with the switch in preservatives was $300,000. The after tax legal and other costs incurred in contesting the governments ban were $500,000 in 1974 and $75,000 in 1975.

During the fourth quarter of fiscal year 1975 the QPI management decided to use a 13-year depreciation life for a certain class of equipment used extensively in the company's food operations. Previously this class of equipment had been depreciated on a ten-year basis. This decision applied only to equipment purchased after March 1, 1975. This decision increased the fourth quarter after tax profits by $200,000 over what they would have been if a ten-year life had been used.

In April 1975, QPI reached an out-of-court settlement with a consumer protection group which had brought a class action against the company on behalf of a number of individuals who claimed a QPI product had been injurious to their health. This action which had been in litigation since 1970, was settled for an aftertax cost of $250,000. Originally, the plaintiffs for the class had sought $100 million in damages. Since the company could not reasonably estimate what their ultimate loss might have been from this claim, no provisions for this possible loss had been made in prior years. In addition, QPI did not have a general litigation loss reserve, since the company believed its industrial and general insurance covered most of the expected types of claims that might be made against the company. This $250,000 settlement was not covered by insurance.

In the fourth quarter of fiscal 1975, an unseasonal and usually severe tornado destroyed the QPI central grain facility in Kansas. The company estimated that its aftertax loss from this catastrophe was $135,000 more than QPI would recover from its facilities insurance claim.

Soon after the new management took over control of the company, it conducted a survey to identify redundant and surplus assets that might be sold to raise funds to finance the company's operations. Among the assets identified as potential candidates for sale were several pieces of industrial land purchased in the early 1950s as possible factory or distribution center sites. After several months of trying, QPI sold two of these sites in May 1975 for an aftertax gain of $750,000.

During the prior three quarters of fiscal year 1975 the company had not reported any extraordinary items, discontinued operations, or accounting changes in its interim financial statements.

Some Considerations

The terms of the sizable long-term promissory note indebtedness of QPI placed a restriction upon the payment of dividends to common stockholders. In general the dividends paid or declared after May 31, 1964, could not exceed 85 percent of consolidated net earnings since that date. At May 31, 1974, $30,411,380 of retained earnings was free of this restriction.

Management was very much aware of its position in the competitive environment in which it operated. Selected information for several firms in the milling and consumer foods industries is shown in Exhibit 4.

EXHIBIT 4

Selected Industry Data*

	Sales†	Net Income after Taxes*	Earnings per Sales Dollar	Earnings per Share	Dividends per Share	Price Range High	Price Range Low
Quality Products:							
1970	$ 527,701	$12,235	2.3%	$1.63	$1.00	$ 23	$19
1977	529,820	14,694	2.8	1.98	1.00	30	20
1972	545,998	16,817	3.1	2.26	1.00	38	30
1973	537,818	11,515	2.1	1.46	1.15	34	24
1974	575,512	12,832	2.2	1.63	1.20	39	31
Processors United:							
1970	$ 331,362	$ 4,006	1.2%	$2.02	$1.25	$ 22	$20
1971	350,610	5,641	1.6	2.90	1.25	37	21
1972	359,657	7,913	2.2	3.70	1.25	50	37
1973	373,818	6,541	1.8	3.03	1.40	47	32
1974	384,962	7,911	2.1	3.62	1.40	77	44
Parker Foods:							
1970	$ 438,261	$14,569	3.3%	$2.28	$0.80	$ 31	$23
1971	493,527	17,468	3.5	2.71	1.00	52	25
1972	530,571	17,784	3.4	2.74	1.20	52	42
1973	527,816	18,915	3.6	2.76	1.20	45	39
1974	581,042	19,908	3.4	3.03	1.35	45	39
National Foods:							
1970	$ 971,334	$42,399	4.4%	$1.81	$1.95	$ 25	$20
1971	1,008,897	48,397	4.8	1.99	2.00	40	24
1972	1,052,964	54,145	5.1	2.21	2.30	54	37
1973	1,087,076	61,071	5.6	2.48	2.60	75	62
1974	1,160,177	66,821	5.8	2.69	2.10	108	69
Consumer Products:							
1970	$1,432,319	$44,058	3.1%	$3.18	$1.80	$ 39	$33
1971	1,451,245	45,544	3.1	3.27	1.80	50	38
1972	1,605,725	49,362	3.1	3.51	1.95	54	46
1973	1,667,176	50,667	3.0	3.59	2.00	66	45
1974	1,790,834	50,211	2.8	3.51	2.00	79	59

* Fiscal year endings for the companies are: Quality Products and Processors United Company, May 31; Parker Foods Company, September 30; National Foods, Inc., March 31; and Consumer Products Corporation, December 31.

† In thousands. All data adjusted for stock splits and dividends.

In mid-April 1975, the market price of QPI's common stock had dropped to $28 after being in the middle 30s in the last few months of 1974. Although sales for the six months ended November 30, 1974, had exceeded those of the corresponding period for the previous year, earnings per share had declined to $0.55 from $0.75 for the same period. At the end of the third quarter of fiscal year 1975 market analysts were anticipating that earnings for the year ending May 31, 1975, would just cover the $1.20 annual dividend and that in the longer run the stock price would recover to the 1974 levels.

Perhaps the most important single factor considered by management in choosing the method of reporting Feed Division liquidation losses was the anticipated effect upon stockholder and prospective investor attitudes toward the company. Throughout its entire history, QPI had maintained an ideal relationship with its stockholders, and the new management would not consider any reporting alternative which stockholders would be likely to interpret as improper or uninformative. Management was aware that the amount of net income reported for the fiscal year ending May 31, 1975, might have an effect upon the market price of the company's common stock. Not only was there a concern to preserve the position of present stockholders, but there was a strong possibility that in the near future additional issues of common might be offered to facilitate further acquisitions for expansion in the area of convenience foods. Management was therefore anxious to avoid any reporting practice which might have a significant, continuing adverse effect upon its relations in the stockholder and financial communities.

Questions

1. How should the liquidation of the Feed Division be reflected in the company's financial statements?
2. How should the company account for the other items on the audit committee's agenda?
3. Assume that the QPI's 1975 profit after taxes before considering the "other agenda items" on the audit committee's agenda will be $9.5 million, prepare the company's 1975 income statement, starting with the line "Income from continuing operations." The $9.5 million includes the estimated 1975 operating losses of the Feed Division, but not the items included in Exhibit 3.
4. How do you think existing and potential investors might react to the 1975 income statement treatment of the items on the audit committee's agenda?

Chapter 11

EARNINGS PER SHARE

Earnings-per-share data are the key financial statistics for most investors. These ratios represent, on a per-share basis, the common stockholder's equity in a company's current profits after considering preferred stock dividends and potential dilution by senior convertible securities, warrants, and options. Typically, this calculation involves some adjustments to the net income figure shown on the income statement. However, it is important to note that these adjustments are made only for the purpose of calculating earnings per share. The net income figure shown on the statements is not affected by these adjustments.

Depending on its capital structure, a company may present two earnings-per-share figures: "primary" and "fully diluted" earnings per share. Furthermore, if the company's earnings computation involves extraordinary items, each of the two earnings-per-share figures will also be presented for both the "income before extraordinary items" and "net income" amounts.

Earnings-per-share data can be very useful, together with other data, in evaluating management's past performance and predicting future earnings potential. However, overreliance on published earnings-per-share figures has several pitfalls. First, the earnings-per-share data tend to be accepted without examining the details of the income statement. This can lead to misleading inferences. Second, the emphasis on a single share earnings figure tends to shift the investor's attention away from the enterprise's total operations.

Opinion No. 15 deals exclusively with the computation of earnings per share and is covered in this chapter. This *Opinion* superseded Part II of *Opinion No. 9*, in which the APB first recommended that dual earnings-per-share figures be presented.

DUAL PRESENTATION: SUMMARY

In addition to the problems related to what income figure should be used to calculate earnings-per-share data, another class of problems relates to the question of what should properly be included in the earnings-per-share divisor. For a number of years some financial analysts believed that the earnings-per-share figures of companies with complex capital structures involving convertible securities, warrants, or stock options were misleading unless they reflected the potential dilutive effect of all of these securities. Others believed that the divisor should at least include all securities that were in substance equivalent to common stock, because of their terms, the circumstances under which they had been issued, or the way the market valued the securities.

The APB initially, in Part II of *Opinion No. 9,* and subsequently, in *Opinion No. 15,* accepted both of these points of view. In addition, after trying unsuccessfully for many years to deemphasize the significance of earnings per share in accounting reports, the APB switched its position in Part II of *Opinion No. 9* and required these data to be displayed on the earnings statement.

The factors contributing to this decision were: *(a)* the widespread use of these data; *(b)* the importance people attached to them; *(c)* the apparent misleading use of this figure by certain companies to boost their stock prices through the issuance of securities with common stock characteristics which did not enter into the earnings-per-share calculation; *(d)* the increasing use of warrants and convertible securities which had the potential effect of diluting earnings per share; and *(e)* the apparent unwillingness of other accounting authorities to deal forcefully with the inconsistencies, confusion, and abuses in this area.

In contrast to the then current practice, Part II of *Opinion No. 9* stated that the primary earnings-per-share computation must give consideration to the existence of all of a company's common stock and common stock equivalents.[1] It also stated that when this primary earnings-per-share calculation was subject to future dilution from the conversion of senior securities, a second earnings-per-share figure should be published showing the full effect of this dilution. Prior to *Opinion No. 9* these computations of earnings-per-share data were seldom presented, except in prospectuses and proxy statements.[2]

Henceforth, companies with complex capital structures had to present with equal prominence on the face of the income statement the company's primary earnings-per-share and fully diluted earnings-

---

[1] *Opinion No. 9* used the term "residual securities" to describe similar security issues referred to as "common stock equivalents" in *Opinion No. 15.* As will be explained later, the test for a common stock equivalent was different, in *Opinion No. 9,* from that eventually adopted in *Opinion No. 15.*

[2] *ARB No. 43* had earlier suggested that the divisor include common stock and other residual securities. A residual security was defined as a security other th an common stock which could be considered the substantial equivalent of common stock. This residual security concept was seldom followed in practice, however.

per-share amounts.[3] Both of these statistics represented new interpretations of the earnings-per-share concept.[4]

Primary earnings per share was defined by *Opinion No. 15* as the amount of earnings attributable to each share of issued common stock and common stock equivalent. A common stock equivalent was defined as any security which, because of its terms or the circumstances under which it was *issued,* was in substance equivalent to common stock.[5]

Fully diluted earnings per share was defined in *Opinion No. 15* as the amount of current earnings per share reflecting the maximum dilution that would result from the conversion of convertible securities and exercise of warrants and options that individually would decrease earnings per share and in the aggregate would have had a dilutive effect. All such issuances are assumed to have taken place at the beginning of the period (or at the time the contingency arose, if later).[6]

Opinion No. 15 specified that the term "earnings per common share" should be used without qualifying language *only* when *no* potentially dilutive convertible securities, options, warrants or other agreements providing for contingent issuances of common stock were outstanding. In all other cases, qualifying language (such as the word "primary") must be used with the term "earnings per share."

Finally, even if some securities are regarded as common stock equivalents, they should not be included in the computation of primary or fully diluted earnings per share if their inclusion will have the effect of increasing the earnings per share or decreasing the loss per share otherwise computed. This effect is referred to as being "antidilutive."

Opinion No. 15 is a very controversial opinion. Several prominent accounting authors have described it as reading like an episode from "Alice in Wonderland." Some of its critics believe the APB should never have issued the *Opinion*, since the subject matter is one of financial analysis, not accounting principles. Others disagree with the novel concepts and methods introduced in this *Opinion* and the prominence it gives to the earnings-per-share figure in income statements. In addi-

---

[3] *Opinion No. 9* referred to this earnings data as "pro forma earnings per share." The term "fully diluted" was first used in *Opinion No. 15*.

[4] Previously, the single earnings-per-share figure presented in annual reports was a company's net profits after taxes less preferred dividends, if any, divided by the number of common shares held by stockholders. This figure represents the equity of common stockholders in current earnings. Until such time as the holders of convertible securities convert their securities and the holders of warrants and options exercise their rights, they have no claim on these earnings.

[5] See later discussion entitled "At Issue" for further clarification.

[6] See later discussion entitled "Fully Diluted Earnings per Share" for further clarification.

tion, others believe that the *Opinion's* recommendations are inconsistent and do not reflect the ways investors calculate and use earnings-per-share data.

Because the fully diluted earnings-per-share calculation reduces the earnings per share of a company to the lowest figure possible, a number of analysts tend to use this figure in preference to primary earnings per share. In addition, some analysts claim that the fully diluted data is more indicative of a company's future earnings-per-share potential. However, a number of other analysts believe the APB's definition of common stock equivalents is arbitrary and has little practical justification. Hence, they consider the resulting earnings-per-share data meaningless for the purpose of predicting long-term market values.

Legal Considerations

The new requirements for calculating earnings per share presented in *Opinion No. 15* did not change in any way the legal rights of the various security holders. Thus, the long-term capital section of the balance sheet still reflects the legal relationships between the various classes of securities. Also, the interest expense related to convertible debt shown as an expense in the computation of net income remains unchanged regardless of how the related debt securities are treated for earnings-per-share calculation purposes.

OPINION NO. 15

Opinion No. 15 was issued in May 1969. It sets forth some general standards and specific methods for (1) computing earnings per share in a consistent manner and (2) presenting this data in a meaningful manner in reports to stockholders.

Opinion No. 15 concluded that the extent of the earnings-per-share data shown on the face of the income statement and the captions used should vary with the complexity of the company's capital structure. Accordingly, the *Opinion* distinguished between companies with simple and complex capital structures. The primary and fully diluted earnings-per-share concepts introduced by the *Opinion* apply only to companies with complex capital structures.

Simple Capital Structures

In the case of companies with relatively simple capital structures, a single presentation of earnings per share is appropriate. Such cases include companies whose capital stock consists only of common stock and includes none or very few other securities, options, or warrants that upon conversion could materially dilute earnings per share.

The so-called 3 percent test is used to determine if a company should make a dual presentation. The required reporting of earnings-per-share data depends on the materiality of the amount of dilution produced by securities which enable their holders to obtain common stock in the future. Aggregate dilution from all such securities which is less than 3 percent of earnings per common share outstanding need not be reported for either primary or fully diluted earnings per share, since such dilution is not considered to be material. Thus, if both the primary and fully diluted amounts are more than 97 percent of earnings per common share outstanding, earnings per share may be based on only common shares outstanding.

The 3 percent provision applies to fully diluted earnings per share compared to earnings per common share outstanding, not compared to primary earnings per share. Antidilutive securities are not dilutive by definition and should be excluded in computing aggregate dilution. An antidilutive security is a security which when included in the earnings-per-share calculation would result in an increase in the amount reported as earnings per share or a decrease in the amount reported as net loss per share. A dilutive security has the opposite effect on earnings per share.

The 3 percent provision also applies to the reporting of any other earnings-per-share information, such as supplementary data.

Aggregate dilution of less than 3 percent generally should be reported when it is anticipated that earnings-per-share data for a period when the provision applies might subsequently be included in a comparative income statement in which the following period reflects dilution of 3 percent or more. Otherwise, dilution in the following period would appear greater than it was in fact.

Illustration 11–1 presents the disclosure of earnings-per-share data for a company with a simple capital structure. (This and all subsequent exhibits in Chapter 11 assume that *Opinion No. 15* was effective for all periods covered.) The numbers of shares assumed for Illustration 11–1 are as follows:

	1975	1974
Common stock outstanding:		
Beginning of year	3,300,000	3,300,000
End of year	3,300,000	3,300,000
Issued or acquired during year	None	None
Common stock reserved under employee stock options granted	7,200	7,200
Weighted average number of shares	3,300,000	3,300,000

The shares issuable under employee stock options are excluded from the weighted average number of shares on the assumption that their effect is not dilutive (i.e.; that it is less than 3 percent).

ILLUSTRATION 11–1

Example of Disclosure of Earnings per Share; Simple Capital Structure
Conclusion of Income Statement
(in thousands, except per-share data)

	1975	1974
Income before extraordinary item	$ 9,150	$7,650
Extraordinary item—gain on sale of property, less applicable income taxes	900	—
Net Income	$10,050	$7,650
Earnings per common share:		
Income before extraordinary item	$2.77	$2.32
Extraordinary item	0.28	—
Net Income	$3.05	$2.32

In Illustration 11–1, the claims of senior securities, such as nonconvertible preferred stock or other securities that have preferential rights and are not a common stock or common stock equivalent, should be deducted from net income and income before extraordinary items before computing earnings per share. Dividends on cumulative preferred stock should be deducted from net income or loss irrespective of whether or not they are earned. If the claims of senior securities are payable only if earned, then the amount deducted should be limited to the extent income is available therefore.

Complex Capital Structures

Corporations with complex capital structures are required by *Opinion No. 15* to present on the face of the income statement two types of earnings-per-share data with equal prominence. If a company had no common stock equivalents, the *Opinion* suggested that it use the titles:

"Earnings per common share, assuming no dilution."
"Earnings per common share, assuming full dilution."

If common stock equivalents are present, the titles are to read approximately as follows (exact titles were not prescribed in the *Opinion*):

"Earnings per common and common equivalent share."
"Earnings per common and common equivalent share, assuming full dilution."

The *Opinion* described these data as follows:

The first presentation is based on the outstanding common shares and those securities that are in substance equivalent to common shares and have a dilutive effect. The second is a pro-forma presentation which reflects the dilution of earnings per share that would have occurred if all contingent issuances of common stock that would individually reduce earnings per share had taken place at the beginning of the period (or time of issuance of the convertible security, etc., if later). For convenience in this Opinion, these two presentations are referred to as "primary earnings per share" and "fully diluted earnings per share," respectively, and would in certain circumstances be supplemented by other disclosures and other earnings-per-share data.

In practice, the terms "primary earnings per share" and "fully diluted earnings per share" have been adopted extensively.

At Issue

The APB concluded that the determination of whether or not a convertible security is a common stock equivalent should be made at the time of issuance and that as long as the security is outstanding it retains this status. The tests for determining a convertible stock's status are:

Convertible securities should be considered common stock equivalents if the cash yield to the holder at time of issuance[7] is significantly below what would be a comparable rate for a similar security of the issuer without the conversion option. Recognizing that it may frequently be difficult or impossible to ascertain such comparable rates, and in the interest of simplicity and objectivity, the Board has concluded that a convertible security should be considered as a common stock equivalent at the time of issuance if, based on its market price, it has a cash yield[8] of less than 66⅔% of the then current bank prime interest rate.[9] For any convertible security which has a change in its cash interest rate or cash dividend rate scheduled within the first five years after issuance, the lowest scheduled rate during such five years should be used in determining the cash yield of the security at issuance.

The Board believes that the current bank prime interest rate in general use for short-term loans represents a practical, simple and readily available basis on which to establish the criteria for determining a common stock equivalent, as set forth in the preceding paragraph.

The Board recognizes that there are other rates and averages of interest rates relating to various grades of long-term debt securities and preferred

---

[7] This is generally the date when agreement as to terms has been reached and announced, even though such agreement is subject to certain further actions, such as directors' or stockholders' approval.

[8] Cash yield is the cash received by the holder of a security as a distribution of accumulated or current earnings or as a contractual payment for return on the amount invested, without regard to the par or face amount of the security. As used in this *Opinion,* the term "cash yield" refers to the relationship or ratio of such cash, to be received annually, to the market value of the related security at the specified date. For example, a security with a coupon rate of 4 percent (on par of $100) and a market value of $80 would have a cash yield of 5 percent.

[9] If convertible securities are sold or issued outside the United States, the most comparable interest rate in the foreign country should be used for this test.

stocks which might be appropriate or that a more complex approach could be adopted. However, after giving consideration to various approaches and interest rates, the Board has concluded that since there is a high degree of correlation between such indices and the bank prime interest rate, the latter is the most practical rate available for this particular purpose.

Investment Value Test Rejected

The adoption of this "at issue" test marked a significant departure from the test for common stock equivalents recommended in Part II of *Opinion No. 9,* which was based on a comparison of the current market price and the investment value of the security throughout its existence whenever earnings-per-share data were presented. According to *Opinion No. 9:*

> When more than one class of common stock is outstanding or when an outstanding security has participating dividend rights with the common stock, or when an outstanding security clearly derives a major portion of its value from its conversion rights or its common stock characteristics, such securities should be considered (common stock equivalents) and not "senior securities" for purposes of computing earnings per share.

According to the typical interpretations of the "major-portion-of-value" test of *Opinion No. 9,* a security was a common stock equivalent if it "derived more than half its value from its common stock characteristics." Thus, a $1,000 convertible bond that was selling in the market for $2,000 was clearly a common stock equivalent. However, in practice this test was interpreted differently if the bond was selling between $1,500 and $1,999. Also, changes in the equity and debt market conditions could affect the security's price, and hence its common stock equivalent status, at any particular time. For example, if a $1,000 convertible bond price fell from $2,500 to $1,200, it would shift from the common stock equivalent category to the senior security class. Subsequently, if its price again rose to $2,100, it would once more be classified as a common stock equivalent.

These difficulties led the APB to replace the *Opinion No. 9* test of common stock equivalents with the at issue test presented in *Opinion No. 15.* Henceforth, irrespective of what happened to the market price of a convertible security after issue, if its effective yield at issue was, say, 3 percent and the prime rate 7 percent, it would always be classified as a common stock equivalent, since its yield at issue was less than 66⅔% of the prime bank rate.

Fully Diluted Earnings per Share

The purpose of the fully diluted earnings-per-share presentation is to indicate on a prospective basis the maximum potential dilution of current earnings per share. Securities whose conversion, exercise, or other contingent issuance would have an antidilutive effect are excluded from this computation.

Fully diluted earnings-per-share data are required to be shown on the face of the income statement for each period presented:

. . . if shares of common stock (a) were issued during the period on conversions, exercises, etc., or (b) were contingently issuable at the close of any period presented and if primary earnings per share for such period would have been affected (either dilutively or incrementally) had such actual issuances taken place at the beginning of the period or would have been reduced had such contingent issuances taken place at the beginning of the period. The above contingencies may result from the existence of (a) senior stock or debt which is convertible into common shares but is not a common stock equivalent, (b) options or warrants, or (c) agreements for the issuance of common shares upon the satisfaction of certain conditions (for example, the attainment of specified higher levels of earnings following a business combination). The computation should be based on the assumption that all such issued and issuable shares were outstanding from the beginning of the period (or from the time the contingency arose, if after the beginning of the period). Previously reported fully diluted earnings-per-share amounts should not be retroactively adjusted for subsequent conversions or subsequent changes in the market prices of the common stock.

Earnings Data Adjustments: Convertible Securities

The new concepts of earnings per share introduced by *Opinions No. 15* and *No. 9* require adjustments, for the earnings-per-share calculation *only*, of a company's profit after taxes, preferred dividends, and interest expense. This is necessary to reflect the fact that the reporting company's net income before and after preferred dividends includes payments that are deducted in arriving at these figures but which would be avoided if these securities were converted as is assumed in the earnings-per-share calculations.

Two possible approaches were considered by the APB to handle interest charges and preferred dividends applicable to the common stock: namely, the "if-converted" and the "two-class" methods of computation. The if-converted method is a method of computing earnings-per-share data that assumes conversion of convertible securities as of the beginning of the earliest period reported (or at time of issuance, if later). The two-class method is a method of computing primary earnings per share that treats common stock equivalents as though they were common stocks with different dividend rates from that of common stock.

Opinion No. 15 expressed a preference for the if-converted method in the case of most convertible securities. The *Opinion* described these two methods and their application:

The "if converted" method recognizes the fact that the holders of convertible securities cannot share in distributions of earnings applicable to the common stock unless they relinquish their right to senior distributions. Conversion is assumed and earnings applicable to common stock and common stock equivalents are determined before distributions to holders of these securities.

The "if converted" method also recognizes the fact that a convertible issue can participate in earnings, through dividends or interest, either as a senior security or as a common stock, but not both. The two-class method (see below) does not recognize this limitation and may attribute to common stock an amount of earnings per share less than if the convertible security had actually been converted. The amount of earnings per share on common stock as computed under the two-class method is affected by the amount of dividends declared on the common stock. . . .

Although the two-class method is considered inappropriate with respect to [most convertible securities] . . . its use may be necessary in the case of participating securities and two-class common stock. This is the case, for example, when these securities are not convertible into common stock.

Under the two-class method, common stock equivalents are treated as common stock with a dividend rate different from the dividend rate on the common stock and, therefore, conversion of convertible securities is not assumed. No use of proceeds is assumed. Distributions to holders of senior securities, common stock equivalents and common stock are first deducted from net income. The remaining amount (the undistributed earnings) is divided by the total of common shares and common share equivalents. Per share distributions to the common stockholders are added to this per share amount to arrive at primary earnings per share.

Computation Examples

To illustrate the recalculations of earnings per share as required by *Opinion No. 15,* assume the ABC Company has a net income of $60,000 after interest and taxes, but before preferred dividends of $10,000; paid a dividend of $0.30 per common share; and had the following long-term capital structure:

Convertible 4% bonds (convertible into 100,000 common shares) . . . . $ 500,000
Convertible 2½% preferred stock (convertible into 50,000
    common shares)   400,000
Common stock (250,000 shares authorized, 50,000 outstanding)   2,000,000

The if-converted method recommended by *Opinion No. 15* is initially used in these examples. Later, the same example is used to illustrate the two-class method.

First, assume that the ABC Company has a simple capital structure. That is, the yield at issue of *neither* the convertible bonds *nor* the convertible preferred was such as to require these securities to be classified as common stock equivalents. The computation of the ABC

Company's "earnings per share, assuming no dilution," according to *Opinion No. 15*, is:

$$\text{Earnings per Share, Assuming No Dilution} = \frac{\text{Net Profit after Taxes} - \text{Preferred Dividends}}{\text{Weighted Average Number of Common Stock Outstanding}}$$

$$= \frac{\$60,000 - \$10,000}{50,000 \text{ Shares}}$$

$$= \$1 \text{ per Share}$$

Now, assume that the convertible preferred stock, but *not* the convertible debt, had been classified at issue as a common stock equivalent. This would give the ABC Company a complex capital structure. As a result, the computation of the company's primary earnings per share (or earnings per common and common equivalent shares) is:

$$\text{Primary Earnings per Share} = \frac{\text{Profit after Taxes before Preferred Dividends}}{\text{Common Stock Outstanding} + \text{Common Stock Equivalent of Preferred Stock}}$$

$$= \frac{\$60,000}{(50,000 + 50,000) \text{ Shares}}$$

$$= \$0.60 \text{ per share}$$

This calculation reflects the fact that if the convertible preferred stock were converted, the need to pay preferred dividends would be eliminated.

Continuing with the same ABC Company complex capital example, the company's fully diluted earnings per share (or earnings per common and common equivalent share, assuming full dilution) is calculated as follows:

$$\text{Fully Diluted Earnings per Share} = \frac{\text{Profits after Taxes before Preferred Dividends} + \text{Aftertax Equivalent of Convertible Debt Interest}}{\text{Common Shares Outstanding} + \text{Common Stock Equivalent of Convertible Preferred Stock Plus Common Stock Potentially Issuable to Convertible Debt Holders}}$$

$$= \frac{\$60,000 + \$10,000}{(50,000 + 50,000 + 100,000) \text{ Shares}}$$

$$= \frac{\$70,000}{200,000 \text{ Shares}}$$

$$= \$0.35 \text{ per Share}$$

This last calculation reflects the elimination of the preferred dividends and the interest cost after the assumed conversion of the convertible preferred and debt issues.

Two-Class Method

The two-class method seeks to determine an earnings base that reflects (1) the fact that the common stock equivalent (convertible preferred in the ABC Company complex capital example) has a disproportionate preference to earnings relative to the common stock and (2) that actual amounts were paid to the holders of these common stock equivalents based on the stock's actual relationship, preference, and privileges. Accordingly, the following calculation is based on the assumption that amounts already paid to the common stock equivalent holders cannot logically be attributed to any other security during the current period. Continuing to use the same ABC Company complex capital example, the ABC Company's primary earnings per share calculated by the two-class method would be:

$$
\begin{aligned}
\frac{\text{Primary}}{\text{Earnings}}\ \text{=} & \ \frac{\substack{\text{Earnings after Distribu-}\\ \text{tion to Senior Securities,}\\ \text{Common Stock Equivalents}\\ \text{and Common Stock}}}{\substack{\text{Common Stock and}\\ \text{Equivalents}}} + \substack{\text{Per-Share Common}\\ \text{Stock Cash}\\ \text{Distributions}} \\[2mm]
\text{=} & \ \frac{\$(60,000 - 10,000 - 15,000)}{(50,000 + 50,000)\ \text{Shares}} + \$0.30\ \text{per Share} \\[2mm]
\text{=} & \ \$0.65\ \text{per Share}
\end{aligned}
$$

As noted earlier, the two-class method may be required to compute earnings per share in the case of companies whose capital structure includes:

a. Securities which may participate in dividends with common stocks according to a predetermined formula with, at times, an upper limit on the extent of participation.
b. A class of common stock with different dividend rates or voting rights from those of another class of common stock, but without prior or senior rights.

In addition, some of these securities may be convertible into common stock. In the case of convertible securities the two-class method may be used only if it results in greater dilution than the if-converted method.

To illustrate the application of the two-class method for nonconvertible securities, assume that a corporation had 5,000 shares of $100 par value nonconvertible preferred stock and 10,000 shares of $50 par value common stock outstanding during 1975 and had a net income of $65,000. The preferred stock is entitled to a noncumulative annual dividend of $5 per share before any dividend is paid on common. After common has been paid a dividend of $2 per share, the preferred stock then participates in any additional dividends on a 40:60 per-share ratio with common. That is, after preferred and common have been paid dividends of $5 and $2 per share respectively, preferred participates in any additional dividends at a rate of two thirds of the additional amount paid to common on a per-share basis. Also assume that for 1975, preferred shareholders have been paid $27,000 (or $5.40 per share) and common shareholders have been paid $26,000 (or $2.60 per share).

Under the two-class method for nonconvertible securities, earnings per share for 1975 would be computed as follows:

Net income		$65,000
Less dividends paid:		
Preferred	$27,000	
Common	26,000	53,000
Undistributed 1975 earnings		$12,000

Allocation of undistributed earnings:

5,000 Shares Preferred	*10,000 Shares Common*	
0.4	0.6	
2,000	+ 6,000	= 8,000 "equivalent shares"

$$\frac{2,000}{8,000} \times \$12,000 = \$3,000 \qquad \frac{6,000}{8,000} \times \$12,000 = \$9,000$$

$$\frac{\$3,000}{5,000} = \$0.60 \text{ per share} \qquad \frac{\$9,000}{10,000} = \$0.90 \text{ per share}$$

Earnings per share:

	Preferred	*Common*
Distributed earnings	$5.40	$2.60
Undistributed earnings	0.60	0.90
	$6.00	$3.50

Because of the great variety of features which these participating and two-class common stock securities have in practice, the *Opinion* did not set detailed specific guidelines for determining when they should be considered common stock equivalents. Rather, it stated simply:

Dividend participation does not per se make a security a common stock equivalent. A determination of the status of one of these securities should be based on an analysis of all the characteristics of the security including the ability to share in the earnings potential of the issuing corporation on substantially the same basis as the common stock.

Earnings Data Adjustments: Options and Warrants

Options, warrants, and similar arrangements, such as securities with a low cash yield that require payment of cash upon conversion, are regarded by *Opinion No. 15* as common stock equivalents at all times. Typically, these securities have no cash yield and whatever value they have is derived from their right to obtain common stock at a specific price during a specified time period. Accordingly, the *Opinion* maintains that primary earnings per share should reflect the assumption that these securities have been exercised.

The earnings-per-share effect of such securities is computed by the "treasury stock" method. This approach assumes (1) that the warrants and options are exercised at the beginning of the period (or at time of issuance, if later); and (2) that any proceeds received by the issuing company are used to purchase its common stock, up to 20 percent of the outstanding stock, at the average market price during the period.[10] If funds from assumed exercises of options and warrants are still available after this 20 percent limit is reached, their assumed application must follow specific rules outlined in paragraph 38 of the *Opinion* (see below). These computations should not, however, reflect the exercise or conversion of any security if its effects on earnings per share is antidilutive, except as indicated in paragraph 38 of the *Opinion*.

As a practice, the APB recommended that the assumed exercise not be reflected in primary earnings-per-share data until the market price of the common stock obtainable had been in excess of the exercise price for substantially all of three consecutive months,[11] ending with

---

[10] For example, if a corporation has 10,000 warrants outstanding exercisable at $54 and the average market price of the common stock during the reporting period is $60, the $540,000 which would be realized from exercise of the warrants and issuance of 10,000 shares would be an amount sufficient to acquire 9,000 shares; thus, 1,000 shares would be added to the outstanding common shares in computing primary earnings per share for the period.

[11] The *Opinion* does not define "substantially all." Presumably, 11 weeks would be substantially all of a 13-week quarter. Therefore, the computation would be made for any quarter after the market price has once been above the exercise price for any 11 weeks during a quarter.

Note that this is a one-time test. Exercise need not be assumed for the computations until the test has been met in a particular quarter. However, once the test is met, the average market price would be computed thereafter unless the market prices are clearly antidilutive.

The test applies for both primary and fully diluted computations. But after the test has once been met, an ending market price which is above the exercise price is used for the fully diluted computation even though the average market price is below the exercise price.

the last month of the period to which earnings-per-share data relate. Therefore, under the treasury stock method, options and warrants have a dilutive effect (and are, therefore, reflected in earnings-per-share computations) only when the average market price of the common stock obtainable upon exercise during the period exceeds the exercise price of the options of warrants. Previously reported earnings-per-share amounts should not be retroactively adjusted, in the case of options and warrants, as a result of changes in market prices of common stock.

The APB recognized that the funds obtained by issuers from the exercise of options and warrants are used in many ways, with a wide variety of results that cannot be anticipated. Application of the treasury stock method in earnings-per-share computations is "not based on an assumption that the funds will or could actually be used in that manner" required by this method. Nevertheless, the APB believed it represented a practical approach to reflecting the dilutive effect that would result from the issuance of common stock under option and warrant agreements at an effective price below the current market price.

The APB concluded, however, that the treasury stock method can be inappropriate, or should be modified, in certain cases. For example, some warrants contain provisions that permit, or require, the tendering of debt (usually at face amount) or other securities of the issuer in payment for all or a portion of the exercise price. The terms of some debt securities issued with warrants require that the proceeds of the exercise of the related warrants be applied toward retirement of the debt. Also, some convertible securities require cash payments upon conversion and are, therefore, considered to be the equivalent of warrants. In all of these cases, the if-converted methods should be applied as if retirement or conversion of the securities had occurred and as if the excess proceeds, if any, had been applied to the purchase of common stock under the treasury stock method. However, exercise of the options and warrants should not be reflected in the primary earnings-per-share computation unless (a) the market price of the related common stock exceeds the exercise price or (b) the security which may be (or must be) tendered is selling at a price below that at which it may be tendered under the option or warrant agreement and the resulting discount is sufficient to establish an effective exercise price below the market price of the common stock that can be obtained upon exercise. Similar treatment should be followed for preferred stock bearing similar provisions or other securities having conversion options permitting payment of cash for a more favorable conversion rate from the standpoint of the investor.

The methods described above should be used to compute fully diluted earnings per share also if dilution results from outstanding options and warrants. However, in order to reflect maximum potential dilution, the market price at the close of the period reported upon should be used to determine the number of shares which would be assumed to be repurchased if this market price is higher than the average price used in computing primary earnings per share. Common shares issued on exercise of options or warrants during each period should also be included in fully diluted earnings per share from the beginning of the period, or from date of issuance of the options or warrants if later. In addition, the computation for the portion of the period prior to the date of exercise should be based on market prices of the common stock when exercised.

Computation Example

For example, assume the following data:

Net income for year	$2,000,000
Shares outstanding	1,000,000
Warrants and options to purchase equivalent shares	
(outstanding for full years)	100,000
Exercise price per share	$15
Average price	$20
Year-end market price	$25

Then primary earnings per share would be computed as:

$$\left(\frac{20 - 15}{20}\right) \times 100{,}000 = 25{,}000 \text{ Shares}$$

$$\frac{\$2{,}000{,}000}{1{,}000{,}000 + 25{,}000} = \$1.95$$

Fully diluted earnings per share would be:

$$\left(\frac{25 - 15}{25}\right) \times 100{,}000 = 40{,}000 \text{ Shares Issued}$$

$$\frac{\$2{,}000{,}000}{1{,}000{,}000 + 40{,}000} = \$1.92$$

Paragraph 38: Twenty Percent Test

The treasury stock method of reflecting use of proceeds from options and warrants may not adequately reflect potential dilution when options or warrants to acquire a substantial number of common shares are outstanding. Accordingly, the APB concluded in paragraph 38 of *Opinion No. 15:*

. . . if the number of shares of common stock obtainable upon exercise of outstanding options and warrants in the aggregate exceeds 20% of the number of common shares outstanding at the end of the period for which the computation is being made, the treasury stock method should be modified in determining the dilutive effect of the options and warrants upon earnings-per-share data. In these circumstances all the options and warrants should be assumed to have been exercised and the aggregate proceeds therefrom to have been applied in two steps:

(a) As if the funds obtained were first applied to the repurchase of outstanding common shares at the average market price during the period but not to exceed 20% of the outstanding shares: and then

(b) As if the balance of the funds were applied first to reduce any short-term or long-term borrowings and any remaining funds were invested in U.S. government securities or commercial paper, with appropriate recognition of any income tax effect.

The results of steps (a) and (b) of the computation (whether dilutive or anti-dilutive) should be aggregated and, if the net effect is dilutive, should enter into the earnings-per-share computation.

ILLUSTRATION 11–2

Application of Paragraph 38

	Case 1	Case 2
Assumptions:		
Net income for year	$ 4,000,000	$ 2,000,000
Common shares outstanding	3,000,000	3,000,000
Options and warrants outstanding to purchase		
equivalent shares	1,000,000	1,000,000
20% limitation on assumed repurchase	600,000	600,000
Exercise price per share	$ 15	$ 15
Average and year-end market value		
per common share to be used	$ 20	$ 12
Computations:		
Application of assumed proceeds ($15,000,000):		
Toward repurchase of outstanding common		
shares at applicable market value	$12,000,000	$ 7,200,000
Reduction of debt	3,000,000	7,800,000
	$15,000,000	$15,000,000
Adjustment of net income:		
Actual net income	$ 4,000,000	$ 2,000,000
Interest reduction (6%) less 50% tax effect	90,000	234,000
Adjusted net income (A)	$ 4,090,000	$ 2,234,000
Adjustment of shares outstanding:		
Actual outstanding	3,000,000	3,000,000
Net additional shares issuable		
(1,000,000 − 600,000)	400,000	400,000
Adjusted shares outstanding (B)	3,400,000	3,400,000
Earnings per Share:		
Before adjustment	$ 1.33	$ 0.67
After adjustment (A ÷ B)	$ 1.20	$ 0.66

Illustration 11–2 demonstrates the application of paragraph 38. Case 2 in the illustration shows a dilutive effect despite a market price below exercise price.

Contingent Issues

Some agreements call for the further issuance by companies of shares either directly or from escrow accounts contingent on such conditions as the attainment of specific earnings levels. Such contingent issuable shares should be considered as outstanding in both the primary and fully diluted earnings computations if the conditions for their issuance are currently being attained. If these conditions are not being met, they should be included only in the fully diluted earnings calculation.

The number of shares contingently issuable may depend on some future market price of the stock. In such cases the current earnings-per-share computations should use the number of shares that would be issuable based on the market price of the stock at the close of the period. If the number of shares issued or contingently issuable subsequently changes because of market price changes, the earnings per share reported for prior periods should be restated. A similar approach should be used if the number of shares contingently issuable is dependent on both future earnings and future stock prices.

Securities of Subsidiaries

In some cases warrants, options, or securities issued by subsidiaries must be considered as common stock equivalents when computing consolidated and parent company earnings per share which reflect the subsidiary's results of operations through consolidation or the use of the equity method. Circumstances requiring this approach and the appropriate rule to follow in reporting consolidated or parent company earnings include:

a.   Certain of the subsidiary's securities are common stock equivalents in relation to its own common stock.

In this case, the earnings per share should include the portion of the subsidiary's income that would be applicable to the consolidated group based on its holdings and the subsidiary's primary earnings per share.

b.   Other of the subsidiary's convertible securities, although not common stock equivalents in relation to its own common stock, would enter into the computation of its fully diluted earnings per share.

Under these conditions, only the portion of the subsidiary's income that would be applicable to the consolidated group based on its holdings and the fully diluted earnings per share of the subsidiary should be included in consolidated and parent company fully diluted earnings per share.

c. The subsidiary's securities are convertible into the parent company's common stock.

Such securities should be considered as issued and treated the same way as the related parent stock in the computation of primary and fully diluted earnings per share.

d. The subsidiary issues options and warrants to purchase the parent company's common stock.

These rights should be considered as common stock equivalents by the parent company.

Further Requirements

The complexity of the earnings-per-share calculation requires additional disclosures to explain (a) the pertinent rights and privileges of the various securities outstanding and (b) the assumptions and adjustments made to calculate primary and fully diluted earnings per share. The disclosure of rights and privileges should include: dividends and liquidation preferences, participation rights, call prices and dates, conversion or exercise prices or rates and pertinent dates, sinking fund requirements, and unusual voting rights.

The disclosure of how the earnings-per-share amounts were obtained should not be shown in such a manner as to imply that an earnings-per-share amount which ignores the effect of common stock equivalents constitutes an acceptable presentation of primary earnings per share. In addition, earnings-per-share data are required to be presented for all periods covered by the statement of income or summary of earnings. If it is necessary to restate previous periods' income, the prior periods' earnings-per-share data must also be restated.

Dividends-per-share presentations in comparative statements should reflect the actual dividends declared during the appropriate period adjusted for any subsequent stock splits or dividends. Following a pooling of interest, the dividends-per-share presentation for periods prior to the pooling creates a problem. In these cases, the typical practice is to disclose the dividends declared per share by the principal constituent.

Weighted Average Computations

The divisor for the earnings-per-share calculation should be the weighted average of the number of common shares and, if any, common share equivalents outstanding during each period presented.

This number is determined by relating (a) the portion of time within a reporting period that a particular number of shares of a certain security has been outstanding to (b) the total time in that period. Thus, for example, if 100 shares of a certain security were outstanding during the first quarter of a fiscal year and 300 shares were outstanding during the balance of the year, the weighted average number of outstanding shares would be 250. The use of a weighted average is necessary so that the effect of changes in the number of shares outstanding is related to the operations during the portion of the accounting period affected.

If the company reacquires its shares, these shares should be excluded from the weighted average calculation from the date of their acquisition.

Computations of earnings-per-share data should give retroactive recognition in all periods presented to changes in the capital structure due to stock splits, stock dividends, or reverse stock splits. If the capital structure is changed by such events after the close of the period but before the completion of the financial report, the per-share calculations for the period should be based on the current capitalization. This presumes that the reader's primary interest is related to the current capitalization.

When a business is acquired for stock, the transaction can be accounted for as either a purchase or a pooling of interest depending on the particular circumstances. When a business combination is accounted for as a purchase, the new shares should be included in the computation of earnings per share only from the acquisition date. In the case of a pooling of interest, the computation should be based on the aggregate of the weighted average outstanding shares of the merged business, adjusted to the equivalent shares of the surviving business for all periods presented. These computations reflect the difference in accounting for income under the two methods of accounting for business combinations. (In a purchase, the income of the purchaser includes the income of the purchased company only from the date of acquisition. In a pooling of interest, the net incomes of the two companies are combined for all periods presented.)

Using the treasury stock method to include options and warrants in the per-share calculations can complicate the computation of the various quarterly, year-to-date and annual earnings-per-share figures. The following paragraphs set forth some of the rules that apply to the computation of these per-share figures when options and warrants are outstanding.

Dilutive options or warrants which are issued during a period or which expire or are cancelled during a period are reflected in both primary and fully diluted earnings-per-share computations for the time they were outstanding during the period being reported upon. The common equivalent shares to be considered enter earnings-per-share computations as part of the weighted average number of shares.

A "period" is the time for which net income is reported and earnings per share are computed. However, when the treasury stock method or any method requiring the computation of an average market price is used and the reporting period is longer than three months, a separate computation is made for each three-month period.

A weighted average of shares is computed based on the average market prices during each three months included in the reporting period. Thus, if the period being reported upon is six months, nine months, or one year, a weighted average of shares is computed for each quarter. The weighted averages for all quarters are then added together, and the resulting total is divided by the number of quarters to determine the weighted average for the period.

When the ending market price of common stock is higher than the average market price for the period, the ending market price is used for the fully diluted computation to reflect maximum potential dilution. The use of different market prices for primary and fully diluted earnings-per-share computations naturally results in different numbers of shares for the two computations. The use of a higher ending market price for fully diluted computations may also result in the assumption of exercise for fully diluted earnings per share but not for primary earnings per share. Year-to-date computations for fully diluted earnings per share may also be more complex when market prices of common stock increase and then decrease during the year, since the share computation is then made two ways and the greater number of shares is used in computing year-to-date fully diluted earnings per share.

Common stock issued upon the exercise of options or warrants is included in the weighted average of outstanding shares from the exercise date. The treasury stock method is applied for exercised options or warrants from the beginning of the period to the exercise date. For primary earnings per share, the computation for the period prior to exercise is based on the average market price of common stock during the period the exercised options or warrants were outstanding (if the result is dilutive). Incremental shares are weighted for the period the options or warrants were outstanding, and shares issued are weighted for the period the shares were outstanding. For fully diluted earnings per share, however, the computation for the period prior to exercise is based on the market price of common stock when the options or warrants were exercised regardless of whether the result is dilutive or antidilutive. Incremental shares are weighted for the period the options or warrants were outstanding, and shares issued are weighted for the period the shares are outstanding.

Retroactive adjustment or restatement of previously reported earnings-per-share data are not made when the incremental number of shares determined by applying the treasury stock method changes. The APB realized that the total of four quarters' earnings per share might not equal the earnings per share for the year when market prices change and the treasury stock method is applied.

Computations for each quarter or other periods are independent. Earnings-per-share data should not either be restated retroactively nor adjusted currently to obtain quarterly (or other period) amounts to equal the amount computed for the year or year to date.

Effective Date

The effective date of *Opinion No. 15* was for fiscal periods beginning after December 31, 1968. It applied to all primary, fully diluted, and supplementary earnings-per-share data regardless of when the securities involved in the computations were issued, except for securities issued prior to June 1, 1969, entering into the computation of primary per-share data.

In the case of securities issued prior to June 1, 1969, the following election could be made with respect to these securities in computing earnings per share: they could either be classified according to the common stock equivalent tests established in *Opinion No. 15,* or they could be classified according to the tests included in *Opinion No. 9* regardless of how they would be classified in *Opinion No. 15.* If the *Opinion No. 15* tests were elected, the provisions of *Opinion No. 15* should be used in the computation of both primary and fully diluted earnings-per-share data for all periods presented.

The APB also recommended that in comparative statements in which the information for some periods is subject to *Opinion No. 15* and for others is not, the *Opinion* be applied to all periods covered, based on the conditions existing in the prior periods.

CONFLICTING VIEWPOINTS

Opinion No. 15 has been criticized widely. In fact, the *Opinion* was not wholeheartedly endorsed by 8 of the 18 members of the APB (three "dissented" and five "assented with qualification"). The principal reservations of these eight APB members, as well as the viewpoints of others not endorsing *Opinion No. 15*, are:

1.   The required dual presentation of earnings per share dignifies one figure above all others. This practice runs counter to the profession's position that fair presentation of financial condition and results of operations is achieved by the whole presentation, not by the specific location of any item. Accordingly, the *Opinion* should not be so specific on the location of the dual presentation of earnings per share.

2.   The determination of common stock equivalence is a subjective one which cannot be accommodated within prescribed formulas or mathematical rules. This determination, however, does begin with the one factually determinable figure of earnings per actual outstanding common share. Therefore, it does not serve the interests of meaningful disclosure to deny corporations the right to report on the face of the income statement as a basis for investor pro forma per-share calculations this one factually determined figure. Given this figure as a base, plus adequate disclosure of information related to capital structure that falls within the present bounds of fair disclosure, the calculation of pro forma common stock equivalence should be left to the investor to do in a way that he believes best serves his purpose. Accounting should not preempt the investor's judgment.

3.   Investors have a right to view the primary earnings-per-share data as a realistic attribution of the earnings of the issuer to the various complex elements of its capital structure based on the current economic realities—not those existing years earlier when securities were issued. Investment value tests such as proposed by *Opinion No. 9* are a more realistic test of common stock equivalence, since they reflect current conditions. In addition, the at-issue test disregards the fact that both the issuers and holders of newly issued convertible securities that are not classified as common stock equivalents at issue recognize the possibility that as the value of the underlying common stock increases, the convertible features become increasingly significant. Therefore, the common stock equivalent concept should have validity at issuance and subsequently.

4.   The use of the bank prime rate for the cash-yield test does not differentiate among types of security issued and the credit standing of the issuers.

5.   It is erroneous to attribute earnings to securities that do not currently, and may never, share in those earnings, particularly when part or all of those earnings may have already been distributed to others as dividends. Furthermore, until convertible securities are converted, the common stockholders are in control of earnings distributions. Therefore, to show an amount per share which assumes conversion is improper.

6.   It is potentially baffling to investors that convertible debt is debt in the statement of earnings but is common stock equivalent in the statement of earnings per share, and that dividends per share are based on the actual numbers of shares outstanding while earnings per share are based on a different and larger number of shares. Others go further and claim that the source of potential confusion is the fact that there is no such category as "common stock equivalent" in reality and the concept involves assumptions and intricate determinations which result in figures of questionable meaning which are more confusing than enlightening.

7.   The argument that the investment value test and its application subsequent to issue has a "circular" effect[12] does not recognize the fact that analysts give appropriate recognition to the increasing importance of the common stock characteristics of convertible securities as the market rises or falls. Therefore, it is the argument against the investment value test that is illogical, not the test.

8.   A third approach—the market parity method—to determining the common stock equivalence of securities has been proposed by some. This approach compares a convertible security's market value with its conversion value. If the two values are substantially equivalent and in excess of redemption price, the convertible security is considered to be a common stock equivalent. The advantage of this method as compared to the investment value test, which requires an estimate of investment value, is that it uses amounts that are readily available and ascertainable.

9.   The financial statements should be consistent with the method used to determine earnings per share. Accordingly, the convertible debt considered to be the equivalent of common stock should be classified in the balance sheet in a combined section with common stock under a caption such as "equity of common stockholders and holders of common stock equivalents." In addition, in the income statement the interest paid on common stock equivalents should be shown as a distribution of income with a caption such as "distributions to holders of common stock equivalents."

10.   Similarly, it is considered inconsistent and misleading by some that the income of subsidiaries reflected in consolidated and parent company statements disregards the existence of the subsidiary's common stock equivalents, whereas the earnings-per-share calculation reflects these securities.

11.   The requirement that options and warrants whose exercise price is at or above the market price of related common stock be taken

---

[12] The reported earnings per share influence the market price, which, in turn, influences the classification of the security's status, which, in turn, influences the computation of earnings per share, which, in turn, influences the market.

into account in the computation of primary earnings per share destroys the usefulness of the dual presentation of primary and fully diluted earnings per share. It fails to disclose the magnitude of the contingency arising from the outstanding warrants and options. Also, it is inconsistent with the determination of the status of convertible securities at time of issuance only, since it is an apparent recognition of the fact that market conditions subsequent to issuance can determine the status of a security.

12. The 20 percent limitation on the use of the treasury stock method of applying proceeds from the assumed exercise of options and warrants is arbitrary and unsupported.

13. It is inconsistent, in computing fully diluted earnings per share, to measure potential dilution by the treasury stock method in the case of most warrants and to assume conversion in the case of convertible securities. This inconsistency results in required recognition of potential dilution attributable to all convertible securities and at the same time, through the use of the treasury stock method, understatement or no recognition of potential dilution attributable to warrants.

14. The treasury stock method is unsatisfactory, and other methods are preferable. One alternative proposed is that the number of equivalent shares be computed by reference to the relationship between the market value of the option or warrant and the market value of the related common stock. This method results in options and warrants having an impact on earnings per share whenever they have a market value, and not only when the market price of the related common stock exceeds the exercise price, as in the treasury stock method.

15. Some argue that the treasury stock method is improper since it (a) fails to recognize dilution unless the market price of the common stock exceeds the exercise price and (b) assumes substantial blocks of treasury stock can be acquired without influencing the current market price, which is based on current actual trades.

16. There are more preferable approaches to the uses of funds assumed to be received from the exercise of outstanding warrants and options. Other uses proposed include the application of these funds to (a) reduce short- or long-term borrowings, (b) invest in government obligations or commercial paper, (c) invest in operations of the issues, or (d) fulfill other corporate purposes.

17. The inclusion of stock issuable in connection with a business combination on a purely contingent basis should not be included in the computation of primary earnings per share if its issuance is wholly dependent upon the future movement of market prices. As a general practice, it is unsound for the determination of earnings to depend on the fluctuations of security prices, since it makes earnings per share a

function of market price movements. The earnings per share should affect market price, and not vice versa.

18.   Finally, there are some who claim that no matter how long the APB (now the FASB) labors to solve the problems associated with computing earnings per share, no real progress will be made until the APB (now the FASB) develops a sounder definition of net income.

SUGGESTED FURTHER READING

BALL, J. T.   *Computing Earnings-per-Share*. New York: American Institute of Certified Public Accountants, 1970.

CASES

CASE 11-1. GENERAL POWER CORPORATION
Weighted Average Number of Shares

The General Power Corporation had 25,000 shares of common stock outstanding during a year and also had granted options which resulted in the following incremental shares, computed using the treasury stock method: 500 in the first quarter; none in the second quarter, because they would have been antidilutive; 1,400 in the third quarter; and 1,000 in the fourth quarter.

Question

Compute the weighted average of shares for computing the company's annual primary earnings per share.

CASE 11-2. WILEY COMPANY
Calculating Incremental Stock Issues

The Wiley Company has 100,000 common shares outstanding, and 10,000 warrants outstanding which are exercisable at $20 per share to obtain 10,000 common shares. Assume also the following market prices per share of common stock during a three-year period:

Quarter	Year 1 Average	Year 1 Ending	Year 2 Average	Year 2 Ending	Year 3 Average	Year 3 Ending
1	$18*	$22	$24	$25	$20	$18
2	20*	21	22	21	18	22
3	22	19	20	19	24	21
4	24	23	18	17	22	25

* Assume market prices had been more than $20 for substantially all of a previous quarter.

Questions

1. Compute the number of incremental shares related to the warrants to be included in each quarter's calculation of *(a)* primary earnings per share and *(b)* diluted earnings per share.
2. Compute the number of incremental shares included in the year-to-date weighted average for calculating *(a)* primary earnings per share and *(b)* fully diluted earnings per share.

CASE 11-3. THE THOMAS COMPANY
Calculation of Earnings per Share

The Thomas Company was located in Boston, Massachusetts. Its stock was traded in the local over-the-counter market. Trading seldom reached a thousand shares a day. Certain data related to the company's earnings, capital structure, and security prices are presented below:

Market Price of Common Stock. The market price of the common stock was as follows:

	1970	1969	1968
Average price:			
First quarter	$50	$45	$40
Second quarter	60	52	41
Third quarter	70	50	40
Fourth quarter	70	50	45
December 31 closing price	72	51	44

Cash Dividends. Cash dividends of $0.125 per common share were declared and paid for each quarter of 1968 and 1969. Cash dividends of $0.25 per common share were declared and paid for each quarter of 1970.

Convertible Debentures. Four percent convertible debentures with a principal amount of $10 million due in 1988 were sold for cash at a price of $100 in the last quarter of 1968. Each $100 debenture was convertible into two shares of common stock. No debentures were converted during 1968 or 1969. The entire issue was converted at the beginning of the third quarter of 1970 because the issue was called by the company.

Convertible Preferred Stock. At the beginning of the second quarter of 1969, 600,000 shares of convertible preferred stock were issued for assets in a purchase transaction. The annual dividend on each share of this convertible preferred stock was $0.20. Each share was convertible into one share of common stock. This convertible stock has a market value of $53 at the time of issuance, and the bank prime rate was 5.5 percent.

Holders of 500,000 shares of this convertible preferred stock converted their preferred stock into common stock during 1970. (Assume even conversion throughout the year.)

Warrants.   Warrants to buy 500,000 shares of common stock at $60 per share for a period of five years were issued along with the convertible preferred stock mentioned above. No warrants have been exercised.

Common Stock.   The number of shares of common stock outstanding was as follows (in thousands):

	1970	1969
Beginning of year	3,300	3,300
Conversion of preferred stock	500	—
Conversion of debentures	200	—
End of year	4,000	3,300

Net Income.   The 1969 and 1970 net income before dividends on preferred stock was (in thousands):

1969:	Net income	$10,300
1970:	Income before extraordinary item..	12,900
	Net income	13,800

Taxes in 1969 were 48 percent; in 1970 they were 52.8 percent.

Questions

1. Compute the company's primary and fully diluted earnings per share for 1970 and 1969. The prime rate was 6 percent in 1968.
2. Starting with the "income before extraordinary item" line of the comparative 1970 and 1969 statements, complete the remaining portion of the bottom of the income statement for presentation in the company's annual report. (The last line should disclose the company's net income per share, assuming full dilution.)
3. Prepare the footnote to accompany the per-share data presented in the 1970 income statement.
4. Does paragraph 38 of *Opinion No. 15* apply in this case?

CASE 11–4. MOREHEAD CORPORATION
Two-Class Method

The Morehead Corporation had 10,000 shares of Class A common stock (the "ordinary" common) and 5,000 shares of Class B common stock outstanding during 1969 and had a net income of $65,000. Each share of Class B is convertible into two shares of Class A. The Class B is entitled to a noncumulative annual dividend of $5 per share. After Class A has been paid a dividend of $2 per share, Class B then participates in any additional dividends on a 40 to 60 per-share ratio with Class A. For 1969, the Class A shareholders have been paid $26,000 (or $2.60 per share) and the Class B shareholders have been paid $27,000 (or $5.40 per share).

Questions

1. Compile the earnings per share for 1969 (*a*) under the "if converted" method and (*b*) under the two-class method.
2. Could the two-class method be used in this case to report earnings per share?
3. Which method do you think results in the better measure of earnings per share?

PART VI

Asset Valuation and Expense Determination

Chapter 12

ACCOUNTING FOR INCOME TAXES

Income taxes are an expense of doing business, and should be allocated to income and other accounts in the same fashion as other expenses. However, a number of companies report items of income and expense for income tax purposes on a basis different from that followed for financial reporting to stockholders and creditors. This raises a fundamental accounting question: Should the annual income tax expense reported in the published income statement be based on the taxable income reported to the Internal Revenue Service on the company's tax return for that year, an amount computed on the basis of the pretax income reported on the financial statements, or some other amount? *Opinion No. 11* of the Accounting Principles Board discusses this issue.

ORIGINS OF THE PROBLEM

The income tax allocation controversy is a direct outgrowth of the federal government's increasing use of income taxes as a positive or negative stimulus in the economy. The use of taxes as a stimulus takes a variety of forms:

1. "Across the board" stimulus, in the form of general changes in the tax rate.
2. Specific modifications to the continuing rules of determining taxable income, such as exemptions of certain revenues from taxable income.
3. Changes in the pattern of payment of the tax liability.
4. Changes in the timing of recognizing taxable revenues or tax deductible expenses.

There is general agreement that it is appropriate to reflect the effects of the changes specified above in the first two categories directly in the income statement during the period in which they occur. Such changes are, by law and regulation, directly relatable to items entering currently into the determination of income subject to tax.

The third type of stimulus—changes in the pattern of tax payments—affects a company's funds flow rather than income pattern. The delay in the payment of the tax increases the taxes payable liability account, and as such represents a source of funds. The eventual payment, which draws down the Cash account, is a use of funds. The size of the tax expense is unaffected. To the extent that corporate tax payments are moving closer to a pay-as-you-go basis, an important source of funds from delayed tax payments is being taken away from business executives.

The tax allocation accounting issue arises when the government employs the fourth category of stimuli; that is, it allows a different timing pattern for revenues and expenses on tax returns from that employed in the financial accounting reports.

Permanent and Timing Differences

Differences between the income reported in the financial statement and that reported on the tax return may be either (1) permanent or (2) related to timing differences. *Permanent* differences arise due to specific statutory concessions or exclusions of the tax code. For example, expenses required for financial reporting, such as premiums on officers' life insurance or amortization of goodwill, may not be deducted in the computation of taxable income.

Timing differences arise from the recognition in the financial reports and tax returns of income and expense in different periods. For example, a retailer may be required under *Opinion No. 10* to use in his published financial reports the accrual method, which recognizes income from installment sales at the time of sale. However, for tax purposes the retailer may elect to use the installment method, which recognizes the profit from the sale proportionately as the installment debt is paid. Another common example of timing differences is the use of straight-line depreciation in financial reports but accelerated depreciation in tax returns.

There are four general types of timing differences. The individual transactions giving rise to these timing differences originate in one period and reverse themselves in subsequent periods:

1. Revenues are included in taxable income later than they are included in pretax accounting income, as in the installment sales example.
2. Expenses are deducted later in determining taxable income than in determining financial statement income, as in the case of war-

ranty costs, which are deductible from taxable income only when incurred.

3. Revenues are included earlier in taxable income than in pretax accounting income. For example, rent payments received in advance may be reported when received for tax determination, but as earned for financial reporting purposes.

4. Expenses or losses are deducted in determining taxable income earlier than in determining pretax book income, such as in the case of store opening expenses that may be deducted immediately on a tax return but amortized in the financial statements over several years.

The major accounting problem arising from the timing differences is the method of recognizing the tax effects of timing differences. Permanent differences between pretax accounting income and taxable income present no problem, since, under applicable tax laws and regulations, current differences are not offset by corresponding differences in later periods.

Timing differences which reverse or turn around in later periods result in an equivalent reversal of the tax effects. Often the impact of the reversal of these differences is indefinitely postponed as similar new transactions balance out the reversal. A basic question develops as to whether the tax effect of timing differences should be recognized in view of the possibility of indefinitely postponing the actual payment of the tax.

THREE APPROACHES

Three methods of recognition of the tax effects arose in response to this problem. One widely held concept is that the income tax expense of a period should equal the tax payable for the period. Advocates of this "flow-through" method argue that there is no tax liability created until a later period; thus, there is no need to create an additional tax expense applicable to the current book pretax income.

Others argue for the "comprehensive allocation" method of reporting the income tax expense. This point of view holds that the tax expense reported in the financial statements should be the same as if the book profit were the profit actually reported for tax purposes. Any difference between this tax calculation and the tax currently due to the Internal Revenue Service is recorded as a potential tax liability labeled "deferred tax liability."[1] *Opinion No. 11* requires this approach.

---

[1] If a company's taxable income reported to the IRS is greater than its book profits before taxes and the difference is due to timing differences, a "deferred tax asset" results.

A third view is expressed by proponents of "partial allocation." They would recognize in the determination of current income only those taxes deferred that are reasonably certain to be paid during, say, the next three to five years.

EXAMPLE

The problem of recognizing timing differences is illustrated in the following example. In early January 1968, retailer Smith sold a TV set for $360 on an installment sale basis. The installment sales contract called for no down payment and 36 payments of $10 per month plus interest on the unpaid balance. The retailer's gross margin was 20 percent of the sales price. (The interest and any carrying charges related to the installment payments can be ignored in this discussion.)

According to Accounting Principles Board *Opinion No. 10* (December 1966), the retailer must use the so-called accrual method of handling the transaction *on his books,* rather than the installment method, since the circumstances of the sale were such that the collection of the sales price was reasonably assured. Therefore, Smith must recognize the full pretax profit of $72 at the time of the sale. If he had been able to use the installment approach, he would have shown a $2 before-tax profit at the time each $10 installment payment was received. The timing of the pretax profit recognition under the two methods is compared in Illustration 12–1.

ILLUSTRATION 12–1

Accrual versus Installment Treatment of Pretax Profit

	Accrual	*Installment*
1968	$72	$24
1969	—	24
1970	—	24
Total	$72	$72

First-Year Taxes

For calculating his tax payments, however, the retailer still has the option of using either the accrual or the installment method. If, in order to conserve his cash, Smith decides to use the installment method for tax purposes, he creates a tax deferral situation: he has recorded on his books the full $72 profit at the time of the sale, but for tax purposes he defers the actual payment of taxes on this profit until the time of the collection.

The aftertax profit consequences of using the accrual method for book purposes and the installment basis for tax purposes would depend on whether Smith uses the flow-through treatment for handling the tax deferral or the comprehensive allocation method. (Of course, in practice Smith would be required by *Opinion No. 11* to use the comprehensive tax allocation approach in this situation. The purposes of this illustration is to show the differences between the two approaches to tax expense accounting. It is important to understand the two approaches since management in some circumstances can elect to follow one or the other method. These special cases are discussed later.)

The flow-through approach records for book purposes the current year's tax payment actually shown on the retailer's tax return. If we assume a 50 percent tax rate, its application in this case would lead to the incremental effect on profits shown in Illustration 12–2.

ILLUSTRATION 12–2

Flow-Through Tax Accounting Illustrated

	Pretax Profit	*Tax**	*Net Profit*
1968	$72	$12	$60
1969	—	12	(12)
1970	—	12	(12)
Total	$72	$36	$36

* 50 percent of the 20 percent profit included in the installments collected.

Given the pretax profit of $72 on the company's books in the year of sale, the comprehensive allocation approach leads to a profit of $36 after taxes. This treatment puts the profit effect of the installment sale on the same basis as an equivalent cash sale. The difference between the $36 tax expense shown on the books and the actual tax of $12 paid to the Internal Revenue Service in 1968 is set up as a deferred tax account of $24 on the liability side of the balance sheet. This account is reduced incrementally each subsequent year by the amount of taxes paid on the profit from the installment payments received during that year. So, in this example, the deferred tax account would be reduced by $12 each year over the remaining two-year installment payment period. The income statement is not affected by these subsequent tax payments or installment collections.

The accounting entries for the tax effect would be:

Comprehensive Allocation

Year 1:

Tax Expense	36	
Taxes Payable		12
Deferred Tax Liability		24

Years 2 and 3:

Deferred Tax Liability	12	
Taxes Payable		12

Flow-Through

Year 1:

Tax Expense	12	
Taxes Payable		12

Years 2 and 3:

Tax Expense	12	
Taxes Payable		12

A comparison of the results obtained from applying the flow-through and the comprehensive allocation methods, when Smith uses different book and tax income recognition timing, is shown in Illustration 12–3. (The cash flow effect of this sale depends on whether the retailer sells for cash or on an installment basis and on the method he chooses to use on his tax return to recognize the profit from the sale. The financial accounting handling of the deferred taxes, if any, does not change his cash flow.)

ILLUSTRATION 12–3

Flow-Through versus Comprehensive Tax Accounting: Aftertax Book Profits

	Flow-Through	Comprehensive	Differential
1968	$60	$36	$24
1969	(12)	—	(12)
1970	(12)	—	(12)
Total	$36	$36	$ 0

Second-Year Taxes

In addition to realizing a first-year profit differential of $24, the flow-through approach provides an opportunity to offset the $12 reduction in second-year profits (see Illustration 12–3). Smith can accomplish this by making a similar $360 TV set installment sale in 1969. Again, the aftertax profit differential between the flow-through and comprehensive allocation treatment would be $24. But he would offset this amount with the second-year $12 profit reduction associated with the 1968 sale. So the net differential in the second year would be $12. This effect is shown in Illustration 12–4.

ILLUSTRATION 12–4

**Flow-Through versus Comprehensive Tax Accounting:
Aftertax Book Profits**

	Flow-Through	Comprehensive	Differential
1968	$60	$36	$24
1969	48	36	12
1970	(24)	—	(24)
1971	(12)	—	(12)
Total	$72	$72	$ 0

If the retailer in the second example is using the comprehensive allocation approach, the deferred tax item appearing on the balance sheet at the end of the first year would be $24. This deferral would rise to $36 at the end of the second year (the $24 difference between the tax payment recognized by the second-year sale handled on an accrual versus an installment basis, less the $12 reduction for taxes related to the first-year sale's actual tax payments made during the second year). If Smith sells one $360 TV set each year on a three-year installment sale basis, his deferred tax will remain at $36. If he increases his installment sales volume, the deferred tax item will increase. It is this so-called permanent deferral that the partial allocation advocates claim should be included in earnings.

So far we have looked only at recognizing the full book profits at the time of sale. Let us go back to the original one TV set sale example and lay aside for a moment the APB's earlier 1966 accrual basis decision. If the retailer, Smith, had handled his installment sale in exactly the opposite way to the previously assumed method—that is, if he reported the sale on an accrual basis for tax purposes and on an installment basis for book purposes—the sale would have the aftertax effect on book profits shown in Illustration 12–5. The first-year pretax profits on the installment method are $24, and the taxable income on the accrual method reported to the government is $72. In years 2 and 3 the book pretax profit is $24 each year. There is no profit reported on the tax return since it was all recognized in year 1. In Illustration 12–5, if

ILLUSTRATION 12–5

**Flow-Through versus Comprehensive Tax Accounting:
Aftertax Book Profits**

	Flow-Through	Comprehensive	Differential
1968	$(12)	$12	$(24)
1969	24	12	12
1970	24	12	12
Total	$ 36	$36	$ 0

comprehensive allocation were applied, the deferred tax item would show up on the asset side of the balance sheet, since the first-year profit recorded for taxes would be greater than the profit recorded for financial accounting purposes. In a sense, the company has overpaid, or prepaid, some taxes.[2]

OPINION NO. 11

In December 1967, after many years of debate, the Accounting Principles Board issued *Opinion No. 11*, requiring comprehensive tax allocation for income taxes. The APB concluded:

. . . that comprehensive interperiod tax allocation is an integral part of the determination of income tax expense. Therefore, income tax expense should include the tax effects of revenue and expense transactions included in the determination of pretax accounting income. The tax effects of those transactions which enter into the determination of pretax accounting income either earlier or later than they become determinants of taxable income should be recognized in the periods in which the differences between pretax accounting income and taxable income arise and in the periods in which the differences reverse. Since permanent differences do not affect other periods, interperiod tax allocation is not appropriate to account for such differences.

The Board has concluded that the deferred method of tax allocation should be followed since it provides the most useful and practical approach to interperiod tax allocation and the presentation of income taxes in financial statements.

The tax effect of a timing difference should be measured by the differential between income taxes computed with and without inclusion of the transaction creating the difference between taxable income and pretax accounting in-

---

[2] Situations giving rise to deferred tax assets include those where rents or royalties are taxed as collected but deferred in the accounts to later periods; and the sale of carved-out production payments, where the tax is due when the sale is made but for book purposes the income from the sale is reported as the underlying minerals are produced.

come. The resulting income tax expense for the period includes the tax effects of the transaction entering into the determination of results of operations for the period. The resulting deferred tax amounts reflect the tax effects which will reverse in future periods. The measurement of income tax expense becomes thereby a consistent and integral part of the process of matching revenues and expenses in the determination of results of operation.

THE CONTROVERSY

Flow-Through Method

Advocates of the flow-through method recognize as taxes only those amounts immediately payable based upon the current tax returns. They believe that only the current taxes are a legal liability and that to recognize future taxes results in undesirable income normalization. Further, since, in the case of many companies, tax deferrals are unlikely to be paid in the foreseeable future, continuation of the policy of deferring taxes may result in an ever-increasing amount on the liabilities side of the balance sheet which does not represent a legally enforceable claim against the corporation.

Comprehensive Allocation

Comprehensive allocation proponents base their arguments on the accounting convention that profits result from matching revenues and related costs. They argue that tax expenses should be recorded in the same accounting period as that in which the related revenue and expense items are recognized for book purposes.

Given this approach, when there is a timing difference between the recognition and payment of taxes, the logic of the debit-credit mechanism requires a deferred balance to be placed on the appropriate side of the balance sheet. Thus, a credit entry to offset the debit to tax expense is made to the liability account, deferred taxes. This liability item, they argue, is only a "residual" entry, and as such does not have all the usual characteristics of a liability or an asset.

Advocates of comprehensive allocation argue that the fact that reversal of timing differences may be more than offset by new timing differences does not alter the fact that the reversals do occur, and may be readily identified as to their tax effect. Accounting principles, they state, cannot be predicated on a reliance that these offsets will continue. They therefore conclude that the fact that the tax effects of two transactions happen to go in opposite directions does not invalidate the necessity of recognizing separately the tax effects of the transactions as they occur.

Partial Allocation

The partial allocation concept is often considered a modification of the flow-through method. The flow-through approach recognizes only those taxes which are payable in the current period. Partial allocation proponents would modify this approach to include those deferred taxes which are reasonably certain to become payable in the immediate future, as, say, within three to five years. Holders of this view believe that when recurring differences between taxable income and pretax accounting income give rise to an indefinite postponement of an amount of tax payments or to continuing tax reductions, tax allocation is not required, since taxes not reasonably expected to be payable should not affect net income. Furthermore, partial allocation advocates believe that indefinite postponement of taxes involves contingencies which are at best remote, and the inclusion of such taxes in the determination of the current book tax expenses results in a misstatement of that expense and of net income. For example, it is argued, comprehensive tax allocation will result in an understatement of net income in the case of a company with a relatively stable or growing investment in depreciable assets which uses straight-line depreciation in determining pretax accounting income but an accelerated method in determining taxable income as it will continue to defer taxes so long as it continues to invest in capital equipment.

Those who favor partial allocation also argue that it is misleading to show the full tax allocation, since it does not represent a legally enforceable claim by outsiders on the company's assets. Therefore, since it is not a liability, it should not be included in the balance sheet. This position should be modified only in those instances in which specific nonrecurring differences between taxable income and pretax accounting income would lead to a material misstatement of income tax expense and net income. If such nonrecurring differences occur, income tax expense of a period for financial accounting purposes should be adjusted to include those amounts expected to be paid within the immediate four- to five-year period.

Opponents of partial allocation believe that partial allocation artificially inflates income; that it does not follow the matching concept; and that it leaves to management judgment the computation of income tax expense, which can, in fact, be directly determined in an objective manner.

Deferred Taxes: A Liability?

Whether or not deferred taxes are a liability has been the focus of much of the controversy over deferred tax accounting. This argument has created problems for the proponents of both partial and comprehensive allocation, since neither has been able to satisfactorily explain the nature of the deferred tax item.

Advocates of partial allocation and flow-through methods correctly claim that the deferred tax item does not satisfy the traditional asset or liability conventions. Some believe the weakness of this argument is exposed by the partial allocation advocates' admission that they would set up a deferred tax item on the balance sheet in certain cases. Also, it is pointed out, partial allocation proponents offer no explanation of what their limited deferral item is, beyond saying that it is that portion of postponed taxes which might have to be paid in the near future. Some comprehensive allocation advocates argue that the "no liability" argument is not relevant, since the conventional definition of a liability is outmoded by current financial reporting practices. In addition to deferred taxes, for example, such items as deferred profits on sale-and-leaseback transactions and pension accruals appear as liabilities, although they do not fit the conventional definition of a liability.

In the past, supporters of comprehensive allocation also have failed to develop an adequate explanation of the deferred tax item on the balance sheet. This has subjected this method to continuing criticism. Business executives have been concerned that users of financial statements might include deferred tax credits as debt in the debt-equity or the working capital ratios, despite the fact that these deferrals do not have the characteristics of debt. This apprehension has made it difficult for many to see how comprehensive allocation produces fairer, more useful results than partial allocation.

Measurable Funds Effect

The partial allocators maintain that under certain circumstances income tax payments postponed can be permanently deferred, and that these deferred taxes cannot be construed to be liabilities. They argue that the government does not tax individual items of revenue or give offsetting refunds for the tax impact of individual expense items. The tax is levied on the results of bringing individual revenues and expense items together. Given this fact, they claim it is possible to offset the eventual tax impact of particular tax deferral transactions by recurring transactions of a similar nature. Thus, the accumulated tax effect of revenues not yet included in tax returns and expenses taken into tax returns at a faster rate than on the financial statements are theorized out of existence.

Legally, the income tax liability is a function of the net profit item shown on the tax return. However, this figure is a *net* result of a multitude of taxable revenue and tax deductible expense items, each of which has a calculable impact on the ultimate tax assessment. The individual elements which created the tax and the actual tax payment are inextricably tied together. It would be misleading to consider each element of the tax calculation without regard to its ultimate tax effect either in (1) making decisions which give rise to revenues and expenses or (2) evaluating the financial results of these decisions. The fact that the individual revenue and expense items shown on the tax return might be brought together at a different time than on the accounting reports does not—assuming the typical case of a profitable entity—remove the calculable tax effect which they create individually.

Another line of reasoning followed by critics of comprehensive allocation also fails to reflect the way business executives look at the tax impact of individual decisions. Their permanent deferral claim glosses over the fact, well recognized among business executives, that revenues recognized now, but not included in current tax returns, will create an upward push on the amount of future income taxes. Also, business executives typically assume that exercising the privilege of taking some deductions for certain expenses on the current year's income tax returns will most likely cause an upward push on future income taxes. Fewer future effects are more predictable than these events in the company with reasonable prospects for future profits. It is a natural result and in line with the common business practice which relates, for decision-making purposes, the tax effects with the individual transactions which collectively determine taxable income, such as in capital investment appraisals.

Extending the Argument

Extending the "permanent deferral" argument to other items on the balance sheet leads to clearly unacceptable results. For example, the accounts receivable and accounts payable balances of most companies have some part which is permanent in amount and is "rolling over" constantly. Applying the permanent deferral approach to these items would mean sales would have to be reduced by the amount of funds related to the "permanently" deferred accounts receivable, which, of course, would not be shown on the balance sheet. Similarly, the "permanent" portion of the funds derived from accounts payable would be left off the balance sheet and expenses reduced to the extent these payables were related to expense items.

Of course, supporters of the flow-through type of approach argue against these "roll-over" objections by claiming that items like accounts payables involve real invoices and real creditors. This is true. However, are they that different a source of funds from deferred taxes?

In fact, from a business executive's point of view, deferred taxes are an even more valuable source of funds, since no direct, immediate creditor claim exists. Some claim this is an important reason for showing this special source of funds on the balance sheet.

Income Measurement

Proponents of comprehensive allocation believe that net income measures principally how effectively management has added to the capital of the business through operations utilizing the capital already invested in the enterprise. Exercise by management of the privilege afforded by the income tax code to postpone taxes does not, in their opinion, constitute improved operating performance, no matter how long may be the prospect of continuing the tax postponement. They view tax postponement as providing an opportunity to perform better in the future as a result of being able to conserve funds currently for use in the business.

Consequently, they state that this funds retention benefit should be reflected in terms of a favorable capital "funds flow," rather than in terms of an immediate increase in income from operations, as proposed by the partial allocators. Furthermore, the income benefits flowing from the deferral of tax payments should be reflected in income only as management earns profits through reducing financial charges or improving operations as a result of using effectively the funds retained.

Many comprehensive tax advocates feel that a standard recognizing income as earned only through "honest-to-goodness" operating efficiency is vital to maintaining some semblance of integrity in the earnings figures as a measure of performance. The partial allocation method fails to meet this objective. For example, the partial allocation approach would permit a company in expanding investment situations, simply by using straight-line depreciation on its books and accelerated depreciation on its tax returns, to get credit for an additional profit improvement equal to 52 percent of the difference in expense charges between these two methods when the tax rate is 48 percent.

Similarly, a retailer with increasing sales who sells on the installment basis would show higher profits than another retailer with identical sales who sells for cash. To achieve this result, the credit sales would be recorded on the accrual basis for book purposes and the installment basis for tax purposes. Obviously, any accounting procedure that permits higher aftertax gross margin profits from credit sales than from cash sales is undesirable since it substitutes the illusion of performance for the realities.

Those favoring comprehensive allocation believe that postponement of tax payments is equivalent in practice to an interest-free loan from the government which should be disclosed in the balance sheet. In contrast, the partial allocation approach does not show this source as an identifiable item on the balance sheet. Rather, it is included as an unidentified part of the source of funds from profitable operations, since income will be higher in most cases using the partial allocation, due to the lower tax expense shown. Thus, an important source of funds is not fully disclosed.

Present Value Approach

Accounting Research Study No. 9, "Interperiod Allocation of Corporate Income Taxes," proposed that certain long-term tax allocation accounts be presented on a present value basis. Laying aside the practical difficulties of determining the discount rate and period, advocates of this proposal claim it reflects the correct accounting theory approach to liabilities and is consistent with conventional accounting theory related to long-term debts.

The advocates of the nondiscounting approach believe their point of view reflects the emphasis business executives place on the amount of funds obtained currently from tax deferrals rather than on the amount owed. Using this approach, they argue, there is no need to determine and report the deferrals on a discounted basis. It is of little interest and relevance. Consequently, in their opinion, the practice supported by the APB, which does not report discounted deferred taxes, is correct.

Rate Changes

The appropriate handling of changes in the corporate income tax rate which occur after the establishment of the original tax deferrals on the balance sheet presents a thorny problem. The APB's solution was to adopt the so-called deferred method. Under this approach there is no adjustment to deferred tax accounts for subsequent rate changes or subsequent tax law changes.

Effective Tax Rate Reduction?

Some authorities believe that the change in the timing for recognition of taxable revenues and deductions is essentially similar to a change in the pattern of payment of the tax liability. Both change the timing of tax payments. Both are changes in the sources of funds created by the government's decision to allow corporations to delay payments. Neither reduces the ultimate tax expense.

Those who hold this view believe comprehensive allocation to be consistent with the facts of the situation. Representatives of the Treasury during the late 1960s disagreed with this view of the nature of the timing differences. They argued that this kind of tax stimulus, which permits timing differences, represents a reduction in the effective tax rate to the corporation taking advantage of the timing difference provisions of the code. Comprehensive allocation, they claim, masks the effect of rate reduction due to timing differences and as such, gives a misleading picture of the administration's tax policy. Also, by reducing the profits of corporations (compared to the flow-through and partial allocation methods), comprehensive allocation leads to an unnecessary understatement of corporate profits, and a consequent understatement of the economy's health.

Those who disagreed with the Treasury's point of view believed that, first, if deferral of tax payments constitutes a rate reduction in taxes, speeding up the payment schedule must be the equivalent of a rate increase. They felt it was doubtful that the Treasury would agree to this extension of their position. Second, the Treasury argument was based upon a cash-flow approach to financial accounting. Corporate reporting had long abandoned cash basis reporting systems for the more useful and fair accrual method. Third, it was suspected that the Treasury Department might have been seeking to fashion corporate reporting principles for political ends. Adoption of noncomprehensive methods would tend to soften the impact of increased corporate tax rates and give the impression of greater growth in the economy than had actually occurred.

PUBLIC UTILITIES

A number of public utilities subject to rate-making processes have elected to use accelerated depreciation on their income tax returns and straight-line depreciation on their reports to stockholders. In these circumstances, some regulatory commissions have permitted the public utility neither to record deferred taxes in their accounts nor include deferred taxes as an allowable cost for rate-making purposes.[3] In these cases, most of the affected public utilities follow flow-through accounting for reporting their current tax expense to stockholders. This creates several problems for public accountants: Should an unqualified opinion be given on financial statements that do not provide for deferred taxes? What constitutes full and fair disclosure when flow-through accounting is used?

---

[3] In a regulated industry, the price of the product is determined by a formula which permits the utility to recover from its operating revenues its operating costs plus a fair return on the cost or fair market value of property used in the public service.

Paragraph 8 of *Accounting Research Bulletin No. 44* (revised) provides that comprehensive tax allocation need not be followed by public utilities with transactions involving timing differences "if it may be reasonably expected that the increased future income taxes resulting from the earlier deduction of declining-balance depreciation, for tax purposes only, will be allowed in future rate determinations." Consequently, the public accountant does not qualify his opinion on the statement of "flow-through" public utilities if there is basis for a reasonable expectation that taxes deferred will be allowed in the future as a recoverable cost in rate determinations.

There is no common understanding or objective standard for determining what constitutes the basis for a "reasonable expectation" in this public utility exception to comprehensive tax allocation accounting. Many accountants assume that if current regulatory commissions do not allow deferred taxes for rate-making determination, future commissions will continue to support this practice and will allow increased taxes in the future when the annual tax return accelerated depreciation charges are lower than the straight-line charges used in the accounts. Some accountants believe this is a dangerous assumption, since future commissions may not necessarily be bound by the decisions of prior commissions. Also, in the opinion of some accountants, the public utility expectation of *ARB No. 44* (revised) is based on an untenable concept that accounting resulting from rules prescribed by rate-making bodies may be unconditionally approved by public accountants notwithstanding the fact that the accounting result of applying the rule is not in accordance with generally accepted accounting practices.

Those public utilities regulated by "flow-through" commissions claim that in their circumstances either to force them to use deferred tax accounting in their accounts or to require the public accountant to issue a qualified opinion would be misleading to users of their reports and unfair to the issuer. For example, assume that, according to the applicable rate formula, a utility is allowed a return of $2 million on its net worth ($1,750,000 for common dividends plus $250,000 for retained earnings), in addition to its allowable operating costs and interest expense. If such a company is forced by its public accountants to include in its accounts a deferred tax cost of $400,000 which is not allowed for rate determination purposes, its common dividends will not be covered out of current profits. This is an intolerable position for such companies. On the other hand, those opposed to paragraph 8 of *ARB No. 44* claim that if deferred taxes are not provided for in the accounts, retained earnings will be overstated to the extent of this cost.

Flow-through accounting for regulated utilities covered by paragraph 8 is opposed by some accountants on the ground that it encourages regulatory commissions to adopt rate determination formulas that transfer costs to future customers that are properly applicable to current customers. Costs currently deducted for tax purposes exert an upward pressure on taxes in future years, since these deductions are unavailable in future years. Therefore, it is argued, the decision allows the tax deferment benefit arising from the use of accelerated depreciation for tax purposes to flow to the current customers. This also increases the risk to security holders, since it is possible that these deferred tax costs may not be allowed in future rate determinations, or that if they are allowed the revenues realized may not be sufficient to cover them and interest costs.

Paragraph 20 of APB *Opinion No. 6*, issued in October 1965, sets the standards for disclosure for "flow-through" utilities:

> When a company subject to rate-making processes adopts the declining-balance method of depreciation for income tax purposes but adopts other appropriate methods for financial accounting purposes in the circumstances described in Paragraph 8 [*ARB No. 44* (revised)] and does not give accounting recognition to deferred income taxes, disclosure should be made of this fact.

This disclosure requirement differed from an earlier one set forth in paragraph 9 of *ARB No. 44*. It required that "full disclosure should be made of the *amount* of deferred income taxes." Several members of the APB objected to the removal of this requirement by the APB in *Opinion No. 6*, on the grounds that "the Accounting Principles Board is inappropriately sponsoring the viewpoint that investors and other users of financial statements should be told of the practice but need not be furnished the information to judge its significance." The "flow-through" segment of the public utility industry agreed with the APB's decision. In their opinion, to disclose the current amount of taxes deferred may cause some investors to erroneously discount current earnings in the belief that the tax deferment is a current cost. Such investor action could adversely affect the utilities' ability to raise common equity.

Tax Reform Act

The Tax Reform Act of 1969 contained a major innovation in tax policy for utilities, in that henceforth the availability of an accelerated tax depreciation method is dependent on the rate practice of the regulatory commission and the utility's accounting policy. This policy was adopted to avoid a federal revenue loss projected to be between $1.5 and $2 billion annually, as additional utilities were being forced by rate-making bodies to shift to flow-through accounting for book and rate determination purposes.

This provision of the act established "normalization" as the preferred standard for public utilities in this country. (A utility is using the normalization method of accounting if it includes any deferred taxes in current expenses for accounting *and* rate purposes, *and* records any accumulated deferred taxes in a balance sheet reserve account.) Henceforth, public utilities, as defined in the act, would be limited to the use of straight-line tax depreciation unless they normalize or unless they had already established conditions specified in the act by August 1969 which would classify them as being flow-through companies.

LOSS CARRY-BACK—CARRY-FORWARD CREDITS

Where an operating loss for income tax calculation purposes occurs, a corporation may offset the loss against the taxable income of the preceding three years to the extent that the entire loss is offset. This is accomplished by filing amended tax returns for the prior years. The difference between tax liability on the amended and original returns can be claimed by the corporation as a tax refund.

If taxable income during the previous three years is less than the current year's loss, the unabsorbed portion of the current year's loss may be carried forward seven years to reduce taxable income. Where two loss years occur, the amount of the first loss is offset in full before the second loss is matched retroactively or prospectively against taxable income.

The carry-back and carry-forward provisions of the tax code create an accounting problem, since the realization of the benefits of the loss carried forward generally is not assured in the loss periods. The issue is: Should the tax reductions resulting from the carry-forwards be included in net income for the year in which the tax benefit is realized, or should they be applied to the prior year in which the losses occurred, as a partial recovery of such losses?

The Accounting Principle Board's conclusions on this topic (including its views on the proper accounting for loss carry-backs) is contained in paragraphs 44–47 of *Opinion No. 11*. The APB concluded that:

1.   The tax effects of any realizable loss carry-backs should be recognized in the determination of net income of the loss periods. The tax loss carry-back and the related tax refund claim are measurable and realizable in the current period.

2.   The tax effects of loss carry-forwards should not be recognized until they are realized, since realization of the tax benefits of the loss periods is dependent on future income.

3.   In certain unusual circumstances, the loss carry-forward tax benefit may

be recognized in the loss period when future realization of these benefits is assured beyond any reasonable doubt at the time the loss carry-forwards arise.

4. When tax benefits of loss carry-forwards are not recognized until realized in full or in part in subsequent periods, the tax benefits should be reported as extraordinary income items.

5. In contrast, in those rare cases where the tax benefit of the carry-forward is recognized in the loss period, the tax benefit should be included in the determination of the results of operations. The offsetting asset (and the tax benefit) should be computed at the corporate tax rates expected to be in effect at the time of realization. If the applicable tax rates should change from those used to compute the amount of the asset, the effect of the rate change should be accounted for in the period of the change as an adjustment to the asset account and the current income tax expense.

6. Disclosure should be made of the amounts of any loss carry-forwards not recognized in the loss period and the expiration date of such carry-forwards.

Prior to the issuance of *Opinion No. 11,* the accounting for tax carry-backs and carry-forwards varied considerably among companies. While recognizing that the opinion filled a need for greater uniformity in this area, some of its critics claim that the handling of realized tax loss carry-forwards as extraordinary items does not result in the most meaningful financial statement presentation. In their opinion, proper matching of costs and revenues requires that the tax benefits of carry-forwards of operating losses be related to the years in which the losses occurred. Also, since the loss carry-forward represents a potentially valuable asset, it should be recorded on the face of the balance sheet in preference to being disclosed only in a footnote. This point of view places greater emphasis on the "matching" concept than the "realization" concept supported by the APB in *Opinion No. 11.*

STATEMENT PRESENTATION

Deferred taxes are part of the tax expense recognized in the determination of current income. Therefore, the portion of taxes deferred should not be included in the balance of the stockholders' equity. This practice is supported by the Accounting Principles Board and the Securities and Exchange Commission, even though some accounting authors and many business executives argue that the portion of income taxes deferred indefinitely should be considered as part of the stockholders' equity.

Despite the fact that deferred taxes do not represent receivables or payables in the traditional sense, they should nevertheless be presented in a manner that is consistent with the customary distinction between current and noncurrent items. The general rule is that deferred taxes should be classified in the balance sheet in the same manner as the related assets and liabilities giving rise to the deferred taxes. For example, that portion of deferred taxes arising from the use of different plant depreciation methods should be classified as a long-term liability. This corresponds to the plant's classification as a long-term asset.

The authority for this practice is *Accounting Series Release No. 102,* issued in December 1965 by the Securities and Exchange Commission, and *Opinion No. 11,* issued by the Accounting Principles Board in December 1967.[4] *Release No. 102,* which dealt specifically with the classification of deferred income taxes related to installment receivables, stated:

The classification of deferred income taxes related to installment receivables as noncurrent is significant when considered in light of the practice of classifying assets and liabilities as current or noncurrent in accordance with the normal operating cycle of the business. In Regulation S–X the Commission recognized the operating cycle treatment in the determination of working capital.

The installment receivables and related deferred income taxes pertaining to the same operating cycle clearly are both either current or noncurrent. There is no justification from the standpoint of either proper accounting or fair financial reporting for the use of the operating cycle approach for installment receivables and not for the related deferred income taxes. Obligations for items which have entered into the operating cycle and which mature within the operating cycle should be included in current liabilities when the related receivables are included in current assets, in order to present fairly the working capital position.

In *Release No. 102* the SEC did not accept the theory advanced by some that the deferred taxes related to installment sales should be offset against the installment receivables as a contra item. In the Commission's opinion, the current value of the receivable is not affected by the amount of the tax deferral. The deferral is not a valuation reserve (such as reserves for anticipated bad debts). Rather, it is a credit or liability item, representing cash retained in the business by the deferral of tax payments.

The opposed point of view argued that it was preferable to deduct the deferred tax from the installment receivable. According to Arthur Andersen & Company:

Such a practice would recognize that the particular asset arises from the same transactions as does the income being deferred for tax purposes and that

---

[4] A similar conclusion was included in the exposure draft of *Opinion No. 6* of the Accounting Principles Board. This portion of the draft was deleted from the final opinion issued in October 1965. Subsequently, Arthur Andersen & Company filed a petition with the Securities and Exchange Commission requesting the Commission to issue an accounting release supporting this deleted portion of the exposure draft of *Opinion No. 6.* The Commission responded favorably to this request and issued *Accounting Series Release No. 102.*

the asset includes the uncollected amount which is not yet taxable. Therefore, the real asset is the receivable less the future tax to be paid. Likewise, if the income on installment sales were deferred for both book and tax purposes, there would be no deferred tax, and the preferable practice in such a case would be to deduct the deferred income from the related receivables.

Deferred taxes become a definite tax liability when and as the receivables are collected, since prior to that time there is only a provision for payment of future taxes. Therefore, if such deferred taxes are deducted from the related asset, the deferred taxes should be transferred to current liabilities as the receivables are collected.

Income Statement

The components of the tax expense shown on the current income statement should be disclosed by the following categories:

1. Taxes estimated to be payable currently.
2. Tax effects of timing differences.
3. Tax effects of operating losses.

These amounts should be allocated to (a) income before extraordinary items and (b) extraordinary items.

In addition, the APB recommends that significant variations in the normal ratio of income tax expense and pretax accounting income that are not otherwise apparent from the company's financial statements or business activities should be explained.

SPECIAL AREAS

Undistributed Earnings of Subsidiary Companies

The APB in *Opinion No. 23* concluded that including undistributed earnings of a subsidiary[5] in the pretax accounting income of a parent company, either through consolidation or the equity method, may result in a timing difference that may or may not reverse depending on the intent of the parent. For example, if the subsidiary is a foreign company that pays little or no foreign taxes, whether or not the parent ever pays U.S. taxes on the subsidiaries will depend on whether or not the parent decides to repatriate the subsidiary's profits. If the profits are repatriated to the U.S.A., the parent pays U.S. taxes on them, less a tax credit for any foreign taxes paid.

With respect to subsidiary earnings, *Opinion No. 23* makes the presumption that the timing difference will reverse. Therefore, deferred tax accounting should be used. However, this presumption can be

---

[5] Investor company owns more than 50 percent of the investee company.

overcome, and no income taxes need be accrued if the parent can demonstrate that the subsidiary has or will reinvest the undistributed earnings overseas indefinitively or that the earnings will be remitted to the U.S.A. in a tax-free liquidation. Thus, in the case of a foreign subsidiary with a low local tax rate on its local earnings, if the parent can present evidence to its CPA to overcome the *Opinion*'s presumption, the parent may pick up its share of the subsidiary's earnings with only the foreign tax expense being associated with the income.

Joint Ventures

Opinion No. 23 concluded that the tax accounting principles that applied to subsidiaries would apply also to joint venture investments. As indicated in Chapter 18, under *Opinion No. 18* such investments have to be accounted for by the equity method.

Other Equity Method Investments

Opinion No. 24 required comprehensive tax allocation accounting be used for all intercorporate equity investments (other than those in subsidiaries and joint ventures) accounted for by the equity method in accordance with *Opinion No. 18*. These are situations where the investor company owns less than 50 percent, but more than 20 percent, of the investee company. In such cases the APB believed the investor corporation did not have the ability to exercise significant influence over the dividend policies of investee companies since the investor corporation owned less than 50 percent of the investee's equity. In contrast, in *Opinion No. 23,* the APB took a somewhat different approach because it recognized that a parent did have the ability to control the dividend policy of subsidiaries and joint ventures because it owned 50 percent or more of the investee's equity. Therefore, it was possible for a parent to decide whether or not the earnings of a subsidiary would be reinvested for indefinite periods.

Domestic International Sales Corporation (DISC)

In order to encourage exports, Congress changed the tax code to permit corporations to funnel their exports through a DISC, which would be required to pay taxes immediately on only part of its profits. The payment of taxes on the remainder of the profits was deferred so long as the untaxed profits were used for export purposes. Should these profits subsequently be used for nonexport purposes, the deferred tax payment would become payable.

In *Statement No. 9* the FASB decided that if the parent of the DISC believes that the deferral of the tax payments is permanent, the parent need not accrue taxes currently in anticipation of eventually paying the deferred taxes.

The APB's conclusions on undistributed earnings of subsidiaries and joint ventures also applies to the portion of a DISC's earnings that is eligible for tax deferral. Thus, if management wishes to use flow-through tax accounting for the deferred tax payment, it simply declares to its public accountant that the profits giving rise to the deferred payment will be "reinvested permanently" in the DISC. On the other hand, if management wishes to build up a "tax cushion" for book purposes, it will state that the reinvestment of the profits creating the tax deferral will not be "permanent" and a deferred tax provision would be made currently for the anticipated future tax payment.

Savings and Loan and Stock Life Insurance Companies

Opinion No. 23 concluded that no income taxes need to be accrued for the difference between taxable income and pretax accounting income attributable to the policyholders' surplus of stock life insurance companies and the "bad debt" reserves of savings and loan associations. In both cases the APB believed that the timing difference may exist for an indefinite period.

Oil and Gas Producing Companies

The intangible development costs of oil and gas producing companies are usually capitalized for financial accounting purposes and then amortized over the productive periods of the related wells. For tax purposes these same costs are commonly deducted in the same period in which the costs are incurred. These practices raised the following accounting issue: Should the tax effects of the current deduction of these costs for tax purposes be deferred and amortized over the productive period of the wells to which the costs relate.

Few companies practiced tax allocation with respect to intangible and development costs. The principal reason being that these companies believed the tax deferral was a permanent one due to the fact that the percentage depletion allowed for tax purposes over the life[6] of the property was expected to exceed the intangible costs that were capitalized and amortized in the determination of pretax accounting income.

---

[6] Percentage depletion is a tax accounting method only. Under the tax code this is a deductible expense. It is computed as a percentage of gross income from a natural resource independent of the cost of the asset or its book amortization charge. The amount of percentage depletion allowance deductible for tax purposes is limited to a percentage of the taxable income.

The Tax Reduction Act of 1975 changed the favorable tax treatment of intangible development costs. This act substantially reduced or eliminated percentage depletion as a federal income tax deduction for many oil and gas producing companies as of January 1, 1975.

In response to the change in the tax code, the FASB issued *Statement No. 9, "Accounting for Income Taxes—Oil and Gas Producing Companies,"* in October 1975. This Statement—

requires the allocation of income taxes for timing differences arising from intangible drilling and development costs and other costs associated with the exploration for and development of oil and gas reserves that are charged to expense in income statements in one period but deducted for income tax purposes in a different period.

The Statement is effective with respect to financial statements issued on or after Dec. 1, 1975, but earlier application is encouraged.

Commencing Jan. 1, 1975, oil and gas producing companies that have not allocated taxes with respect to these costs must begin doing so using the prospective net method of accounting. The prospective net method requires the allocation of income taxes on the net change in timing differences originating in the period and the reversal during the period of similar differences that arose in prior periods.

The Statement provides for an election that permits oil and gas producing companies to take interaction with percentage depletion into account when using the prospective net method.

Prior to 1975, certain oil and gas producing companies allocated income taxes in accordance with the provisions of Accounting Principles Board Opinion No. 11 without recognizing interaction with percentage depletion. FASB Statement No. 9 permits a company wishing to change to that accounting method to do so, but if it does, the company must apply the method retroactively by restating prior period financial statements.

Disclosure

The income tax expense note in annual reports includes a reconciliation of the differences between the book tax expense, expressed as a percentage of pretax profit, and the statuatory corporate tax rate. Common causes of this difference are: the inclusion of equity method income on an aftertax basis in the pretax income; *Opinion No. 23—* type flow-through tax elections by management; and investment tax credits. Another item included in the note related to income tax expense is an explanation of the causes and tax effect of the timing differences that created the deferred tax portion of the current tax expense. Other disclosures are: the company's accounting for the investment tax credit; the status of the company's tax audits; and a breakdown of the deferred and current portions of the tax expense between domestic, foreign, and state income taxes.

Continuing Controversy

Following the issuance of *Opinion No. 11*, most of the topics discussed in this chapter no longer represent a problem in practice. However, the subject of deferred income tax accounting continues to be controversial and is of deep interest to those interested in the development of generally accepted accounting principles.

SUGGESTED FURTHER READING

AMERICAN INSTITUTE OF PUBLIC ACCOUNTANTS. "Accounting Interpretations of APB." *Opinion No. 11*. New York, 1972.

BEVIS, DONALD, and PERRY, RAYMOND E. *Accounting for Income Taxes: An Interpretation of APB Opinion No. 11*. New York: American Institute of Certified Public Accountants, 1969.

BLACK, HOMER, A. "Interperiod Allocation of Corporate Income Taxes." *Accounting Research Study No. 9*. New York: American Institute of Certified Public Accountants, 1966.

COMMERCE CLEARING HOUSE. *Master Tax Guide, 1976*. New York: Commerce Clearing House, 1976.

CASES

CASE 12–1. FRANKLIN STORES, INCORPORATED
Accounting for Income Tax Expense

In June 1975, the board of directors of Franklin Stores, Inc., a large chain of discount stores, approved a recommendation from the company's president, Joe Franklin, that Franklin Stores offer its customers the opportunity to purchase goods on an installment sales basis. Prior to this time, all of Franklin Stores' sales had been on a cash basis.

As part of this decision, the board had to consider a recommendation concerning the accounting treatment of the installment sales made by Peter Lewis, the company's financial vice president. Lewis recommended that Franklin account for its installment sales by the installment sales method for tax purposes. That is, the profit from the sale would be recognized as collections were made from the customer, or when the installment sales contract was sold to a finance company. He claimed that this method would defer the payment of income taxes arising from the sales and, thus, help the company's cash position. He likened the deferred taxes to an "interest-free loan from the government."

Lewis told the board that APB rules required Franklin to adopt the accrual method for public reporting purposes, however. The accrual method, he said, recognized the profit on the transaction at the time the goods giving use to the installment sales contract were sold.

Following Lewis's recommendation, the board approved the use of the installment method for tax purposes, principally because their public accountant had recommended it. However, several directors asked Lewis to explain the nature of the deferred tax account created by the use of the installment method for the calculation of income taxes and the accrual method for determining profit in the financial reporting to stockholders.

Several other directors questioned the appropriateness of using the accrual method for book purposes, since the company had no prior experience on which to base its estimate of the collections from installment sales. Excerpts from this conversation are presented later in the case.

Franklin Stores, Inc.

Franklin Stores, Inc., was founded in 1957 by Joe Franklin, his brother William, and Peter Lewis to sell television sets at a deeply discounted price on a cash and carry basis. The company's merchandising policy was an instant success—so much so that customers began to ask the store to obtain other appliances for them at a discount. As a result of these requests, the founders decided to expand their business to include a full line of household appliances. Initially, this move met with opposition from some manufacturers and local department stores. However, this was eventually overcome and, by 1965, the company was the largest retailer of appliances in its market area.

In 1968 the founders decided to expand their operations to include other cities. Accordingly, during the next five years they established new Franklin Stores in three cities. Also during this same period, Franklin stores expanded its operations to include records, home furnishings, musical instruments, toys, and a variety of other goods. This expansion was financed by a large public stock offering. Eventually, Mr. Franklin hoped to have Franklin Stores in every major city of the nation.

Beginning in the early 1970s the company began to experience greater competition from other discount stores and department stores. The competing discount stores cut heavily into Franklin's sales by improving their store layouts, installing more attractive displays, and granting liberal credit terms. The department stores became more competitive by lowering their prices to meet the discounted items, offering better service on the goods sold, and granting more liberal and varied credit terms.

These industry trends forced Franklin in 1975 to adopt an installment sales plan. The plan was a fairly simple one: Customers could purchase merchandise by paying as little as 10 percent of the purchase price at the time of purchase and then paying the outstanding balance over the next 12, 24, or 36 months in equal installments. A service charge of 2 percent of the outstanding balance was charged each month. Under this plan, Franklin continued to hold title (reduced by the buyer's equity as established by payments) to the merchandise until the final payment. Before a customer could use the installment plan, he was checked out by the company's credit bureau to see if he was able to comply with the terms of the installment sales contract.

June Board Meeting

After the decisions concerning installment sales were made, the following discussion related to deferred taxes occurred at the June board of directors meeting.

Lewis: Let me begin by saying that whenever you report items of income and expense for income tax purposes on a basis different from that followed for financial accounting purposes, the provision for the income tax expense does not represent the taxes actually paid, but the taxes properly allocated to the profit shown in the income statement.

Let me illustrate this problem with an example: Suppose we sold a freezer unit for $800 on August 1, 1975. The customer paid $80 down and agreed to pay $720 in equal installments over the next 36 months. Furthermore, let us assume the freezer cost us $600. So, we made $200 on the sale. As a percentage of the sales price, this represents a 25 percent gross margin.

Now here's how we'd account for the sale using the installment method.

On August 1 we'd record the sale, the creation of an installment receivable, and the initial down payment thus:

Installment Receivable 800
    Inventory[1] 600
    Deferred Gross Profit on Installment Sales 200

Cash 80
    Installment Receivable 80

Now, on September 1, and monthly thereafter for 36 months as the payments are received, the following entries will be made:

Cash 20
    Installment Receivables 20

Of course, there'd be an entry recognizing the service charge, but for the purposes of this example let's not worry about it.

Next, at the close of the fiscal year during which the sale was made we'd recognize the profit on the collections. Here's the journal entry:

Deferred Gross Profit on Installment Sales 40
    Recognized Gross Profit on Installment Sales 40

The $40 is the sum of the payments received times the percentage gross margin on the sale: that is, $160 × 25 percent.

Now the entries for the same transaction are . . . [Lewis went on to explain the accounting for the accrual method and to demonstrate how the deferral and actual taxes were calculated].

Small (director, retired business executive): That was an excellent explanation. However, I still don't understand why we have to provide for deferred taxes.

Lewis: Well, it is the generally accepted way to handle such situations by business executives and the public accounting profession. In fact, the general principle of income tax allocation is required by *Opinion No. 11* of the Accounting Principles Board.

Small: Oh, yes. I recall you mentioned that at our last meeting. Nevertheless, I think we ought to have some good business reasons for following this deferred tax method. Irrespective of how much authority such statements

---

[1] Franklin Stores, Inc., maintained perpetual inventory records.

may have among accountants, I don't see why we should blindly follow them.

Franklin: You may have a good point there, but I think we have no alternative. I have another question for Peter: Where is this deferred tax item carried on the balance sheet?

Lewis: It ought to be reported as a current liability, since the installment receivables giving rise to the deferred taxes are covered as current assets. The SEC insists upon this approach for registered companies.

Small: It seems silly to carry as a current liability an item that will in aggregate never be paid. Are there some alternative ways?

Lewis: No. However, in the past people have proposed the following: first, as a deduction from the related asset; second, below current liabilities, but above long-term debt; and finally, below long-term debt, but above stockholders' equity.

Murphy (director, president of utility company):   At one time didn't American Electric Power Company try to show as part of net worth the deferred taxes arising from using different depreciation policies for tax and book purposes?

Lewis: Yes. They claimed it was part of the stockholders' equity. However, the Securities and Exchange Commission issued a "Statement of Administrative Policy" stating they considered classifying the deferred tax liability as part of common stock equity was misleading for financial statement purposes. The AICPA also issued a similar pronouncement. After discussions with the SEC and the AICPA, a compromise was reached. The item was placed by this utility between net worth and long-term debt. In addition, all parties agreed the amount was to be considered as neither long-term debt nor common stock equity.

Franklin: Clearly, this question of the location of deferred taxes on the balance sheet is of some importance, since it will have a direct impact on our financial ratios. I think we ought to direct the executive committee to look further into this deferred tax business and make a recommendation as to how we should explain it and its impact on earnings and balance sheet ratios over the next few years to our stockholders. Are there any other questions related to this topic you want the executive committee to consider?

Peterson (vice president, public relations):   Yes, as I said earlier when the recommendation was first made, I'm not at all convinced we ought to use the accrual method in published statements for installment sales. Now, after listening to this discussion of deferred taxes, I'm even less convinced. It seems to me that we can avoid this whole deferred tax business by using the installment method in our published statements. And, unlike Peter, I happen to think the installment method does match costs and revenues. In my opinion, when we make an installment sale, we don't make a profit until at least about 80 percent of the monthly collections are made. In previous discussions with Peter, he tells me that some opinion of the Accounting Principles Board requires that we should use the accrual sales method. However, we are new at the installment sales business, and without any track record to guide us in estimating the probability of collections, I think we ought to be very conservative in recognizing income.

Franklin: Any other items for the executive committee?

Small: Yes, Peter's example was very helpful, but it dealt with only one sale. As I see it, our installment sales volume is going to continue growing over the years and I'm curious just how big this deferred tax account is going to be in say, 1978. Are we talking of $1 million or $10 million?

Lewis: I'll get that figure to you by the next board meeting.

Lorenz: I'd like to know what our auditors say about this. Also, do they think we should indicate in the annual report what we estimate the present value of this liability to be?

Franklin: Of course, we have been discussing this matter with our auditors. In fact, it's clear to me now that I made a mistake by not asking Frank Towle [the audit partner in charge of the Franklin Stores account] to come to this meeting. I'll make sure he comes to the next executive committee meeting, however. . . .

Questions

1. Complete the freezer example Peter Lewis presented to the board. What are the accounting entries for the installment sale, using the accrual and the installment methods? Assuming a 50 percent income tax rate, what will be the related actual tax payments for 1975, 1976, 1977, and 1978? What will be the deferred tax accounting entries during these years?

2. The following projections of Franklin Stores' operations are available (all amounts are millions of dollars):

| | Sales | | | Cash Collected on Installment Receivables | Selling and General Expense |
	Install-ment	Cash	Total		
1975	$ 8	$20	$28	$ 2.8	$4.2
1976	18	22	40	9.5	6.0
1977	24	26	50	18.2	7.5
1978	30	30	60	24.1	9.0

Assuming a constant 25 percent gross margin and a 50 percent income tax rate, and ignoring service charges, compute the amounts of net income after taxes, income taxes payable, deferred gross profit on installment sales, and deferred income taxes at the close of each year, 1975 through 1978, under each of these alternatives:

a. The accrual method is used for financial reporting and for income tax purposes.

b. The installment method is used for financial reporting and for income tax purposes.

c. The accrual method is used for financial reporting, and the installment method is used for income tax purposes.

3. How would you explain the deferred tax items on the balance sheet and income statement to the stockholders?

4. Should Franklin use the installment or accrual method in its public financial statements? Why?

5. Which net income figure is more relevant for valuing the Franklin Stores common stock? The net income computed in a comprehensive tax allocation basis or a flow through basis? Using the accrual or installment sale basis?

CASE 12–2. ALLIS-CHALMERS MANUFACTURING COMPANY
Accounting for Losses Carried Forward

In the first few paragraphs of his letter to stockholders in the 1968 annual report, the new president of Allis-Chalmers Manufacturing Company, David C. Scott, outlined the company's situation:

We began in September 1968 to take decisive action that will place this company in the forefront of American industry. Included in these actions are steps to face financial reality, build a new management team, reorganize along decentralized lines, market new products and negotiate new ventures. . . .

Sales totaled $767 million in 1968, compared with the company's sales volume of $821 million in 1967. The net loss reported for 1968 is $54 million, divided into (1) $22 million from regular operations, (2) $19 million identified as new charges and reserves, and (3) $13 million from extraordinary and nonrecurring charges. As explained in Note 6 to the financial statements, in 1968 the company changed its method of computing depreciation and extended the application of tax allocation accounting procedures. These changes had the effect of reducing the net loss for the year by $8.9 million. In 1967, net income totaled $5 million. . . .

Our 1968 operating results were adversely affected by reduced sales and extraordinary expenses involving costs and reserves related to closing down unprofitable plants for optimum utilization of manufacturing space and cutting out slow moving inventory not associated with profitable product lines. . . .

The 1968 income statement presented in the 1968 annual report is shown in Exhibit 1. Notes 3 and 6 read as follows:

NOTE 3: Special Reserves and Income Taxes. During the last quarter of 1968 a major change took place in the company's management. The new management made an extensive study of the company's operations, products, and markets. This study resulted in changes in company philosophy and policies relating to organization, products and production facilities, marketing,

EXHIBIT 1

ALLIS-CHALMERS MANUFACTURING COMPANY
Statement of Income (loss)
Allis-Chalmers Manufacturing Company and Consolidated Subsidiaries

	Year Ended December 31	
	1968	*1967**
Sales and Other Income:		
Sales	$767,313,100	$821,764,535
Discounts, interest earned, and other income	11,152,147	6,428,597
Income of finance subsidiaries	9,901,233	6,893,641
	$788,366,480	$835,086,773
Costs and Expenses:		
Materials, plant payrolls, and services (Note 3)	$703,041,018	$689,225,155
Depreciation (Note 6)	16,024,167	18,713,666
Selling, general, and administrative expense (Note 3)	131,352,862	100,216,572
Discount and interest on receivables sold to finance subsidiaries..........................	21,662,133	11,158,812
Other interest expense	9,380,927	9,590,531
	$881,461,107	$828,904,736
Income (loss) before income taxes and extraordinary charges	$ (93,094,627)	$ 6,182,037
Federal, state, and Canadian income taxes (Notes 3 and 6).............................	51,942,000	(1,180,200)
Income (loss) before extraordinary charges	$ (41,152,627)	$ 5,001,837
Extraordinary charges, net of income taxes of $15,057,211 (Note 3).........................	(13,437,093)	—
Net Income (Loss) for the Year	$ (54,589,720)	$ 5,001,837

* 1967 has been restated to conform with the current year's classifications.

and relations with dealers and customers. The company has estimated that implementation of these policy changes will result in substantial costs and losses for *(a)* parts replacement, warranty costs, repossession losses, and price allowances; and *(b)* relocation and discontinuance of facilities and products. Provisions were recorded in the last quarter of 1968 to establish special reserves totaling $68,754,410 for these anticipated costs and losses. Of this amount, $28,494,304 ($13,437,093 net of taxes), associated with relocation and discontinuance of products and facilities, is shown as an extraordinary charge in the consolidated statement of income (loss). The remaining provisions, totaling $40,260,106, were charged to sales ($5,627,178); materials, plant payroll, and services ($28,190,928); and selling, general, and administrative expenses ($6,442,000).

Although the costs and losses to be charged to the special reserves cannot be finally determined at the present time, management believes, based on the company's extensive studies and evaluations which were reviewed in depth by the independent auditors, that the provisions recorded in 1968 represent a fair and reasonable determination of the amounts required.

The net loss for the year has been determined after giving recognition to income taxes recoverable ($14,345,721) from carry-back to prior years of operating losses and to estimated future tax benefits ($50,900,000) of unused losses, including $6,836,276 relating to an accounting change described in Note 6 to the financial statements. The amounts recoverable from carry-back to prior years are included in current assets in the consolidated balance sheet, together with 1968 tax refunds receivable of $3,970,000 and estimated future income tax benefits of $17,303,304 relating primarily to normal book-tax timing differences applicable to amounts included in current assets and liabilities. The realization of estimated future income tax benefits which total $60,275,704 is dependent upon the company's ability to generate future taxable income. This amount is included in the financial statements because, in the opinion of management, the realization of such tax benefits is assured beyond any reasonable doubt.

The company has unrecorded investment tax credit carry-forwards of $6,098,722, applicable to the years 1962 through 1968, which may be used to reduce income taxes payable in future years.

NOTE 6: Accounting Changes. The company has adopted, for financial reporting purposes, the straight-line method of computing depreciation for substantially all plants and equipment. These fixed assets were previously depreciated on an accelerated basis. This change, effective January 1, 1968, reduced depreciation expense by $4,505,109 and decreased the net loss by $2,126,411, equal to $0.21 per common share.

In 1968, the company extended the application of tax allocation accounting procedures to certain reserve accounts to comply fully with new tax accounting requirements effective this year. The extension of these procedures decreased the net loss by $6,836,276, equal to $0.66 per common share.

An article entitled "A Bit of Rouge for Allis-Chalmers" appeared in the May 1969 issue of *Fortune.* It stated:

The accounting that appears in annual reports sometimes serves a cosmetic purpose—it is there not so much to inform stockholders as to help management keep them happy, or at least quiet, by touching up blemishes and brightening beauty spots. When a company is not doing well, and at the same time is trying to fend off unwanted merger, the cosmeticians of accountancy can sometimes perform wonders—even when they are limited to shades of red. Quite a number of companies in this year's directory used bookkeeping devices of various kinds to brighten their results. But Allis-Chalmers Manufacturing outdid them all at the rouge pot.

As 1968 ended, long-suffering Allis-Chalmers, No. 130 among the 500, found itself with some conflicting needs and desires. It presumably wanted to put the best possible face on 1968 results in order to maintain stockholder support in a bitter battle against a takeover by White Consolidated Industries, No. 143. But the new president of Allis-Chalmers, David C. Scott, who took office September 1, wanted to write off at once the tremendous charges associated with past mistakes and thereby turn the company around. To do that, he had to slap stockholders with some very bad news just when White Consolidated's onslaught was hotting up.

Allis-Chalmers resolved this conflict with some intricate accounting that let it accept Scott's write-off while minimizing the bad news that had to be reported to stockholders. The published results were still pretty dismal: on sales of $767,313,100, the company reported a loss of $54,589,720. That was, however, a whole lot better than the $121,588,931 that the company *actually* lost last year.

To understand how an actual loss of $122 million can become a reported loss of $55 million requires some comprehension of tax accounting. It is well known, of course, that a corporate dollar earned is roughly 50 cents lost to the tax collector. The converse is also true, i.e., *a dollar lost is 50 cents earned.* Allis-Chalmers simply claimed a credit on its profit-and-loss statement for the taxes that it saved by achieving a loss. The company said, in effect: "If Uncle Sam deserves his slice of profits, he also deserves his slice of the losses. We cannot be said to have lost $122 million when we thereby hung on to something over $60 million in taxes that we otherwise would have had to pay."

Allis-Chalmers had deducted from its operating loss of $93,094,627 "federal, state and Canadian income taxes" of $51,942,000. Part of this was provided by a loss carry-back of $14,345,721, effectively refunding taxes paid in 1965, 1966, and 1967. The remainder was supplied by potential carry-forward benefits. The company listed as a current asset "income tax refunds and future income tax benefits" of $35,619,025, and an additional asset, between current and long-term assets "estimated future income tax benefits" of $42,972,400 (see Exhibit 2).

APB *Opinion No. 11* (effective for periods beginning after December 31, 1967) had stated:

> If operating losses are carried backwards to earlier periods under provisions of the tax law, the tax effects of the loss carry-*backs* are included in the results of operations of the loss period, since realization is assured. If operating losses are carried forward under provisions of the tax law, the tax effects usually are not recognized in the accounts until the periods of realization, since realization of the benefits of the loss carry-*forwards* generally is not assured in the loss periods. The only exception to that practice occurs in unusual circumstances when realization is assured beyond any reasonable doubt in the loss periods. Under an alternative view, however, the tax effects of loss carry-*forwards* would be recognized in the loss periods unless specific reasons exist to question their realization.

The auditor's opinion on the 1968 financial statements read:

> . . . As explained in Note 3 to the financial statements, in the last quarter of 1968 the Company recorded substantial amounts associated with *(a)* reserves for anticipated costs and losses, and *(b)* estimated income tax benefits expected to be realized in the future. Although these reserves and anticipated tax benefits reflect the best current judgment of the Company's management,

we cannot determine at this time the amounts of costs and losses which ultimately will be charged against the reserves, and the amounts of future tax
benefits which ultimately will be realized.

In our opinion, subject to the effect of any adjustments which may result
from ultimate determination of the matters referred to in the preceding paragraph, the accompanying consolidated financial statements examined by us
present fairly the financial position of Allis-Chalmers Manufacturing Company
and its subsidiaries at December 31, 1968 and the results of their operations
for the year, in conformity with generally accepted accounting principles

EXHIBIT 2

ALLIS-CHALMERS MANUFACTURING COMPANY
Assets

	December 31	
	1968	1967*
Current Assets:		
Cash	$ 23,483,905	$ 32,778,384
Receivables, less reserves of $16,171,800 and		
$12,990,000, respectively	126,836,883	125,835,967
Inventories, at lower of approximate cost (10%		
valued at Lifo) or market, less progress pay-		
ments of $14,286,644 and $13,816,887,		
respectively	234,115,066	231,107,182
Income tax refunds and future income tax		
benefits (Note 3)	35,619,025	21,590,000
Other current assets	3,997,779	4,496,240
Total Current Assets	$424,052,658	$415,807,773
Estimated future income tax benefits (Note 3)	42,972,400	—
Investments and Other Assets:		
Investment in finance subsidiaries, at equity		
in net assets	$ 53,498,936	$ 46,594,803
Investment in other subsidiaries, at cost, less		
reserves (Note 1)	18,524,117	23,748,137
Intangible assets arising from acquisition		
(Note 2)	7,389,935	7,389,935
Other investments, assets, and deferred		
charges (Note 5)	6,366,775	5,244,786
	$ 85,779,763	$ 82,977,661
Plants and Equipment at Cost:		
Land and buildings	$110,168,287	$103,163,467
Machinery and equipment.....................	190,005,484	180,635,390
Tools and fixtures	32,212,797	29,925,202
Furniture and fixtures	7,136,070	6,391,647
	$339,522,638	$320,115,706
Accumulated depreciation and amortization		
(Note 6)	186,714,838	178,989,166
	$152,807,800	$141,126,540
	$705,612,621	$639,911,974

EXHIBIT 2 *(continued)*

Liabilities and Equity

	December 31	
	1968	*1967**
Current Liabilities:		
Notes payable and current maturities of long-term debt..............................	$106,382,295	$ 50,797,500
Accounts payable and payrolls	68,970,051	69,978,681
Federal, state, and Canadian income taxes........	883,458	4,072,998
Reserves for completion of contracts and product corrections and current portion of special reserves	69,486,985	12,611,115
Other current liabilities	20,606,507	19,237,153
Total Current Liabilities..................	$266,329,296	$156,697,447
Special Reserves (Note 3):		
Estimated costs of parts replacement, warranty costs, repossession losses, and price allowances	$ 40,260,106	—
Estimated costs and losses associated with relocation and discontinuance of facilities and products	28,494,304	—
	$ 68,754,410	—
Less amount included in current liabilities	48,000,000	—
	$ 20,754,410	—
Long-Term Debt (Note 4):		
Notes payable	$ 66,000,000	$ 69,000,000
Sinking fund debentures	45,000,000	45,000,000
Other long-term debt..........................	3,361,924	4,228,487
	$114,361,924	$118,228,487
Deferred income taxes	—	$ 1,449,260
Share Owners' Equity (Notes 5 and 9):		
Preferred stock, $100 par value, 500,000 shares authorized, 134,594 shares, 4.20% cumulative convertible series outstanding in 1967..	—	13,459,400
Common stock, $10 par value, 12,500,000 shares authorized, 10,410,292 and 9,881,481 shares outstanding after deducting 42,869 and 82,869 shares held in treasury, respectively	$104,102,920	98,814,810
Capital in excess of par value of capital stock	122,548,752	113,198,182
Earnings retained.............................	77,515,319	138,064,388
Total Share Owners' Equity	$304,166,991	$363,536,780
	$705,612,621	$639,911,974

* 1967 has been restated to conform with the current year's account classifications.

applied on a basis consistent with that of the preceding year, except for the changes in accounting for depreciation and income taxes as explained in Note 6 to the financial statements.

The 1969 first quarter earnings were $11.7 million, less a provision for taxes, for a net profit of $5.1 million. The tax carry-forward benefit had been taken completely in 1968 for book purposes. Hence, it was not available for 1969. In contrast, the actual tax payment benefits could only be realized as future profits were reported for tax purposes.

Questions

1. Appraise the current and prospective corporate implications of the corporate reporting decisions discussed in the Allis-Chalmers case.
2. Comment on the appropriateness of these decisions from the point of view of "fairness" and "generally accepted accounting principles."
3. What is your appraisal of the comments included in the *Fortune* article?
4. What is your evaluation of the auditor's opinion?

Chapter 13

FIXED ASSET ACCOUNTING

Tangible fixed assets include all of those assets of a physical substance with a life of more than one year that are used in operations but are not intended for sale as such in the ordinary course of business. Tangible fixed assets can be classified in three different categories: *(a)* those subject to depreciation, such as plant and equipment; *(b)* those subject to depletion, such as natural resources; and *(c)* those not subject to depreciation or depletion, such as land. Fixed assets are normally carried at their original cost, less any accumulated depreciation. Depreciation, the process of allocating the cost of fixed assets over the useful life of the asset so as to match the cost of an asset with the benefits it creates, is covered in Chapter 14. This chapter focuses on the measurement of investments in fixed assets.

Fixed assets are shown on the balance sheet as follows:

Fixed Assets:
Plant and equipment (original cost) xxxx
   Less: Allowance for depreciation xxxx
      Net Plant and Equipment xxxx

Ordinarily no mention is made of a fixed asset's market value. However, the SEC does require certain companies to indicate their productive assets' replacement cost in the notes on a new and net basis.

CAPITALIZATION CRITERIA

Considerable judgment is sometimes required to determine whether or not an expenditure related to fixed assets should be capitalized or expensed as incurred. Generally, those expenditures whose usefulness is expected to extend over several accounting periods or that extend the useful life of a fixed asset are capitalized. Conversely, expenditures should be expensed when they neither extend the useful life of a fixed asset beyond the original estimates nor

352

generate benefits beyond the current accounting period. Companies usually establish minimum cost limits below which all amounts are expensed, even if they might otherwise be properly capitalized. The minimum amount selected should be set at that point which still results in fair financial reporting but which does not place an unreasonable burden on the accounting system.

COST BASIS

Unless otherwise indicated, the cost of a purchased fixed asset is the price paid for the asset plus all of the costs incidental to acquisition, installation, and preparation for use. Judgment must be applied to assure the inclusion of all material identifiable elements of cost, such as purchasing, testing, and similar items. All available cash discounts irrespective of whether or not they are taken should be excluded from the amount capitalized. Discounts not taken should be charged as a current financial expense.

Fixed assets may be acquired by manufacture or by exchange. The cost of assets manufactured for use in the business generally includes the materials, labor, and manufacturing overhead directly related to the construction. How much, if any, of the general factory overhead is included in the construction cost depends on whether or not the plant constructing the asset is operating at or below capacity.

When the plant is operating at or near capacity, the use of the scarce productive facilities to construct an asset for internal use reduces the opportunity to produce regular items for sale. Because of this lost profit opportunity, a fair share of general manufacturing overhead is typically charged to an asset construction project, thereby relieving the income statement of costs that, in the absence of the construction, would have generated some offsetting revenue.

Under below-capacity conditions, it is debatable whether or not a fair portion of general manufacturing overhead should be charged to the cost of assets constructed for a company's own use. The arguments for charging a portion of general manufacturing overhead include: (a) the current loss from idle capacity will be overstated unless a cost for the idle capacity used for construction is capitalized; (b) the construction will have future benefits, so all costs related to acquiring these benefits should be deferred; and (c) the construction project should be treated the same as regular products, which are charged with general overhead.

The principal arguments opposing this point of view are: (a) the cost of the asset should not include general overhead costs that would still have been incurred in the absence of the construction; (b) the general overhead was probably not considered as a relevant cost in making the decision to construct the asset for the company's own use, since the costs would be incurred irrespective of whether or not the asset was constructed; *(c)* by capitalizing part of the general overhead, current income will increase due to construction rather than the production of salable goods; and *(d)* it is more conservative not to capitalize general overhead.

Increasingly, the practice of charging fixed assets constructed for a company's own use with general overhead on the same basis and at the same rate as regular goods produced for sale is being adopted, irrespective of the prevailing capacity conditions. This trend reflects a movement away from conservatism for its own sake and a growing concern for the proper allocation of costs to reduce distortions of periodic income due to undervaluation of assets.

Assets manufactured for a company's own use may cost less than their purchase price. This saving should not be recorded as profit at the time the asset is completed, since profits result from the use of assets, not their acquisition. The advantage of the saving will accrue to the company over the life of the asset through lower depreciation charges than would have been incurred if the asset had been purchased.

Assets costing more to construct than their purchase price are sometimes recorded at their purchase price in the interests of conservatism. The difference between construction cost and purchase price is charged to income upon completion of the asset.

As indicated in Chapter 9, *Opinion No. 29*, the cost of a nonmonetary asset acquired in exchange for another nonmonetary asset is the fair value of the asset surrendered to obtain it, and a gain or loss should be recognized on the exchange if the exchange is essentially the culmination of an earnings process. However, if the exchange is not the culmination of an earnings process, the accounting for an exchange of a nonmonetary asset between an enterprise and another entity should be based on the book value of the nonmonetary asset relinquished and no gain or loss recognized on the exchange.

Trade-in allowances on exchanged assets are often greater than their market value. Consequently, the use of trade-in allowances to value a newly acquired asset may lead to misleading results through an overstatement of its cost and subsequent depreciation charges. Caution must be exercised in trade-in situations, since assets acquired through exchanges should not be recorded at a price greater than would have been paid in the absence of a trade-in.

For income tax purposes, "no gain or loss is recognized if the taxpayer exchanges property held for productive use in his trade or business, together with cash, for other property of like kind for the same use." The depreciation base of the newly acquired property is the book value shown for tax purposes of the exchanged property plus the cash payment.

For many years the interest cost on funds borrowed for construction could also be capitalized as part of the fixed asset cost. However, in 1974 the SEC prohibited the further use of this accounting practice until the FASB reached its decision on accounting for interest costs. The SEC moratorium did not apply to public utilities.

Donated assets should be recorded at their fair market value.

EXPENDITURES SUBSEQUENT TO ACQUISITION AND USE

After a fixed asset is acquired and put into use, a number of expenditures related to its subsequent utilization may be incurred. The manager must decide whether or not these expenditures should be capitalized as part of the asset cost or expensed as incurred. The general practice is to capitalize those expenditures that will generate future benefits beyond those originally estimated at the time the asset was acquired. However, if there is substantial uncertainty as to whether the benefits will ever be realized, such expenditures are charged to current income. Also, all expenditures related to fixed assets that are necessary to realize the benefits originally projected are expensed.

Repairs and Maintenance

Maintenance and repair costs are incurred to maintain assets in a satisfactory operating condition. When these expenditures are ordinary and recurring, they are expensed. Significant expenditures made for repairs which lead to an increase in the asset's economic life or its efficiency beyond the original estimates should be charged to the allowance for depreciation. This effectively raises the asset's book value. In addition, the asset's depreciable rate should also be changed to reflect the new use, life, and residual value expectations. Extraordinary expenditures for repairs that do not prolong an asset's economic life or improve its efficiency probably represent the cost of neglected upkeep of the asset, and as such should be charged to income as incurred.

Repairs made to restore assets damaged by fire, flood, or similar events should be charged to loss from casualty up to the amount needed to restore the asset to its condition before the damage. Expenditures beyond this amount should be treated like any other expenditure that prolongs the economic life of an asset.

When some assets are acquired, it is anticipated that unusually heavy maintenance costs, such as repainting, may be incurred at different points during their lives. In these situations, some managers establish an "Allowance for Repairs and Maintenance" account to avoid unusually large charges against income. This practice, which is permissible, charges income with a predetermined periodic maintenance expense based upon management's estimate of the total ordinary and unusual maintenance costs over the asset's life. The credit entry is to the liability account, Repairs and Maintenance Allowance. When the actual expenditures for the anticipated maintenance are incurred, the allowance account is charged with this amount. Since the allowance represents a future charge to current assets, it is sometimes treated as a current liability. In other cases, it is reported as a contra account to fixed assets, along with the allowance for depreciation account. Credit balances are deducted from original cost in determining book value. Debit balances are regarded as temporary additions, and as such increase book value. For income tax purposes, only the actual expenditures for maintenance are deductible. Therefore, the establishment of an allowance usually has deferred tax accounting implications also.

Betterments, Improvements, and Additions

Expenditures for betterments and improvements, such as replacing wooden beams in a building with steel girders, usually result in an increase in an asset's economic life or usefulness. As such, these expenditures are properly capitalized and subsequently charged to the related asset's allowance for depreciation. Also, the asset's depreciation rate should be redetermined to reflect the economic consequences of the expenditure. Minor expenditures for betterments and improvements are typically expensed as incurred.

Additions to existing assets, such as a new wing to a plant, represent capital expenditures, and as such should be recorded at their full acquisition cost just like the original investment in fixed assets.

LAND

Land is a nondepreciable asset, since its life is assumed to be indefinitely long. Land should be shown separately on the balance sheet.

The cost of land includes the purchase price, all costs incidental to the purchase, and the costs of permanent improvements, such as clearing and draining. Expenditures made for improvements with a limited life, such as sidewalks and fencing, should be recorded in a separate account, Land Improvements, and written off over their useful lives.

If land is held for speculative purposes, it should be captioned appropriately and reported separately from the land used for productive facilities. The carrying costs of such land can be capitalized, since the land is producing no income and the eventual gain or loss on the sale of the land is the difference between the selling price and the purchase price plus carrying charges. For income tax purposes, the carrying charges can be either capitalized or deducted as incurred.

WASTING ASSETS

Mineral deposits and other natural resources that are physically exhausted through extraction and are irreplaceable are called "wasting assets." Until extracted, such assets are classified as fixed assets. The cost of land containing wasting assets should be allocated between the residual value of the land and the depletable natural resource. If the natural resource is discovered after the purchase of the land, it is acceptable to reallocate the original cost in a similar way.

Companies in the business of exploiting wasting assets on a continuing basis incur exploration costs to replace their exhausted assets. As indicated in Chapter 16, these exploration costs can be either expensed or capitalized. Because of the great uncertainty associated with the extractive industry, the typical practice is to capitalize only those costs identifiable with the discovery and development of productive properties and expense the rest as incurred.

There are two basic approaches to the capitalization of discovery and development costs. These are commonly called the "full cost" and "field cost" methods. In practice these methods are applied in a variety of different ways.

The field cost method assigns the costs of discovery and development to specific fields of wasting assets, such as a specific oil or gas field in Oklahoma. If the exploration and development activities related to that field are unsuccessful, the costs are expensed. If the field proves to be successful, the costs are capitalized and written off against the production of the field on a units of production basis. If the costs exceed the value of the field's reserves, the costs are capitalized only to the extent they can be recovered from the sale of the reserves. Should a field be abandoned, any capitalized costs are written off immediately.

The full cost method assigns costs of discovery and development to regions of activity, such as the North American continent. These regions may include one or more fields in which the company is active. The full cost method follows the same capitalization-expense rules as the field method. However, since the area for measuring reserves is now a larger region, the costs of discovery and development in unsuccessful fields can be lumped together with the costs of successful efforts and written off against the total region's production.

HISTORICAL COSTS AND ACCOUNTABILITY

The general practice of recording fixed assets at cost can lead to situations where there is a conflict between adherence to the cost principle and management accountability for the use of the assets at their disposal. In some rare cases where this conflict arises, it is permissible to depart from the cost principle. In most cases, however, it is not permissible. *Opinion No. 6* discussed the accounting for appreciation:

The Board is of the opinion that property, plant and equipment should not be written up by an entity to reflect appraisal, market or current values which are above cost to the entity. This statement is not intended to change accounting practices followed in connection with quasi-reorganizations or reorganizations. This statement may not apply to foreign operations under unusual conditions such as serious inflation or currency devaluation. However, when the accounts of a company with foreign operations are translated into United States currency for consolidation, such write-ups normally are eliminated. Whenever appreciation has been recorded on the books, income should be charged with depreciation computed on the written up amounts.

ALTERNATIVE PROPOSALS

Historical cost is the only accepted base for measuring plant and equipment and related depreciation charges in published financial statements. A number of other approaches have been proposed by accounting authors. These include: making the carrying value of assets more responsive to their current market values, adjusting the historical cost base to reflect price level changes, and the use of replacement costs as the basis for calculating annual depreciation charges.

Those who oppose the use of historical costs to value fixed assets do so principally on the ground that it does not, in their opinion, lead to useful financial statements. For many years those who supported alternative approaches to the historical cost convention did not challenge the desirability of historical costs in terms of objectivity and feasibility over other alternative methods for measurement of fixed assets. However, in recent years these two qualities have been increasingly questioned as to their validity.

The supporters of historical cost argue that this basis is useful and part of the discipline of management: it holds management responsible for the funds invested in fixed assets. Also, the users of financial reports are fully aware that historical costs do not represent value but merely unexpired costs. The weight of convention, experience, and acceptance is clearly on the side of historical costs; therefore, it is argued, the burden of proving some alternative basis more useful rests with those who oppose the use of historical costs to measure assets.

The *essence of the price level and market value approaches* can be illustrated as follows: A farmer's sole business asset is land purchased 15 years ago for $8,000. The current appraisal of the land's market value is $300,000. Based upon this appraisal, the farmer obtained a mortgage loan of $350,000 for the construction of a new shopping center on the land, the total value of which will be $650,000. During the 15 years the farmer held the land, the prive levels doubled.

An historical cost statement for this farmer just prior to the bank loan would show assets of $8,000 and net worth of $8,000 (other items excluded). If price level adjustments were made, the statement would show assets of $16,000 and a similar amount for net worth. If market values were used, the statements would show assets at $300,000 and net worth at $300,000, which would consist of $8,000 original investment plus $292,000 appreciation by reason of holding the land in a rising market. If the price level and market value approaches were combined, the assets would remain the same, but net worth would now consist of the $8,000 original investment, the $8,000 price level gain, and the $284,000 appreciation in the market value of the land after adjusting for price level changes.

Price level adjustment attempts to state historical costs incurred in different years in terms of a current and common monetary unit of equivalent purchasing power. It is not a valuation method. In countries with rapidly rising price levels, it is common practice to adjust the historical acquisition costs of fixed assets for general price level changes. This results in a measurement of fixed assets and their related depreciation charges in terms of the general purchasing power invested and expiring. Under conditions of rapid inflation, few question the wisdom of this practice. However, many, including the Accounting Principles Board, argued that the annual rate of inflation in the United States had not been high enough to justify converting the historical costs invested in assets during prior years to current dollars having the same purchasing power. Nevertheless, in those cases where management believes price level adjusted statements are more meaningful than historical-cost-based statements, the Accounting Principles Board encouraged the use of supplemental disclosure of the price level adjusted data. Price level accounting and the recent developments in this area are covered in greater detail in Chapter 15.

The case for the *market value method* of asset valuation is expressed as follows: Assets are recorded at cost initially, because this is the economic measure of their potential service value. After acquisition, the accounting goal should continue to be the expression of the eco-

nomic value of this service potential. This is difficult to measure directly. However, the current market price others are willing to pay for
similar assets approximates in most cases this value. Therefore, to the
extent that market values are available they should be used to measure
fixed asset carrying values and their subsequent consumption in the
production of goods and services. Property values are more useful to
managers and stockholders than historical costs because market values
determine the collateral value of property for borrowing purposes, fix
liability for property taxes, establish the basis for insurance, and reflect
the amount an owner might expect to realize, upon sale of the
property.

The principal objection to market value is that it is often difficult to
determine objectively. The proponents of market value answer this
argument by indicating that the notion of market value has some important qualifications. For example: recognition should only be given
to fairly determined market values when the disparity between market
value and cost is likely to prevail for a fairly long period of time.
Furthermore, recognition of market value should occur only when
there is reliable evidence as to the market value of the asset involved.
Also, the notion of market value probably has little relevance to
nonstandardized equipment, or special fixed assets for which no readily available market exists. Historical costs must suffice in these cases.

The market value approach has significant implications for the income statement. The market value advocates claim that management
continually faces the alternative of using or disposing of assets. Income
statements based on historical cost do not show how well management
has appraised this alternative, since in no way is the "cost" of the
alternative foregone included in the statements. In a case where the
market value of an asset is greater than its historical cost, historical-
cost-based depreciation leads to an overstatement of the incremental
benefit gained by using rather than selling, since the book depreciation basis is understated. The reverse is true when the market value is
less than the book value. It is claimed that market-value-based depreciation would overcome this weakness. The incremental benefit of
continuing to use the asset would be determined after a depreciation
charge based on the "cost" of the income foregone by not disposing of
the asset.

There is a difference of opinion among market value supporters as
to how changes in the carrying value of the assets should be recorded.
Some would treat the increases or decreases in stockholder's equity in
much the same way as appraisal adjustments are recorded. Others
propose including the changes as part of the income determination, in
a fashion similar to the adjustments to income for gains or losses on
foreign exchange.

The *replacement cost approach* advocates carrying assets at the cost of reproducing equivalent property, not identical property, as some critics of replacement cost assume. This approach is based on a concept of income which maintains that no profit is made until adequate provision through depreciation charges is made for the eventual cost of replacing the capacity represented in the existing assets with an asset of more modern design. Based on this theory, in periods of rising replacement costs, traditional depreciation, which recovers original cost from revenues, does not adequately provide for future replacement and so leads to an overstatement of profits. As a result, excessive dividends, wages, and income taxes may be paid, to the detriment of the company's ability to maintain its current level of capacity.

The replacement cost approach involves the application of specific price indexes to an asset's original cost. The result approximates the replacement cost of an asset derived through an appraisal. Such price indexes are available and widely accepted for specific categories of assets. The replacement cost proponents argue that their method has the advantage of the objectivity associated with recording the original cost of the asset at acquisition, plus minimizing the role of judgment in subsequent revaluations. Thus, the net result of their approach, they argue, is a more useful income figure without any sacrifice in objectivity.

Accounting Research Bulletin No. 43 recognizes the potential erosion of capital inherent in applying cost-based depreciation in periods of rising replacement costs, but concludes that increasing depreciation charges against income is not an appropriate solution. It recommends "annual appropriations of net income or surplus in contemplation of replacement of such facilities at higher price levels" as a more satisfactory solution.

In 1976 the SEC required that the value of productive assets and their related depreciation computed on a replacement cost basis be presented in the notes to the financial statements. The SEC defined the replacement cost of a productive asset as the current expenditure that would be required to acquire a new asset with productive or functional capability equivalent to that currently held using management's normal approach to replacement taking into account price changes and other current economic conditions. This requirement could move financial statements closer to a current value basis.

INVESTMENT TAX CREDIT

To encourage investment in productive assets, the Revenue Act of 1962 allowed taxpayers a credit against income taxes of up to 7 percent of the acquisition cost of certain tangible personal property used in business operations. Originally, taxpayers qualifying for the investment credit were required for income tax purposes to reduce the depreciation basis of the property to which the credit related by the amount of the credit. This requirement was eliminated in the Revenue Act of 1964. In October 1966, the credit was suspended by Congress. It was restored again in May 1967. The 1969 Tax Reform Act abolished the investment tax credit. The Revenue Act of 1971 restored the investment tax credit. Later, in 1975 the investment tax credit was raised to 10 percent for some assets.

To illustrate the calculation of the investment tax credit, assume a qualified piece of machinery with a ten-year life and zero salvage is purchased for $200,000. The company's profits before taxes, but after depreciation, on all other items except the new machinery is $1,320,000. Therefore, the company's taxable income is:

Profit after all depreciation, but before taxes and
    depreciation on new equipment $1,320,000
      Less: Depreciation on new machinery ($200,000 × 0.10) 20,000

Taxable income $1,300,000

The effect of the purchase and a 7 percent tax credit on the company's tax payment is:

Income taxes before investment credit
    (50% of taxable income) $650,000
      Less: Investment Credit ($200,000 × 0.07) 14,000

Tax payment due $636,000

It is important to note that the investment tax credit is a direct reduction of the tax otherwise payable.

The granting of the investment tax credit created a serious accounting problem. Although most people[1] agreed that the credit was a factor which influenced the determination of net income, they could not agree on how the credit increased income.

A number of business executives and accountants supported the flow-through method for handling the credit. Under this method, the investment tax credit was considered as being in substance a selective reduction in taxes which otherwise would have been payable and which were related to the taxable income of the year in which the

---

[1] It was argued by some that the credit was in effect a subsidy by way of a contribution to capital and, hence, should be so recorded directly as an increase in owners' equity. This position was not considered by the Accounting Principles Board, since it ran counter to the widespread belief that the credit increased income.

credit was granted. This approach considered the credit as being related to taxable income rather than to the cost of using assets. Also, since the credit was not relatable to, or dependent on, future revenues, the flow-through advocates maintained that the credit was earned during the period in which it was obtained.

The supporters of the deferral approach believed that the investment tax credit should be put on the balance sheet as deferred income and reflected in earnings as a separately identifiable item as the related asset was used and depreciated. They rejected the flow-through approach, principally on the ground that the credit did not enhance the integrity of the earnings figure if earnings could be increased simply by buying an asset.

To illustrate the effect of these different approaches to handling the investment credit, assume that the Hampton Company bought a new piece of equipment costing $100,000. The expected life of the equipment was ten years. Consequently, the company qualified to receive an investment tax credit of $7,000. Handling the credit on a flow-through basis would improve aftertax profits by the full $7,000 in the year of purchase, but on a deferral basis by only $700. In both cases, the cash flow would be the same. However, the use of the flow-through method would boost the Hampton Company aftertax profits by $6,300 over using the deferral method. Alternatively, the adoption of the deferral method would result in future profits for each of the next nine years being $700 higher than they would have been if the flow-through method had been adopted.

In December 1962 the Accounting Principles Board issued *Opinion No. 2*, "Accounting for the 'Investment Credit'," which supported the deferral method and explicitly rejected the flow-through approach. Later, in January 1963, the Securities and Exchange Commission, in *Accounting Series Release No. 96*, indicated that the Commission would accept statements using either the deferral or the flow-through approach, principally because of the substantial diversity of opinion among responsible people as to the appropriate accounting for the credit. As a result of the Commission's decision and the significant number of companies adopting the flow-through method, the Accounting Principles Board issued *Opinion No. 4*, which amended *Opinion No. 2* to approve both the flow-through and deferral methods. However, the APB still expressed a preference for the deferral approach.

Subsequently, in 1967, the APB issued an exposure draft of *Opinion No. 11*, which again proposed that the deferral method be adopted as the only acceptable way to account for the investment credit. This proposal aroused the ire of many corporate executives, accountants, and government officials and was withdrawn from the final draft of the opinion for further study.

Later, in 1971 in anticipation of the reinstatement of the investment tax credit the APB with the backing of the SEC again issued an exposure draft proposing that the new investment tax credit be accounted for by the deferral method. Considerable pressure was brought by business executives on the Congress and the administration to veto the APB proposal. These efforts were successful, and the 1971 Revenue Act specifically stated that "no taxpayer shall be required, without his consent, to use, for purposes of his financial reports, any particular method of accounting for the credit." This decision by Congress meant that a corporation could account for the tax credit in any fashion it choose to adopt. This was an intolerable situation. So, the IRS and the APB agreed to limit the acceptable alternatives to the deferral and flow-through methods.

SUGGESTED FURTHER READING

SPROUSE, ROBERT T., ed. *The Measurement of Property, Plant and Equipment in Financial Statements*. Boston: Harvard University, 1964.

CASES

CASE 13–1.   BRAZOS PRINTING COMPANY
Problems in Fixed Asset Transactions

The Brazos Printing Company was founded as a one-man job printing firm in a small southwestern town. Shortly after its founding, the owner decided to concentrate on one specialty line of printing. Because of a high degree of technical proficiency, the company experienced a rapid growth.

However, the company suffered from a competitive disadvantage in that the major market for this specialized output was in a metropolitan area over 300 miles away from the company's plant. For this reason, the owner 12 years later decided to move nearer his primary market. He also decided to expand and modernize his facilities at the time of the move. After some investigation, an attractive site was found in a suburb of his primary market, and the move was made.

A balance sheet prepared prior to the move is shown in Exhibit 1. The transactions that arose from this move are described in the following paragraphs.

1.   The land at the old site together with the building thereon was sold for $35,000. The land had originally cost $5,000. The building appeared on the company's books at a cost of $76,000, and a depreciation allowance of $45,000 had been accumulated on it.

2.   Certain equipment was sold for $4,500 cash. This equipment appeared on the books at a cost of $16,700 less accumulated depreciation of $9,700.

3.   New bindery equipment was purchased. The invoice cost of this equipment was $20,000. A 2 percent cash discount was taken by the Brazos Company, so that only $19,600 was actually paid to the seller. The Brazos Company also paid $80 to a trucker to have this equipment delivered. Installation of this equipment was made by Brazos workmen, who worked a total of 40 hours. These men received $1.50 per hour in wages, but their time was ordinarily charged to printing jobs at $4 per hour, the difference representing an allowance for overhead ($2.10) and profit ($0.40).

365

EXHIBIT 1

BRAZOS PRINTING COMPANY
Condensed Balance Sheet

Assets

Current Assets:
Cash		$ 91,242
Other current assets		69,720
Total Current Assets		$160,962

Fixed Assets:
Land....................................		5,000
Buildings	$76,000	
Less: Accumulated depreciation	45,000	31,000
Equipment	$65,822	
Less: Accumulated depreciation	42,340	23,482
Total Assets		$220,444

Equities

Current liabilities.......................	$ 41,346
Common stock.........................	100,000
Retained earnings	79,098
Total Equities	$220,444

4.   The city to which the company moved furnished the land on which the new plant was built as a gift. The land had an appraised value of $20,000; the appraisal had been made recently by a qualified appraiser. The company would pay property taxes on its assessed value, which was $15,000.

5.   The Brazos Company paid $4,000 to have an old building on the gift plot of land torn down. (The value of this building was not included in the appraised or assessed values named above.) In addition, the company paid $2,000 to have permanent drainage facilities installed on the new land.

6.   A new strip caster with an invoice cost of $4,500 was purchased. The company paid $3,000 cash and received a trade-in allowance of $1,500 on a used strip caster. The used strip caster could have been sold outright for not more than $1,200. It had cost $3,000 new, and accumulated depreciation on it was $1,200.

7.   The company erected a building at the new site for $90,000. Of this amount $70,000 was borrowed on a mortgage.

8.   After the equipment had been moved to the new plant, but before operations began there, extensive repairs and replacement of parts were made on a large paper cutter. The cost of this work was $1,100. Prior to this time, no more than $100 had been spent in any one year on the maintenance of this paper cutter.

9. Trucking and other costs associated with moving equipment to the new location and installing it there were $1,400. In addition, Brazos Company employees worked an estimated 120 hours on that part of the move that related to equipment.

10. During the moving operation, a piece of equipment costing $3,000 was dropped and damaged; $400 was spent to repair it. Mr. Timken believed, however, that the salvage value of this equipment had been reduced to $200. Up until that time, the equipment was being depreciated at $240 per year, representing a 10 percent rate after deduction of estimated salvage of $600. Accumulated depreciation was $960.

Questions

1. Analyze the effect of these transactions on the items in the balance sheet.
2. In your opinion, should the transactions which affect net worth in the case be accounted for in the profit and loss account or carried directly to retained earnings? If in the profit and loss account, where should these items appear in the profit and loss statement?

CASE 13–2. PROFESSOR F. WINGER
Investment Tax Credit and Accounting Rule-Making

Professor F. Winger, an authority on capital markets, tax legislation, and corporate reporting on the faculty of a leading Californian law school felt compelled by the controversy over the appropriate accounting for the investment tax credit proposed in the Revenue Act of 1971 to speak out on the issue. As a first step he asked several of his friends who had previously expressed their opinions in letters to the APB, key congressmen, and the Secretary of the Treasury to send him copies of their letters. In turn, Professor Winger promised to send his comments on each of these letters to the respective authors. In addition, Professor Winger intended to send a letter to all of the interested parties stating his position on this issue and the reasons for this conclusions.

APB Decision and Congressional Reaction

On October 6, 1971, the House of Representatives passed a tax bill that included a 7 percent "job development tax credit."

In response to this action the APB issued a draft of a proposed *Opinion* on the appropriate accounting for investment tax credits on

October 22, 1971. This *Opinion* stated that "the benefits arising from the investment tax credits be accounted for as reductions of income tax over the periods in which the cost of the related property is charged to income."

Subsequently in November 1971 the Senate in its version of the tax bill voted that "no taxpayer shall be required, without his consent, to use, for purposes of his financial reports, any particular method of accounting for the credit and a taxpayer shall disclose, in any financial report made by him, the method of accounting for the credit used for purposes of such report."

According to an Undersecretary of the Treasury the Senate action was justified because the relatively lower profits that would be reported under the deferral method "might operate to diminish the job-creating effect of the credit" since business executives would "have less motivation to purchase new equipment."

Investment Banker's Letter

The first letter Professor Winger received was a copy of a letter sent to the APB on October 2 by an investment banker friend who was a partner of a major underwriting firm. The letter stated:

I am sure that you have been deluged with comments about the airline industry and the flow-through of investment credit. From an accounting and a security analyst standpoint I can well understand your position, but I think you are taking on a lot of responsibility in which, by the farthest stretch of the imagination, you have no authority. By this I mean you are forcing changes in market share for various companies.

I am sure you are well aware of the $1.487 billion difference in retained earnings that the major trunks told Mr. Ackley that they would not have if they were forced to amortize the investment credit. Metropolitan Life and Chase Manhattan, which have been two of the leading lenders, have in times of severe problems been willing to give the carriers straight debt equal to 1.5 times the sum of convertibles plus net worth. Make it just one-to-one and you will see you are preventing carriers from buying $3 billion worth of equipment over the next decade. The gross plant of the entire industry is only $5 billion.

In the interests of conversatism, or perhaps fear of the SEC, do you really want to have that much control over companies' fortunes? Also, are you sure you have considered the disservice you are doing to the American traveling public by withholding the benefits of improved service and possible lower fares from them?'

Enough is enough!

Another Professor's Response

One of Winger's fellow professors sent to him a copy of a letter he had written in mid-November to an Undersecretary of the Treasury.

This letter commented on a letter sent by this official in early November to the APB in which he had supported the flow-through approach because the tax credit was in essense a reduction of the corporate income tax rate. The law professor said:

This letter is to take issue with the Treasury Department position, expressed in your letter of November 8 to the Accounting Principles Board, on accounting for income taxes.

It seems to me that the Treasury Department letter misses the point as to what the accountants' problem is. Economists tend to think in macroeconomic terms about aggregate cash flows, and from that point of view, perhaps, the investment credit is something like a rate reduction. But the accountants' problem is to give a meaningful report of the results of operation of a particular firm during a particular period on a basis that can be intelligently compared with similar reports for other firms or for other periods. From that viewpoint there is all the difference in the world between a reduction in the rate of tax imposed on income and a credit against tax measured by something wholly unrelated to income in the current period. Neither the purpose nor the effect of the credit can be altered by referring to its association with the capital asset to which it relates as "artificial," or as a mere "mechanical method by which [a rate] reduction is measured or implemented in the statute." What the credit is and was intended to be is a form of subsidy for capital investment; what is artificial, and a mere mechanical method by which the subsidy is implemented, and a source of seemingly interminable semantic confusion, is the fact that the credit was incorporated into the income tax law instead of being separately enacted as a subsidy measure.

Allocation of taxes between current expense and capital account is a recurring and commonplace accounting procedure. Real estate taxes are charged to current expense or to plant accounts according to whether the plant is in service or under construction. Sales taxes on goods used for plant construction are charged to plant account.

If the federal government were to impose an excise tax on the purchase of airplanes, for example, that would be treated as part of the cost of the airplane and charged off over its useful life, not all at once. The investment credit is in purpose and effect much more nearly a negative exercise tax on capital investment than a reduction of rate of tax on income, and as such, it should be reflected, like a positive excise, over the useful life of the asset in question.

I am, perhaps, most troubled by the following sentence in the Treasury letter: "Furthermore, a mandate to defer the benefit arising from the investment credit could well blunt its effectiveness as an incentive to modernization and expansion."

I can find nothing in any part of the description of the intended incentive affect of the credit that depends in any way upon the credit being immediately reflected in income. The whole analysis was in terms of a rather sophisticated consideration of discounted cash flows, in which the credit was regarded essentially as reducing the cost of a capital investment without affecting the projected yield. The only way I can imagine that the accounting treatment would affect the incentive to invest is that under a flow-through method of accounting a management would see the investment credit as presenting an opportunity to show higher immediate earnings—or to cover up a drop in earnings—by making an otherwise undesirable capital investment and having the credit reflected immediately as a decrease in current income tax expense. This form of added inducement seems to me to involve a higher cost in terms of honesty and integrity of corporate financial reporting that we should be willing to pay.

The last sentence of the Treasury letter says that it would be unfortunate for the accounting profession to be bound by "ad hoc characterizations" of tax benefits. I agree wholeheartedly with that sentiment, but it seems to me that what is ad hoc about the investment credit is its incorporation into the income tax law, not its association with capital investment.

Security Analyst's Response

On November 19, 1971, the president of the Financial Analysts Federation sent to key members of Congress the following telegram. Professor Winger received his copy from the Federation's president several days later.

THE FINANCIAL ANALYSTS FEDERATION WISHES TO FILE AN OBJECTION TO THE AMENDMENT TO THE TAX BILL H.R. 10947, PARAGRAPH C, PAGE 5, BY THE SENATE, GIVING COMPLETE FREEDOM TO CORPORATIONS IN THE METHOD OF ACCOUNTING FOR THE INVESTMENT TAX CREDIT IN THEIR FINANCIAL RE-PORTING. WE URGE THAT THIS PROVISION BE STRICKEN FROM THE BILL IN THE CONFERENCE COMMITTEE.

THE FINANCIAL ANALYSTS FEDERATION IS THE PROFES-SIONAL ORGANIZATION OF 13,000 SECURITY ANALYSTS AND INVESTMENT MANAGERS WHO REPRESENT, DIRECTLY OR INDIRECTLY, A LARGE SEGMENT OF ALL INSTITUTIONAL AND INDIVIDUAL INVESTORS IN THE UNITED STATES.

OUR OBJECTIONS TO THIS PROVISION ARE TWOFOLD. FIRST, WE DO NOT BELIEVE ACCOUNTING AND REPORTING STANDARDS SHOULD BE ESTABLISHED BY LEGISLATION, ESPECIALLY WITH-OUT OPPORTUNITY FOR HEARING FROM INVESTORS WHO ARE AFFECTED BY SUCH STANDARDS. THIS PROVISION UNDERCUTS THE ESTABLISHED AUTHORITY OF THE SECURITIES AND EX-CHANGE COMMISSION AND THE ACCOUNTING PRINCIPLES BOARD FOR THE DETERMINATION OF ACCOUNTING STANDARDS. WE FEAR THAT THIS ACTION, IF FINALLY ADOPTED BY THE CON-GRESS, WILL ENCOURAGE SPECIAL INTEREST GROUPS TO AT-TEMPT TO BRING ABOUT OTHER CHANGES IN ACCOUNTING STANDARDS FOR THEIR BENEFIT THROUGH THE LEGISLATIVE PROCESS. WE BELIEVE THIS WILL RESULT IN A GROWING LOSS OF CONFIDENCE IN CORPORATE FINANCIAL REPORTING TO THE DETRIMENT OF INVESTORS.

SECOND, THE PROVISION PERMITS A VARIETY OF ACCOUNTING TREATMENTS OF THE TAX CREDIT. OUR FEDERATION HAS FOR MANY YEARS WORKED TO NARROW OR REDUCE THE NUMBER OF ALTERNATIVE ACCOUNTING METHODS. ANY MOVE TOWARD INCREASING THE NUMBER OF ALTERNATIVE METHODS IS A BACKWARD STEP IN REPORTING TO INVESTORS, RESULTING IN MISLEADING COMPARISONS OF THE FINANCIAL RESULTS OF PUBLIC CORPORATIONS.

THE CONGRESS HAS ALWAYS SHOWN GREAT CONCERN FOR THE PROTECTION OF THE INVESTOR. WE URGE THAT THIS PROVISION IN H.R. 10947 IN REGARD TO FINANCIAL REPORTING OF THE TAX CREDIT BE RECONSIDERED FOR ITS AFFECT ON INVESTORS. WE BELIEVE THAT THE CONTINUOUS LONGTERM IMPROVEMENT IN CORPORATE REPORTING TO INVESTORS IS BEING SACRIFICED FOR THE SHORTRUN BENEFIT OF A LIMITED NUMBER OF CORPORATIONS AND THAT A DANGEROUS PRECEDENT IS BEING ESTABLISHED.

Treasury Response to FAF

In early December an Undersecretary of the Treasury responded to the FAF letter. Knowing of Winger's interest in the FAF position, he sent a copy to Winger (see below).

This is in response to your telegram dated November 19, 1971, to Senator Long and Representative Mills, a copy of which was sent to me, relating to the Senate amendment to H.R. 10947 concerning the financial accounting treatment of the Job Development Investment Credit.

The Treasury Department supports the actions of the Senate in providing that a corporation shall retain the option of accounting for the credit in its financial statements on either the "flow-through" or the "deferral" method.

The Department's primary concern in seeking the credit is to stimulate the economy and create jobs by encouraging the purchase of new machinery and equipment. We believe that a requirement that corporations may only amortize the benefits of the credit over the service life of the asset in their financial statements may have an adverse impact on the intended effects of the credit.

When the Administration decided to press for the enactment of the Job Development Investment Credit, one of the factors that was considered was the manner in which such a credit would affect corporate reported earnings. The decision to request a restoration of the credit was based, in part, on the assumption that the present optional treatment of the credit for financial accounting purposes would be continued.

The Treasury Department has often stated that it believes that the establishment of accounting principles is solely within the province of the accounting profession and the Securities and Exchange Commission. However, because of the exceptional circumstances surrounding the accounting treatment of the credit and because of its critical relationship to the stimulation of the economy through the Job Development Investment Credit, we are compelled to support the actions of the Senate in dealing with the financial accounting treatment of the credit.

The Treasury Department strongly supports the efforts of the accounting profession to narrow the range of permissible accounting practices. Furthermore, we hope that our support for the Senate's action is in no way interpreted as a precedent for any future efforts to legislate financial accounting principles. Nevertheless, the strategic importance of the credit in the overall economic program—to create jobs through the stimulation of capital investment—requires that the Treasury Department support the efforts of the Senate to retain the present optional accounting treatment of the Job Development Investment Credit.

If you have any further questions, please feel free to contact us.

Questions

1. What comments on their position would you send back to the authors of the various letters and telegrams?
2. What is your position on the accounting principle, investment, economic development, and public responsibility issues raised by this controversy?

Chapter 14

DEPRECIATION ACCOUNTING

The term depreciation, as used in accounting, refers to the process of allocating the cost of a depreciable tangible fixed asset to the accounting periods covered during its expected useful life to a business. Some of the difficulties encountered in connection with depreciation result from failure to recognize the meaning of the term in this accounting sense. Outside the area of accounting, depreciation is generally used to denote a reduction in the value of property; misunderstandings are caused by attempts to substitute this concept for the more specialized accounting definition.

Depreciation was defined by the American Institute of Certified Public Accountants in its *Accounting Terminology Bulletin No. 1:*

Depreciation accounting is a system of accounting which aims to distribute the cost or other basic value of tangible capital assets, less salvage (if any), over the estimated useful life of the unit (which may be a group of assets) in a systematic and rational manner. It is a process of allocation, not of valuation.

Depreciation for the year is the portion of the total charge under such a system that is allocated to the year. Depreciation can be distinguished from other terms with specialized meanings used by accountants to describe asset cost allocation procedures. Depreciation is concerned with charging the cost of man-made fixed assets to operations (and not with determination of asset values for the balance sheet). Depletion refers to cost allocations for natural resources such as oil and mineral deposits. Amortization relates to cost allocations for intangible assets such as patents and leaseholds. The use of the term depreciation should also be avoided in connection with valuation procedures for securities and inventories.

COMPUTING DEPRECIATION

Depreciation expense for a period of operations can be determined by a variety of means, all of which satisfy the general requirements of consistency and reasonableness. Depreciation accounting requires the application of judgment in four areas: (1) determination of the cost of the asset depreciated (covered in Chapter 13), (2) estimation of the useful life of the asset, (3) estimation of the salvage value at the end of expected useful life, and (4) selection of a method of computing periodic depreciation charges.

Estimating the Useful Life of Fixed Assets

The estimated useful life of most fixed assets is expressed in terms of a period of calendar time. For example, a time basis for determining depreciation charges is suitable for general-purpose assets like buildings. The useful life of an asset might be expressed in units other than time, however. For instance, the life of a motor vehicle could be estimated as 100,000 miles, while the life of a unit of specialized machinery could be estimated as 200,000 units of output or as 5,000 operating hours.

The estimated life of an asset should be the period during which it is of use to the business. Thus, the estimate should take into account such factors as the use of the asset, anticipated obsolescence, planned maintenance, and replacement policy. The period of useful life may be less than the entire physical life of the asset. For example, machinery with an expected physical life of ten years under normal conditions will have a useful life for depreciation purposes of six years if company policy is to trade or dispose of such assets after six years or if technological improvements are expected to make the machine obsolete in six years.

Salvage value of fixed assets represents estimated realizable value at the end of the expected life. This may be the scrap or junk proceeds, cash sale proceeds, or trade-in value, depending upon the company's disposition and replacement policies.

Depreciable cost is determined by subtracting salvage value from the cost of the fixed asset. This depreciable cost is the amount allocated to the operating periods comprising the asset's useful life.

DEPRECIATION METHODS

Any depreciation method which results in a logical, systematic, and consistent allocation of depreciable cost is acceptable for financial accounting purposes. The procedures most commonly used are based upon straight-line, declining-balance, sum-of-the-years'-digits, and units-of-production (or service-life) depreciation methods. The commonly used depreciation methods are illustrated and discussed separately below. Several rarely used and comparatively complex depreciation methods which take into account the imputed earning power of investments in fixed assets will not be discussed. This group includes the annuity and sinking fund methods.

Straight-Line Depreciation

The most simple method of computing depreciation is the straight-line method. For purposes of illustration, a machine with a cost of $6,000 and estimated salvage value of $1,000 at the end of its expected five-year useful life is assumed. Depreciation expense for one year is computed thus:

Cost of machinery	$6,000
Less: Estimated salvage value	1,000
Depreciable cost	$5,000

$$\frac{\text{Depreciable Cost}}{\text{Estimated Life}} = \text{Depreciation Expense}$$

$$\frac{\$5,000}{5 \text{ Years}} = \$1,000 \text{ per Year}$$

The straight-line method's strongest appeal is its simplicity. Until accelerated depreciation methods were permitted for income tax purposes, this method was used almost universally. Objections to the straight-line method center on the allocation of equal amounts of depreciation to each period of useful life. Identical amounts are charged in the first year for use of a new and efficient machine and in the later years as the worn machine nears the salvage market.

Accelerated Depreciation

Accelerated depreciation methods provide relatively larger depreciation charges in the early years of an asset's estimated life and diminishing charges in later years. The double-declining-balance method and the sum-of-the-years'-digits method are the two best known methods.

Double-declining-balance depreciation for each year is computed by multiplying the asset cost less accumulated depreciation by twice the straight-line rate expressed as a decimal fraction. Using the earlier example—machinery with a cost of $6,000 and a five-year estimated useful life, which is equal to 20 percent per year—depreciation is computed as follows:

First year:	$6,000 × 0.40	$2,400
Second year:	($6,000 − $2,400) × 0.40	1,440
Third year:	($6,000 − $3,840) × 0.40	864
Fourth year:	($6,000 − $4,704) × 0.40	518
Fifth year:	($6,000 − $5,222) × 0.40	311
Total		$5,533

Note that estimated salvage value is not used directly in these computations, even though the asset has salvage value. Since the double-declining-balance procedure will not depreciate the asset to zero cost at the end of the estimated useful life, the residual balance provides an amount in lieu of scrap or salvage value. Ordinarily, however, depreciation is not continued beyond the point where net depreciated cost equals a reasonable salvage value. Also, it is common practice to switch from double-declining-balance depreciation to straight-line depreciation over the remaining life of an asset when the annual depreciation charge falls below what the charge would have been if straight-line depreciation had been used on the remaining cost of the asset.

Sum-of-the-years'-digits depreciation for the year is computed by multiplying the depreciable cost of the asset by a fraction based upon the years' digits. The years' digits are added to obtain the denominator $(1 + 2 + 3 + 4 + 5 = 15)$, and the numerator for each successive year is the number of the year in reverse order.

The formula for determining the sum-of-the-years' digits is:

$$SYD = n \left(\frac{n+1}{2} \right)$$

Again using the facts for the illustration of straight-line depreciation, annual depreciation computed by the sum-of-the-years'-digits method would be:

First year:	$5,000 × 5/15	$1,667
Second year:	$5,000 × 4/15	1,333
Third year:	$5,000 × 3/15	1,000
Fourth year:	$5,000 × 2/15	667
Fifth year:	$5,000 × 1/15	333
	Total........................	$5,000

Accelerated depreciation methods provide larger depreciation charges against operations during the early years of asset life, when the asset's new efficient condition contributes to greater earnings capacity. Further, the increasing maintenance and repair costs in the later years of asset use tend to complement the reducing depreciation charges, thereby equalizing the total cost of machine usage. Therefore, it is claimed that accelerated depreciation methods more properly match income and expense than does the straight-line method.

Units-of-Production Depreciation

The units-of-production depreciation method is based upon an estimated useful life in terms of units of output, instead of a calendar time period. Units-of-production (or service-life) methods are appropriate in those cases where the useful life of the depreciable asset can be directly related to its productive activity.

Under the units-of-production method, depreciation is determined by multiplying the actual units of output of the fixed asset for the operating period by a computed unit depreciation rate. This rate is calculated by dividing the depreciable cost by the total estimated life of the asset expressed in units of output. A $6,000 machine is estimated to have a $1,000 salvage value after producing 100,000 units of output. The depreciation rate for the machine is:

$$\frac{\$5,000}{100,000 \text{ Units}} = \$0.05 \text{ per Unit}$$

And, the depreciation charge for a year in which 25,000 units are produced upon this machine is $1,250 (25,000 units × $0.05 per unit).

The units-of-production depreciation method relates fixed asset cost directly to usage. It is argued this method best matches depreciation costs and revenues. However, the life of an asset is not necessarily more accurately estimated in units of output than in terms of time. Further, this depreciation method requires a record of the output of individual assets, which may not be readily available without significant additional effort and cost.

A hybrid straight-line and production method is sometimes used by companies in cyclical businesses. The straight-line portion is treated as a period cost and is the minimum depreciation charge. In addition, when production increases beyond a "normal" operating level, an additional depreciation charge is made to reflect the use of assets which are idle at normal production levels.

ACCOUNTING FOR DEPRECIATION

Regardless of the method chosen for computing depreciation, the accounting entry required to record depreciation applicable to a period of operations is:

```
Depreciation Expense .................................................. xxx
    Accumulated Depreciation .......................................        xxx
```

In addition, both account titles should indicate the type of fixed assets involved, that is, buildings, machinery, office equipment, and so on. This aids in proper handling of the accounts in the financial statements.

Depreciation expense can be listed in the income statement as a single item or according to the nature of the fixed asset giving rise to the depreciation. Depreciation expense on factory machinery can be included in factory overhead, while depreciation on office equipment can be included among the administrative expenses.

Accumulated Depreciation (sometimes called Allowance for Depreciation or labeled with the outdated title of Reserve for Depreciation) is deducted from the related fixed asset account on the balance sheet. This account's credit balance is increased as assets are depreciated in successive accounting periods. Of course, the allocation of fixed asset cost could be accomplished by crediting the amount of depreciation directly to the fixed asset accounts. This procedure is not recommended because the cost of the fixed asset is merged with estimated depreciation charges, and the users of financial statements would be denied information about fixed asset investment and depreciation policies.

Depreciation charges are continued systematically until the asset is disposed of or until the asset is depreciated to its salvage value. Fully depreciated assets remaining in service are carried in the accounts until disposition. From time to time, significant changes in a company's circumstances may require a switch from one depreciation method to another.

Group Depreciation

Depreciation is frequently computed for a group of assets owned by a business. In preceding illustrations, it was assumed that depreciation was calculated separately for each fixed asset; such procedures are called unit methods. If the asset units can be grouped together in some general category, such as machinery, delivery equipment, or office equipment, it may be desirable to compute depreciation for the total of each group. This practice minimizes detailed analyses and computations. Also, errors in estimates of useful life and salvage value tend to balance out for the group. Estimated useful life is established for the entire group of assets, and depreciation is computed on the basis of weighted-average or composite rates.

Both unit and group methods will theoretically achieve the same results of charging fixed asset costs to operations during the period of expected useful life.

Depreciation and Federal Income Tax

Federal income tax laws recognize depreciation as an expense in the computation of taxable income. The law permits a deduction of a reasonable allowance for the "exhaustion," "wear and tear," and "obsolescence" of property used in a business. As a general rule, the taxpayer bears the burden of proof to justify depreciation charges claimed.

There is no requirement that the same depreciation methods be used for both tax and financial reporting purposes. It is not uncommon for a business to adopt an accelerated depreciation method for tax purposes while using the straight-line depreciation method for financial reporting. Material differences in depreciation charges under this procedure will require appropriate deferred tax accounting in the financial statements.

In recent years, the tax laws related to depreciation have been modified so as to stimulate the economy by encouraging investment in fixed assets. For example, in 1954, the law for the first time specifically described and permitted the use of accelerated depreciation under either the declining-balance or sum-of-the-years'-digits methods for subsequent tax years. In 1958, a special additional 20 percent bonus depreciation was permitted in the year of acquisition on certain fixed asset purchases, up to a total of $10,000 fixed asset cost for each taxpayer.

In mid-1962, the Treasury Department issued new depreciation guidelines and rules which generally permitted more generous depreciation deductions by reducing prescribed estimated lives for groups of assets with similar physical characteristics.

In the 1971 Revenue Act, Congress introduced the Asset Depreciation Range System (ADR) to accelerate the capital recovery from depreciation of American businesses. This acceleration narrowed, but did not eliminate, the advantage provided by even faster capital recovery allowed to industry in other highly industrial nations. The principle element of the ADR regulation permitted companies to use for tax purposes depreciable lives that are 20 percent shorter than the guideline lives.

Depreciation Schedule Revisions

Depreciation schedules are based upon management's best estimate of the future utilization of an asset at the time it is acquired. During the life of the asset, these estimates may prove to be improper due to circumstances that indicate that either the asset's useful life or the disposal value, or both, should be revised. Under these conditions, the approach specified in *Opinion No. 20* is leave the book value as it is and alter the rate of future depreciation charges.[1] The changes are made prospectively, not retroactively.

For example, assume a company depreciating a $11,000 asset on a

---

[1] Chapter 10 discusses the accounting for changes in accounting estimates and policies in greater detail.

straight-line basis over ten years decided after five years that the assets remaining useful life was only going to be two years, rather than five years. In addition, the previous $1,000 estimate of the salvage value was now thought to be erroneous. The new salvage value was estimated to be zero. The prior depreciation schedule was $1,000 per year ([$11,000 − $1,000] ÷ 10). Therefore, after five years the book value of the asset would be $6,000 ($11,000 − [5 × $1,000]). Before the change in the estimated life and salvage value, the annual depreciation charge over each of the next five years would have been $1,000. Now, based on the revised estimates, the annual depreciation charge over the next two years will be $3,000 per year ([$6,000 − $0] ÷ 2).

Depreciation Method Changes

In recent years a number of companies have changed their depreciation method. Typically, the shift has been from an accelerated to a straight-line depreciation method. In *Opinion No. 20* the APB recommended that when a company changes its depreciation accounting policy, the change should be recognized by including in the net income of the period of the change the cummulative effect based on a retroactive computation, of changing to the new depreciation principle.

For example, assume a company decides in 1974 to adopt the straight-line method of depreciation for new acquisitions as of January 1, 1974, as well as for previously acquired plant equipment, which in previous years had been on an accelerated method. Furthermore, assume the effects of the change are limited to the effect on depreciation and related tax provisions.

The following table shows the excess of accelerated depreciation over what would have been the straight-line depreciation changes prior to 1974 if the existing equipment had been depreciated on a straight-line basis.

Year	Excess of Accelerated Depreciation over Straight-Line Depreciation	Effects of Change Less Direct Tax Effect
Prior to 1969	$ 20,000	$ 10,000
1970	80,000	40,000
1971	70,000	35,000
1972	50,000	25,000
1973	30,000	15,000
Total at beginning of 1974	$250,000	$125,000

The manner of reporting the change in two-year comparative statements[2] is:

	1974	1973
Income before extraordinary item and cumulative effect of a change in accounting principles......................................	$1,200,000	$1,100,000
Extraordinary item (description)..................	35,000	—
Cumulative effect on prior years (to December 31, 1973) of change to a different depreciation method............................	125,000	—
Net Income	$1,290,000	$1,200,000

The current year's income figure of $1,200,000 figure is calculated using the straight-line depreciation method to determine the 1974 depreciation expense. Last year's net income of $1,100,000 is the net income reported originally in the 1973 statement. It was derived after depreciating the assets on an accelerated basis. The aftertax cumulative excess of accelerated depreciation figure of $125,000 relates to the years prior to 1974.

Additions

For depreciation purposes, an addition to fixed assets should be depreciated over its own economic life or that of the original asset, whichever is shorter.

Donated Assets

Fixed assets donated on a conditional basis to a company raise a difficult issue: Should income be charged with depreciation on such assets before full title is obtained? Since the company does not own the asset, it can be argued that depreciation should not be charged. On the other hand, the economic life of an asset is not dependent on who owns it. Therefore, if depreciation is not charged until title is obtained, the full depreciation charge must be applied to the economic life of the asset remaining after this event. This practice, which relates depreciation to ownership rather than the period of use, results in a misleading variation of income charges during two similar operating periods.

---

[2] In addition, *Opinion No. 20* requires the disclosure of certain pro forma income and earnings-per-share data showing what the 1974 and 1973 earnings would have been if the depreciation change would have been applied retroactively. For a full example of an accounting change disclosure and statement format, see Chapter 10.

Therefore, it is argued the depreciation for such assets should be charged to operations during the full period of use.

Asset Write-Downs

Should it become clear to a company that it cannot recover through sale or productive use its remaining investment in a fixed asset, the asset should be written down to its net realizable value and current income changed with the write-down amount.

Written-Up Assets

As noted in Chapter 13, the writing up of assets is not an acceptable practice. However, as *Opinion No. 6* indicated, it may happen under certain circumstances in the accounts of foreign subsidiaries. If such a company wrote up its assets, it would use the following depreciation accounting.

The write-up of depreciable assets requires, in addition to the recognition of appraisal capital, an adjustment to the depreciation accounts. The related allowance for depreciation must be increased to reflect the fact that inadequate depreciation has been taken in the past. The amount added to the Appraised Capital account is the net difference between the appraised value and the original cost minus the adjustment to the Allowance for Depreciation account. In addition, if the asset's appraised life remaining is different from the remaining life implicit in the book value of the asset, the past depreciation allowance based on cost should also be adjusted to reflect the new estimated life.

To illustrate, assume the following information related to a manufacturing plant: cost, $100,000; estimated life, 50 years; period used, 20 years; allowance for depreciation, $40,000. An appraisal of the plant indicates that it would cost $200,000 to replace the plant with an identical new plant. (This amount is the so-called reproduction cost.) The estimated actual depreciation to date is $100,000 based upon the reproduction cost. Hence, the sound value or reproduction cost less estimated actual depreciation to date based on this value is $100,000. Therefore, the estimated actual depreciation is 50 percent, rather than the 40 percent assumed in the company's books.

The appraisal indicates that the accounts should be adjusted as follows:

a.   The depreciation allowance based on cost must be increased by $10,000 to reflect the fact that 50 percent of the asset's life has been consumed in operations. The new allowance for depreciation is $50,000. The accounting entries are:

Depreciation Expense—Adjustment for Understatement
   of Prior Period Depreciation Charges 10,000
     Allowance for Depreciation   10,000

b. The $100,000 original cost of the asset must be increased to its
$200,000 reproduction cost. In addition, the allowance for de-
preciation must be increased to 50 percent of the reproduction cost.
Therefore, since the Allowance for Depreciation account is now
$50,000, after adjusting it for accumulated depreciation charges
based on original cost, an additional $50,000 must be added. The
net result is the new book value, equal to the asset's sound value.
The entries are:

Building—Appraisal Increase 100,000
   Allowance for Depreciation of
     Building—Appraisal Increase   50,000
   Appraisal Capital—Building   50,000

Opinion No. 6 indicates that when appreciation is entered on the
books, the company is obliged to make periodic depreciation charges
that are consistent with the increased valuation rather than the historical cost basis.

Accounting for Retirements

The accounting for asset retirement is fairly straightforward. At the
time an asset is retired, its original cost is credited to the appropriate
asset account and the related accumulated depreciation is charged to
the accumulated depreciation account. Any gain or loss on the retirement after adjusting for the cost of removal and disposition should be
recognized as an extraordinary gain or loss.

To illustrate, assume the Cleveland Company purchased a piece of
equipment for $100,000. After two years, the company sold the
equipment for $50,000. At the time of the sale the asset's book value
was $60,000 and the related accumulated depreciation was $40,000.

The entries to record the purchase are:

Machinery 100,000
   Cash   100,000

The entries to record the subsequent sale are:

Cash 50,000
Accumulated Depreciation 40,000
Loss on Sale of Machinery 10,000
   Machinery   100,000

If the group method of depreciation had been in use, there would
have been no loss and Accumulated Depreciation would have been
reduced by $50,000.

Capital Investment Decisions

Some fault current depreciation accounting on the ground that it does not lead to a measurement of return on investment which matches the economic concept of return on investment used by many companies in making asset investment decisions.

To illustrate, assume a company approves a proposed investment of $1,000, which is estimated to earn $250 *cash* per year after taxes for five years and therefore is expected to earn 8 percent on the amount, at risk, as indicated by Illustration 14–1. The economic return on this

ILLUSTRATION 14–1

Year	Total Earnings (a)	Return at 8% on Investment Outstanding (b)	Balance Capital Recovery (c) = (a) − (b)	Investment Outstanding End of Year (d)
0	—	—	—	$1,000
1	$250	$80	$170	830
2	250	66	184	646
3	250	52	198	448
4	250	36	214	234
5	250	19	231	3*

* Due to rounding.

investment is 8 percent, since the investor's principal is recovered over the life of the investment and each year he receives an 8 percent return on the principal balance outstanding.

Assuming a straight-line depreciation method, this investment will be reported for financial accounting purposes as shown in Illustration 14–2. From this illustration it is clear that the financial reports in no year show a return of 8 percent. This problem is eliminated if the periodic cost-based depreciation of an asset is shown as the difference

ILLUSTRATION 14–2

Year	Gross Assets	Average Net Assets*	Net† Income	Computed Return On Gross	Computed Return On Net
1	$1,000	$900	$50	5%	5.5%
2	1,000	700	50	5	7.1
3	1,000	500	50	5	10.0
4	1,000	300	50	5	16.7
5	1,000	100	50	5	50.0

* Beginning and ending book values divided by two.
† Cash earnings, $250, minus depreciation, $200. Income taxes are included in the calculation of net earnings.

between the present value of the related future service benefits at the beginning and end of the accounting period discounted by the internal rate of return[3] calculated in the purchase decision analysis. In practice, it is difficult to measure the future service benefits accurately enough to apply this approach with confidence, so managers resort to using the various depreciation methods discussed above.

Depletion

Depletion is the process of allocating the cost of an investment in natural resources through systematic charges to income as the supply of the physical asset is reduced through operations, after making provision for the residual value of the land remaining after the valuable resource is exhausted.

There are two depletion methods: the production method and percentage method. The production method is acceptable for accounting purposes, whereas the percentage method is not. It is commonly used for computing income tax payments, however.

The production method establishes the depletion rate by dividing the cost of the depletable asset by the best available estimate of the number of recoverable units. The unit costs are then charged to income as the units are extracted and sold. The unit can be the marketing unit (ounces of silver) or the extractive unit (tons of ore), although the marketing unit is preferred. It is permissible to adjust the depletion rate when it becomes apparent that the estimate of recoverable units used to compute the unit cost is no longer the best available estimate.

To illustrate the cost-based depletion method, assume a coal mine containing an estimated profitable output of ten million tons of coal is developed to the point of exploitation at a cost of $1 million. Furthermore, during the first year of operations, 500,000 tons of coal are mined and 450,000 tons are sold. The depletion unit charge is the total development cost divided by the estimated profitable output, or 10 cents per ton, that is, $1 million/10 million tons. The total depletion charged to the inventory in the first operating year is $50,000, that is, total production (500,000 tons) times the depletion unit cost ($0.10). The depletion charged to income as cost of goods sold during this period is $45,000, that is, total production sold (450,000 tons) times the depletion unit cost of ($0.10). Consequently, $5,000 of the year's depletion charge is still lodged in the inventory account.

Depletion differs from depreciation in several respects: depletion charges relate to the actual physical exhaustion of an asset, and as such are directly included in inventory costs as production occurs. In con-

---

[3] The internal rate of return is the discount rate which reduces the present value of the future benefits to the present value of the investment.

trast, depreciation recognizes the service exhaustion of an asset and is allocated to periodic income, except for depreciation related to manufacturing facilities, which is included in inventory costs on an allocated basis.

The percentage or statutory method, which is permissible for tax purposes only, computes depletion as a fixed percentage of the gross income from the property. The percentage varies according to the type of product extracted and is specified in the Internal Revenue Code and Regulations. The depletion deduction is limited to 50 percent of the net income from the property before consideration of depletion, however. This method, which can result in depletion deductions greater than the original cost of the property, is applicable to all mineral investments for tax purposes. The cost method is also permissible for determining income tax payments. Companies are not obliged to use the same depletion method for book and tax purposes. In 1975 Congress eliminated or reduced the use of percentage depletion for tax purposes for many oil and gas producing companies.

Replacement Depreciation

In 1975 the SEC required that certain large companies under its jurisdiction state in their notes the estimated current cost (new) of replacing their productive capacity together with a depreciation expense based on this value and the current net replacement cost represented by the depreciable, depletable, and amortizable assets on hand at the end of each fiscal year for which a balance sheet is presented. This requirement is discussed in greater detail in Chapter 15.

Depreciation Decisions

The accounting criteria for choosing one depreciation method rather than another in any particular situation are fuzzy.

The decision to use one of the depreciation methods over another should be made on the basis of a close examination of the asset's characteristics and the way management viewed these characteristics in their investment decision. Empirical and theoretical evidence suggests that most productive assets tend to become less and less valuable over time. Maintenance costs rise and the quality of the asset's service declines as time goes on. Also, as technological advances are made, the quality of the existing equipment declines relative to alternative more modern equipment, even though quality does not deteriorate absolutely. Based on this evidence, it is believed by some that productive equipment in most cases depreciates on an accelerated basis rather than, as thought for a long time, on a straight-line basis. Similar studies indicate straight-line depreciation is a reasonable approximation of the depreciation rate of buildings and plant structures.

When an asset is utilized in a project whose future success is more uncertain than the typical situation, some managements believe it is prudent to use accelerated depreciation. Others object to this practice on the ground that the high depreciation charges in the early years will increase the likelihood that the project will be viewed as unsuccessful due to the lower profits. Thus, the action taken to reflect the excessive risk involved contributes to the worst fears of management being realized.

More often than not, depreciation accounting is used as an instrument of management's financial reporting policy. Management selects the depreciation method or mix of methods that contributes to the desired financial results they hope to achieve over time. For example, in some cases accelerated depreciation methods have been used to hold earnings down and conserve funds by reducing stockholder pressure to increase dividend distributions. It also provides an argument against pay increases. In other situations, straight-line depreciation has been utilized to smooth earnings. And, in times of depressed profits, some companies have switched from accelerated to straight-line depreciation to boost earnings with the hope that this will maintain the market price of the company's stock. The choice of service life can also be used in a similar way to further the achievement of management's financial objectives.

The different nature of assets argues for retaining the present wide range of permissible depreciation methods. However, the apparent use of depreciation as a tool of financial policy, due to the difficulty in practice of determining which method is the most appropriate for any given asset, has led some to conclude that depreciation methods should be standardized for similar categories of assets. To date, nobody has seriously pursued this proposal. However, unless some managements adopt a more responsible attitude towards depreciation accounting, some action limiting management's flexibility in this area may be necessary.

SUGGESTED FURTHER READING

GRANT, EUGENE L., and NORTON, PAUL T., JR. *Depreciation*. New York: Ronald Press Co., 1955.

CASES

Selection of Appropriate Depreciation Methods

United States Steel Corporation is the nation's largest steel producer, with approximately 25 percent of United States producers' shipments. The corporation's operations are highly integrated; it produces a substantial portion of its required stock of coal, iron ore, limestone, and electric power. Additionally, it operates steamships, barges, and stock facilities for the transportation of raw materials and steel products.

The following discussion pertains only to U.S. Steel's depreciation accounting policies and its treatment of the investment credit between 1946 and 1968.

The Environment (1947)

For a number of years prior to 1947, the management of U.S. Steel had been concerned with the effects of the steady rise in the general price level on the company's capital replacement program. This concern arose from the realization that the amounts being deducted from earnings as depreciation and amortization of plant and equipment were insufficient to provide for the replacement of worn-out or obsolete physical facilities. Depreciation was based on the original cost of plant and equipment, despite the fact that general price levels and replacement costs had risen markedly. U.S. Steel executives believed that failure to take action on this well-recognized problem would be failure to discharge a major management responsibility to corporate stockholders: the preservation of the company's capital.

The management of U.S. Steel believed that unless price, wage, and dividend policies were predicated upon a full recognition of the need to replace worn-out plant and equipment, the company would dissipate capital in the course of normal operations. First, selling prices, based on cost, would be insufficient to recover the real costs of wear and exhaustion of facilities (i.e., replacement costs). Second, the

388

misleading net profit figure might be used as the argument for higher wage or dividend payments than were actually justified.

The relaxation of governmental price controls in late 1946 and early 1947 resulted in an immediate surge in prices, further aggravating the problem of providing for plant and equipment replacement. The effect of these price increases is indicated in Exhibit 1, which shows the

EXHIBIT 1

	Increase, 1947 over 1940
Wire drawing machine	91%
Standard electric crane	105
Reheating furnace	108
Blast furnace	105
By-product coke ovens	150
Mine locomotive	44
Large electric motor	50
Continuous rolling mill	84
Concrete construction	124
Brick construction	250

increase in price for typical equipment and services purchased by U.S. Steel during the period. In the same period, the wholesale price of iron and steel rose 50 percent and that of finished steel 39 percent.

As a step toward stating depreciation in an amount which would recover in current dollars of diminished buying power the same purchasing power represented by the original plant expenditure, the company deducted, in arriving at net income for 1947, an amount of $26.3 million over and above its regular depreciation charge (based on the straight-line method). Although the federal tax authorities would not allow the extra depreciation as a deduction in arriving at taxable income for that year, the company's executives considered it essential to recognize this element of cost in arriving at a measure of income to be used in other matters of company management.

In its 1947 annual report, the management stated that while awaiting accounting and tax acceptance, U.S. Steel believed that it was prudent for it to give some recognition to increased replacement costs rather than to sit idly by and witness the unwitting liquidation of its business should inadequate recording of costs result in insufficient resources to supply the tools required for sustained production.

The additional depreciation charge was shown in the company's income statement as a separate item in the section under "Wear and Exhaustion of Facilities" and labeled, "Added to Cover Replacement Cost"; it was shown in the balance sheet, on the liability side, as "Reserve for Replacement of Properties." The sum of $26.3 million, which amounted to approximately 30 percent of the regular depreciation based on original cost, was arrived at partly on the basis of cost increases actually experienced by the company and partly through study of construction cost index numbers (notably the *Engineering News-Record Index*). The management pointed out that, although the amount was actually much less than that which could be substantiated by actual cost increases, it was all that was deemed appropriate in view of the newness of the application of such a method of computing depreciation.

The company's independent auditors noted that the 1947 financial statement lacked consistency, since the corporation had included in costs additional depreciation of $26.3 million "in excess of the amount determined in accordance with the generally accepted accounting principle heretofore followed of making provision for depreciation on the original cost of facilities."

U.S. Steel was not alone in its concern over the effect of rising prices. In the late 1940s, several other large corporations, among them Crane Company, E. I. du Pont de Nemours & Company, and Libbey-Owens-Ford Glass Company, also made accounting provisions for replacement costs.

Carman G. Blough, director of research of the American Institute of Certified Public Accountants (at that time the American Institute of Accountants), commented on this practice as follows:

> There can be no argument but that a going concern must be able to replace its productive assets as they are used up if it is to continue to do business. It is also important for management to understand that the difference between cost and estimated replacement value may be significant in determining production and pricing policies. It does not follow, however, that the excess of the cost of replacement over the cost of existing assets should be accounted for as current charges to income. All who have dealt with appraisal values know how very difficult it is just to determine current replacement costs, but the most striking difficulty in this respect is the impossibility of predicting what will be the eventual cost of replacing a productive asset. How many men are prepared to state what the price level will be two years from today, to say nothing of trying to guess what it will be five or ten years hence when many of these assets are to be replaced?[4]

The AICPA Committee on Accounting Procedure issued in late 1947, *Accounting Research Bulletin No. 33* (later restated as *APB No. 43*, Chapter 9, Section A, paragraphs 4–9), in which it stated that it disapproved of immediate write-downs of plant cost by charges against

---

[4] Replacement and Excess Construction Costs," *Journal of Accountancy*, vol. 84 (October 1947), p. 335.

current income in amounts believed to represent excessive or abnormal costs occasioned by current price levels. However, the committee calls attention to the fact that plants expected to have less than normal useful life can properly be depreciated on a systematic basis related to economic usefulness.

1948

United States Steel Corporation continued through the first three quarters of 1948 its practice of charging additional depreciation to cover higher costs of replacing worn-out facilities, and in view of the continued increase in the cost of facilities during 1948, advanced the additional charge from 30 to 60 percent of the depreciation based on original cost.

In the release of its quarterly statements for the third quarter of 1948, however, the company stated that in view of the position taken by the AICPA and the discussions between the corporation and the Securities and Exchange Commission, further study was being made in an effort to agree upon principles satisfactory to the commission for "determining and reflecting additional wear and exhaustion cost."

In its annual report for 1948, U.S. Steel announced that it was abandoning the policy adopted in 1947 of charging to costs an amount over and above the regular depreciation on original cost and was substituting in its place a method of charging "accelerated depreciation on cost." The following quotation from the notes to the financial statements in the 1948 annual report provides a brief description of the formula to be used in determining the amount of annual charge for accelerated depreciation:

The accelerated depreciation is applicable to the cost of postwar facilities in the first few years of their lives when economic usefulness is greatest. The amount thereof is related to the excess of current operating rates over U.S. Steel's long-term peacetime average rate of 70 percent of capacity. The annual accelerated amount is 10 percent of the cost of facilities in the year in which the expenditures are made and 10 percent in the succeeding year, except that this amount is reduced ratably as the operating rate may drop, no acceleration being made at 70 percent or lower operations. The accelerated depreciation is an addition to the normal depreciation on such facilities, but the total depreciation over their expected lives will not exceed the cost of the facilities.

This method was made retroactive to January 1, 1947, and there was included in the $55,335,444 deducted for accelerated wear and exhaustion of facilities for 1948 an amount of $2,675,094 to cover a deficiency in the $26,300,000 sum reported in 1947 as "depreciation added to cover replacement cost." In other words, the new method when applied to the 1947 situation resulted in a deduction that exceeded the figure actually reported in 1947. It was again pointed out at this time that the accelerated depreciation was not "presently deductible for federal income tax purposes."

The company's independent auditors apparently interpreted the concept of accelerated depreciation as being within AICPA standards as a "systematic basis related to economic usefulness"; for they stated in their report to the stockholder for 1948 that they "approved" the new policy.

The management's convictions on the change in policy were, however, clearly set forth by the chairman of the board of directors in the following quotation from the company's annual report for 1948:

U.S. Steel believes that the principle which it adopted in 1947 and continued in 1948 is a proper recording of the wear and exhaustion of its facilities in terms of current dollars as distinguished from the dollars which it originally expended for those facilities. However, in view of the disagreement existing among accountants, both public and private, and the stated position of the American Institute of Certified Public Accountants, which is supported by the Securities and Exchange Commission, that the only accepted accounting principle for determining depreciation is that which is related to the actual number of dollars spent for facilities, regardless of where or what buying power, U.S. Steel has adopted a method of acceleration based on cost instead of one based on purchasing power recovery.

1949 to 1952

U.S. Steel continued its policy of charging accelerated depreciation through 1952; more than $201 million was deducted from income on the 1946–52 financial statements. Deduction of the "excess portion" (above straight-line) was not permitted in computing taxable income.

In its annual report for 1949, U.S. Steel restated its belief that:

. . . a manufacturer should be able to recover out of receipts from customers through depreciation and through income remaining for reinvestment after equitable dividends, an amount sufficient to replace and keep modern his plant and equipment so as continuously to retain his productive capacity on a competitive basis.

In its annual report for 1952, management commented:

. . . so long as depreciation that is deducted for tax purposes is measured by the relatively smaller number of dollars of greater buying power expended in an earlier period, it will be inadequate to recover the original purchasing power invested in the facilities consumed in production. Real wear and exhaustion costs are thus understated, real profits are overstated, and there results an erosion of capital through taxation.

Although the continuing concern for capital replacement provision was expressed in 1952, U.S. Steel was deducting from both taxable and reported income substantial additional amounts of depreciation under "certificates of necessity."

To increase productive capacity necessary for the support of the Korean War, the Internal Revenue Code of 1950 provided for a 60-month amortization of "emergency facilities" constructed under (and evidenced by) "certificates of necessity," regardless of the facility's probable economic life.

The AICPA through an accounting research bulletin strongly recommended that users of the 60-month amortization period for tax purposes carefully consider whether these facilities should be depreciated over a longer period for financial purposes.

. . . Sound financial accounting procedures do not necessarily coincide with the rules as to what shall be included in the "gross income" or allowed as a deduction therefrom, in arriving at taxable net income. It is well recognized that such rules should not be followed for financial accounting purposes if they do not conform to generally accepted accounting principles. . . .

The APB recommended, for the first time, the deferral of differences in income tax resulting from the differing treatment of depreciation for financial and tax purposes:

In those cases in which the amount of depreciation charged in the accounts on that portion of the cost of the facilities for which certificates of necessity have been obtained is materially less than the amount of amortization deducted for income-tax purposes, the amount of income taxes payable annually during the amortization period may be significantly less than it would be on the basis of the income reflected in the financial statements. In such cases, after the close of the amortization period, the income taxes will exceed the amount that would be appropriate on the basis of the income reported in the statements. Accordingly, the committee believes that during the amortization period, where this difference is material, a charge should be made in the income statement to recognize the income tax to be paid in the future on the amount by which amortization for income-tax purposes exceeds the depreciation that would be allowable if certificates of necessity had not been issued. The amount of the charge should be equal to the estimated amount by which the income tax expected to be payable after the amortization period exceeds what would be so expected if amortization had not been claimed for income-tax purposes in the amortization period. The estimated amount should be based on normal and surtax rates in effect during the period covered by the income statement with such changes therein as can be reasonably anticipated at the time the estimate is made. . . .

In accounting for this deferment of income taxes, the committee believes it desirable to treat the charge as being for additional income taxes. The related credit in such cases would properly be made to an account for deferred income taxes. . . .[5]

1953 to 1954

In 1953, U.S. Steel accelerated depreciation, stating in a note to the 1953 financial statement:

Since 1946, U.S. Steel has followed the policy of reflecting accelerated depreciation on the cost of new facilities in the first few years of their lives when the economic usefulness is greatest. The amounts charged to income for accelerated depreciation have been related to U.S. Steel's rate of operations.

Under the Internal Revenue Code, that portion of the cost of facilities certified by the Defense Production Administration as essential to the defense effort is covered by a Certificate of Necessity and can be written off for tax·purposes at the rate of 20 percent per year. The effect of amortization of these facilities is to charge to income a greater portion of their cost in the earlier years of life and, therefore, follows the principle of accelerated depreciation.

U.S. Steel has included in wear and exhaustion in 1953, as a measure of the accelerated depreciation for the year, $105,137,893, representing amortization on its facilities covered by Certificates of Necessity.

In commenting on the effect of accelerated amortization and the tax laws, management pointed out that it had to be regarded as a temporary expedient, since "for many companies the addition of amortization on new facilities to 'so-called' regular depreciation on old facilities may approximate, temporarily, a truer total of wear and exhaustion on all facilities based on current dollar value. But it automatically guarantees something of a *future crisis*." (Emphasis added.)

Management noted in 1954 that the new methods of accelerated depreciation first allowed for tax purposes in 1954 would ease the future crisis, but even these provisions, applicable to new assets only, would fall far short of providing adequate depreciation on the relatively more numerous and older existing facilities.

1956

In its 1956 report, U.S. Steel included a chart (see Exhibit 2) comparing "wear and exhaustion recorded" with "wear and exhaustion needed." To calculate "Total Wear and Exhaustion Needed," as shown in the chart, the following statistical procedure was followed: excluding the amount of nontax-deductible accelerated depreciation from 1947 through 1952 (see Exhibit 3), and including only regular depre-

---

[5] *Accounting Research Bulletin No. 43*, chap. 9, sec. C.

EXHIBIT 2

Wear and Exhaustion Recorded versus Wear and Exhaustion Needed

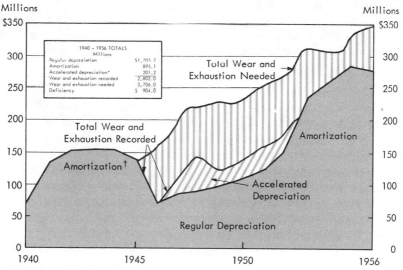

Millions   Millions

1940 - 1956 TOTALS	
	Millions
Regular depreciation	$1,705.7
Amortization	895.1
Accelerated depreciation*	201.2
Wear and exhaustion recorded	2,802.0
Wear and exhaustion needed	3,706.0
Deficiency	$ 904.0

Total Wear and Exhaustion Needed

Total Wear and Exhaustion Recorded

Amortization

Amortization†

Accelerated Depreciation

Regular Depreciation

1940   1945   1950   1956

* Not deductible for tax purposes.
† Additional amortization due to ending of emergency period allocated to years 1941–45.

ciation on emergency facilities, the amount of wear and exhaustion previously recorded for each year included in the chart was subdivided according to the acquisition years of the assets being depreciated. Each yearly subdivision was then adjusted to reflect the change in the *Engineering News-Record*'s index of construction costs from the various earlier acquisition years to any given year included in the chart. The sum of that year's adjusted depreciation amounts gave the "Total Wear and Exhaustion Needed" for that year. The process was repeated for every year in the chart. Notice that each year's deficiency is in dollars of the buying power that prevailed in *that* year.

1957 to 1958

Evidence of the "future crisis" of declining allowable depreciation on emergency facilities first appeared in 1957, and was far more obvious in 1958 (see Exhibit 3). Amortization of emergency facilities, which reached a peak of $147.7 million in 1955, had declined to $57.2 million by 1958.

1959

In 1959, management noted the approaching exhaustion of emergency amortization:

This [depreciation] deficiency has been aggravated by the running out of five-year amortization permitted on varying percentages of the total costs of certain defense and defense supporting facilities covered by Certificates of Necessity. The need for revision of the tax laws as they relate to depreciation . . . continues to be most vital to the maintenance of existing and the addition of new productive capacity.

In the spring of 1959, the representatives of the United Steelworkers of America and the major steel companies met to negotiate a new wage contract to replace the contract expiring in June. The union requested sizable increases in wages and fringe benefits, contending that large steel profits would permit these increases without affecting the prices of finished steel. The steel industry spokesman argued this was not possible; any *sizable* wage increase would have to be passed along in the form of higher prices. There was considerable government pressure for a settlement without the need for a price increase in order to avoid the threat of further inflation.

EXHIBIT 3

Selected Financial Statistics, 1946–1967
(millions of dollars)

	Net Income	Depre- ciation	Capital Expen- ditures	Investment Tax Credit Taken	Investment Tax Credit Deferred
1967	$172.5	$354.7	$547.7	$33.4	$26.0
1966	249.2	344.3	440.7	20.8	16.6
1965	275.5	324.5	353.6	13.7	12.4
1964	236.8	335.8	292.6	0.6	12.8
1963	203.5	307.8	244.7	0.6 (est.)	12.0
1962	163.7	265.9	200.6	0.4 (est.)	8.2
					Amortization of
					Emergency Facilities
1961	190.2	210.5	326.8		
1960	304.2	208.4	492.4		$ 13.7
1959	254.5	189.9	366.1		22.2
1958	301.5	204.9	448.1		57.2
1957	319.4	276.0	514.9		115.8
1956	348.1	277.6	311.8		140.2
1955	348.1	285.2	239.8		147.7
1954	195.4	261.8	227.4		142.8
1953	222.1	236.6	361.4		105.1
1952	143.6	176.9	469.2		46.2
1951	184.3	162.1	352.4		12.8
1950	215.5	143.9	179.3		—
1949	165.9	119.7	179.1		—
1948	129.6	146.0	275.2		—
1947	127.1	114.0	206.6		—
1946	88.6	68.7	201.0		—

In May of 1959, the union paid for a series of full-page newspaper advertisements stating its position. A portion of one of these ads, which cites financial data from the United States Steel Corporation's 1952 and 1958 annual reports, is reproduced as Exhibit 4.

EXHIBIT 4

STEELWORKERS' SHARE OF STEEL INDUSTRY'S INCOME
HAS NOT INCREASED SINCE 1952

TRUE, there have been wage increases, but because fewer men are making more steel, the total labor costs have remained the same.

Please examine these LABOR COSTS*

| 1952 | 42.1¢ of each sales dollar |
| 1958 | 42.8¢ of each sales dollar |

(notice they are about the same)

Now examine the NET PROFITS

| 1952 | $143,678,740 |
| 1958 | 301,558,231 |

(profits have DOUBLED)

	1952	1958
* Sales (millions)	$3,137.4	$3,472.2
Number of employees	294,263	223,490
Employment costs (millions)	$1,322.1	$1,488.5

Source: *Wall Street Journal*, May 14, 1959. Reproduced by permission.

Because neither side would compromise its position, a nationwide steel strike resulted, lasting from July until mid-November. The union's advertisement, while failing to arouse sufficient public reaction to prevent the strike, raised some questions about the financial accounting practices of the United States Steel Corporation.

On December 8, 1959, J. S. Seidman, president of the AICPA, released to the press a statement explaining the issues in the steel strike:

The (steel) industry's contention was that under conventional accounting, depreciation is calculated based on original dollar cost, and that this is inadequate because it fails to give effect to the tremendous change that has taken place in the purchasing power of the dollar, as a result of which it would cost many more dollars today to replace the plant than were originally spent. The industry maintains that realistic profits should be figured by reference to replacement figures. On that basis, the industry's profits are one-half of what the financial statements show.

The labor officials contend that original cost is all that should be recovered, and that anything in excess of that is a profit. Furthermore, they say that the original cost should be spread over the expected period in which the plant will be used. However, the companies have been following the tax laws in the way they write off depreciation, and the tax laws have allowed a higher write-off to be bunched in early years and counterbalanced by a lower write-off in later years. The figures presented by the steel industry cover the earlier years where there is the higher write-off. The labor people say that the depreciation amounts should be reduced by this excess write-off in the early years. Reducing the depreciation would result in an increase in profits.

All of this raises a question as to whether the conventional accounting use of historical dollars is meaningful in an inflationary period.

In commenting on the problem, he expressed a personal opinion that when inflation is significant, managements should issue two financial statements, one in the conventional form based on historical cost and the other adjusted to show the effects of inflation on earnings and financial position. "Basically," he said, "the problem is disclosure." The American Institute's accounting procedures committee had encouraged in 1948 and again in 1953 the use of supplementary financial statements showing the need for retention of a substantial portion of current income (or procurement of funds otherwise) to maintain assets at the same level of productivity. Mr. Seidman felt, in his personal opinion, that the supplementary statements should indicate the effects of inflation on every aspect of financial statements, including bank balances, long-term liabilities, lease commitments, and other items.

Mr. Seidman stated that historical and price level statements side by side would be useful to indicate what part of the affairs of a business was due to "managing" and what part to government fiscal factors.

The U.S. Steel 1960 annual report contained the following comment related to depreciation:

. . . Past and prospective dollar debasement is now a continuing—and often overriding—concern of business and government. It intrudes upon, complicates, and warps all business, saving, investing, wage, and tax decisions. It has introduced immeasurable injustice. . . .

Illustrative of the seriousness of these matters are the facts of U.S. Steel. For the postwar years, 1946–1960, U.S. Steel's recorded wear and exhaustion—sometimes called depreciation—aggregated $2,872 million. Of this amount $2,671 million was deductible in determining taxable income. If, each year, depreciation had been sufficient to recover the appropriate buying power—not just the number—of dollars originally expended, the total would have been $4,276 million. The deficiency from this amount needed to stay even was $1,605 million, on which taxes were levied as though it were income. Tax destruction to the flow of dollars that maintains the nation's tools of production in their status quo not only darkens the prospect that new jobs will be created by productive investment, it threatens continuation of existing jobs. It directly handicaps all corporations having depreciable property and especially those corporations heavily invested in long-life facilities. It indirectly handicaps all other enterprises who do business with them as their capabilities as customer or supplier are undermined.

In former times when the tax rate on corporate income was smaller and inflation was not a big factor, these same injustices and impediments to growth were present but not of as great moment. But with the enormous increases in the tax rate until it is now over 50 percent—some *three* times the prewar rates—they are indeed worthy of most serious consideration and correction if we are to have economic growth.

1962 to 1967

In 1962, U.S. Steel obtained some relief in its continuing struggle with the problem of inadequate depreciation. Inflationary pressure on the economy was diminishing; the adoption of Revenue Ruling 62–21 by the Internal Revenue Service set forth new guideline lives for depreciable assets, frequently shorter than the lives previously used; and U.S. Steel added $44 million to the wear and exhaustion amounts previously determined, as a direct result of the new guideline procedures.

In addition, the investment tax credit provided by the Revenue Act of 1962 (later amended and liberalized in the Revenue Act of 1964) provided for U.S. Steel an immediate reduction of $8.2 million in federal income taxes. The investment tax credit was intended to stimulate capital investment; it allowed a credit directly against the company's federal income tax liability of 7 percent of the cost of "qualified" depreciable property. A sliding scale of eligibility for the credit was established on the basis of the life of the property. Assets with a life of eight years or more received the full credit; assets with a life of less than four years were not eligible. U.S. Steel's 1962 annual report stated:

> The guideline procedure and the investment credit against federal income tax are recognitions of the vital depreciation problem that exists. They serve currently to lift total wear and exhaustion to an amount more nearly approaching true depreciation based on current dollars. However, they fall short in dealing with the fundamental facility replacement problem arising from inflation, since total depreciation over the lives of the facilities is still limited to original cost.

The enactment of the investment tax credit raised certain accounting questions regarding the timing for recognition of the benefit in reported income. Two methods evolved for financial statement recognition of the immediate cash benefit from the reduction in the tax liability, based on differing interpretations of the nature of the credit.

Proponents of the belief that the credit was a selective reduction in taxes recognized the full amount of the credit in the year of property acquisition—the "flow-through" method; the other group believed the credit to be a reduction in a cost chargeable to future accounting periods, and thus deferred the benefit over the life of the assets being depreciated—the "deferral" method.

The Accounting Principles Board of the AICPA, in March 1964, issued *Opinion No. 4* (superseding its *Opinion No. 2* of December 1962), which, although continuing to find the deferral method preferable, recognized the flow-through method as acceptable. This opinion was in harmony with the Securities and Exchange Commission's *Accounting Series Release No. 96,* issued in January 1963, recognizing both methods.

Following the issuance of APB *Opinion No. 4,* many steel companies adopted the flow-through method of accounting for the investment credit, and also in 1964 recognized the portion of the credit deferred in earlier years. *Barron's* commented, on February 1, 1965:

> Some of the corporate reports issued last month call for close analysis . . . steel companies . . . differed widely in the treatment of the investment tax credit. In other instances, investors will have to scrutinize annual reports to learn how management has tailored "profits."

In its 1964 annual report, U.S. Steel continued to defer the investment credit:

> . . . The investment tax credit provided for in the Revenue Act of 1962, as amended in 1964, amounted to $12.0 million in 1963 and $13.4 million in 1964. The amount for 1963 was included in wear and exhaustion of facilities in that year and added to the reserve for depreciation; because of amendment of the law, the amount for 1964 was included in a provision for income taxes and established as a deferred investment credit to be amortized over the lives of the property acquired. . . .

Bethlehem Steel Corporation, the second largest steel producer, reported in its annual report for 1964 (see Exhibit 5):

> . . . Net income for 1964 reflects a reduction in the provision for federal income taxes equal to the 1964 investment tax credit of approximately $18,300,000 plus $6,300,000 representing that portion . . . of the investment tax credit that was applicable to 1962 and 1963 which was deferred in those years.

Another large steel producer, Republic Steel, reported:

> . . . The credits for investments in depreciable property . . . for the current year amounting to $5,295,000 and the deferred credits for 1962 and 1963 amounting to $3,837,000 were applied in 1964 as a reduction of the provision for federal taxes on income. . . .

EXHIBIT 5
Selected Financial Statistics, 1955–1967
(millions of dollars)

	Net Income	Depreciation	Capital Expenditures	Investment Tax Credit Taken	Investment Tax Credit Deferred
1967	$130.4	$214.8	$338.3	$10.1	—
1966	170.9	212.0	265.1	20.4	—
1965	150.0	196.1	377.6	20.6	—
1964	147.9	181.2	385.7	18.3*	$(6.3)*
1963	102.5	163.7	177.3	4.1	4.4
1962	88.7	155.5	144.5	2.2	2.4
1961	122.4	98.1	114.3	—	—
1960	121.2	94.2	169.9	—	—
1959	117.2	97.6	86.7	—	—
1958	137.7	108.7	91.4	—	—
1957	191.0	110.6	209.0	—	—
1956	161.4	102.4	211.6	—	—
1955	180.2	102.6	98.5	—	—

* A total of $24.6 million was taken in 1964, which is the sum of $18.3 million applicable for 1964 and $6.3 million eliminated as deferrals from prior years.

Of the major steel producers, only U.S. Steel and Inland Steel continued to defer the investment tax credit.

1968

In early 1968, economic pressures on steel producers began to increase. The labor contract with the U.S. Steelworkers expired August 1, 1968. There was widespread expectation that a strike would ensue, and steel users stockpiled inventories heavily. The high volume of ordering resulted in capacity operations, requiring the use of less efficient, marginal productive facilities. In addition, foreign imports of steel were growing substantially.

When the labor contract was settled in July without dispute, production fell sharply. Steel users began to reduce their heavy inventories and industry analysts anticipated, in September, that a normal pattern of ordering would not be resumed until January 1969. Further downward pressure on steel production resulted from continued importation of foreign steels at prices as much as $35 a ton lower than domestic producer prices.

The cumulative effect of these pressures was to sharply reduce third-quarter profits for most steel producers located in the United States. Profit declines for the third quarter of 1968 as compared with the third quarter of 1967 were reported in the *Wall Street Journal* as:

U.S. Steel	....	− 70%
Bethelehem	....	− 6
Republic	....	− 31
Jones & Laughlin	....	− 86
Inland	....	+ 20
Youngstown Sheet & Tube	....	− 57
Armco	....	+ 51

U.S. Steel's third-quarter earnings declined despite an increase in third-quarter sales in 1968. Earnings dropped from the 1967 figure of $36.2 million ($0.67 a share) to $11 million ($0.21 a share) in 1968.

The apparent effect of the decreased third-quarter activity for most manufacturers of steel would have been more severe except for changes made by the majority of the firms in their depreciation policies and in accounting for the investment credit. Exhibit 6 shows the company's earnings for the three- and nine-month periods ended September 30, 1968, under two alternative depreciation methods.

EXHIBIT 6

A. Operating Earnings for Three Months Ended September 30, 1968 (millions)

	Accelerated Depreciation		Straight-Line Depreciation	
	Earnings	*EPS*	*Earnings*	*EPS*
Bethlehem	—	—	$21.7	$0.49
Republic...............	$8.2	$0.53	11.3	0.72
Jones & Laughlin	(3.48)*	(0.29)*	0.8	0.05
Inland	9.1†	0.49†	13.7‡	0.75‡
Youngstown	N.A.	N.A.	2.5	0.24
U.S. Steel	11.0†	0.21†	33.0	0.61

B. Operating Earnings for Nine Months Ended September 30, 1968 (millions)

	Accelerated Depreciation		Straight-Line Depreciation	
	Earnings	*EPS*	*Earnings*	*EPS*
Bethlehem	—	—	$115.3	$2.53
Republic	$ 56.1	$3.55	65.0	4.11
Jones & Laughlin	22.5	2.71	26.8	3.25
Inland	50.6†	2.77†	63.7	3.49
Youngstown	N.A.	N.A.	26.8	2.51
U.S. Steel	139.5†	2.58†	205.6	3.80

* Loss.
† Amortizing investment credit.
‡ Does not include nonrecurring gain from property sale of $4.1 million at $0.22 per share.
Source: Computed from *Wall Street Journal* articles of October 1968.

Bethelehem changed from accelerated to straight-line depreciation on new acquisitions in 1968; equipment acquired in prior periods continued to be depreciated by accelerated methods. Firms changing from accelerated to straight-line depreciation on all depreciable assets included National Steel, Republic Steel, and Youngstown Sheet & Tube. Inland Steel changed to straight-line depreciation on all assets and, additionally, flowed through the investment credit generated by 1968 capital acquisitions. The deferred investment credit for prior acquisition continued to be amortized on a straight-line basis.

At the end of the third quarter of 1968, among the major producers, only U.S. Steel continued to defer the investment credit over the life of the related assets and to use accelerated depreciation for all assets.

In October 1968, U.S. Steel management stated:

In view of the announced changes by other companies in the industry, U.S. Steel is studying its situation to determine whether it also should change its procedures so as to avoid the possibility of improper conclusions being drawn by attempts to compare operating results that are not comparable.

U.S. Steel said that if it had adopted the depreciation and investment credit accounting methods used by other companies, its earnings would have been significantly higher, increasing earnings to $33 million or $0.61 a share from the third quarter, and $205.6 million or $3.80 a share for the year to date, from $0.21 per share for the third quarter and $2.58 for the year to date previously reported.

Acquisition Challenge

One factor which was considered by many to have a bearing on the accounting change made by the steel companies was the take-over of Jones & Laughlin by Ling-Temco-Vought. Many of the smaller steel producers were considered attractive acquisitions because of their high cash flows, understated assets, low earnings per share, and depressed price-earnings ratios.

As an admitted direct response to this potential problem, Armco Steel had changed to straight-line depreciation methods during the first half of 1968. This change had added $0.46 to earnings per share for the first half of the year. By consolidation of European operations, an additional $0.19 per share had been obtained; earnings for the first six months thus ran 25 percent above the comparable period in 1967.

Questions

1. Comment on U.S. Steel's accounting for depreciation between 1946 and 1968.

2. Should U.S. Steel change to straight-line depreciation in 1968?
3. How should U.S. Steel account for the investment tax credit?

CASE 14–2. SHERATON CORPORATION OF AMERICA
Depreciation of Appreciating Assets

In May 1946, Sheraton Corporation and United States Realty Improvement Company were merged to form the Sheraton Corporation of America. By 1962 the Sheraton Corporation of America, through its numerous subsidiaries, owned and operated a number of properties including a multiple hotel system, several office and industrial buildings, and other assorted real estate.

From time to time, Sheraton's management claimed that conventional financial statements failed to present an earnings figure which truly measured Sheraton's performance. Most of management's discontent stemmed from the way in which traditional accounting handled depreciable assets—their valuation, amortization, and sale. Repeatedly, Mr. Ernest Henderson, the president of Sheraton Corporation of America, had complained of:

. . . , the difficulty in presenting an accurate picture of a hotel company through the medium of conventional financial statements, which are so often interpreted in the light of the needs of manufacturing or merchandising companies. The discrepancy between book values and fair market value—becomes very significant for a company such as [Sheraton]. The extent of the heavy deductions from reported earnings resulting from large depreciation reserves, while the properties are quite consistently increasing in value, is a factor peculiar to [the hotel] industry. Conventional financial statements fail to reflect the change in value of hotels until an actual sale is made. A poorly maintained property may shrink in value to an extent that may exceed depreciation reserves, while a well managed and well maintained hotel can and does appreciate in value so significantly that the reported earnings reflect little of the economic progress achieved during the year.

Sheraton's Business

The bulk of Sheraton's income came from its hotel operations, which involved the construction, purchase, operation, modernization, and sale of hotel properties. In all, the corporation operated some 68 hotels in 1962.

These 68 hotels, Sheraton's officers believed, were "skillfully managed and soundly financed." These conditions were in contrast to the real estate operations of 20 and 30 years ago, when according to Sheraton's management, "inept management and haphazard financing" had destroyed most of the public's confidence in real estate securities.

Between 1946 and 1962, Sheraton bought and sold a number of hotel properties. The general goal underlying these hotel real estate transactions was to establish the Sheraton name in the principal cities of the United States and Canada—wherever possible, with the best hotel in each city. On occasions when the company had been able to secure a better hotel in a given city where a Sheraton hotel was located already, Sheraton often sold the original hotel. Also, many hotels were sold during this period to secure funds for the acquisition of new properties. As a result, hotels acquired by Sheraton did not always represent a permanent investment.

Another integral part of Sheraton's business was the modernization of its properties. Since 1946, Sheraton had reinvested a substantial portion of its earnings, as well as funds derived from other sources, in the improvement of hotels. Management believed these expenditures tended to increase a hotel's earning power and, hence, its value. For instance, it was commonly believed among Sheraton executives that for every $1 invested in such modernization programs as the installation of air conditioning, the fair market value of the improved property was increased by about $2.

The management of Sheraton characterized these fixed assets of the company as seasoned, income-producing real estate for which a ready cash market existed. As a result, because "experience had shown that hotels are readily salable," Sheraton's management viewed the company's fixed assets as being in some respects more liquid than some of the current assets of, say, manufacturing companies, which under average conditions might be difficult to convert into cash.

Sheraton's complete financial statements for 1961–62, as presented in the corporation's 1962 annual report, are included in Exhibits 1, 2, and 3.

Financial Reporting Practices and Problems

Faced with the inadequacies of conventional accounting statements, Sheraton's management used a variety of accounting techniques, some of them unconventional, to measure, describe, and communicate to the public the "true earnings" resulting from management's efforts. Discussed below are seven accounting practices related to depreciable assets employed by Sheraton's management during the period of 1946–62.

These practices included:

1. Earnings per share, including capital gains.
2. Fair market value of fixed assets, presented as supplemental information.
3. Estimated net asset value per share.
4. Accelerated depreciation, for book and tax purposes.
5. Cash flow.
6. Economic gain or "gainings."
7. "Adjusted earnings."

1. *Earnings per Share.* The Sheraton Corporation of America always included capital gains in its reported earnings per share. Generally, these capital gains resulted from an outright sale of a real estate property, although on at least one occasion capital gains were included which resulted from a sale-and-leaseback transaction. In Sheraton's 1949 annual report Mr. Henderson said:

> In accordance with previous custom, your company reports earnings from operation only, as well as the total earnings including capital gains or losses. In this connection we point out that unlike mercantile or manufacturing corporations, which may occasionally report such profits or losses as isolated transactions, that this corporation in addition to the operation of hotels and office buildings is also actively engaged in the business of acquiring real estate properties for the purpose of improving their physical condition, rental income, and operating economies with a view to selling such properties at a profit. It is significant to note that substantial capital gains were registered in all but one of the past ten semi-annual reporting periods of Sheraton [Corporation] indicating that the creation of gains through the sale of improved properties is an important factor in the operations of this company. Such gains have an additional advantage in that they are subject to a lower rate of Federal Income Tax than are earnings secured from operations.

However, in 1960, Mr. Henderson announced a modification of his original policy related to the sale of hotels:

> . . . It is not our policy to sell properties merely because appreciation in their value would enable us to record capital gains. Since 25 percent of the gain would be payable in taxes, we would consider the realization of such a gain as representing a loss in "net worth" to the extent of the capital gains tax. In earlier years when cash flow was at a lower level and when the Company was less able to sell debentures, sales of some properties involving the realization of capital gains were necessary to obtain financing for desirable new projects or new acquisitions. The present financial condition of the Company no longer makes this procedure necessary, and therefore it is unlikely the Company will dispose of properties unless it deems it desirable to sell them for other reasons. During the year ended April 30, 1960, Sheraton made no such sales of property and therefore reports no substantial capital gains or capital gains tax.

2. *Fair Market Value of Fixed Assets.* Another practice Sheraton followed consistently, since 1947, was to include in its annual and semiannual reports a "conservative" estimate of the current fair market value of Sheraton's fixed assets. Management adopted this practice because it believed conventional financial statements based on historic costs did not reflect the fair market values of Sheraton's underlying properties.

The estimated value of the corporation's fixed assets was based on either the best judgment of Sheraton's officers or actual offers to purchase specific properties. Prior to 1954, the management appraisals were derived by using the commonly accepted method in the hotel industry of valuing income producing real estate by multiplying its earnings before interest, depreciation, and income taxes[6] by a factor varying between 8 and 10; the factor depending principally on the age of the building, its location, probable future competition, available financing, and other conditions which might affect the value.

After the introduction of the 1954 Internal Revenue Code and the widespread adoption among real estate holders of accelerated depreciation methods, another yardstick of valuation was also used which gave "roughly the same evaluation" as the earlier formula. The new method assumed that a hotel subject to mortgage debt was worth ten times its earnings after interest and an allowance for "reasonable depreciation," rather than the usually higher accelerated depreciation reported in the accounts. It should be noted that no allowance was made in either method, for the capital gains taxes which might be payable if the properties were actually sold.

In 1961, management commented upon the reliability of these estimates:

> Sales of company property over a long period of years were always made at sales prices in excess of the latest estimated values determined prior to the sales.

The limits of the Sheraton's total debt was closely related to this estimate of the fair market value of the corporation's fixed assets. The 1959 annual report stated:

> Sheraton has always made an effort to maintain a conservative debt structure with a ratio of total long-term debt, including income debentures, of not over 50% of the fair market value of all assets. It should be pointed out that fair market value is a sounder criterion than book value. Book value being an historical factor may and often does not have any relation to the price for which a property may be bought or sold. A debt structure of not over 50% of fair

---

[6] Referred to in the real estate industry as "free and clear" or "basic" earnings.

market value carried an adequate margin of safety against any depression that is likely to be encountered in the visible future.[7]

3. *Estimated Net Asset Value per Share.*

Each year since 1947, the officers of the Sheraton presented also a figure labeled "estimated net asset value."[8] When presented on a per common share basis, this figure was regarded by management as a better measure of Sheraton's accomplishments than the traditional earnings-per-share and book value-per-share calculations.

Estimated net asset value represented the common stockholders' residual equity in Sheraton based upon the officers' appraised value of Sheraton's total assets, after deducting all known liabilities, minority interests, and preferred stock interests. An increase in the "estimated net asset value" could result from such favorable factors as:

a. The sale of several real estate properties at prices in excess of the value at which they had been carried in previous appraisals.
b. Payment of dividends to stockholders in amounts substantially less than was earned by the company.
c. ᴵThe purchase of minority interests in subsidiary corporations at prices below the calculated asset value of such shares.
d. The repurchase of preferred shares of the company at a discount.
e. The sale of treasury stock at more than acquisitions cost.
f. The indicated increase in value of certain office buildings and hotels based on increased earnings, offset in part by reduction in indicated value of several hotels.

Periodically, when no more advantageous use of the corporation's funds could be found, Sheraton repurchased some of its own outstanding shares. Typically, Sheraton's stock was traded at a substantial "discount" from "estimated net asset value." Such purchases, management noted, were to the shareholders' advantage since they resulted in an immediate increase in the estimated net asset value of the remaining publicly held shares.

4. *Accelerated Depreciation.*

In 1954 following the revision of the Internal Revenue Code, Sheraton shifted to accelerated depreciation for both tax and book purposes, although the code did not require specifically that the same depreciation method be used for both book and tax reporting.

Sheraton had a very large investment in buildings, furniture, and so on, in relation to its sales. The matter of depreciation, therefore, had an

---

[7] Between 1947 and 1962, the ratio of Sheraton's debt to the fair market value of its fixed assets ranged between 30.3 percent to 47.3 percent. For the last four years, the ratio was 38.7 percent, 1962; 38.9 percent, 1961; 40.7 percent, 1960; and 45.8 percent, 1959.

[8] Sometimes called "indicated net asset value," in the early annual reports of the corporation.

important bearing on the company's reported earnings. In 1956, Sheraton management expressed the following general thoughts related to depreciation.

. . . Sheraton has consistently devoted its principal energies to creating earnings for succeeding years rather than to establishing immediately reportable earnings. We plan to continue this policy. We therefore set aside each year the highest depreciation reserves allowable—even though relatively little deterioration or obsolescence takes place. The consistent upward trend in the market value of our properties suggests that a large portion of the depreciation reserves deducted each year might well be considered a part of the current earnings of the Company.

In 1957, management stated:

. . . Depreciation reserves are of course set aside as a deduction from earnings to allow for possible shrinkage in the value of assets due to obsolescence, deterioration, etc.

Real estate firms are given considerable latitude as to the number of years over which depreciation may be calculated and the methods of determining such deductions. Companies can use their best judgment as to whether or not advantage should be taken of provisions in the new tax law permitting in some instances 200% depreciation subject to declining balances. This flexibility in selecting methods and rates of depreciation provides considerable leeway with respect to reported earnings which of course rise or fall in inverse ratio as depreciation reserves are increased or diminished. Sheraton has consistently elected to take the maximum depreciation deductions believed to be allowable under the provisions of the revenue laws, and considered consistent with good accounting practice. Although this policy can affect reported earnings adversely, it increases "cash flow," and therefore adds to the financial strength of the Company.

Subsequently, in 1959, Sheraton's management said:

. . . Sheraton believes that with propriety its depreciation reserves could be reduced by several million dollars—in part by eliminating accelerated depreciation, and in part by taking into account improvements which add more than their cost to the value of these properties, thereby reducing the need for as much depreciation. If reductions in depreciation reserves had been made, reported earnings might conceivably have been twice as large. Unfortunately, such procedure would require added income taxes.

Later, in 1960, management noted:

. . . While depreciation in theory is a deduction from income to compensate for aging and obsolescence of fixed property, the real estate investor has come to look on depreciation deductions in part as a "tax shelter" permitting tax free cash which is not offset by a corresponding loss or expense.

Three new measures of management's performance were included in Sheraton's annual reports beginning in 1954, namely, "cash flow," "economic gain," and "adjusted earnings." All three calculations were attempts by management to report Sheraton's performance without the bias of accelerated depreciation.

5. Cash Flow. About 1954, Sheraton's management gave increasing weight to "cash flow" in its annual report to the stockholders. According to the company's 1958 annual report:

Cash flow, as referred to by Sheraton, represents reported operating earnings to which depreciation allowances have been added back. Since Sheraton's depreciation allowances are calculated to a considerable extent on an accelerated basis, the large depreciation reserves mean that cash flow differs markedly from reported earnings.

For fiscal 1958, the cash flow of $17,895,506 compares with reported operating earnings of only $3,731,883.

Cash flow provides a more realistic measure of our Company's activities than so-called reported earnings, particularly since properties are meticulously maintained and since accelerated depreciation is involved.

Cash flow has customarily been the principal basis for determining values preferred by the majority of those who invest in income bearing real estate.

When properties for any one of several reasons tend to *appreciate* rather than *depreciate* each year, the elimination of deductions for depreciation becomes worthy at least of some consideration when attempting to present a more realistic picture of a company's progress than is provided by reported earnings from which large deductions for depreciation have been made. For these and other reasons, Sheraton places more emphasis on cash flow than on reported earnings from operations. Reported capital gains are of little significance for they merely record previously existing appreciation.

6. Economic Gain, or "Gainings." In 1955, Ernest Henderson introduced in his annual letter to Sheraton's stockholders a new measure of management's accomplishments labeled "economic gain" (sometimes called "economic performance" or "gainings"). This measure, Henderson claimed, was an improvement upon "cash flow."

The 1958 Sheraton annual report had this to say about "economic gain":

"Economic gain" as used by Sheraton, is a measure that provides an even more inclusive yardstick of performance than does cash flow, for it gives weight each year not only to the Company's cash flow, but also to the net change—either shrinkage or gain—in the value of the Company's assets during the year under review. Such net gain or loss, when added to its cash flow, represents what we refer to as *economic gain.*

Expressed in other words, the total economic gain (or loss) represents the total changes during the year in the net worth of the Company which would have been recorded if market values rather than book values were used in the balance sheet, after adding back any cash dividends that may have been paid during the year. Under this concept, any actual depreciation would be deducted, or appreciation (if any) added to the cash flow, in order to reflect such change in the Company's properties as they have occurred during the year. This would be in lieu of the customary practice of deducting as depreciation a specific amount each year arrived at by using one of the accepted formulae dictated by currently accepted accounting practice. Depreciation would thus reflect the exact shrinkage in assets, if any, which actually occurred. If, on the other hand, either as a result of improvements to the properties which produce values which exceed their cost, or perhaps as a result of inflationary forces, or because of improved earnings power, the aggregate value of Sheraton properties increased (as had almost invariably been the case) then during that year no deduction for depreciation would be necessary. Instead, an allowance for appreciation would be added to the cash flow to reflect the extent of this appreciation. The cash flow plus appreciation would thus be reported as economic gain.

Prior to 1962, "economic gains" had been to a large extent the result of increases in the "estimated market value of properties." These gains, according to management, were brought about in part by generally rising real estate values, and in part by the effectiveness of improvement projects financed to a considerable extent by the "reinvestment of the company's depreciation reserves."

During 1962, Sheraton for the first time reported an "economic loss" (see Exhibit 5).

7. Adjusted Earnings. In 1962, Sheraton adopted a new yardstick to recognize the effect of its depreciation policy on the reported earnings of the company. The new yardstick, "adjusted earnings," was defined as earnings from operations after income taxes and after all other fixed charges, except that for this purpose depreciation was computed on the basis of 6 percent of gross sales. The 6 percent figure was the average percentage of depreciation charges to gross sales for the hotel industry over the last five years.

Management sought through the "adjusted earnings" calculation to restate reported earnings on a basis more comparable to industrywide practices, and likewise to record these earnings on a basis comparable with Sheraton's pre-1954 earnings (when no accelerated depreciation was involved and Sheraton's depreciation reserves as a percentage of sales were similar to the rest of the hotel industry). In 1962, Sheraton estimated its annual depreciation charges were some 65 percent greater than the estimated annual depreciation customarily charged in the hotel industry.

According to management, the advantage of "adjusted earnings" over other concepts previously adopted, such as "economic gains," was that it was "less subject to possible fluctuations from year to year in the market value of real estate." It was also more "appropriate than 'reported earnings' since the latter are heavily penalized by Sheraton's policy of high depreciation reserves which has been in effect since 1954."

The notion of "adjusted earnings" was first presented to Sheraton's shareholders by Ernest Henderson in a special mailing entitled "Sheraton's 'True' Earnings," dated March 1962. The entire report is included as Exhibit 4.

"Adjusted earnings" on a gross and per-share basis for the years 1947–62 are shown in Exhibit 5. Also presented in Exhibit 5 are statistics related to the other measures of management performance discussed previously.

Questions

1. Comment on the various income measurement approaches proposed by the Sheraton management?
2. Why was Mr. Henderson objecting to the traditional approach to income measurement?
3. How ought the income of a company like Sheraton be measured?

EXHIBIT 1

SHERATON CORPORATION OF AMERICA

Assets

	April 30, 1962	April 30, 1961
Current Assets:		
Cash:		
Demand deposits	$ 11,422,577	$ 14,690,933
Restricted deposits	975,738	345,045
On hand	1,594,558	1,561,147
	$ 13,992,873	$ 16,597,125
Securities—marketable—at cost:		
U.S. Treasury bonds	$ 247,872	$ 328,275
Other (Note 2)	1,096,041	64,645
(market values $1,157,608 and $377,874)	$ 1,343,913	$ 392,920
Accounts and notes receivable	$ 18,994,348	$ 17,026,292
Less: Estimated uncollectible accounts and notes	656,546	606,522
	$ 18,337,802	$ 16,419,770
Accrued interest receivable	$ 48,763	$ 54,245
Mortgages receivable—payments due within one year (below)	168,779	744,277
Inventories—at cost	6,938,637	5,837,055
Prepaid expenses	2,662,910	2,643,814
Total Current Assets	$ 43,493,677	$ 42,689,206

EXHIBIT 1 *(continued)*

	April 30, 1962	April 30, 1961
Investments—at cost (Notes 1 and 2):		
Securities—other than marketable	$ 1,557,186	$ 3,973,409
(officers' estimated values $1,391,203 and $3,919,299)		
Securities of subsidiaries—not consolidated	619,906	619,906
(estimated values $646,000 and $738,000)		
Mortgages receivable	2,037,619	7,261,666
(officers' estimated values $2,986,798 and $8,899,767)		
Less: Mortgage payments due within one year		
(above)	(168,779)	(744,277)
Total Investments	$ 4,045,932	$ 11,110,704
Property, Plant, and Equipment (Notes 1 and 3):		
Land and leaseholds.....................................	$ 54,078,879	$ 50,954,545
Buildings and improvements	194,905,639	181,919,270
Leasehold improvements	7,359,101	5,456,237
Furniture and equipment	84,377,150	78,742,413
	$340,720,769	$317,072,465
Less: Depreciation to date	113,961,337	99,701,085
Total Property, Plant, and Equipment................	$226,759,432	$217,371,380
(officers' estimated values $341,500,000 and $340,500,000)		
Other Assets:		
Options and deposits on contracts	$ 30,000	$ 5,000
Notes and contracts receivable—due after one year	338,719	304,989
Unamortized debt discount and expense (Note 10)	3,121,025	2,944,835
Security and other deposits	729,834	763,836
Life insurance—cash surrender value	292,683	276,921
Other (Note 1)	1,768,485	1,274,437
Total Other Assets	$ 6,280,746	$ 5,570,018
Total Assets	$280,579,787	$276,741,308

See Notes to Consolidated Financial Statements. (Not reproduced.)

Liabilities, Capital Shares, and Surplus

	April 30, 1962	April 30, 1961
Current Liabilities:		
Notes and contracts payable (Note 2)	$ 23,237,782	$ 23,033,371
Less: Payments due after one year (below)	14,851,639	17,119,692
	$ 8,386,143	$ 5,913,679
Accounts payable	14,240,793	11,483,066
Accrued liabilities:		
Interest	1,789,955	1,661,554
Federal, Canadian, and state taxes	1,842,139	1,622,804
Other	6,479,523	6,697,168
Bonds and mortgages payable—payments due within one year (below):		
Capital income sinking fund debentures	992,200	768,700
Other bonds and mortgages	7,094,654	7,417,916
Total Current Liabilities.............................	$ 40,825,407	$ 35,564,887

EXHIBIT 1 *(concluded)*

	April 30, 1962	April 30, 1961
Long-Term Indebtedness (Notes 2, 3, 4, and 5):		
Bonds and mortgages payable (except capital debentures)	$140,967,826	$143,956,367
Less: Payments due within one year (above)	7,094,654	7,417,916
	$133,873,172	$136,538,451
Notes and contracts payable—due after one year (above)	14,851,639	17,119,692
Federal and state taxes payable	465,221	1,140,591
	$149,190,032	$154,798,734
Capital income sinking fund debentures (1989)	$ 32,743,600	$ 24,800,200
Less: Payments due within one year (above)	992,200	768,700
	$ 31,751,400	$ 24,031,500
Total Long-Term Indebtedness	$180,941,432	$178,830,234
Total Liabilities	$221,766,839	$214,395,121
Minority Interests	$ 1,679,663	$ 1,640,388

Capital Shares and Surplus:

	Shares			
	April 30, 1962	April 30, 1961		
Capital Shares (Notes 4 and 5):				
Preferred, par $100:				
Authorized	100,000	100,000		
Issued and outstanding—				
4% cumulative convertible ..	15,120	15,120	$ 1,512,000	$ 1,512,000
Common—par $0.50:				
Authorized	10,000,000	10,000,000		
Issued and issuable	5,447,425	5,329,780		
Less: In treasury	145,533	67,185		
Outstanding	5,301,892	5,262,595	2,650,946	2,631,298
Total Capital Shares			$ 4,162,946	$ 4,143,298
Surplus (Notes 5 and 6):				
Paid-in surplus			39,033,291	38,193,244
Earned surplus			12,294,305	16,602,912
Surplus from consolidation (Note 1)			1,642,743	1,766,345
Total Capital Shares and Surplus			$ 57,133,285	$ 60,705,799
Total Liabilities, Capital Shares and Surplus			$280,579,787	$276,741,308

EXHIBIT 2

SHERATON CORPORATION OF AMERICA
Comparative Consolidated Income Statement, 1961–1962

	For the Year Ended	
	April 30, 1962	April 30, 1961
Gross Operating Income:		
Hotels:		
Rooms	$ 75,646,165	$ 73,298,337
Food and beverages	81,203,612	76,465,179
Other	15,562,077	14,759,658
	$172,411,854	$164,523,174
Commercial buildings	3,608,306	3,694,415
Apartment buildings	1,529,530	1,599,883
Thompson Division	31,229,345	29,730,948
Other	5,938,451	5,250,532
Total	$214,717,486	$204,798,952
Operating Costs and Expenses:		
Departmental costs and expenses	$100,792,246	$ 94,446,930
Administrative and general	14,772,502	14,625,991
Advertising and promotion	6,138,070	5,892,371
Heat, electricity, and water	6,851,146	6,129,072
Repairs and maintenance	8,313,589	8,495,807
Rent	3,437,481	3,031,623
Real estate and personal property taxes	7,836,119	7,121,119
Insurance	213,265	198,574
Bad debts expense	699,436	668,903
Thompson Division:		
Cost of sales	24,396,277	24,386,540
Other	2,907,100	2,602,946
Other	6,394,844	5,701,580
Total	$182,752,075	$173,301,456
Operating income	$ 31,965,411	$ 31,497,496
Other Income:		
Dividends and interest	474,833	893,780
Other	7,031	8,221
Total (referred to as "basic earnings")	$ 32,447,275	$ 32,399,497
Other Deductions from Income:		
Depreciation	$ 19,276,038	$ 18,181,468
Interest and debt expense	10,345,448	10,170,789
Total	$ 29,621,486	$ 28,352,257
Ordinary income	$ 2,825,789	$ 4,047,240

EXHIBIT 2 *(continued)*

	For the Year Ended	
	April 30, *1962*	*April 30,* *1961*
Income Taxes:		
Federal and Canadian.......................................	$ 1,862,402	$ 1,654,519
State	180,307	199,799
Total	$ 2,042,709	$ 1,854,318
Net income before profit from capital transactions	$ 783,080	$ 2,192,922
Profit from capital transactions	$ 407,014	$ 1,575,635
Less: Income taxes thereon	90,116	409,493
Net profit from capital transactions	$ 316,898	$ 1,166,142
Income and profits for the year	$ 1,099,978	$ 3,359,064
Net income and profits applicable to minority interests	152,980	124,914
Net Income and Profits for the Year	$ 946,998	$ 3,234,150

See Notes to Consolidated Financial Statements. (Not reproduced.)

EXHIBIT 3

SHERATON CORPORATION OF AMERICA
Consolidated State of Surplus
April 30, 1962

Paid-In Surplus

Consolidated paid-in surplus April 30, 1961		$38,193,244
Additions:		
Portion of earned surplus transferred to paid-in surplus in connection with August 1, 1961, 2% common stock dividend (100,221 shares at $18.50 per share)	$1,854,089	

Excess of amounts received over par value of 16,842 shares
of common stock issued at $8.333 per share upon the exercise
of warrants and cash paid in lieu of fractional shares

	Amounts Received	
Paid by—		
6% debenture bonds	$ 10,000	
Cash	130,360	
Total	$140,360	
Par value of shares issued and cash paid in lieu of fractional shares	8,446	131,914

Excess of par value of 4¾% sinking fund convertible debentures surrendered for conversion over par value of 582 shares of common stock issued therefore and cash paid in lieu of fractional shares	8,685	
Proceeds of sale of warrants to purchase 158,800 shares of common stock at $50 per share to November 1976	119,100	
		2,113,788
		$40,307,032
Deduction:		
Excess of amount paid over par value of 78,348 shares of common stock purchased (total cost $1,312,915)		1,273,741
Consolidated Paid-in Surplus April 30, 1962		$39,033,291

EXHIBIT 3 *(continued)*

Earned Surplus

Consolidated earned surplus April 30, 1961		$16,602,912
Addition:		
Net income and profits for the year ended April 30, 1962		946,998
		$17,549,910
Deductions:		
2% common stock dividend (Note 1)		
100,221 shares at $19.00 per share	$1,904,199	
Cash in lieu of fractional shares	95,809	
	2,000,008	
Cash dividends:		
Preferred—$4.00 per share	60,480	
Common—$0.60 per share	3,195,117	
		5,255,605
Consolidated Earned Surplus April 30, 1962		$12,294,305

Note 1. The charge to Earned Surplus represents the closing sales price on June 30, 1961, date of record, on the New York Stock Exchange. The Capital Shares account was credited with $0.50 per share, the par value, and Paid-In Surplus was credited with the balance of $18.50 per share.

See Notes to Consolidated Financial Statements.

EXHIBIT 4
Sheraton's "True" Earnings

There may still remain some confusion in the minds of investors and security analysts as to the real earnings of Sheraton.

The more conventional yardsticks of performance used for reporting progress are the following:

1. Ordinary reported earnings after depreciation reserves.
   Depreciation was increased to $18,181,000 for the 1961 fiscal year and is expected to be higher in fiscal 1962. This compares with only $4,500,000 in 1954. Since various forms of accelerated depreciation are presently used, most analysts recognize that high depreciation probably obscures some of the true earnings.
2. Our reported cash flow.
   This measure is likewise not acceptable to many analysts since no reserve for depreciation is provided in these figures.

Sheraton's reported earnings from operations per share after depreciation were 39¢ for fiscal 1961, whereas cash flow per share was $3.84. Since the true earnings doubtless lie somewhere between these two limits, the problem arises how to determine just how much depreciation should be deducted in order to measure the Company's true earnings. Since there are both ups and downs from year to year, a depreciation figure that represents a reasonable "average" over the years is desirable, rather than one geared to an especially good or bad year.

Sheraton shares with the electric utility industry the accounting problems that relate to depreciation reserves. There is an interesting analogy in Sheraton's experience to that of the Potomac Electric Power Company. Potomac has total assets of over $500,000,000 compared with an estimated $400,000,000 for Sheraton. Potomac Electric sales are $88,000,000, considerably less than the $200,000,000 reported by Sheraton. The Potomac Electric Power Company, using schedules established by the District of Columbia Public Utility Commission, sets up straight-line depreciation of 2.7% of its investment in depreciable property when reporting to shareholders. This amounts to $10,955,000 for the 1960 calendar year and covers considerably more property than is held by Sheraton. A footnote in the Potomac Electric annual report indicates that for income tax purposes close to $18,100,000 (including some accelerated depreciation) was

EXHIBIT 4 *(continued)*

actually charged off. The difference of some $7,000,000 provides a $3,500,000 tax saving. Earnings reported to shareholders are thus increased by $7,000,000.

Similarly Sheraton also charged off some $18,100,000 of depreciation last year for income tax purposes, but used approximately the same amount in determining the earnings reported to shareholders, even though, as was the case with Potomac, some of Sheraton's earnings were doubtless included in the high depreciation reserves reported for tax purposes. Sheraton's reported earnings to shareholders are therefore relatively small.

A year ago Sheraton's depreciation on hotel properties was 10% of gross sales and is currently running at this rate; whereas according to both Horwath & Horwath and Harris, Kerr, Forster & Company, leading hotel accounting firms, depreciation averaged 6% of gross sales for the industry for the past five years. The industry figure of 6% which is based on the experience of several hundred hotels may even be somewhat overstated, since Sheraton hotels with unusually high depreciation reserves are included in the computation of the industry averages.

Clearly some of Sheraton's earnings are absorbed in the nearly nineteen millions of depreciation currently being charged off. Actually asset value computations by Company officers indicate that in the entire 25-year hotel history of Sheraton and likewise during the past ten years, there has been more "appreciation" than shrinkage in the value of Sheraton properties. This may not apply to individual years or individual properties, especially in recent years when greater competition is being encountered.

To meet the problem of providing what we consider a better yardstick for reporting financial performance, we have evolved the concept of "adjusted earnings." Under this theory, reported earnings from operations are modified by including in "adjusted earnings" those depreciation charges that are in excess of the average amount customarily used in the hotel industry. The revised deduction for depreciation would be determined by applying to Sheraton the same ratio of depreciation to total sales as the five-year average for the hotel industry amounting to 6%, according to Harris, Kerr, Forster & Company and Horwath & Horwath. Amounts applicable to Sheraton's Thompson Division, a manufacturing operation, would of course be excluded from the computation of excess depreciation.

"Adjusted earnings" can, we believe, provide a satisfactory compromise between "cash flow" and "reported earnings" for measuring income available for common shares. In determining dividend policy, adjusted earnings may well be taken into account by the directors, both as a measure of the performance of the Company, as well as of the amount of available funds for such payments available from current operations.

It is our present belief that depreciation reserves adjusted to hotel industry averages will provide during the next ten years considerably more protection than is likely to be required for obsolescence and shrinkage in real estate values. Should Sheraton hotel sales remain constant over the next ten years, depreciation reserves, even if adjusted to 6% of sales, would still amount in ten years to nearly $120,000,000, considerably more than seems necessary for Sheraton's well maintained properties. Even such reduced reserves might be a substantial source of potential added growth in the Company's net worth.

Attached hereto are statements for recent years showing "adjusted earnings" together with the percentage of such earnings paid out each year in dividends. These figures of adjusted earnings, I believe, will be more acceptable to security analysts than other more conventional measures of performance which we will continue to present as heretofore in our financial reports.

With respect to dividends, Potomac Electric pays out 40% of earnings after scaling downward by some $7,000,000 the depreciation reserves used for income tax purposes. Sheraton, following a similar though theoretical scaling down of depreciation reserves by $6,833,000 in order to conform with hotel industry ratios, paid out 35½ percent of the resulting "adjusted earnings" in cash dividends last year. Sheraton's policy of emphasizing adjusted earnings is not too different from the procedures of recent publicly financed real estate corporations.

Our current 60¢ dividend actually approximates 35% of our present "adjusted earnings." In my opinion, the level of adjusted earnings should be a more important factor in

EXHIBIT 4 *(continued)*

influencing dividend policy in a company such as Sheraton, than are the reported earnings. It is not unusual for real estate companies with relatively high depreciation reserves to pay dividends nowadays even though they may show no reported earnings whatsoever.

In order to achieve the maximum possible increase in adjusted earnings, it would be desirable to see depreciation reserves increase if and when cash earnings increase, in order that income taxes should not rise. Otherwise it would take two dollars of increased pre-tax earnings to provide—after taxes—an extra dollar of increased "adjusted earnings."

Our Room Rate Revision Program

Two years ago we decided to extend greater values to our customers by reducing room rates and by extending the privilege of free parking in the majority of Sheraton hotels.

Our rate reduction program has been costly. Extending over a second year, it has slowed down our rate of progress to an extent that must have been discouraging to many shareholders. The next few years will, we believe, show that the program was quite constructive. Giving effect to an actual rate reduction of 5.2% in the past two years, and to the policy of not raising rates during the past two years by at least 1½% a year required to offset higher costs, this intentional narrowing of profit margins is estimated to have cost us $5,600,000 during the past two years. This loss—since our basic earnings (earnings before interest, depreciation and income taxes) have remained fairly constant—apparently has been largely recouped by economies, and by profitable additions and acquisitions financed principally by some $35,000,000 of depreciation reserves available to us during the course of the past two years. Since further rate reductions are unlikely, and since some rate increases seem presently justified, the reinvestment of our depreciation reserves should—as seems to have been the case in all but the last two or three years—maintain a satisfactory growth pattern, one that has been matched by few if any companies now listed on the New York Stock Exchange if viewed over a period of twenty years.

The question has been asked—with rate reductions, free parking in most hotels, and after absorbing payroll increases, burdens amounting in all to some $2,800,000 a year for each of the past two years—how was it possible to maintain basic earnings at close to $32,000,000. This question is especially pertinent in the face of losses associated with the recent major renovation program in Oklahoma City, heavy starting up expenses at the Sheraton-Chicago and extensive competition in certain areas.

Fortunately we were able to meet these rate reduction costs because of various favorable aspects of the Company. These include:

1. Our Belt-Tightening program.
2. A small increase in occupancy since 1959 (68.8 to 70.0) in the face of a heavy decline in the industry.
3. Progress in the office buildings.
4. Profitable reinvestment of our depreciation reserves.
5. Recovery of earning power in Montreal following heavy losses from competition three years ago from a new Montreal hotel.
6. Improved performance in Dallas, Binghamton, Portland, Princess Kaiulani in Hawaii, and other new hotels that caused initially a heavy drain on earnings.

Whereas basic earnings (earnings before depreciation, interest and income taxes) remained fairly constant at close to $32,000,000 for the past two years, and is continuing close to this level for the current fiscal year, the same seems to be true of our cash flow (basic earnings after deducting interest and income taxes). Although interest charges have been rising, income taxes are down due to larger depreciation reserves.

Our cash flow in the $3.80 per share range for the last two years is still running close to this level in fiscal 1962, although reported earnings will be substantially lower. In other words, the adjustment of some $5,600,000 in room rates and in other concessions designed to improve our competitive position has been almost entirely made up as far as cash flow is concerned by means of economies and other newly created earning power.

EXHIBIT 4 *(continued)*

Comparison of Cash Flow with Hilton Hotels Corporation

Our cash flow (after income taxes and exclusive of capital gains) compared with that of Hilton Hotels for the past four years has been as follows:

	Sheraton	*Hilton*
Sheraton 1961*	$20,249,476	
Hilton 1960		$18,285,557
Sheraton 1960*	$19,656,353	
Hilton 1959		$19,167,175
Sheraton 1959*	$17,494,180	
Hilton 1958		$18,104,357
Sheraton 1958*	$17,895,506	
Hilton 1957		$16,726,716

* Year ended April 30.

A year ago we indicated that our fiscal 1962 goal called for a 10% to 12% increase in cash flow. This we did not achieve. A second round of rate reductions for fiscal 1962, amounting for the year to a sacrifice in rates estimated at $2,800,000 appears to have prevented the growth in cash flow and adjusted earnings normally anticipated from the profit improvement projects financed by our depreciation reserves. Such added earnings, the source of our anticipated fiscal 1962 growth, were required to make good a large portion of the cost of our second round of rate reductions effected in fiscal 1962. Since we have now achieved relatively satisfactory occupancy levels some eight percentage points higher than is indicated for the industry, we do not anticipate the need for any substantial further rate reductions. Accordingly, after progress was delayed for a second year which ends this April thirtieth, we are looking forward to the resumption of an upward trend of cash flow, and more significantly to an uptrend in what we call "adjusted earnings." Fiscal 1963 should determine whether or not our calculations are correct. No increase in dividends is likely even to be contemplated unless a rise in "adjusted earnings" can be realized.

Conclusion

Having established a sound room rate structure, we feel that we are now in a strong position to meet future competition. With free parking presently available in the majority of our hotels, we believe we have considerably more to offer the public than do most motels.

Recognizing the importance, however, of "convenience" parking, we have converted some twelve of our smaller hotels into Sheraton Motor Inns. These, together with the motor inns which we have built or acquired, give us presently a total of 16 motor hotels. This number will rise to 22 by July 1962. We are becoming an important factor in this field, and we are growing.

Our 1963 fiscal year begins next May 1. It will determine, we believe, the correctness of our costly two-year "investment" estimated at $5,600,000 in rate reductions. This represents a loss of rooms income which, capitalized at 11% would have represented a reduction of about $50,000,000 in asset value, had not this loss due to reduced rooms revenue fortunately been replaced to a large extent through the creation of new earning power and increased sales volume. We believe we have now acquired at considerable expense, a strong foundation upon which future growth can be built.

ERNEST HENDERSON, *President*
Sheraton Corporation of America

Boston, Massachusetts
March 17, 1962

EXHIBIT 4 (continued)

SHERATON CORPORATION OF AMERICA AND SUBSIDIARIES
Adjusted Earnings
(Note 1)

	Years Ended April 30					Nine Months Ended January 31	
	1961	1960	1959	1958	1957	1962	1961
Basic earnings (before depreciation, interest, and income taxes)	$32,339,497	$32,961,601	$29,266,654	$29,405,274	$28,150,379	$23,718,790	$23,930,213
Deduct:							
Interest and debt expense	10,170,789	9,829,272	7,292,032	6,849,261	5,979,133	7,765,120	7,610,718
Income taxes	1,854,318	3,126,873	3,914,563	4,105,214	4,783,000	1,580,000	1,490,000
Minority interests	124,914	349,103	565,879	555,293	720,606	107,706	109,072
Cash flow	20,249,476	19,656,353	17,494,180	17,895,506	16,667,640	14,265,964	14,720,423
Deduct—depreciation	18,181,468	16,833,225	14,144,378	14,163,623	11,919,759	13,645,373	13,140,448
Ordinary reported earnings	$ 2,068,008	$ 2,823,128	$ 3,349,802	$ 3,731,883	$ 4,747,881	$ 620,591	$ 1,579,975
Add—depreciation in excess of average for hotel industry	6,833,473	5,875,230	5,068,425	5,408,244	3,818,353	5,046,633	4,782,924
Adjusted earnings (Note 1)	$ 8,901,481	$ 8,698,358	$ 8,418,227	$ 9,140,127	$ 8,566,234	$ 5,667,224	$ 6,362,899
Adjusted earnings per share	$1.65	$1.65	$1.70	$1.83	$1.72	$1.05	$1.18
Cash dividends	$ 3,159,281	$ 2,957,576	$ 2,811,160	$ 2,753,542	$ 2,365,666	$ 2,430,065	$ 2,339,695
% of adjusted earnings	35.5%	34.0%	33.4%	30.1%	27.6%	42.9%	36.8%

Note 1. Adjusted earnings represent the reported earnings from operations adjusted by adding back the excess of depreciation deductions over the average for the hotel industry. This is accomplished by using a figure equal to 6% of gross hotel sales in lieu of the depreciation reserves actually set up. This 6% figure corresponds to the five year average for the hotel industry based on computations by Harris, Kerr, Forster & Company and Horwath & Horwath, hotel accountants and consultants. Amounts applicable to the Thompson Division, a manufacturing operation, are excluded in computing excess depreciation.

EXHIBIT 4 *(continued)*

Adjusted Earnings Showing Reported Earnings Plus Excess Depreciation

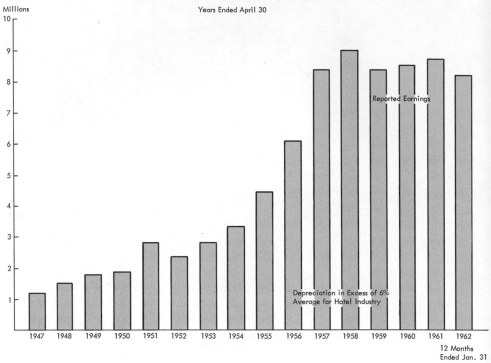

Note: No excess depreciation shown for years prior to 1955 (tax law changed in 1954).

EXHIBIT 4 *(concluded)*

Impact on Basic Earnings* of Rate Reductions

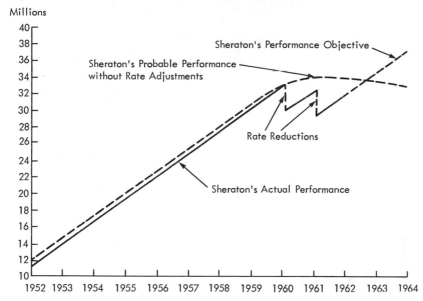

* Before depreciation, interest, and income taxes.

EXHIBIT 5
Financial Statistics, 1947–1962

A. Growth Consolidated in Thousands of Dollars

Years Ended April 30	Total Assets at Estimated Values (a)	Total Assets at Book Values	Gross Income	Depreciation	Cash Flow (b)	Basic Earnings (c)	Reported Net Operating Income and Other Credits (d)	Net Profits on Capital Transactions (d)	Total Reported Net Income and Net Profits (d)	Net Worth Profit (loss) (a)(e)(f)	"Adjusted" Earnings (a)(d)(g)
1962	$393,984	$280,580	$215,199	$19,276	$19,906	$32,447	$ 630	$ 317	$ 947	($ 8,222)	$7,911
1961	400,445	276,741	205,701	18,181	20,249	32,399	2,068	1,166	3,234	8,469	8,901
1960	390,620	273,401	204,882	16,833	19,656	32,962	2,823	270	3,093	18,854	8,698
1959	346,910	245,503	171,474	14,144	17,494	29,267	3,350	2,001	5,351	19,651	8,418
1958	304,007	217,325	159,014	14,164	17,896	29,405	3,732	1,101	4,833	7,257	9,140
1957	304,645	219,866	153,792	11,920	16,668	28,150	4,748	654	5,402	18,263	8,566
1956	243,697	172,468	121,672	8,098	12,534	21,748	4,436	2,215	6,651	18,239	6,104
1955	193,033	134,543	89,376	5,390	9,504	16,622	4,114	4,760	8,874	23,111	4,634
1954	132,520	89,568	72,771	4,507	7,924	14,302	3,417	1,878	5,295	11,261	3,417
1953	129,475	91,313	68,142	3,857	6,772	12,625	2,915	1,007	3,922	11,295	2,915
1952	113,524	82,459	62,773	3,490	6,062	11,096	2,896(i)	1,196	4,182	7,174	2,986(i)
1951	101,861	74,982	56,071	3,253	6,156	10,629	3,719(i)	1,191	4,910	16,701	3,719(i)
1950	87,874	73,029	39,739	2,626	4,594	7,898	2,107(i)	1,457	3,564	13,440	2,107(i)
1949	60,279	54,541	31,605	1,795	3,698	5,779	1,903	1,470	3,373	2,723	1,903
1948	55,710	47,643	28,663	1,569	3,177	5,389	1,608	68	1,676	2,378	1,608
1947	49,860	42,332	21,511	1,128	2,141	3,946	1,013	1,161	2,174	7,924	1,013

B. "Economic performance" per common share*

Years Ended April 30	Estimated Net Asset Values (a) (h)	Cash Flow (b)	Quoted Market Price	Depreciation	Cash Dividends Paid During Year	Increase or (decrease) in Estimated Net Asset Value during Year	"Economic Performance" i.e., Asset Value Increase Plus Dividends Paid (includes estimated appreciation)	"Adjusted" Earnings (a) (e) (g)	Price Cash Flow Ratio (shows ratio of market price of shares to cash flow)	Reported Net Operating Income and Other Credits (e)	Net Profits on Capital Transactions (d)	Total Reported Net Income and Net Profits (e)
1962	$30.20*	$3.74	$14.75	$3.53	$0.60	($1.85)	($1.26)	$1.48	3.9	$0.11	$0.06	$0.17
1961	32.06*	3.77	17.40	3.39	0.59	0.99	1.58	1.65	4.6	0.38	0.22	0.60
1960	31.07*	3.72	17.78	3.19	0.57	2.78	3.35	1.65	4.8	0.53	0.05	0.58
1959	28.29*	3.53	17.43	2.85	0.56	3.03	3.59	1.70	4.9	0.68	0.40	1.08
1958	25.26*	3.59	10.51	2.84	0.55	0.87	1.42	1.83	2.9	0.75	0.22	0.97
1957	24.39*	3.34	11.43	2.39	0.47	2.98	3.45	1.72	3.4	0.95	0.13	1.08
1956	21.41*	2.50	10.17	1.61	0.40	3.11	3.51	1.22	4.1	0.89	0.44	1.33
1955	18.30*	1.89	11.44	1.97	0.27	2.75	3.02	0.92	6.0	0.82	0.95	1.77
1954	15.55	1.56	5.29	0.89	0.21	2.02	2.23	0.67	3.4	0.67	0.37	1.04
1953	13.53	1.30	4.31	0.74	0.18	2.00	2.18	0.56	3.3	0.56.	0.20	0.76
1952	11.53	1.14	3.60	0.66	0.17	1.19	1.36	0.56(i)	3.1	0.56(i)	0.23	0.79
1951	10.34	1.18	2.98	0.63	0.17	3.05	3.22	0.71(i)	2.5	0.71(i)	0.23	0.94
1950	7.29	0.86	2.32	0.50	0.12	2.46	2.58	0.39(i)	2.7	0.39(i)	0.28	0.67
1949	4.83	0.68	1.60	0.34	0.12	0.40	0.52	0.34	2.3	0.34	0.28	0.62
1948	4.43	0.58	1.74	0.30	0.12	0.53	0.45	0.28	3.0	0.28	0.01	0.29
1947	4.10	0.38	2.07	0.21	0.10	1.59	1.49	0.17	5.4	0.17	0.22	0.39

* Adjusted for stock dividends and stock split-ups, and estimated net asset values at April 30, 1955, to 1962 allow for exercise of warrants and conversion of 4¾% Debentures.
(a) Estimated by company officers.
(b) Net operating income plus depreciation.
(c) Before interest, Depreciation and income taxes.
(d) After minority interests.
(e) After minority interests and preferred dividends.
(f) Represents total net income and profits including charges in estimated net asset values and differences arising from sales and purchases of common stock at more or less than estimated net asset values.
(g) Represents net operating income adjusted by adding back the excess of depreciation deductions over the estimated average for the hotel industry.
(h) After liabilities, minority interests, and preferred stock.
(i) Includes other credits in 1950, 1951, and 1952 of $139,000, $816,000, and $414,200, respectively; or $0.03, $0.16, and $0.08 per share, respectively.
Source: 1962 Annual Report.

Chapter 15

PRICE LEVEL AND REPLACEMENT COST ACCOUNTING

Inflation is a condition of overall rising prices. There is widespread concern throughout the world over the future purchasing power of local currencies. The extent of this interest and the degree of inflation varies from country to country. For example during 1975 the purchasing power of the Argentine Peso declined about 280 percent, whereas the United States dollar in the most inflationary period in recent years depreciated only 12 percent in 1974. This chapter briefly covers some of the basic technical questions about how inflation and purchasing power are measured by economists and accountants.

In the U.S.A. inflation accounting is governed by APB *Statement No. 3*, which sets forth the guidelines for publishing on a voluntary basis as a supplement to a company's regular statements financial statements adjusted for changed in the general level of prices, and SEC *Release No. 190*, which requires certain companies to disclose in their notes the current replacement cost of their inventories and productive assets as well as the expenses arising from the consumption of these assets.

MEASURES OF INFLATION

Statisticians and economists measure inflation by selecting a sample of goods and services representative of the economy and recording their price movements, each item being weighted by its relative importance in terms of its total volume of sales related to the sales of all items. Next, a base year is selected and the index number 100 is assigned to represent that year's composite price. The sample's composite price index for subsequent years can then be compiled and compared to the base year to measure changes in the price level index.

The Consumer Price Index prepared monthly by the Bureau of

Labor Statistics of the United States Department of Labor is generally used as one of the indicators of general price level changes in the United States. The base period for this index is 1967. This index is a weighted average of the prices paid by the public for some 400 consumer products in 56 regions of the U.S.A. The Consumer Price Index is often used in escalator clauses in wage and lease contracts. It is also recognized by the courts.

A broader and perhaps better measure of the changes in the overall general level of prices is the Implicit Price Deflator for the Gross National Product. It is calculated by dividing gross national product in current prices by gross national product in constant prices. This price index, published by the Office of Business Economics, United States Department of Commerce, is used to translate the gross national product from current prices to constant prices. Its base period is 1958.

Another commonly used price index is the Wholesale Price Index compiled by the Bureau of Labor Statistics. It measures price changes in primary producers' markets. Because of its limited coverage, this index is not considered a good measure of inflation.

According to the Consumer Price Index, the average annual increase in consumer prices in the United States between 1971 and 1974 was 6.9 percent. In contrast, the GNP Implicit Price Deflator Index suggests prices rose annually on the average 3.2 percent during this same period. Thus, these two measures of price level changes indicate different rates of inflation between 1971 and 1974. This difference has led to controversy over which index is the more reliable measurement of inflation. The Implicit Price Deflator reflects broader price changes than the Consumer Price Index, since it includes a wider range of goods and services. However, it is apparently not as sensitive as the Consumer Price Index is to short-run price changes.

The principal virtue of the Consumer Price Index is the fact that it is more easily understood by the general public. The principal criticism of it is that it does not adequately take into account changes in product quality. Nevertheless, quality is not ignored, and over the years this index has generally proved to be a reasonably adequate measure of inflation.

In addition to the indices that measure general shifts in prices, there are a number of indices published by private companies and government agencies that measure the changes in the prices of specific items, such as the costs of construction, services, durables, electrical motors, and steel wire.

BUSINESS CONSIDERATIONS

During inflationary periods, business executives try to minimize their company's purchasing power losses and maximize its purchasing power gains so as to at least maintain the purchasing power equivalent of their stockholders' equity. The ways to do this are well known to business executives. The problem is to achieve them in practice.

Cash, accounts receivable, and similar monetary assets are all exposed to purchasing power losses in an inflationary economy. For example, a $10,000 check deposited in a bank on January 1, 1974, would have bought fewer goods on December 31, 1974, since the price level index rose 12 percent during this period. The same is true of accounts and loans receivable held during the same period.

Accounts payable, long-term debt, and similar monetary liabilities are exposed to purchasing power gains. To the extent that these liabilities are extinguished with "cheaper" currency than originally obtained through the incurring of the liability, a company is better off.

Consequently, most business executives during inflationary times seek to maintain a net monetary liability balance (i.e., monetary liabilities in excess of monetary assets), or at least the minimum net monetary asset balance possible.

To the extent feasible, managers operating in inflationary conditions shift their resources from monetary assets to physical assets, such as inventory, plant, or equipment. They assume that raw materials and finished goods inventories are protected against inflation as long as the prices of raw materials and finished goods keep pace with the rate of inflation. Similarly, fixed assets are protected to the extent that their resale or replacement value rises with inflation and their cost of replacement is recovered through increases in the prices of the goods and services produced with these assets.

ACCOUNTING REQUIREMENTS

Financial statements are prepared initially in terms of historical costs, and it is assumed that the local currency is a constant unit of measure. However, inasmuch as the amounts shown in the statements result from many transactions occurring at different times, the purchasing power equivalent of these various amounts will not be the same if inflation has taken place during the period when these transactions occurred. Also, the expenses charged for the consumption of inventories and productive assets will not be the same as the cost of replacing these assets.

In countries with extreme inflation, it is generally agreed that it is desirable to restate historical cost-based statements to some basis that reflects the impact on the reporting company of specific price changes and inflation. However, in the United States until the mid-1970s the annual rate of inflation had been relatively mild and there was little support of the proposals made that financial statements ought to be restated to reflect changes in the purchasing power of the dollar and the prices of specific assets. As a result in the mid-1970s, the practice was not to adjust statements, although a few companies did publish supplemental statements showing the impact of inflation on their business.

The 1974 inflation changed this situation. As a result, in 1974 the FASB put forth a proposal that would have required mandatory publication of supplementary financial statements adjusted for changes in the purchasing power of the dollar as measured by changes in the Gross National Product Implicit Price Deflator. Subsequently, in 1976 the SEC issued *Accounting Series Release No. 190* that required the disclosure of certain replacement cost information by large nonfinancial companies under its jurisdiction. This approach rejected the use of general price level indexes in favor of restating inventories and productive assets to reflect the changes in the prices of the specific assets. In 1976 the FASB withdrew its proposal. However, should companies wish to publish supplemental statements adjusted for general price level changes, *Statement No. 3* of the APB is still an authoritative guide to the preparation of these statements.

General Purchasing Power Restatement: APB and FASB Approach

The goal of restatement for inflation and price changes adopted by the APB and favored by the FASB in its withdrawn Exposure Draft is to express the financial statements in terms of the purchasing power measured by some general price level index at the most recent balance sheet date so as to measure both the purchasing power gains and losses on holding monetary items and the ability of the company to recover the purchasing power invested in the assets consumed during the current period. As a practical matter, the process used to restate financial statements in stable amounts having the same purchasing power can be complicated or simple, depending on the particular company involved or the degree of precision sought. In all cases, however, the amounts are restated through the use of an index of changes in general level of prices.

Restatement is a statistical procedure independent of other accounting principles and procedures. It starts with the historical cost data and the company's particular accounting policy. Consequently, the restatement process is independent of the accounting principles selected to prepare the statements.

The general rule for restating is to multiply the historical cost figure by the price level index at the end of the accounting period divided by the price level index at the time of the transaction. For example, if a

$1,000 sale takes place on January 1 and the price level index rises from 100 to 110 between January 1 and the end of the fiscal period on December 31, the end-of-year purchasing power equivalent of this sale is $1,100 ($1,000 × 110/100).

For the purpose of restatement, all items in the financial statements are classified as either being monetary or nonmonetary items. Monetary items are those normally carried in the accounts at current cash values, such as cash, accounts receivable, accounts payable, and long-term debt. The remaining items are classified as nonmonetary. They include inventories, plant and equipment, and capital stock.

Monetary items are worth their face value. Consequently, monetary items held at the balance sheet date do not need to be restated. They are automatically stated in current dollars. The purchasing power of these items does change, however. Consequently, monetary assets held during periods of inflation lose purchasing power, whereas holding monetary liabilities leads to a gain in purchasing power. One of the principal objectives of restatement is to measure this net gain or loss from holding monetary items.

Nonmonetary items are restated in terms of the currency equivalent of the purchasing power at the time of their acquisition. As noted above, this is achieved by multiplying the item's historical dollar cost by the current price level index divided by the price level index for the period of the original transaction. For example, using the Implicit Price Deflator index to obtain the 1974 current dollar equivalent of the original cost of an asset purchased in 1960, the original cost would be multiplied by the 1974 index or 170.2 divided by the 1960 index or 103.3, approximately 1.54. Thus, the difference in the amounts shown for nonmonetary assets on the historical-cost-based statements and the restated statements is due entirely to change in the measuring unit. No profit or loss results from this process. The adjustment simply restates the original investment in terms of the current purchasing power situation.

If the nonmonetary accounts and the beginning owners' equity balance are restated in current purchasing power terms and the monetary accounts are unchanged, the two sides of the balance sheet will be out of balance. This difference is the gain or loss from holding monetary items for the accounting period.

Illustration 15–1 presents a simple illustration of this procedure. It goes one step further, however. It illustrates the adjustment of comparative statements. The Bahia Corporation, a Brazilian company, has been in business one year. Its principal asset is land held for future developments, and the company has no transactions during the year. All of the items on the year-end balance sheet have been held for one year, a period during which the local price level index has doubled from 100 to 200. This movement reflects a 50 percent depreciation in the local currency's purchasing power.

ILLUSTRATION 15–1

BAHIA CORPORATION
A. Historical Cost Statements
(in cruzeiros)

Beginning Balance Sheet		*Ending Balance Sheet*
Assets		
Cash	10,000	10,000
Land	20,000	20,000
Total	30,000	30,000
Liabilities and Net Worth		
Notes payable	5,000	5,000
Capital	25,000	25,000
Total	30,000	30,000

B. Beginning Balance Sheet Adjusted to Year-End Cruzeiros (price index at beginning of year 100 and 200 at end of year)
(in cruzeiros)

Beginning Balance Sheet in Historical Cruzeiros		*Adjustments*	*Beginning Balance Sheet in Year-End Purchasing Power Equivalents*
Assets			
Cash	10,000	× 2.0	20,000
Land	20,000	× 2.0	40,000
Total	30,000		60,000
Liabilities and Net Worth			
Notes payable	5,000	× 2.0	10,000
Capital	25,000	× 2.0	50,000
	30,000		60,000

C. Ending Balance Sheet Adjusted to Year-End Cruzeiros (price Index rose from 100 to 200 during the year)
(in cruzeiros)

Ending Balance Sheet in Historical Cruzeiros		*Adjustments*	*Ending Balance Sheet in Year-End Purchasing Power Equivalents*
Assets			
Cash	10,000	—	10,000
Land	20,000	× 2.0	40,000
			50,000

ILLUSTRATION 15–1 *(continued)*

Liabilities and
  Net Worth

Notes payable	5,000	—	5,000
Capital	25,000	× 2.0	50,000
Loss from net monetary assets	—	—	⟨5,000⟩
			50,000

D. Comparative Beginning and Year-End Balance Sheets
Expressed in Year-End Purchasing Power Equivalents
(in cruzeiros)

Beginning Balance Sheet in Year-End Purchasing Power Equivalents	*Ending Balance Sheet in Year-End Purchasing Power Equivalents*
Assets	
Cash 20,000	10,000
Land 40,000	40,000
Total 60,000	50,000

Liabilities and Net Worth	
Notes payable 10,000	5,000
Capital 50,000	50,000
Loss from net monetary assets . . . . —	⟨5,000⟩
Total 60,000	50,000

Illustration 15–1A shows the Bahia Corporations statements expressed on a historical cost unadjusted for inflation basis at the beginning and end of the year. These comparative statements conform to the assumptions outlined above.

Next, Illustration 15–1B presents the beginning historical balance restated to its end-of-year purchasing power equivalent. Since the price level index moved from 100 to 200, the cash held at the beginning of the year would have purchased twice as much at the beginning of the year as it did at the end of the year. Therefore, to express the CR $10,000 at its end-of-year purchase power equivalent, the Cr $10,000 must be multiplied by 200/100 or a factor of 2.0, which is the price level index at the beginning of the year expressed in end of the period prices. (The end of year factor is 1.0.) All of the other accounts must be adjusted in a similar fashion.

Illustration 15–1C shows the ending balance sheet adjusted to end-of-year purchasing power equivalents. Since the Cr $10,000 cash and Cr $5,000 notes payable are monetary items, these end of period accounts are already stated at their end-of-year purchasing power equivalent. No restatement is necessary. The land and capital must be restated, however. These nonmonetary assets and capital items must be multiplied by the price level index at the end of the year (200) divided by the price level index at the beginning of the year (100), or multiplied by a factor of 2.0. When this is done, the sum of the notes payable and capital amounts is greater than the sum of the cash and land. As a result, the basic accounting equation is out of balance. To achieve a balance, Cr $5,000 must be deducted from the right-hand side of the balance sheet. This amount is a loss in purchasing power caused by Bahia having a net monetary asset position during the year (cash less notes payable).

Illustration 15–1D presents comparative beginning and end-of-year balance sheets expressed in their end-of-year purchasing power equivalents. This comparison shows the source of the Cr $5,000 monetary loss. The Bahia Corporation lost Cr $10,000 of end-of-year purchasing power on its cash balance. Offsetting this loss was a Cr $5,000 gain on the notes payable. The Cr $5,000 loss is the difference between this gain and loss.

If the Bahia Corporation had not been able to offset its monetary asset balance by the notes payable, the company's monetary loss would have been Cr $10,000. This assumes that the beginning owners' equity would have had to be Cr $30,000 to make the two sides of the unadjusted balance sheet balance. Therefore, the restated capital balance would have been Cr $60,000 before recognizing the monetary loss of Cr $10,000.

The gains and losses applicable to monetary items can be calculated directly on a monetary item-by-item basis. The Cruzeiro Corporation example describes this procedure. It also shows how to restate sales, expenses, assets, liabilities, and capital.

AN EXAMPLE: THE CRUZEIRO CORPORATION

The unadjusted statements of the Cruzeiro Corporation, a Brazilian company, are presented in Illustrations 15–2 and 15–3.[1] They will be used to illustrate the technique for adjusting for price level changes.

The following price index for the period 1960–70 reflects the changes in the year-end Braziliam government's wholesale price index. To speed up the restatement of past years to 1970 purchasing power equivalents, the index has been restated to show 1970 as the base year (1.0 = base period). This restatement is achieved by dividing the price level index for 1970 by the price level index for the past

---

[1] This example is based on material presented in "A Practical Approach to Accounting for the Effects of Price-Level Changes in Brazil" by Thomas Y. S. Summer published in the December 31, 1963, issue of the Arthur Andersen *Chronicle*.

ILLUSTRATION 15–2

CRUZEIRO CORPORATION
Comparative Balance Sheets, December 31, 1970, and 1969
(in cruzeiros)

Assets	1969	1970	Liabilities	1969	1970
Cash	10	20	Accounts payable	60	92
Accounts receivable	100	150			
Inventory	120	185			
Plant and equipment			*Stockholders' Equity*		
(at cost)	260	280			
Less: Accumulated			Common stock	200	200
depreciation	(112)	(138)	Retained earnings	118	205
Total	378	497	Total	378	497

ILLUSTRATION 15–3

CRUZEIRO CORPORATION
1970 Income Statement
(in cruzeiros)

Sales	900
Cost of goods sold	(690)
Gross margin	210
Depreciation	26
Other expenses	97
Net Income	87

year. For example, the price level index for 1970 (1252) divided by the price level index for 1969 (864) gives a factor of 1.45. These factors will be used to adjust the company's statements to a common purchasing power equivalent.

December	Price Index	Factor*
1970	1252.0	1.00
1969	864.1	1.45
1968	566.5	2.21
1967	420.1	2.98
1966	309.9	4.04
1965	228.5	5.48
1964	220.0	5.69
1963	174.9	7.16
1962	150.3	8.33
1961	123.2	10.16
1960	100.0	12.52

$$* \frac{\text{Price Index for 1970}}{\text{Price Index for the year}}.$$

The price level factors for the last four months of 1969 and 1970 are:

	1969	1970
September	1.63	1.17
October	1.57	1.13
November	1.50	1.06
December	1.45	1.00

The company's unadjusted balance sheets at the beginning (December 31, 1969) and at the end (December 31, 1970) of the calendar year 1970 are not comparable because the units of measurement in these balance sheets are cruzeiros of different dates and therefore of different purchasing power. Therefore, to make these balance sheets comparable, they will be adjusted to a common unit of measurement, namely, the cruzeiro (Cr $) as of December 31, 1970.

Monetary assets and liabilities at the end of 1970 are already stated in cruzeiros as of the closing balance sheet date. However, the monetary assets and liabilities at the beginning of the year must be translated into year-end cruzeiros so they may be compared with year-end balance sheet figures. The restatement of December 31, 1969, monetary assets and liabilities is shown in Illustration 15–4. The adjustment factor of 1.45 is based on the 45 percent increase in the general price level that occurred between December 31, 1969, and December 31, 1970.

ILLUSTRATION 15–4
Net Monetary Assets

December 31, 1969 Balances	Before Adjustment	Adjustment Factor	After Adjustment
Cash	Cr $ 10	1.45	Cr $ 14
Receivables	100	1.45	145
Accounts payable	(60)	1.45	(87)
Net Monetary Assets	Cr $ 50		Cr $ 72

The company's inventories are stated at cost in terms of cruzeiros as of date of purchase. To make the beginning and year-end inventory figures comparable, it is necessary to translate them into year-end cruzeiros. Assuming that inventories are valued on the first-in, first-out method and that they represent purchases made during the last months of each year, their restatement to the December 31, 1970, price level is accomplished as shown in Illustration 15–5. The adjustment factors applied are based on increases in the price level from date of purchase to December 31, 1970, as shown by the monthly price level index.

ILLUSTRATION 15–5
Inventories

	Before Adjustment	Adjustment Factor	After Adjustment
December 31, 1969, Balance			
Purchases:			
October 1969	Cr $ 30	1.57	Cr $ 47
November 1969	40	1.50	60
December 1969	50	1.45	73
Year-end inventory	Cr $120		Cr $180
December 31, 1970, Balance			
Purchases:			
September 1970	Cr $ 25	1.17	Cr $ 29
October 1970	45	1.13	51
November 1970	55	1.06	58
December 1970	60	1.00	60
Year-end inventory	Cr $185		Cr $198

Typically, the greatest distortion due to inflation is found in the property, plant, and equipment accounts. In order to adjust the property accounts and the related reserves for depreciation to the year-end price level, it is necessary first to analyze the accounts by dates of acquisition. In this example we will assume all acquisitions were made

ILLUSTRATION 15–6
Plant and Equipment

	Before Adjustment		Adjustment Factor	After Adjustment	
	Cost	Depr.		Cost	Depr.
December 31, 1969					
Investments:					
1964	Cr $180	Cr $ 90	5.69	Cr $1,024	Cr $512
1965	50	20	5.48	274	110
1968	20	2	2.21	44	4
1969	10	—	1.45	14	—
Plant and equipment	Cr $260	Cr $112		Cr $1,356	Cr $626
December 31, 1970					
Investments:					
1964	Cr $180	Cr $108	5.69	Cr $1,024	Cr $614
1965	50	25	5.48	274	137
1968	20	4	2.21	44	9
1969	10	1	1.45	14	1
1970	20	—	1.00	20	—
Plant and equipment	Cr $280	Cr $138		Cr $1,376	Cr $761

at year-end for cash. The appropriate restatement factors are then applied to the cost and reserve balances as shown in Illustration 15–6. Combining the above price level adjustments calculations, the adjusted balance sheets are shown in Illustration 15–7.

ILLUSTRATION 15–7

CRUZEIRO CORPORATION

Comparative Balance Sheets, December 31, 1969, and 1970
(in cruzeiros)

	Before Adjustment		After Adjustment	
	1969	1970	1969	1970
Cash	10	20	14	20
Accounts receivable	100	150	145	150
Accounts payable	(60)	(92)	(87)	(92)
Net monetary assets	50	78	72	78
Inventory	120	185	180	198
Plant and equipment (at cost)	260	280	1,356	1,376
Less accumulated depreciation	(112)	(138)	(626)	(761)
Stockholders' equity	318	405	982	891
Reconciliation of stockholders' equity, beginning of year	—	318	—	902
Net income	—	87	—	(91)*
End of year	—	405	—	891

* Assume for the moment that this is a balancing figure. Derivation and proof are presented in Illustration 15–9.

In addition, the 1970 cost of goods sold must be restated to December 31, 1970, cruzeiros:

	Before Adjustment	Adjustment Factor	After Adjustment
Opening inventory	Cr $ 120	(See Ill. 15–5)	Cr $ 180
Purchases	755	1.225	925
Closing inventory	(185)	(See Ill. 15–5)	(198)
Cost of goods sold	Cr $ 690		Cr $ 907

To simplify our calculations, purchases have been adjusted by the average adjustment factor for the year: (1.45 + 1)/2 = 1.225.

For the sake of convenience, 1970 sales and other expenses are also adjusted by the average adjustment factor for the year (this implicitly assumes these items were evenly distributed throughout the year):

	Before Adjustment	Adjustment Factor	After Adjustment
Sales	Cr $900	1.225	Cr $1,103
Other expenses	97	1.225	119

In order to adjust the 1970 income statement to year-end 1970 cruzeiros, the 1970 depreciation expense must be stated. Therefore, using the adjusted data determined above, the 1970 depreciation expense is:

	Before Adjustment	After Adjustment
Cost of plant and equipment at December 31, 1970	Cr $280	Cr $1,376
Less December 31, 1970 addition not depreciated	20	20
Total	Cr $260	Cr $1,356
1970 depreciation (at 10% rate)	Cr $ 26	Cr $ 135

To complete the adjustment of the financial statements to common year-end cruzeiros, it is necessary to calculate the loss for the year on the monetary items and to restate each item in the conventional income statement.

Monetary assets (such as cash, receivables, and deposits) and liabilities (such as bank loans and accounts payable), are stated in fixed cruzeiro amounts. As the price level rises, monetary assets lose purchasing power and liabilities become payable in cruzeiros of decreasing purchasing power. The excess of monetary assets over liabilities represents the "exposure to inflation." The inflation loss may be computed on the basis of the average "exposure to inflation" as shown in Illustration 15–8.

The income statement before and after the price level adjustments explained above is summarized in Illustration 15–9. In this example, the results of operations reported in accordance with generally ac-

ILLUSTRATION 15–8
Exposure to Inflation

	Balance	
	Beginning of Year	End of Year
Cash	Cr $ 10	Cr $ 20
Receivables	100	150
Accounts payable	(60)	(92)
	Cr $ 50	Cr $ 78
Add: Cash used to acquire property in December 1970	—	20
	Cr $ 50	Cr $ 98

Average exposure, $\dfrac{50 + 98}{2}$ .... Cr $74

Loss on exposure to 45% inflation, 74×0.45 ... Cr $33

ILLUSTRATION 15–9

CRUZEIRO CORPORATION
Income Statement

	Before Adjustment	After Adjustment
Sales	Cr $900	Cr $1,103
Cost of goods sold	690	907
Gross margin	Cr $210	Cr $ 196
Depreciation	26	135
Other expenses	97	119
Loss on net monetary assets		33
Net Income (loss)	Cr $ 87	Cr $ (91)

cepted accounting principles indicated a profit, but a loss after price level adjustments. In addition, the balance sheet financial ratios before price level adjustments are changed significantly after the price level adjustments are made.

Degree of Restatement

There are three major points of view as to the degree to which financial statements in the United States should be restated in current dollars. These are: no restatement, limited restatement, and complete restatement showing monetary gains and losses.

Those advocating no price level restatement argue that despite the inflationary problems of the mid-1970s, inflation has typically been mild in the United States and as such has not resulted in any gross misstatements of income in most years. In addition, they point out: that price level adjusted statements would be confusing to the users of financial statements. For example, the monetary gains from a net monetary liability position may be misleading, since a near bankrupt company with excessive debt might appear to be profitable simply because of its large monetary gains. Price level adjustments are not acceptable for determining income tax liability. And, there is little demand for price level adjusted statements by investors, bankers, or creditors. Other arguments include: there is no practical, easy method for making reliable price level adjustments. The cost principle is easily understood and has proved a useful convention in practice. And, business executives would not voluntarily adopt price level accounting that resulted in lower profits, unless they were public utilities seeking to prove that their reported unadjusted cost-based income was overstated for rate-making decisions.

The proponents of limited price level adjustments support restatement of only the inventory, cost of goods sold, fixed asset, and depreciation accounts. Generally, these people are sympathetic to the "no-restatement" point of view. However, they feel limited restatement might demonstrate to the taxation authorities the extent to which income taxes confiscate capital in times of inflation. Other advantages claimed for limited restatement are that it will provide management with cost data in current dollars for financial decisions, as well as indicate to stockholders whether or not a company's financial policy is designed to prevent an impairment of capital due to price level changes. The limited restatement advocates also believe their approach avoids confusing readers of financial statements with the notions of losses and gains on monetary items.

The complete restatement supporters claim that their approach is necessary to avoid having net income measured partly in historical dollars and partly in current dollars, which might result from limited restatement. Also, they believe widespread adoption of their proposal would better increase the chances of some income tax relief. More importantly, however, they argue that matching revenue and expenses in current dollars and showing all balance sheet items in similar dollars would be more useful for measuring performance and judging the effectiveness of financial policies. In addition, the complete restatement proponents claim that the cumulative effect of inflation in the United States over the life of most long-lived assets and liabilities has been far from "mild," and that the notion of gains and losses on monetary items is well understood by most users of financial statements.

APB *Statement No. 3*

In June 1969, the APB published *Statement No. 3*, "Financial Statements Restated for General Price Level Changes." It recommended that comprehensive price level statements be published as a supplement to historical cost statements. Specific procedures suggested for price level restatement were:

1. Both price level statements and historical dollar statements should embody the same accounting principles.
2. An index of the general price level should be used—the GNP Implicit Price Deflator was suggested for the United States (except that the Bureau of Labor Statistics' Consumer Price Index might be used as a basis of approximating the GNP Implicit Price Deflator on a monthly basis).
3. General price level financial statements should be presented in terms of the general purchasing power of the dollar at the latest balance sheet date.
4. Monetary and nonmonetary items should be distinguished for the

preparation of price level financial statements. The statement presentation should emphasize that general price level gains and losses arise from holding monetary items. Distinguishing monetary and nonmonetary items, the APB believed, would allow *(a)* restatements of nonmonetary items in terms of general purchasing power and *(b)* recognition of general price level gains and losses on monetary items. Those assets and liabilities that have both monetary and nonmonetary characteristics (debentures held as investment and convertible debt) should be classified as monetary or nonmonetary according to the purpose for which they are held.

5. Nonmonetary items should be restated to dollars of current purchasing power at the end of the period. In the case of inventory, the lower-of-cost-or-market rule should be applied to the restated cost.

6. Monetary assets and liabilities should be stated in dollars of *current* purchasing power. Therefore, for comparative purposes, prior period monetary assets would be updated to dollars of current general purchasing power.

7. The income statement items should be restated to the end-of-period current purchasing power.

8. General price level gains and losses should be included in current net income, as a separate, clearly identified item.

9. General price level statements of earlier periods should be updated to dollars of purchasing power at the end of each subsequent period for which they are presented as comparative information. (The APB noted that this "rolling forward" of prior restated results should be carefully described as an updating rather than a restatement of previous information.)

10. Restatement of financial statements of foreign branches or subsidiaries in combined or consolidated financial statements should be based on an index of general price levels in the United States. Foreign branch or subsidiary statements should be stated on an historical basis before restatement for general purchasing power of the U.S. dollar.

11. All general price level information should be based on complete price level calculations. As a minimum, the results presented should include sales, net general price level gains and losses on monetary items, net income, extraordinary items, and common stockholders' equity.

12. The basis of preparation of general price level information and what it purports to show should be clearly explained in the notes to the general price level financial statements or other appropriate places. The explanation should include the following points:

a. The general price level statements (or information) are sup-
    plementary to the basic historical dollar financial statements.
b. All amounts shown in general price level statements are
    stated in terms of units of the same general purchasing power
    by use of an index of changes in the general purchasing
    power of the dollar.
c. The general price level gain or loss in the general price level
    statements indicates the effects of inflation (or deflation) on
    the company's net holdings of monetary assets and liabilities.
    The company gains or loses general purchasing power as a
    result of holding these assets and liabilities during a period
    of inflation (deflation).
d. In all other respects, the same generally accepted accounting
    principles used in the preparation of historical dollar state-
    ments are used in the preparation of general price level
    statements (or information).
e. The amounts shown in the general price level statements do
    not purport to represent appraised value, replacement cost,
    or any other measure of the current value of assets or the
    prices at which transactions would take place currently.
f. The general price level statements (or information) of prior
    years presented for comparative purposes have been up-
    dated to current dollars. This restatement of prior years' gen-
    eral price level statements is required to make them compa-
    rable with current information. It does not change the prior
    periods' statements in any way except to update the amounts
    to dollars of current general purchasing power.
13. Disclosure involving the following items should also be made:
    a. The difference between the balance of retained earnings at
        the end of the preceding year in beginning-of-the-year dol-
        lars and at the beginning of the year in end-of-the-year dol-
        lars, which arises in the roll-forward process discussed in
        item 9 above should be explained as follows:

Retained earnings at the beginning of the year:
  Restated to general purchasing power at the beginning of
    the year xxx
  Amount required to update to general purchasing power
    at the end of the year xxx
  Restated to general purchasing power at the end of the year xxx

    b. The fact should also be disclosed that when assets are used or
        sold, federal income taxes are based on cost before restate-
        ment for general price level changes, since inflation is not
        recognized in the Internal Revenue Code.

Replacement Cost: SEC Approach

In March 1976 the SEC issued *Accounting Series Release No. 190,* which required beginning in 1976 the disclosure of certain replacement cost information in notes or a separate section of the financial statements included in Form 10-K filings. In contrast to APB *Statement No. 3,* the SEC approach focuses on the changes in the prices of specific goods and services consumed by the reporting company, rather than on the impact of changes in the general level of prices. In addition, the SEC *Release* only requires restatement of inventories, cost of goods sold, productive assets, and their related current charge for the impact of price changes. It does not include monetary gains and losses.

The purpose of the new rule was "to provide information to investors which will assist them in obtaining an understanding of the current cost of operating the business . . . [and] information which will enable investors to determine the current cost of inventories and productive capacity as a measure of the current economic investment in these assets." This *Release* applies to companies registered with the SEC whose total inventories and gross land, plant, and equipment are $100 million or more and exceed 10 percent of total assets.

The SEC defined replacement cost as "the lowest amount that would have to be paid in the normal course of business to obtain a new asset of equivalent operating or productive capability." The SEC *Release* does not require that any particular method be used for calculating replacement cost. The *Release* suggests it might be done by using indexes, such as a published price index or index developed internally by the reporting company, or appraisal. The replacement cost may be determined for individual or groups of similar assets and transactions. The method used to compute replacement costs must be disclosed.

The specific disclosures required are: the current replacement cost of inventories based on current buying prices considering normal order quantities and supply conditions. The approximate cost of sales using the replacement cost of goods and services at the time the sales were made. The estimated current cost of newly replacing the productive capacity at year-end and the depreciated cost of this productive capacity. Productive capacity includes the operating assets generally represented by fixed assets and assets held under financing leases,[2] but excludes monetary assets, goodwill, investments held for monetary gain rather than operating use, and land not consumed in the productive process. The approximate amount of straight-line depreciation, depletion, and amortization based on the current depreciable lives and average current replacement cost of productive capacity.

---

[2] As defined in SEC *Accounting Series Release No. 147.* See Chapter 20.

These disclosures are required for the two most recent fiscal years. These replacement cost data may be labeled "unaudited." However, the independent auditor must be "associated" with these disclosures. The SEC did not define what it meant by "associated." Rather, it urged the AICPA to develop appropriate standards applicable to the auditor in the case of such association.

Concurrent with its release requiring replacement cost disclosure, the SEC proposed a "safe harbor" for registrants which would limit their liability under the antifraud provisions of the securities laws if their disclosure (1) is prepared with reasonable care, (2) has reasonable factual basis and represents management's good faith judgment, and (3) is accompanied by a statement disclosing the basis of calculation and its inherent imprecision.

One of the major accounting firms in a staff release[3] presented the following illustration of the required replacement cost disclosure in the Form 10-K:

Estimated Replacement Cost Information (unaudited)

The following replacement cost information for certain of the Company's assets has been estimated by management. Such information does not purport to represent amounts at which the assets could be sold.

	Estimated Replacement Cost (1)	Comparable Historical Cost (2)
	(000 omitted)	
December 31, 1976:		
Inventories:		
Finished products and work in process	$ 307,000	$ 299,300
Raw materials and supplies	129,000	122,000
	$ 436,000	$ 421,300
Plant and equipment:		
Buildings	$ 584,000	$ 324,440
Machinery and equipment	1,148,000	890,672
	$1,732,000	$1,215,112
Less: Accumulated depreciation	914,000	641,231
	$ 818,000	$ 573,881
Year ended December 31, 1976:		
Cost of sales	$1,830,000	$1,756,200
Depreciation:		
Included in cost of sales	$ 65,000	$ 43,600
Other	33,000	22,100
	$ 98,000	$ 65,700

---

[3] Ernst & Ernst, Financial Reporting Developments, April 1976, pp. 4–6.

1. The replacement cost of inventories and buildings and equipment was estimated as follows:

> Catalog and other published prices for the quality, quantity, and terms at which the company generally purchases these items were used to price approximately 60 percent of raw materials and supplies. Current replacement cost for the remainder of such items was estimated by applying an index of relevant purchase prices to the historical cost of such items.
>
> Finished goods and work in process have been estimated on the basis of standard costs adjusted to reflect current material, labor, and overhead variances as well as replacement cost depreciation of buildings, machinery, and equipment determined on a straight-line basis.
>
> Where practicable, the replacement cost of machinery and equipment was estimated on the basis of current quoted market prices (approximately 70 percent of such assets in the United States and 40 percent elsewhere) for new machinery of equivalent capacity. With one exception, the replacement cost of remaining machinery and equipment was estimated by applying index numbers which were derived from recent cost data for items of similar productive capacity. The exception consists of production and materials handling equipment in one plant which is scheduled to be phased out of use in 1978 and replaced by fully automated facilities with a 30 percent greater capacity. The current quoted acquisition prices of the new equipment have been reduced by the portion estimated to be applicable to the additional capacity.
>
> The replacement cost of buildings acquired within the last ten years was estimated by applying published construction cost indexes to the acquisition prices of the buildings. For older buildings, current estimated construction cost to obtain equivalent floor space was used

The replacement cost of sales and provision for depreciation were estimated as follows:

> Replacement cost of sales was estimated through adjustment of historical costs for the approximate three-month time lag between incurring inventory costs and their subsequent conversion into sales revenues. Average production costs increased by approximately 1 percent a month during 1976.
>
> Depreciation based on the replacement cost of productive capacity has been estimated on a straight-line basis using the same estimates of useful life and salvage value utilized in preparing the historical cost financial statements. Average replacement cost of productive capacity at the beginning and end of the year, exclusive of 1976 additions, was used in determining the basis upon which depreciation expense was computed. Depreciation expense for current year additions is stated at historical cost.

2. The comparable historical cost amounts are reconciled to those shown in the accompanying consolidated balance sheet shown on following page.

Although replacement of productive capacity with technologically superior equipment generally results in some efficiencies, such as a reduction in required direct labor per unit of produced output, there are frequently additional costs associated with asset replacement, such as additional costs solely to comply with environmental regulations. Accordingly, it is not practicable to estimate any related effects on other costs which would result from replacement of existing productive capacity. Similarly, it is not practicable to quantify the extent to which replacement may result in identical units of produced output which are of superior quality to those which are now produced.

The company has maintained an approximately constant rate of gross profit on sales for a period of several years. Price increases have generally been timed to coincide with income statement recognition of increased inventory costs. Although manage-

	Inventories	*Property, Plant, and Equipment**
	(000 omitted)	
Amounts for which replacement cost data are provided	$421,300	$1,215,112
Present value of future rentals for noncapitalized financing leases as determined at inception of the leases (deduction)	—	(104,912)
Obsolete and discontinued inventory items—at net realizable value	17,900	—
Land—at cost	—	25,600
Assets in foreign countries outside the European Economic Community—at cost	11,800	44,800
Total as shown on the accompanying consolidated balance sheet	$451,000	$1,180,600

* Before deduction of accumulated depreciation.

ment presently anticipates its continued ability to compensate for cost increases by adjusting sales prices so as to maintain an approximately 25 percent historical cost gross margin on sales, there can be no assurance that competitive or other factors will not adversely affect continuance of this practice.

The example of the Form 10-K replacement cost disclosure might be presented in the annual shareholders report as follows:

Asset Replacement Costs (unaudited). The impact of inflation on the Company's production costs was generally greater than the corresponding change in the general price-level. However, the Company has historically been able to compensate for cost increases by increasing sales prices in an amount sufficient to maintain an approximately constant gross profit percentage on sales.

Replacing items of plant and equipment with assets having equivalent productive capacity has usually required a substantially greater capital investment than was required to purchase the assets which are being replaced. The additional capital investment principally reflects the cumulative impact of inflation on the long-lived nature (approximately 10 years for machinery and 25 years for buildings) of these assets.

The Company's annual report on Form 10-K (a copy of which is available upon request) contains specific information with respect to year-end 1976 replacement cost of inventories and productive capacity (generally buildings, machinery, and equipment), and the approximate effect which replacement cost would have had on the computation of cost of sales and depreciation expense for the year.[4]

As the above Form 10-K note indicates more than one approach may be used to determine replacement costs. The actual computation of

[4] Ernst & Ernst, Financial Reporting Developments, April 1976, p. 11.

these costs can be complex and require judgment. To illustrate, using an example presented by Arthur Andersen & Co.:

Assume, for example, that a company constructed a general-purpose building in 1970 when an applicable index of construction costs was 125. The base year of the index was 1967 (i.e., 1967 = 100). The building cost $1,250,000 in 1970. At December 31, 1975, the index was 190. The estimated replacement cost of the building at December 31, 1975, would be $1,900,000, calculated as follows:

$$\$1,250,000 \times (190 \div 125) = \$1,900,000$$

If it is assumed that the building was constructed in 1967 (index = 100) for $1,000,000 and was purchased by the company in 1970 (index = 125) for, say, $1,500,000, the indicated replacement cost at December 31, 1975, would be about $2,280,000 as follows:

$$\$1,500,000 \times (190 \div 125) = \$2,280,000$$

This is $380,000 more than the replacement cost calculated on the assumption that the building was constructed in 1970. The excess, of course, represents the premium (adjusted for inflation) over "pure" construction costs which the company paid in 1970 to acquire an existing structure. This illustrates the need to consider carefully the applicability of an index to a particular asset. In this illustration, the factors which caused the company to be willing to pay a premium for the building in 1970 may still be valid; thus, they should be reflected in a higher estimate of replacement costs. But, maybe because of business changes, today's best estimate of replacement cost is the $1,900,000, even though the net realizable value of the building is greater than $2,280,000. This is indicative of the complex judgments which companies will have to make in developing replacement-cost data.

In this example, the related adjustment to the historical cost depreciation to place depreciation on a replacement cost basis might be computed by multiplying the historical cost depreciation expense by the ratio of the replacement cost of the asset to the historical cost of the asset.

The following simple example shows how the annual replacement cost depreciation, accumulated depreciation, and depreciated replacement cost are compiled. Note, the accumulated depreciation is not the sum of the annual depreciation charges:

	Year		
	1	2	3
Replacement cost of new asset having three-year life:			
Beginning of year	$100	$140	$160
End of year	140	160	200
Average for the year	120	150	180

Question:
What are replacement cost depreciation expense and accumulated depreciation for each of the three years?

Interpretive response:
The amounts are as follows:

	Year		
	1	*2*	*3*
Depreciation expenses (computed as ¹/₃ of average replacement cost for the year)	$ 40	$ 50	$ 60
Accumulated depreciation (computed as proportion of end of year replacement cost which has expired, i.e., ¹/₃, ²/₃, ³/₃)	47	107	200
Depreciated replacement cost (end of year replacement cost less accumulated depreciation)	93	53	-0-

One approach to adjusting to a replacement cost basis of a Fifo material inventory and the material content of the cost of goods sold is illustrated below.[5] Similar calculations would be required to adjust the labor and overhead content of these accounts:

Assume the following historical cost information for a company which uses the Fifo inventory method:

	Material (in thousands of dollars)
Average inventory	$41,000
Year-end inventory	37,000
Cost of sales (including depreciation of $7,000,000)	90,000

Through analysis of production costs and a sample of representative material prices, the company has determined that specific cost increases during 1976 for material was approximately 12 percent. Sales, purchases of material, production of finished goods, and specific price increases were spread evenly throughout the year.

Cost of Sales

1. Compute inventory turnover:

	Material
Cost of sales (A)	$90,000,000
Average inventory (B)	41,000,000
Inventory turnover (A ÷ B)	2.20

---

[5] Based upon an example in Ernst & Ernst, *Financial Reporting Developments,* April 1976, pp. 17–19.

2. Determine the percentage adjustment for specific price increases during the approximate time lag between incurring cost and the time of sale:

	. *Material*
Annual percentage price change (A)	12%
Inventory turnover (B)	2.20
Adjustment for specific price increases during the time lag between incurring cost and the time of sale (A ÷ B)	5.45%

3. Determine the cost of sales adjustment from the percentage adjustment determined above:

	Material
Cost of sales	$90,000,000
	—
	90,000,000
Approximate adjustment	5.45%
Adjustment to cost of sales for specific price change	$ 4,905,000

Inventory

4. Determine year-end inventory adjustment for approximate time lag in recognizing price changes:

Year-end inventory excluding depreciation	$37,000,000
Approximate adjustment (at one-half of the cost of sales rate)*	2.73%
Adjustment to year-end inventory for price change	$ 1,010,000

> * Based on 2.20 inventory turns, material cost of sales did not recognize specific cost increases for about 5½ months (12 ÷ 2.20). However, inventories reflect cost increases ratably during the production cycle. For example, material purchases during the last month of the year reflect current costs. However, the material acquired about five months earlier (the earliest inventory not yet recognized in cost of sales) would be stated at costs which trail price increases by the full 5.45 percent. An estimate of the extent to which material inventory costs trail current prices is therefore 2.73 percent (½ × 5.45 percent).

Accounting Series Release No. 190 represents an initial step away from the traditional historical cost model of accounting toward a model that measures the impact of inflation and price changes on a business. The SEC limited the applicability of this *Releases* requirement, since it believed time was needed to experiment with this new approach before requiring widespread adoption and issuing more specific rules.

At the time that the SEC issued *Release No. 190* it did not believe that its new requirement was competitive with the FASB proposal which would have required financial statements to include supplemental data in which historical costs were adjusted for changes in the general price level. Apparently, the FASB thought otherwise and withdrew its proposal. The FASB's withdrawal statement noted that the SEC had not discouraged companies from using data regarding changes in general price level as part of the analysis of reasons for changes in replacement costs. The FASB also noted that the SEC required companies in their annual reports to shareholders to discuss the impact of inflation on the business, which might include a discussion of the impact of inflation on monetary items as well as the changes in the prices of specific goods and services. Therefore, since the SEC position did not preclude publication of the type of inflation data favored by the FASB, the FASB believed that it was wiser not to burden corporations with the cost of two alternative inflation accounting approaches.

SUGGESTED FURTHER READING

AMERICAN INSTITUTE OF CERTIFIED PUBLIC ACCOUNTANTS. "Reporting the Financial Effects of Price Level Changes." *Accounting Research Study No. 6.* New York, 1963.

BRUNS, WILLIAM J., JR., and VANCIL, RICHARD F. *A Primer on Replacement Cost Accounting.* Glen Ridge, N.J.: Thomas Horton and Daughters, 1976.

FINANCIAL ACCOUNTING STANDARDS BOARD. *Reporting the Effects of General Price Level Changes in Financial Statements.* Stamford, Conn.: Financial Accounting Standards Board, 1974.

JONES, RALPH. *Effects of Price-Level Changes on Business Income, Capital and Taxes.* Columbus, Ohio: American Accounting Association, 1956.

———. *Price Level Changes and Financial Statements—Case Studies of Four Companies.* Columbus, Ohio: American Accounting Association, 1955.

MASON, PERRY E. *Price Level Changes and Financial Statements.* Columbus, Ohio: American Accounting Association, 1956.

CASES

CASE 15–1. HOLDEN CORPORATION
Calculating the Effect of Price Level Changes

The Holden Corporation was a two-year-old merchandising firm. During this period the price level index changed as follows:

Opening of business 150
First year, average 160
First year, end 175
Second year, average 190
Second year, end 200

The company business was such that all of its revenues and expenses were earned or incurred fairly evenly throughout the year. The only exceptions to this generalization were depreciation and that portion of the merchandise sold represented by the beginning inventory. Inventory was priced on a first-in, first-out basis. Dividends were declared and paid at the end of each year.

The company's plant and equipment was acquired on the first day of business and at the end of the first year. All of the plant and equipment was depreciated on a straight-line basis over a ten-year life. The land on which the plant was located was held under a long-term lease agreement.

At the beginning of the company's second year, management paid off in cash $50,000 of the company's $350,000 long-term liabilities. The remaining $300,000 was converted to capital stock.

Exhibit 1 presents the company's income statements on a historical basis for each of its first two years of operations. Exhibit 2 shows the unadjusted statement of retained earnings for the same periods. Holden's balance sheets at the opening of business and at the end of each year's operations are presented in Exhibit 3.

At the end of the second year's operations, the management wanted the company's statements restated in "current dollars" to determine whether or not the company had experienced a monetary gain or loss to date. Management also wanted to know how much of this accumulated gain or loss related to the second year of operations.

Question

Restate the company's statements for its first two years' operations in current dollars. (Note: If you are using the Cruzeiro Corporation example as a guide, the example does not include long-term liabilities whereas the Holden Corporation case does.)

EXHIBIT 1

HOLDEN CORPORATION

Comparative Income Statement—Historical Basis
(in thousands)

	Year 1	Year 2
Sales	$800	$1,000
Operating Expenses:		
Cost of goods sold	$470	$ 600
Depreciation	30	40
Other expenses (including income tax)	280	300
Total Operating Expenses	$780	$ 940
Net Profit from Operations	$ 20	$ 60

EXHIBIT 2

HOLDEN CORPORATION

Comparative Statement of Retained Earnings—Historical Basis
(in thousands)

	Year 1	Year 2
Retained earnings, beginning of year	$ ..	$15
Net profit from operations	20	60
Total	$20	$75
Dividends to stockholders	5	10
Retained Earnings, End of Year	$15	$65

EXHIBIT 3

HOLDEN CORPORATION
Comparative Balance Sheet—Historical Basis
(in thousands)

Assets

	Opening of Business	End of Year 1	End of Year 2
Cash, receivables, and other monetary items	$200	$195	$235
Inventories..	250	300	200
Plant and equipment	300	400	400
Less: Accumulated depreciation		(30)	(70)
Total Assets	$750	$865	$765

Liabilities and Stockholders' Equity

Liabilities:			
Current liabilities	$100	$200	$100
Long-term liabilities	350	350	...
Total Liabilities	$450	$550	$100
Stockholders' Equity:			
Capital stock	$300	$300	$600
Retained earnings	...	15	65
Total Stockholders' Equity	$300	$315	$665
Total Liabilities and Stockholders' Equity	$750	$865	$765

CASE 15–2. DRAGO CHEMICAL
Impact of Price Level Changes on Management Performance Evaluation

In October 1974, Mr. Ralph Reeves, managing director of Drago Chemical, was reviewing his financial director's proposal for changes in the company's management control system. The proposed changes, prepared at Mr. Reeves's request, made explicit provision for inflation accounting.

Drago Chemical's manufacturing was centered in southern England. The company's major products included PVC, plasticizers, polyethylenes, surfactants, and herbicides. The heads of the five manufacturing divisions and the several staff departments reported to the managing director. Over 30 percent of the company's sales were outside the United Kingdom (although mostly within the EEC).

The capital investments of each division were carefully reviewed at the corporate level; in most respects, however, each division manager was free to pursue his business objectives. For control purposes, a division was organized as an investment center. Each was expected to steadily improve current performance while pursuing long-term viability. In August 1974, all divisions had a positive ROI. Nevertheless, there were wide variances in their returns; the two least profitable divisions had ROIs of 2 percent and 4 percent.

In mid-1974, although pleased with Drago's current financial performance (Exhibits 1 and 2), Ralph Reeves had become concerned about the impact of inflation on the firm's profitability (Exhibit 3). Accordingly, he had asked his financial director to study the internal impact of inflation. He knew the subject of external reporting was under active study in the U.K. (Exhibit 4). However, he felt that Drago's approach to this issue for management control and for performance appraisal should be independent of statutory requirements for external reporting and for the Inland Revenue Service.

Mr. Reeves was impressed by the simplicity and comprehensive approach of the financial director's report (Appendix). Nonetheless, he wondered if the proposed procedures would adequately reflect what happened to his stocks[6] of raw materials, works in process, and finished goods. During the last 18 months, this stock had dropped about 2 percent in tonnage, although the mix of products had remained almost the same. In the same 18 months, however, the rapid rise in the prices of raw materials had inflated the value of his stock from slightly over £6.6 million of £11.6 million (£8.5 million on February 28, 1974). (As was common in the U.K., stock was valued on a first-in, first-out basis.) This stock represented about 60 days of purchases.

Mr. Reeves was also mindful of a recent chance conversation with the head of Drago's most important union. The union head had been complimentary about the company's recent results (Exhibit 1), which he had just seen. Then he had expressed the hope that all who had helped to achieve those results could share amicably in the obviously ample rewards.

Of equal concern to Mr. Reeves was a recent letter that Drago's chairman had sent to the stockholders. The chairman had hailed the firm's record performance in sales and earnings; he added that he intended to pay an increased dividend for the year, "up to the maximum" then permitted. Mr. Reeves was partly reassured, since Drago's pretax profit of £2,960,000 came only after deduction of a special one-time contribution of £900,000 to the corporate pension fund. (This was to recognize the fund's increased liabilities, "an inevitable consequence of inflationary pressures upon remuneration.")

---

[6] Inventories.

For that reason, Mr. Reeves felt that the company's real earnings were somewhat higher than the announced figure.

Mr. Reeves had a further bit of relevant information: in the last six months, Drago had incurred a tax liability of £1,598,000 as a result of operations. However, the company had acquired considerable new equipment during the same period. Since the associated tax credits were large enough to balance the liability, no tax would have to be paid.

Questions

1. How much inflation-adjusted profit do you believe Drago earned during the last 18 months?
2. Should this inflation-adjusted profit figure be the basis for calculating the firm's profits and return on investment?
3. What are the pros and cons of using inflation-adjusted data in evaluating the company's investment centers?

EXHIBIT 1
Profit and Loss

	Full-Year Ending February 28, 1974 (£000)	Half-Year Ending August 31, 1974 (£000)
Turnover*	48,002	40,080
Trading profit before following deductions	4,604	3,806
Depreciation	980	492
Interest charges	802	354
Profit before tax	2,822	2,960
Tax	1,524	1,599
Profit after tax	1,298	1,361

* Sales.

EXHIBIT 2
DRAGO CHEMICAL
Balance Sheet

Assets

	March 1, 1973 (£000)	February 28, 1974 (£000)
Cash	103	158
Debtors (accounts receivable)	9,614	11,413
Stock (inventory)	6,614	8,512
Fixed assets	8,684	9,103
	25,015	29,186

Liabilities and Net Worth

	March 1, 1973 (£000)	February 28, 1974 (£000)
Accounts payable	8,276	12,109
Short-term debt	2,010	1,400
Long-term debt	5,040	5,040
Net worth	9,689	10,637
	25,015	29,186

EXHIBIT 3
Inflation in the United Kingdom, 1963–1973

Year	Retail Price Index	Annual Inflation	Cumulative Inflation
1963	100		
1964	103	3%	3%
1965	108	5	8
1966	112	4	12
1967	115	3	15
1968	121	5	21
1969	127	5	27
1970	135	6	35
1971	148	10	48
1972	158	7	58
1973	173	10	73

EXHIBIT 4
The State of Inflation Accounting in the United Kingdom—October 1974[*]

In London, the Sandilands Committee on Inflation Accounting is hard at work in an attempt to produce its recommendations by early 1975. Last May, the Institute of Chartered Accountants published its provisional statement of standard accounting practice No. 7 (SSAP 7). This contains proposals for adapting conventional historic cost accounts to conditions of inflation. The statement supports the current purchasing power or general price level method of adjustment. *The accountants point out that management must be able to appreciate the effects of inflation on costs, profits, distribution policies, dividend cover, borrowing power, return on investment, and cash requirements.*

Although the Institute opinion supports the current purchasing power method, the Sandilands Committee is still analyzing the advantages and disadvantages of the replacement cost method. The replacement cost method has many supporters in industry who argue that it is better to use a more complex system in an effort to approach the truth than to use a rigid, easy to apply formula which will always be inaccurate.

The ease of applying the current purchasing power system for the company and the ease of auditing it for the accountant make the system an attractive one. Although the Sandilands Committee has made no disclosures on which way it is leaning, many feel that they will attempt a synthesis of the two methods. There is currently a loophole in SSAP 7 allowing companies to revalue assets as well as to apply a rigid index to their original purchase cost. If the Sandilands Committee decides to support this decision, the controversy over the two systems may become irrelevant.

---

* *Financial Times,* October 3, 1974.

APPENDIX

DRAGO CHEMICAL

To: Mr. Ralph Reeves, managing director
From: Mr. John Thompson
Date: October 7, 1974

Pursuant to our discussion of last month, I have investigated the feasibility of incorporating an inflation accounting approach into our on-going Management Control System. It is my opinion that while many aspects of an inflation accounting approach are counter-balancing insofar as their ultimate impact on the firm's profit, the overall impact on profits could be sufficiently significant that we should move to an inflation accounting approach for internal purposes, effective January 1. The rest of this memorandum details the approach I believe we should follow with Exhibit A showing how these procedures would have impacted our stated earnings for the year ending February 28, 1974, and the half year ending August 31, 1974, and Exhibit B showing the critical calculations in depth.

Debtors, Creditors, Stock, and Fixed Assets are all subject to inflation adjustments, which will affect the company's real profitability. Accordingly I plan to process these items each quarter to take into account the impact of inflation during the quarter. *The Economist* Intelligence Unit's index (E.I.U.)[1] will be used on an annual basis to revalue our Fixed Assets. The Retail Price Index (R.P.I.) will be used on other assets and liabilities.

Quarterly, all Assets and Liabilities will be adjusted for inflation using only the Retail Price Index (the base value of Fixed Assets being the calculated E.I.U. values as of March 1 each year). If anything, we are understating the specific effect of inflation on the company since chemical industry raw material prices have soared in the past 12 months. The table below gives a brief feel for the magnitude of the changes in our plant values as a result of using the E.I.U. index.

---

[1] E.I.U. Index is an industry replacement value index created by *The Economist* Intelligence Unit of *The Economist* magazine. The E.I.U. produces 16 indices for various industries. An industry index is established by selecting a number of different types of standard equipment representative of the industry. The number of deliveries of a piece of equipment determines its relative importance. The change in the manufacturer's sale price over a certain period of time is then considered and weighted according to the relative importance of each piece of equipment to determine the E.I.U. The weighting of the various pieces of equipment is revised as the items become obsolete.

	Net Book Value	
	Historical (*£000)*	*Current Purchasing Power as of August 31, 1974* (*£000)*
Plant A	1,538	2,392
Plant B	452	820
Plant C	360	604

The specific procedure for calculating the effect of inflation is as follows, and the impact worked out in detail for the year ending February 28, 1974, in Exhibit B.

A. *Net Monetary Assets (i.e., debtors less creditors)*
     The closing Retail Price Index is divided by the opening Retail Price Index. The percentage uplift multiplied by the value of the opening net monetary assets is the loss (profit if net monetary liability) to be offset against the historically recorded profits.

B. *Stock*
     The index to be used for the opening stock must be backdated to allow for the period over which that stock was purchased (if two months' stock in hand, then the opening index is the average index of those two months). This index is divided into the closing index, etc., as above.
     The closing stock, on a similar basis, would yield a constant purchasing power profit in the period: that is,

$$\frac{\text{RPI @ Closing Date}}{\text{RPI @ Average of Last Two Months}} \times \text{Value of Closing Stock}$$
$$- \text{Value of Closing Stock} = \text{Purchasing Profit in Period}$$

C. *Fixed Assets*
     The depreciation charge is to be uplifted by the proportion the historical costs is to the current value.

Impact of Inflation on Company Accounts

	Year Ending February 28, 1974 (£000)	Half-Year Ending August 31, 1974 (£000)
Profits before tax per conventional accounts	2,822	2,960
—Taxes	1,524	1,599
Profit after tax conventional accounts	1,298	1,361

Adjustments

1. Stocks (restatement of stocks at beginning and end of year)	(638)	(668)
2. Depreciation (additional depreciation due to adjusting fixed asset values)	(457)	(304)
3. Monetary items (again due to excess of monetary liabilities over monetary assets)	573	278
Net adjustments	(522)	(694)
Profit before tax expressed in £'s of current purchasing power at the end of the period ...	2,300	2,266
—Taxes	1,524	1,599
Profit after tax in £ current purchasing power	776	667

EXHIBIT B

**Calculation of Change in Corporate Profits Moving from
Historical Cost Accounting to Inflation Adjusted Accounting
March 1, 1973 February 28, 1974**

1. *Summary Balance Sheet Data from Exhibit 2*

	March 1, 1973	February 28, 1974
Net monetary assets (cash + debtors —creditors—short-term debt —long-term debt)	(5,609)	(6,978)
Stock	6,614	8,512
Net book value—fixed assets	8,684	9,103

2. *Retail Price Index*

December 31, 1972	158
January 31, 1973	160
February 28, 1973	160.6
December 31, 1973	173
January 31, 1974	175
February 28, 1974	177

3. *Fixed Assets adjusted by E.I.U. Index*

March 1, 1973	11,550
February 28, 1974	12,106

4. *Calculation of Impact of Inflation on Profits* — *Gain/(loss)*

Net monetary assets	$5,609 \times \dfrac{177}{160.6} - 5,609 =$	573
Opening stock	$6,614 \times \dfrac{177}{(158 + 160.6) \times .5} - 6,614 =$	(735)
Closing stock	$8,512 \times \dfrac{177}{(173 + 177) \times .5} - 8,512 =$	97
Depreciation	$\dfrac{11,550}{8,684} \times 980 \times \dfrac{177}{160.6} - 980 =$	457

Chapter 16

INTANGIBLE ASSETS

Intangible assets are expenditures for special rights, privileges, or competitive advantages which will lead to increased revenues or earnings. They include expenditures for franchises, patents, and similar items having no physical existence, but which nevertheless can reasonably be expected to contribute to earnings beyond the current accounting period.

Intangible assets are often thought to be less deserving of being shown as an asset than physical assets because of their nonphysical character. This is incorrect, since accounting regards an asset as being an economic quantum. Whether or not it is represented by a physical item is incidental to the issue of whether or not an expenditure with potential future income benefits should be capitalized. The principal reason for associating asset quanta with specific physical or intangible items is to clarify for communication purposes the kinds of resources in which management has invested the firm's funds.

Accounting for intangible assets raises the same kinds of troublesome questions encountered when accounting for tangible long-lived assets. Namely: What should be the asset's carrying cost? How should the asset cost be charged to income under normal business conditions? How should a substantial and permanent decline in the value of the asset be reflected in the financial statements?

Solving these problems in practice is complicated by the characteristics of an intangible asset: its lack of physical qualities makes evidence of its existence elusive, its value is often difficult to estimate, and its useful life may be indeterminable. If the intangible asset is purchased, identifiable, and can be given a reasonably descriptive name, such as a patent, the task is somewhat easier than if the intangible is an unidentifiable acquired intangible, such as goodwill, or an internally developed intangible asset. In the case of identifiable purchased intangibles there is less uncertainty because a specific sum is usually paid and the buyer has an idea of the future benefits that should flow from the acquired asset.

A number of managements and accountants believe conservatism should govern the accounting for intangibles. Therefore, they adopt the general presumption that intangible asset costs should be written off as incurred or, if capitalized, amortized over a relatively short period of time. Increasingly, however, there is a growing belief that conservatism alone should not justify such actions which might eliminate a valid business asset from the accounts. Rather, the goal of accountancy should be to provide as accurate a record of costs and cost expiration as possible.

A business may acquire intangible assets from others or develop them itself. In theory the accounting for these intangible items should be the same. This is not always the case, however. In practice, acquired identifiable and unidentifiable intangible assets are recorded as an asset and amortized over two or more accounting periods. In contrast, internally developed identifiable intangibles are typically expensed as incurred, rather than capitalized. Unidentifiable internally generated intangible assets, such as internally generated goodwill, are always expensed as incurred.

The practice of expensing as incurred the costs of internally generated intangibles is often justified on the grounds that it is difficult to determine as the expenditures for a potential intangible are being made whether or not future benefits will result from these expenditures. Also, some companies are continually making expenditures for internally developed intangibles, which management considers to be a regular, recurring expense of doing business and, hence, properly charged to income as incurred. In addition, it is sometimes difficult to determine the specific costs related to developing an intangible asset. Under these circumstances, the usual course of action is to expense the costs as incurred on the ground that only those costs that can be specifically identified with an item being capitalized should be recorded as assets.

AUTHORITATIVE SOURCES

APB *Opinion No. 17*, "Intangible Assets," and FASB *Statement No. 2*, "Accounting for Research and Development Costs," are the most authoritative statements dealing with intangible assets. Prior to the publication in October 1974 of *Statement No. 2*, some companies classified their research and development expenditures as intangible assets. *Statement No. 2* prohibits this practice. It requires that all research and development costs be expensed as incurred. Earlier, in August 1970, APB *Opinion No. 17* concluded that a company should record as assets the costs of intangible assets acquired from others, including goodwill acquired in a business combination, and record as expenses the costs to develop intangible assets which are not specifically identifiable. The APB also concludes that the cost of each type of intangible asset should be amortized by systematic charges to income over the period estimated to be benefited and that the period of amortization should not exceed 40 years.

Opinion No. 17

In *Opinion No. 17* the APB requires that a company record as assets at the date of acquisition the costs of intangible assets acquired from others. However, the costs of internally developing, maintaining, or restoring intangible assets which are not specifically identifiable, have indeterminate lives and relate to the enterprise as a whole should be expensed when incurred.

The cost of an acquired asset is the amount of cash distributed, the fair value of other assets exchanged, the present value of amounts to be paid for liabilities incurred, or the fair value of stock issued. If intangible assets are acquired as part of a group of assets, the cost of the identifiable intangible and tangible assets should be based on their individual fair values. The difference between costs assigned to the identifiable intangible and tangible assets should be assigned to the unidentifiable intangible assets acquired. Chapter 18 describes in greater detail the process for assigning the purchase price of an acquired company to the individual assets and liabilities acquired.

The cost of an intangible asset should be amortized by systematic charges to income over the period expected to benefit from the asset. However, the amortization period must not exceed 40 years. If the expected life of the intangible is more than 40 years, the 40-year write-off period must be used, not an arbitrary shorter period. APB *Opinion No. 17* states that the period of amortization should be determined after a consideration of these factors:

a.   Legal, regulatory, or contractual provisions may limit the maximum useful life.
b.   Provisions for renewal or extension may alter a specified limit on useful life.
c.   Effects of obsolescence, demand, competition, and other economic factors may reduce a useful life.
d.   A useful life may parallel the service life expectancies of individuals or groups of employees.
e.   Expected actions of competitors and others may restrict present competitive advantages.
f.   An apparently unlimited useful life may in fact be indefinite and benefits cannot be reasonably projected.
g.   An intangible asset may be a composite of many individual factors with varying effective lives.

The APB concluded that the straight-line method of amortization should be applied to intangible assets, unless another systematic amortization method can be demonstrated to be more appropriate.

Statement No. 2

In October 1974 the FASB issued *Statement No. 2*, "Accounting for Research and Development Costs." This *Statement* required that all research and development costs be charged to expense when incurred. The *Statement* defined research and development as follows:

a. *Research* is planned search or critical investigation aimed at discovery of new knowledge with the hope that such knowledge will be useful in developing a new product or service or a new process or technique or in bringing about a significant improvement to an existing product or process.
b. *Development* is the translation of research findings or other knowledge into a plan or design for a new product or process or for a significant improvement to an existing product or process whether intended for sale or use. It includes the conceptual formulation, design, and testing of product alternatives, construction of prototypes, and operation of pilot plants. It does not include routine or periodic alterations to existing products, production lines, manufacturing processes, and other on-going operations even though those alterations may represent improvements and it does not include market research or market testing activities.

This *Statement* does not apply to the prospecting, acquisition of mineral rights, exploration, drilling, mining, and related mineral development activities that are unique to the extractive industries. However, it does apply to the research and development activities of the extractive industries that is comparable to that undertaken by other enterprises. The costs of contract research and development conducted for others is also excluded from this *Statement*.

Statement No. 2 listed the following activities that typically would be included in research and development.

a. Laboratory research aimed at discovery of new knowledge.
b. Searching for applications of new research findings or other knowledge.
c. Conceptual formulation and design of possible product or process alternatives.
d. Testing in search for or evaluation of product or process alternatives.
e. Modification of the formulation or design of a product or process.
f. Design, construction, and testing of pre-production prototypes and models.
g. Design of tools, jigs, molds, and dies involving new technology.
h. Design, construction, and operation of a pilot plant that is not of a scale economically feasible to the enterprise for commercial production.

i. Engineering activity required to advance the design of a product to the point that it meets specific functional and economic requirements and is ready for manufacture.

The costs of materials, equipment, or facilities that are acquired or constructed for a particular research and development project that have no other alternative future use should be expensed as research and development costs at the time the costs are incurred. If the materials, equipment, or facilities have alternative future uses in research and development or other projects, the expenditures should be capitalized as tangible assets when acquired or constructed. The portion of the cost of these tangible assets consumed in research and development activities should be expensed as the assets are used for this purpose. These same rules apply to acquired or constructed intangible assets used in research and development.

Salaries, wages, and other related costs of personnel engaged in research and development activities are research and development costs and must be expensed as incurred. Also included in research and development costs are the costs of services performed by others in connection with research and development activities. The research and development costs should include a reasonable allocation of indirect costs. However, general and administrative costs that have little relationship to research and development should not be classified as research and development costs.

The FASB reached the conclusion that research and development costs should be expensed as incurred because it believed that—

1. There is normally a high degree of uncertainty about the future benefits of individual research and development projects.
2. There is a lack of casual relationship between expenditures for research and development and the benefits received.
3. The capitalization of research and development costs is not useful in assessing the earnings potential of a company or the variability of this earnings potential.

Statement No. 2 requires that the total research and development cost charged to income in each period be disclosed in the notes for each period for which an income statement is presented.

INCOME TAX TREATMENT

Intangible property which definitely has a limited life and is used in the business or production of income can either be written off as incurred or capitalized and amortized for tax purposes. However, these items cannot be amortized using the declining-balance and sum-of-the-years'-digits methods. Goodwill, trade names, and other intangibles with indefinite useful lives cannot be amortized for tax purposes, although certain organization costs can be amortized against taxable income over a period of not less than five years.

If a company accounts for its intangibles differently for book and tax purposes, deferred tax accounting must be used. The exceptions to this rule are those intangibles, such as purchased goodwill, with indefinite lives that cannot be deducted as expenses for tax purposes but must be amortized over a 40-year period for book purposes. In these situations there is a permanent timing difference. So, no deferred tax item is recognized. As a result, for financial reporting purposes the pretax charge is not reduced by a deferred tax credit in the determination of net income.

SPECIFIC INTANGIBLE ASSETS

Patents

Patents are granted by the United States Patent Office. They give holders the exclusive rights to control their invention for a period of 17 years. The actual period of control may be extended by obtaining additional patents on improvements to the original item. Patent rights may be sold or granted to others on a royalty basis.

The cost of an internally generated patent usually includes legal fees, patent fees, costs of models and drawings, and related experimental and development costs that can reasonably be identified with the patent. Since the registration of a patent is no guarantee of protection, it is usually necessary to defend the patent in court tests. Accordingly, the costs of successful court tests are generally included in the costs of the patent. When litigation is unsuccessful, the costs of litigation and the other costs of the affected patent should be written off immediately.

In the case of successful litigation, the costs of the patent should be amortized over the useful economic life of the patent. Because of technological or market obsolescence, this period is typically shorter than the patent's legal life. However, if a patent's effective economic life can be extended by an additional patent, it is permissible to write the unamortized balance of the cost of the old patent over the economic life of the new one.

The classification of patent amortization charge depends on the nature of the patent. For instance, patents related to manufacturing activities are charged to manufacturing expenses. Patents used in shipping are charged as selling expenses.

Copyrights

A copyright gives its owner the exclusive right to sell literature, music, and other works of art. The copyright period is 28 years, with the option to renew for another 28 years. The costs of obtaining a copyright are nominal. Therefore, the cost is often written off as incurred. However, the cost of a purchased copyright may be substantial. The common practice is to write such costs off against the income from the first printing or its equivalent.

Franchises

A franchise may be either perpetual, revocable at the option of the grantor, or limited in life. The costs of a franchise includes fees paid to the grantor and legal and other expenditures incurred in obtaining the franchise. When the franchise is perpetual, these costs should be amortized over 40 years. If the franchise is for a specific period of time, the franchise costs should be systematically amortized over the franchise period or 40 years whichever is the shorter. The costs of revocable franchises, in the absence of a specific time limit on the life of the franchise, are usually accounted for as perpetual franchises, although some accounting authorities believe it is prudent to amortize the costs of such franchises over a relatively short period of time.

Trademarks and Trade Names

Trademarks, trade names, and distinctive symbols, labels, and designs used to differentiate products and brands can be protected from infringement by registering them with the United States Patent Office. Proof of prior and continuous use is required to retain the right to the trade name or trademarks registered. Protection of trademarks and names that cannot be registered can be sought through common law.

The cost of a trademark includes legal fees associated with successful litigation, registry fees, and all developmental expenditures that can be reasonably associated with the trademark. The cost of a purchased trademark is its purchase price.

As long as they are used continuously, trademarks have an unlimited life. Therefore, they can be written off over a 40-year period. However, in practice, their costs are often amortized rapidly, since the economic life of a trademark depends on the tastes of consumers.

Leasehold Improvements

Lessees often make alterations or improvements to the property they are leasing. At the end of the lease, such leasehold improvements revert to the lessor. Therefore, the lessee only has the right to use his improvements during the period of this lease. Consequently, leasehold improvements are amortized over the remaining life of the lease or their useful life, whichever is shorter.

Organization Costs

Organization costs include incorporation fees, legal fees, promotion expenditures, and similar costs associated with the initial organization of a company. These costs benefit the corporation during its entire life, which for accounting purposes can be considered to be unlimited, and as such written off over a 40-year period. Others agree that initial organization costs should be capitalized to avoid starting a business with a deficit, but argue that these costs should be amortized rapidly, since they have no ultimate disposal value. Hence, they should be written off against income before the ultimate income created by the business enterprise is determined. Others justify rapid amortization on the ground of conservatism.

Intangible Development Costs

In the oil and gas industry, all drilling costs, excluding the pipe and equipment used to complete a well, are classified as intangible development costs. Other intangible costs include drill site preparation, roads to the location, grading, logging (electrical well surveys conducted with special downhole instruments), perforating, cementing, and formation stimulation. Such costs are classified as being intangible since they do not give rise to an asset with physical substance or salvage value.

Some companies expense these costs as incurred. Increasingly the prevalent practice is to capitalize these costs and amortize them over the life of the related productive wells. Most companies expense these costs as incurred for tax purposes.

Those companies deducting their intangible development costs as incurred for accounting purposes do so to be conservative or to conform with their treatment of these expenditures for tax purposes, even though this is not necessary to qualify the cost for tax deductibility. Others write these costs off as incurred since they believe that the annual charges approximate the amortization charges that would be recognized if a capitalization policy had been followed in earlier years.

In the opinion of many, capitalization of intangible development costs results in a proper matching of costs and revenues, since these costs are very similar in nature to capital expenditures. A few companies capitalize all of their intangible development costs on the ground that unsuccessful development activities are a necessary part of developing successful wells. The total pooled costs are then written off over the life of the productive wells. However, the more common practice is to capitalize only those intangible development costs associated with wells that appear productive. Intangible development costs for "dry holes" are expensed as exploration costs in the year the well is abandoned.

Some oil and gas companies capitalize all of their costs of discovering and developing oil or gas reserves. This method, which capitalizes dry hole costs, is called "full costing." In contrast, the "successful efforts" method capitalizes only those discovery and development costs that result directly in the discovery and development of oil or gas reserves.

Capitalizing intangible development costs in the accounting records and expensing them for tax purposes creates a timing difference which requires the application of interperiod tax allocation. Prior to 1975 most oil and gas companies did not provide for deferred taxes because of the percentage depletion tax rules. This situation was changed by Congress in 1975 when it substantially reduced or eliminated percentage depletion as a federal tax reduction for many oil and gas producing companies after January 1, 1975. As a result, those companies that had not previously provided for deferred taxes were now required to do so. To cover this transition the FASB issued *Statement No. 9* in 1975.

Statement No. 9 permitted companies to elect one of two alternative methods for computing their deferred taxes. Under the retroactive restatement method, past financial statements can be restated as if deferred taxes had been provided in earlier years. The prospective net method allows companies to provide for deferred income taxes only to the extent of the net change since January 1, 1975, in the capitalized intangible drilling and development account. No retroactive restatement is required.

ROLE OF JUDGMENT

The appropriate accounting for intangible assets is very dependent on the particular circumstances of each situation, perhaps more so than in any other areas of accounting. Seldom does an exhaustive analysis of the facts lead to a clear-cut answer. Therefore, selecting the best approach usually requires the exercise of management judgment.

The public accountant faces the same judgmental situation in deciding what form his opinion statement will take. Sometimes his problem is aggravated, when he is not fully satisfied with management's treatment of the item but is not absolutely convinced that his preferred alternative treatment is the only possible answer. In these situations, the public accountant usually resorts to a "subject to" type of opinion. This warns the reader of the statement that the auditor has some reservations about management's handling of the intangible, but the auditor feels management's position has merit. Of course, if the auditor believes management's treatment is inappropriate and management insists on using its approach, the auditor will issue a more drastic form of opinion, or he may even terminate his audit arrangement.

Businesses change over time, and often their past accounting practices and estimates become inappropriate for their new conditions. This is particularly true of accounting for intangibles. However, it is seldom clear at what precise point in time a change in accounting policy or estimate is justified. Again, responsible management judgment must be exercised. Unfortunately, in most cases changes in accounting for intangibles are made long after the events justifying a change have occurred. Also, a decline in profitability is often the event that appears to prompt the decision to change accounting methods. Changes under these circumstances inevitably raise questions about the integrity of management's statements.

Profit Impact of Shift

It is important to note that when a management changes from expensing to capitalizing the cost of an internally generated intangible, the favorable impact on profit may spread well beyond the year of the change. While there are many possible variations of this impact, depending on the direction and size of the annual expenditures, the following simple example should be sufficient to illustrate the point:

The Viking Chemical Company has a very stable business. The management plans to continue its practice of spending $1 million per year to purchase patents over the next ten years. In 1975 the company changed its accounting for purchased patents from expensing as acquired to capitalization and amortization over five years.

What will be the impact on profits of this decision over the next five years? Illustration 16–1 supplies the answer.

Inappropriate Practices

It is often difficult to determine whether or not an intangible asset expenditure will be recovered out of future revenues. Typically, this problem of uncertainty is resolved on the basis of conservatism, by expensing the cost as incurred. In the case of many well-established companies run by responsible managers, this treatment is often un-

ILLUSTRATION 16–1

Profit Impact Illustration
(in thousands)

	Old Policy: Expense Patents as Purchased 1975	New Policy: Capitalize Patents and Amortize over Five Years					
		1975	1976	1977	1978	1979	1980
Profits before taxes and Patent expenses	$4,000	$4,000	$4,000	$4,000	$4,000	$4,000	$4,000
Patent expenses	1,000	200	400	600	800	1,000	1,000
	$3,000	$3,800	$3,600	$3,400	$3,200	$3,000	$3,000
Income taxes (50%) .	1,500	1,900	1,800	1,700	1,600	1,500	1,500
Net profit after taxes and all charges	$1,500	$1,900	$1,800	$1,700	$1,600	$1,500	$1,500
Annual profit improvement	—	400	300	200	100	—	—
Deferred patent asset (balance sheet item) ..	—	800	1,400	1,800	2,000	2,000	2,000

necessarily followed. This can result in an improper matching of costs and revenues and the omission of a valid business asset from the balance sheet. On the other hand, marginal firms often resort to capitalizing intangible asset costs of dubious future value in order to boost earnings. Thus, in practice, the inappropriate treatment is the one most often adopted.

SUGGESTED FURTHER READING

FINANCIAL ACCOUNTING STANDARDS BOARD. *Accounting for Research and Development and Similar Costs.* FASB Discussion Memorandum. Stamford, Conn.: Financial Accounting Standards Board, 1973.

GELLEIN, OSCAR S., and NEWMAN, MAURICE A. "Accounting for Research and Development Expenditures." *Accounting Research Study No. 14.* New York: American Institute of Certified Accountant, 1973.

CASES

CASE 16–1. MILWAUKEE BRAVES, INCORPORATED

Milwaukee Braves, Inc., was incorporated under the laws of the state of Delaware on November 15, 1962, to operate the Milwaukee Braves baseball team of the National League. This case deals with the Milwaukee Braves's accounting for the costs of the player contracts acquired from a predecessor corporation and the subsequent costs incurred by the company for player development and acquisitions.

Players

The competitive success of a baseball club, which bears a strong relationship to its financial success, depends primarily upon the skill of players under contract to the club. In 1963, the policy of the Braves was to rely primarily upon players who were recruited and developed through the company's own player replacement program in the seven-club farm system it operated. During the period 1958–62, the National League Baseball Club of Milwaukee, Inc., spent about $6.6 million for the cost of scouting and team replacement, including the farm system, bonuses, schools, and tryouts. Occasionally, players' contracts were also acquired in major league trades or purchases. These costs were entirely written off as an expense in the respective years paid.

Forty-three players made up the Braves major league roster as of February 1, 1963. In 1963, Warren Spahn, with 327 major league wins, held the National League record for most games won by a left-handed pitcher and had two no-hit games. Also, he was a member of the National League All Star team 14 times. Frank Bolling led the league in fielding at his position in 1961 and 1962 and was a member of the National League All Star team in those years. Del Crandell led National League catchers in fielding in 1958, 1959, 1960, and 1962, and had been a member of the All Star squad eight times. Eddie Matthews had hit 399 home runs in his major league career and had played on the All Star team nine times. He ranked eighth on the all-time list of major league home-run hitters. Hank Aaron led the league in total bases in 1956, 1957, 1959, 1960, and 1961, and was on the All Star team eight years. His lifetime major league batting average was .319, which was second highest among all active National League players in 1963.

The Braves controlled approximately 160 additional baseball player contracts. Player contracts were acquired through the services of 15 full-time scouts and 19 part-time scouts who covered the United States, Canada, and Latin America.

Player Acquisition

Young players often required at least three to five years' experience in the minor leagues before acquiring the skills needed to perform in the major leagues. In 1963 the Braves owned and operated two minor league clubs and in addition had working agreements with five other minor league clubs.

Once a player had signed a professional baseball contract with one of the clubs comprising the farm system of the Braves, his contract remained subject to the control of the Braves until such time as it was traded or sold to a club outside the Braves system, or until he was given an outright and unconditional release from his contract, or unless he was selected by another major league club in what was popularly called the baseball draft.

Most major league clubs often were interested in the same young baseball players. As a result of this tremendous competition, the practice developed on the part of many clubs to pay large bonuses to induce free-agent players to sign their first contract.

Capitalization and Amortization of Player Acquisition and Development Costs

On November 16, 1962, the Milwaukee Braves entered into an agreement to purchase all of the outstanding capital stock of the National League Baseball Club of Milwaukee from Perini Corporation. On the closing date for this transaction, November 26, 1962, the National League Baseball Club of Milwaukee was liquidated and its assets and liabilities were transferred to the Milwaukee Braves.

The total cost of the acquisition, including broker's commission, was $6,218,480; the cost was allocated to player contracts ($6,168,480) and league membership ($50,000).

Prior to the acquisition, the predecessor company, the National League Baseball Club of Milwaukee, had expensed all costs in connection with the acquisition and development of players.

Starting with the 1963 season, for financial reporting purposes, the Milwaukee Braves intended to capitalize the total cost of developing players, including the net income or expense from purchase and sale of player contracts. The amounts so capitalized were to be amortized against operating income "over a period equivalent to the actual playing careers of major league players." The cost of player contracts acquired from the predecessor company were to be amortized against operating income "over a period estimated to reflect replacement through future player development expenditures."

For income tax purposes, the company intended to deduct future team replacement expenditures from income as incurred. The cost of player contracts acquired from the predecessor company were to be amortized over a ten-year period, which represented the major league

EXHIBIT 1

MILWAUKEE BRAVES, INC.

Pro Forma Statement of Income from Baseball Operations
For the Year Ended October 31, 1962

	Historical Statement	Pro Forma Adjustments*	Pro Forma Statement
Operating income	$3,670,417		$3,670,417
Operating Expenses:			
Team, park, games, and concessions .	$2,263,706	$ (60,032)[a]	$2,203,674
Team replacement, including net income or expense from purchase and sale of players	599,433	(599,433)[b]	......
Amortization of player costs	......	601,777[c]	601,777
Scouting salaries and expense	274,278		274,278
General and administrative	336,718		336,718
	$3,474,135		$3,506,447
Income from baseball operations	$ 196,282		$ 163,970
Interest expense	3,567	150,000[d]	153,567
Net income applicable to baseball operations before income taxes .	$ 192,715		$ 10,403
Provision for income taxes, applicable to baseball operations† ...	104,000	(100,600)[e]	3,400
Net Income Applicable to Baseball Operations	$ 88,715		$ 7,003

* Explanation of pro forma adjustments:

† On a pro forma basis, amortization of player contracts and future team replacement costs for tax purposes will exceed the amortization recorded in the income statement, and, consequently, there will be no income tax currently payable.

[a] Restatement of rental costs under terms of the new stadium lease.

[b] Reduction in operating expenses for the amount of team replacement expense to be capitalized and amortized over the estimated playing career of major league players.

[c] Amortization of player contracts capitalized upon acquisition of the club and of amounts expended for team replacement subsequent to acquisition.

[d] Annual interest charges estimated at 5 percent on the term note payable to bank.

[e] Adjustments in the provision for income taxes to reflect the foregoing adjustments.

experience of the players of the National League Baseball Club of Milwaukee.

Exhibit 1 is an operating statement for 1962 prepared by the Milwaukee Braves. This statement shows the effect of certain adjustments to be made by the Milwaukee Braves. In the opinion of the company, these adjustments, when applied to the historical statements related to the baseball operations of the National League Club of Milwaukee, fairly presented the results of operation on a pro forma basis for the year ended October 31, 1962.

Questions

1. Do you agree with the decision to capitalize *(a)* the costs of the player contracts acquired from the National League Baseball Club of Milwaukee and *(b)* future player acquisition and development costs?
2. Do you approve of the company's policies covering the amortization of the costs referred to in Question 1? What accounting techniques do you recommend that the company adopt to achieve its goal of amortizing *(a)* the acquired player contract costs "over a period estimated to reflect replacement through future player development expenditures" and *(b)* the future player development and acquisition costs "over a period equivalent to the actual playing careers of major league players"?
3. Comment on the allocation of the purchase price ($6,218,480) between player contracts ($6,168,480) and league membership ($50,000).

CASE 16–2. WALT DISNEY PRODUCTIONS
Accounting for Film Inventories

"Our product is practically eternal," declared Roy Disney, president, Walt Disney Productions.[1] The most profitable example of this statement was "Snow White and the Seven Dwarfs," Walt Disney Productions' first feature-length movie. It cost $1.4 million to make. The picture's initial release, in 1937, resulted in a profit of $3.8 million. Its first reissue, in 1944, and its second, in 1951, netted Disney another $3 million. The movie was again reissued in 1958. The master negatives of "Snow White" and all of the other Disney films were kept in a specially built two-story concrete "vault" at the Disney Studios in Burbank, California. This case deals with the company's accounting policies related to the amortization of the costs of these film inventories.

_____
[1] Exhibit 1 shows the company's inventory balances and results of operations from 1957 to 1964.

Walt Disney Productions

During fiscal year 1964, Walt Disney Productions earned $7 million profit on a gross income of $87 million. The company's principal sources of income were: theatrical film rentals, television film rentals, and Disneyland Park. In addition, the names, characters, music, and other creative values flowing from the company's theatrical motion pictures, television shows, and Disneyland Park were marketed on records, merchandise, and comic strips by the divisions, subsidiaries, or agents of the company in practically every country in the world.

Over the years, Walt Disney Productions had produced a number of outstanding films for theatrical and television release. The company's film inventory included full-length cartoon features such as "Snow White," "Pinocchio," "Alice in Wonderland," and "The 101 Dalmatians"; full-length live features, including "Treasure Island," "Robin Hood," "Old Yellow," and "The Absent-Minded Professor"; full-length "true-life" pictures, such as "Living Desert" and "Nature's Half-Acre"; and about 500 short subjects, consisting mostly of cartoons and travel pictures which were produced before 1954. In addition to the theatrical features, the company's inventory also included films produced for television, such as the "Zorro" adventure episodes and the films prepared for the Mickey Mouse Club and "Walt Disney's

EXHIBIT 1
Selected Inventory and Operating Data
(in millions of dollars, except earnings per share)

	1964	1963	1962	1961	1960	1959	1958	1957
Inventories (at lower of cost or market):								
Production in process	10.8	13.6	16.9	15.2	15.1	15.4	20.4	14.5
Completed production, less amortization	12.3	11.1	7.6	8.8	14.0	14.0	5.0	4.4
Story rights and pre-production costs	1.3	0.9	0.8	0.4	0.6	0.5	0.3	0.3
Merchandise, materials, and supplies	1.9	1.7	1.7	1.8	2.7	2.7	2.2	1.4
Less provision for possible excess over estimated realizable amounts	—	—	—	—	—	(1.0)	(0.5)	(0.3)
Total Inventories	26.3	27.3	27.0	26.2	32.4	31.6	27.4	20.3
Total theatrical films and television revenues	46.1	49.2	46.8	46.3	23.4	35.3	29.1	24.4
Amortization of theatrical and television production costs	14.5	16.1	15.6	19.2	14.6	19.4	13.7	12.3
Net income after taxes	7.1	6.6	5.3	4.5	(1.3)	3.4	3.9	3.7
Earnings per share	$3.96	$3.81	$3.14	$2.75	$(0.83)	$2.15	$2.51	$2.44

Wonderful World of Color." Except for a few commercial productions, Walt Disney Productions owned the master negatives of all the films the company had ever produced.

Accounting for Production Costs

The Walt Disney Productions 1964 annual report to stockholders included the following data in the current asset section of the consolidated balance sheet:

Inventories at the lower of cost or market (Note 2):	
Productions in process	$10,830,987
Completed productions, less amortization	12,341,914
Story rights and preproduction costs	1,245,824
Merchandise, materials, and supplies	1,905,382
Total Inventories	$26,324,107

Note 2 accompanying the financial statements stated:

Note 2—Inventories and Amortization. Costs of completed theatrical and television productions are amortized by charge to the income account in the proportion that the producer's share of income (less distribution, print, and advertising costs) received by the company for each production bears to the estimated total of such income to be received. Such estimates of total income are reviewed periodically and amortization is adjusted accordingly.

For accounting purposes, Walt Disney Productions maintained three major inventory categories for production costs: story right and preproduction costs, productions in process, and completed productions. Most productions began with the acquisition of a story property. Once acquired, the property was assigned an account number and all preproduction costs associated with the story were collected under this account number. These costs included the salary of the writer responsible for preparing the screen version of the story, and any other charges directly related to this activity. Indirect studio overhead was allocated between story accounts on the basis of direct dollar costs, including employee benefits. Should a story be abandoned before going into production, the costs accumulated in the story's account were written off to current income.

Once it was decided to produce a film based upon the story, the story account was closed out and the accumulated costs transferred to a production account. The number assigned to this production account remained with the production throughout its lifetime. Again, all of the costs directly associated with the production were charged to the production, and studio overhead was allocated between productions on the basis of direct dollar costs. Direct cost included such items as the salaries of actors, directors, cameramen, and set designers, as well as the wages of electricians, carpenters, and stagehands. Studio overhead included all those studio costs which could not be directly allocated to a specific production.

The cost of each feature production was charged to income in the proportion the income received[2] during the production's first release bore to the estimated total to be received. This practice was referred to as the "flow-of-income" method. For example, assume a film cost $1 million to produce and management estimated it would earn "net rentals" of $2 million during its first release. In this case, for every dollar of "net rental" from the film included in the income of the current period, 50 cents of production costs would be amortized. "Net rentals" were gross rentals less distribution, print, and advertising costs. These costs were about 40 percent of every gross rental dollar. Only the rental income associated with the production was included in the amortization calculation.

The production costs of films produced for television release were written off at the time the film was first shown on television. In those cases where a film previously released for theatrical showing was re-issued for use on "Walt Disney's Wonderful World of Color," the costs associated with preparing the film for use on television were charged to income during the period in which the film was first run on television. Examples of theatrical releases later shown on television were "Johnny Tremain" and "The Miracle of the White Stallions."

Thus, the entire production costs of a film were amortized during the film's first release. Unlike several other movie producers, the company did not assign any residual value to its film inventory. These other companies assigned residual values to their theatrical releases based upon the expected revenues from the sale of the rights to the film for subsequent use on television. Walt Disney Productions did not follow this practice, since it was the company's policy not to sell the rights to its old theatrical releases to the television networks. Because of the nature of its product, the company believed it was more profita ble to reissue its films for theatrical rather than television distribution. Also, while management intended that every film it produced would be reissuable, they nevertheless recognized that their product was

---

[2] Walt Disney Productions recorded domestic film rental income upon actual receipt of remittances. Similarly, the company recorded foreign income at the time of receipt of remittances in United States dollars or at the time of expenditures of foreign currencies abroad for the account of the company. In the case of feature theatrical films released on a national basis, these receipts were typically over a three- to four-year period, with between 70 and 80 percent of the total revenues realized during the first 12 months. About 256 key theaters out of a total 10,000 possible outlets accounted for about 80 percent of these revenues.

subject to public acceptance, and that no true feeling of reissue possibilities could be estimated at the time a film was first released.

The company's inventories were carried at the "lower of cost or
market." For this purpose, "market" was defined as estimated net
rentals. For example, assume a film cost $1 million to produce and,
based upon the initial public reaction, management estimated the film
would generate net rentals to the producer of only $600,000 during its
first release. In this case, the inventory value of the film would be
written down to $600,000, $400,000 would be charged to income in
the current period, and the remaining $600,000 cost would be amor-
tized on the basis of $1 of cost for each $1 of net rental received.

The management of Walt Disney Productions had achieved a high
level of competence in estimating film receipts. When a production
was completed, key administrative and sales personnel submitted
their estimates of the production's revenues. These estimates gave the
company an initial feel for the production's income potential. Once the
production was released, the company collected detailed statistics on
the number of showings, admissions, and cash receipts. These results
were then compared to similar statistics for earlier releases. The comparisons, tempered by experienced judgment and adjusted to reflect
the actual release schedule, were then used to project the current
release's estimated revenues for both financial accounting and cash
management purposes. In the case of new releases, these estimates
were prepared during the six-week period between the initial release
date and the receipt of the first rental income.

Three or four times each year, management reappraised their income estimates. If a production's revenues were likely to fall materially below the prior estimate, the production's inventory value was
written down and the loss charged to current income. On the other
hand, if it appeared that the production's receipts were going to be
materially larger than anticipated, the production's unamortized costs
would be written off on the basis of the new income estimate.

1965 Motion Picture Product

It was generally anticipated that fiscal year 1965 would be a banner
year for Walt Disney Productions. Based upon early record-shattering
box-office receipts, "Mary Poppins" promised to be the most widely
acclaimed of all Walt Disney motion pictures. In addition, the company planned to release the classic cartoon feature, "Cinderella."
Other 1965 full-length theatrical releases included "Emil and the De-
tectives," "The Tattooed Police Horse," "Those Calloways," and "The
Monkey's Uncle." Scheduled for release in Christmas 1965 was "That
Darn Cat." Other features in process included "Jungle Book," "Lt.

Robin Crusoe," "Follow Me Boys," "A Son-in-law for Charles McCready," "Bullwhip Griffin," "The Gnomobile," and "The Happiest Millionaire."

Questions

1. Should the company capitalize story right and preproduction costs? Production costs?
2. What amortization policy should the company follow for deferred film costs?
3. Do you agree with the company's policy of reporting its film inventory on a lower-of-cost-or-market basis?

CASE 16–3. R. G. BARRY CORPORATION
Human Resources Accounting

The R. G. Barry Corporation had sales and earnings for 1969 of $25,310,588 and $700,222 respectively. For the ten years ending with 1969, Barry's sales grew at a 20 percent compounded annual rate while earnings increased at a 21.5 percent rate.

Barry produced and marketed a broad line of leisure footwear and related products. Its markets were characterized by intense price and style competition, which dictated that management have good internal controls. As part of its controls, Barry introduced in 1967 a "human asset accounting" concept.

The president's letter in the 1967 annual report stated under the subtitle "Organizational Assets":

> As managers we are entrusted with the care of three types of assets: physical assets, organizational assets, and customer loyalty assets. Each manager is responsible for effective utilization of these assets to create a profit for the organization while preserving the financial soundness of the business.
>
> If people are treated abusively, short-term profits will be derived at the expense of the company's organizational assets.
>
> Managers now work with accounting data which reflect the condition of physical assets and changes in these assets over a period of time. The assets of human resources and customer loyalty do not appear in dollar terms on the balance sheets. To employ effectively all three types of assets, and realize the objectives of R. G. Barry, equally reliable accounting instruments are required to reflect the condition of organizational assets and customer loyalty and changes in these assets over time.
>
> To fulfill these objectives we are now in the process of developing and installing a Human Resource Accounting system to measure in dollar terms the organizational assets and changes in these assets over time.

In later sections of the 1967 report "people—the human resources of the company" are referred to as that asset "without which all other assets become meaningless in terms of potential and future growth."

The initial development of this human asset accounting system was a joint effort by Barry and the University of Michigan's Institute for Social Research.

Barry's commitment to human asset accounting was further articulated throughout its 1968 annual report:

We set ambitious goals for profitable growth in 1968. We achieved these goals in the principal result areas of the business, namely, (1) to generate a profit on total resources employed, (2) to protect and improve the value of the financial, physical, organizational, and customer loyalty resources of the company, and (3) to manage profits to insure a sound financial position.

The resources of the business are: (1) the financial resources available to the corporation; (2) the technological resources such as buildings, equipment, and production technology; (3) the human resources in terms of the skills and abilities possessed by the people who comprise the organization; (4) the proprietary resources such as corporate name, brand names, copyrights, and patents; (5) the information resources of the business which provide reliable data upon which to make timely decisions.

The 1968 report went on to define the basic objectives of Barry's human resource accounting system as being:

1.   To provide Barry managers with specific feedback information on their performance in managing the organizational resources and customer loyalty resources entrusted to their care so that they can make proper adjustments to their pattern of operations to correct adverse trends or further improve the condition of these resources.

2.   To provide Barry managers with additional information pertaining to human resources to assist in their decision making.

3.   To provide the organization with a more accurate accounting of its return on total resources employed, rather than just the physical resources, and to enable management to analyze how changes in the status of the resources employed affect the achievement of corporate objectives.

Barry clearly noted that the human resource accounting system was a "first pioneering step" and that it lacked refinement. Additionally, Barry stressed that, "The human resource capital accounts are used for internal informational purposes only and are not reflected, of course, in the financial data presented in this report."

The 1969 Barry annual report devoted 2 of its 24 pages to human resource accounting. (See Exhibit 1.) This material was introduced with a disclaimer which cautioned the reader that:

The figures included regarding investments and amortization of human resources are *unaudited* and you are cautioned for purposes of evaluating the performance of this company to refer to the *conventional certified* accounting data further on in this report. [Italics added.]

Question

Comment on the efforts of R. G. Barry to measure in dollar terms the organizational assets and changes in these assets over time. What alternative measurement or disclosure approaches might the company have used to achieve the same end?

EXHIBIT 1

R. G. BARRY CORPORATION AND SUBSIDIARIES
Excerpt from 1969 Annual Report
Balance Sheet

Assets

	Financial and Human Resource	Financial Only
Total current assets	$10,003,628	$10,003,628
Net property, plant, and equipment	1,770,717	1,770,717
Excess of purchase price of subsidiaries over net assets acquired	1,188,704	1,188,704
Net investments in human resources	986,094	—
Other assets	106,783	106,783
Total Assets	$14,055,926	$13,069,832

Liabilities and Stockholders' Equity

	Financial and Human Resource	Financial Only
Total current liabilities	$ 5,715,708	$ 5,715,708
Long-term debt, excluding current installments	1,935,500	1,935,500
Deferred compensation	62,380	62,380
Deferred federal income taxes as a result of appropriation for human resources	493,047	—
Stockholders' Equity:		
Capital stock	879,116	879,116
Additional capital in excess of par value	1,736,253	1,736,253
Retained earnings:		
Financial	2,740,875	2,740,875
Appropriation for human resources	493,047	—
Total Stockholders' Equity	5,849,291	5,356,244
Total Liabilities and Stockholders Equity	$14,055,926	$13,069,832

EXHIBIT 1 *(continued)*

Statement of Income

	Financial and Human Resource	Financial Only
Net sales	$25,310,588	$25,310,588
Cost of sales	16,275,876	16,275,876
Gross profit	$ 9,034,712	$ 9,034,712
Selling, general, and administrative expenses	6,737,313	6,737,313
Operating income	$ 2,297,399	$ 2,297,399
Other deductions, net	953,177	953,177
Income before federal income taxes	$ 1,344,222	$ 1,344,222
Human resource expenses applicable to future periods	173,569	—
Adjusted income before federal income taxes	$ 1,517,791	$ 1,344,222
Federal income taxes	730,785	644,000
Net Income	$ 787,006	$ 700,222

The information presented in this exhibit is provided only to illustrate the information value of human resource accounting for more effective internal management of the business. The figures included regarding investments and amortization of human resources are unaudited and you are cautioned for purposes of evaluating the performance of the company to refer to the conventional certified accounting data further on in this report.

Human Resource Accounting

During the past year work continued on the development of Barry's Human Resource Accounting System. The basic purpose of the system is to develop a method of measuring in dollar terms the changes that occur in the human resources of a business that conventional accounting does not currently consider.

Basic Concept

Management can be considered as the process of planning, organizing, leading, and controlling a complex mix of resources to accomplish the objectives of the organization. Those resources, we believe, are: physical resources of the company as represented by buildings and equipment, financial resources, and human resources which consist of the people who comprise the organization and proprietary resources which consist of trademarks, patents, and company name and reputation.

In order to determine more precisely the effectiveness of management's performance it is necessary to have information about the status of investments in the acquisition, maintenance, and utilization of all resources of the company.

Without such information, it is difficult for a company to know whether profit is being generated by converting a resource into cash or conversely whether suboptimal performance really has been generated by investments in developing the human resources which we expensed under conventional accounting practice.

Definition

Human Resource Accounting is an attempt to identify, quantify, and report investments made in resources of an organization that are not presently accounted for under conventional accounting practice. Basically, it is an information system that tells management what changes over time are occurring to the human resources of the business. It must be considered as an element of a total system of management—not as a separate "device" or "gimmick" to focus attention on human resources.

EXHIBIT 1 (continued)
Objectives

Broadly, the Human Resource Accounting Information System is being designed to provide better answers to these kinds of questions: What is the quality of profit performance? Are sufficient human capabilities being acquired to achieve the objectives of the enterprise? Are they being developed adequately? To what degree are they being properly maintained? Are these capabilities being properly utilized by the organization?

As expressed in our 1968 Annual Report, our specific objectives in development of human resource accounting are . . . [see case for description].

Approach

The approach used has been to account for investments in securing and developing the organization's human resources. Outlay costs for recruiting, acquiring, training, familiarizing, and developing management personnel are accumulated and capitalized. In accordance with the approach conventional accounting employs for classification of an expenditure as an asset, only those outlays which have an expected value beyond the current accounting period deserve consideration as investments. Those outlays which are likely to be consumed within a twelve-month period are properly classified as expense items. The investments in human resources are amortized over the expected useful period of the investment. The basic outlays in connection with acquiring and integrating new management people are amortized over their expected tenure with the company. Investments made for training or development are amortized over a much shorter period of time. The system now covers all management personnel at all locations of the corporation.

Research and development of the system began in late 1966. . . .

Applications

There are many potential applications for human resource accounting. Considering outlays for human resource investments which have a useful life over a number of years would have an impact upon the current year's revenue. Recognizing investments in human resources and their useful lives, losses resulting from improper maintenance of those resources can be shown in dollar terms. Estimating the useful lives of investments also provides a basis for planning for the orderly replacement of human capabilities as they expire, supplementing conventional manpower planning. Finally, recognizing investments in human resources will allow management to calculate dollar return on investment on a more comprehensive resource base for a particular profit center.

Summary

From the standpoint of management, knowledge of the human resource investments, maintenance, and returns is necessary for proper decision making and planning long-range corporate growth. As industry becomes increasingly technical, and management becomes progressively more complex, we believe conventional accounting practice will come to recognize human resource accounting in financial reporting.

At this stage, the Human Resource Accounting System at R. G. Barry is best regarded as a potentially important tool of the overall management system. It is not an end in itself, and needs continuing refinement and development.

EXHIBIT 1 *(concluded)*

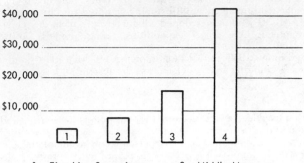

Typical Investments
in Individuals

1 – First Line Supervisor   3 – Middle Manager
2 – Industrial Engineer   4 – Top Level Manager

Chapter 17

INVENTORY PRICING

The selection of a method for pricing inventories represents an important management decision. The procedure selected will have a major impact on the measurement of net income and net working capital.

Inventories include all tangible items held for sale or consumption in the normal course of business for which the company holds title, wherever they might be located. Typically, inventories can be placed in one of four categories: finished goods, goods in process, raw materials, and manufacturing supplies. There are several generally accepted methods for pricing inventories. The significant problems in the area of inventory valuation result from the difficulties involved in allocating costs between periods and products, and the failure of selling prices and costs to move together.

The American Institute of Certified Public Accountants' pronouncement on inventory pricing appears in *Accounting Research Bulletin No. 43*, Chapter 4. This chapter, originally issued in 1947 as *Accounting Research Bulletin No. 29*, sets forth the general principles applicable to the pricing of inventories of mercantile and manufacturing enterprises.

Periodic and Perpetual Inventory Systems

Inventory value is determined by multiplying the quantity of inventory on hand by the price per unit. There are two systems for determining the quantity of inventories: the periodic inventory system and the perpetual inventory system. Irrespective of the system used, it is necessary periodically to inspect physically inventories.

The periodic inventory system involves a periodic determination of beginning inventory, purchases for the period, and ending inventory. These totals are determined by actual count. From these counts the cost of goods sold may be determined by deduction. The basic formula is:

Beginning Inventories + Purchases − Ending Inventories
= Cost of Goods Sold

The perpetual inventory system involves the keeping of a running record of all the additions and subtractions to the inventory.

Pricing Bases

Depending on the circumstances, the bases for pricing inventories may be: cost; cost or market, whichever is lower; or selling price. The major objective underlying the selection of a pricing basis in a particular case should be the fairest determination of periodic income.

COST METHODS

Cost is the principal basis for pricing inventories. *Accounting Research Bulletin No. 43*, Chapter 4 states:

> The primary basis for accounting for inventories is cost . . . as applied to inventories, cost means in principle the sum of the applicable expenditures and charges directly or indirectly incurred in bringing an article to its existing condition and location.

The inventory prices of manufacturing and merchandising companies reflect the different functions of these two classes of business activity. Manufacturing companies convert raw materials into finished goods. Consequently, their inventory prices reflect the cost of raw materials, direct labor, and factory overhead. Those costs associated with the product are referred to as product costs and are charged against revenues when the products are sold. All other costs, such as general administration and selling costs, are classified as period costs and are charged to the period in which they were incurred. Typically, merchandising businesses do not incur conversion costs. As a result, their inventory prices are the same as the prices the company paid for the products it sells.

Every well-run business maintains some record of its costs. These costs may be collected and recorded on the basis of either individual jobs (a job cost system) or the various production processes (a process cost system). The costs assigned to the various finished and partially finished products may be predetermined standard costs or actual costs. If a standard cost system is used, the common practice is to assign any small difference between actual and standard costs to cost of goods sold. If the variance is relatively large, however, some effort may be made to allocate the variance between the cost of goods sold and ending inventory accounts. In practice, a number of methods are used to allocate overhead costs to inventories. Most cost systems use a standard manufacturing overhead rate which allocates a fixed amount of overhead per unit to finished or partially finished goods, based upon the amount of, say, direct labor dollars embodied in the inventory. Other common bases for absorbing overhead are machine-hours and direct labor hours.

The exclusion of all factory overheads from inventory costs does not constitute an accepted accounting procedure for financial or tax accounting. Some argue that the inclusion of fixed factory overhead in inventory prices (and cost of goods sold) is misleading, since it tends to make a profit a function of production rather than sales since a buildup of inventory means more overhead will be charged to inventory and less will be charged to the current accounting period. These people advocate "direct costing," a procedure which includes in the inventory price only variable manufacturing costs. The fixed manufacturing costs are treated as period costs and are charged against income during the period in which they are incurred. Irrespective of the method used in financial reports, direct costing can be used for internal accounting purposes.

Often more than one product is produced from the same raw material. In the case of common products and by-products, raw material costs are typically allocated between the products on the basis of relative sales value, although a variety of other methods are permissible as long as the results are not misleading. Often, for example, if the by-products represent a relatively minor portion of the total production, the "by-product cost method" is used. Under this method, the by-product is initially valued at selling price less disposition costs. The total cost of the primary product is then reduced by this net amount. As a result, the profits and losses of the company are recorded on the sale of the primary product.

INVENTORY METHODS

There are a number of generally acceptable methods based on historical costs for determining the price of inventories.

Illustration 17–1 will be used to illustrate briefly a number of these cost-based methods (how the actual unit costs were determined will be ignored in these examples).

Specific Identification

The specific identification procedure associates the actual costs to the particular items in inventory. For example, if by inspection the ABC Company determined that its ending inventory consisted of purchases 1 and 3, the ending inventory would be valued at $23. Con-

ILLUSTRATION 17–1
ABC COMPANY

	Units	Unit Cost	Total
Beginning inventory	2	$10	$20
Purchases:			
1	1	11	11
2	1	10	10
3	1	12	12
4	1	13	13
Cost of goods available for sale			$66
Total quantity available for sale	6		
Total sold during period	4		
Ending inventory	2		

sequently, the cost of goods for the period would be $43 (total goods available for sale less ending inventory). While this method may directly relate revenues and costs, it is impractical for most businesses. However, it is sometimes used for "big ticket" items, for example, autos.

Last Invoice Price

The last invoice price method values the ending inventory at the most recent invoice price paid. Under this method, the two units in the ABC Company's ending inventory would be priced at $26 and the cost of goods sold expense would be $40. For those companies with a rapid turnover of inventory and where older inventory items are used first, this method gives inventory prices which are a close approximation of those determined by the specific identification method. This method is not widely used.

Simple Average

The simple average method prices the ending inventory as follows:

$$\frac{\text{Sum of Invoice Prices per Unit}}{\text{Number of Invoices}} \times \frac{\text{Number of Units}}{\text{in Ending Inventory}}$$

In the case of the ABC Corporation, this method would lead to an ending inventory value of $22.40 if the beginning inventory value per unit was included as an "invoice price." As a result, the cost of goods sold would be $43.60. The principal weakness of this procedure is that it gives equal weight to the invoice prices of large and small purchases. However, like some of the other methods discussed in this section, because of its simplicity it is used by small businesses.

Weighted Average

The weighted average method assigns to the ending inventory the average cost of the units available for sale during the period. The weighted average cost of the ABC Company's ending inventory is $22, and its cost of goods sold expense for the period is $44:

Cost of goods available for sale $66
Total units available for sale 6
Average cost $11
Ending inventory price (2 units × $11) $22

Moving Average

The moving average method computes the average unit price of the inventory after each purchase. The use of a moving average reduces the extent of the possible lag between inventory price and selling prices associated with the weighted average method. Given a perpetual inventory system, the cost of goods sold of the ABC Company is $42.22 and the value of the ending inventory is $23.78 (see Illustration 17–2).

ILLUSTRATION 17–2

| Date | Physical Units | | | Dollar Costs | | |
	Additions to Stock	Reductions in Stock	Balance	Additions to Stock	Reductions in Stock	Balance
April 1	—	—	2	—	—	$20.00
6	1	—	3	$11	—	31.00
7	—	2	1	—	$20.66	10.34
15	1	—	2	10	—	20.34
16	1	—	3	12	—	32.34
25	—	2	1	—	21.56	10.78
27	1	—	2	13	—	23.78

First-In, First-Out

The first-in, first-out (Fifo) method assigns the costs to inventory that reflect the most recent purchases. In the case of the ABC Company, the price of the ending inventory using the Fifo procedure is $25 (i.e., the sum of the costs of purchases 3 and 4). As a result, the cost of goods expense is $41.

Last-In, First-Out

The last-in, first-out (Lifo) method assumes the most recent purchase costs are related to current revenues. As a result, the ending
inventory reflects the oldest costs.

Lifo inventories consist of a series of "cost layers." The initial layer
includes the quantities and related prices existing at the time when
Lifo was adopted. The ending inventory is the base cost layer plus the
older layers of inventory required to equal the quantity of goods at the
balance sheet date. In the case of the ABC Company, if Lifo had been
adopted before the beginning of the period, the initial cost layer
would be two units at $10 (i.e., the beginning inventory). The next
layer would have been purchase 1. Under the Lifo method, ABC's
ending inventory determined by a *periodic* inventory system is $20[1]
and the resulting cost of goods sold expense is $46. Since unit reduc-
tions in inventory equaled purchases, the two units in the ending
inventory are valued at the $20 shown for the two units in the begin-
ning inventory. (In practice Lifo inventory accounting is more complex than suggested by the ABC Company example. These complexities will be discussed later.)

A company can adopt the Lifo method for income tax purposes only
on the condition that it use this method in its published financial
statements. If the ABC Company used Lifo accounting, its taxable
profits would be less under Lifo than Fifo, since the Lifo cost of goods
would be higher ($46) than the Fifo figure ($41).

Lifo versus Fifo

The Lifo and Fifo methods are among the most popular inventory
pricing procedures. In practice, each is considered an equally acceptable alternative. However, their impact on working capital and net
income can be significantly different. For example, in the ABC situation, the Lifo procedure led to an ending inventory valued at $20,
whereas the Fifo method resulted in an ending inventory valued at
$25. The cost of goods sold for the period also reflected the different
procedures: Lifo led to a cost of goods sold expense of $46 and Fifo
resulted in a cost of goods sold expense of $41. The extent of the cost
differential in this illustration should not be considered typical. How-

---

[1] Illustration 17–2 shows that on April 7 the ABC Company reduced its inventory to
one unit, which is less than the Lifo layer of two units at the beginning of the year. The
same thing occurred on April 25. Since the determination of the value of Lifo inventory
is made at year-end, if the depleted Lifo layers are replaced by year-end the fact that the
company "dipped into" its Lifo basis during the year has no impact on the cost of goods
sold.

ever, it does highlight the relationship between the inventory pricing procedure, the inventory value, and the cost of goods sold expense.

The adoption of Lifo as an acceptable inventory method caused considerable controversy. The advocates of Lifo argued that this procedure stated the cost of goods sold in current dollars. As a consequence, they noted, costs and revenues would be matched in terms of relatively similar dollars, irrespective of the direction of the trend in prices. This result, the advocates of Lifo argued, overcame a major weakness of Fifo, namely, that in periods of rising prices it leads to an "overstatement" of profits, since a portion of these profits have to be used to replace the consumed inventories at higher costs. Similarly, in periods of falling prices, the proponents of Lifo stated, Fifo leads to an "understatement" of profit, since inventories produced or bought during an earlier period of higher prices would be matched with current lower selling prices.

Those who opposed Lifo argued that Lifo leads to an unrealistic balance sheet presentation of inventory. Except in some rare situations, Lifo did not correspond to the actual flow of goods, and Lifo did not necessarily result in an improved matching of costs and revenues. If a Lifo inventory consisting of very old cost layers was depleted, the Lifo opponents argued, the current profits would be misleading, since current revenues would be matched in part against these old unrealistic costs.

While not necessarily agreeing that Lifo is a sound accounting method, a number of people became reconciled to Lifo because it represented a partial recognition of price level changes for the purpose of determining income. Others accept Lifo because of the tax advantage it gives to users of Lifo in periods of inflation. Those who use Fifo may recognize these tax and income measurement advantages of Lifo, but still be reluctant to adopt it because of the uncertainty as to the impact of reporting lower profits under Lifo on their stock prices. The efficient market theory suggests that this concern is naive, on the grounds that the market sees through the Lifo-based profits to the underlying economic reality, which in periods of inflation is more favorable to Lifo companies, since they pay less taxes than Fifo companies. The results of specific research as to whether or not the market "sees through" Lifo profits to the underlying economic reality are inconclusive.

Disclosure

Statement users can use the data in the notes related to inventories to adjust a Lifo company's income and inventory values to a Fifo basis. Similarly beginning in 1976 income and inventory of certain Fifo companies registered with the SEC can be adjusted to a Lifo basis. Here are the disclosure rules that make these analyses of the income and balance sheet effect of different inventory accounting possible:

. When a company shifts from Fifo to Lifo accounting, the impact of the change on earnings in the year of change must be disclosed. However, because of IRS rules, this earnings difference cannot be disclosed in subsequent years. If such a disclosure is made, the company would be denied the use of Lifo for tax purposes.

. If a company already on Lifo for some of its inventories decides to extend the use of Lifo to other inventories, the effect of Lifo extension on earnings must be disclosed. Again, the IRS permits this disclosure only in the extension year.

. Lifo companies must disclose in their notes to the financial statements for each period presented the difference between the Lifo and current cost values of their inventories. This disclosure, which is sometimes called the "Lifo reserve," is useful in two ways: First, this amount can be added to the Lifo inventory value shown on the face of the statement to obtain an approximation of the company's Fifo inventory value. Second, the change in the Lifo reserve from one year to another is equivalent to the before-tax effect on earnings of using Lifo rather than Fifo accounting.

. Sometimes Lifo companies at year-end dip into, or "invade," one of their Lifo inventory's old cost layers. Typically, this boosts earnings, since current revenues are matched with costs from a period when unit costs were considerable lower than the current replacement cost. The effect on earnings of Lifo layer invasions must be disclosed.

. Beginning in 1976 the SEC required about 1,000 of the larger companies registered with it to disclose the replacement cost of their inventories and related cost of goods sold.[2] Thus, the Fifo companies that must comply with this rule will provide the data needed to restate their earnings to a Lifo basis. In the case of most Lifo companies, their income for all practical purposes is already based on a replacement cost of goods sold valuation.

Typically, Lifo companies do not use Lifo accounting for their overseas inventories, since in most foreign countries this accounting method is not available for tax purposes. In addition, only a part of a company's domestic inventories may be accounted for by the Lifo method. When more than one inventory method is used, the proportion of inventory accounted for by each of the principle methods should be disclosed.

---

[2] The end-of-year inventory priced at end-of-year prices will give the replacement cost for SEC purposes. The cost of goods sold should be priced at the replacement cost at the time of sale. This can be accomplished by multiplying the historical cost of the item by its price index at the time of sale divided by its price index at the time of purchase.

Lifo Methodology

Lifo inventory accounting can be applied to raw materials, finished goods, or some component of finished goods. It may be used to account for some inventories and not others. Or, it may be used to account for one item or a collection of items grouped into so-called dollar value pools. Pools are often formed around natural business unit inventories, product lines, or geographical locations.

There are two basic approaches to Lifo accounting. The specific identification method and the dollar value method.

Specific Identification Method

In the year for which Lifo is adopted, the beginning Lifo inventory is valued at cost and all units combined to form the basic Lifo "layer."

Should the inventory at the end of the year exceed the beginning inventory, then the additional inventory is priced at the current year's cost. This can be first purchase costs, last purchase costs, or the average for the year. Frequently each purchase (or the average of a month's worth of purchases) is applied in order of acquisition until the inventory increase is accounted for in full. An average of the costs making up this increase is taken and treated as one Lifo layer.

If the inventory at the end of the year is less than the beginning inventory, then the layers are reduced by the most recent acquisitions. Illustration 17–3 illustrates the specific identification method.

In practice the specific identification method is infrequently used, except in firms which have only a few raw materials or manufactured goods. The ease and simplicity of its calculation is outweighed in most enterprises by the need to protect income from inflationary profits which could be brought about through inventory decreases, material substitution, or product changes which charge low-priced Lifo layers to cost of goods sold in the year the inventory is reduced. The use of dollar value pools which incorporate a variety of items minimize these problems.

Dollar Value Method

For each inventory pool that is formed, the cost of beginning inventory of every item in the pool is determined for the year Lifo is adopted. This sum of these costs is termed the "base-year cost" for that pool.

A number of dollar value methods are used for valuing inventories at the end of the first and subsequent years. The two most common are the "double extension" method and the "link-chain" method. The latter uses a cumulative index of beginning and ending costs in each

ILLUSTRATION 17–3

Sample Lifo Calculation: Specific Identification Method

The Situation:

Time	Item	Quantity	Current Unit Cost	Total Current Cost
Beginning of year 1	A	2,000	$5.00	$10,000
(base year)	B	5,000	4.00	20,000
				$30,000
End of year 1	A	2,000	5.25	$10,500
	B	6,000	4.50	27,000
				$37,500
End of year 2	A	3,000	5.50	$16,500
	B	5,000	5.00	25,000
				$41,500
End of year 3	A	4,000	5.30	$21,200
	B	-0-	—	-0-
	C	4,000	4.00[1]	16,000
				$37,200

[1] Base year cost estimated at $3 per unit.

Specific Identification Method Illustration:

Time	Item	Quantity	Value		Total
End of year 1	A	2,000	$5.00		$10,000
	B	5,000	4.00	$20,000	
	Addition year 1	1,000	4.50	4,500	24,500
					$34,500
End of year 2	A	2,000	5.00	$10,000	
	Addition year 2	1,000	5.50	5,500	$15,500
		3,000			
	B	5,000	4.00		20,000
					$35,500
End of year 3	A	2,000	5.00	$10,000	
	Addition year 2	1,000	5.50	5,500	
	Addition year 3	1,000	5.30	5,300	$20,800
		4,000			
	C	4,000	4.00		16,000
					$36,800

pool to value successive layers. It is not considered further here. The double extension method is discussed below.

In the "double extension" method the year-end inventory pool is valued (a) at "current," year-end costs and (b) at the cost it would have had (with its current composition) at the beginning of the base year. If an item was not in inventory in the base year, its base year cost is estimated.

Each year's increment to the Lifo inventory is determined:

a. By calculating the base year cost of the total ending inventory in the pool.
b. Subtracting from this total the base year cost of the inventory at the beginning of the year. The difference is a Lifo layer attributable to this year at base level cost.
c. Multiply this current layer by the ratio of the current year's cost to the base year's cost. This gives the Lifo layer in current dollars, and it is added to the beginning inventory.

Decrements to a Lifo inventory occurs when the ending inventory in terms of base year costs is less than the base year cost of the beginning inventory. This decrement is removed from the most recent Lifo layers. Illustration 17–4 presents a double extension inventory calculation.

The advantages of a dollar value method stem from the treatment of a number of inventory items as one pooled unit. In a Lifo pool, substitution of new materials for old ones or new products for discontinued ones does not necessarily result in the older costs being charged against sales since either permanent or temporary reduction in inventory of one item in the pool can be offset by an increase in others.

The disadvantages are clerical costs and the difficulty in double pricing every item in current and base year terms. This is mitigated to some extent in the "link-chain" method since only year-to-year price changes must be calculated.

Indices can also be used based on pool samples, although the samples in practice tend to include a substantial fraction of the pool.

Base Stock

The base or "normal" stock method assumes that a business needs a minimum or basic inventory quantity to carry on normal operations. For example, if the ABC Company needed an inventory of two units to carry on normal operations, the two units could be regarded as the base stock. In a sense, it is argued, this base stock is similar to the company's fixed assets. If the company is to continue operations, the base stock must be preserved. Therefore, the argument continues, if the

ILLUSTRATION 17–4

Sample Lifo Calculation: Double Extension Method

The Situation:

Same as Illustration 17–3.

Double Extension Method:

	(A) Total Base Year Cost	(B) Total Current Cost	(C) Ratio B ÷ A
Beginning of year 1	$30,000	$30,000	1.0000
End of year 1	34,000[2]	37,500	1.1029
End of year 2	35,000[3]	41,500	1.1857
End of year 3	32,000[4]	37,200	1.1625

$$\begin{array}{lll} & A & B \\ {}^{(2)}(2,000*5) + (6,000*4) = & \$10,000 + \$24,000 = \$34,000 \\ {}^{(3)}(3,000*5) + (5,000*4) = & 15,000 + 20,000 = 35,000 \\ & & C \\ {}^{(4)}(4,000*5) + (4,000*3) = & 20,000 + 12,000 = 32,000 \end{array}$$

	Total Base Cost	Ratio	Total Lifo Cost
End of year 1:			
Base year inventory	$30,000	1.0000	$30,000
Layer No. 1	4,000	1.1029	4,412
	$34,000		$34,412
End of year 2:			
Base year inventory	$30,000	1.0000	$30,000
Layer No. 1	4,000	1.1029	4,412
Layer No. 2	1,000	1.1857	1,186
	$35,000		$35,598
End of year 3:			
Base year inventory	$30,000	1.0000	$30,000
Layer No. 1	2,000	1.1029	2,205
	$32,000		$32,205

replacement cost of the minimum inventory rises, the increase in these costs should not be reflected in higher income. To avoid this effect, the base stock is priced at a cost well below current market. In this respect, the base stock method is similar to the Lifo method. Both seek to match current costs with current revenues.

The inventory in excess of the base stock can be valued by Lifo, Fifo, or some other method. Should a company cut into its base stock and intend to replace the deficient quantity later, a replacement provision is established equal to the difference between the base price and the current market price of the deficient units. When the units are replaced, they are replaced at the base price and the provision offset by the difference between the base price and the actual cost of the deficient units.

The base stock method is generally accepted for financial accounting purposes. It is not approved for income tax purposes, however. Outside of some companies engaged in processing basic raw materials, this method is not widely used.

COST OR MARKET, WHICHEVER IS LOWER

A basic rule of accounting is that losses should be recorded as charges to income as soon as they are discovered. This rule takes precedence over the matching of costs with revenue rule. So, any inventory losses should be recognized currently to the extent that they can be determined, and the cost of inventory in excess of its utility should be charged to income and not carried forward as an asset. The lower-of-cost-or-market rule applies to such situations and provides a guide to the proper accounting treatment. *Accounting Research Bulletin No. 43,* Chapter 4 states:

A departure from the cost basis for pricing the inventory *is required* when the utility of the goods is no longer as great as its cost. Where there is evidence that the utility of goods, in their disposal in the ordinary course of business, will be less than cost, whether due to physical deterioration, obsolescence, changes in price levels, or other causes, the difference should be recognized as a loss of the current period. This is generally accomplished by stating such goods at a lower level commonly designated as *market.*

The lower-of-cost-or-market rule is based on the assumption that costs and selling prices move together. Thus, a decrease in the replacement cost of an inventory item signals a potential selling price decline and a decline in the utility of the inventory on hand. However, if the sales price does not decline and the inventory on hand will be sold at the normal margin, there will be no loss of utility. Conversely, if selling prices decline but the replacement cost does not, a less than "normal" margin will be earned. This is also a signal that the utility of the inventory has decreased.

The word "cost" in the rule means the cost of replacing the inventory on hand by purchase in the open market or reproduction in the company's own factories. The purchase price includes all of the costs of bringing the goods to their usual location. The reproduction cost includes all of the direct and indirect costs associated with manufacturing the goods.

The term "market" is a technical word that has a very special meaning in the context of this rule. It is an indication of the utility of the inventory as measured by the relationship between replacement cost, selling price, and normal margin. As used in the rule, "market" also means current replacement cost, but with two provisos:

1. Market should not exceed net realizable value (estimated selling price less costs of completion and disposal); and
2. Market should not be less than net realizable value reduced by an allowance for an approximately normal profit margin. This figure is often referred to as the "market floor."

Thus, determining market requires comparing three values: replacement cost, net realizable value, and the "market floor." If net realizable value is lower, it is market: if replacement costs is lower, it is market *unless* its use would result in a larger than normal profit margin; in that event, the "market floor" is market.

Illustration 17–5 illustrates the application of the lower-of-cost-or-market rule.

ILLUSTRATION 17–5

Cost or Market, Whichever Is Lower Rule*

	Illus. 1	Illus. 2	Illus. 3	Illus. 4
Cost	$1.00†	$1.00	$1.00	$1.00
Replacement or reproduction cost	1.05	0.98†	0.99	0.94
Net realizable value	1.25	1.15	0.95†	1.10
"Market floor": Net realizable value less a normal profit	0.99	0.91	0.75	0.95†
Inventory write-down amount	–0–	0.02	0.05	0.05

Net realizable value and net realizable value less a normal profit are determined as follows:

	Illus. 1	Illus. 2	Illus. 3	Illus. 4
Selling price	$1.30	$1.20	$1.00	$1.25
Less: Cost of completion and disposal	0.05	0.05	0.05	0.05
Net realizable value	$1.25	$1.15	$0.95	$1.20
Normal profit (20% of selling price)	0.26	0.24	0.20	0.25
Net realizable value less a normal profit	$0.99	$0.91	$0.75	$0.95

*Philip L. Defliese, Kenneth P. Johnson, and Roderick K. MacLiod, *Montgomery's Auditing* (New York: The Ronald Press Co., 1975), p. 387.
† Represents the value to be used for inventory purposes.

Retail Method

The retail inventory method is used as an approximation of the cost or market method by retailers and others who keep their inventory records on a selling price basis. In order to apply this method, records must be maintained of purchases and returns to manufacturers, showing cost and selling prices; and of customer sales and returns, showing selling prices. The cost of the ending inventory is calculated as follows:

1. Add the purchases during the period at cost to the opening inventory at cost.
2. Add the purchases at retail to the opening inventory at retail.
3. Subtract these two totals. The difference is the so-called cumulative mark-on in dollars. Calculate this amount as a percentage of the total retail price of the goods available for sale during the period.
4. Subtract actual sales from the total retail price of goods available for sale (determined in 2 above) to obtain computed inventory at retail.
5. Multiply the ending inventory at retail by the mark-on percentage (computed in 3 above) and subtract from inventory at retail to determine inventory at cost.

The retail method is widely used in the retail business, since it reduces the clerical work and permits cost to be omitted from price tags.

The following procedure is used to state retail inventories on a Lifo basis:

1. Inventory at retail value is calculated for all items in a department at inventory date.
2. The total department inventory at retail is reduced to a base year value by applying the appropriate indices published by the Bureau of Labor Statistics for this purpose which covers that department's merchandise. This base level value is then separated into Lifo layers attributable to each year.
3. A layer is added if ending inventory is greater than beginning inventory. If it is less, the more recent layers in beginning inventory are moved to cost of goods sold.
4. Each layer in ending inventory is reduced to *cost* by using the average gross markup in that department appropriate to the year that layer was acquired.
5. The result is ending inventory at Lifo cost.

SELLING PRICE

Another basis for pricing inventories is selling price. According to *Accounting Research Bulletin No. 43*, Chapter 4:

Only in exceptional cases may inventories properly be stated above cost. For example, precious metals having a fixed monetary value with no substantial cost of marketing may be stated at such monetary value; any other exceptions must be justifiable by inability to determine appropriate approximate costs, immediate marketability at quoted market price, and the characteristic of unit interchangeability. When goods are stated above costs this fact should be fully disclosed.

If the selling price basis is used, the cost of disposition should be deducted. The principal arguments for the application of the selling price basis are: first, the inventory is readily marketable at known market prices and, second, production is the critical business activity, rather than selling. In general, the inability to determine cost is the weakest argument for pricing inventories on a selling price basis.

STATEMENT PRESENTATION

Typically, inventories are shown in the current asset section of the balance sheet, immediately after accounts receivable. According to *Accounting Research Bulletin No. 43*, Chapter 4:

The basis of stating inventories must be consistently applied and should be disclosed in the financial statements; whenever a significant change is made therein, there should be disclosed the nature of the change and, if material, the effect on income.

The Securities and Exchange Commission's Regulation S–X requires disclosure of the inventory pricing basis:

The basis of determining the amounts shall be stated. If a basis such as "cost," "market," or "cost or market whichever is lower" is given, there shall also be given, to the extent practicable, a general indication of the method of determining the "cost" or "market": e.g., "average cost," "first-in, first-out," or "last-in, first-out."

SUMMARY

The valuation of inventories is critical to the periodic measurement of net working capital and net income. The importance of inventories is further reflected in the prominence this item receives in internal control systems and audit programs. There are many different accepted procedures for valuing inventory, most of which are cost-based. Management should select the inventory pricing method which leads to the fairest determination of periodic income. The discussion of inventories involves considerable controversy: some argue that the number of acceptable inventory procedures should be reduced. Others contend that particular inventory methods are misleading. A number of people believe that the disclosure of inventories is inadequate. Clearly, this is an important area for all those who prepare, audit, or use accounting statements.

SUGGESTED FURTHER READING

ACCOUNTING INTERNATIONAL STUDY GROUP. *Accounting and Auditing Approaches to Inventories in Three Nations: Stock in Trade and Work in Progress in Canada, the United Kingdom and the United States.* London: St. Clements Foot & Cross Ltd., 1968.

HOFFMAN, RAYMOND A., and GUNDERS, HENRY. 2d ed. *Inventories: Control, Costing, and Effect upon Income and Taxes.* New York: The Ronald Press Co., 1970.

CASES

CASE 17–1. GSC, INC.
Adopting Lifo Inventory Valuation

In mid-January 1975 Terry O'Neil, controller of GSC, Inc., was examining the consequences of GSC's adopting a last-in, first-out (Lifo) method of valuing raw material. He was meeting the next afternoon with Gregory Spencer, president of GSC, and Christ Scott, GSC's auditor, to evaluate the impact of adopting Lifo on GSC's cash-flow operating results, and financial position. Terry was hopeful that the meeting would result in a decision so that he could get GSC's 1974 financial statements and the 1975 financial projections ready for his end-of-January meeting with the Shipman Bank & Trust Company—the holder of GSC's equipment mortgage and line-of-credit notes.

The Corporation

GSC, Inc., was formed in 1967 to manufacture a high-quality line of plastic-based kitchen and household accessories—spice racks, bookends, geometric shapes, and so on. These products are produced by taking Forclon, a chemical powder, and processing it in a fairly capital intensive facility. The company has grown steadily, and in 1974 had an after-tax profit of $67,000 on sales of $1.7 million—Exhibits 1 and 2. For 1975, sales are estimated to be $2.4 million, and if expenses hold constant, such a sales volume will produce a pretax profit of $452,000 according to GSC's profit forecasting chart—Exhibit 3. This profit forecasting chart was based on the "contribution" reporting system that Greg Spencer and Terry O'Neil have used from the very beginning of their business. This system separates fixed and variable costs and reports the *contribution* to profit and fixed costs of both the manufacturing and selling activities—see Exhibit 1. GSC prepared expected, pro forma, financial statements in the same contribution format each year and submitted them and the profit forecasting chart to the bank in January. The bank also receives financial statements on actual results at the end of each quarter. These same projected statements are used internally to monitor the progress of GSC.

Inventory Pricing

The raw material inventory was composed almost entirely of Forclon, and this material is an important component of GSC's costs— some 80 percent of the variable and 45 percent of the total manufacturing costs. GSC had experienced substantial price increases in 1974, and the cost of Forclon had risen from 23 cents a pound under price controls in early 1974 to 57 cents a pound in December. Currently it was 59 cents a pound and expected to remain close to this level for at least the first half of 1975. The rapid price increase in 1974 caused O'Neil and Scott to recommend a look at Lifo to save income taxes.

Scott proposed that GSC consider raw materials to be one Lifo "pool" and lump together the raw material inventory with the raw material component of finished goods. (There is, essentially, no work in process inventory.) To isolate this inventory pool, Scott prepared an inventory movement analysis in both physical and dollar terms— Exhibit 4—using the existing first-in, first-out inventory pricing system. Scott also prepared a summary of key financial ratios using Fifo—Exhibit 5—and gave both documents to O'Neil. O'Neil was now engaged in calculating the impact of Lifo and preparing a recommendation and the necessary supporting analyses for his meeting with Greg Spencer and Chris Scott the next day.

Questions

1. Calculate the beginning and ending inventories and the cost of materials in goods sold under the assumption that 1974 is the first year for GSC on a Lifo inventory basis?

2. Fill in the financial ratio's on Exhibit 5 under Lifo. (Note, income tax on the first $25,000 of income is 22 percent and is 48 percent on the remainder.)

3. What recommendation would you make, and what issues must be considered in preparing for your meeting with Spencer?

EXHIBIT 1

GSC, INC.
Statement of Operations
For the Twelve Months Ending December 31, 1974

	Variable $	Variable %	Fixed	Total
Sales	1,843,979			$1,843,979
Less: Sales discounts	70,919			70,919
Net sales	1,773,060	100.0		$1,773,060
Cost of Sales:				
Materials	583,622			$ 583,622
Less: Increase in finished goods inventory	(37,599)			(37,599)
Raw materials in cost of sales	546,023	30.80		$ 546,023
Manufacturing Expenses:				
Plant labor	110,592	6.24	$ 71,678	$ 182,270
Payroll taxes	6,177	0.35	5,052	11,229
Group health insurance			7,968	7,968
Utilities			39,242	39,242
Depreciation			268,326	268,326
Rental expense on land and building			55,161	55,161
Insurance and fire and casualty			23,073	23,073
Freight-out	62,728	3.54		62,728
Truck expense—out			15,191	15,191
Factory repairs			37,998	37,998
Factory supplies	25,267	1.42		25,267
Factory miscellaneous—administration			9,628	9,628
Cost of manufacturing	204,764	11.55	$533,317	$ 738,081
Less addition to finished goods inventory	3,800	.22	9,896	13,696
Manufacturing cost of goods sold	200,964	11.33	$523,421	$ 724,385
Cost of sales	746,987	42.13		$1,270,408
Gross contribution from manufacturing	1,026,073	57.87		$ 502,652
Salaries			$ 90,186	$ 90,186
Commissions	76,627	4.32		76,627
Payroll taxes			5,899	5,899
Advertising and sales promotion			13,789	13,789
Auto expense			2,599	2,599
General taxes			11,739	11,739
Insurance—key man			3,252	3,252
Telephone and telegraph			10,770	10,770
Travel and entertaining			44,420	44,420
Professional services			15,967	15,967
Other expenses			22,621	22,621
Total S and A	76,627	4.32	$221,242	$ 297,869
Other Income and Expense:				
Interest expense			88,198	88,198
Total S and A and Other	76,627	4.32	$309,440	$ 386,067
Net Operating Contribution	949,446	53.55		$ 116,585
Less: Fixed expense	832,861	46.97	$832,861	
Pretax profit	116,585	6.58		$ 116,585
Income tax				49,461
Net Profit after Tax				$ 67,124

EXHIBIT 2

GSC, INC.
Statement of Financial Position
December 31, 1974

Assets

Current Assets:

Cash		$ 10,713	
Accounts receivable net of reserve for doubtful accounts		245,867	
Notes receivable		16,517	
Other receivables		2,008	
Inventory:			
Raw materials	$157,081		
Finished goods	102,783	259,864	
Prepaid expenses		25,896	
Total Current Assets			$ 560,865

Property, Plant, and Equipment:

Leasehold additions and improvements		$ 22,929	
Machinery and equipment...................		2,123,434	
Office equipment		30,867	
Autos and trucks		21,766	
		$2,198,996	
Less: Reserve for depreciation		727,720	
Total Property, Plant, and Equipment ...			1,471,276
Total Assets			$2,032,141

Equities

Current Liabilities:

Accounts payable		$ 307,007	
Notes payable to bank		120,000	
Accrued payroll and related taxes withheld		58,300	
Accrued expenses		17,876	
Federal income and state property taxes		53,728	
Total Current Liabilities..............		$ 557,811	
Long-term debt (less current portion)		952,472	
Total Liabilities			$1,510,283

Stockholders Equity:

Cumulative preferred stock		$ 76,750	
Common stock.............................		41,890	
Paid in surplus		35,089	
Retained earnings		368,129	
Total Stockholders Equity			521,858
Total Equity			$2,032,141

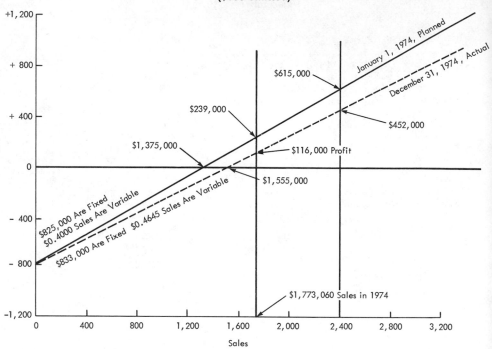

EXHIBIT 3
Break-Even Chart
For the Twelve Months Ending 12-31-74
($000 omitted)

EXHIBIT 4
Raw Materials Movement and Position
During the Calendar Year Ending December 31, 1974

Beginning Inventory on January 1, 1974:				
	140,650 lbs at $0.220		$ 30,943	
	142,000 lbs at 0.230		32,660	
	282,650 lbs			$ 63,603
January—March:				
Purchased + 75,000 lbs at .230			$ +17,250	
Used −303,040 lbs				
	140,650 lbs at 0.220	$ 30,943		
	162,390 lbs at 0.230	37,350	−68,293	−51,043
Balance 54,610 lbs				$ 12,560
April—June:				
Purchased +700,000 lbs				
	100,000 lbs at 0.230	$ 23,000		
	200,000 lbs at 0.295	59,000		
	300,000 lbs at 0.350	105,000		
	100,000 lbs at 0.375	37,500	$+224,500	

EXHIBIT 4 *(continued)*

Used	−488,170 lbs					
		154,610 lbs at	0.230	$ 35,560		
		200,000 lbs at	0.295	59,000		
		133,560 lbs at	0.350	46,746	−141,306	+83,194
Balance	266,440 lbs					$ 95,754

July—September:

Purchased	+350,000 lbs					
		250,000 lbs at	0.425	$106,250		
		100,000 lbs at	0.467	46,700	+152,950	
Used	−403,230 lbs					
		166,440 lbs at	0.350	$ 58,254		
		100,000 lbs at	0.375	37,500		
		136,790 lbs at	0.425	58,136	−153,890	−940
Balance	213,210 lbs					$ 94,814

October—December:

Purchased	+520,000 lbs					
		200,000 lbs at	0.515	$103,000		
		150,000 lbs at	0.550	82,500		
		170,000 lbs at	0.570	96,900	$+282,400	
Used	−453,790 lbs					
		113,210 lbs at	0.425	$ 48,114		
		100,000 lbs at	0.467	46,700		
		200,000 lbs at	0.515	103,000		
		40,580 lbs at	0.550	22,319	−220,133	+62,267
Balance	279,420 lbs					$157,081

Ending Inventory Reconciliation

109,420 lbs at 0.550	$ 60,181
170,000 lbs at 0.570	96,900
279,420 lbs	$157,081

Cost of Raw Materials Used

1st quarter	303,040 lbs	$ 68,293
2d quarter	488,170 lbs	141,306
3d quarter	403,230 lbs	153,890
4th quarter	453,790 lbs	220,133
	1,648,230 lbs	$583,622

Raw materials in beginning finished goods inventory (82,020 lbs)	18,040
Raw materials in goods available for sale (1,730,250 lbs)	$601,662
Less raw materials in ending finished goods inventory (105,279)	55,639*
Cost of raw materials in sales (1,624,971)	$546,023

*	64,699 lbs at 0.515	$33,320
	40,580 lbs at 0.550	22,319
	105,279 lbs	$55,639

EXHIBIT 5

Key Financial Ratios
For the Calendar Year Ending 12-31-74

		Fifo	*Lifo*
Ending raw material		$212,720	
In raw material inventory	$157,081		
In finished goods	55,639		
Cost of raw materials used		$546,023	
Net operating contribution		$949,446	
Pretax profit		$116,585	
Income tax expense		$ 49,461	
Net profit after tax		$ 67,124	
Working capital		$ 3,054	
Current ratio		1.005/1	
Inventory turnover—raw material component		3.71	
Times interest earned		2.32	
Return of stockholders equity (average)		0.14	

CASE 17–2. CHRYSLER CORPORATION
Adoption of Fifo Inventory Valuation

In late February 1971, Larry Polk and an analyst with a medium-sized mutual fund made an appointment to discuss with one of his former professors the letter to stockholders which his firm had recently received from Chrysler.

The letter, addressed "To Our Shareholders," was a multilith copy of a typewritten three-page letter from Lynn Townsend, chairman, and John Riccardo, president of Chrysler together with a typewritten copy of the financial statements of both Chrysler Corporation (and consolidated subsidiaries) and Chrysler Realty Corporation, as audited by Touche Ross & Company. Both the letter and the auditor's opinion were dated February 9, 1971.

The first three paragraphs of the letter outlined the essential communication to the stockholders:

Sales of Chrysler Corporation and consolidated subsidiaries throughout the world in 1970 totaled $7.0 billion, compared with $7.1 billion in 1969. Operations for the year resulted in a net loss of $7.6 million or $0.16 a share, compared with net earnings of $99.0 million or $2.09 a share in 1969.

Net earnings for 1969 are restated to reflect a retroactive change in the company's method of valuing inventories, from a Lifo (last-in, first-out) to a

Fifo (first-in, first-out) cost basis, as explained in the notes to financial statements. The Lifo method reduces inventory values and earnings in periods of rising costs. The rate of inflation in costs in 1970 and for the projected short-term future is so high that significant understatements of inventory values and earnings result. The use of the Lifo method in 1970 would have reduced inventory amounts at December 31, 1970, by approximately $150 million and did reduce inventory amounts reported at December 31, 1969, by approximately $110 million. Also, the use of the Lifo method in 1970 would have increased the loss for the year by approximately $20.0 million, and its use in 1969 reduced the earnings as reported for that year by $10.2 million. The other three U.S. automobile manufacturers have consistently used the Fifo method. Therefore the reported loss for 1970 and the restated profit for 1969 are on a comparable basis as to inventory valuation with the other three companies. Prior years' earnings have been restated to make them comparable.

Results of operations for the first three quarters of 1970 were previously reported on the Lifo method of valuing inventories. The restated results, on the Fifo method of valuing inventories, for the four quarters of 1970 are as follows:

	Net Earnings (loss) (millions)	Earnings (loss) a Share
1st quarter	$(27.4)	$(0.57)
2d quarter	10.1	0.21
3d quarter	2.1	0.05
4th quarter	7.6	0.15
1970	$ (7.6)	$(0.16)

The letter stressed the economic conditions that had led to the losses for Chrysler. The total sales of the company's passenger cars, trucks, and tractors, both domestic and overseas, had increased slightly in 1970. However, the management stated:

. . . the United States economy during 1970 experienced a combination of inflation and recession, high employment, high interest rates, and restricted growth. Consumer confidence was weakened by economic and social problems at home, and by serious crises in the Middle East and Southeast Asia. A major strike in the automotive industry cut North American vehicle production and added to the consumers lack of confidence. As a result, United States automobile industry sales for the year reached their lowest point since 1962.

The letter pointed out that these economic factors were reflected in the company's financial statements, and further revealed that there was a drop in North American factory sales of 64,339 cars and trucks, as well as a shifting in consumer demand toward smaller, less expensive automobiles, resulting in a less profitable product mix. Further, the company had experienced increased costs not recoverable through increased selling prices.

The company's response to the economic pressures was described as review and reduction of operating expense and capital expenditures, realignment of the organization to produce a more direct system of operational controls, and improvements in the marketing and product programs, both short and long term.

The letter stressed that "Chrysler Corporation has operated at a profit for the nine-month period since April 1, 1970."

Competitive Situation

Chrysler, ranked third among U.S. auto manufacturers, was not the only major auto company to find 1970 a difficult year. General Motors had experienced a 23 percent drop in sales; 1970 sales were $18.8 billion in contrast to $24.3 billion in 1969. Consequently, profits fell from 1969's $1.7 billion to $670 million. This represented a decline in net income as a percentage of sales to 3.2 percent from the usual level of 7 percent. Earnings per share of $2.09 failed to cover a dividend reduced to $3.40 from the prior $4.30 level. The 1969 earnings per share had been $5.95. General Motors attributed the decline in company sales and profit partially to U.S. inflation, and particularly to the strike which had halted production for more than ten weeks primarily in the fourth quarter of the calendar year. Stock prices reflected the company's problems; from a high of $72 in 1968 the stock had fallen to $26 in February. (See Exhibit 6.)

Ford Motor Company had fared better in the inflationary economy. Fourth-quarter introduction of the Pinto had reversed the trend of declining retail car sales, and total sales for 1970 were $15 billion, a slight increase over 1969's sales of $14.8 billion. The impact of inflation could be viewed in corporate profits, which had fallen to $516 million from 1969's $547 million. The annual dividend was held at $2.40 in both years; 1969 earnings per share had been $5.03, and, 1970, $4.77 (selected statistics for the three major auto companies are included in Exhibit 5).

Accounting Policies

The accounting policies of the three companies were generally considered to be conservative by security analysts. All three companies expensed research and development expenses as incurred. All deferred the investment tax credit over the life of the equipment which gave rise to the credit. GM and Chrysler used accelerated depreciation for all fixed assets; Ford followed a similar policy for 78 percent of its plant and equipment accounts.

Due to union contracts, pension costs were major expenses of all major auto manufacturers. All three companies funded current pension provisions costs; past service costs were amortized over 30 years.

Up until 1970, the primary differences in accounting were in the treatment of goodwill and inventory. Chrysler alone was on Lifo; the others used Fifo or lower of cost or market. Neither Ford nor Chrysler amortized goodwill; GM amortized goodwill over 20 years.

Chrysler's Problems, 1970

Beyond the general inflation and labor problems common to all auto manufacturers, Chrysler Corporation had a number of other problems in 1970. Among these were:

. Unexpectedly low fourth-quarter sales. Profits were $7.6 million, rather than $20 million expected by security analysts. Typically, the fourth quarter was the profit setter for auto companies.
. Net loss of $7.9 million on overseas sales of $1.6 billion. In 1969 Chrysler had earned $19 million on $1.5 billion sales.
. A substantial change in sales by product lines. Compact cars accounted for 34 percent of Chrysler sales in 1970.
. A drop in U.S. factory sales of nearly 100,000 units in 1970.
. Due to lower 1969 profits and 1970 losses, pressure on working capital, especially cash.

The Accounting Change

In Mr. Polk's conference, two key issues in the 1970 accounting change were pointed out, namely, the change in inventory valuation policy and the allocation of income taxes. These were described in footnotes to the financial statements:

Inventories—Accounting Change

Inventories are stated at the lower of cost or market. For the period January 1, 1957, through December 31, 1969, the last-in, first-out (Lifo) method of inventory valuation had been used for approximately 60% of the consolidated inventory. The cost of the remaining 40% of inventories was determined using the first-in, first-out (Fifo) or average cost methods. Effective January 1, 1970, the Fifo method of inventory valuation has been adopted for inventories previously valued using the Lifo method. This results in a more uniform valuation method throughout the Corporation and its consolidated subsidiaries and makes the financial statements with respect to inventory valuation comparable with those of the other United States automobile manufacturers. As a result of adopting Fifo in 1970, the net loss reported is less than it would have been on a Lifo basis by approximately $20.0 million, or $0.40 a share. Inventory amounts at December 31, 1969, and 1970 are stated higher by approximately $110.0 million and $150.0 million, respectively, than they would have been had the Lifo method been continued.

The Corporation has retroactively adjusted financial statements of prior years for this change. Accordingly, the 1969 financial statements have been restated resulting in an increase in Net Earnings of $10.2 million, and Net Earnings Retained for Use in the Business at December 31, 1969, and 1968 have been increased by $53.5 million and $43.3 million, respectively.

For United States income tax purposes the adjustment to inventory amounts will be taken into taxable income ratably over 20 years commencing January 1, 1971.

Taxes on Income

Taxes on income as shown in the consolidated statement of net earnings include the following:

	1970	1969
Currently payable:		
United States taxes (credit)	$(81,800,000)	$50,000,000
Other countries	44,300,000	36,300,000
Deferred taxes	16,100,000	(6,000,000)
As previously reported		80,300,000
Adjustment in deferred taxes for		
change in inventory valuation		11,400,000
Total taxes on income		
(credit)	$(21,400,000)	$91,700,000

The change in inventory valuation resulted in a reduction in income taxes allocable to the following year of approximately $56.0 million at December 31, 1969.

Reductions in taxes resulting from the investment credit provisions of the Internal Revenue Code are being taken into income over the estimated lives of the related assets. The amounts of such credits which were reflected in net earnings were $6,300,000 in 1970 and $5,400,000 in 1969.

The change in inventory valuation method was made as of January 1, 1970; thus it included a retroactive adjustment to Chrysler's 1969 retained earnings. The Chrysler financial statements are shown in Exhibits 1 (net earnings), 2 (retained earnings), 3 (source and application of funds), and 4 (balance sheet).

From this information, it was suggested that Mr. Polk could estimate Chrysler's 1970—

1. Pretax loss.
2. Loss reported to the IRS.
3. The benefit of changing inventory valuation methods.

First Quarter, 1971

On April 19, 1971, Chrysler management reported that company had earned $0.22 a share, as compared with a net loss of $0.57 a year earlier. A condensed financial report is included as Exhibit 7.

Questions

1. Why did Chrysler change accounting methods?
2. What was the cost to Chrysler of using a Lifo inventory method in 1970? In 1969? In 1965?
3. What was the cost to Chrysler of changing from Lifo to Fifo?
4. Approximate Chrysler's 1970 reported income for federal tax purposes. What does it tell you? Can you reconcile this amount with the reported $7.6 million loss?

EXHIBIT 1

CHRYSLER CORPORATION AND CONSOLIDATED SUBSIDIARIES
Consolidated Statement of Net Earnings
For Years Ended December 31, 1969, and 1970

	1970	1969*
Net sales	$6,999,675,655	$7,052,184,678
Equity in net earnings (loss) of unconsolidated subsidiaries	(6,210,013)	(6,286,309)
Other income and deductions	(19,962,022)	23,261,424
	$6,973,503,620	$7,069,159,793
Cost of products sold, other than items below	$6,103,250,974	$5,966,732,377
Depreciation of plant and equipment	176,758,139	170,305,745
Amortization of special tools	172,568,348	167,194,002
Selling and administrative expenses	386,041,866	431,706,851
Pension and retirement plans	121,406,136	114,577,630
Interest on long-term debt	46,998,713	31,702,530
Taxes on income (credit)	(21,400,000)	91,700,000
	$6,985,624,176	$6,973,919,135
Net earnings (loss) including minority interest	$ (12,120,556)	$ 95,240,658
Minority interest in net loss of consolidated subsidiaries	4,517,536	3,730,564
Net Earnings (loss)	$ (7,603,020)	$ 98,971,222
Average number of shares of common stock outstanding during the year	48,693,200	47,390,561
Net earnings (loss) a share	$(0.16)	$2.09

* Restated to reflect the change made in 1970 in accounting for inventories and to conform to 1970 classifications. The 1969 net earnings and net earnings a share, as previously reported, were $88.8 million and $1.87 respectively. See Inventories—Accounting Change note.

See notes to financial statements.

EXHIBIT 2   •

CHRYSLER CORPORATION AND CONSOLIDATED SUBSIDIARIES
Consolidated Statement of Additional Paid-In Capital
For Years Ended December 31, 1969, and 1970

	1970	1969
Balance at beginning of year	$ 455,739,253	$ 421,184,933
Excess of market price over par value of newly issued shares of common stock sold to the thrift-stock ownership programs (1,556,843 in 1970; 927,276 in 1969)	28,281,685	33,796,320
Excess of option price over par value of shares of common stock issued under the stock option plans (none in 1970; 25,172 in 1969)	—	758,000
Balance at End of Year	$ 484,020,938	$ 455,739,253

Consolidated Statement of Net Earnings Retained for Use in the Business
For Years Ended December 31, 1969, and 1970

	1970	1969*
Balance at beginning of year	$1,399,028,028	$1,351,453,762
Adjustment (for the years 1957 through 1968)		43,309,750
As restated		$1,394,763,512
Net loss	(7,603,020)	
Net earnings as restated		98,971,222
	$1,391,425,008	$1,493,734,734
Cash dividends paid ($0.60 a share in 1970 and $2.00 a share in 1969)	29,193,336	94,706,706
Balance at End of Year	$1,362,231,672	$1,399,028,028

* Restated to reflect the change made in 1970 in accounting for inventories.
See notes to financial statements.

EXHIBIT 3

CHRYSLER CORPORATION AND CONSOLIDATED SUBSIDIARIES
Consolidated Source and Application of Working Capital
For Years Ended December 31, 1969, and 1970

	1970	1969*
Additions to Working Capital:		
From operations:		
Net earnings (loss)	$ (7,603,020)	$ 98,971,222
Depreciation	176,758,139	170,305,745
Amortization of special tools	172,568,348	167,194,002
Decrease (increase) in income taxes allocable—noncurrent	10,163,405	(9,242,610)
Proceeds from long-term borrowing	241,550,761	91,062,485
Proceeds from sale of common stock	38,011,954	40,507,120
Retirement of property, plant, and equipment	14,856,466	23,414,707
Total Additions	$646,306,053	$ 582,212,671
Dispositions of Working Capital:		
Cash dividends paid	$ 29,193,336	$ 94,706,706
Increase in investments and advances	107,570,466	32,587,326
Expenditures for property, plant, and equipment	173,792,798	374,534,311
Expenditures for special tools	241,745,805	271,761,847
Payments on long-term borrowing	37,449,055	39,391,567
Decrease in other liabilities	19,896,695	6,877,073
Other	3,712,747	2,231,075
Total Dispositions	$613,360,902	$ 822,089,905
Increase (decrease) in Working Capital during the Year	$ 32,945,151	$(239,877,234)

* Restated to reflect the change made in 1970 in accounting for inventories and to conform to 1970 classifications.

See notes to financial statements.

EXHIBIT 4

CHRYSLER CORPORATION AND CONSOLIDATED SUBSIDIARIES
Consolidated Balance Sheet
For Years Ended December 31, 1969, and 1970

Assets

	1970	1969*
Current Assets:		
Cash	$ 95,807,393	$ 78,768,440
Marketable securities—at cost and accrued		
interest	60,607,134	230,562,926
Accounts receivable (less allowance for		
doubtful accounts: 1970—$15,700,000;		
1969—$13,400,000)	438,852,496	477,880,423
Refundable United States taxes on income	80,000,000	—
Inventories (see inventories—accounting		
change note)	1,390,681,228	1,335,198,128
Prepaid insurance, taxes, and other expenses ..	83,299,833	80,087,753
Income taxes allocable to the following year ..	17,415,554	27,186,281
Total Current Assets	$2,166,663,638	$2,229,683,951
Investments and Other Assets:		
Investments in and advances to associated		
companies outside the United States	$ 24,907,266	$ 15,496,619
Investments in and advances to unconsolidated		
subsidiaries	675,212,687	577,052,868
Income taxes allocable—noncurrent	22,301,845	32,465,250
Other noncurrent assets	44,971,952	55,814,937
Total Investments and Other Assets	$ 767,393,750	$ 680,829,674
Property, Plant, and Equipment:		
Land, buildings, machinery, and equipment...	2,949,256,417	2,825,623,645
Less Accumulated depreciation	1,593,482,362	1,451,750,556
	$1,355,774,055	$1,373,873,089
Unamortized special tools	447,449,636	379,153,112
Net Property, Plant, and Equipment	$1,803,223,691	$1,753,026,201
Cost of investments in consolidated		
subsidiaries in excess of equity	78,491,382	78,184,245
Total Assets	$4,815,772,461	$4,741,724,071

* Restated to reflect the change made in 1970 in accounting for inventories.
See notes to financial statements.

EXHIBIT 4 *(continued)*

Liabilities and Shareholders' Investment
For Years Ended December 31, 1969, and 1970

	1970	*1969**
Current Liabilities:		
Accounts payable and accrued expenses	$1,095,984,194	$1,116,607,970
Short-term debt	374,186,273	477,442,371
Payments due within one year on long-term debt	34,572,552	39,825,038
Taxes on income	43,136,332	9,969,436
Total Current Liabilities	$1,547,879,351	$1,643,844,815
Other Liabilities:		
Deferred incentive compensation	$ 2,726,641	$ 7,493,823
Other employee benefit plans	63,462,301	55,575,476
Deferred investment tax credit	21,774,580	25,598,022
Unrealized profits on sales to unconsolidated subsidiaries	49,280,076	47,336,034
Other noncurrent liabilities	68,733,595	89,870,533
Total Other Liabilities	$ 205,977,193	$ 225,873,888
Long-Term Debt:		
Notes and debentures payable	$ 671,053,172	$ 466,951,466
Convertible sinking fund debentures	119,999,000	119,999,000
Total Long-Term Debt	$ 791,052,172	$ 586,950,466
International operations reserve	35,500,000	35,500,000
Minority interest in net assets of consolidated subsidiaries	79,742,516	95,149,271
Shareholders' Investment:		
Represented by—		
Common stock—par value $6.25 a share: Authorized 80,000,000 shares; issued and outstanding 49,498,979 shares at December 31, 1970, and 47,942,136 shares at December 31, 1969	$ 309,368,619	$ 299,638,350
Additional paid-in capital	484,020,938	455,739,253
Net earnings retained for use in the business	1,362,231,672	1,399,028,028
Total Shareholders' Investment	$2,155,621,229	$2,154,405,631
Total Liabilities and Shareholders' Investment	$4,815,772,461	$4,741,724,071

* Restated to reflect the change made in 1970 in accounting for inventories.
See notes to financial statements.

EXHIBIT 5

Selected Statistics—Major Auto Manufacturers (in millions)

	1970	1969	1968	1967	1966	1965
FORD MOTOR CO.						
Sales (millions)	$14,979.9	$14,755.6	$10,515.7	$12,240.0	$11,536.8	$ 9,670.8
Net income before tax	1,006.2	1,115.1	1,291.3	133.5	1,183.1	1,319.1
Tax provision	479.8	554.4	656.5	44.5	555.9	610.2
Net income (millions)	515.7	546.5	626.6	84.1	621.0	703.0
Capital expenditure	563.6	553.5	462.4	661.1	692.5	629.1
Depreciation—special tools	413.6	385.2	366.1	344.7	307.9	267.5
Expenditure—special tools	483.5	424.3	416.9	374.8	358.9	366.6
Amortization	409.9	418.5	382.1	331.3	322.5	267.4
Balance Sheet:						
Deferred tax and ITC	216.0	169.9	111.0	.109.2	74.0	57.3
Prepaid tax	317.2	246.4	220.2	227.7	167.5	142.9
Earnings per share ⎱ dollars	4.77	5.03	5.73	0.77	5.63	6.3
Dividends ⎰	2.40	2.40	2.40	2.40	2.40	2.1
Net income/sales	3.5%	3.8%	4.5%	0.8%	5.1%	6.2%
GENERAL MOTORS						
Sales	$18,752.4	$22,295.1	$22,755.4	$20,026.3	$20,208.5	$20,734.0
Net income before tax						
Tax provision	169.4	1,743.3				
Net income	609.1	1,710.7	1,731.9	1,627.3	1,793.4	2,125.6
Capital expenditure	1,134.2	1,043.8	860.2	912.6	1,188.1	1,322.0
Depreciation—special tools	841.5	765.8	729.1	712.6	654.1	556.7
Expenditure—special tools	1,148.6	863.1	865.8	881.2	890.8	729.8
Amortization	677.3	891.8	853.1	839.6	860.8	744.7

Balance Sheet:

Deferred tax and ITC	133.8	162.9	N.A.	N.A.	N.A.	N.A.
Prepaid tax	—	—	N.A.	N.A.	N.A.	N.A.
Earnings per share ⎱ dollars	2.09	5.95	6.02	5.66	6.24	7.41
Dividends ⎰	3.40	4.30	4.30	3.80	4.53	5.25
Net income/sales	3.2%	7.0%	7.6%	8.1%	8.9%	10.3%

CHRYSLER*

Sales	$ 7,000	$ 7,052	$ 7,445	$ 6,213	$ 5,650	$ 5,300
Net income before tax and minority interest	(21)	165	611	367	356	448
Tax provision	(8)	80	321	169	164	213
Net income	174	89	291	200	189	233
Capital expenditure	177	375	217	191	306	292
Depreciation—special tools	242	170	162	153	130	102
Expenditure—special tools	173	272	205	201	200	157
Amortization		167	187	161	173	148
Balance Sheet:						
Deferred taxes and ITC		25.6†	23.9†	35.4†	50.1	38.4
Prepaid tax	—	83.7	85.2	67.0	40.5	35.4
Inventory reserve		20	24	6	10	12
E.P.S. (dollars)	(0.16)	1.87	6.23	4.35	4.16	5.44
Dividends (dollars)	0.60	2.00	2.00	2.00	2.00	1.25
Net income/sales	(0.2)%	1.2%	3.9%	3.2%	3.4%	4.4%

* As reported on a Lifo basis, except for 1970 which is on Fifo.

† ITC only. Other deferred taxes not separately stated.

EXHIBIT 6

Selected Auto Manufacturers Stock Prices and Price Earnings Ratio, 1965–1970

	Ford		*General Motors*		*Chrysler*	
	Stock Price Range	*P/E Ratio*	*Stock Price Range*	*P/E Ratio*	*Stock Price Range*	*P/E Ratio*
1970	56–37	8.5	81–59	33.9	35–16	—
1969	54–40	9.7	83–65	12.5	57–31	24.2
1968	60–48	9.5	89–72	13.5	72–48	9.8
1967	55–39	9.4	89–67	13.9	57–31	10.2
1966	57–38	9.9	108–65	13.9	61–29	11.0
1965	62–50	10.1	113–91	13.8	62–41	10.1

EXHIBIT 7

CHRYSLER CORPORATION AND CONSOLIDATED SUBSIDIARIES

Consolidated Statement of Net Earnings

Three months ended March 31, 1971, and 1970

(in millions of dollars)

	1971	1970
Net sales	$1,846.4	$1,511.4
Equity in net earnings (loss) of unconsolidated subsidiaries	(0.7)	(7.2)
Other income and deductions	(5.0)	(6.1)
	$1,840.7	$1,498.1
Cost of products sold, other than items below	$1,580.0	$1,331.3
Depreciation of plant and equipment	43.8	46.1
Amortization of special tools	46.1	42.9
Selling and administrative expenses	96.2	103.5
Pension and retirement plans	39.2	29.9
Interest on long-term debt	12.8	8.7
Taxes on income (credit)	11.3	(32.1)
	$1,829.4	$1,530.3
Net earnings (loss) including minority interest	$ 11.3	$ (32.2)
Minority interest in net (income) loss of consolidated subsidiaries	(0.5)	4.8
Net Earnings (loss)	$ 10.8	$ (27.4)
Average number of shares of common stock outstanding during the period (in thousands)	49,673	48,106
Net earnings (loss) a share	$0.22	$(0.57)

EXHIBIT 7 (continued)

Condensed Consolidated Balance Sheet
March 31, 1971, and 1970
(in millions of dollars)

Assets	1971	1970
Cash and marketable securities	$ 195.6	$ 414.4
Accounts receivable	550.3	555.9
Inventories	1,352.0	1,290.5
Prepaid expenses	78.5	152.7
Income taxes allocable to the following year	16.3	12.8
Total Current Assets	$2,192.7	$2,426.3
Investments and other assets	780.4	689.3
Property, plant, and equipment	2,975.7	2,860.5
Less Accumulated depreciation	1,633.9	1,490.9
	$1,341.8	$1,369.6
Unamortized special tools	440.1	398.6
Net property, plant, and equipment	$1,781.9	$1,768.2
Cost of investments in consolidated subsidiaries in excess of equity	78.5	78.5
Total Assets	$4,833.5	$4,962.3

Liabilities and Shareholders' Investment	1971	1970
Accounts payable	$ 734.9	$ 662.0
Accrued expenses	430.2	411.3
Short-term debt	328.8	641.5
Payments due within one year on long-term debt	31.9	31.7
Taxes on income	37.2	—
Total Current Liabilities	$1,563.0	$1,746.5
Other liabilities	211.7	183.4
Long-Term Debt:		
Notes and debentures payable	654.5	657.2
Convertible sinking fund debentures	120.0	120.0
International operations reserve	35.5	35.5
Minority interest in net assets of consolidated subsidiaries	80.2	90.3
Shareholders' Investment:		
Common stock—par value $6.25 a share (outstanding shares at March 31: 1971—49,858,287 and 1970—48,279,144)	311.6	301.8
Additional paid-in capital	491.4	463.2
Net earnings retained	1,365.6	1,364.4
Total Shareholders' Investment	$2,168.6	$2,129.4
Total liabilities and Shareholders' Investment	$4,833.5	$4,962.3

1970 has been restated to reflect the change in accounting for inventories. Accordingly, the net loss for the first quarter of 1970 is restated at $27.4 million or $0.57 a share, compared to the previously reported net loss of $29.4 million or $0.61 a share.

Chapter 18

INTERCORPORATE INVESTMENTS AND BUSINESS COMBINATIONS

Frequently corporations acquire interests in other corporations ranging from a few shares of capital stock to 100 percent ownership. The reasons for these acquisitions vary from temporary short-term investments of excess funds to permanent investments made to control and direct all operations of the company acquired. The corporation in which an interest is acquired usually continues in existence, but in some instances it may be dissolved by merger into the acquiring company.

As indicated briefly in Chapter 5, the investments of investor companies in the equities of investee companies typically are accounted for by the equity method if the investor owns more than 20 percent of the investee's common stock. Investments of less than 20 percent are accounted for as marketable securities.

Initially, this chapter discusses the accounting for corporate investor holdings of common stock in other companies. Then the topic of business combinations is covered. The principal authoritative statements on the accounting for intercorporate investments and business combinations are: *Opinion No. 10*, "Omnibus Opinion;" *Opinion No. 16*, "Business Combinations"; *Opinion No. 17*, "Intangible Assets"; *Opinion No. 18*, "Equity Method for Investments in Common Stock"; FASB *Statement No. 10*, "Extension of 'Grandfather' Provisions for Business Combinations"; and FASB *Statement No. 12*, "Accounting for Certain Marketable Securities."

EQUITY INVESTMENTS

Opinion No. 18, issued in March 1971, clarified the applicability of the equity method of accounting for investments in the common stock of corporate joint ventures and certain other investments in common stock. Previously, in December 1966, the APB in *Opinion No. 10* made the use of the equity method in consolidated statements mandatory for reporting investments in unconsolidated domestic subsidiaries. *Opinion No. 18* extended the use of the equity method of accounting to all intercorporate investments in voting stock, if the investment in voting stock gave the investor the ability to exercise significant influence over the operating and financial policies of the investee company (even though the investor holds 50 percent or less of the voting stock). The presumption that such control existed must be made, according to the *Opinion,* when an investor's investment in the investee represents 20 percent or more of the investee's voting stock.

Prior to *Opinion No. 18* the cost method was typically used to report such investments. After *Opinion No. 18* the cost method could only be used if the investor could demonstrate that it did not have the ability to significantly influence the investee company. The accounting for investments in marketable equity securities that are not reported by the equity method is set forth primarily in FASB *Statement No. 12.*

Ownership Interests of Less than 20 Percent

Ownership interests of less than 20 percent are typically reported in the same fashion as marketable securities: that is, at cost or market whichever is lower. An investment of less than 20 percent of the voting stock of an investee leads, according to *Opinion No. 18,* to a presumption that the investor does not have the ability to exercise significant influence over the operating and financial policies of the investee. However, if the investor can demonstrate such an ability, then the use of the equity method is permissible.

Initially, stock acquisitions of less than 20 percent are recorded by charging an asset investment account for the investment cost, which includes the purchase price plus all incidental acquisition costs such as broker's commissions. Dividends received as a distribution of earnings subsequent to acquisition are recognized at the time of receipt as dividend income.

Presentation of these investments of the balance sheet and their effect upon current income depends upon whether the investment is made for temporary, short-term reasons or for the purpose of creating some longer term relationship.

FASB *Statement No. 12* requires that if the market value of a portfolio of marketable equity securities is below the portfolio cost at the balance sheet date, the portfolio should be written down to its market value. The amount by which the aggregate cost of the portfolio exceeds the market value is accounted for as a valuation allowance.

That is, the portfolio is presented at cost less the valuation allowance in the balance sheet. If a company classifies some of its marketable securities as current and others as noncurrent, a separate determination of whether or not the portfolio's market value is less than its cost should be made for each of the current and noncurrent portfolios. If marketable equity securities are included in an unclassified balance sheet, the portfolio should be accounted for in the same way as a portfolio classified as a noncurrent asset.

Changes in the valuation allowance for a marketable equity security portfolio classified as a current asset must be included in the determination of net income in the period in which the change occurs. Accumulated changes in the valuation allowance for a marketable equity security portfolio included in the noncurrent assets should be included in the equity section of the balance sheet as an identifiable item. Should the market value of a current or noncurrent portfolio of marketable equity securities rise above the portfolio's cost and eliminate any previously recorded valuation allowance, no unrealized gain above the cost is recognized. Unrealized gains can only be recorded up to the amount of the valuation allowance.

If a security's current-noncurrent classification is changed, the security is transferred at the lower of its cost or market value at the transfer date. If the market value of the security is less than its cost, the market value becomes the new cost basis and the difference between the new and old cost basis is included in the determination of net income.

Ownership Interests of More than 20 Percent

Since *Opinion No. 18*, ownership interests of more than 20 percent are accounted for by the equity method on the statements of the investor company. These ownership interests can fall into a number of different categories. These categories determine whether or not the investment should be fully consolidated or not in consolidated statements and whether or not comprehensive tax allocation may be required when reporting the investor's share of the investee's undistributed earnings.

The acquisition of more than one half of the voting capital stock of a corporation creates a parent and subsidiary relationship. The company owning the controlling interest is the parent (or holding) company, and the controlled corporation is the subsidiary company. In this case, if the subsidiary qualifies for full consolidation (see Chapter 5), the investment will be reported on a fully consolidated basis in the consolidated statements of the investor company.

On the other hand, investments of 50 percent and less (but more than 20 percent) do not qualify for full consolidation. They are accounted for by the equity method on both the investee's parent company statement and the investee's consolidated statement.

As indicated in Chapter 12, a tax accrual for an investor's share of 50 percent or more in an investee's undistributed earnings may or may not be required, depending on whether or not the undistributed profits are reinvested by the investee for an indefinite time. In contrast, tax accrual accounting is required for interests of less than 50 percent, irrespective of the investee's retained earnings policy.

Cost and Equity Methods Illustrated.   An investor corporation records the acquisition of an equity interest in an investee by charging the cost of the stock purchased to an investment account. Cost is the cash price paid or the fair market value of the property exchanged. Subsequent to acquisition, the relationship with the subsidiary may be recorded by the parent using either (1) the cost method or (2) the equity method, depending on whether or not the equity method reporting criteria of *Opinion No. 18* are met.

The cost method maintains the separate legal distinction between corporate entities. This method gives no recognition to the subsidiary company's earnings or losses in the parent's records. The investment account includes only the amounts invested in the investee by the investor corporation. Dividends from the subsidiary are credited to income at time of receipt.

After the initial acquisition cost has been entered in the parent's investment account, the *equity method* subsequently adds or subtracts from this amount the parent's proportional share of the changes in the subsidiary's retained earnings. The investment account increases as the parent's share of the subsidiary's reported earnings is credited to an income account. Dividends received from the subsidiary reduce the investment account. As a result of these entries, the investment account reflects initial cost plus or minus the parent's share of the change in the subsidiary's retained earnings subsequent to acquisition.

Illustration 18–1 summarizes the accounting entries in the parent's books applying the cost method and the equity method.

Under the equity method, it is mandatory that the parent charge against the income from the subsidiary a portion of the difference between the cost of the parent's investment in the subsidiary and the net worth of the subsidiary represented by the parent's investment. If a parent purchased a subsidiary company with net worth of $1.5 million for $2 million, the $500,000 differential must be amortized against that portion of the subsidiary's income recognized in the parent's accounts over a reasonable period. However, the parent should not recognize appreciation in the subsidiary's net worth, except that provided by earnings.

ILLUSTRATION 18–1

Cost and Equity Methods of Accounting for Intercorporate Investments

Transaction	Investor Owns Less than 20%—Cost Method		Investor Owns More than 20%—Equity Method	
(a) Investor acquires part of investee company's stock for $200,000	(a) Investment .... Cash	200,000 200,000	(a) Investments .... Cash	200,000 200,000
(b) Investee reports $40,000 earnings	(b) No entry		(b) Investments .... Income	32,000 32,000
(c) Investee pays $20,000 in dividends	(c) Cash .... Dividend Income	3,800* 3,800	(c) Cash .... Investments	16,000 16,000
(d) Investee reports $20,000 loss	(d) No entry		(d) Income .... Investments	16,000† 16,000†

* $20,000 × 0.19 (assumes 19 percent ownership).
† $20,000 × 0.80 (assumes 80 percent ownership).

The APB *Opinion No. 18* noted that the difference between consolidation and the equity method lay in the details reported in the financial statements, not in the stockholders' equity and income determination goal. Therefore, the equity method should be applied in such a way as to produce the same stockholders' equity and net income as would be the case in consolidation.[1] Accordingly, to achieve this result the *Opinion* set forth the following detailed procedures that must be followed by investors in applying the equity method to investments which qualify for the equity method:

a. Intercompany profits and losses should be eliminated until realized by the investor or investee as if a subsidiary, corporate joint venture or investee company were consolidated.

b. A difference between the cost of an investment and the amount of underlying equity in net assets of an investee should be accounted for as if the investee were a consolidated subsidiary.

c. The investment(s) in common stock should be shown in the balance sheet of an investor as a single amount, and the investor's share of earnings or losses of an investee(s) should ordinarily be shown in the income statement as a single amount except for the extraordinary items as specified in (d) below.

d. The investor's share of extraordinary items and its share of prior-period adjustments reported in the financial statements of the investee in accordance with APB *Opinions No. 9* (and *No. 30*) should be classified in a similar manner unless they are immaterial in the income statement of the investor.

e. A transaction of an investee of a capital nature that affects the investor's share of stockholders' equity of the investee should be accounted for as if the investee were a consolidated subsidiary.

f. Sales of stock of an investee by an investor should be accounted for as gains or losses equal to the difference at the time of sale between selling price and carrying amount of the stock sold.

g. If financial statements of an investee are not sufficiently timely for an investor to apply the equity method currently, the investor ordinarily should record its share of the earnings or losses of an investee from the most recent available financial statements. A lag in reporting should be consistent from period to period.

h. A loss in value of an investment which is other than a temporary decline should be recognized the same as a loss in value of other long-term assets. Evidence of a loss in value might include, but would not necessarily be limited to, absence of an ability to recover the carrying amount of the investment or inability of the investee to sustain an earnings capacity which would justify the carrying amount of the investment. A current fair value of an investment that is less than its carrying amount may indicate a loss in value of the investment. However, a decline in the quoted market price below the carrying amount or the existence of operating losses is not

---

[1] The equity method is sometimes referred to as "one-line consolidation."

necessarily indicative of a loss in value that is other than temporary. All are factors to be evaluated.

i. An investor's share of losses of an investee may equal or exceed the carrying amount of an investment accounted for by the equity method plus advances made by the investor. The investor ordinarily should discontinue applying the equity method when the investment (and net advances) is reduced to zero and should not provide for additional losses unless the investor has guaranteed obligations of the investee or is otherwise committed to provide further financial support for the investee. If the investee subsequently reports net income, the investor should resume applying the equity method only after its share of that net income equals the share of net losses not recognized during the period the equity method was suspended.

j. The guides for income taxes on undistributed earnings of subsidiaries in consolidation should apply.

k. When an investee has outstanding cumulative preferred stock, an investor should compute its share of earnings (losses) after deducting the investee's preferred dividends, whether or not such dividends are declared.

l. An investment in voting stock of an investee company may fall below the 20 percent level of ownership from sale of a portion of an investment by the investor, sale of additional stock by an investee, or other transactions and the investor may thereby lose the ability to influence policy. An investor should discontinue accruing its share of the earnings or losses of the investee for an investment that no longer qualifies for the equity method. The earnings or losses that relate to the stock retained by the investor and that were previously accrued should remain as a part of the carrying amount of the investment. The investment account should not be adjusted retroactively. However, dividends received by the investor in subsequent periods which exceed his share of earnings for such periods should be applied in reduction of the carrying amount of the investment.

m. An investment in common stock of an investee that was previously accounted for on other than the equity method may become qualified for use of the equity method by an increase in the level of ownership (i.e., acquisition of additional voting stock by the investor, acquisition or retirement of voting stock by the investee, or other transactions). When an investment qualifies for use of the equity method, the investor should adopt the equity method of accounting. The investment, results of operations (current and prior periods presented), and retained earnings of the investor should be adjusted retroactively in a manner consistent with the accounting for a step-by-step acquisition of a subsidiary.

n. The carrying amount of an investment in common stock of an investee that qualifies for the equity method of accounting as described in subparagraph (m) may differ from the underlying equity in net assets of the investee. The difference should affect the determination of the amount of the investor's share of earnings or losses of an investee as if the investee were a consolidated subsidiary. However, if the investor is unable to relate the difference to specific accounts of the investee, the difference should be considered to be goodwill and amortized over a period not to exceed forty years, in accordance with APB *Opinion No. 17.*

Ability to Influence.   Whether or not an investor has the ability to exercise significant influence over the operating and financial policies of an investee could be difficult to determine in practice. In order to achieve a reasonable degree of uniformity in the application of *Opinion No. 18,* the APB concluded that a direct or indirect investment of 20 percent or more in the voting stock of an investee should lead to the presumption that in the absence of evidence to the contrary an investor has the ability to exercise a significant influence over an investee.

An investor's voting stock interest in an investee is based on the current outstanding stock held by stockholders who have voting privileges. Potential voting privileges which may become available to holders of securities of an investee are disregarded. Furthermore, an investor's share of the earnings or losses of an investee is based on the shares of common stock held by an investor, without recognition of securities of the investee which are designated as "common stock equivalents" under APB *Opinion No. 15.*

If, despite a holding of more than 20 percent of an investee's voting stock, an investor can present evidence that suggests that the presumption of ability to influence is not warranted, the investor can use the cost method to account for the investment. Such a situation may arise in the case of an investor company that owns 30 percent of an investee but for antitrust reason has entered into an agreement with the government not to participate in the investee's affairs. Similarly, these are some examples of investor companies that have used the equity method to account for their investments in companies where their equity interest was less than 20 percent of the investee's voting stock. Usually in these cases the investor controls the board of directors, despite the small stock holding.

Disclosure.   Typically, when the investment in other company's common stock is significant relative to the investor's financial position and net income, the following disclosures are appropriate:

a.   Financial statements of an investor should disclose parenthetically, in notes to financial statements, or in separate statements or schedules (1) the name of each investee and percentage of ownership of common stock, (2) the accounting policies of the investor with respect to investments in common stock, and (3) the difference, if any, between the amount at which an investment is carried and the amount of underlying equity in net assets and the accounting treatment of the difference.

b.   For those investments in common stock for which a quoted market price is available, the aggregate value of each identified investment based on the quoted market price usually should be disclosed. This disclosure is not required for investments in common stock of subsidiaries.

c. When investments in unconsolidated subsidiaries are, in the aggregate, material in relation to financial position or results of operations, summarized information as to assets, liabilities, and results of operations should be presented in the notes or separate statements should be presented for such subsidiaries, either individually or in groups, as appropriate.

d. When investments in common stock of corporate joint ventures or other investments of 50% or less accounted for under the equity method are, in the aggregate, material in relation to the financial position or results of operations of an investor, it may be necessary for summarized information as to assets, liabilities, and results of operations of the investees to be presented in the notes or in separate statements, either individually or in groups, as appropriate.

e. Conversion of outstanding convertible securities, exercise of outstanding options and warrants and other contingent issuances of an investee may have a significant effect on an investor's share of reported earnings or losses. Accordingly, material effects of possible conversions, exercises or contingent issuances should be disclosed in notes to the financial statements of an investor.

BUSINESS COMBINATIONS: TWO APPROACHES

A business combination occurs when two or more businesses are joined together as one entity to continue the same business activities each had carried on previously. Business combinations include all those changes in corporate ownership which are termed mergers, purchases, consolidations, poolings, amalgamations, and acquisitions. The financial accounting issue raised in recording and reporting business combinations centers upon the valuation of the assets which are brought together in a business unit. The two methods used to record business combinations are: (1) the purchase method and (2) the pooling of interest method.

Purchase Method

Under the purchase method of recording a business combination, the assets of the acquired entity are recorded at their fair market value on the books of the acquirer. This alternative treats the acquisition as if the dominant business had bought the net assets of another business and established a new cost basis for these acquired assets. All acquisitions of other companies except those involving an exchange of common stock which meets all of the restrictive conditions for a pooling of interest set forth in *Opinion No. 16* must be recorded by the purchase method. (Those that meet these specific conditions for a pooling of interest *must* be accounted for by the pooling of interest method, as indicated later.)

Purchase Method Illustration. The accounting for purchases can be illustrated by a relatively simple example of a business combination.

Company A acquired Company B intending to continue the operations of both companies as a single unit. Company B's financial position at the date of acquisition was as follows:

	Book Value	Fair Market Value
Net current assets	$100,000	$100,000
Fixed assets	400,000	700,000
Total	$500,000	$800,000
Capital stock	$300,000	
Retained earnings	200,000	
Total	$500,000	

Company A paid $900,000 cash for Company B. The accounting entry in Company A's records is:

Net Current Assets	100,000	
Fixed Assets	700,000	
Excess of Purchase Price over Net Assets Acquired	100,000	
Cash		900,000

This transaction is clearly a purchase of Company B by Company A. The previous owners of Company B received cash and retained no ownership in the new business unit. Consequently, subsequent operations will be charged with depreciation based on fixed asset costs of $700,000, which is the fair market value of the assets acquired. The excess of the purchase price over the assets acquired is typically called goodwill. It is first recorded as an asset and subsequently charged to operations over a period of years not to exceed 40, as specified in *Opinion No. 17.* It is important to note that income from the acquired company will be included in Company A's accounts only from the date of acquisition, and Company B's retained earnings at acquisition are not carried over to Company A.

Pooling of Interest Method

Under the pooling of interest method, all assets of the newly combined group are valued at the same amounts at which they were previously carried in the accounts of the individual predecessor businesses. Underlying this alternative is the presumption that no new business entity had been created. Instead, it is assumed that ownership groups have merely contributed assets (or pooled resources) to carry on operations in an organization which is substantially a continuation of the preceding entities. Therefore, there is no reason to change asset values from those carried by the predecessor businesses.

Pooling of Interest Illustration. Using the example presented earlier, assume that Company A issued its own capital stock with a par value of $200,000 and a fair market value of $900,000 in payment for Company B, instead of paying $900,000 cash. In this transaction, the choice of the pooling of interest method can be strongly supported. The new entity is owned jointly by all stockholders of the previously separate corporations. The total assets and liabilities and retained earnings are undiminished and unchanged by the combinations. The stockholders of two corporations have merely pooled assets and liabilities and retained pro rata ownership in the new entity.

The combination would be entered on Company A's records as follows:

Net Current Assets	100,000	
Fixed Assets	400,000	
Capital Stock		200,000
Capital in Excess of Par Value		100,000
Retained Earnings		200,000

It should be noted that subsequent operations of the combined companies will be charged with depreciation based upon the original $400,000 book value of Company B's fixed assets. Also, no goodwill is recognized and no related problems of subsequent amortization or write-off are encountered. Further, the retained earnings of Company B are carried over into the combination, and the paid-in capital accounts are adjusted to reflect any differences between the par value of Company B stock and the par value of stock issued by Company A.

Company A's statement of results of operations for the accounting period in which Company B was acquired will include the combined results of operations of the constituent interests for the entire annual accounting period in which the combination was effected.

OPINION NO. 16, "BUSINESS COMBINATIONS"

In August 1970, the APB issued *Opinion No. 16,* "Business Combinations" to clarify criteria for using the purchase and pooling methods to account for business combinations. It concluded that both methods were acceptable in accounting for business combinations, but not as alternatives under the same conditions. A business combination meeting specified conditions *required* the pooling of interest method. All other combinations were *required* to use the purchase method. Furthermore, a single method must be applied. Therefore such transactions as a part purchase, part pooling were no longer acceptable.

Conditions Requiring Pooling Treatment

Pooling of interest was defined in *Opinion No. 16* as the presentation as a single interest of two or more common stockholder interests that were previously independent and the combined rights and risks represented by those interests. The use of this method showed that the combining stockholder groups neither withdrew nor invested assets, but simply exchanged voting common stock in a ratio that determined their respective interests in the combined corporation.

The pooling of interest method could only be used if the transaction met all of the conditions specified in the opinion. In fact, if all of these conditions were met, the pooling of interest method had to be used. These basic conditions fall under three categories:

1. With Respect to the Combining Companies

a. Each of the combining companies is autonomous and has not been a subsidiary or a division of another company within two years before the plan of combination is initiated.

b. Each of the combining companies is independent of the other companies. (Independence existed if neither of the combining companies held as intercorporate investments more than 10 percent in total of the outstanding voting common stock of the other combining company.)

2. With Respect to the Manner of Combining of Interests

a. The combination is effected in a single transaction or is completed in accordance with a specific plan within one year after the plan is initiated.

b. A corporation offers and issues only common stock with rights identical to those of the majority of its outstanding voting common stock in exchange for substantially all of the voting common stock interest of another company at the date the plan of combination is consummated.

c. None of the combining companies changes the equity interests of the voting common stock in contemplation of effecting the combination, either within two years before the plan of combination is initiated or between the dates the combination is initiated and consummated; changes in contemplation of effecting the combination may include distributions to stockholders and additional issuances, exchanges, and retirement of securities.

d. Each of the combining companies reacquires shares of voting common stock only for purposes other than business combinations, and no company reacquires more than a normal number of shares between the dates the plan of combination is initiated and consummated.

e. The ratio of the interest of an individual common stockholder to those of other common stockholders in a combining company remains the same as a result of the exchange of stock to effect the combination.

f. The voting rights to which the common stock ownership interests in the resulting combined corporation are entitled are exercisable by the stockholder; the stockholders are neither deprived nor restricted in exercising those rights for a period of years.

g. The combination is resolved at the date the plan is consummated, and no provision of the plan relating to the issue of securities or other considerations is pending.

3. With Respect to the Absence of Planned Transactions

a. The combined corporation does not agree directly or indirectly to retire or reacquire all or part of the common stock issued to effect the combination.

b. The combined corporation does not enter into other financial arrangements for the benefit of the former stockholders of a combining company, such as a guaranty of loans secured by stock issued in the combination which in effect negates the exchange of equity securities.

c. The combined corporation does not intend or plan to dispose of a significant part of the assets of the combining companies within two years after the combination, other than disposals in the ordinary course of business of the formerly separate companies and to eliminate duplicated facilities of excess capacity.

Originally the APB had proposed to include a size test in *Opinion No. 16*. The first proposal was to limit poolings to acquisitions of companies that were at least 25 percent of the size of the combined company based on the distribution of relative voting rights in the new entity. Later, this test was reduced to 10 percent after considerable opposition by business executives to the original proposal. Eventually, the APB failed to get approval of this more limited size test among its members and, as a result, *Opinion No. 16* did not include a size test.

The 90 Percent Test

The primary source of technical problems in applying these criteria is the definition of "substantially all of the voting common stock" which must be exchanged (see 2*b* above).

The text of *Opinion No. 16* states that substantially all of the voting common stock means "90 percent or more." That is, at the date the combination is consummated, one of the combining companies (issuing corporation) issues voting common stock in exchange for at least 90 percent of the outstanding voting common stock of the other company (combining company).

For the purposes of computing the 90 percent figure, shares of the combining company are excluded if they were (1) acquired before and held by the issuing corporation and its subsidiaries at the date the plan of combination is initiated, regardless of the form of consideration; (2) acquired by the issuing corporation and its subsidiaries after the date the plan of combination is initiated other than by issuing its own voting common stock; or (3) outstanding after the date the combination is consummated.

An investment in the stock of the issuing corporation by a combining company may prevent a combination from meeting the 90 percent criterion, even though the investment of the combining company may not be more than 10 percent of the outstanding stock of the issuing corporation. To determine whether or not an investment by the company being acquired in the stock of the issuing corporation precludes use of the pooling method, this stock investment must be expressed as an equivalent number of shares of the combining company, because the 90 percent of shares exchanged criterion is expressed in terms of shares of stock of the combining company. The procedure for this translation is shown in Illustration 18–2.

ILLUSTRATION 18–2

Reduction of Shares Exchanged Due to Intercorporate Investment

Assume:

1. Company A (issuing company) agrees on March 31, 1970, to issue one share of A stock for each four shares of Company B.
2. Company B on March 31 has 100,000 shares of its own stock outstanding, and holds 2,000 shares of A as an investment.*
3. By March 31, 1971, Company A has issued 24,000 shares of its stock for 96,000 shares of B.

The required computation:

Shares of B exchanged for A	96,000
Shares of A held by B restated on basis of rate of exchange (2,000 shares of A @ 4:1)	8,000
Defined number of shares exchanged	88,000
Number of shares exchanged required for pooling	90,000

* The effect of the computation would be the same is B had purchased all or part of the 2,000 shares for cash after the combination plan had been initiated.

A combination of more than two companies is evaluated essentially as a combination of two companies. The percentage of voting common stock is measured separately for each combining company.

Accounting Mechanics

The pooling of interest method requires that the recorded assets and liabilities of the separate companies be combined at their historical cost basis. However, since the separate companies may have recorded assets and liabilities under differing methods of accounting, it is permissible to adjust the amounts to the same basis of accounting if the change would otherwise have been appropriate for the separate company. Such a change in accounting method to make the accounts conform should be applied retroactively, and financial statements for prior periods should be restated.

The stockholders' equities are also combined as part of the pooling of interests, including the capital stock, capital in excess of par value, and retained earnings or deficits. If the par value of the total outstanding stock exceeds the capital stock of the separate combining companies, the excess is deducted first from contributed capital, then from retained earnings.

If treasury stock is used to effect a combination, this treasury stock should first be treated as retired, and the stock issued in the combination then treated as if it were previously unissued shares.

The treatment of stock of the combining companies held by another company depends on whether the holder is the issuing company or another combining company. If the investment of a combining company is in the common stock of the issuing company, it is, in effect, returned to the resulting combined corporation and should be treated as treasury stock. In contrast, an investment in the common stock of another combining company (not the issuing company) is an investment in stock that is exchanged in the combination for the common stock issued. This stock is in effect eliminated in the combination, and would be treated as retired stock.

Reporting Requirements

A corporation that uses the pooling of interests method of accounting for a combination should report results of operations for the period in which the combination occurs as though the companies had been combined as of the beginning of the period. Results of operations for that period thus comprise those of the separate companies combined from the beginning of the period to the date the combination is consummated, and those of the combined operations from that date to the end of the period. The effects of intercompany transactions on current assets, liabilities, revenues, and cost of sales for the periods presented, and on retained earnings at the beginning of the periods presented, should be eliminated to the extent possible. The nature of an effects on earnings per share of nonrecurring intercompany transactions involving long-term assets and liabilities (such as fixed assets purchased before the combining date), need not be eliminated, but should be disclosed.

The combined corporation should disclose in notes to its financial statements the revenue, extraordinary items, and net income of each of the separate companies from the beginning of the period to the date of combination. In addition, balance sheet and financial information presented for prior years should be restated on a combined basis to furnish comparative information. Such data should clearly indicate the nature of the information.

Expenses incurred in effecting a business combination accounted for as a pooling of interests should be deducted in determining the net income of the combined corporation for the period in which the expenses are incurred. Such expenses include such items as registration fees and costs of furnishing information to stockholders.

Disclosure of Poolings

A combined corporation is required to disclose in its financial statements that a combination which is accounted for by the pooling of interests method has occurred during the period. The basis of the current presentation and restatements of prior periods may be disclosed in the financial statements by captions or by reference to the notes.

Notes to the financial statements of a combined corporation should disclose the following for the period in which a business combination occurs:

1. Name and brief description of the companies combined, except a corporation whose name is carried forward.
2. Description and number of shares of stock issued.
3. Details of the results of operations of the previously separate companies for the period before the combination was consummated that are included in the current combined income. The details should include revenue, extraordinary items, net income, other changes in stockholders' equity, and the amount of and manner of accounting for intercompany transactions.
4. Descriptions of the nature of any adjustments of net assets of the combining companies in order to adopt the same accounting prac-

tices and the effects of these changes on net income reported previously by the separate companies and now presented in comparative financial statements.

5. Details of an increase or decrease in retained earnings from changing the fiscal year of a combining company. The details should include at least revenue, expenses, extraordinary items, net income, and other changes in stockholders' equity for the period excluded from the reported results of operations.

6. Reconciliations of amounts of revenue and earnings previously reported by the corporation that issues the stock to effect the combination with the combined amounts currently presented in financial statements and summaries. A new corporation formed to effect a combination may instead disclose the earnings of separate companies which comprise combined earnings for the prior periods.

Business combinations consummated before the financial statements are issued, but which are either incomplete as of the date of the financial statements or initiated after that date, cannot be included in the statements of the prior period. However, the notes to the financial statements should disclose details of the effects of such combinations. The details should include revenue, net income, earnings per share, and the effects of anticipated changes in accounting methods as if the combination had been consummated at the date of the financial statements.

Purchase Accounting

The principal accounting issues to be decided in mergers required to be accounted for by the purchase method are:

1. Which company is the acquirer?
2. How much did the acquirer pay for the purchase?
3. What adjustments are required to the book values of the individual assets acquired and liabilities assumed so that these values on the acquirer's book reflect their net realizable value or fair market value?
4. How should any differences between the purchase price and those adjusted book values be handled in the accounts of the acquired?

Opinion No. 16 and *No. 17*, which were issued concurrently, discuss these issues.

Acquirer Characteristics.   A corporation which distributes cash or other assets or incurs liabilities to obtain the assets or stock of another corporation is clearly the acquirer. In most cases involving exchanges of stock, the APB concluded that presumptive evidence of the acquiring corporation in combinations effected by an exchange of stock is obtained by identifying the former common stockholder interests which either retain or receive the larger portion of the voting rights in the combined corporation, unless other evidence clearly indicates that another corporation is the acquirer.

Purchase Price Determination.   The responsibility for determining the purchase price rests with the acquiring company. The general principles governing this determination are:

1. Assets acquired by exchanging cash or other assets are recorded at cost, which is the amount of cash disbursed or the fair value of the assets distributed.
2. Assets acquired by assuming liabilities are recorded at cost, which is the present value of the amounts to be paid.
3. Assets acquired by issuing stock are recorded at the fair value of the stock or the fair value of the consideration given up for the stock.

The difficulty of determining the "fair value" of noncash assets or stock given up by the acquirer has led to the rule that their "cost may be determined either by the fair value of the consideration given or by the fair value of the property acquired, whichever is more clearly evident."

Book Value Adjustments.   The acquiring company is responsible for making any required adjustment to the book values of assets acquired and liabilities assumed as a result of the purchase. *Opinion No. 16* presented some guidelines for this assignment of the purchase price. They are:

1. Marketable securities should be recorded at their current net realizable values.
2. The amounts shown for receivables should be the present values of amounts to be received determined at appropriate current interest rates, less allowances for uncollectibility and collection costs, if necessary.
3. Inventories:
    a. Finished goods and merchandise should be recorded at their selling prices less the sum of (1) cost of disposal and (2) a reasonable profit allowance for the selling effort of the acquiring corporation.
    b. Work in process must be valued at the estimated selling prices of finished goods less the sum of (1) costs to complete, (2) costs of disposal, and (3) a reasonable profit allowance for the completing and selling effort of the acquiring corporation based on profit for similar finished goods.
    c. Raw materials have to be restated to their current replacement costs.

4. Plant and equipment: (a) to be used, stated at current replacement costs for similar capacity unless the expected future use of the assets indicated a lower value to the acquirer; (b) to be sold or held for later sale rather than used, adjusted to its current net realizable value; and (c) to be used temporarily, presented at its current net realizable value recognizing future depreciation for the expected period of use.

5. Intangible assets which can be identified and named, including contracts, patents, franchises, customer and supplier lists, and favorable leases, should be recorded at their appraised values.[2]

6. Other assets, including land, natural resources, and nonmarketable securities, must be presented at their appraised values.

7. The amounts shown for accounts and notes payable, long-term debt, and other claims payable should be the present values of amounts to be paid determined at appropriate current interest rates.

8. Similarly, the amounts recorded for liabilities and accruals—for example, accruals for pension cost, warranties, vacation pay, deferred compensation—must be present values of amounts to be paid determined at appropriate current interest rates.

9. Other liabilities and commitments, including unfavorable leases, contracts, and commitments, and plant closing expense incident to the acquisition, should be recorded at the present value of amounts to be paid determined at appropriate current interest rates.

Additional rules are: an acquiring corporation should record periodically as a part of income the accrual of interest on assets and liabilities recorded at acquisition date at the discounted values of amounts to be received or paid (see Illustration 18–3 on page 542). An acquiring corporation should not record as a separate asset the goodwill previously recorded by an acquired company and should not record deferred income taxes recorded by an acquired company before its acquisition. An acquiring corporation should reduce the acquired goodwill retroactively for the realized tax benefits of loss carry-forwards of an acquired company not previously recorded by the acquiring corporation.

GOODWILL

Goodwill purchased as a part of an acquisition must be amortized, according to *Opinion No. 17.* (Previously, the common practice was not to amortize goodwill.) The goodwill amortization can be based on

---

[2] Fair values should be ascribed to specific assets; identifiable assets should not be included in goodwill.

ILLUSTRATION 18–3
Implementation of APB *Opinion No. 16*
Purchase Accounting Using Discounted Values

	Book Value	Basis of Valuation	Value for Purchase Accounting
Current Assets:			
Cash	$ 10,000	Actual	$ 10,000
Accounts receivable (net) ...	90,000	Discounted @ 8%, 1 year* ..	83,340
Fixed assets	400,000	Reproduction cost	700,000
	$500,000		$793,340
Accounts payable	$ 10,000	Actual	$ 10,000
Long-term debt	90,000	Five years @ 8%	61,290
	$100,000		$ 71,290
Net Value of Purchases	$400,000		$722,050

Net Charge against Income:

In year 1:	Income (accounts receivable, 90,000 − 83,340)	$6,660	
	Expense (long-term debt†)	4,860	
	Net Credit to Income	$1,800	

---

* Assume, for the purposes of the example, that accounts receivable are due one year from this date (90,000 @ 0.926).

† Present value of debt @ 8%, payable in 4 years (90,000 @ 0.735) $66,150
Present value of debt @ 8%, payable in 5 years (90,000 @ 0.681) 61,290

Change in present value of debt .... $ 4,860

anticipated loss in value if a logical basis can be determined. Otherwise, it must be amortized over a period not to exceed 40 years on a straight-line basis.

The Nature of Goodwill

It is difficult to give a precise definition of the nature of goodwill, since every business situation gives rise to a different mutation. However, in most situations it can be considered, in the technical sense, as simply being the cost paid for a business in excess of the fair market value of its net tangible and intangible assets for the expectation of earnings in excess of a normal return on these assets. It is only through such a transaction that good will can be recognized on the books of a company. Goodwill is an integral part of a business and cannot be regarded as an asset which is salable independent of the business.

"Negative Goodwill"

Sometimes companies are purchased for a price less than their net book value. In these so-called bargain purchase cases, a "negative goodwill" or an "excess of book value of assets acquired over cost" item is created. If, after adjusting the book value of the assets acquired and liabilities assumed, the sum of the market or appraisal values of the assets acquired less liabilities still exceeds the purchase cost, the values assignable to noncurrent assets acquired (except marketable securities) should be reduced proportionately. Under *Opinion No. 16*, negative goodwill is prohibited unless such long-term assets are reduced to zero value. If such negative goodwill is then recorded, it must be amortized systematically as a credit to income over the period estimated to be benefited, so long as the period is not in excess of 40 years. In addition, the method and period of amortization must be disclosed in the financial statements.[3]

Goodwill Tax Consideration

Under the Internal Revenue Code, the cost of self-developed intangibles and goodwill is deductible in the year paid or incurred, even though it may have a useful life extending beyond the taxable year. Such items are considered to be an ordinary and necessary expense of doing business. In contrast, the cost of a purchased intangible cannot be amortized or depreciated for tax purposes, unless it can be demonstrated that it has a limited life which can be estimated with reasonable accuracy. Under this provision, the purchase price of intangibles such as copyrights, patents, and other contracts of limited duration may be deducted from taxable income. However, purchased goodwill is expressly denied this treatment. The tax code assumes that the life of goodwill cannot be estimated reasonably. Consequently, the asset goodwill must, for tax purposes, be carried as an asset until the business giving rise to this item is sold. At that time the tax basis of the business sold will be the market price paid originally for the business, which included goodwill.

RESEARCH EFFORTS OF THE APB

Over the years the accounting for business combinations deteriorated to the point where it was one of the most controversial unresolved

---

[3] Before *Opinion No. 16* and *No. 17*, to the extent that negative goodwill was attributable to certain depreciable assets, it was allocated to them. This resulted in a corresponding downward adjustment of the assets' related depreciation. Any negative goodwill was either combined with any positive goodwill already on the balance sheet or carried on the right-hand side of the balance sheet and amortized over some appropriate period. The netting approach was defended on the basis of conservatism. However, since there was no logical relationship between the negative and positive goodwill items created in separate transactions, the preferred method became that of crediting the excess to income in future periods on a reasonable and systematic basis.

problem areas in financial accounting in the late 1960s. Most of the controversy centered on two issues: the criteria for a pooling of interests and the treatment of goodwill. Two APB research studies examined these problems.

ARS No. 10

In 1968, Catlett and Olson concluded that business combinations in which a continuing entity survives are in essence purchase transactions and that the pooling of interest method is not appropriate in such combinations. Furthermore, they concluded that in those "relatively rare" combinations where no constituent company clearly emerges as the continuing entity, a new business has in effect been created. In these cases, the accounting should be similar to that for new companies: the assets and rights should be recorded at fair market value and no goodwill recognized. Based on these conclusions, they recommended that the pooling of interest method be discontinued as an acceptable accounting practice.

ARS No. 10 argued that by treating most combinations that then qualified as pooling of interests as purchases, financial statements would be more useful to investors. First, the fair market value of separable assets and property rights would be disclosed. Second, assigning fair market, rather than book, values to acquired assets would result in more realistic depreciation charges. Third, the amount paid for goodwill would be fully disclosed. The goodwill would be charged directly against the retained earnings of the acquiring corporation as an advance payment by the current stockholders for excess future earnings.

ARS No. 5

Earlier, in 1963, Wyatt had reached similar conclusions. He recommended that the pooling of interests concept be dropped and replaced by a "fair-value pooling" concept. He argued that the fair-value pooling treatment should only be applied to those business combinations in which (a) the constituent combinations approximate each other in size; (b) it is difficult to determine which constituent acquired the other; and (c) the facts of the transaction clearly indicate that the combined entity is a new enterprise. All other combinations should be treated as purchases.

The fair-value pooling method records the assets of the new enterprise created through a combination at their fair market value. Normally, because it is essentially a new enterprise, the combined entity would not begin operations with any retained earnings. However, if required for legal or regulatory purpose, the combined entity may record as retained earnings that amount of the constituent companies' retained earnings which is legally available for dividends.

Criticisms

A number of accountants and business executives disagreed with the conclusions of Wyatt, Catlett, and Olson. They argued that pooling of interests and purchase accounting were appropriate methods for accounting for business combinations and that many combinations were in effect pooling of interests. The challenge, they believed, was to identify the proper circumstances when each approach is appropriate.

Some accountants argue that combinations effected by cash are in substance different from those effected by stock, and a different method of accounting should be applied to each. Acquisitions for cash, they argue, should be treated as purchases, since one company gains control over the assets of another. An exchange of shares means that both groups of stockholders continue their ownership interest and a genuine pooling of interests takes place, a fact which the accounting should reflect. While agreeing with this basic position, those who consider continuity of ownership interest as the key criteria for pooling believe purchase accounting is appropriate for combinations if either a material minority interest in a subsidiary company exists after acquisition of the subsidiary or if a material amount of preferred stock, either voting or nonvoting, has been used for the acquisition.

Others question the practicality of the fair-value pooling concept proposed by Wyatt for combinations which in essence create "a new enterprise." In their opinion, the tests for determining whether or not a new enterprise has in fact been created are not clear and, hence, not operational.

The continuing controversy over what is the appropriate accounting for business combinations led the FASB to add the issue to its agenda in 1976.

SUGGESTED FURTHER READING

CATLETT, GEORGE R., and OLSON, NORMAN O. "Accounting for Goodwill." *Accounting Research Study No. 10.* New York: American Institute of Certified Public Accountants, 1968.

FINANCIAL ACCOUNTING STANDARDS BOARD. "Accounting for Business Combinations and Purchased Intangibles." *FASB Discussion Memorandum.* Stamford, 1976.

WYATT, ARTHUR R. "A Critical Study of Accounting for Business Combinations." *Accounting Research Study No. 5.* New York: American Institute of Certified Public Accountants, 1963.

CASES

CASE 18–1. WILLISTON INTERNATIONAL INDUSTRIES
Purchase Accounting

On December 30, 1974, the Williston International board of directors voted to complete the acquisition as of December 30, 1974, of Erikson Machinery, a manufacturer and distributor of similar equipment to that sold by Williston.

Erikson was established by three brothers: Lionel Erikson, the founder, and currently the president, owned 60 percent of the common stock. Peter Erikson, currently vice president and treasurer, owned 25 percent. Of the remainder of the stock, 10 percent was held by Burger Erikson, the only son of Tor Erikson, the third brother, and Williston International held the rest. The two officers had previously agreed to exchange one share of $5 par-value Erikson stock for three shares Williston stock; Burger Erikson had refused to agree to the exchange.

Williston International Industries stock was traded over the counter. In late December the average of bid and ask prices was $50.

Erikson stock had been purchased by Williston when the company was first established. Raymond Stevens, Williston's president at that time, had been a close friend of Lionel Erikson. After Mr. Stevens's death, Williston continued to hold the 5 percent stock interest in Erikson as an investment. There were no intercompany relationships or transactions.

The estimated financial statements of the Erikson Company at December 31, 1974, are presented in Exhibit 1, and of Williston in Exhibit 2.

Questions

1. Which treatment, pooling or purchase, is required? Does Burger Erikson's acquiesence make a difference? What other conditions might affect the purchase/pooling treatment?
2. Account for the acquisition of Erikson by Williston Company in 1974. Prepare a parent company and consolidated statement for the year.

3. After completing Questions 1 and 2, assume that before closing the acquisition deal on December 30, 1974, that the Williston board offered Burger Erikson the choice of either *(a)* a cash payment of $170 for each of his Erikson shares or *(b)* an exchange of stock based on 3.5 shares of Williston for each share of Erikson. How would the acceptance by Burger Erikson on December 30, 1974, of either of these offers effect the accounting treatment of the Erikson acquisition by Williston.

4. As the president of Williston, what accounting treatment would you prefer for this acquisition? (Assume you had an option and the facts are as presented in the case, except that Burger Erikson will accept the one-for-three exchange offer.)

EXHIBIT 1

ERIKSON COMPANY
Income Statement
For the Year Ended December 31, 1974 (estimated)

Sales..		$2,900,000
Cost of sales...............................		1,900,000
		$1,000,000
Less: Selling expense	$250,000	
Administration	384,000	
Interest	6,000	640,000
Profit before taxes		$ 360,000
Taxes: Current...........................	$170,000	
Deferred	10,000	180,000
Net income................................		$ 180,000
Retained Earnings, January 1, 1974		173,000
December 31, 1974		$ 353,000

ERIKSON COMPANY
Condensed Balance Sheet
Book and Appraisal Value (estimated)
December 31, 1974

		Book	Appraisal
Current Assets:			
Cash..		$ 35,000	$ 35,000
Marketable securities, at cost			
(market $350,000)		200,000	350,000
Accounts receivable (net)		178,000	175,000
Inventory		210,000	270,000
Total Current Assets		$623,000	$ 830,000
Long-Term Assets:			
Plant and equipment	$540,000		
Less: Accumulated depreciation	170,000	370,000	800,000
Total—Book		$993,000	
Total Assets—apprasial			$1,630,000

EXHIBIT 1 *(continued)*

Current Liabilities:

Accounts payable	$ 50,000	$ 50,000
Accrued taxes	170,000	170,000
	$220,000	$ 220,000
Deferred taxes	120,000	120,000
Long-term debt, 6%, due 1980	100,000	63,000
		$ 183,000

Stockholders' Equity:

Capital stock ($5 par)	$ 50,000		
Capital in excess of par value	150,000		
Retained earnings	353,000	553,000	
Total—Book		$993,000	
Total Liabilities—appraisal			$ 403,000

EXHIBIT 2

WILLISTON INTERNATIONAL INDUSTRIES, INC.
Condensed Balance Sheet
December 31, 1974
(in thousands)

Cash		$1,261
Marketable securities (at cost, market $500,000)		420
Inventory		1,100
Investments in subsidiaries at equity in net assets		949
Plant, property, and equipment	$2,476	
Less: Accumulated depreciation	226	2,250
		$5,980
Current liabilities		$ 470
Taxes payable		220
Long-term debt		500
Deferred taxes		190
		$1,380

Stockholders' Equity:

Common stock ($1 par)	$1,000	
Capital in excess of par value	500	
Retained earnings*	3,100	4,600
		$5,980

* Estimated after tax net income for 1974, $1,100,000.

CASE 18-2. FOSTER-MARTIN, INCORPORATED
Analysis of Criteria for Pooling of Interest Accounting

Foster-Martin, Inc., a manufacturer of television sets, intends to acquire all the outstanding stock of Comet Tube Company, a manufacturer of television tubes. It is expected that Foster-Martin will issue 175,000 shares of its capital stock in a nontaxable exchange for the net assets of Comet, which will be discontinued as a company and then operated as a division of Foster-Martin. The data in Exhibit 1 are taken

EXHIBIT 1

FOSTER-MARTIN, INC.

Current assets	$2,100,000
Property, plant, and equipment (net)	2,399,000
Other assets	331,700
Current liabilities	852,700
Long-term debt	1,875,000
Capital stock	457,500
Retained earnings	1,645,500
Sales and other revenues	6,582,500
Net income before taxes	687,500
Net income after taxes	394,750
Recent market price	31

COMET TUBE COMPANY

Current assets	$1,317,000
Current liabilities	750,000
Working capital	567,000
Fixed assets, net	574,000
Capital stock	175,000
Retained earnings	966,000
Sales	2,665,000
Other revenues	135,000
Net profit before taxes	775,000
Federal income tax	410,000

from the financial statements of the companies at the close of the most recent fiscal year.

Foster-Martin has 457,500 shares of capital stock outstanding, of which 198,792 shares are owned directly or beneficially by Tom Foster and 118,400 are owned directly or beneficially by Lowell Martin. The remainder of the stock is widely held and is from time to time on the over-the-counter market.

Comet Tube Company was organized in 1955 by Messrs. Thomas and Hinchey, who own 75 and 25 percent of the company, respectively. The company has proved very profitable, net income after taxes having varied from 9 to 14 percent of sales in the past few years.

Comet's product line will complement lines now manufactured by Foster-Martin, and the marketability of the Foster-Martin shares makes the transaction attractive to Thomas and Hinchey. Thomas and Hinchey have agreed not to dispose of any shares acquired in the transaction for a period of 12 months after its consummation.

All of the ownership interest in the original business will be represented in the surviving business. Mr. Thomas, who is now president of Comet, will continue as general manager of these operations and will also be placed on the Foster-Martin board of directors. Hinchey is now production manager of Comet and will continue in that capacity. Foster-Martin intends to sign employment contracts with both men.

Questions

1. Does the case outlined above qualify as a pooling of interests? List the factors to be considered in determining whether a particular transaction is a pooling of interests or a purchase, and apply each of these factors to this case.

2. State whether your conclusion in 1 above would be changed by each of the following changes in facts, and why (changes should be considered individually and not cumulatively):

   a. Comet Tube Company is not liquidated after the acquisition; but because of certain local tax advantages, it is operated as a subsidiary.

   b. Thomas and Hinchey have indicated their intention to sell, shortly after the consummation of the transaction, 50,000 of the shares they acquire thereby and agree to hold the remainder for a period of 12 months.

   c. The 175,000 shares issued to Thomas and Hinchey are a special Class B common stock that differs from the common stock already outstanding only with respect to voting rights, which are one tenth that of the other common shares.

   d. Only 100,000 shares are issued to Thomas and Hinchey, and the remainder of the consideration for the transaction is paid in cash.

3. Assume that Foster-Martin, Inc., publishes an annual report containing comparative financial statements and a ten-year financial summary. If the transaction qualifies as a pooling of interests, what changes if any should be made in the prior year financial statements and the ten-year summary in the next annual report?

4. Assume that Foster-Martin acquired the capital stock of Comet Tube and continues to operate it as a subsidiary. How should the transactions be recorded on the books of Foster-Martin?

5. How should Foster-Martin account for the Comet acquisition if the company were acquired for $5.5 million cash?

CASE 18–3. LAWRENCE PAPER COMPANY
Accounting for Joint Ventures

In 1974, Facts Incorporated and Lehman Paper Corporation jointly formed the Lawrence Paper Company to build and operate a $31 million mill to produce high-quality machine-coated paper.

Under the terms of a long-term purchase contract Facts and Lehman were each obligated to buy one half of the output of the Lawrence Paper Company.

In addition to an initial investment by Facts and Lehman in all of the common stock and some subordinated notes of Lawrence, the new company obtained financing by means of first mortgage bonds issued to four institutional investors. The latter source represented about 60 percent of the initial financing of the mill. The mortgage lenders viewed Facts's and Lehman's long-term purchase contracts with Lawrence as a form of security for the bonds.

The Lawrence Paper Company began operations in June 1976. A $29 million expansion program to add a second paper machine was announced in late 1976 and scheduled for completion by 1981. It was expected that nearly all of the funds for this expansion would be provided by institutional lenders.

Facts Incorporated

Facts Incorporated published *Facts,* several other popular weekly magazines, and a number of trade journals. Early in 1974, Facts entered the book publishing business. Facts had a subsidiary which operated paper and board mills and timberlands in Oklahoma and a paperboard converter facility in South Carolina. Facts also owned several radio and television stations. In reporting the Lawrence joint venture to its stockholders, Facts Incorporated said:

> The Company and Lehman Paper Corporation each own 50% of the capital stock of Lawrence Paper Company (a corporation formed in January 1974, which is constructing a groundwood pulp and paper mill at Lawrence, Texas, at an estimated cost (including working capital) of approximately $31,000,000. Initially, the mill will contain one paper machine designed to produce approximately 78,000 tons of machine coated printing paper annually. Lehman will manage the mill and supply its requirements of bleached chemical pulp. In addition to their stock ownership, the Company and Lehman have made, and have agreed to make in the future, certain loans to Lawrence which will be evidenced by subordinated notes. At December 31, 1974, the total investment of the Company and Lehman in the stock and notes of Lawrence amounted to $5,000,000 and $3,500,000 respectively, and, based on present estimates, the additional cash required from the Company and Lehman for this purpose

during 1975 will be approximately $2,600,000 and $1,300,000, respectively. Lawrence has arranged for additional financing from four institutional investors in the maximum amount of $18,600,000 first mortgage bonds. In the event that (1) funds required for certain purposes by Lawrence should exceed a specified amount, or (2) the corporation's "quick assets" (as defined) should be reduced below a specified amount, or (3) the mill should not be completed, or certain other conditions should not have been met, by stipulated dates, or (4) the corporation should determine not to complete such a mill, the Company and Lehman are obligated on a 50–50 basis to purchase additional subordinated notes or to purchase the then outstanding first mortgage bonds of Lawrence and, under certain of the above-mentioned circumstances, to pay a termination fee to the purchasers of such bonds, as the case may be. The Company is obligated under a long-term contract to purchase paper produced during 50% of the total available operating time of the paper machine or machines at the mill of Lawrence as well as to pay certain shutdown costs. Lehman is similarly obligated. The payments by the Company and Lehman under such paper contracts are to be (1) amounts sufficient to enable Lawrence to recoup all costs, charges and expenses (other than Federal and state income taxes) properly includable in the determination of its net income and not attributable to periods of disability resulting from any act of God, fire, strike or certain other causes, and (2) a fixed annual amount of $500,000 each as long as the mill contains only one paper machine.

Facts's annual report also indicated that the joint venture represented a hedge by Facts against anticipated shortages of the special paper used by Facts; the mill would supply one fifth of Facts's paper requirements; use the most modern equipment available; and was expected to operate at capacity.

The 1974 balance sheet of Facts showed stockholders equity at $88 million, other liabilities at $46 million, long-term debt at $45 million, and current liabilities at $29 million.

Lehman Paper Corporation

Lehman Paper Corporation ranked as one of the world's largest paper companies.

In the president's covering letter for Lehman's 1974 annual report to stockholders, a brief reference was made to the plans for the new mill being built in conjunction with Facts Incorporated noting that it would be completed some time in 1976. The following additional comments were included in the text of this same annual report in a section titled "Sales and Marketing":

. . . In anticipation of the high-quality output of the new mill under construction at Lawrence, Texas, we are developing new markets for the company's coated printing papers in the Midwest, South, and East. The Lawrence mill is owned jointly with Facts Incorporated, which will share its production with Lehman. . . .

In a later section of the 1974 report, titled "Financial Review," the following description of the Lawrence Paper Company was presented:

Lawrence common stock is owned 50% by Lehman and 50% by Facts Incorporated. During the year Lehman purchased 20,000 shares of common stock of this company at a cost of $2 million and made long-term advances of $1.5 million; Facts Incorporated also purchased 20,000 shares of common stock for $2 million and made long-term advances of $3 million. These advances will be secured by subordinated notes.

It is contemplated that Lehman Paper will similarly advance an additional $1.3 million and Facts Incorporated an additional $2.6 million during 1975, and that Lawrence will sell approximately $18.6 million of 25-year, 8% first mortgage and collateral bonds to four institutional investors.

The 1974 balance sheet of Lehman reported the following: stockholders' equity, $378 million; long-term debt, $115 million; and current liabilities, $44 million.

In 1975, the explanation of the Lawrence financing was moved from the text of Lehman's annual report to a footnote to the financial statements. The amount reported to stockholders in 1975 as the investment in Lawrence was $4.8 million. The footnote read as follows:

Investments. The investment in Lawrence Paper Company represents 20,000 shares of common stock (50% of the common stock outstanding) at a cost of $2,000,000 and long-term advances of $2,800,000. Lawrence is constructing a paper mill in Texas which will commence operation early in 1976. Lehman Paper Corporation will manage the mill and has contracts to purchase a portion of the output and to furnish certain amounts of pulp.

Lehman Paper Corporation has also made temporary advances of $1,500,000 to Lawrence which will be repaid from the proceeds of the sale of bonds upon completion of the mill.

In 1976 the company's investment was reported at $4,605,000 and the footnote was similar to the 1975 footnote, except that it indicated the mill had begun operation in May 1976. The company's president, in his letter to stockholders, indicated that the mill was operating on a 24-hour, seven-day week schedule.

The president's letter also included the following comments:

In the growing field of double-coated magazine papers, the new mill owned jointly with Facts Incorporated at Lawrence, Texas, should remain in a start-up status during much of 1977, the first full year of operations, as technological problems are smoothed out. Production and efficiency should steadily improve, and by the end of the year Lawrence paper should contribute to the rise in corporate sales volume, although the mill's high start-up costs will most probably offset any benefits to 1977 earnings.

Questions

1. How should Lehman and Facts account for their investment in the Lawrence Paper Company? Why?
2. How adequate is this method?
3. How should Lehman and Facts account for their long-term purchase contracts with Lawrence?

PART VII

Long-Term Commitments

Chapter 19

LONG-TERM DEBT

Long-term debt includes all creditor claims upon a company that are not payable within 12 months or the normal operating cycle, whichever is longer. These obligations include mortgage notes, bonds, installment payment contracts, and long-term notes. This chapter focuses on those forms of long-term debt issued under formal agreements, such as bonds payable. The accounting for other forms of long-term debt is similar.

CHARACTERISTICS OF LONG-TERM DEBT

Long-term debt issued by corporations to raise funds from credit sources represents a promise (1) to repay the sum of money at a specified future date and (2) to compensate the lender for the use of his money through periodic interest payments. The basic conditions of the debt are printed on the face of the bond certificate. The full details of the contract between the company and the bondholders are contained in the bond indenture, which is held by a representative of the bondholder, who is known as the trustee under the indenture. In bankruptcy, the claims of the bondholders rank ahead of those of stockholders.

Long-term debt may come in a variety of forms. It may be secured or unsecured; if unsecured, it is termed a debenture. Secured debt often takes its name from the character of the collateral pledged. For example, bonds secured by marketable securities are known as collateral trust bonds. Mortgage bonds or notes are secured by all or some of the fixed assets of the borrower. Securities backed by chattel mortgages may be called equipment trust certificates. Within the various categories of long-term debt some debt instruments, such as subordinated debentures, may rank lower than others in their claims upon the company's assets in bankruptcy.

There are many variations in the method and timing of the repay-

ment of the principal amount of long-term debt. The basic bond is
repayable in a lump sum at a specific future date. The sinking-fund
bond is a modification of this form. Its indenture requires the borrower
to make periodic cash payments into a sinking fund. This cash, plus
the accumulated interest on it, is used to retire the bonds at maturity. A
more common type of sinking fund bond indenture calls for payments
to a trustee, who uses the funds accumulated for making periodic bond
retirements. This practice increases the probability that the lender
will be repaid.

Serial bonds are another type of bond with provisions designed to
reduce the risk to the bondholders. These bonds are repayable in a
series over the life of the issue instead of a single maturity date.

Callable bonds give the borrower the option, after a certain period
of time, to redeem all or some of the debt prior to maturity for the
payment of a specified call premium beyond the principal amount.
The call provision gives the borrower greater flexibility in the design
of his capital structure, in that as interest rates change he can replace
old bonds with less expensive new ones.

Long-term debt indentures contain a number of provisions. Some
provisions may restrict the dividend payments of the borrower. These
restrictions often limit the use of additional short- or long-term debt, or
require that the borrower stay within certain debt-to-equity and working capital ratio limits. Other provisions may include the right to convert the bonds to other securities, such as stock.

Typically, the borrower's obligation to pay interest is fixed. It is not
conditional upon company earnings, except for income and participating bonds. The payment of interest on income bonds is conditional
upon the earning of income: if the income is not sufficient to pay
interest, no payments need be made. The interest obligation may or
may not be cumulative (i.e., interest not paid in one year becomes a
lien against future earnings). These bonds usually result from corporate reorganizations, where it is necessary to give old security holders a
less desirable form of security so that new senior securities can be sold.
Participating bonds entitle the holder to share in earnings with the
stockholders in a pro rata or limited way, in addition to the bondholder's usual fixed interest.

Bond Prices

The price of a bond is determined by the relationship between its
nominal rate (the fixed interest payment specified in the terms of the
indenture) and the prevailing market interest rate for the bonds of
similar investment quality. For example, if the Viking Chemical Company issued $1 million worth of 5 percent $1,000 principal bonds re-

payable in ten years and the current market interest rate for comparable bonds was 6 percent, the company would receive $926,000 from the buyers of the bonds or $926 per bond. Assuming interest is paid annually, this sum represents the present value of ten annual payments of $50,000 plus payment of $1 million ten years hence, all discounted at 6 percent. If a bondholder held the Viking bonds to maturity, the return on his investment of $926 per bond would be 6 percent. The computation would be made as shown in Illustration 19–1.

ILLUSTRATION 19–1

	Cash Flow		Times	Equals
Years	Item		P.V. Factor (6%)*	Present Value
1–10	Annual interest payments, $50,000		7.360	$368,000
10	Repayment of principal, $1,000,000		0.558	558,000
Market Value of Total Income				$926,000

* See Tables A and B in Appendix. The PV factor 7.360 is the present value of an annuity of $1 per year for ten years discounted to the present at 6 percent (Table B). The PV factor 0.558 is the present value of a dollar received ten years hence discounted at 6 percent (Table A).

The market price of a bond can vary during its life as the level of interest rates shift or the quality of the company's credit changes. For example, assume that after five years pass, the market rate for bonds similar to the Viking Chemical Company's bonds falls to 4 percent very soon after the fifth interest payment. Since the Viking bond pays a 5 percent nominal rate, the market price for all of this issue of bonds will rise to $1,044,600, which is $1,044.60 per bond. Anyone buying the bonds in the market for this price would get a yield of 4 percent on this investment if the bonds were held over the remaining five years to maturity. Assuming annual interest payments the present value calculations are shown in Illustration 19–2.

ILLUSTRATION 19–2

	Cash Flow		Times	Equals
Years	Item		P.V. Factor (4%)*	Present Value
1–5	Annual interest payments, $50,000		4.452	$ 222,600
10	Principal repayment, $1,000,000		0.822	558,000
Market Value of Total Income				$1,044,600

* See Tables A and B in Appendix. The PV factor 4.452 is the present value of an annuity of $1 per year for five years discounted to the present at 4 percent (Table B). The PV factor 0.822 is the present value of a dollar received five years hence discounted at 4 percent.

Generally, interest payments are made semiannually, but for the sake of simplicity it will be sufficient for the purposes of this chapter to assume annual payments.[1]

Bond tables are available for determining bond prices and yield rates. The tables are based on present value calculations. They consider five elements of a bond: nominal rate, number of periods to maturity, maturity value, market price, and yield rate. Illustration 19–3 reproduces an excerpt from a typical bond table.

ILLUSTRATION 19–3

Bond Value Table (purchase price of a $100 bond at 5% nominal rate, payable semiannually)

	Maturity (years)			
Yield	*4*	*4.5*	*5*	*5.5*
4.8%	$100.72	$100.80	$100.88	$100.96
4.9	100.36	100.40	100.44	100.48
5.0	100.00	100.00	100.00	100.00
5.1	99.64	99.60	99.56	99.53
5.2	99.29	99.21	99.13	99.05

When bonds are bought between interest dates, the purchase price includes the accrued interest.

Registration

Bonds may be registered in one of three ways in the books of the issuer. Some are registered with respect to both principal and interest; that is, the name of the owner is recorded in the issuer's records and checks for interest and principal payments are sent directly to him by the issuer. This protects the bondholder from losses or theft of his certificates, since the transfer of ownership benefits can only be effec-

---

[1] For semiannual payments, the present value results can be computed by halving the annual interest payment and rate and doubling the number of annual periods. For example, if the Viking bonds paid interest on a semiannual basis, the value of the total issue after the interest rates shifted at the beginning of year 6 from 6 to 4 percent would have been $1,044,575. This value was computed as follows:

Periods	*Cash Flow* *Item*	*Times* *P.V. Factor (2%)*	*Equals* *Present Value*
1–10	Semiannual interest payments, $25,000	8.983	$ 224,575
10	Principal repayment, $1,000,000	0.820	820,000
Market Value of Total Issue............................			$1,044,575

tively made by changing the owner's name in the issuer's books. Other bonds are registered as to principal only. This protects the bondholder from loss or theft of principal. Interest is received by detaching on the appropriate interest dates interest coupons attached to the certificate and presenting them to a bank for deposit or collection. Occasionally, bonds are not registered as to either interest or principal and are freely transferable.

Financial Consideration

The long-term fund requirements of corporations are usually satisfied through the issuance of a combination of stocks and bonds and the retention of earnings. Compared to stocks, bonds have some attractive features. The interest payments are deductible as a business expense in determining taxable income, whereas dividends are not. The ownership interest is not diluted when bonds are issued. The earnings on the funds obtained through a bond issue may be greater than the related interest charge, with the result that the earnings per share of the stockholders increase since no additional equity shares are issued. This effect is called "leverage."

The major disadvantage of bonds is the fixed requirement to repay principal and to pay interest periodically. If a corporation fails to meet these obligations, the bondholders may assume control of the company or force it into bankruptcy.

ACCOUNTING PRACTICES

The principal controversy concerning accounting for bonds revolves around the handling of unamortized discount, issue costs, and redemption premiums on bonds refunded. These matters are discussed in APB *Opinion No. 14, No. 21,* and *No. 26* and FASB *Statement No. 4.*

Issuance of Bonds

When bonds are issued, they are recorded at their face value in the long-term liability account. Any difference between the proceeds of the sale and the face value of the bond is put into the liability account Bond Premium or the asset account Bond Discount. The premium or discount balance is then written off to the Bond Interest account over the life of the issue.

The accounting entry to record an issue of one thousand $1,000 bonds at their face value is:

```
Cash ................................................. 1,000,000
    Bonds Payable .....................................        1,000,000
```

If these bonds had been issued at a premium of $100,000, the entry would have been:

Cash 1,100,000
 Bonds Payable   1,000,000
 Bond Premium   100,000

The accounting entry for a $100,000 discount is:

Cash   900,000
Bond Discount   100,000
 Bonds Payable   1,000,000

The costs associated with issuing bonds include underwriting fees, taxes, printing, and engraving. These issuing costs are accounted for as a deferred cost and amortized over the life of the issue.

When there is more than one bond issue, each issue should be listed either separately on the balance sheet or in the notes. Fair disclosure requires that the interest rate, maturity date, collateral data amount, and the number of authorized and issued bonds be shown for each issue. Any convertibility and subordination of long-term debt should also be indicated. In addition, violations of any of the indenture stipulations should be disclosed.

Amortization of Bond Premium and Discount

There are two common methods for amortizing bond premium and discount items. The compound-interest method reduces the discount or premium by the amount needed to make the nominal interest expense equal to the effective rate of interest. The APB requires this approach in *Opinion No. 21*. The straight-line method takes this discount or premium into the interest expense account over the life of the bond in equal amounts. This procedure results in an equal interest charge each period. This method (or any other method) is acceptable as long as the results do not differ materially from those which would result from the compound-interest method.

Illustration 19–4 presents an example of the straight-line amortization method. It assumes a five-year $1 million bond issue with a nominal rate of 5 percent sold at a discount to yield approximately 6 percent paid annually.

Illustration 19–5 demonstrates the compound-interest method, using the same example presented in Illustration 19–4.

Using the amounts in Illustration 19–4 for each interest period, the accounting entries for recording periodic interest payment and adjustment to the bond discount account are:

Bond Interest Expense 58,480
 Cash..   50,000
 Bond Discount   8,480

ILLUSTRATION 19–4

Discount Amortization, Straight-Line Method ($1 million 5-year bonds, nominal rate 5% payable annually, sold at $957,600 to yield approximately 6%)

	A	B	C	D	E
		Bond	*Effective*	*Unamortized Bond*	
Interest	*Cash*	*Discount*	*Interest*	*Discount*	*Bond Carrying*
Payment	*Interest*	*Amortization*	*Expense*	*Balance*	*Value**
Periods	*Payment*	*($42,400/5)*	*(A + B)*	*(D − B)*	*($1 million − D)*
0	—	—	—	$42,400	$ 957,600
1	$50,000	$8,480	$58,480	33,920	966,080
2	50,000	8,480	58,480	25,440	974,560
3	50,000	8,480	58,480	16,960	983,040
4	50,000	8,480	58,480	8,480	991,520
5	50,000	8,480	58,480	—	1,000,000

* Carrying value on the balance sheet if bond discount is treated as a valuation account rather than an asset.

ILLUSTRATION 19–5

Discount Amortization, Compound-Interest Method ($1 million 5-year bonds, nominal rate 5% payable annually, sold at $957,600 to yield approximately 6%)

	A	B	C	D	E
		Effective	*Bond*	*Unamortized Bond*	*Bond Carrying Value* (P.V. of*
Interest	*Cash*	*Interest*	*Discount*	*Discount*	*future interest +*
Payment	*Interest*	*Expense*	*Amortization*	*Balance*	*principal payments*
Periods	*Payment*	*(6% of E)*	*(B − A)*	*(D − C)*	*discounted at 6%)*
0	—	—	—	$42,400	$ 957,600
1	$50,000	$57,456	$7,456	34,944	965,250
2	50,000	57,915	7,915	27,029	973,650
3	50,000	58,419	8,419	18,610	981,650
4	50,000	58,899	8,899	9,711†	990,150
5	50,000	59,711	9,711†	—	1,000,000

* Carrying value on the balance sheet if the bond discount is treated as a valuation account rather than as an asset.
† Slightly more than 6 percent. This small discrepancy is due to rounding in the present value tables. On the final payment, the bond discount account is closed. Whatever balance remains is charged to interest expense.

The entries for amortizing bond premium are similar, except the amortization charge is debited to the bond premium account.

The net carrying amount of debt is the amount due at maturity adjusted for any unamortized premium or discount and the cost of issuance.

Extinguishment before Maturity

Corporations sometimes reacquire their debt securities through the exercise of their call provision or by purchase in the open market.

Bonds acquired by call are usually called at a periodic interest date, after paying and recognizing in the accounts the interest due for the period. Repurchase of debt securities occurs most frequently when interest rates rise and the market value of low nominal rate bonds declines. This provides the corporate issue with the opportunity to reacquire these discounted debt obligations at less than their principal value. Once acquired, the debt security may be retired or used to satisfy sinking-fund requirements.

APB *Opinion No. 26,* "Early Extinguishment of Debt," issued in 1972, concluded that the difference between the reacquisition price and the net carrying value of extinguished debt should be recognized currently in the income of the period of the extinguishment as losses or gains and identified as a separate item.

Subsequently, in March 1975, the FASB in *Statement No. 4,* "Reporting Gains and Losses from Extinguishment of Debt," required that the gains and losses from the extinguishment of debt be classified as an extraordinary item. This conclusion does not apply to gains or losses from cash purchases of debt made to satisfy current or future sinking-fund requirements.

The reacquisition price of debt is the amount paid on early extinguishment, including any call premium and miscellaneous costs of reacquisition. If early extinguishment is achieved by a direct exchange of new securities, the reacquisition price is the total present value of the new securities.

To illustrate the accounting entries, assume that $100,000 par value of bonds with a related discount of $3,000 are retired after paying a call premium of $2,000. The entries to record the call and retirement are:

Bonds Payable	100,000	
Loss on Bond Extinguishment	5,000	
Cash		102,000
Bond Discount		3,000

The accounting entries to record the call and retirement of a similar issue, except that it had originally been sold at a premium of $3,000, are:

Bonds Payable	100,000	
Bond Premium	3,000	
Cash		102,000
Gain on Bond Extinguishment		1,000

Refunding

When interest rates decline, corporations often take advantage of the call provisions of their bonds outstanding to float a new, cheaper issue to obtain funds which are then used to call and retire the outstanding more expensive issue.

Refunding creates an accounting controversy, namely: What is the proper accounting treatment for any (a) unamortized bond discount and issue costs, related to extinguished debt and (b) call premium related to the extinguished issue? For example, assume a $5 million ten-year 5 percent bond issue sold at a $300,000 discount is redeemed after five years at a call price of 104. The issue costs connected with these bonds was $100,000. To finance the redemption of the old issue, a new 15-year 3 percent bond issue is sold. The management must now decide how to account for the following charges related to the old bond issue:

Unamortized discount and issue costs.....	$200,000
Call premium (50,000 shares × $4)	200,000
Total	$400,000

Prior to *Opinion No. 26* and *Statement No. 4* there were four acceptable methods for handling these costs:

1. Write the $400,000 off directly to income as an extraordinary charge.
2. Write the $400,000 directly off to income as a nonextraordinary charge.
3. Amortize the $400,000 over the remaining five-year life of the original issue.
4. Amortize the $400,000 over the 15-year life of the new issue.

Opinion No. 26 and *Statement No. 4* resolved this controversy. In most cases method 1 became the only acceptable accounting method for these costs.

Conversion

In order to make bonds more attractive to buyers, some issues give the bondholder the right under certain conditions to convert his bonds into stock. The conversion terms can vary: the conversion ratio may specify a certain number of shares of stock to be issued for each bond, or it may simply indicate that stock of an equivalent par value to the bond's value may be issued. Sometimes the conversion right can be exercised only after a specific period of time.

Whether or not the bondholder exercises his right to convert depends on a number of factors. For example, a $1,000 bond with a nominal interest rate and yield of 6 percent, convertible into ten shares of stock, will sell as a bond as long as the market value of the stock is less than $100 per share. However, should the market price of the stock rise to $150 per share, the bond's price will reflect the fact that it is equivalent to 10 shares of stock. Under these conditions bondholders would probably not consider converting their bonds into stock until the annual dividends paid on ten shares of stock are greater than the $60 annual interest payments received, or until the bonds reach maturity or conversion is forced by the borrower.

When bonds are converted, the first step is to correct the current balances by recording any accrued interest, and by adjusting, if necessary, the unamortized bond discount or premium accounts. The next step is to record the conversion. This can be done in one of two ways.

The first method records the conversion on a market value basis. The newly issued security is recorded at either its market value or the market value of the bonds, whichever is more readily determinable; the appropriate bonds payable account is reduced by the par value of the bonds converted; and any difference between par value of the bonds and the market value assigned to the new securities is reported as a gain or loss on conversion. This method assumes that the conversion terminates the bond transaction and begins a new one for the stock. Therefore, the relevant value associated with this transaction is the amount that would be received today if the bonds were sold, or if the stock was sold rather than exchanged. If the market values of the bonds and equity differ, the market value of the bonds is the preferred measure of the new equity created.

The alternative approach assumes that the original issue price of the bonds represented in large part a sum paid for the future delivery of stock. Therefore, when conversion occurs, the book value of the bonds should be transferred to the newly issued stock.

To illustrate, the Ronald Company offers bondholders 20 shares of $5 par value stock in exchange for each $1,000 6 percent bond they hold. The market value of the stock is $60 per share and of the bonds $1,200 per bond. All accrued interest has been paid, and the balance of the unamortized premium account is equivalent to $20 per bond. Holders of 600 bonds exercise their conversion right. The accounting entries are:

Market Value Method (based on bonds' market value of $720,000)

Bonds Payable (600 bonds @ $1,000)	600,000	
Bond Premium (600 × $20)	12,000	
Loss on Bond Conversion	108,000	
Common Stock (12,000 shares × $5 par value)		60,000
Premium on Common Stock [600 × $1,200] − $60,000 ...		660,000

Book Value Method (based on bonds' book value of $612,000)

Bonds Payable (600 bonds @ $1,000)	600,000	
Bond Premium (600 × $20)	12,000	
Common Stock (12,000 shares × $5 par value)		60,000
Premium on Common Stock ($612,000 − $60,000)		552,000

The conversion of bonds into other bonds in the same company which are substantially the same, or into stock in accordance with the bond indenture, is considered by the Internal Revenue Service as a nontaxable transaction to the bondholder. All exchanges of bonds for other securities or property are taxable.

Debt Issued with Stock Warrants

The interest rate of bonds issued with warrants is typically lower than the rate for similar quality bonds without warrants. Therefore, the issuer is able to get a higher price for his bonds by adding stock warrant features than he would otherwise. This difference in the proceeds is in substance a payment by the bondholder for a future "call" on the stock of the issuer. The proceeds minus this amount can be considered as the imputed cost of the straight bond portion of the security.

In March 1969, the Accounting Principles Board issued *Opinion No. 14,* "Accounting for Convertible Debt and Debt Issued with Stock Purchase Warrants." In the case of convertible debt and debt issued with stock warrants where the debt must be converted to obtain the advantage of the warrants, the APB recommended that no portion of the proceeds from the issuance be accounted for as attributable to the conversion feature. The APB noted that the inseparability of the debt and conversion feature was the primary difficulty, rather than the practical problems of valuing the conversion feature.

If the debt were issued with detachable stock warrants, the APB stated that the portion of the proceeds allocable to the warrants should be accounted for as a credit to paid-in capital. Since the face value of the debt obligation remains unchanged, the offsetting entry is to the discount or premium on debt accounts, depending upon the relationship between the proceeds of the issue and the face amount of the obligation. This has the effect of recording the discount or premium that would have been recorded if the issue had been sold as straight debt.

Warrants are often traded, and their fair market value can usually be determined by their market price at the issue date. This value is the basis for allocating the proceeds of the issue between the debt obligation and warrants. If no market exists for the warrants, the market value for the debt without warrants must be estimated.

Debt Issued with Conversion Privileges

Beginning December 31, 1966, *Opinion No. 10* of the Accounting Principles Board recommended that the conversion features of debt obligations be accounted for in a similar fashion to debt with detachable warrants, principally because the full extent of the actual discount on the bond portion of the convertible bonds is not recorded at the time of issuance. Since only the difference between the proceeds and the face value is charged as bond discount, the real interest cost of the debt obligation portion of the security is understated compared to similar straight debt, since the proceeds include the value of the future conversion privilege. However, there were a number of practical problems related to estimating the value of the conversion right. Therefore, the APB in *Opinion No. 12* rescinded its recommendation until the question could be studied further. Also, the APB felt that the classification of convertible debt as a residual security for computing primary or fully diluted earnings per share would offset some of the distortion in income measurement resulting from the understatement of bond discount.

Classification of Short-Term Debt Expected to Be Refinanced

Prior to 1975 corporations classified in a variety of ways on their balance sheets short-term obligations that were expected to be refinanced on a long-term basis. For example, commercial paper, construction loans, and the currently maturing portion of long-term debt that was expected to be refinanced was sometimes classified as a current liability, a long-term liability, or as a class of liability distinct from both the current and long-term liabilities. Those who classified these short-term obligations as something other than a current liability did so because the satisfaction of the obligation was not expected to require the use of working capital during the ensuing fiscal year.

Sometimes at the time annual reports were issued the short-term obligations classified as noncurrent liabilities had not been refinanced and the probability that the long-term refinancing would occur varied from not very likely to certain.

During 1975 the FASB became disturbed by the variety of classification practices and the different levels of uncertainty associated with the probability of refinancing. Accordingly, it issued in May 1975, *Statement No. 6*, "Classification of Short-Term Obligations Expected to Be Refinanced." Henceforth, those short-term obligations that are expected to be refinanced can be classified as a noncurrent liability only if the company's intent to refinance the short-term obligation is supported by an ability to consummate the refinancing demonstrated in either of the following ways: After the date of an enterprise's balance sheet, but before the balance sheet is issued, a long-term obligation or equity security has been issued for the purpose of refinancing the short-term obligation on a long-term basis. Or, before the balance sheet date the company has entered into a financing agreement that permits the company to refinance the short-term obligation on a long-term basis on terms that are readily determinable. In addition all of these conditions must be met: The agreement does not expire during the 12 months (or operating cycle, if longer), and during this period the agreement is noncancelable by the prospective lender, except for violation of a provision with which compliance is objectively determinable or measureable. Prior to the issuance of the statements, the agreement has not been violated and no information exists that suggests that it will be violated. The lender is financially capable of honoring the agreement.

Inappropriate Interest Rates

In *Statement No. 21*, "Interest on Receivables and Payables," the APB set forth its views regarding the appropriate accounting when the face amount of a note does not reasonably represent the present value of the consideration given or received in the exchange. Such a transaction may occur when property is exchanged for a long-term noninterest-bearing note, or for a note with artificially low interest.

In these circumstances, unless the note is recorded at its present value, the sales price and profit to the seller in the year of the transaction and the purchase price and cost to the buyer are misstated, and the interest income and interest expense in subsequent periods are also misstated. The present value of the note is determined by discounting all future payments at an imputed interest rate, which is the approximate rate which would have resulted if an independent borrower and an independent lender had negotiated a similar transaction under comparable terms and conditions with the option to pay cash upon purchase or to give a note in the amount of the purchase which bears the prevailing rate of interest to maturity. One guide to the appropriate rate is the prevailing rate for similar instruments of issuers with similar credit ratings.

The discount or premium resulting from the application of *Opinion No. 21* is not an asset or liability that is separable from the note which gives rise to it. Therefore, the discount or premium is reported in the balance sheet as a direct deduction from or addition to the face amount of the note.

The discount or premium is amortized and reported as interest in the income statement over the life of the note.

ACCOUNTING PRACTICES: THE BUYER

Purchase of Bonds

Bonds may be bought at their face value or at a price which represents either a premium or discount from the face value. The accounting entries in the bondholder's books to record the purchase of bonds are:

Investment in Bonds xxx
    Cash xxx

The amount recorded by the purchaser as the asset Investment in Bonds is always the bondholder's cost.

Interest Payments Received

When bonds are bought at their face value, the bondholder records his periodic interest payments by a simple debit to Cash and credit to Interest Income. If the purchase involved a premium or discount and the bondholder intends to hold his bonds as a long-term investment, the accounting is more complex.

The carrying value of a bond bought at a discount gradually rises to par at maturity. Rather than wait until the maturity date to recognize all of this gain over cost, it is customary to record in the bondholder's accounts the increase as it accrues as part of his interest income. Thus, the interest income includes the interest payment received plus the change in the carrying value of the bond. The accounting entries are:

Cash xxx
Investment in Bonds xxx
    Bond Interest Income xxx

This treatment assumes that the discount is analogous to a prepayment of interest by the issuer. It also assumes that the bond will be held to maturity.

The carrying value of a bond purchased at a premium slowly declines to par at maturity. The accounting treatment for recognizing this change in carrying value is the reverse of the bond discount situation. However, the carrying value at any point in time should not be greater than the redemption value at the issuer's next optional redemption date. The accounting entries are:

Cash xxx
    Investment in Bonds xxx
    Interest Income xxx

The change in the carrying value is the difference between the present value of future interest payments and the redemption payment at maturity at the current interest payment date and the date of the prior interest payment. The discount rate used to compute these present values is the yield to maturity rate implicit in the purchase price. If the bondholder's balance sheet date does not match the interest payment date, the accrued interest to date is the difference between the carrying values at the two dates bounding the current accounting period.

To illustrate the calculation of change in carrying value, assume that $1 million of ten-year bonds paying 5 percent annually is bought for $926,000 to yield 6 percent to maturity. Illustration 19–6 reflects the carrying value *after* one year. At the end of this year, the first annual interest payment of $50,000 is received.

ILLUSTRATION 19–6

Calculation of Carrying Value Charge at End of Year 1

Years	Item	Times P.V. Factor (6%)	Equals Present Value
1–9	Annual interest payments, $50,000	6.802	$340,100
9	Principal repayment, $1,000,000 ....,....	0.592	592,000
Present value on first payment date			$932,100
Present value at purchase date			926,000
Change in Bond Investment...			$ 6,100

The accounting entries to record interest income are:

Cash	50,000	
Investment in Bonds	6,100	
Interest Income		56,100*

* More precise present value tables than those used in Tables A and B would have led to the following calculation:

Purchase price of bond	$926,399
Present value of bond at end of year 1	938,983
Increase in bond value	$ 5,584
Nominal interest payment	50,000
Interest expenses	$ 55,584

Verification of interest expense: $926,399 × 6% = $55,584

A similar entry at the end of each period will result in a level effective rate of interest income being recognized on the carrying value of the bond (i.e., $56,100/$926,000 = 6 percent approximately). As the bond approaches maturity, the related interest income will slowly increase to reflect the increasing carrying value.

Alternatively, for convenience, investors often adjust the carrying value of their investment in bonds by an amount equal to the bond discount (or premium) divided by the number of interest periods to maturity. This amount is added or deducted, depending on whether it relates to discount or premium, from the periodic interest payment received to determine interest income. This approach leads to the recognition of a level interest income item over the life of the bonds. However, since the carrying value is slowly increasing as maturity approaches, the effective rate of interest obtained by relating interest income to carrying value declines.

Changes in carrying value are not recognized when the issuer's financial condition makes the collection of par at maturity doubtful. Also, bonds held for short-term investments are carried at cost and are not typically adjusted for changes in carrying value. Such short-term investments are usually reported on the basis of lower of cost or market, but unless a decline in market price is significant and appears to be permanent the carrying value is seldom reduced to market. In all cases, the current market value should be disclosed parenthetically on the balance sheet.

The income tax regulations related to bonds are complicated. However, in most cases, for income tax purposes the investor reports as interest income the interest payments actually received. Upon disposal of the bonds, any difference between the amount received and the purchase price is reported as a taxable gain or loss. In general, the bond's original purchaser will be taxed at ordinary rates on these gains up to the amount of the original discount at the issue date. Other purchasers will pay capital gains rates on gains above their original purchase price. No gains or losses can be recognized before disposal.

RESTRUCTURED DEBT

When debtors have trouble meeting their loan obligations to creditors, the creditor may restructure the loan arrangement to fit the debtors' new circumstances. For example, the creditor may reduce the principle amount due, lengthen the principle repayment period, or reduce the interest. All of these forms of restructuring alter the cash flows of the obligation.

In 1976 the FASB issued a discussion memorandum entitled "Accounting by Debtors and Creditors When Debt Is Restructured." The discussion memorandum outlined these five possible approaches to accounting for restructured debt. Record the restructured obligation at its market value; the present value of its future cash flows using the rate implicit in the original obligation; the present value of its future cash flows using the current market rate; the expected nondiscounted amount of cash into which the restructured obligation will convert; or the initial obligation amount less subsequent amortization of discount or premium. If the value of the restructured debt was different to the value of the original obligation, a gain or loss would result for the debtor and creditor. In late 1976 the FASB proposed that no loss would result from a restructured debt if the nondiscounted cash inflow was more than the value of the original obligation.

VALUE OF REAL ESTATE AND RELATED RECEIVABLES

In May 1976 the Accounting Standards Division of the AICPA issued a proposed SOP on the accounting for any real estate held for sale and loans secured by real estate when the loan collection is doubtful. Typically, the SOP recommended that the real estate and or related loan be valued at the real estates estimated selling price, less the costs to complete and sell it, which include the holding costs to the expected sale date. Interest, based on the average cost of debt and equity capital, should be included in the holding costs. Unless the FASB acts on this issue, a final SOP was expected to be issued in late 1976.

SUGGESTED FURTHER READING

FINANCIAL ACCOUNTING STANDARDS BOARD. *Accounting by Debtors and Creditors When Debt Is Restructured.* Stamford, 1976.
WESTON, J. FRED, and BRIGHAM, EUGENE F. *Managerial Finance.* 5th ed. Hinsdale, Ill.: The Dryden Press, 1975.

CASE

CASE 19–1. PACE CORPORATION
Accounting for Bonds

On June 30, 1971, Pace Corporation issued 8 percent first mortgage ten-year bonds having a maturity value of $3 million. The bonds were issued at a price to yield 7 percent.

The Pace bonds were dated June 30, 1971, and required semiannual interest payments. They were redeemable after June 30, 1976, and before June 30, 1978, at 104; thereafter until maturity they were redeemable at 102. They were also convertible into Pace $10 par value common stock according to the following schedule:

Before June 30, 1976: 60 shares of common stock for each $1,000 bond.
July 1, 1976, to June 30, 1979: 50 shares of common stock for each $1,000 bond.
After June 30, 1979: 40 shares of common stock for each $1,000 bond.

The following transactions occurred in connection with Pace's bonds.

July 1, 1977. Bonds having a maturity value of $500,000 were converted into common stock.
December 30, 1978. Bonds having a maturity value of $500,000 were reacquired by Pace Corporation by purchase on the market at 99¼ and accrued interest. The reacquired bonds were canceled immediately.
June 30, 1979. Pace Corporation called the remaining bonds for redemption. In order to obtain the cash necessary for the redemption and for business expansion, a $4 million issue of 20-year 6 percent sinking fund debenture bonds were issued at a price to yield 6 percent. The new bonds were dated June 30, 1979, and also called for semiannual interest payments.

Questions

1. Determine the amount of the proceeds from the June 30, 1971, bond issue. Illustrate the December 31, 1971, balance sheet disclosure(s) related to this indebtedness. (Use tables at the end of Question 4.)
2. Determine the amount of "interest expense" to be deducted in arriving at the net income for the year ending December 31, 1972.
3. Describe the balance sheet and income statement effects of the July 1, 1977, conversion, including dollar amounts involved.
4. Describe the balance sheet and income statement effects of the June 30, 1979, redemption, including dollar amounts involved.

Present Value of $1

Periods	3%	3.5%	4.0%	4.5%	5.0%	5.5%
10	0.744	0.709	0.676	0.644	0.614	0.585
20	0.554	0.503	0.456	0.415	0.377	0.343
40	0.307	0.253	0.258	0.172	0.142	0.117

Present Value of $1 per Period

Periods	3%	3.5%	4.0%	4.5%	5.0%	5.5%
10	8.530	8.317	8.111	7.913	7.222	7.538
20	14.877	14.212	13.590	13.008	12.462	11.950
40	23.115	21.355	19.793	18.402	17.159	16.046

Chapter 20

ACCOUNTING FOR LEASES

The use of leases to finance asset acquisitions has grown substantially in recent years. This chapter discusses the accounting by lessees and lessors for long-term personal and property leases. Leverage leases and lease agreements involving natural resources are not covered, principally because of their complex and varied nature.

In 1976 the FASB issued an Exposure Draft of a *Statement* dealing with the accounting for leases. As defined in the Exposure Draft, a lease is: ". . . an agreement conveying the right to use property, plant or equipment (land and/or depreciable assets) for a stated period of time." The Exposure Draft does not apply to rights to explore for or to exploit natural resources, nor does it apply to licensing agreements. This *Statement* was intended to supersede the APB lease accounting recommendations expressed in *Opinion No. 5, No. 7, No. 18, No. 27,* and *No. 31.* Until the FASB issues a final lease accounting *Statement,* these APB lease *Opinions* are the authoritative source of lease accounting.

If the FASB Exposure Draft is adopted,[1] a knowledge of the super-

---

[1] After this book was in the hands of the printer, the FASB issued *Statement No. 13,* "Accounting for Leases." This statement was similar to the earlier exposure draft, except for these major changes:

1. The 75 percent life and 90 percent recovery tests for a capital lease were qualified as follows: If the beginning of the lease term falls within the last 25 percent of the total economic life of the leased property, including earlier years of use, this criterion shall not be used for purposes of classifying the lease. (See page 579.)
2. The lessee shall compute the present value of the minimum lease payments using his incremental borrowing rate, unless (i) it is practical for him to learn the implicit rate computed by the lessor and (ii) the implicit rate computed by the lessor is less than the lessee's incremental borrowing rate. If both of these conditions are met, the lessee shall use the implicit rate. (See page 580.)
3. A lessor's initial direct costs related to direct financing leases must be charged to income as incurred. An equal portion of the unearned income from the lease shall be recognized as income in the same period. (See pages 588 and 593.)
4. The difference between the estimated residual and its present value should be included in a lessor's unearned income and recognized in income over the lease term for both sales-type and direct financing leases. (See page 593.)

seded APB lease *Opinions* will still be required since these *Opinions* will still govern for at least four more years after the *Statement*'s effective date the accounting for those leases on the books of lessees and lessors that were entered into prior to the effective date of the FASB *Statement*. The lease accounting of companies under the jurisdiction of the SEC is also governed by SEC *Release No. 147.*

There is a major conceptual difference between the APB and FASB approaches to lease accounting. The APB's lessor and lessee accounting requirements reflected a belief that the nature of the lessor's and lessee's businesses was often sufficiently different to warrant different accounting treatment by the two parties. The FASB rejected this approach. The FASB believed that the characteristics of the leasing transaction, rather than the characteristics of the businesses of the parties to the lease, should determine the appropriate lessee and lessor accounting and that the accounting for a lease by both parties to the lease should be similar.

LEASING PRACTICES

A lease agreement conveys the right to use property in return for a series of specified future rental payments over a definite period.

There are a great many different leasing agreements in practice. A typical lease contract contains provisions covering the following areas:

a. The duration of the lease, which can run from a few hours to the expected economic life of the asset.

b. The options open, if any, to renew the lease or purchase the property at the end of the lease's term. In some cases these renewal or purchase options can be exercised for a nominal consideration.

c. The duties of the lessor to service the leased property. The service duties may range from none to complete maintenance.

d. The restrictions, if any, on the lessee's business activities, such as paying dividends or entering new bank loans.

e. The penalties for early termination of the lease. Often, the cost of termination is the lessor's unrecovered costs plus a penalty payment.

---

5. A gain cannot be recognized immediately on renewals or extensions of sales-type or direct financing leases. (See page 593.)

6. Added this disclosure requirements for direct financing leases: The amount of increased income included in income to offset initial direct costs charged against income. (See page 594.)

7. In the case of an operating lease, the lessor's initial direct costs may be charged as an expense as incurred if the effect is not materially different from deferring and allocating them over the lease term. (See page 594.)

8. The 15 percent limitation established in leases involving real estate was raised to 25 percent. (See page 596.)

f. The consequences of default. Usually, the lease agreement re-
    quires the lessee to pay immediately all future payments in the
    event of default. However, in practice this provision may be dif-
    ficult to enforce since the lessor has an obligation to attempt to
    mitigate his losses.

g. The obligation of the lessor to provide the lessee with "quiet en-
    joyment" of the leased property.

There are a number of advantages and disadvantages to leasing
assets. One of the advantages claimed by leasing companies is that
certain lease obligations do not have to be listed among a company's
liabilities, whereas loan obligations must be recorded. Consequently,
by financing asset acquisitions with leases, rather than borrowing, a
company can report a better debt-equity ratio. As we shall describe,
this advantage would be available to fewer lessees if the FASB recommendations are adopted. Some of the other advantages cited by
leasing companies include: shifting the risks of ownership, such as
technological obsolescence, onto the lessor; freeing of lessee capital to
finance working capital needs; possible tax advantages in certain cases
that makes leasing cheaper on an aftertax basis than owning; and 100
percent financing.

Typically the cost of a lease is slightly higher than the cost of a
direct borrowing to finance the acquisition of an asset. However, in
some cases, due to the tax treatment of leased assets, the lessor may be
willing to lease at a cost less than the lessees' marginal borrowing rate.
For example, the availability to the lessor of investment tax credits and
depreciation write-offs may make his aftertax return from leasing
higher than the return from straight debt. In return for these tax advantages the lessor may give the lessee a lease at a cost that is less than the
lessees' debt cost.

LESSEE'S STATEMENTS

The principle lessee accounting question raised by leasing is: Are
assets and liabilities created on the lessee's books by entering a noncancelable agreement to lease property on a rental basis?

The Accounting Principles Board concluded in *Opinion No. 5* that
unless the lease agreement was in substance an installment purchase
of property, no asset or related liability need be shown on the lessee's
balance sheet. The rental payments of leases that are not in substance
installment purchases should be charged to operations as they become
payable. The APB further stated that financial statements should disclose sufficient information regarding material noncancelable leases
". . . to enable the reader to assess the effect of lease commitments
upon the financial position and results of operations, both present and
prospective, of the lessee."

Opinion No. 5, which dealt with lessee accounting also indicated that leases which were clearly in substance installment purchases of property should be treated as purchases. The APB believed a lease was essentially equivalent to a purchase when the rental payments ran well ahead of any reasonable measure of the expiration of the service value of the property and the lease permitted either a bargain purchase by the lessee or the renewal of the lease during the leased asset's anticipated useful life at bargain rentals. In such cases the lessee is considered to be acquiring a "material equity" in the leased property that will lead to the lessee exercising the bargain options, since the lessee has in essence paid for this privilege during the initial lease term. Finally, the APB recommended that gains and losses on sale-and-leaseback agreements be amortized over the life of the lease as an adjustment to the rental cost.

The FASB in its Exposure Draft reached a different conclusion on the criteria for lease capitalization. It proposed that leases meeting *any one* of the following four criteria be called "capital leases" and be accounted for by lessees as purchased assets and liabilities incurred:

1. Title is transferred to the lessee by the end of the lease term.[2]
2. The lease contains a bargain purchase option.[3]
3. The lease term is at least 75 percent of the leased property's estimated economic life.[4]
4. The present value of the minimum lease payments[5] is 90 percent or more of the fair value of the leased property[6] less any related investment tax credit retained by the lessor.

---

[2] The lease term is defined in the Exposure Draft as the fixed noncancelable term of the lease plus all periods, if any, covered by bargain renewal options but not extending beyond the date a bargain purchase option becomes exercisable.

A bargain renewal option is a provision that allows the lessee, at his option, to renew the lease for a rental that at the inception of the lease is expected to be substantially less than the fair rental of the property at the date the option becomes exercisable.

[3] A bargain purchase option is a provision that allows the lessee, at his option, to acquire the leased asset for a price that at the inception of the lease is expected to be substantially less than the fair market value of the property at the date the option becomes exercisable.

[4] The estimated economic life is the estimated remaining useful life of the leased property in the purpose for which it was intended at the inception of the lease, without limitation by the term of the lease.

[5] The minimum lease payment includes:

    a. The minimum rental payments over the lease term, excluding estimated executory costs.

    b. Any guarantee of the residual value at the expiration of the lease term.

    c. Any payment required for failure to renew or extend the lease at the expiration of the lease term.

    d. The payment called for by a bargain purchase option.

If the lease contains a bargain purchase option, only the rental payments plus the bargain purchase option would be included in the minimum payment computation.

[6] The fair value of the leased asset is the price at which the property could be sold.

A capital lease is recorded initially by the lessee as an asset (capital lease asset) and a liability (obligation under capital lease). The amount of the asset and liability is the present value of the minimum lease payments. (See footnote No. 5.) The present value discount rate is the interest rate implicit in the lease, if the lessee knows this implicit rate *and* it is less than the lessee's incremental borrowing rate. If these two conditions are not met, the lessee's incremental borrowing rate should be used. The capitalized amounts are then accounted for like any other asset which is amortized and interest-bearing debt which is reduced over its term. That is, the asset is amortized in a manner consistent with the lessee's normal depreciation policy over the lease term or, if the lease meets the capital lease criteria No. 1 or No. 2 listed above, over the leased assets estimated economic life. The interest expense on the recorded liability is recognized in proportion to the remaining balance of the obligation.

Leases which do not meet any of the four criteria listed above are classified as "operating leases" by the FASB Exposure Draft. The FASB proposed that no related asset or liabilities are to be recorded at the time the lessee enters into such lease agreement and the rentals for such leases be charged to operations as they become payable. Should the rental payments be not of equal amounts over the lease term, the rental expense should be recognized on the straight-line basis, unless some other systematic method that reflects the benefits derived from the leased asset is more appropriate.

Illustration 20–1 presents the balance sheet classification proposed by the FASB Exposure Draft.

ILLUSTRATION 20–1

LAMBERT DIVERSIFIED PRODUCTS, INC.
Balance Sheet

Assets			*Liabilities*		
	December 31,			*December 31,*	
	1975	*1974*		*1975*	*1974*
Leased Property:			Current:		
Capital leases, less accumulated amortization	XXX	XXX	Obligations under capital leases	XXX	XXX
			Long Term:		
			Obligations under capital leases	XXX	XXX

Accounting Entries

As noted above, when capitalized lease's obligations are recorded on the face of financial statements, an asset account, Capital Lease

Asset, and a liability account, Obligations under Capital Leases, are shown.[7] Subsequently, as the leased property right is "consumed" and the rental payments made, the two balance sheet accounts are amortized. The asset account, is amortized in the same manner as owned property is depreciated. This treatment recognized the fact that depreciation schedules reflect the characteristics of the property, not the means used to finance its acquisition. The liability account is reduced by the principal repayment amount implicit in the rental payment. The remaining portion of the rental payment is charged to the income statement as an interest expense. Typically, rental payments are level. Therefore, in the case of long-term leases, the liability account would be extinguished slowly at first, since the bulk of the rental payment would be interest on the unpaid balance of the obligation. Toward the end of the lease, the opposite would occur, because the unpaid balance and related interest charges would be smaller.

It is important to note that under the capitalization and amortization method, the total expenses charged to the income statement will be the same as under the *Opinion No. 5* accounting for true leases and as the FASB proposed accounting for operating leases. The timing of the expenses during the life of the lease would be different under the capitalization and noncapitalization approaches, however.

In order to illustrate the accounting entries by a lessee, assume that the lessee signs a ten-year lease payable in annual amounts of $1,000. The implicit pretax interest rate of the lease financing is 6 percent.

Under *Opinion No. 5*'s accounting for true leases and the FASB's proposed operating lease accounting the lessee's books simply record the rental payment for the lease as an expense at the time of payment:

Equipment Rental Expense	1,000	
Cash		1,000

If the lease obligation was capitalized, as proposed by the FASB for capital leases or required by *Opinion No. 5* for leases that are in substance installment purchases, the following entries would be made at the time the lease was signed by the lessee to recognize an asset and a related liability:

Capital Lease—Equipment (an asset account)	7,360	
Obligation under Capital Leases (a liability account)		7,360

To recognize the present value of future lease obligations in this case $1,000 a year for ten years at 6 percent.[8]

---

[7] The account titles used are those proposed by the FASB Exposure Draft. Under APB *Opinion No. 5* capitalized leases were equivalent to purchases, so the leased asset was classified as an asset account according to the type of asset acquired. The lease obligation was listed on the liability side of the balance sheet as a capitalized lease obligation.

[8] The present value of a stream of payments or receipts is the amount that would have had to be invested today to generate that cash flow at a given rate of interest. For

The first rental payment would be recorded as follows:

Obligation under Capital Leases 558
Interest Expense (6 percent of $7,360) 442
    Cash 1,000

An additional entry each year should be made to recognize the amortization of the Capital Lease—Equipment asset.

Amortization Expense—Equipment (10 percent of $7,360) 736
    Accumulated Amortization—Equipment 736

The Accumulated Amortization—Equipment account is shown on the balance sheet as a contra account to the Capital Lease—Equipment account.

Next year, the interest expense would be less, since the balance of the rental obligation had been reduced by $558 during the first year. The second-year entries are:

Obligation under Capital Leases 592
Interest Expenses [6 percent of ($7,360 − $558)] 408
    Cash 1,000

In subsequent years, more of the $1,000 lease payment will go to reducing the balance of the Obligation under Capital Leases as the annual interest on the declining balance of this account gets smaller. At the end of the lease period, the capital lease obligation liability account will be reduced by the last lease payment to zero.

Over the life of the lease, the amortization and interest expenses will be equal to the total net lease rental payments. Thus the total cost of a lease is the same irrespective of whether it is classified as a capital or operating lease. However, the sum of the annual lease related interest expense and asset amortization charges for a capital lease will be greater than the annual rental expense for an operating lease in the early years of a lease term. In the later years of the lease the reverse is true.

---

example, if $7,360 were invested today at 6 percent it would return $1,000 per year for ten years to the investor. At the end of that time the investment would be recouped and the return would be 6 percent. Thus, the present value of $1,000 per year for ten years discounted at 6 percent is $7,360. Present value tables that can be used to make this calculation are included at the end of this book.

If the lease rental included executory costs, such as maintenance and real estate taxes paid by the lessor, these amounts would be deducted from the gross rental for the purposes of making the present value capital lease calculation. Only the net rental is capitalized. In this illustration there are no executory costs. If executory costs are included in the lease rental, a separate accounting entry is made to reflect these costs annually as they are paid. The entry is:

Dr Lease Executory Cost Expense xx
    Cr Cash xx

Disclosure

SEC *Release No. 147* makes mandatory the disclosure in notes of the present value of those noncancelable lease commitments where the lessor either recovers during the initial lease period his investment in the leased asset plus a reasonable return or the lease period is equal to 75 percent of the leased asset's economic life. (Such leases are called "financing leases" by SEC *Release No. 147.*) This *Release* also requires the disclosure of what the impact on net income would have been if these "financing leases" had been capitalized. It is anticipated that the SEC will drop this requirement once the FASB adopts its final lease statement.

If adopted, the proposed FASB *Statement on Leases* would expand the required disclosure of lease data in the notes. The proposed lessee disclosure requirements are summarized in Illustration 20–2.

LESSOR'S STATEMENTS

The accounting for leases on the lessor's statements raises several problems: the allocation of the rental revenues and costs to the appropriate accounting periods; the allocation of lease acquisition, operating, and closing costs in a manner which is systematic, fair, and consistent with the revenue recognition method; and the appropriate description and classification of leased assets in the balance sheet.

In late 1976, lessor accounting for lease transaction was determined primarily by APB *Opinion No. 7*, "Accounting for Leases in Financial Statements for Leases," and APB *Opinion No. 27*, "Accounting for Lease Transactions by Manufacturer or Dealer Lessors." If adopted, the FASB Exposure Draft would supersede these APB *Opinions* for all new leases entered into after December 31, 1976.

The APB classified leases into three groups: financial leases, operating leases, and leases involving manufacturer or dealer lessors. The FASB Exposure Draft also classified leases from the lessor point of view in three categories: namely, direct-financing leases, sales-type leases, and operating leases. The classification criteria set forth by the APB and FASB are different.

APB Lessor Accounting

The APB recognized that there were two generally accepted methods of accounting for leases by lessors: the so-called financing and operating methods. The APB believed that the financing method should be used to account for those leases which pass on many of the risks or rewards of ownership, such as maintenance, to the lessee. The APB also recommended that the operating method be used in those

ILLUSTRATION 20–2

Disclosure Requirements Proposed by FASB*

Disclosure	Disclosure Applicable to — Capital Leases	Disclosure Applicable to — Noncancelable Operating Leases of More than One Year	Disclosure Applicable to — All Operating Leases	Disclosure Required for — Each Balance Sheet Presented	Disclosure Required for — Latest Balance Sheet Presented	Disclosure Required for — Each Income Statement Presented
1. General description of lessee's leasing activities including:						
a. Basis for determining contingent rentals.	X	X	X			
b. Existence and terms of renewal or purchase options and escalation clauses.	X	X	X			
c. Dividend or other restrictions.	X	X	X			
2. Gross amount of assets in the aggregate and by major property categories.	X			X		
3. Amount of accumulated amortization in total.	X			X		
4. Separate disclosure of amortization unless it is included in depreciation expense and that fact disclosed.	X					X
5. Minimum future lease payments in the aggregate and for each of the five succeeding fiscal years.	X	X			X	
6. Amount of aggregate future minimum lease payments representing:						
a. Executory costs.	X				X	
b. Imputed interest to reduce to present value.	X				X	
7. Total of minimum future rentals due from noncancelable subleases.	X	X			X	
8. Total contingent rentals actually incurred.	X					X
9. Rental expense with separate amounts for minimum and contingent rentals and sublease rental income.			X			X

* Ernst & Ernst, Accounting for Leases, Financial Reporting Developments, September 1976, p. 12.

instances where the lessor retains the risks and rewards of ownership, such as in the case of automotive equipment leases where the lessor maintains the leased property. In addition, the APB suggested that it was preferable to initially defer the costs of writing leases and then allocate them to expenses over the life of the lease. In those cases where a manufacturer uses leases as part of his marketing activities, the APB recommended that if certain conditions were met, the manufacturer should recognize his normal manufacturing profit when the lease agreement was signed and defer the lease income over the life of the lease, using the financing method. In other cases, the APB recommended that both the manufacturing and lease incomes be deferred and recognized over the lease's life, using the operating method.

Operating Method.   The operating method (sometimes called the rental method) recognizes revenue as each rental receipt is received. Costs related to the lease asset, such as depreciation and executory costs, are expensed as incurred. Thus the lease profit is the difference between the lease rentals received and the related depreciation and executory costs. Under the operating method the leased asset is shown as an asset, less the accumulated depreciation. No receivable recognizing the lessee's future obligation to pay rental is recorded.

Illustration 20–3 illustrates the operating method with different depreciation schedules. The illustration assumes that equipment costing $10,000 is leased for a five-year period with 60 noncancelable monthly payments of $225 each. At the end of five years, the lessee has the option of renewing for one year at a time for a nominal annual rental of

ILLUSTRATION 20–3

Operating Method

		Sum-of-the-Year's Digits		Straight-Line Depreciation	
Year	Lease Payments Received (a)	Depreciation Expense (b)	Gross Profit or (loss) (c) = (a) − (b)	Depreciation Expense (d)	Gross Profit or (loss) (e) = (a) − (d)
1	$ 2,700	$ 3,167	$ (467)	$ 1,900	$ 800
2	2,700	2,533	167	1,900	800
3	2,700	1,900	800	1,900	800
4	2,700	1,267	1,433	1,900	800
5	2,700	633	2,067	1,900	800
6	100	100	0	100	0
7	100	100	0	100	0
8	100	100	0	100	0
9	100	100	0	100	0
10	100	100	0	100	0
Totals	$14,000	$10,000	$4,000	$10,000	$4,000

$100. In the illustration it is assumed that five renewal payments are received and at the end of ten years the equipment is abandoned by the lessor. The total revenue for the ten years is thus $14,000, and the lessor's total gross profit is $4,000. Assuming 95 percent of the equipment cost is amortized during the initial term of the lease, the problem is: How much of the $4,000 gross profit should be recognized each year? Columns *(c)* and *(e)* of Illustration 20–3 show the annual gross profit (or loss) varies with depreciation method and salvage values selected.

The Accounting Principles Board recommended that the operating method be used in those cases where the lessor substantially retains the risks or rewards of ownership in connection with his leased assets. According to *Opinion No. 7:*

. . . there are companies (e.g., the owner-operator of an office building, the lessor of automotive equipment on short-term leases—daily, weekly or monthly) which retain the usual risks or rewards of ownership in connection with their leasing activity. They may also assume responsibilities for maintaining the leased property or furnishing certain related services which will give rise to costs to be incurred in the future. Rental revenues are designed to cover the costs of these services, depreciation and obsolescence, and to provide an adequate profit for assuming the risks involved. In these cases the operating method is appropriate for measuring periodic net income from leasing activities. The operating method is also appropriate if the leasing activity is an integral part of manufacturing, marketing or other operations of a business which generate revenues and costs which must be considered along with revenues and costs from the leasing activities in arriving at appropriate methods for measuring the overall periodic net income (examples are leases of retail outlets with lease provisions deliberately made favorable to induce lessee to handle lessor's product and leases which generate significant servicing revenues and costs). The operating method likewise is appropriate for leasing activities for an otherwise strictly financing institution if such activities are characterized as set forth in this paragraph.

Financing Method.   The financing method (sometimes called financial method) regards the lease as being similar to a sale on credit. That is, the leased asset is removed from the lessor's books as if it were sold and a receivable is recorded in its place. The excess of aggregate rentals over the cost of the leased asset (reduced by estimated residual values) is considered to be the lessor's compensation for financing the property acquisition. This income is then spread over the period of the lease so that the amount of income recognized each period bears the same relationship to the unpaid balance of the loan. The receivable shown as an asset is reduced by the difference between the gross rental receipt and the amount allocated to rental income.

Illustration 20–4 illustrates the application of the financing method

ILLUSTRATION 20–4

Financing Method

Year	Months in Year*	Gross Profit
1	60–49	$1,251
2	48–37	975
3	36–25	700
4	24–13	425
5	12–1	149
6	0	100
7	0	100
8	0	100
9	0	100
10	0	100
Total		$4,000

* The sum of 60 months' digits is 1,830. During the first year the sum of the 49th through the 60th months is 654/1,830, so 35.7 percent of the income is recognized during the first year.

to the same example presented earlier (see Illustration 20–3). In Illustration 20–4, the deferred gross income is recognized over the initial lease period on the sum-of-the-month's-digits basis.[9] This technique approximates compound interest calculations. The income over the renewal periods is equal to the option period payments of $100 per year.

The Accounting Principles Board believed that the financing method is generally appropriate where the lessor does not retain the risks or rewards of ownership. According to *Opinion No. 7:*

The financing method is generally appropriate for measuring periodic net income from leasing activities of entities engaged in, perhaps among other things, lending money at interest—e.g., lease-finance companies, banks, insurance companies or pension funds. Lease agreements of institutions of this kind typically are designed to pass all or most of the usual ownership risks or rewards to the lessee, and to assure the lessor of, and generally limit him to, a full recovery of his investment plus a reasonable return on the use of the funds invested, subject only to the credit risks generally associated with secured loans. Usually, the financing method is similar to the method of accounting for

[9] Rather than actually working out what the unpaid principal amounts to each month, which would require splitting each lease payment into an interest portion and a principal repayment portion, the total amount of gross profit is simply spread over the life of the lease on a declining scale. The method is called "sum-of-the-months' digits," or sometimes, the "rule of 78." Some banks use it for their consumer installment loans; a 12-month loan has 78 months' digits, and during the first month the bank recognizes 12/78 of the total interest charge. This is a reasonable approximation to the result obtained by using a more accurate method based on compound interest, even though it does tend to recognize income slightly earlier than a true compound interest-based method.

revenue already in use for other lending activities of the institutions. The
financing method is also appropriate for a leasing activity of an entity which is
not identified as a financial institution, such as a manufacturer, if the lease
agreements have the characteristics described earlier in this paragraph.

Accounting Entries.   Using the same example as Illustration 20–3,
which assumes that a company purchases an asset for $10,000 and then
leases it, the operating method recognizes the income as the cash from
the $2,700 annual lease rental charge is received. The leased asset
owned by the lessor is depreciated in this case on a straight-line basis
of $1,900 per year. The gross profit is the difference between these
amounts.

Cash..	2,700	
Rental Income...		2,700
Depreciation Expense	1,900	
Allowance for Depreciation		1,900

Based on the gross profit schedule in Illustration 20–4 and the
aggregate lease payments and asset cost in Illustration 20–3, the financing method recognized at the time the lease is signed the following
asset and liability accounts:

Lease Payments Receivable	14,000	
Deferred Profit on Leasing		4,000
Cost of Leased Asset		10,000

The profit is recognized as each $2,700 payment is received:

Cash..	2,700	
Lease Payments Receivable		2,700
Deferred Profit on Leasing	1,251	
Current Profit on Leasing		1,251

The amount of the last entry is the first-year, sum-of-the-months'-digits
figure shown in Illustration 20–4.

Therefore, at the end of the first year, the receivable from leasing
would be $11,300 and the remaining deferred profit $2,749
($4,000 − 1,251). At the end of the second year, the lease receivable
would be $8,600 ($11,300 − 2,700) and the deferred profit account
$1,774 ($2,749 − 975).

Initial Direct Cost.   Leasing companies incur costs, such as commissions and legal fees, which can be directly associated with con-
summating particular leases. For a number of years, it was a common
practice to recognize an immediate recovery of these costs out of expected gross income at the time the lease agreement was signed.
Rather than accelerate the recognition of income, the Accounting
Principles Board expressed a preference for deferring negotiation and
closing costs and amortizing them over the life of the lease.

Leasing by Manufacturers. As part of their regular marketing program, a number of manufacturers are willing to lease, rather than sell, their products to customers. In these cases, the manufacturer receives his normal manufacturing profit margin as well as a return for lease financing, if provided. Depending on the circumstances, the manufacturing profit on leased assets should be recognized at either the time the lease agreement is signed or over the lease period.

APB *Opinion No. 27*, "Accounting for Lease Transaction by Manufacturer or Dealer Lessors," states:

Some lease transactions with independent lessees are in substance equivalent to sales of the property with the sales price collectible over a period of time. A manufacturer or dealer lessor should account for a lease transaction with an independent lessee as a sale if at the time of entering into the transaction (a) collectibility of the payments required from the lessee is reasonably assured, (b) no important uncertainties, surround the amount of costs yet to be incurred under the lease, and (c) any one of the following conditions is present:

(i)   The lease transfers title to the property to the lessee by the end of its fixed, noncancelable term; or

(ii) The lease gives the lessee the option to obtain title to the property without cost or at a nominal cost by the end of the fixed, non-cancelable term of the lease; or

(iii) The leased property, or like property, is available for sale, and the sum of (1) the present value of the required rental payments by the lessee under the lease during the fixed, noncancelable term of the lease (excluding any renewal or other option) and (2) any related investment tax credit retained by the lessor (if realization of such credit is assured beyond any reasonable doubt) is equal to or greater than the normal selling price or, in the absence thereof, the fair value (either of which may be less than cost) of the leased property or like property; or

(iv) The fixed, noncancelable term of the lease (excluding any renewal option) is substantially equal to the remaining economic life of the property. (This test cannot be complied with (1) by estimating an economic life substantially equal to the noncancelable term if this is unrealistic or (2) if a material contingent residual interest is retained in the property.)

A high credit risk frequently presents measurement problems (a) in determining the interest rate that is commensurate with the risk and should be applied in computing the present value of the rental payments or (b) in determining an adequate provision for bad debts. When the credit risk is so high as to preclude reasonable assurance of collection the lease transaction should not be recorded as a sale.

When a lease transaction by a manufacturer or dealer lessor is recorded as a sale, (a) revenue should be recognized in the period of the sale in an amount equal to the present value of the required rental payments by the lessee under the lease during the fixed, noncancelable term (excluding any renewal or other option) of the lease and (b) the cost of the property (not reduced by salvage or residual value) and the estimated related future costs (other than interest) should be charged against income in that period. In some cases this may result in a loss on the transaction.

Operating leases. Important uncertainties may still exist in some lease transactions that otherwise appear to meet the tests for recognition as a sale. For example, the lease may contain commitments by the lessor to guarantee performance in a manner more extensive than the typical product warranty or to effectively protect the lessee from obsolescence. The difficulties of evaluating the future costs, both individually and collectively, and thus the risks under such commitments may be so great that the lease transaction should be accounted for by the operating method.

A manufacturer or dealer lessor should account for a two-party lease transaction that does not meet the criteria for treatment as a sale by use of the operating method set forth in APB Opinion No. 7.

An implicit loss exists and should be recognized by the manufacturer or dealer whenever the rental payments expected to be received from independent lessees over the remaining economic life of the leased property together with its estimated residual value are insufficient to recover the unrecovered costs pertaining to the property, estimated related future costs and any deferred costs relating to leases of the property.

In some instances a manufacturer or dealer lessor sells or assigns a lease, or property subject to a lease, to independent financial institutions and independent leasing companies. In these cases where a third party is participating in the lease transaction the lease transaction should be accounted for as a sale if the original accounting determination of the lease transaction qualifies the lease as being equivalent to a sale. Any profit or loss at the time of the transaction with the financing institution should be recognized at the time of the transaction. According to *Opinion No. 27*—

the sale or assignment of a lease or leased property subject to an operating lease should not be accounted for as a sale unless no important uncertainties exist and either (a) all risks and rewards of ownership in the property are transferred to the purchaser or (b) all risks are transferred but some of the rewards are retained by the manufacturer or dealer and the sum of the present value of the required payments by the purchaser and any related investment tax credit retained by the dealer is equal to or greater than the normal selling price or, in the absence thereof, the fair value of the property. When a sale is recorded, all costs should be charged against income in that period.

A manufacturer or dealer may by various arrangements assure recovery of the investment by the third-party financing institution in some operating lease transactions and thus retain substantial risks of ownership in the property. For example, in the case of default by the lessee or termination of the lease, the arrangements may involve a formal or informal commitment by the manufacturer or dealer (a) to acquire the lease or the property, (b) to substitute an existing lease, or (c) to secure a replacement lessee or a buyer for the property under a remarketing agreement. In these circumstances the manufacturer or dealer has not transferred all risks and should not reflect the transaction as a sale. However, a remarketing agreement by itself should not disqualify accounting for the transaction as a sale if the manufacturer or dealer (a) will receive a reasonable fee, commensurate with the effort involved, at the time of securing a replacement lessee or buyer for the property and (b) is not required to give any priority to the re-leasing or disposition of the property owned by the third party over similar property owned or produced by the manufacturer or dealer. (For example, for this purpose, a "best efforts" or a first-in, first-out, remarketing arrangement is considered to be a priority.)

When the sale to an independent financing institution of property subject to an operating lease is not reflected as a sale, the transaction should be accounted for as a loan and revenue should be recognized under the operating method. Likewise, the sale or assignment by a manufacturer or dealer of lease payments due under an operating lease should continue to be accounted for under the operating method by the manufacturer or dealer and the proceeds should be recorded as a loan. (Transactions of these types are in effect collateralized loans from the financing institution to the manufacturer or dealer.) However, if all risks of ownership in the property are transferred but the transaction does not qualify as a sale because the sum of the present value of the required payments by the purchaser and any related investment tax credit retained by the dealer is less than the normal selling price or, in the absence thereof, the fair value of the property, the proceeds should be classified as deferred revenue and taken into income under the operating method.

Accounting Entries. A manufacturer using leasing as a marketing aid might have the following breakdown for the "sale" of one unit on a ten-year lease contract:

Cost	$ 9,000
Manufacturing profit	1,000
Deferred leasing profit	2,000
Selling price	$12,000

If the conditions listed above were met, the $1,000 profit from manufacturing would be recognized immediately, and the profit from leasing the equipment would be recognized under the financing method.

Under the *financing* method (using the sum-of-the-years' digits), the entries would be:

1. Immediate (to recognize manufacturing profit):

Accounts Receivable	12,000	
Sales		10,000
Deferred Profit on Leasing		2,000
Cost of Goods Sold	9,000	
Inventory		9,000

2. As payment is received (to recognize leasing revenue):

Cash 1,200
    Accounts Receivable 1,200

Deferred Profit on Leasing............................. 360
    Leasing Profit...................................... 360

If there were substantial risk in the lease, recognition under the *operating method* would be required. Accounting entries (in this case under a straight-line method) would be made as each payment is received:

Cash.. 1,200
    Rental Income... 200
    Sales 1,000

Depreciation Expense 900
    Allowance for Depreciation 900

FASB Proposed Lessor Accounting

Leases that would be classified by a lessee as a capital lease are classified from the point of view of the lessor by the FASB Exposure Draft as being either direct-financing leases or sales-type leases provided the lease also meets both of these criteria:

a. Collectibility of the payments required from the lessee is reasonably predictable.
b. No important uncertainties surround the amount of costs yet to be incurred by the lessor under the lease. Important uncertainties might include commitments by the lessor to guarantee performance of the leased property in a manner more extensive than the typical product warranty or to effectively protect the lessee from obsolescence of the leased property. However, it is not intended that the necessity of estimating executory expenses such as insurance, maintenance, and taxes to be paid by the lessor shall constitute an important uncertainty.

Leases that do not meet these criteria are classified as operating leases.

A sales-type lease is similar to the type of lease covered by APB *Opinion No. 27*, since it normally arises in situations where a manufacturer uses leases that are equivalent to a sale as a means of marketing his products. Direct-financing leases usually result when a leasing company's primary mission is to finance the acquisition of property by a lessee. Typically, direct-financing leases would be similar to those classified as financing leases by *Opinion No. 7*.

Direct-Financing Leases. The FASB proposes that a direct-financing lease should be accounted for by the lessor as follows:

a.   The minimum lease payments (net of amounts, if any, included therein with respect to executory costs such as maintenance, taxes, and insurance to be paid by the lessor), plus the unguaranteed residual value accruing to the benefit of the lessor, plus the initial direct costs shall be recorded as the gross investment in the lease.

b.   The difference between the gross investment in the lease in (a) above and the cost or carrying amount, if different, of the leased property shall be recorded as unearned income. The net investment in the lease shall consist of the gross investment less the unearned income. The unearned income shall be amortized to income over the lease term so as to produce a constant periodic rate of return on the net investment in the lease. The initial direct costs shall be amortized in the same proportion as the unearned income. The net investment in the lease shall be subject to the same considerations as other assets in classification as current or noncurrent assets in a classified balance sheet. Contingent rentals, including rentals based on variables such as the prime interest rate, shall be credited to income when they become receivable.

The estimated residual value, if any, should be classified in the balance sheet as part of the investment in direct-financing leases.

The accounting entries for a direct-financing lease are similar to those illustrated earlier for a financing lease.

Sales-Type Lease. According to the FASB Exposure Draft, a sales-type lease should be accounted for the lessor as follows:

a.   The minimum lease payments (net of amounts, if any, included therein with respect to executory costs such as maintenance, taxes, and insurance to be paid by the lessor) plus the unguaranteed residual value accruing to the benefit of the lessor shall be recorded as the gross investment in the lease.

b.   The difference between the gross investment in the lease in (a) above and the sum of the present values of the two components of the gross investment shall be recorded as unearned income. The discount rate to be used in determining the present values shall be the interest rate implicit in the lease. The net investment in the lease shall consist of the gross investment less the unearned income. The unearned income shall be amortized to income over the lease term so as to produce a constant periodic rate of return on the net investment in the lease. The net investment in the lease shall be subject to the same considerations as other assets in classification as current or noncurrent assets in a classified balance sheet. Contingent rentals, including rentals based on variables such as the prime interest rate, shall be credited to income when they become receivable.

c.   The present value of the minimum lease payments (net of executory costs), discounted at the interest rate implicit in the lease, shall be recorded as the sales price. The cost or carrying amount, if different, of the leased property, plus any initial direct costs, less the present value of the unguaranteed residual value accruing to the benefit of the lessor shall be charged against income in the same period.

The estimated residual value, if any, should be presented in the balance sheet as part of the investment in sales-type leases.

The accounting entries for this type of lease are similar to those presented earlier for a manufacturer's lease that is equivalent to a sale.

Operating Leases. The accounting for an operating lease proposed by the FASB is:

a. The leased property shall be included with or near property, plant, and equipment in the balance sheet. The property shall be depreciated following the lessor's normal depreciation policy, and in the balance sheet the accumulated depreciation shall be deducted from the investment in the leased property.

b. Rent shall be reported as income over the lease term as it becomes receivable according to the provisions of the lease. However, if the rentals depart from a straight-line basis, the income shall be recognized on a straight-line basis unless another systematic and rational basis is more representative of the time pattern in which use benefit from the leased property is diminished, in which case that basis of income recognition shall be considered as justified by the circumstances.

c. Initial direct costs shall be deferred and allocated over the lease term.

The accounting entries for an operating lease are similar to the *Opinion No. 7* operating lease accounting entries illustrated earlier.

Disclosure. If the FASB Exposure Draft is adopted the following information with respect to leases would be disclosed in lessor's financial statements:

a. For sales-type and direct financing leases:
   i. The components of the net investment in sales-type and direct financing leases as of the date of each balance sheet presented:
     a. Future minimum lease payments to be received, with separate deductions for (i) amounts representing executory costs included in the minimum lease payments and (ii) the accumulated allowance for uncollectible minimum lease payments receivable.
     b. The unguaranteed residual values accruing to the benefit of the lessor.
     c. The unamortized balance of initial direct costs. (For direct financing leases only.)
     d. Unearned income (see paragraphs 16(b) and 17(b)).
   ii. Future minimum lease payments to be received for each of the five succeeding fiscal years as of the date of the latest balance sheet presented.
   iii. Total contingent rentals included in income for each period for which an income statement is presented.
b. For operating leases:
   i. As of the date of the latest balance sheet presented: the cost or carrying amount, if different, of property on lease and the cost of that held for leasing, separately; their combined cost by major classes of prop-

erty according to nature or function; and the amount of accumulated depreciation in total.

ii. Minimum future rentals on noncancelable leases as of the date of the latest balance sheet presented, in the aggregate and for each of the five succeeding fiscal years.

iii. Total contingent rentals included in income for each period for which an income statement is presented.

c. A general description of the lessor's leasing arrangements.

RELATED PARTIES

The FASB proposal, if adopted, would require leases between related parties[10] to be classified in accordance with the proposed capital and operating lease criteria in the separate financial statements of the related parties. In consolidated statements or in financial statements in which an investment in an investee is accounted for on the equity basis, any profit or loss on lease transactions with a related party should be eliminated.

APB *Opinion No. 10* requires that subsidiaries whose principal business is leasing assets to its parent or other affiliated entities should be consolidated.

LEASES INVOLVING REAL ESTATE

The FASB in its Exposure Draft divided leases involving real estate into four categories: (1) leases involving land only, (2) leases involving land and buildings, (3) leases involving real estate and equipment, and (4) leases involving only part of a building or building complex.

A lease involving land only would be classified as a capital lease only if the lease contained a bargain purchase option or the lease transfers the land to the lessee at the end of the lease term. All other leases involving land only would be classified as operating leases. A land-only capital lease would not be amortized, since the assumption is that the lessee would acquire the land. A lessor could account for a capital land-only lease as a direct-financing or sales-type lease if the lessor criteria for this treatment were met.

---

[10] The FASB proposal defines related parties in leasing transactions as follows:

"A parent company and its subsidiaries, an owner company and its joint ventures (corporate or otherwise) and partnerships, and an investor and its investees, provided that the parent company, owner company, or investor has the ability to exercise significant influence over operating and financial policies of the related party, as significant influence is defined in APB *Opinion No. 18*. In addition to the examples of significant influence set forth in the opinion, in a leasing arrangement significant influence may be exercised through guarantees of indebtedness, extensions of credit, or through ownership of warrants, debt obligations, or other securities. When two or more entities are subject to the significant influence of a parent, owner company, or investor, those entities shall be considered related parties with respect to each other."

A lease involving land and buildings which transfers the leased assets to the lessee at the end of the lease term or provides for a bargain purchase should be broken into two parts—a land capital lease and building capital lease. The division of the capitalized value of the total lease between its two parts should be based on the relative values of the land and the buildings. In this situation only the building capital lease should be amortized. The lessor would account for this lease as a single lease.

Other leases involving both land and buildings would be classified as capital or operating leases according to the appropriate criteria. If the land's value is less than 15 percent of the total property's value and the capital lease criteria are met, both the lessee and lessor would treat the lease as a single lease and the lessee would amortize the entire capitalized amount. If the value of the land is 15 percent or more of the total property's fair value, both the lessor and lessee should divide the lease into a land lease and a building lease. However, in these circumstances, the land lease should always be classified as an operating lease.

The equipment portion of a lease involving both real estate and equipment should be accounted for separately from the real estate by both the lessee and lessor.

In general, if the leased property is part of a building or building complex, both the lessee and lessor should classify and account for the lease according to the method proposed for leases involving land and buildings.

SALE AND LEASEBACK

The sale and leaseback is a financing device whereby the owner of property sells it and simultaneously leases it back from the buyer. The lease portion of the transaction presents no accounting problem. The lease is treated like any other lease. A lessee accounting problem arises when there is a gain or loss on the sale of the asset, however.

The FASB Exposure Draft treats a sale and leaseback as a single transaction and proposes that seller-lessees classify leases arising from sale-and-leaseback transactions as either capital or operating leases. Irrespective of the classification, any loss on the sale would be recognized as a loss at the time of the sale. The Draft proposes that gains be deferred. The actual treatment of this deferred gain depends on the lessee classification of the lease. If the leaseback lease meets any one of the criteria for a capital lease, any gain on the sale of the leased-back property would be deferred and amortized over the lease term in proportion to the amortization of the capital lease asset. The deferred gain is presented on the balance sheet as a deduction from the capital lease asset. When the lease is an operating lease, any gain on the sale of the asset is amortized in proportion to the rental payments over the time the asset is expected to be used.

If the lease meets the bargain purchase or asset transfer criteria for a capital lease, the purchaser-lessor should record the transaction as a purchase and a direct financing lease; otherwise, the purchaser-lessor should record the transaction as a purchase and an operating lease.

TRANSITION

The FASB proposed that its lease accounting *Statement* be effective for new leases and revisions to old leases entered into on or after January 1, 1977, except for lease renewals or new leases entered into under agreements existing or committed at December 31, 1976. Retroactive application of the *Statement* would be encouraged, but not required. If retroactive application was not adopted, those leases existing at the effective date that are capitalized in accordance with *Opinion No. 5* would be considered as capital leases, and those existing leases at the effective date that are accounted for as operating leases would continue to be considered as operating leases. If any of these operating leases met the capital lease criteria, separate disclosure should be made in the notes of what the income and balance sheet effect would be if these leases were treated as capital leases. Similar transition disclosure rules were established for lessors following *Opinion No. 7*.

For all annual and interim periods beginning after December 31, 1980, retroactive application of the proposed *Statement* is mandatory for financial statements at least back to December 31, 1976.

THE CONTROVERSY

As long as *Opinion No. 5* governed lessee accounting, nearly all of the companies leasing property or equipment did not list lease property rights and rental obligations in their balance sheets. The Accounting Principles Board approved this practice, principally because it viewed leases as being similar to executory contracts. According to *Opinion No. 5:*

It seems clear that leases covering merely the right to use property in exchange for future rental payments do not create an equity in the property and are thus nothing more than executory contracts requiring continuing performance on the part of both the lessor and the lessee for the full period covered by the leases. The question of whether assets and liabilities should be recorded in connection with leases of this type is, therefore, part of the larger issue of whether the rights and obligations that exist under executory contracts in general (e.g., purchase commitments and employment contracts) give rise to assets and liabilities which should be recorded.

The rights and obligations related to unperformed portions of executory contracts are not recognized as assets and liabilities in financial statements under generally accepted accounting principles as presently understood. Generally accepted accounting principles require the disclosure of the rights and obligations under executory contracts in separate schedules or notes to the financial statements if the omission of this information would tend to make the financial statements misleading. The rights and obligations under leases which convey merely the right to use property, without an equity in the property accruing to the lessee, fall into the category of pertinent information which should be disclosed in schedules or notes rather than by recording assets and liabilities in the financial statements.

This reasoning was used by some to argue against the FASB proposal. In addition, others have objected to the FASB proposed showing of leases in lessee balance sheets for some of the following reasons: the rental obligation does not represent a liability to repay borrowed funds; and it is simply a commitment for future rent expenses. Also the legal rights of the lessor are different from those of lenders in bankruptcy. Others argue that the right to use leased property is not the same as ownership, and hence the lease right is not an asset. According to this point of view, assets are rights acquired irrevocably, whereas a lease provides for services yet to be rendered and which may not be performed. Another argument against recording lease rights and obligations is that if some companies were forced to capitalize leases, they would default under their present loan indentures. Thus, a change in accounting would precipitate action on the part of creditors and investors to the detriment of the reporting company, despite the fact that the basic financial condition of the company had not changed.

Those who support the recording on lessee financial statements of lease rights and obligations claim that leasing is a form of financing which has many similarities to conventional debt financing, rather than executory contracts. Typically, the proponents of lease capitalization claim that the lessor essentially completes his part of the agreement when he delivers the leased property. Consequently, the lease agreement is different from the typical executory contract, since no significant future service is to be performed by the lessor. In addition, those supporting capitalization claim that the lessee is committed to making a series of fixed cash payments which reduce his ability to meet a similar obligation to other creditors. Accounting, they point out, is interested in presenting a useful report of the company's financial condition. Given this purpose, it is indefensible, the argument runs, to omit a significant asset and liability simply because its inclusion in the balance sheet would hurt the company.

Two points of view of a lease arrangement underlie the proposal of the FASB. These two concepts, which some FASB members gave greater weight to some aspects of rather than others, are:

Under the first concept the substance of a lease from an accounting standpoint is viewed essentially as follows:

The important characteristic of a lease is the transfer for its term of possession and control of use of property by the lessor to the lessee, subject to any restrictions in the lease. As a result of the transfer, the lessee has acquired a resource representing the potential service to be obtained from using the property. The lessee has agreed to pay for that resource through periodic payments. Financial statements should report as assets the resources being used in the business and as obligations the agreement to pay for them.

The lessor has relinquished service potential inherent in the property. He has disposed of a resource at a price. Financial statements should report the result of substituting one resource for another.

A lease is different from some take-or-pay contracts and other kinds of executory contracts where neither party has performed, that is, where neither property nor service has been transferred.

In viewing the transfer of service potential and the concurrent contractual agreement for the payment and receipt of cash as the essential elements to be recorded in accounting for leases, it is acknowledged that those essential elements are present in most lease arrangements. It is recognized, however, that only in limited circumstances have lessees accounted for the results of lease arrangements in a manner that reflects those essential elements. The adoption of the [classification] criteria [for capital leases] together with the disclosures required represent, under this view a practical advance in recognizing in financial statements the essential nature of the resources of lessees and lessors and the obligations of lessees.

Under the second concept a lease that transfers substantially all of the benefits and risks incident to ownership of property should be accounted for as an acquisition of a tangible asset by the lessee and as a sale or financing by the lessor. All other leases are in substance executory contracts and should be accounted for in a manner consistent with that accorded other executory contracts, namely, as operating leases.

It is recognized that all noncancelable leases convey some portion of the benefits and risks incident to the property. However, it is only in those leases that transfer all, or a sufficiently large proportion, of the benefits and risks, that the economic effect on the parties closely approaches that of an installment purchase. It is that economic effect, and that alone, which justifies the classification of some leases as capital leases by the lessee and as sales-type or direct financing leases by the lessor.

The classification criteria set forth are viewed in this concept as appropriate for the identification of those leases in which substantially all of the benefits and risks have been transferred to the lessee. The fact that the lease term need be for only 75 percent of the economic life of the property or that the lessor may retain a residual value of up to 25 percent is not inconsistent with the concept of "substantially all."

The parallel accounting for leases by lessees and lessors that the FASB believed flowed from its concept of a lease transaction is a break with past lease accounting practices. Those opposed to this conclusion believe that the accounting for a transaction should reflect the nature of the transaction, the circumstances of company, and the reporting management's view of the transaction. One objection raised to the FASB proposal by those who support its general thrust was that the retroactive application of the *Statement* should be mandatory. They argue that if the new requirements are not applied retroactively, similar leases will be accounted for differently. Old leases may be treated as operating leases whereas identical new leases would be recorded as capital leases.

SUGGESTED FURTHER READING

FINANCIAL ACCOUNTING STANDARDS BOARD. *FASB Discussion Memorandum Accounting for Leases.* Stamford, 1974.

CASES

CASE 20–1. DRAXSON INDUSTRIES
Accounting for Sale and Leasebacks and Lessee's Lease Commitments

In May 1970, the officers of Draxson Industries were considering the presentation of the company's lease transactions in the 1970 financial statements.

Draxson Industries was incorporated in Pennsylvania in 1947 as the successor to a family-owned business formed two decades earlier. The company sold supplies and equipment to the commercial dry-cleaning and laundry industries.

The Company

In 1969, sales and net income reached all-time highs of $16.4 million and $343,000, respectively. Stockholders' equity at the close of that year totaled $2.6 million.

Operations of the company had always been profitable. In the ten-year period from 1960 to 1969, net income had ranged from 9 to 22.8 percent of shareholders' equity at the beginning of the year. Book value per share of stock had climbed from $2.68 to $10.54 during the same period. A ten-year summary of selected operating and financial information is shown in Exhibit 1.

From its earliest years, Draxson Industries sought to build a reputation for offering its customers a full line of high-quality equipment and operating supplies. The dry-cleaning and laundry industries in the nationwide market looked to Draxson leadership in the development of new equipment, accessories, and specialized consumable supplies.

The company acted primarily as a national distributor for a number of relatively small manufacturers and as exclusive representative for others in limited geographic areas. About 90 percent of the products sold by Draxson were manufactured by others. The balance, consisting of replacement parts for standard laundry and dry-cleaning equipment

601

EXHIBIT 1

Ten-Year Summary (figures in thousands of dollars except percentages and per share figures)

	1969	1968	1967	1966	1965	1964	1963	1962	1961	1960
Operations:										
Net sales	16,418	15,222	13,056	11,659	10,516	10,099	9,340	7,711	6,246	5,379
Income before federal income tax	750	539	507	286	246	375	402	308	183	188
Percentage of sales	4.3%	3.5%	3.9%	2.5%	2.3%	3.7%	4.3%	4.0%	3.0%	3.5%
Net income to shareholders	343*	259	240	134	118	178	183	145	90	77
Percentage of sales	2.1%	1.7%	1.9%	1.1%	1.1%	1.8%	1.9%	1.9%	1.4%	1.4%
Per share†	$1.39	$1.16	$1.09	$0.60	$0.53	$0.80	$0.82	$0.65	$0.41	$0.34
Dividends paid in cash	94	14	7	2	2	15	—	15	15	15
Financial position:										
Current assets	4,633	4,423	3,490	2,915	2,742	2,634	2,345	1,978	1,566	1,278
Current liabilities	1,988	2,289	1,415	1,282	1,201	1,164	1,156	995	865	647
Working capital	2,645	2,134	2,075	1,633	1,541	1,470	1,189	983	701	631
Current ratio	2.3	1.9	2.5	2.3	2.3	2.3	2.0	2.0	1.8	1.9
Long-term debt	371	424	472	262	390	428	315	441	186	178
Shareholders' equity	2,605	2,036	1,852	1,552	1,420	1,305	1,127	801	672	597
Percentage of net income to shareholders' equity at beginning of year	16.8%	14.0%	15.5%	9.6%	9.0%	15.8%	22.8%	21.6%	15.0%	14.3%
Book value per share†	$10.54	$9.16	$8.33	$6.99	$6.39	$5.87	$5.07	$3.61	$3.02	$2.68

* Does not include income tax refund of 23 cents per share.
† Based on 247,000 shares outstanding at December 31, 1969, and 222,000 shares outstanding in 1968 and prior years.

such as belts, padded rollers, and chemically treated press covers, were manufactured in the company's Philadelphia plant.

In 1958, following the death of the company's president and principal stockholder, the management of the company changed. The new management embarked upon an aggressive expansion program. Existing branches were strengthened by adding sales personnel and increasing inventories. The company's geographic sales coverage became nationwide as branches were established in new cities.

Funds for Draxson's expansion program had been obtained from several sources. The largest part of increased working capital requirements was internally generated. Minimum dividends were paid to stockholders during the expansion period. In 1959, capital stock sold to several members of the new management team provided about $100,000. The balance was obtained by borrowing on long-term notes, which were refinanced late in 1967. In 1969 the company's working capital position was improved by the sale of 25,000 additional shares of capital stock to the general public. At the close of 1969, Draxson's stock was held by about 600 stockholders.

Draxson's Lease Activities

Since 1947, the company had signed a number of lease agreements involving real estate. In 1970 a sale-and-leaseback arrangement was used to acquire a building to house the New York branch. Also in 1970, management was considering the leasing of automobiles needed in company operations.

Real Estate Leases.   Since 1947, Draxson had leased all of the physical facilities used in operations. In 1947, when the home office and plant space requirements exceeded its Philadelphia building, the company sold its plant and moved into leased property.

Branch operations had always been conducted in leased facilities. In most cases, new branches were established in very low-rent districts under three- to five-year leases. After sufficient sales volume was obtained, the branches were moved to larger and better buildings. At the close of 1969, all of Draxson's operations except the New York branch were housed in fairly new, modern buildings. A schedule of the company's real estate leases is shown in Exhibit 2.

Draxson's management had subscribed to a principle of leasing real estate to conserve working capital for inventory and accounts receivable expansion. Early in 1969 the company's treasurer said,

> We have always leased, but I would be inclined to say that leasing is not an industry practice. Many of our competitors, I know, own their own buildings, but this may well be one of the reasons that they have failed to expand from more than one or two locations.

EXHIBIT 2

Real Estate Leases at May 28, 1970

	Philadel-phia	New York	Chicago	Cleve-land	Atlanta	Kansas City	Dallas	Los Angeles	Seattle
Date of lease	5-1-68	11-1-60	2-1-66	5-1-67	10-1-69	9-1-67	7-1-69	4-1-68	8-1-67
Length of lease	20 yrs.*	10 yrs.	25 yrs.	10 yrs.	5 yrs.	5 yrs.	10 yrs.§	10 yrs.	5 yrs.
Probable life of property (from date of lease)	50 yrs.	30 yrs.	30 yrs.	50 yrs.	30 yrs.	20 yrs.	50 yrs.	50 yrs.	20 yrs.
Option to buy at a nominal price?	No	No	No	No	No	No	No	No	No
Cancellation provisions	None	None	None	None	None	None	None	None	None
Amount of annual rental	$45,400*	†	$18,000	$13,900	$9,600	$3,600	$12,600	$13,500	$5,800
Other payments by lessee?									
Taxes	Yes	No‡	No	No‡	No‡	No	No‡	Yes	No
Insurance	Yes	No‡	No	No	No	No	No	Yes	No
Maintenance	Yes	Yes	Yes	Yes	Yes	Yes	Yes	Yes	Yes
Heat	Yes	Yes	No	Yes	Yes	Yes	Yes	Yes	Yes
Light	Yes	Yes	Yes	Yes	Yes	Yes	Yes	Yes	Yes

* Plus four five-year renewal options with annual rentals of $24,100, $22,900, $22,900, and $22,900 respectively.
† $39,700 for first five years and $40,700 for second five years.
‡ Payments required by lessee equal to increases over the initial base year of the lease.
§ Plus two five-year renewal options.

All our leases are negotiated at the best possible price to the company. We do not know exactly what percentage of net income the lessor receives on his investment, but we assume it to be in the 6 to 10 percent range. As our annual report for 1969 indicates, we earned 16.8 percent on our shareholders' money, using it for trading purposes.

No attempt has been made to compare the cost of leasing either with long-term debt or equity capital. These are studies that probably should have been made, but I doubt that they would have seriously altered the company's leasing program. Any method of obtaining equity or long-term capital immediately requires some extra strings on management. This is a factor that we are reluctant to assume, especially when any resultant savings is hit by high income tax rates and earnings at present are satisfactory.

Planned Sale and Leaseback. For a number of years, Draxson had been planning to move its New York City branch to better facilities in a more desirable location. The lease on the New York premises was to terminate November 1, 1969.

After exhausting all efforts to find suitable existing space, arrangements were completed early in 1970 to obtain required facilities through a sale-and-leaseback transaction. Unimproved land was purchased at a cost of $300,000. A contract had been signed with a New York contractor for the construction of a one-story building on the site. Interim financing had been obtained from the company's Philadelphia bank. The building scheduled for completion early in September 1971 was to cost $500,000, including all financing and related costs. The completed building, together with the land, was to be sold to the Old Quaker Life Insurance Company of Philadelphia for $750,000 and immediately leased by Draxson for a period of 25 years at a monthly lease rental of $4,500. The lease provided that Draxson would pay all costs of maintaining the property as well as periodic amounts equal to the property taxes and insurance costs. At the expiration of the lease, Draxson was to have the option of purchasing the property for $250,000. It was estimated that the steel and masonry building would have a physical life of 40 years.

Automobile Leasing. In May 1970, management of Draxson Industries was considering the adoption of a policy of providing automobiles for certain key sales personnel in all branches. Currently, company-owned automobiles were used only by executives at Philadelphia. Under the contemplated plans, a fleet of about 20 automobiles would be leased from a national firm of automotive equipment lessors. The plan, if adopted, would probably be effected later in 1970 when 1971 model autos became available.

Approximate costs were available, although the lessor had not submitted his detailed proposals. Under a typical lease arrangement, the lessor would provide new autos at the estimated fleet cost price of about $3,500 for periods of two years. In addition to a monthly payment of $100 per unit, the lessee would pay an annual charge for insurance, taxes, and licensing, depending upon the location of the auto's use. The lessee would, of course, pay all costs of operation and normal maintenance. The leases would be noncancelable. If Draxon did not lease the cars, it planned to borrow funds at 6 percent from a local bank to finance the purchase.

London Subsidiary.   In late 1969 the Draxon management decided to expand their business overseas. Their plan was to acquire a well-established British company in the same field as Draxon. In February 1970, Draxon located a desirable company and entered into negotiations for its acquisition. The British company's two owners were willing to sell their business to Draxon for Draxon stock. However, for tax and cash-flow reasons they wanted Draxon to lease, rather than buy, the company's buildings. The two owners would also retain title to the company's land assets. In May 1970 Draxon was considering a proposed 25-year noncancelable net lease which called for an annual rental or $30,000. The estimated remaining economic life of the building was 30 years. The proposed lease included a five-year renewal option at a $15,000 rental. The lease did not include a provision for Draxon to acquire the property, since the two owners wished to transfer the ownership of the land and building to their heirs as part of an estate tax planning scheme. Draxon's management tentatively had concluded that this lease arrangement was acceptable. Draxon intended to borrow from English banks the funds needed to finance the working capital of its new English subsidiary. The current interest rate for long-term corporate debt in England was 8 percent.

Questions

1. How would Draxon account on the face of its 1970 financial statements for its existing and contemplated leases under each of these conditions:
   a. *Opinion No. 5* governs lease accounting?
   b. The FASB proposal, with no mandatory retroactive application? (Assume the FASB proposal became effective at the beginning of the year.)
   c. The FASB proposal, with mandatory retroactive application? (Assume the FASB proposal became effective at the beginning of the year.)
2. How should the sale and leaseback of the New York property be reflected in the 1970 statements?

CASE 20–2. TELTRONICS SERVICES INC.
Lessor Accounting

"The irony of life is that what one person thinks is conservative another feels is downright misleading," said Ed Beagan, chairman of the board and president of Teltronics. "We want to tell our financial story as it is, show the Ericsson Corporation we are profitable, the banks we are solvent, and reflect to prospective clients we will continue to be in business in spite of the fact that a number of large companies have dropped out of the interconnect business. Everyone seems to believe that accounting for long-term leases on the operating basis is the conservative approach, but I don't think that this method accurately portrays the operations of this company and I think it deludes our present investors."

Ed Beagan made the above comment in late July during an executive committee meeting devoted to determining the way in which the company would report its earnings for the first half of 1974. Although the selection of an accounting method for the interim report would not preclude the use of alternative methods at year-end, the executive committee felt strongly that switching methods six months from now would damage the company's credibility in the investment community.

BACKGROUND ON THE COMPANY

Teltronics Services was incorporated in late 1971 and began operating in 1972. It provides business telephone systems to organizations in the greater New York metropolitan area. Teltronics product line included telephone switching equipment called PABX's (Private Automatic Branch Exchange) located on the customer's premises and connected to ATT's trunk lines, telephone instruments, and telephone-type intercom systems.

The Industry

The industry in which Teltronics operates is known as the interconnect market which was given its start by the landmark Federal Communications Commission's Carterfone decision in 1968. This ruling required AT&T to permit private telephone equipment to be attached to operating telephone companies' circuits. Since that decision, the interconnect business has grown from 59 systems in 1970 to 2,935 in 1973 and is estimated by the New York State Public Service Commission to grow to 5,000 systems in 1974 and to 63,000 by 1984.

The potential of the interconnect market attracted many firms, but the small initial size of the market and the inappropriate strategies used to deal with it caused such firms as Litton, Norelco, G.E., Plessy, Arcata, and Teleprompter to withdraw after sustaining losses from $1 million to $40 million. At present Teltronics has over 45 percent of the metropolitan New York interconnect market. The balance is distributed 14 percent to ITT, which is down nationwide from 15 to 2 offices; 8 percent to Stromberg-Carlson, which has closed over 20 offices; and 32 percent to some 20 small companies.

Of the factors contributing to the failure of so many firms, Ed Beagan believes the following to be the most significant:

. Direction of initial sales effort to the Fortune 500 companies which put the firms in head-to-head competition with AT&T without first demonstrating the credibility of their product through smaller systems in companies where AT&T's influence is less pervasive.
. The relatively small size of the initial market could only support one or two firms.
. Attempting to sell nationwide at standard prices in a country where local tarriffs make individual pricing policies mandatory.
. Installing a variety of equipment in a dispersed geographical area which makes the high level of service that must be provided very difficult and very, very expensive.
. The disinclination of equipment manufacturers who sell primarily to independent telephone companies to compete aggressively and thus jeopardize a significantly larger market for their products.
. The undercapitalization of small firms that limited their ability to finance customer systems and the tendency of larger firms to utilize ex-telephone company personnel who were less than familiar with rough and tumble competitive situations.
. Differing union wage structures which, for some companies, resulted in installation and service rates double those of others.

Teltronics's Strategy

Teltronics viewed the interconnect market as a classic situation in which penetration would initially occur in small- to medium-sized firms and then move to the Fortune 500. That this was indeed true has been borne out by Teltronics average sale increasing from $8,000 in 1972 to $15,000 in 1973 and $22,000 in the first half of 1974. This increase in size coupled with a growth in the number of systems installed has produced a 50 percent annual growth rate in sales in Teltronics's four-year history.

The second major strategy was financial. Teltronics was formed with the realization of the need to go public as soon as possible in order to have the capital necessary to offer a lease program which, in Ed Beagan's words, "is essential for successful marketing of telephone equipment. A lease program effectively counters the Telephone Company's argument to customers that 'interconnect companies will sell you the equipment and then walk away.' However lease programs require substantial capital because of the investment required in equipment and installation and the delayed return of cash in the form of rental payments spread, in Teltronics leases over three to nearly ten years."

To implement its financial strategy, Teltronics looked to the financial markets. In July 1972 it received an offer from a New York Stock Exchange member firm to make a $1 million private placement. Teltronics turned it down but accepted a $100,000, three-year convertible note[1] with a firm letter of intent for a subsequent public offering. In January 1973 the company sold 200,000 shares of common stock to the public at $10 a share, netting $1,670,000. These funds and the close connections the company has maintained with the banking community—four of the six company officers were formerly employed in financial positions—allowed Teltronics to maintain a cash balance of nearly $500,000. "A customer often has a vision—often implanted by a Telephone Company salesperson—that interconnect firms are going to sell the equipment and disappear. When they see a half million in cash on the balance sheet, the sale is half made." In 1972 and 1973 the company entered into an arrangement with the Chemical Bank of New York to "sell" them customer leases at "prime plus 2½ percent" with a minimum of requirements—a restricted recourse cash fund amounting to 3 percent of the aggregate unpaid balance of these contracts. This amounted to an effective interest rate of about 11 percent a year in 1974.

In personnel, Teltronics has recruited only successful Telephone salespersons for marketing and recruits its technical people primarily from the computer industry because of both their technical expertise which is relevant to the modern equipment Teltronics installs and the mental attitude towards their job that the computer industry engendered and that by and large the telephone industry fails to produce. Teltronics's installation personnel are represented by the Communications Workers of America—the same union representing Telephone Company personnel.

Teltronics's market area has been restricted to metropolitan New York. Teltronics's management estimates that 20 percent of the world's PABX equipment is located within 75 miles of New York City, 98

---

[1] The convertible notes carry a 7 percent coupon and mature in August 1975. The conversion price is $5.

percent supplied by AT&T. New York telephone rates are presently 40 percent higher than telephone rates in all other states. Thus any ultimate expansion will depend on rate increases in other areas—which Teltronics's management estimates to be five to ten years away.

Teltronics's relationship with the L. M. Ericsson Company of Sweden provides it with a strong product line and increased financial strength. Ericsson's worldwide sales in 1973 were $1.2 billion with $204 million in private exchanges and telephone instruments. Less than 2 percent of Ericsson's sales are in the United States. Teltronics serves as Ericsson's PABX marketing arm in the New York metropolitan area. The closeness of this relationship is exemplified by Ericsson agreeing to guarantee a forthcoming Teltronics five-year bank loan to fund its rental program. The Ericsson product line is complete ranging from small telephone systems to huge computer controlled switching systems. In Europe, Ericsson's computer switch dominates the market against such competition as IBM's 3750 Telephone System. Ericsson's downtime is estimated to be 2 hours every 40 years versus the weekly interruptions accepted in conventional computer-based systems. Though higher priced, 20 percent above competition, Teltronics believes Ericsson's superior quality overcomes any market resistance the price may produce and accounts for Ericsson being the second largest telephone equipment manufacturer in the world—next only to Western Electric.

PRESENT SITUATION

The Market

Teltronics offers equipment to customers for purchase or for lease. The leasing terms normally range from three to ten years with the provision that the customer has the right to buy the equipment at the end of the lease at its then market value. In an environment of constantly increasing rates charged by New York Telephone—an average rate increase over the last five years of 10 percent a year—the equipment has actually been increasing in value. As Paul Dominick, vice president operations, stated, "The telephone business is a peculiar one, our old equipment goes up in value each year. It takes 40 years to wear out and, as the cost to manufacture it steadily increases with Ma Bell continually receiving rate increases, we can keep releasing most of what we have for the next 25 or so years."

Teltronics installs the equipment free, generally including one-year free service, and offers service on a low fixed-rate contract or a time-and-materials basis for the life of the lease. As Melvin Silverstein, vice president, marketing, put it, "We are happy to use our service contract as a loss leader; the installing equipment is the key to this business, and you'd be amazed how well customers respond to a guaranteed rental rate and essentially free service." The reliability of the equipment is attested to by the fact that maintenance expenses run some 2 percent of operating expense.

Customer choice between outright purchase and leasing (rental) has been changing—see Exhibit 1. The current shift toward leasing has been due in part to Teltronics sales efforts, in part the nature of the economy, but it is also attributable to the larger systems Teltronics is now selling. "It is much easier for the communications manager to get top level approval—or to even avoid going to the top altogether—on a telephone equipment rental contract than for a capital expenditure. After all, companies have to have telephone service and they always rented it. If you ask a manager what his phone system is worth, he has a hard time deciding even a ballpark number. 'We get it from Ma Bell free, don't we?' is a typical response. We are flexible however and we will try to accommodate the customer in any way that is appropriate—cash purchase, lease funding, investment tax credit, depreciation—you name it."

The Economics

Teltronics rates for telephone equipment are approximately 20 percent under those of the New York Telephone Company. In spite of the flexibility in the terms available, most customers either purchase for cash or take a lease, now tending toward five years in length, that provides for a series of monthly payments with an extra one in the first month and another in the last. Thus a five-year lease would have 59 equal payments plus a double payment in the first month and an extra one at the end. Teltronics uses a 16-plus percent interest rate to calculate the monthly payments which, with the two extra payments, approximates the 18 percent interest charged by banks to finance competitor's interconnect installations. This rate is caused both by the high current interest charges and the dropouts experienced in the interconnect business. Using interest tables, the monthly factor for five years is 0.0245. This times the cash selling price yields the monthly payment.[2] For a system with a cash selling price of $32,000 and a five-year lease (see Exhibit 2) the comparative rate would be $784 per month (0.0245 × $32,000) versus $940 per month for the New York

---

[2] The factor is calculated as that number which equates a stream of rental payments at the end of each month for five years with the present lump-sum cash price at an interest rate of 16.34 percent.

Telephone Company. The average cost of sales to Teltronics has been 55 percent including installation.[3] Teltronics pays a sales commission of 10 percent of the cash sales price. The $32,000 system cited above, if sold for cash, would produce a direct contribution of $11,200 calculated as follows:

Sales revenue		$32,000
Cost of sales:		
Equipment	$15,000	
Installation	2,600	17,600
Sales commission		3,200
Direct contribution		$11,200

In 1973 Teltronics increased its sales to $1,549,000 from $1,061,000 in 1972. During the year the company's owners became divided over whether or not Teltronics should go into manufacturing. The issue was resolved at a stockholder's meeting with a subsequent buyout of the former president. The year 1973 saw Teltronics with an operating loss due in part to the dissention that existed, and in part to the write-off of the manufacturing project's study costs—see Exhibit 3 and 4 for the 1973 financial statements. The stock, issued at $10, had fluctuated between $9.50 and $11 per share until June 1973 when the underwriting firm was suspended from the New York Stock Exchange. This resulted in the release of a substantial number of Teltronics's shares onto a relatively thin and, in general, a declining market. As a result, the stock dropped to $3 within ten days and has stayed between $1¾ and $3 ever since. In July 1974, a class action lawsuit was filed by a group of stockholders to recover the $10 purchase price of their stock. Teltronics Services Inc., sees no merit in the action and believes it has good and meritorious defenses to the claims asserted against it.

The 1973 customer installations were mostly in the form of leases which Teltronics turned around and "sold" to Chemical Bank at an average of 9¾ percent interest annually and the provision of the 3 percent recourse account. These advantageous terms were due to Teltronics's solid financial position and a history of many lease placements with essentially a no-default record. Chemical discounted the lease payments and put the money in Teltronics bank account. Teltronics recorded the cash received from the bank as sales revenue in the same way it did cash from customers. If in the Exhibit 2 example a

[3] The average cost of equipment has been going down—45 percent (excluding installation fee) in 1974 and 30 percent estimated in a few years. This is because Teltronics has been selling both new and used equipment. While Teltronics is currently acquiring very little used equipment, the company is anticipating reacquiring equipment through conversions of customers to larger systems and reinstalling this equipment elsewhere at essentially zero cost.

lease were signed and then sold to the bank, sales revenue would be recorded at $38,685 and the direct contribution is $17,885 as calculated below.

Sales revenue (discounted at 0.008125 per month)	$38,685
Cost of sales—equipment	15,000
—installation	2,600
Sales commission	3,200
	$17,885

The few leases not "sold" were accounted for on a monthly operating basis. In addition, customers are continually adding instruments and features to their systems they have purchased or leased. Each year this business totals approximately 10 percent of the installed equipment base and produces a 40 percent profit on sales.

The First Six Months of 1974

In the first half of 1974, Teltronics increased the number of placements and the dollar value of each over the same 1973 period. While the number sold for cash increased, Teltronics also began to increase the number of leases it held and thus to reduce from 60 percent to 35 percent the number of leases sold Chemical Bank. In effect, Teltronics was using its own cash and its general credit to finance its sales, and this was expected to continue as Teltronics financial structure increases its capacity to finance the leases and as Chemical Bank has indicated a rate increase by the end of the year. This shift in the nature of the sales arrangement and the prediction of its future trend—see Exhibit 1—called for a reconsideration of the method for recording "lease placements."

THE EXECUTIVE COMMITTEE MEETING

In preparation for the executive committee meeting, Robert Chanda vice president finance, projected that equipment placements, priced on a cash sales basis, would be about $2 million in 1974—better than a 50 percent increase over 1973—divided between cash sales, retained leases, and leases sold to Chemical on a 40-30-30 basis. When asked what he forecasted Teltronics's profit would be, Bob Chanda replied, "'That depends."—An answer which required the following explanation:

There is no problem when we record a cash sale. We show the cash price as revenue, the costs of equipment, installation, and sales commission as expenses and the difference is a profit contribution—and we get the cash.

In the past, when we signed a customer to a lease, we would take it to Chemical Bank and get cash for it. Thus we have always recorded as sales revenue the cash the lease provided without having to worry about interest income. Then we deducted the equipment and commission costs and showed a profit—one higher than cash sales because of the 16 percent to 18 percent interest rate built into our leases. When we kept an occasional lease we used the operating method. In the past this problem just wasn't worth worrying about.

This year we are beginning to keep as many leases as we sell to the bank, and we will be keeping all of them in a few years. Thus Ed [the chairman and president] wanted us to review the way we record profit on the leases we keep since we don't immediately get much in the way of cash.

One way to do this is to record profit on the so-called *operating method* in which we would show only the lease payments we receive each year as revenue, write off the sales commission as expense, and depreciate the cost of equipment and installation over its useful life.

A second way is known as the *financial method*. This method treats a lease as really being a sale. With the finance method you determine the selling price by calculating the present value of the lease payments. We could make the sales revenue on a lease equal to the cash sales price by discounting the lease at the 18¾ percent rate we charge our customers. Then we treat all the costs as we do with a cash sale and we would show the same operating profit whether we leased or sold—and our "financial profit" would show the 18¾ percent interest revenue.

The third alternative is also the *financial method* but doing what we do now—discounting the lease at the 11 percent bank rate. With this method, the sales revenue on a leased placement is greater than on a cash sale. If you look at the first sheet in front of you (Exhibit 5) you will see for our lease example the profit pattern we would report if it was a cash sale and if it was a lease under each accounting alternative.

Following Bob Chanda's explanation of the financial alternative a rather heated discussion ensued:

Sal Lo Bianco (vice president, leasing):   The way I look at it is that we are in two businesses: marketing and banking. We make a profit on both, and we have the market savvy and the cash to do both. I can't see why we should get one marketing profit on a sale and another one on a lease. My salespeople get the same 10 percent. The critical element in this business is installing our equipment. How it is financed is a secondary consideration. We check the customer's credit, and if it is OK, we will make any deal he wants in order to make a sale. If we think rental is the only way to overcome his skepticism to non-Bell equipment, we will rent to him and I'll write the lease to best suit the customer's objectives. To me a sale is a sale, and I say show the same profit on every transaction.

Paul Dominick (vice president, operations):   I don't agree, Sal. There is something different about a lease. The customer doesn't own the equipment—we do—and it is good for 20 or more years. Further we don't get the cash the first year so how can we take the profit. Let's use the operating method but depreciate the leases we keep over 25 years. In five years we know we are going to get back a perfectly usable, solid telephone system which you tell me, Sal, we can lease out at least 75 percent of a new one—and that could be 125 percent of the old price. I think our business is renting out equipment for three- to ten-year periods; let's show our profit that way—and you can't call me conservative since my method will show more total profit in five years than yours will. You know, our present accounting method is too conservative for the people who invested in our company.

Ed Beagan (chairman and president):   One thing, Bob, about the financial method is that you never lose sight of sales on an annual basis. With the operating method there is a guaranteed income stream, and thus people can rest on previous efforts and it takes you a while to see the slowdown. You see it right away when you present value the lease.

   Bob, what does the accounting profession have to say about lease accounting; IBM and others surely face this problem.

Bob Chanda: In a way, Ed, our problem is to decide if we are in the equipment or the banking business. The accounting rules offer some basic guidelines to help decide, but in the end we have to choose—along with our auditors. Generally we should look at the nature of our leasing activity, the terms of the lease relative to its useful life, the renewal and purchase options of the lease, the probability that these options will be exercised, and the risks and rewards of ownership. This last factor relates to who "really" worries about the equipment. For example, if the equipment became totally obsolete, who is stuck with it; or if a major repair was necessary, who pays the bill; or if the rates that Ma Bell charges for this sort of equipment are doubled, who benefits from the rate increase.

   If we want to treat these leases on a financing basis, the accounting profession has set down some minimum criteria to be met; these include the following:

1. Collectibility of rents must be highly certain.
2. Any further costs that have to be incurred with regard to the leased equipment must be known or accurately estimated.
3. And at least one of the following conditions must hold:
    a. Title of the equipment transfers to the lessee at the end of the lease.
    b. The lease term runs the full economic life of the equipment.
    c. A "favorably" priced option to purchase or renew exists—so that it is highly likely to be exercised.
    d. The present value of the rent payments is greater than usual selling price or the fair value of the equipment.

   As to the interest rate used to generate the sales revenue, it is often suggested that the rate normally used by the person leasing the equipment is appropriate.

Sal Lo Bianco: That would be the 18 percent we charge them.

Melvin Silverstein (vice president, marketing): Oh come on Sal, you know the only reason we can charge 18 percent is that Ma Bell charges so much and has so conditioned people to believe that telephone rental is the only way to go. Prime plus a few points depending on their credit rating would be a better estimate.

I like 11 percent, it is near prime and it makes Teltronics profits look the best. We use the fact that we are a public company in our sales presentations. Customers in this industry have seen enough "red ink." Our customers are sophisticated, yet I am afraid they would not be able to perceive that Teltronics is running an efficient organization if its profits are way down as they would be under the operating method. I don't think our salespeople have the expertise necessary to explain the differing effects of accounting. Let's show our profits on the financial basis and use 11 percent. Isn't that the rate at which we sell our leases to the bank? Don't we want to be consistent and isn't that what our auditors keep talking about?

Paul Dominick: I don't know what accountants talk about but I think our investors and even our customers should be sophisticated enough to realize the possible distortions that can occur in reporting on an operating basis. I don't want to go too far by comparing Teltronics to IBM, but wouldn't we face exactly the opposite problem that IBM has been warning its shareholders about for years if we use the financing method. When the placement mix shifts at IBM from leasing to outright cash sales, they record a large chunk of profits immediately—the full gross margin to be precise—and thus "lose" the future rental profits they would otherwise have. Every year they've been warning the shareholders that outright sales make the company look highly profitable now, but should not be expected to continue at that level particularly if the mix shifts back to leasing. Our problem will be just reversed if we decide to use the present value method of reporting. Because of the interest rate differential between what we charge and what we use for discounting, every time we sign a lease we will record more immediate profit than if we sold it outright. Thus a shift from leasing hurts our current year profits while at IBM it boosts it. Which is fair? Sounds to me like one of us would have an inaccurate accounting method.

Bob Chanda: I have made up some projected financials under four methods for 1974. Maybe it's time for me to hand them out—Exhibit 6. You will notice that I kept our accounting for cash sales constant. The only difference is in the way we handle the leases. The income statements are based on the same assumptions underlying the cash-flow figures on the next page—Exhibit 7—and reflect the fact that 35 percent of the leases we will retain have come in the first six months—the rest will come in from now until December. As for our cash flows in future years, they will be increased by 1975 sales and so on. We haven't had enough unsold leases in the past to make any difference. I personally believe we should adopt the operating method for *all* leases—the stock market is really lousy right now; good earnings won't help us and bad earnings won't hurt us. If we adopt the operating method, we will have built up a nice "kicker" which can help us out in future years and it hasn't cost us a thing.

IBM and Teltronics are two different animals. We are four years old in a brand-new industry which did not exist a few years ago; is characterized by a high dropout rate; and is dominated by the most widely known, government sanctioned monopoly in North America. We serve as a marketing arm of a billion dollar foreign telephone manufacturer. How much profit would we make if a couple of lessees decide they like Ma Bell better than us. Sure we can sue for collection, but all that would bring us would be legal bills and headaches. As long as that lease is in force we bear the risk of ownership. It's not at all like making a sale. I really think we can prove that the operating method is best, given what happened to other companies in this industry. And besides, think of the future.

Paul Dominick: Wait a minute, Bob. I want operating but not on the leases we sell Chemical. We haven't any defaults on our leases to speak of, and the one or two we have had the equipment was worth more than the balance of the contract. Besides, if the customer has two bills to pay—the IRS and the telephone—guess which one he will pick. He will pay us and call up the IRS to discuss the problem. Chemical gets its cash from our customers, and they gave us ours. I say it would be a real crime to hide that money from profits. We are in a cash-flow business, let's record the profits when we get the money.

Sal Lo Bianco: Bob, the operating method is just too conservative, I like the thinking behind the numbers in column C. They show our profits when we earn them, when we put the equipment in, and that is the story of our business. The gross profit is due to operations, and it doesn't change with differing financial terms; the financial profit is shown separately where it should be.

Mel Silverstein: Well I like the financial method too; but one thing I don't like about your proposal, Sal, is all the financial profit it shows. I say use the prices we charge as the sales revenue and show Ericsson we are great equipment salespersons and not just efficient bankers. If we didn't have a price list you couldn't use the 18 percent but would take the rate we borrow at to produce the sales figure—that's what column D shows and that is what is right.

Ed Beagan: Bob, I think these income statements, the cash-flow streams, and the examples of what happens in each year are helping us to put the problem in the proper perspective. I don't think the operating method fairly reflects this company for its current accounting period because it doesn't show the future effects of today's transactions—the company's sales. In effect future stockholders will be buying earnings subsidized by previous losses. That's not even conservative; that is unfair. The present stockholders are also deluded into making decisions based on a distorted picture of operations. Bob, I appreciate your strategic view; Mel, I understand your wanting to see figures that reflect sales efforts, and Sal and Paul I understand your concerns for cash and for equipment placements. What we want to do is to show this business as it is. Now let's take a look at the options again and see how they match up to the way we really operate Teltronics.

Questions

1. Which revenue recognition method should Teltronics adopt?
2. What criteria should be considered in selecting this method?
3. How well does the method you selected meet these criteria?
4. How does this method you selected compare with the lessor accounting rules of the APB and the FASB view of leasing?

EXHIBIT 1

Nature of Equipment Placements

Year	Outright "Cash" Sale	Lease Placements Retained	Lease Placements Sold to Banks
1972	20%	—	80%
1973	30	10%	60
1974 (first half)	40	25	35
1975 (estimate)	40	40	20
1979 (estimate)	33	67	—
1981 (estimate)	25	75	—

EXHIBIT 2

Typical Contract

Cash sales price $32,000
Cost equipment $15,000
Cost installation 2,600

Lease terms:
$32,000 × 0.0245 = $784 per month for 5 years

Cash flow—contract effective 1/1/74. Rents are received on the first day of each month.

Year	January	February	March		December	Total Payments
1974	$1,568	$784	$784	....	$ 784	$10,192
1975	784	784	784	....	784	9,408
1976	784	784	784	....	784	9,408
1977	784	784	784	....	784	9,408
1978	784	784	784	....	1,568	10,192
Total						$48,608

Present value of cash stream to equal cash price of $32,000 is about 18¾ percent. Cost of the equipment, installation, and selling commission ($3,200) is recovered in two years and two months.

EXHIBIT 3

TELTRONICS SERVICES INC.
Consolidated Statement of Operations
Year Ended December 31, 1973
(000 omitted)

Sales revenues	$1,570
Cost of goods sold	863
Total Gross Margin	$ 707
Selling, general, and administrative expense	934
Nonrecurring write-offs	133
Profit before income tax (loss)	$ (360)
Income taxes:	
Federal	(70)
State and local	(29)
Net Income (loss)	$ (261)
Earnings per share	($0.47)

EXHIBIT 4

TELTRONICS SERVICES INC.
Consolidated Balance Sheet
December 31, 1973
(000 omitted)

Cash and certificates of deposit	$ 868
Accounts receivable (net of estimated losses)	105
Inventory	489
Property and equipment:	
Leased to customers (net)	69
Operating (net)	49
Other Assets	22
Total	$1,602
Notes payable	$ 5
Accounts payable and accrued liabilities	79
Customer deposits	38
7% convertible notes payable	100
Common stock and capital in excess of par	1,748
Retained earnings (deficit)	(168)
Less treasury stock at cost	(200)
Total	$1,602

EXHIBIT 5
Alternative Accounting for Leases

Cash sales price $32,000
Cost (including installation of $2,600) 17,600
Sales commission 3,200

	1974	1975	1976	1977	1978	Total
			Cash Sale			
Revenue	$32,000	—	—	—	—	$32,000
Cost of equipment	17,600	—	—	—	—	17,600
Commission	3,200	—	—	—	—	3,200
Profit before Taxes	$11,200	–0–	–0–	–0–	–0–	$11,200
			Operating Lease			
Revenue	$10,192	$9,408	$9,408	$9,408	$10,192	$48,608
Cost of equipment depreciation, 10 years including installation	1,760	1,760	1,760	1,760	1,760	8,800
Commission	3,200	—	—	—	—	3,200
Profit before Taxes	$ 5,232	$7,648	$7,648	$7,648	$ 8,482	$36,608
			Financial Lease (18¾%)			
Revenue	$32,000	—	—	—	—	$32,000
Cost of equipment	17,600	—	—	—	—	17,600
Commission	3,200	—	—	—	—	3,200
Interest income	5,318	$4,535	$3,538	$2,337	$ 880	$16,608
Profit before Taxes	$16,518	$4,535	$3,538	$2,337	$ 880	$27,808
			Financial Lease (11%)			
Revenue	$37,631	—	—	—	—	$37,631
Cost of equipment	17,600	—	—	—	—	17,600
Commission	3,200	—	—	—	—	3,200
Interest income	3,684	3,022	2,282	1,458	531	10,977
Profit before Taxes	$20,515	$3,022	$2,282	$1,458	$ 531	$27,808

EXHIBIT 6

Estimated Profit for 1974
(000 omitted)

	Operating Method		Financial Method	
	All Leases (A)	Re-tained Leases (B)	18¾% (C)	11% (D)
Sales Revenue:				
Cash sales	$ 800	$ 800	$ 800	$ 800
Retained leases	70	70	610	770
Sold leases	70	770	610	770
Total Sales Revenue	$ 940	$1,640	$2,020	$2,340
Cost of Sales:				
Cash sales	$ 440	$ 440	$ 440	$ 440
Retained leases	33	33	330	330
Sold leases	33	330	330	330
Total Cost of Sales	$ 506	$ 803	$1,100	$1,100
Sales gross margin	$ 434	$ 837	$ 920	$1,240
Financial Profit:				
From banks*	—	30	200	30
Interest income	—	—	47	25
Total Gross Margin	$ 434	$ 867	$1,167	$1,295
Less:				
Sales commission	200	200	200	200
General and administrative expense	650	650	650	650
Net Profit before Taxes	$ (416)	$ 17	$ 317	$ 445
Income Taxes:				
Federal	$ (170)	$ 7	129	182
State and local	(62)	3	8	67
	$ (184)	$ 7	$ 140	$ 196
Earnings per share	$(0.37)	$ 0.01	$ 0.28	$ 0.40

* The difference in present value of the leases sold to the bank calculated at Teltronics rate, 18¾ percent or 11 percent, and the bank rate—which averaged 9¾ percent.

EXHIBIT 7

Estimated Cash Flow from 1974 Equipment Placements
(000 omitted)

Year	Cash Sales	Leases Kept	Leases Sold
1974	$800	$ 70	$800
1975		150	
1976		140	
1977		135	
1978		130	
1979		120	
1980		120	
1981		120	
1982		100	
1983		80	

Chapter 21

PENSION COSTS

A pension plan is an arrangement whereby a company provides for retired employees' benefits which can be determined in advance. The major accounting controversy involves the timing of the charge of the cost of these plans to income and the measurement of the pension liability. Other related issues involve accounting for changes in the actuarial assumptions, appreciation of the pension fund assets, and revisions to the plan.

The passage of the Social Security Act in 1935 created considerable public interest in pensions. During World War II, pension benefits were exempt from wage stabilization controls. From 1949 onwards, following a federal court ruling, pensions were wages and hence bargainable issues; organized labor has vigorously presented demands for expanded private pension coverage. At the same time, employers have increasingly used pension plans as part of their personnel policy to attract, motivate, and hold better qualified workers and executives. This trend was motivated in large part by the tax inducements offered to employers by the federal government to encourage the creation of "qualified" pension plans. The Employee Retirement Income Security Act of 1974 (ERISA) gave added protection to employees covered by private pension plans.

Pension costs are an important cost of doing business. Except in rare cases, when a company commits itself to pay pensions to its employees upon their retirement, the cost of those pensions may be expected to continue as long as the company has employees. Furthermore, year-by-year pension cost should not be greatly out of line with the size or compensation of the employee group. (For example, it does not appear reasonable for a company with a stable or growing employee group to have pension costs of $50,000 one year, $100,000 the next, and $10,000 the next. This could happen, for instance, if the company followed the policy of only charging as its periodic pension expense an amount equal to its annual cash contribution to the pension fund.)

The accounting for pension plans is governed by *Opinion No. 8*, published by the APB in 1966. In this *Opinion* the APB decided that pension costs, included the related administration expense, should be accounted for on an accrual basis, based on an assumption that the employer will continue to provide benefits. This assumption implied in the APB *Opinion* a long-term undertaking, the cost of which should be recognized annually whether or not funded. Therefore, the accounting for pension costs should not be discretionary. This was a break from past practice when some major companies recognized pension costs only to the extent cash payments were made to pensioners or to a pension trust fund.

FASB *Interpretation No. 3* covers the accounting for the cost of pension plans subject to the Employee Retirement Income Security Act of 1974.

In 1976 the FASB was reviewing the accounting for pension plans. It anticipated issuing a *Statement* on this topic in late 1977.

PENSION PLANS

A full understanding of the accounting for pension costs requires an appreciation of the variety of actuarial valuation techniques and funding instruments, agencies, and methods involved in determining the financial provisions for pension benefits. Therefore, the discussion of the accounting for pension costs is preceded by a brief description of pension plans.

Valuation

Actuarial valuation is the process of determining the amounts needed to finance a pension plan. This process relies on three principal concepts. First, the valuation is for a closed group of employees. Second, the ultimate cost of the plan is primarily the present value, as of the valuation date, of the expected future benefit payments. Third, the valuation is merely an approximation, since the assumptions underlying the calculations (actuarial assumptions) involve considerable uncertainty. The valuation of a pension plan is sometimes separated, after it is determined, into two portions: past service costs and normal costs. Past service costs are those pension costs assigned on account of services rendered in years prior to the inception or current modification of the pension plan. Normal costs are those pension benefits based on service after the inception or current modification of the plan. In making the actuarial valuation, however, the past service and normal costs are not considered separately.

At a particular valuation date, in contrast to the inception or modification date of a pension plan, pension costs may be classified as prior service costs. Prior service costs are pension costs assigned to years prior to the particular valuation date.[1]

Assumptions

When estimating the cost of pension plans, actuaries must make a number of difficult assumptions regarding uncertain future events. For example, estimates are made of the expected rate of return on the pension fund, the fund's administrative expenses, and the amounts and timing of future benefits. The future benefit estimates, in turn, may involve estimates of future employee compensation levels, cost-of-living indices, mortality rates (both before and after retirement), retirement ages, employee turnover, vesting privileges, and social security benefits.

Clearly, it is most unlikely that the actuarial assumptions will be realized in practice. Therefore, it is necessary to review and change the actuarial assumptions from time to time. If the original assumptions turn out to have been conservative in terms of actual events, the pension fund may become overfunded and an actuarial gain results. If the assumptions turn out to have been optimistic, there will be an actuarial deficiency.

The net adjustment for actuarial gains and losses is handled by actuaries in one of two ways when revising valuations and contribution patterns. The so-called immediate method applies the net actuarial gain to reduce the next employer contribution. This method is typically not used for net losses. The spread method spreads the net gain or loss over the present and expected future contributions. Some actuaries use the immediate method for handling net gains and the spread method for losses.

Funding Instruments and Agencies

Typically, employers make some financial provision for the current and future benefits payable under pension plans. There are a variety of funding instruments, the most popular being contracts with life insur-

---

[1] Past service costs and prior service costs are often confused. Past service costs represent the present value of future benefits already earned under the pension scheme at its inauguration by employees because of their past service. After the pension plan has been in effect for some time, the actuary must compute the value of the pension obligation. This value will include any unfunded past service cost as well as any unfunded normal costs incurred between the inception of the plan and the valuation date. This obligation is the prior service cost.

ance companies (insured plans) and trust agreements (trust fund plans).

Insured plans cover a variety of arrangements. For example, individual policies providing death and retirement benefits may be issued to a trustee for each employee. A similar arrangement is a group annuity contract issued to the employer. Both of these arrangements specify the premiums and benefits.

Other popular insured funding arrangements are deposit administration contracts and immediate participation guarantee contracts. Essentially, both of these plans require the employer to open an account with an insurance company and make regular contributions to this account. The insurance company in turn adds interest to the account at an agreed rate. When the employee retires, the insurance company issues an annuity providing the stipulated benefits and the annuity premium is withdrawn from the employer's account.

Trust fund plans require the employer's contributions to be made to a trustee who invests the funds and pays retirement benefits according to the terms of the trust agreement. Trustees may be an individual, a bank, or a group of individuals. The terms of trust agreements may give the trustee full power to select investments or he may be subject to the general direction of the employer.

Funding Methods

Once an employer adopts a pension plan he has wide choice of funding alternatives. Some of the more common methods are:

Unit credit method.
Entry age normal method.
Individual level premium method.
Aggregate method.
Attaining age normal method.

Each of these methods produces varying periodic contribution patterns.

The unit credit method funds future service benefits as they accrue. The normal annual cost under this method is the present value of the units of future benefit credited to employees for service during the year. The total annual contribution ordinarily comprises two parts: (1) the normal cost and (2) an amount for past service cost, which may include the interest on the unfunded past service cost as well as an amount to reduce the unfunded past service cost balance.

In contrast to the unit credit method, which looks only at services performed, the entry age normal method apportions to past, present, and future periods the estimated cost of an employee's projected benefits, without regard to the timing of the service giving rise to the benefits. This method assumes that (1) every employee entered the plan at the earliest possible time and (2) contributions have been made from the time of entry into the plan to the actuarial valuation date. In theory, the normal costs under this plan are level amounts. The sum of these payments plus accumulated interest should provide fully for the employee's pension at retirement. The entry age normal method can be applied on an aggregate or individual basis.

The individual level premium method requires the payment of a level annual amount over the period from the employee's actual entry into the plan until his retirement. This method is commonly used where the funding instrument is individual insurance or annuity plans.

When the level premium method is applied on a collective basis, it is called the aggregate method. The aggregate method implicitly amortizes past service costs over the average remaining service life of the participants, whereas the individual level premium method amortized the implicit past service costs over the expected remaining life of the participants.

The attained age normal method is similar to the aggregate method, except the past service cost is specifically determined at the beginning of the plan as it is under the unit credit method. As in the unit cost and entry age methods, the past service cost may be amortized through a variety of contribution patterns.

Income Tax Considerations in Plan Selection

Most pension plans are designed so that the employer contributions are deductible for tax purposes during the year contributed. To qualify for this status, pension plans must meet certain requirements specified by the Internal Revenue Code and the Internal Revenue Service.

There are several other tax aspects which should be noted. First, the tax treatment of pension costs follows cash, rather than accrual, accounting. Second, the earnings of qualified trust plans are tax free. Third, employer contributions to the fund are not taxable income to employees until distributed as retirement benefits.

Summary

The variety of pension agreements, funding arrangements, and the different relevance of the income tax consideration to individual companies results in a wide variety of pension obligations among businesses. This leads to numerous accounting variations for pension costs since the accounting reflects the actuarial method and assumptions of each plan.

ACCOUNTING CONSIDERATIONS

The accounting controversy over pension costs revolves around these fundamental questions: What constitutes adequate accrual accounting? What actuarial method should this accrual basis follow? What disclosure standards should be applied to pension plans and costs? Other related questions include: How should one account for changes in pension plans? What is the proper accounting treatment of actuarial gains and losses? What is the correct way to account for unrealized appreciation (or depreciation) of pension funds? How should one account for possible pension costs related to employees who may become eligible for coverage at a later date? How should potential liabilities for future pension obligations be shown on the face and notes of financial statements?

OPINION NO. 8

Opinion No. 8, "Accounting for the Cost of Pension Plans," supports the accrual approach to pension accounting. The pension cost may be determined by an actuarial cost method which is rational, systematic, and consistent with the accrual approach to accounting. Both the accounting method and the actuarial cost method should be consistently applied from year to year. *Opinion No. 8* places limits on the maximum and minimum annual provision for pension costs.

In developing APB *Opinion No. 8,* the APB agreed unanimously concerning the need (1) to eliminate fluctuations in annual pension costs that can result from cash based methods and (2) to prescribe the accrual basis for accounting for pension costs.[2]

The following accounting entries illustrate the accrual approach to accounting for pension expense. Assume a new pension plan with a first-year normal cost of $100,000 (including interest on the unamortized past service cost). The past service cost is $300,000.

a. At the time the plan is established: No accounting entry is made to record the past service liability.

---

[2] Three technical terms mentioned earlier in the text that will be unfamiliar to most readers are used repeatedly throughout this portion of the text. To avoid confusion the definitions of these terms are repeated here:

Normal cost. The annual cost assigned, under the actuarial cost method in use, to years *subsequent to* the inception or current modification of a pension plan.

Past service cost. Pension costs assigned, under the actuarial cost method in use, to years *prior to* the inception or current modification of a pension plan.

Prior service cost. Are the pension costs assigned to years *prior to* the date of a particular *actuarial valuation?* Prior service cost includes any remaining past service cost.

b. After the first year the actuarially determined payment that should be made to the fund is $100,000.

Pension Expense 100,000
    Pension Payment Liability   100,000

c. The company makes an actual cash payment of $50,000 to the pension fund (the company intends to fund the remaining $50,000 sometime during the next accounting period):

Pension Payment Liability 50,000
    Cash   50,000

It is important to note: No entry in the company's books is made to record the past service cost at the time the plan is established. Also the pension expense was recorded as $100,000, even though only $50,000 cash was paid to the pension fund in the current accounting period. The difference between the expense and the cash payment was recorded as a pension liability.

An Overview

The basic accounting for pension plans required in the *Opinion* is relatively straightforward: the provision for pension cost should be based on an actuarial cost method that gives effect, in a consistent manner, to employee group data, pension benefits, pension fund earnings, investment gains or losses, and other assumptions regarding future events. The actuarial cost method selected should result in a systematic and rational allocation of the total cost of pensions among the employees' years of active service. If the actuarial cost method selected includes past service cost as an integral part of normal cost, the provision for pension cost should be the pension cost adjusted for the effect on pension fund earnings of differences between amounts accrued and amounts funded. If the actuarial cost method deals with past service cost separately from normal cost, the provision for pension cost should include normal cost, an amount for past service cost, and an adjustment for the effect on pension fund earnings of differences between amounts accrued and amounts funded.

Pension Costs: Maximum and Minimum Limits

The APB encountered considerable disagreement as to the appropriate definition of pension costs. Most members agreed that the annual pension cost should include normal cost. The principal difference between the members' views was in the accounting for past service costs.

The APB agreed that past service costs relate to periods subsequent to the adoption or amendment of a plan and should not be charged against retained earnings as something applicable to the past, since the benefits to the company from this form of employee compensation are available for future periods.

Some members of the APB believed past service cost should be specifically recognized in annual provisions over a period of years, although there were some differences in views concerning the appropriate period to use. Other members believed it unnecessary to make specific provisions for past service cost if all benefit payments could be met on a continuing basis by annual provisions representing normal cost plus an amount equivalent to the interest on unfunded prior service cost.[3]

There is merit to both positions. Although the APB stated a preference for past service cost being amortized, it concluded, due to differing opinions as to the real long-run costs of pensions, that it should not at this time rule out either approach as an acceptable measure of pension costs. Accordingly, in order to substantially narrow the difference in accounting for the cost of pension plans, the APB expressed its opinion in terms of a minimum method based on the normal cost plus interest concept, and a maximum method based upon the amortization of past service cost concept. One result of this conclusion is that any period may be selected for the amortization of past service cost, as long as the total annual provision falls between the minimum and maximum. As the *Opinion* is written, it allows a company to fit its

---

[3] In many places, the *Opinion* refers to "amounts equivalent to interest" or "interest equivalents." As used in the *Opinion* and in the actuarial profession, "interest" is a simple way of referring to the earnings, assumed or actual, of a pension fund. The need to take interest equivalents into account in computing the pension cost provision arises when the actual pension fund differs from a theoretical fund and when the amounts funded differ from the amounts which have been recorded for accounting purposes.

Under the present-worth basis used for pension cost accounting, it is assumed that amounts equivalent to prior service cost and normal cost will be contributed to a fund and that the fund will produce earnings (interest) at an assumed rate. If contributions for these amounts are not made, they will not be available to produce earnings, and it becomes necessary to make an additional provision equivalent to what the earnings would have been if the contributions had been made. This assumption is extended to past service cost even though it is known at the outset that the amounts will not be funded until sometime in the future.

For this reason, the *Opinion* calls for the pension cost provision to include an amount equivalent to interest on unfunded prior service cost. Such interest may be included as a separate component of the provision or it may be included in the amortization of the past service cost. Whenever past service cost is being amortized and the prior year pension cost provisions have not been funded, an amount equivalent to interest on the unfunded provisions should be added to the provision for the year in addition to any amount included in the amortization. Conversely, when the amounts funded exceed the prior year pension cost provisions, a reduction of the provision for the year is needed to reflect the interest equivalents on the excess amounts funded.

accounting for the cost of its pension plan to the facts and circumstances in its particular case.

Opinion No. 8 defines the minimum and maximum methods as follows:

Minimum method. The total of normal cost and interest equivalent[4] on unfunded prior service cost.

Maximum method. The sum of normal cost, 10 percent of past service cost until fully amortized, 10 percent of any increases or decreases in prior service costs arising from amendments of an existing plan until fully amortized, and interest equivalents on the difference between cumulative amounts expensed and cumulative amounts funded.

A provision for vested benefits must also be included in the computation of the minimum amount. Vested benefits are pension benefits that accrue to an employee irrespective of whether or not the employee continues in the source of its employer. Vested benefit accounting is discussed later.

It is important to note that the 10 percent limitation applies separately to past service cost at the adoption of a plan and to changes in prior service cost that result from amendments of the plan. For example, disregarding interest equivalents, if a company adopts a pension plan with past service cost of $100,000, the maximum accounting provision would be normal cost plus $10,000 (10 percent of $100,000) of past service cost. If the company later amends the plan to increase benefits, and the cost of the increased benefits related to service prior to the amendment is an additional $50,000, the maximum would be normal cost plus $15,000 (10 percent of the total $150,000) until such time as the original past service cost has been fully amortized; after that time the maximum becomes normal cost plus $5,000 (10 percent of the $50,000 increase). This can be significant when there is a series of increases in benefits over a period of time.

Under the maximum method, when the funding differs from the cost provision, the cost provision must be increased or decreased by interest equivalents on the difference between the amount provided and the amount funded. An illustration may be helpful. When a company adopts a pension plan, it may fund immediately all of the past service cost in order to gain the advantage of the tax-free income from the investment of the funds by the pension trust. Because the pension cost provision with respect to the past service cost is limited to 10 percent, there will be a deferral on the balance sheet for the other 90 percent. Again taking past service cost of $100,000, $10,000 would be

---

[4] See footnote 3 for discussion of "interest equivalent."

included in the pension cost provision for the year and the other $90,000 would appear as a deferred charge on the asset side of the balance sheet. In this situation, the accrual for the following year would be reduced by the earnings on the funded $90,000. If the assumed interest rate was 4 percent, the cost provision for the succeeding year would be reduced by $3,600.

Conversely, if the company decides to make the maximum pension cost provisions but does not immediately make contributions to the fund or makes contributions in smaller amounts than provided, there will be an accrued pension liability for the unfunded amount on the balance sheet. The pension cost provision for subsequent years should include an amount equivalent to interest on whatever amount is shown as an accrual on the balance sheet.

In two frequently used actuarial cost methods, the "individual level premium" and "aggregate" methods, past service cost is not measured separately. That is, it is included in normal cost. Because there is no separately computed amount for past service cost, the defined minimum and maximum are the same under these methods.

On the other hand, in many other frequently used actuarial cost methods, such as the unit credit (accrued benefit), entry age normal, and attained age normal methods, past service cost is measured separately. It is only when methods such as these are used that there is a difference between the defined minimum and maximum. However, if the past service cost has been fully amortized, there is no difference between the defined minimum and maximum.

Opinion No. 8 assumes that the defined minimum, the defined maximum, and the provision for the year will all be computed using the actuarial cost method selected by the reporting corporation. For example, if the pension cost provision is based on the unit credit method, the defined maximum should also be based on that method and not on the entry age normal method, which usually would give a greater maximum amount.

The *Opinion* also contemplates that in all cases, the provision for pension cost will be based on an acceptable actuarial cost method, with all variable factors consistently applied. Furthermore, the treatment of actuarial gains and losses, the actuarial assumptions, and the like should conform with the recommendations of the *Opinion*, and should be applied consistently from year to year (see below).

As to past service cost, except for a special vested-interest provision, the *Opinion* assumes the company will select the interest-only or some amortization plan (not exceeding the 10 percent limitation) and apply whatever it selects consistently. If this is done, pension cost provisions will not fluctuate greatly from year to year, unless caused by such factors as major changes in the size, composition, or compensation of the employee group. If the vested-benefit provision is required, it could cause some variations from year to year. However, the effect is not likely to be material.

Vested Benefits

After an employee has worked for a company for a certain amount of time, which is defined in the Employee Retirement Income Security Act, the employee must acquire a vested right to a part of his or her pension benefits. The right of the employee to receive these vested benefits is not contingent on the employee continuing in the service of the employer. The value of these vested benefits is computed on a present-value basis, giving effect to the usual probability assumptions concerning mortality and retirement, but not to turnover or future changes in the level of compensation.

The APB believed that a company's pension cost provisions should anticipate in an orderly way the creation of a pension fund and balance sheet accrual at least equivalent to the actuarially computed value of its vested benefits. After much discussion of how to achieve this result, the APB developed a complex rule which requires the accounting provision for vested benefits to be the least of—

1. Five percent of the excess of vested benefits over the total of the pension fund and the balance sheet accrual at the beginning of the period.
2. The amount needed to reduce the beginning excess by 5 percent.
3. An amount that would make the total pension cost provision equal to that which would result if 40-year amortization of past service cost were used.

Illustration

Illustration 21–1 presents an application of the defined maximum method. The example assumes the plan was adopted at the beginning of year 1 and amended to increase its benefits at the beginning of year 4. Pension-cost provisions, benefit payments, and contributions are assumed to be made at the end of the year in computing "interest." The assumed "interest" rate is 4 percent; and there are no variations from this or any other actuarial assumptions.

Illustration 21–2 (pages 636–37) uses these same data to illustrate the defined minimum method. This example also includes a provision for vested benefits.

ILLUSTRATION 21–1

A Defined-Maximum Method

			Year			
	1	*2*	*3*	*4*	*5*	
Prior Service Cost:						
Beginning	$88,000	$ 90,000	$100,000	$110,000	$164,000	A
Increase at amendment of plan				40,000		B
"Interest" growth	3,200	3,600	4,000	6,000	6,560	4% of A + B
Normal cost	8,000	8,000	8,000	11,500	11,500	C
(Less) benefits paid	(1,200)	(1,600)	(2,000)	(3,500)	(4,000)	D
Ending	$90,000	$100,000	$110,000	$164,000	$178,060	
Pension Fund:						
Beginning	$ –0–	$ 14,800	$ 25,792	$ 36,824	$ 74,797	E
Earnings	–0–	592	1,032	1,473	2,992	4% of E
Contribution	16,000	12,000	12,000	40,000	25,000	F
(Less) benefits paid	(1,200)	(1,600)	(2,000)	(3,500)	(4,000)	D
Ending	$14,800	$ 25,792	$ 36,824	$ 74,797	$ 98,789	
Balance Sheet:						
Beginning	$ –0–	$ –0–	$ 4,000	$ 8,160	$ (8,014)	G
Provision for pension cost	16,000	16,000	16,160	23,826	23,179	H
(Less) contribution	(16,000)	(12,000)	(12,000)	(40,000)	(25,000)	F
Ending	$ –0–	$ 4,000	$ 8,160	$ (8,014)	$ (9,835)	
Pension-Cost Provision for the Year:						
Normal cost	$ 8,000	$ 8,000	$ 8,000	$ 11,500	$ 11,500	C
10% of past service cost	8,000	8,000	8,000	8,000	8,000	10% of A, Yr. 1
10% of prior service cost on amendment of plan				4,000	4,000	10% of B, Yr. 4
"Interest" on difference between accruals and funding			160	326	(321)	4% of G
Provision for the year	$16,000	$ 16,000	$ 16,160	$ 23,826	$ 23,179	H

Income Taxes

In most cases, the maximum annual pension cost defined in the *Opinion* is the same as the maximum allowed for federal income tax purposes. Generally speaking, the Internal Revenue Service will allow an annual deduction for the normal cost of a qualified plan plus not more than 10 percent of the past service cost.

Other Considerations

Actuarial Gains and Losses. Some companies can make substantial reductions in their annual pension expense when investment gains are realized by the pension fund; the estimated future earning rate of the fund is increased; or accumulated appreciation in pension fund investments is recognized in the actuarial valuation. All of these events are "actuarial gains." The APB concluded that actuarial gains—and, in like manner, actuarial losses—"should be given effect in the provision for pension cost in a consistent manner that reflects the long-range nature of pension cost." The recommended way to accomplish this was to "spread" or "average" actuarial gains and losses over a period of years.

Funding. Accrual accounting is based on the assignment of costs among years on the basis of the economic benefits derived from the incurrence of the cost. Funding arrangements may not, and often do not, follow the pattern of economic benefits. The amounts funded frequently varied widely from year to year because of working capital availability, tax considerations, and other factors. Funding is a matter of financial management. Beyond the legal requirements of ERISA, it may be discretionary and as such is not a matter of accounting principles.

Change in Method. In the case of a change from one acceptable method to another (such as in the actuarial cost method employed, and in the treatment of past or prior service costs or of actuarial gains and losses) the Accounting Principles Board believed that prior cost should be left unchanged; the effect of the change should be applied prospectively (i.e., to future periods). Similarly, if a change is made to an acceptable method, any unamortized prior service cost (computed under the actuarial cost method to be used for accounting purposes in the future) may be treated as an amendment of the plan on the date of change, rather than on the date of adoption or amendment of the plan.

Deferred Taxes. If pension costs are recognized for tax purposes in a period other than the one in which it is recognized for financial reporting, consideration should be given to allocation of income taxes among accounting periods.

ILLUSTRATION 21-2

Defined-Minimum Method and Vested Benefit Tests

	Year 1	2	3	4	5	Ref
Prior Service Cost:						
Beginning	$80,000	$90,000	$100,000	$110,000	$164,000	A
Increase at amendment of plan				40,000		B
"Interest" growth	3,200	3,600	4,000	6,000	6,560	C — 4% of A + B
Normal cost	8,000	8,000	8,000	11,500	11,500	
(Less) benefits paid	(1,200)	(1,600)	(2,000)	(3,500)	(4,000)	D
Ending	$90,000	$100,000	$110,000	$164,000	$178,060	
Pension Fund:						
Beginning	$ —0—	$ 10,000	$ 20,000	$ 30,200	$ 44,628	E
Earnings	—0—	400	800	1,208	1,785	4% of E
Contribution	11,200	11,200	11,400	16,720	16,744	F
(Less) benefits paid	(1,200)	(1,600)	(2,000)	(3,500)	(4,000)	D
Ending	$10,000	$ 20,000	$ 30,200	$ 44,628	$ 59,157	G
Unfunded Prior Service Cost:						
Beginning	$80,000	$ 80,000	$ 80,000	$119,800	$119,372	H = A + B-E
"Interest" thereon	$ 3,200	$ 3,200	$ 3,200	$ 4,792	$ 4,775	I = 4% of H
Balance Sheet:						
Beginning	$ —0—	$ —0—	$ 200	$ 428	$ 469	J
Provision for pension cost	11,200	11,400	11,628	16,761	17,581	S
(Less) contribution	(11,200)	(11,200)	(11,400)	(16,720)	(16,744)	F
Ending	$ —0—	$ 200	$ 428	$ 469	$ 1,306	K
Actuarially Computed Value of Vested Benefits:						
Beginning	$10,000	$ 19,000	$ 28,750	$ 40,000	$ 75,000	L
Increase at amendment of plan				20,000		M
"Interest" growth	400	760	1,150	2,400	3,000	4% of L + M
Benefits vested during year	9,800	10,590	12,100	16,100	17,200	
(Less) benefits paid	(1,200)	(1,600)	(2,000)	(3,500)	(4,000)	D
Ending	$19,000	$ 28,750	$ 40,000	$ 75,000	$ 91,200	N

Excess of Vested Benefits over Pension Fund and Balance Sheet Accrual:

Beginning excess	$10,000	$ 9,000	$ 8,550	$ 9,372	$ 29,903	$O = L \cdot E \cdot J$
Ending excess before additional provision for vested benefits	9,000	8,750	9,800	30,372	32,043	$P = N-G-K+R$
Decrease (increase) during year	$ 1,000	$ 250	$ (1,250)	$ (21,000)	$ (2,140)	Q

Calculation of Additional Provision for Vested Benefits:

Test 1: 5% of beginning excess	$ 500	$ 450	$ 428	$ 469	$ 1,495	(1) = 5% of O
Test 2: Amount needed to reduce beginning excess by 5% (Not less than —0—)	$ —0—	$ 200	$ 1,678	$ 21,469	$ 3,635	(2) = (1)-Q
Test 3: 40-year amortization of past service cost of $80,000	$ 4,041	$ 4,041	$ 4,041	$ 4,041	$ 4,041	
40-year amortization of prior service cost of $40,000 arising on amendment of the plan				2,021	2,021	
"Interest" on difference between accruals and funding	—0—	—0—	8	17	19	4% of J
Total	4,041	4,041	4,049	6,079	6,081	
"Interest" on unfunded prior service cost	3,200	3,200	3,200	4,792	4,775	I
Additional provision under Test 3	$ 841	$ 841	$ 849	$ 1,287	$ 1,306	(3)

Additional provision for vested benefits— Least of tests 1, 2, or 3	$ —0—	$ 200	$ 428	$ 469	$ 1,306	R

Pension-Cost Provision for Year:

Normal cost	$ 8,000	$ 8,000	$ 8,000	$ 11,500	$ 11,500	C
"Interest" on unfunded prior service cost	3,200	3,200	3,200	4,792	4,775	I
Additional provision for vested benefits	—0—	200	428	469	1,306	R
Total Provision	$11,200	$ 11,400	$ 11,628	$ 16,761	$ 17,581	S

Disclosure.   *Opinion No. 8* required the following disclosure:

1.   A statement that such plans exist, identifying or describing the employee groups covered.
2.   A statement of the company's accounting and funding policies.
3.   The provision for pension cost for the period.
4.   The excess, if any, of the actuarially computed value of vested benefits over the total of the pension fund and any balance sheet pension accruals, less any pension prepayments or deferred charges.
5.   The nature and effect of significant matters affecting comparability for all periods presented, such as changes in accounting methods (actuarial cost method, amortization of past and prior service cost, treatment of actuarial gains and losses, etc.), changes in circumstances (actuarial assumptions, etc.), or adoption or amendment of the plan.

An example of appropriate disclosure was presented in *Opinion No. 8:*

The company and its subsidiaries have several pension plans covering substantially all of their employees, including certain employees in foreign countries. The total pension expense for the year was $———, which includes, as to certain of the plans, amortization of prior service cost over periods ranging from 25 to 40 years. The company's policy is to fund pension cost accrued. The actuarially computed value of vested benefits for all plans as of December 31, 19—, exceeded the total of the pension fund and balance sheet accruals less pension prepayments and deferred charges by approximately $———. A change during the year in the actuarial cost method used in computing pension cost had the effect of reducing net income for the year by approximately $———.

Employee Retirement Income Security Act of 1974

The Employee Retirement Income Security Act of 1974 (ERISA) became law on September 2, 1974. ERISA prohibited pension plans from establishing eligibility requirements of more than 1-year service, or an age greater than 25, whichever is later. Employers were also required to fund annually the full cost for current benefit accruals and amortize past service benefit liabilities over 30 to 40 years. Another section of the law established minimum standards of vesting and created an insurance scheme funded by employers to cover vested benefits. In addition, the law imposed on an employer a liability to reimburse this insurance fund for any insurance benefits that are paid if the company's plan fails. The amount of this liability is limited to 30 percent of the net worth of the employer. ERISA also set reporting standards for employers and pension trusts.

The new legal obligations of employers under ERISA led to questions being raised as to what now constituted appropriate pension cost accounting. The FASB in *Interpretation No. 3* addressed these concerns.

Interpretation No. 3 concluded that any change in pension cost resulting from compliance with the new law should enter into the determination of the company's pension costs subsequent to becoming subject to the act's participation, vesting, and funding requirements.

Based on an analysis of information presently available, the APB did not believe that the act created a legal obligation for unfunded pension costs that warrants accounting recognition as a liability, except in the following two situations: First, an enterprise with a plan subject to the act must fund a minimum amount annually unless a waiver is obtained from the Secretary of the Treasury. If a waiver is not obtained, the amount currently required to be funded shall be recognized as a liability by a charge to pension expense for the period, by a deferred charge, or by a combination of both. Second, in the event of the termination of a pension plan, the act imposes a liability on an enterprise. When there is convincing evidence that a pension plan will be terminated, evidenced perhaps by a formal commitment by management to terminate the plan, and the liability on termination will exceed fund assets and related prior accruals, the excess liability must be accrued. If the amount of the excess liability cannot be reasonably determined, disclosure of the circumstances must be made in the notes to the financial statements, including an estimate of the possible range of the liability.

As a result of ERISA, the FASB decided to place the overall subject of pension accounting, including the accounting and reporting by pension trusts, on its agenda.

Continuing Controversy

Opinion No. 8 succeeded in eliminating wide fluctuation in the annual pension costs of companies. However, there are many accounting commentators who would like to see the differences in current practice still further reduced. The complexity of the area and the great diversity of company practices will make this difficult for the FASB to achieve.

SUGGESTED FURTHER READING

AMERICAN INSTITUTE OF CERTIFIED PUBLIC ACCOUNTANTS. "Accounting for the Cost of Pension Plans." *Accounting Interpretations of APB Opinion No. 8.* New York, 1968.

FINANCIAL ACCOUNTING STANDARDS BOARD. *Accounting and Reporting Employee Benefit Plans.* Stamford, 1975.

HICKS, ERNEST R.   "Accounting for the Cost of Pension Plans." *Accounting Research Study No. 8.* New York: American Institute of Certified Public Accountants, 1965.

CASES

Computation of Normal Cost, Past Service Cost, and Prior Service Cost

The treasurer of the Hesper Company was asked by management to compute the approximate normal, past service, and prior service costs associated with the pension plan of a private company that Hesper was considering as a potential merger partner. The vice president in charge of acquisitions gave the treasurer the following information:

Memorandum

To: Corporate Treasurer.
From: Vice President, Acquisitions.
Re: Potential Acquisition's Pension Costs—Computational Assumptions and Guidelines.

To avoid the need to consider employee turnover and longevity, you may assume that all employees work exactly 40 years, from age 25 to age 65, retire, and live for exactly 10 more years, up to age 75. Each employee earns $10,000 per year, payable at year-end. In addition, each employee is entitled to a pension upon retirement and $100 per year of service, or $4,000 per year based on 40 years of service, also payable at year-end. Thus, each employee receives 40 wage payments of $10,000, retires, and receives 10 pension payments of $4,000. Pension benefits vest upon retirement.

There are 4,000 employees working and 1,000 employees retired as of December 31, 1971. For convenience, employees are divided into groups of 100. For any year, one employee group attains age 26 at year-end, a second employee group attains age 27 at year-end, a third employee group attains age 28 at year-end, and so forth; the 40th employee group attains age 65 at year-end and retires, but a new employee group just attains age 25 at year-end and is hired. Similarly, once the retired work force matures, for any year, one retired employee group attains age 66 at year-end, a second retired employee group attains age 67 at year-end, a third retired employee group attains age 68 at year-end, and so forth; the 10th retired employee group dies just before attaining age 75 at year-end, but a new group just attains age 65 at year-end and retires. Thus, the age distributions of both the active and retired work forces are constant at year-end. The annual wage expense is $1,000,000 per active employee group or $40,000,000 for the entire active work force; each active employee group is entitled to a pension of $10,000 per year of service, or $400,000 per year of service for the entire active work force. Similarly, the annual pension payment is $400,000 per retired employee group or $4,000,000 for the entire retired work force.

The pension plan commenced on December 31, 1949, just after one employee group retired without pension benefits and another employee group was hired; the remaining 39 employee groups receive full credit for services performed prior to the inception of the plan. Accordingly, the first pension payments total $400,000 payable on December 31, 1951, to the first employee group that retires under the plan on December 31, 1950. Ten groups have retired by December 31, 1959; pension payments total $4,000,000 on December 31, 1960, and subsequent years.

The treasurer decided to assume that the company used the unit credit method. Appendix A of *Opinion No. 8* describes this actuarial cost method as follows:

Under the unit credit method, future service benefits (pension benefits based on service after the inception of a plan) are funded as they accrue—that is, as each employee works out the service period involved. Thus, the normal cost under this method for a particular year is the present value of the units of future benefit credited to employees for service in that year (hence unit credit). For example, if a plan provides benefits of $5 per month for each year of credited service, the normal cost for a particular employee for a particular year is the present value (adjusted for mortality and usually for turnover) of an annuity of $5 per month beginning at the employee's anticipated retirement date and continuing throughout his life.

The past service cost under the unit credit method is the present value at the plan's inception date of the units of future benefit credited to employees for service prior to the inception date.

The annual contribution under the unit credit method ordinarily comprises (1) the normal cost and (2) an amount for past service cost. The latter may comprise only an amount equivalent to interest on the unfunded balance or may also include an amount intended to reduce the unfunded balance.

As to an individual employee, the annual normal cost for an equal unit of benefit each year increases because the period to the employee's retirement continually shortens and the probability of reaching retirement increases; also, in some plans, the retirement benefits are related to salary levels, which usually increase during the years. As to the employees collectively, however, the step-up effect is masked, since older employees generating the highest annual cost are continually replaced by new employees generating the lowest. For a mature employee group, the normal cost would tend to be the same each year.

Question

Complete the treasurer's assignment.

CASE 21–2. ALLEN CORPORATION
Accounting for a New Pension Plan

On January 1, 1973, the Allen Corporation discontinued its informal pension arrangement for hourly rated employees and adopted a formal plan of retirement under which the actuarially determined costs of past and current services were to be funded through a qualified pension trust. Management considered a formal plan necessary to maintain good employee relations (there was no union) and to obtain the advantages which a funded pension plan offered in comparison with the predecessor "pay-as-you-go" plan.

Previously, the company charged income with the cost of the annual pension benefits paid to retired employees. Retired employees received $235,000 in 1972 and will receive the same amount of 1973 and 1974; pension benefits are paid on December 31. The present value of the past service cost for the 435 retired employees was actuarially estimated to be $1,934,000 as of January 1, 1973, and will be funded immediately upon adoption of the formal plan. In addition, the present value of the past service cost for the 3,500 present employees was actuarially estimated at $4,614,000 as of January 1, 1973, and will be funded in 12 equal annual installments of $472,723[1] beginning January 1, 1973. Current (normal) service cost for the 3,500 present employees was actuarially estimated at $220,000 annually as of January 1 of each year and will be funded on January 1 as incurred. A 4 percent discount rate was assumed throughout, and all interest equivalents are computed as of January 1 of the appropriate year.

Selected financial data for Allen Corporation follow:

Total assets	$47,098,000
Total liabilities	5,480,000
Capital stock	14,120,000
Retained earnings	27,498,000
Sales	57,199,000
Net income	2,009,000

Management proposed the following financial reporting for the formal pension plan:

1. Charge retained earnings with the present value of the past service cost for the 435 retired employees, net of taxes, since it related to wages of prior periods.

---

[1] Given the fact that the implied obligation for past service cost increases periodically due to the interest factor, an amount greater than $1/12$ would have to be funded each year in order to fully fund the entire $4,614,000 past service cost of present employees over a 12-year period. Assuming a 4 percent interest factor, the company would fund $4,614,000/9.7604767 or $472,723 each January 1 for 12 years, where 9.7604767 is the present value of an annuity in arrears for 12 periods at 4 percent.

2. Amortize past service cost for present employees over a 25-year period, which is the estimated average remaining service life of these employees.
3. Charge income with current (normal) cost.

The $6,548,000 past service cost of retired and present employees was to be deducted for federal income tax purposes 10 percent per year until fully amortized. A flat 40 percent tax rate was assumed throughout.

Questions

1. Is the proposed accounting acceptable? Why?
2. Compute the defined minimum, the defined maximum, and any tax effects related to each for 1973 and 1974.
3. What information should be included in the balance sheet of Allen Corporation as of December 31, 1973, and December 31, 1974?
4. Five years after the adoption of the plan, an actuary makes a new study of the assumptions on which the estimated pension costs are based. The study indicates that due to higher than anticipated interest rates on investments and favorable mortality experience, the pension fund balance at the end of five years exceeds the balance originally expected at the end of this period. Since the company's earnings for that year are poor and its cash position is low, management decides that no contribution is to be made into the pension fund. What is the impact of this funding policy change on the company's financial statements for this year?

PART VIII

Stockholders' Equity

Chapter 22

EQUITY CAPITAL TRANSACTIONS

The owners' equity or net worth section of the balance sheet shows the accumulated investment of the owners of the corporation, the stockholders. The stockholders' investment may be made "directly" through purchase of common or preferred stock, or "indirectly" through the corporations' retention of earnings which might have been paid out to stockholders. The net worth represents the "book" or residual value of the corporation; this residual is the assets less the liabilities.

In its balance sheet, the corporation discloses the sources and nature of equity capital, including the types of stock authorized and outstanding and any statutory or contractual limitations. To use this data effectively, the reader of the report must understand the accounting, legal, and financial distinctions between the various accounts comprising the equity section.

OWNERS' EQUITY

The stockholders' investment in the corporation is represented by either common or preferred stock. More than one type of each kind of stock may be issued. If there is more than one class of stockholder, the equity interests of each class should be disclosed fully in either the financial statements or the accompanying footnotes. Accounting treats both classes of stock in a similar fashion.

Owners of preferred stock have certain privileges ahead of the common stockholders, such as a preference in dividends or liquidation. Preferred stock dividends are usually fixed in amount and can be noncumulative or cumulative; usually no dividend can be paid on the common stock until preferred dividends previously earned but not declared are paid. Preferred shares may be classified as participating. That is, the owners can participate in dividend distribution with the

647

common shareholders once a specified level of dividends has been paid to the common shareholders. In liquidation, after the claims of creditors have been settled, preferred stockholders have a preferred fixed claim on assets relative to the common stockholders. Typically, preferred stock does not carry voting rights. Most preferred stock is redeemable under certain conditions, at the corporation's option, at a specified price schedule which usually includes a special premium. Sometimes preferred stockholders are granted the privilege of converting their stock into shares of common stock. The conversion ratio and conditions vary from issue to issue, but the intent of the company is usually the same: to make the preferred stock more attractive to potential purchasers.

Common stock represents the residual ownership interest in a company after recognizing the preferred stockholders' preferred position. Common stockholders elect directors, share in the profits of the business after preferred dividends are paid, and in liquidation share in the residual assets of the company after the claims of all creditors and preferred stockholders have been settled. Usually, common stockholders have the option to purchase any new common shares issued by their company in proportion to their holdings. This is called a "preemptive" right.

The common stockholders' investment in a company is typically shown in three parts:

1. Capital stock.
2. Capital in excess of par value.[1]
3. Retained earnings.

The capital stock account shows the par or stated value of the common shares issued. It is customary to disclose the number of shares authorized by the board of directors for the company, the number issued, and the number owned by the company as treasury stock, if any. The par value of a share bears no relationship to actual value. It is simply the amount engraved on the face of the stock certificate. This practice satisfies a legal requirement and indicates the limit of the stockholders' liability for the debts of the company. To limit legal liability and lessen certain stock transfer taxes, the par value is usually arbitrarily set as low as possible. Some states permit companies to issue no-par stock. In these cases, the no-par stock is assigned an arbi-

---

[1] Alternative names for this account found in older balance sheets are: "other contributed capital," "paid-in surplus," and "capital surplus." The term "surplus" is discouraged because of the misleading inferences naive readers of financial statements may draw from its use. Even today, however, accountants in conversations will use for the sake of convenience the term "capital surplus" rather than the preferred, but longer caption "capital in excess of par value."

trary value and recorded on the books at this stated value, which is usually very low.

Typically, shares are issued at a price in excess of their par or stated value. In these cases, the excess amount is shown in the capital in excess of par value account. In addition, the value of any capital received by the company which did not involve issuing shares, such as donated assets, is included in this account. Other transactions which are described later that could affect the capital in excess of par values account include: treasury stock transactions, stock dividends, and stock splits. The adjustments to the capital in excess of par value account associated with accounting for "pooling of interest" has been discussed previously.

The accounting entries for a new stock issue are fairly straightforward. For example, assume the Lawson Corporation issued at a price of $25 per share 10,000 new common shares with a par value of $5 per share. The underwriting costs were $15,000. Consequently, the net proceeds to the company from the issue were $235,000. The accounting entries are:

```
Cash ..................................................  235,000
    Capital Stock.......................................          50,000
    Capital in Excess of Par Value.....................         185,000
```

None of these transactions, including the underwriting costs, affect net income. It is the preferred practice to show the increase in the capital accounts net of the costs associated with the stock issue.

Retained earnings represents the accumulated earnings of the company less dividends. It also includes the cumulative effect of any special credits and charges, such as prior period income adjustments, not included in the income computation. If there is no capital in excess of par value available, the retained earnings account may properly be charged with those items normally absorbed by the capital in excess of par value account. Also, under some circumstances, such as the declaration of a stock dividend, a portion of the retained earnings account may be transferred to the capital accounts. It is not considered good practice to add to retained earnings the net worth increments created by reappraisal of assets or the purchase of other companies at less than their book value. These increments should be clearly segregated from retained earnings and their source indicated by an appropriate account title.

Treasury Stock

Treasury stock is a company's own stock which has been issued and subsequently reacquired by the company but not yet retired formally. Treasury stock is shown as a deduction at cost from capital, rather than as an asset since legally a company can only reacquire its own stock with unrestricted capital. Treasury stock does not have voting privileges and does not enter into the computation of earnings per share.

When treasury stock is retired, the capital account is reduced by its par or stated value. The number of shares authorized remains unchanged, but the number of shares issued is reduced by the stock retired. Any difference between the retired treasury stock's cost and the amount charged to the capital account is deducted from the capital in excess of a par value account applicable to the retired class of shares. If the capital in excess of par value account is inadequate to absorb the full excess of cost over par value, any remaining excess is charged to retained earnings.

When treasury stock is resold, the capital in excess of par value account is adjusted to reflect any difference between the stock's cost and selling price. As far as accounting is concerned, such transactions do not give rise to corporate profits or losses.

Dividends

Dividends are pro rata distribution to stockholders of retained earnings. They can be in the form of cash, stock, or property. Generally, corporations can only declare dividends out of earnings, although some state laws and corporate agreements permit the declaration of dividends from sources other than earnings.

The declaration of dividends in cash or property by the board of directors legally binds the company to pay the dividends, unless the decision is rescinded by the stockholders receiving the dividends. Therefore, at the time dividends in cash or property are declared, retained earnings is charged with the amount of the dividend and a current liability account, Dividends Payable, is established. When the dividends are distributed, this account is reduced accordingly. Typically, when property is distributed as dividends, the retained earnings account is reduced by the book value of the property.

Sometimes the directors of a company may segregate in a separate account in the owners' equity section of the balance sheet a portion of the retained earnings account and label it as being a restricted or appropriated reserve. This practice indicates that the reserved amount is not legally available for distribution to stockholders as dividends until the restrictions are removed. When the conditions leading to the segregation of retained earnings no longer exist, the reserve should be eliminated and credited to retained earnings directly. Irrespective of whether or not a special reserve is created, any restrictions of retained earnings as to dividend distributions should be fully disclosed in footnotes or parenthetical notation.

Ordinarily, dividends are not paid on treasury stock.

Stock Dividends and Splits

Stock dividends and splits are treated differently for accounting purposes, although they arc generally regarded as being essentially the same from the financial point of view, since they both leave the shareholders' proportional share of equity unchanged.

Accounting Research Bulletin No. 43 distinguishes between stock dividends and stock splits as follows. A stock dividend "is prompted mainly by a desire to give the recipient shareholder some ostensibly separate evidence of a part of their respective interests in accumulated corporate earnings without distribution of cash or other property which the board of directors deems necessary or desirable to retain in the business." In contrast, a stock split-up "is prompted mainly by a desire to increase the number of outstanding shares for the purpose of effecting a reduction in their unit market price and, thereby, of obtaining wider distribution and improved marketability of the shares."

Accounting practice and the Internal Revenue Service do not regard a stock dividend or split as income to the recipient. The rationale for this position was cited in *Eisner* v. *Macomber* (252 U.S. 189), wherein it was held that stock dividends are not income under the Sixteenth Amendment. The court ruled:

A stock dividend really takes nothing from the property of the corporation and adds nothing to the interests of the stockholders. Its property is not diminished and their interests are not increased . . . the proportional interest of each shareholder remains the same. The only change is in the evidence which represents that interest, the new shares and the original shares together representing the same proportional interests that the original shares represented before the issue of the new ones.

Since a shareholder's interest in the corporation remains unchanged by a stock dividend or split-up except as to the number of share units constituting such interest, the cost of the shares previously held should be allocated equitably to the total shares held after receipt of the stock dividend or split-up. When any shares are later disposed of, a gain or loss should be determined on the basis of the adjusted cost per share.

Nevertheless, accounting practice does treat a stock dividend on the books of the issuing company as if it were a dividend to the recipient, principally because many recipients appear to regard it as such. *ARB No. 43* states:

A stock dividend does not, in fact, give rise to any change whatsoever in either the corporation's assets or its respective shareholders' proportionate interests therein. However, it cannot fail to be recognized that, merely as a consequence of the expressed purpose of the transaction and its characterization as a *dividend* in related notices to shareholders and the public at large, many recipients of stock dividends look upon them as distributions of corporate earnings and usually in an amount equivalent to the fair value of the additional shares received. Furthermore, it is to be presumed that such views of recipients are materially strengthened in those instances, which are by far the most numerous, where the issuances are so small in comparison with the shares previously outstanding that they do not have any apparent effect upon the share market price and, consequently, the market value of the shares previously held remains substantially unchanged.

The Committee on Accounting Procedure believed that where these circumstances existed, the company must "in the public interest" account for the transaction by transferring from retained earnings to the permanent equity capital accounts (i.e., the capital stock and capital in excess of par values accounts) an amount equal to the "fair value" of the additional shares issued. For example, to account for the issuance of 10,000 shares with a par value of $5 and fair value of $25 as a stock dividend, the following entries would be required.

Retained Earnings	250,000	
Capital Stock		50,000
Capital in Excess of Par Value		200,000

Unless this approach was used, the CAP believed "the amount of earnings which the shareholder may believe to have been distributed to him will be left, except to the extent otherwise dictated by legal requirements, in earned surplus subject to possible further similar stock issuances or cash distributions."[2]

Where the number of additional shares issued as a stock dividend was so great that it had, or may reasonably be expected to have, the effect of materially reducing the market value per share, the CAP believed that the dividend income implications and possible other constructions stockholders attributed to stock dividends were not likely to occur. Under these circumstances, the nature of the transaction clearly indicates it is a stock split. Consequently, the CAP required there was no need to capitalize retained earnings, other than to the extent required by law. For example, assume a company split its stock two for one, issued 100,000 new shares, and reduced its par

---

[2] The accounting for stock dividends recommended by the CAP will in most cases result in capitalization of retained earnings in an amount in excess of that called for by the laws of the state of incorporation. Such laws usually require capitalization of the par value of the shares issued. However, these legal requirements are minimum requirements and do not prevent the capitalization of a larger amount.

value per common share from $5 to $2.50. Under these circumstances, no accounting entries would be required. The capital stock account would remain unchanged. However, compared to the situation before the split, the footnotes to the capital section of the balance sheet would now show twice as many authorized and outstanding shares and a par value per share of half the original value. Now, assume the company did not reduce its par value per share. In order to reflect the fact that the par value of the stock issued had increased by $500,000, the following entries would be required:

Retained Earnings... 500,000
    Capital Stock...   500,000

In addition, when the circumstances indicated that a stock split had occurred, the CAP required that the use of the word "dividend" should be avoided in related corporate resolutions, notices, and announcements. In those cases where because of legal requirements this could not be done, the CAP required that the transaction be described as a "split-up effected in the form of a dividend."

The problem of resolving at what point a stock dividend becomes so big as to constitute a stock split was resolved by *ARB No. 43* as follows:

Obviously the point at which the relative size of the additional shares issued becomes large enough to materially influence the unit market price of the stock will vary with individual companies and under differing market conditions and, hence, no single percentage can be laid down as a standard for determining when capitalization of earned surplus in excess of legal requirements is called for and when it is not. However, on the basis of a review of market action in the case of shares of a number of companies having relatively recent stock distributions, it would appear that there would be few instances involving the issuance of additional shares of less than, say 20% or 25% of the number previously outstanding where the effect would not be such as to call for the procedure [described for accounting for stock dividends].

Bulletin No. 43 does not indicate the appropriate date for determining the fair market value of stock dividends. Typically, the declaration date is used, although in practice the ex-dividend and payment dates have also been used.

Noncompensatory Plans to Issue Stock to Employees

Many companies have employed stock purchase plans which seek to encourage employee ownership of the company's shares by allowing the employee to purchase shares at prices slightly below the current market price. The hope is that the share ownership will lead to a better relationship between the employee and the company. The primary interest of such plans is not to compensate employees.

In *Opinion No. 25*, "Accounting for Stock Issued to Employees," the APB concluded that employer corporations need not recognize an element of employee compensation expense for the services of employees who acquire stock through such noncompensatory plans as long as the plan had at least four criteria: namely, substantially all full-time employees after meeting limited employment qualifications can participate; the stock is offered to eligible employees equally or based on a uniform percentage of salary or wages; the time permitted for exercise of an option or purchase right is limited to a reasonable period; and the discount from the market price of the stock is no greater than would be reasonable in an offer of stock to stockholders. Any employee stock acquisition plan or agreement that does not possess these four characteristics is classified for accounting purposes as a compensatory plan.

Compensatory Stock Option and Purchase Plans

In order to compensate managers and to increase their interest in their company's activities, companies sometimes issue to managers on a selective basis nontransferable rights entitling them to buy a stated number of shares of stock at a specific price during some limited time period. These plans do not have the characteristics of noncompensatory plans.

If the fair market value of a stock option is more than the option price at the time the option is granted, any gain the recipient realizes at the time the option is exercised may be taxed as ordinary income. Consequently, the option price is usually close to the market price at the time the right is granted.

The hope of those granting stock options is that through the efforts of those receiving them the price of the company's stock will rise above the option price. If this expectation is realized, the stock option recipient regards the increase in value of his stock purchase right as additional compensation.

For a number of years, there was considerable accounting controversy as to how to measure such compensation and over what period to expense it. For example:

On January 1, 1970, John Lester, the president of a publicly owned company, is granted the right to purchase 10,000 shares of the company's $5 par value stock at a price of $10 per share. The earliest time he can exercise this right is December 1, 1970. His right expires on December 31, 1973. The market price of this stock on January 1, 1970, was $12 per share. By December 31, 1970, the price had reached $20 per share. On January 25, 1973, John Lester exercised his right and was issued 10,000 shares at $10 per share. The current market price was $35 per share.

To ignore the compensation element of these events would lead to an overstatement of the company's income and an understatement of John Lester's cost of services. The problem is how to measure the compensation. Is it the difference between the grant price and the market price at the grant date? The difference between the grant price and the market price at the time the option is exercised? Or, the difference between the grant price and the price of the stock when the grantee sells it?

Opinion No. 25 concluded that in the case of compensatory plans, such as the John Lester one cited above, compensation for services should be measured by the difference between the quoted market price of the stock and the amount, if any, the employee is required to pay at the measurement date, which is the first date both the number of shares that an individual employee is entitled to receive and the option price are known. If a quoted market price is unavailable, then an estimate of the market value must be made.

The measurement date in the John Lester example is the grant date. Also, since the market value of the optioned stock at that date is $12 per share and the option price is $10 per share, compensation must be recognized.

If compensation is involved in a stock option plan, the amount of the compensation should be charged to income in some reasonable manner consistent with the facts of the situation in the period during which the services of the employee covered by the plan are rendered. Sometimes the stock option plan states that the employee can exercise the option only if he agrees to stay with the company for a specified period of time. In this case, it is reasonable to charge the compensation to income during this specified period. The offset to the income charge should be a credit to the Accumulated Credit under Stock Option Plan account, which is shown in the owners' equity section of the balance sheet. When the stock option is exercised, the credit item is eliminated.

Using the John Lester example, the accounting entries would be:

a. When the option was granted:

Additional Compensation	20,000	
Accumulated Credit under Stock Option Plan*		20,000

    * 10,000 shares times the difference between the option price and the market price at the grant date.

b. When the option was exercised:

Cash	100,000	
Accumulated Credit under Stock Option Plan	20,000	
Common Stock, $5 par value		50,000
Capital in Excess of Par Value		70,000

Issuance of 10,000 shares at $10 per share pursuant to stock option plan.

If a stock option is not exercised because an employee fails to meet all of his obligations, any related accrued compensation expense should be adjusted by decreasing compensation expense in the period of forfeiture. If an option is not exercised before the expiration date of the option, a similar accounting entry is made. In both cases the related accumulated credit is added to owners' equity.

Should a company obtain a tax benefit under an employee stock option plan, the amount of the tax benefit allocated to income should be limited to the tax benefit related to the compensation cost recognized in income for accounting purposes. The balance of the tax benefit, if any, should be considered as a capital transaction.

Convertible Securities

A number of companies have issued bonds and other debt obligations which have future implications for the stockholders' equity accounts because they are either convertible into stock or carry detachable warrants to purchase stock. Chapter 19 indicated the appropriate accounting for these conversion privileges and warrants.

SUGGESTED FURTHER READING

MELCHER, BEATRICE. *Stockholders' Equity.* New York: American Institute of Certified Public Accountants, 1973.

CASE

CASE 22–1. KEMP FOODS CORPORATION
Accounting for Changes in Net Worth Accounts

"Here's the entire mess," said Ed McCowan, as papers of various sizes and colors fluttered from the large manila envelope and spread over the desk of Dan Conner, CPA. "I bought 40 shares of Kemp Foods common last year in May. Since then I've received proxy statements, notices of stock splits, stock certificates, quarterly financial statements, and a few dividend checks. When this thick annual report came in yesterday's mail, I called you. I knew what to do with those little dividend checks, but to tell the truth I don't know what the rest of this means. I thought the annual report would explain things, but I don't see any relationship between my 40 shares and the big numbers and big words in the report."

"It appears that you saved everything, Ed," said Dan Conner. "Let's see if we can list things as they happened from the beginning." He made these notes on a desk pad as he selected papers from the assortment before him.

May 5, 1974, bought 40 common at 38 plus commission	$1,539.60
July 20, 1974, received cash dividends, 40 at 25¢	10.00
Oct. 20, 1974, received cash dividends, 40 at 25¢	10.00
Oct. 25, 1974, received 2 shares, common stock dividend.	
Jan. 20, 1975, received cash dividends, 42 at 25¢	10.50
Mar. 15, 1975, received 21 shares, 3 for 2 stock split.	
Apr. 20, 1975, received cash dividends, 63 at 20¢	12.60

"Now, let's look at the quotations in today's *Wall Street Journal* and see how you've made out over the past year. Here it is on the Pacific Coast Exchange. The June 10 closing price was 28½. Now we'll look at the April 30, 1975, annual report together and see what it tells us."

This case concerns corporate financial reporting for changes in stockholders' equity and its meaning to the investor.

The Company

Kemp Foods Corporation was established in Illinois in 1937 to acquire and operate three small vegetable canning plants. Operations were expanded to include canning of fruits and frozen fruit processing. The growth of these newer activities in the late 1950s was responsible for transfer of company headquarters to California. In 1975 the company had 15 canning and processing plants throughout the Midwest and on the West Coast.

Kemp's operations had always been profitable. Earnings per share of common reached an historic high of $2.27 in the fiscal year ended April 30, 1975. Net income for the year was $1.3 million on sales of almost $59 million. Stockholders' equity at April 30, 1975, exceeded $13 million. The company's comparative balance sheets at the close of the two most recent years are shown in Exhibit 1. An analysis of common stock, paid-in surplus, and retained earnings is shown in Exhibit 2.

Most of the funds needed to finance the company's growth had been provided internally. Modest cash dividends had been paid quarterly without interruption since 1956, when the common stock was split three for one. In 1962, after a public offering of preferred and common stock, a policy of supplementing the regular cash dividends with stock dividends to common stockholders was adopted. Five percent stock dividends were declared in each year thereafter except for 1965 and 1966, when stock dividends were 20 percent and 10 percent respectively. The 4 percent preferred stock was gradually being retired as it became available in the market at an attractive price. Some funds had been obtained by the use of long-term debt and future expansion was to be financed more extensively in this way.

The price of Kemp Foods' common stock had risen steadily since the early 1960s. For example, the price had ranged from a low of 12¾ to a high of 18⅝ in the year 1969 and reached an all time high of 43½ in 1974.

Questions

1. Evaluate Ed McCowan's investment at June 10, 1975.
2. Examine the stockholders' equity section of Kemp Foods' balance sheet to:
   a. Determine how each item was originally created.
   b. Explain changes during the year ended April 30, 1975.
3. Contrast Kemp's methods of reporting preferred treasury stock and common treasury stock.

4. What is the effect of Kemp's acquisition of treasury stock upon investor McCowan's holdings?
5. Suggest improvements Kemp might make in reporting stockholders' equity information on its balance sheet.
6. How does the issuance of stock options to the management change the company's net worth accounts at *(a)* date of issuance, *(b)* date the options are first exercisable, and *(c)* date exercised? Assume options to buy 2,000 shares are first exercisable in 1975. (These were issued originally at a price equal to the then current market price of 20.) What would be the accounting entry for these options if they were exercised during 1975, when the market price of Kemp stock was 26? How did the company originally account for the granting of these options?

EXHIBIT 1

KEMP FOODS CORPORATION

Comparative Balance Sheets, April 30, 1975, and 1974

Assets

	1975	1974
Current Assets:		
Cash	$ 996,020	$ 1,124,588
Receivables (net)	5,076,894	5,084,087
Inventories, at the lower of cost (Fifo basis)		
or market	10,440,509	8,708,578
Total Current Assets	$16,513,423	$14,917,253
Prepaid expenses	133,434	230,002
Plant and Equipment:		
Land	$ 290,349	$ 346,319
Buildings and leasehold improvements	4,200,760	4,719,515
Machinery and equipment	3,916,508	4,275,927
Automotive equipment	601,393	586,030
Construction in progress	2,033,324	—
	$11,042,334	$ 9,927,791
Less: Accumulated depreciation		
and amortization	5,038,251	4,532,968
Net Plant and Equipment	$ 6,004,083	$ 5,394,823
Total Assets	$22,650,940	$20,542,078

Liabilities

	1975	1974
Current Liabilities:		
Bank loans	$ 2,192,500	$ 1,350,000
Current maturities of long-term debt	170,790	163,478
Accounts payable and accrued liabilities	2,187,440	1,770,026
Income taxes	1,014,527	936,889
Dividends payable	126,811	102,554
Total Current Liabilities	$ 5,692,068	$ 4,322,947
Long-term debt, noncurrent portion	3,660,223	3,831,013
Deferred income taxes and other expenses	273,850	174,225
	$ 9,626,141	$ 8,328,185

EXHIBIT 1 (continued)

Stockholders' Equity:	1975	1974
Cumulative 4% preferred stock, par value $100; authorized 15,000 shares, issued 8,995 shares less 198 shares in treasury	$ 879,700	
Common stock, par value $5; authorized 1,000,000 shares, issued 590,552 shares, (4,482 shares in treasury, see below)	2,952,760	
Capital in excess of par value (Exhibit 2)	2,853,702	
Retained earnings (Exhibit 2):		
Reserve for plant expansion	1,466,676	
Unappropriated*	4,997,457	
	$13,150,295	
Less: Treasury stock, common (4,482 shares at cost)	125,496	
Total Stockholders' Equity	$13,024,799	12,213,893
Total Liabilities	$22,650,940	$20,542,078

* Under terms of the long-term debt agreement $2,330,808 of retained earnings at April 30, 1975, is restricted against payment of cash dividends on or purchase of common stock.

EXHIBIT 2
Common Stock, Paid-In Surplus, and Retained Earnings
For the Year Ended April 30, 1975

	Common Stock		Capital in Excess of Par Value	Retained Earnings	
	Shares	Par Value		Reserve for Plant Exp.	Unappro-priated
Balance at May 1, 1974	375,130	$1,875,650	$3,197,277	$3,500,000	$2,742,831
Add:					
Net income for the year	—	—	—	—	1,376,871
Gain on sale of 600 shares common treasury stock ...	—	—	17,716	—	—
Discount on 245 shares of preferred stock purchased	—	—	4,003	—	—
Reduction in reserve for plant expansion	—	—	—	(2,033,324)	2,033,324
Total	375,130	$1,875,650	$3,218,996	$1,466,676	$6,153,026
Add or (deduct):					
Transfer to common stock in connection with 3 for 2 stock split	196,690	983,450	(983,450)	—	—
Cash dividends:					
Preferred ($4 per share) ..	—	—	—	—	(35,386)
Common ($0.95 per share)	—	—	—	—	(408,367)
5% stock dividend, recorded at fair market value of $38 per share	18,732	93,660	618,156	—	(711,816)
Balance at April 30, 1975	590,552	$2,952,760	$2,853,702	$1,466,676	$4,997,457

PART IX

Special Accounting Problems

Chapter 23

ACCOUNTING FOR FOREIGN OPERATIONS

Multinational corporations operate in a number of different currencies. Typically, their overseas subsidiaries maintain their accounting records in the local currency. For equity method accounting and consolidation purposes, these different currency statements must be restated to a common currency, which in the case of American-controlled multinationals is the U.S. dollar.

The process of translation remeasures in dollars the foreign currency denominated assets and liabilities of a company. *No actual conversion* of assets or liabilities from one currency to another takes place. If the exchange rate between the dollar and the local foreign currency changes, this accounting procedure can give rise to an unrealized dollar exchange gain or loss due to translation. Realized exchange gains or losses can also result from the *actual* conversion of foreign currency or the settlement of a receivable or payable denominated in a foreign currency at a rate different from that at the time when the item was recorded.

FASB *Statement No.* 8 issued in 1975 established the accounting and reporting standards for translating statements from one currency to another. This *Statement* also governs the reporting of foreign currency transactions.

EXCHANGE RATES

The exchange rate is the amount of a currency which must be exchanged for one unit of another. For example $1 (Australian) is equivalent to $1.25 (U.S.). Conversely, one would have to pay $0.80 (Australian) to purchase $1 (U.S.). Since each country has its own currency, there are a multiplicity of exchange rates. The rates for the major countries involved in international trade are published daily in most of the leading newspapers.

At any moment, more than one exchange rate may exist between two currencies. For example, the "spot" or immediate currency delivery rate is usually different from the forward rate for delivery in, say, 90 days. Sometimes, countries use different rates for financing different types of goods and services. Also, in some cases, a black market rate might exist alongside the official government rate.

The supply and demand for foreign currencies is influenced by international movements involving goods, services, and investments as well as speculative activities in foreign currencies. For example, when United States residents export goods or services overseas they receive payment in U.S. dollars. To obtain these U.S. dollars, the foreign importers must exchange some foreign currency. Thus, the U.S. exports increase the supply of foreign currency and the demand for U.S. dollars in the foreign exchange market. The reverse situation exists when U.S. residents import goods or services from overseas.

In a free market, the exchange rate will tend to stabilize at the point where the supply and demand for a currency are in balance. This balance can be influenced by a variety of factors. Since a country's exports and imports often reflect its internal cost-price structure, changes in the domestic purchasing power of different currencies may influence their relative exchange rates. The exchange rate in free markets is also influenced by the fact that not all imports and exports are bought on price alone. For example, consumer preferences for certain imports and inelastic demand situations can complicate the adjustment mechanism. Also, if any discrepancies between foreign exchange markets exist, arbitrage activities by foreign currency traders will soon eliminate the discrepancies.

In the early 1970s the major trading countries moved away from a policy which supported fixed exchange rates to one that permitted freely fluctuating exchange rates. To minimize the possibility that freely fluctuating rates could cause distortions in a country's balance of payments and internal economy, governments use a number of devices that increase the supply or decrease the demand for their currency to keep their exchange rates fairly stable and at a desired level. These include selling or adding to foreign exchange reserves, establishing foreign exchange controls, imposing import controls, subsidizing exports, and reducing foreign aid programs.

Restrictions upon the free exchange of currencies can lead to a currency being overvalued. In these cases, it becomes desirable to shift funds from the overvalued currency to the more normally valued currencies. In order to halt this flight from the overvalued ("soft") currency to the normally valued ("hard") currencies, the soft currency can be declared inconvertible by its government. Thus, the currency cannot be freely exchanged for other currencies. Countries can make their currencies wholly inconvertible for all people, or for residents but not foreigners; for some but not all other currencies; and for certain types of transactions only.

At times, governments with serious adverse balance of payments problems are unable to maintain their currency's exchange rate. The classical solution to this problem is to let the currency devalue. It is hoped that this step will improve the balance of trade by making it more expensive for citizens to import goods and less expensive for foreigners to buy exports. Successful devaluation requires an increase in exports and, since local prices of imported goods will rise, an antiinflationary domestic fiscal policy must be instituted. However, since trade is only one part of the total international payments system, currency speculation, foreign investments, and military aid may also affect the payments balance.

TRANSLATION OF STATEMENTS

Managers and stockholders of U.S. companies with overseas subsidiaries generally measure the success of these overseas operations in terms of the changes in the U.S. dollar equivalent of their net worth determined in accordance with generally accepted accounting principles. In order to do this, the local currency statements of the foreign subsidiary must be restated to their U.S. dollar equivalent. No actual cash changes hands in this process. It is simply a work sheet adjustment. For example, to convert a balance sheet account in Australian dollars to U.S. dollars, most items on the Australian statement are multiplied by 1.25, since $1 (Australian) equals $1.25 (United States). If there has been a change in the exchange rate, as explained later, some items on the balance sheet and statement of retained earnings will be multiplied by an old rate and some by the current rate. Thus, when each item is converted to dollars, the statements will most probably be out of balance. The balancing item is the translation gain or loss.

Once each of the items on the right-hand side of the following equation have been converted from local currency to U.S. dollars, the translation gain or loss can be computed as follows:

Translation Gains or Losses = Assets − (liabilities
+ beginning net worth + profit
− dividends)

If the answer is a negative amount, then a loss has occurred. It must be deducted from the owners' equity portion of the right-hand side of the balance sheet to bring the right and left sides into balance. That will occur if after translation:

Assets < (liabilities + beginning net worth + profit − dividends)

Conversely, if the assets are greater than the right-hand side of the equation, a translation gain will occur.[1]

The way to translate each of the items in the equation from local currency to U.S. dollars is specified by *Statement No. 8,* which accepted the so-called "temporal method." *Statement No. 8* also required that the translation gain or loss calculated by this method be included in the determination of income for the period in which the gain or loss occurs. Translation gains of losses arising in an interim period should be included in the net income calculation for that interim period.

Temporal Method

Statement No. 8 adopted the "temporal method" for translating foreign currency denominated statements into U.S. dollars. This approach recognizes the different items are affected differently by exchange rate changes. It groups the balance sheet accounts into categories which reflect their responsiveness to exchange changes.

The first category is those accounts denominated in a foreign currency that represent either money and claims to money or are stated at the current market price. Cash, accounts receivable, and investments in securities carried at market fall into this category. These accounts are translated at the current rate, which is the exchange rate prevailing on the date of the statement.

The second category includes all of the other balance sheet items. These accounts are translated at the so-called historical rate, which is the rate of exchange existing on the date the transaction took place that created the item. For example, in the case of fixed assets, the historical rate would be the rate prevailing at the time the company acquired the assets.

Foreign currency denominated revenue and expense transactions are translated into dollars at the rate on the day the transaction occurred. Since separate translation of each transaction is usually impractical, an average rate for a period, such as a month or quarter, is used to translate the revenue and expense transactions of that period.

The exceptions to this general income statement approach are revenues and expenses that relate to assets and liabilities that are translated at historical rates. These income statement items are translated at the historical rates used to translate the related assets or liabilities. For example, the depreciation expense, which relates to the plant and

---

[1] The translation gain or loss can be calculated directly. The procedure is essentially the same as the direct computation of the monetary gain or loss described in Chapter 15, "Price Level and Replacement Cost Accounting."

equipment asset, is translated at the same historical rate used to translate the related asset.

Illustration 23–1 lists the rates used to translate assets and liabilities.

The selection of the appropriate current rate presents problems in those cases where multiple rates exist or the currency is not freely convertible. When multiple rates are encountered, the rate for remitting dividends to U.S. shareholders is often used, since the ultimate

ILLUSTRATION 23–1

Rates Used to Translate Assets and Liabilities

	Translation Rates	
	Current	Historical
Assets		
Cash on hand and demand and time deposits	x	
Marketable equity securities:		
Carried at cost		x
Carried at current market price	x	
Accounts and notes receivable and related		
unearned discount	x	
Allowance for doubtful accounts and notes		
receivable	x	
Inventories:		
Carried at cost		x
Carried at current replacement price of		
current selling price	x	
Carried at net realizable value	x	
Carried at contract price (produced under		
fixed price contracts)	x	
Prepaid insurance, advertising, and rent		x
Refundable deposits	x	
Advances to unconsolidated subsidiaries	x	
Property, plant, and equipment		x
Accumulated depreciation of property, plant,		
and equipment		x
Cash surrender value of life insurance	x	
Patents, trademarks, licenses, and formulas		x
Goodwill		x
Other intangible assets		x
Liabilities		
Accounts and notes payable and overdrafts	x	
Accrued expenses payable.....................	x	
Accrued losses on firm purchase commitments ...	x	
Refundable deposits	x	
Deferred income.............................		x
Bonds payable or other long-term debt	x	
Unamortized premium or discount on bonds or		
notes payable...........................	x	
Convertible bonds payable	x	
Accrued pension obligations	x	
Obligations under warranties	x	

objective of doing business overseas is to return profits in the form of dividends to the U.S. investors.

An Illustration: Overseas Incorporated

Illustration 23–2 presents the worksheet for translating a company's foreign subsidiary's balance sheet and income statement into dollars. The company, Overseas Incorporated, started business on January 1,

ILLUSTRATION 23–2

Foreign Statement Translation Example—Overseas Incorporated

	1977 Financial Statement (local currency)	Translation Factor	1977 Financial Statement (dollars)
Assets			
Cash and receivables	40	0.125	5
Inventory	24	0.167	4
Plant	80	0.250	20
Less: Accumulated depreciation	⟨8⟩	0.250	⟨2⟩
Total Assets	136		27
Liabilities			
Current liabilities	56	0.125	7
Long-term debt	24	0.125	3
Capital stock	24	0.250	6
Beginning retained earnings	0	—	0
Plus net income	32	Income before translation gain or loss—see below	5
			21
		Translation gain	6
		(plug, 27 − 23)	
Total Liabilities and Owners' Equity	136		27
Income Statement			
Sales	400	0.167	67
Less: Cost of sales	200	0.167	33
Depreciation	8	0.250	2
Other expenses	160	0.167	27
Net Income	32		
		Income before translation gain or loss	5
		Translation gain	6
		Net Income	11

1977. The example assumes plant is bought at the beginning of the year; sales, purchases of raw materials, and expenses are evenly spread throughout the year; inventory is priced at its average cost for the year; plant is depreciated on a straight-line basis over ten years; and no dividends are paid. On January 1, 1977, the exchange rate was four local units to $1 (U.S.). During the year the currency steadily devalued relative to the dollar so that on the last day of the year, December 31, 1977, the exchange rate was eight local units to the U.S. dollar. The average rate for the year was six local units to the U.S. dollar.

The historical rate for translating Overseas Incorporated's plant, and capital stock in Illustration 23–2 is four local currency units to the dollar. Thus, the dollar equivalent of these local currency balances in these accounts can be obtained by multiplying the foreign currency balance by 0.25 (1 U.S. dollar/4 local currency units). Since the exchange rate changed evenly throughout the year, a factor of 0.167 (1 U.S. dollar/6 local currency units) can be used to translate the revenues, expenses, and purchases that occurred evenly throughout the year. On the last day of the year the exchange rate is eight local currency units to the dollar. Consequently, a factor of 0.125 (1 U.S. dollar/8 local currency units) can be used to convert those account balances that must be translated at the current or balance sheet date rate.

When Overseas Incorporated's foreign currency statements were translated into U.S. dollars, the balance sheet translation process led to a translation gain of 4 U.S. dollars since the company had an excess of liabilities translated at the current rate over assets translated at the current rate and the local currency devalued. The gain is not reported in the foreign currency statements. It is shown only on the translated statements.

The Rationale

The rationale underlying the translation processes illustrated in Illustration 23–2 is discussed below. From the point of view of the U.S. investor, the dollar equivalent of the foreign currency (cash) and claims to receive a fixed number of local currency units (accounts receivable) decrease immediately when devaluation of the local currency occurs. Consequently, the current rate of exchange gives the best translation for such financial assets expressed in foreign currency.

Similarly, the dollar equivalent of local currency liabilities is also affected by a change in the exchange rate. The effect is the reverse of the financial asset situation, however. Following devaluation, debts payable in local currency can be satisfied with local currency which is the equivalent of fewer dollars. Again, because the dollar equivalent of these financial items is immediately affected by changes in the exchange rate, the current rate is used to translate liabilities.

Local currency values denominated assets, such as inventory and plant, are often regarded as being unaffected by exchange rate changes. Therefore, they are translated at the relevant historical rate (i.e., the rate prevailing at the time the particular asset was acquired). Underlying this practice is the assumption that devaluation is usually the consequence of inflation within the foreign country and that the local selling prices of the inventory and the other goods or services which will eventually be produced from using the fixed assets will increase sufficiently to offset the devaluation.

Local currency profits of the foreign subsidiary accrue as local sales are recognized and the related costs are incurred. Local currency revenues are recorded in current funds and hence are usually translated at the prevailing exchange rate at the time they are recorded in the company's books.

The local currency costs used to determine local profits can be of two kinds: those using current funds, such as wages and expenses; and those using funds incurred in previous periods, such as depreciation which relates to fixed assets acquired in prior periods. Those involving current funds, such as salary and utilities expenses, are translated at the average rate for the month during which the expenses were incurred. Depreciation, cost of goods sold, and other expense items related to fund expenditures made in prior periods are translated at the historical rate at the time the related assets were recorded during the prior period.

The difference between the translated local revenue and translated local costs is the dollar equivalent of the local profit before considering translation gains or losses arising from the company's balance sheet position. When the local currency is devaluing relative to the U.S. dollar, the dollar equivalent of the local currency profits declines. The reverse is true when the local currency is appreciating relative to the dollar.

As indicated earlier, no gain or loss on translation has occurred if after translation the sum of the assets equals the liabilities plus net worth accounts. If the translated assets are greater than the translated right-hand side of the balance sheet, a translation gain has occurred. This gain is the amount needed to make the sum of the liabilities and net worth equal to the total assets. On the other hand, if the right-hand side is greater than assets, the amount needed to bring it into balance with the assets is the translation loss.

The translation gain or loss balancing figure represents the change in the U.S. investor's dollar equity in the foreign company due to exchange rate changes. Irrespective of whether they are realized or not in terms of actual currency transfers, translation gains and losses are included in the dollar consolidated statements in the accounting period during which the exchange rate changes.

Net worth includes capital stock and retained earnings. Capital items are translated at their historical rate to maintain consistency with the parent company's records. Retained earnings include an accumulation of the amounts added in each of the prior years. Each of these amounts (annual profit less dividends) is translated at the rate originally used at the time of its addition to retained earnings. The current period's addition to the translated retained earnings account is the dollar profit equivalent obtained from the translated income statement less any dividends translated at the rate prevailing at the time declared.

Managerial Response

The risks of being exposed to local currency devaluation losses can be minimized if the local foreign operating unit's manager keeps the unit's net exposed assets (assets translated at the current rate minus liabilities translated at the current rate) in as big a net negative position as possible, since devaluation of the local currency relative to the dollar reduces the dollar value of local financial assets. Conversely, these same changes reduce the dollar equivalent needed to extinguish local debts. The opposite is true in those cases where appreciation in the local exchange rate is anticipated. In this case an excess of exposed assets over liabilities is the goals.

Local managers can also protect themselves against the risk of translation losses by converting exposed financial assets that are translated at the current rate into physical assets, since physical assets are translated at their appropriate historical rate except when this assumption that local prices can be increased to recover devaluation losses is not realistic. No translation gain or loss occurs when there is a change in the exchange rate. On the other hand, if they anticipate an appreciation in the exchange rate, they can gain from this event by shifting funds from physical assets into financial assets.

Sales create cash and accounts receivables. Therefore, in a year when the local currency is devaluing, the local manager should take whatever steps he can, consistent with sound business practices, to minimize the increase in financial assets created by sales, since the profits earned on the sales may be reduced by the translation losses on the related financial assets.

Inventories

Statement No. 8 requires that foreign currency denominated inventories be translated at their historical rate. In addition, it specifies that the inventory in foreign currency statements be carried in translated statements at the lower of cost or market, which is the lower of translated historical cost or translated market. The historical rate is used to determine the translated cost. However, since the temporal method translates items that are stated at their market price at the current rate, the current rate is applied to the market price to obtain the translated market value.

The following example, based on two examples included in *Statement No. 8,* summarizes two situations involving a foreign subsidiary and illustrates the application of this rule. In Situation 1 the lower-of-cost-or-market rule requires the company to value its inventory at market on the local currency balance sheet. In contrast the dollar statements use the translated cost value. Situation 2 is the reverse.

	Situation 1	*Situation 2*
Exchange rate at date of purchase ..	$2.40	$2.40
Cost expressed in units of foreign currency	500	500
Exchange rate at balance sheet date .	$3.00	$1.80
Market at balance sheet date expressed in units of foreign currency	450	600
Carrying amount in untranslated foreign balance sheet	450 (market)	500 (cost)
Translated market (450 × $3 and 600 × $1.80)	$1,350	$1,080
Translated historical cost (500 × $2.40)	$1,200	$1,200
Carrying amount in translated balance sheet....................	$1,200 (cost)	$1,080 (market)

Deferred Taxes

In general, deferred taxes are translated at the same rate as the item giving rise to the deferred tax. For example, deferred taxes that relate to assets or liabilities translated at the current rate, such as accrued losses on firm purchase agreements, are translated at the current rate also.

Equity Method

The foreign statements of an investee that are accounted for by the equity method should be first translated into dollars before applying the equity method.

Prior to *Statement No. 8*

Prior to *Statement No. 8* a variety of translation methods were used. Many companies used the temporal method, which was often called the monetary-nonmonetary method. Another widely used approach was the current-noncurrent method. This translated all current assets and liabilities at the current rate. The principal difference between this approach and the temporal method was that it treated inventory as a monetary item and consequently translated it at the current rate. Very few U.S. companies used the current rate method, which is popular overseas. This method translates all of the balance sheet accounts, except capital stock and retained earnings, at the current rate.

After *Statement No. 8* became effective in 1976, none of these approaches were acceptable for American companies. The companies that used these methods had to adopt the temporal method, which most did on a retroactive basis.

FORWARD EXCHANGE CONTRACTS

Frequently, corporations with overseas operations enter into forward exchange contracts to hedge either a foreign currency commitment or a foreign currency exposed net asset or exposed net liability position or to speculate in anticipation of a gain. *Statement No. 8* sets forth the accounting for these contracts. It distinguishes between contracts that are hedges of identifiable commitments and other hedges. At the balance sheet date, no gain or loss is recognized on open contracts that are hedges of identifiable commitments. In the case of open contracts that do not fall into this category, any unrealized gains or losses as of the balance sheet date must be included in income for the period ending with that balance sheet.

EXCHANGE GAINS OR LOSSES

Exchange gains or losses can also arise when a company converts foreign currency or settles receivables or payables denominated in a foreign currency and the exchange rate changes. *Statement No. 8* specifies that all such gains or losses should be included in determining net income for the period in which the rate changes.

SEPARATING PRICE LEVEL AND TRANSLATION GAINS AND LOSSES

Inflation and currency depreciation can differ with respect to timing and magnitude. Using the translation method discussed previously, this fact can create distortions in the translated net worth of subsidiaries in economically unstable countries.

In situations where significant inflation exists, it may be useful to separate the impact on both shifts in the local price level and exchange rate on translated profits. This can be done as follows: first, adjust the local statements for changes in the local price levels in order to determine whether a purchasing power "gain" or "loss" has occurred. After this adjustment, all of the items on the local statements will be in local units of current purchasing power. Next, translate the price level adjusted local statements into dollars using the current rate method, that is, translate all of the local statement items at the current rate except the equity capital and retained earnings accounts which are translated at the historical rate. This step gives a translation gain and loss figure, which is the adjustment on the right-hand side of the translated balance sheet needed to balance the left- and right-hand sides of the balance sheet.

MEASUREMENT AND MOTIVATION

Local managers in economically unstable countries are often held responsible for translated profits after translation gains and losses. This measure of performance puts pressure upon them to take, with the cooperation of the parent company, whatever steps are possible to reduce their exposure to exchange gains and losses. In inflationary economies, many of these same steps also protect against inflation eroding the U.S. stockholders' investment.

The interest a manager shows in taking particular steps to reduce his exposure to devaluation may be biased somewhat by the translation method used for internal management measurement purposes. For example, the temporal method biases a manager toward shifting funds from cash to inventories because inventories are translated at the historical rate and, hence, are not exposed to local currency devaluation. On the other hand, cash is translated at the current rate, which means it is exposed to local currency devaluation losses. The current asset method translates both cash and inventories at the current rate. So, if the current method is as used for internal measurement purposes, the local manager is biased by this method toward being indifferent between holding cash or inventories. Under this approach, they both are translated at the current rate and, hence, are exposed to local currency devaluation losses. Of course, to the extent the local manager believes local prices for his products will rise after devaluation, he will be biased by this measurement approach toward preferring to hold inventory rather than cash. He can recapture some of his devaluation loss through these higher prices.

There are other possible measures of management performance. Some companies, for example, use the profit shown on the local currency statements. This can be a misleading indication of management's performance, since the rising local profit margins may be inadequate to offset local currency devaluation of the U.S. stockholders' dollar equity in the subsidiary. If the local manager has no responsibility for the financial aspects of his business, he may be measured in terms of translated profits before translation gains and losses.

Regardless of how the local manager is measured and the degree of control he has over his company's financial activities, someone in the organization must be responsible for seeing that the company's exposure to devaluation is minimized. This requires active, continuous planning and an aggressive approach to financial management.

SUGGESTED FURTHER READING

FINANCIAL ACCOUNTING STANDARDS BOARD. "An Analysis of Issues Related to Accounting for Foreign Currency Translation." FASB *Discussion Memorandum.* Stamford, 1974.

LORENSON, LEONARD, and ROSENFIELD, PAUL. "Reporting Foreign Operations of U.S. Companies in U.S. Dollars." *Accounting Research Study No. 12.* New York. American Institute Certified Public Accountants, 1972.

CASES

CASE 23–1. HEMISPHERE TRADING COMPANY
Translation of Foreign Currency Statements

On January 1, 1976, the Hemisphere Trading Company, with head-quarters offices in New York, established the Overseas Company. This new wholly owned subsidiary located in a foreign country was to carry on its merchandising activities entirely within that country. Hemisphere's investment of $60,000 (exchanged for the foreign country's currency, pintos, at the rate of 5 pintos for $1) was paid into the Overseas Company for all of its authorized capital stock.

Immediately, on January 1, Overseas borrowed 400,000 pintos from a local bank on a five-year note with a 20 percent interest rate. Fixed assets were purchased at a cost of 600,000 pintos, merchandise was acquired from local suppliers, and operations began on the same date.

Overseas's operations were spread evenly through the year. Interest on the long-term note was paid on the last day of each month. Overseas paid no dividends in 1976.

The following information about the price level index in the foreign country and the official rate of exchange was available.

	Price Level Index	Exchange Rate, Pintos to U.S. $
January 1, 1976	100	5.0 to 1
July 1, 1976	125	5.5 to 1
December 31, 1976	150	6.0 to 1

Changes in price levels and exchange rates occurred at a constant rate throughout 1976 and were expected to continue in 1977 and thereafter.

At the close of the 1976 year, the Overseas Company submitted the income statement and balance sheet shown in Exhibits 1 and 2 to Hemisphere Trading Company.

EXHIBIT 1

OVERSEAS COMPANY
Income Statement for the Year Ended December 31, 1976
(in thousands)

	Pintos	*Rate*	*U.S. Dollars*
Sales	1,000		
Cost of sales:			
Purchases	800		
Less inventory	200		
Cost of sales	600		
Gross profit	400		
Expenses:			
Depreciation	60		
Interest	80		
Other expenses	120		
Total	260		
Net income before taxes	140		
Income taxes	70		
Net Income after Taxes	70		

EXHIBIT 2

OVERSEAS COMPANY
Balance Sheet, December 31, 1976
(in thousands)

Assets

	Pintos	*Rate*	*U.S. Dollars*
Cash	80		
Accounts receivable	300		
Inventories	200		
Fixed assets	600		
Accumulated depreciation ...	(60)		
Total Assets	1,120		

Liabilities

	Pintos	*Rate*	*U.S. Dollars*
Accounts payable	280		
Taxes payable	70		
Notes payable	400		
Capital stock	300		
Retained earnings	70		
Total Liabilities	1,120		

Questions

1. Using space provided in Exhibits 1 and 2, translate Overseas's statements into U.S. dollars. (Do not make any price level adjustments prior to translation.)
2. After you have completed Question 1, consider the effect that the following transactions would have upon translation:
   a. Overseas borrowed funds from its U.S. parent.
   b. Overseas borrowed locally, but its U.S. parent guaranteed the loan.
   c. Dividends were declared by Overseas on December 31, 1976, but were not remittable to its parent until June 30, 1977, because of exchange control restrictions.
   d. Purchases of equipment and merchandise for dollars were made from the parent, rather than purchasing locally.
3. Should price level be taken into account before translating into dollars? For what purposes would this be useful?

CASE 23–2. RAMADA INNS
Statement No. 8 and Management Reaction

On April 26, 1975, Carl D. Long, Ramada Inn's group vice president and chief financial officer, sent the following letter to the FASB, which was reviewing comments on the Exposure Draft of its proposed statement dealing with the translation of foreign currency transactions and foreign currency statements. The Exposure Draft recommended the use of the temporal translation method, which was similar to the monetary-nonmonetary translation method used currently by a number of companies. The Draft also proposed that translation gains and losses be included in the determination of income in the accounting period in which they arise. Mr. Long's letter is reproduced in Exhibit 1.

Questions

1. Does the method of financing foreign operations which Ramada has adopted make good economic sense?
2. Ramada says it has not adopted the current rate method because it was not permissible. Can you, however, verify that the balance sheet exposure would be "long" by $7,600,000 under that method?
3. If the average of all foreign currencies in which Ramada-Europe has borrowed devalued 10 percent versus the dollar in 1976, approximate the translations gain or loss which Ramada Europe would report in 1975

under the monetary-nonmonetary method? the current rate method? the current-noncurrent method?

4. Consider the "gains and losses" shown in the Ramada response. If you were part of Ramada's management, how would you explain these "gains and losses" in your reports to shareholders and lenders?

5. With the adoption of FASB *Statement No. 8*, what actions *should* Ramada take? What actions do you think they *will* take?

EXHIBIT 1

Long's Letter

Dear Sirs:

Following is our response to the Exposure Draft "Accounting for the Translation of Foreign Currency Transactions and Foreign Currency Financial Statements." Specifically our response discusses and illustrates what we consider to be a mismatching of revenue and expenses which can occur through the application of current rates to long-term debt, in conjunction with the use of historical rates for fixed assets.

I. Effect of Exposure Draft Policies on Ramada's Reported Profits

The effect is shown in the following paragraphs using Ramada's European operations (Ramada Europe) as an example. Ramada translates its foreign currency financial statements into U.S. dollars using the current-noncurrent method and any resulting translation gains or losses are included in current net income. As of February 28, 1976, Ramada Europe's Consolidated balance sheet and its balance sheet exposure (stated in equivalent U.S. dollars and based on the current-noncurrent translation method) was as follows:

	Balance Sheet (at 2-28-75)	Exposure Unexposed	Exposure Exposed
Cash, receivables	$ 2,777		$2,777
Inventory, prepaids	317		317
Net fixed assets	35,434	$35,434	
Deferred and other	1,490	1,490	
	$40,018	$36,924	$3,094
Short-term payables	$ 3,091		$3,091
Long-term debt:			
Swedish kronor	5,465		
German DM	16,090		
French francs	2,751		
Belgian francs	5,026		
	$29,332	$29,332	
Equity and dollar debt	$ 7595	7,595	
	$40,018	$36,927	$3,091
Net Exposure (long)			$ 3

Several points are apparent from the above balance sheet and exposure report:

1. Ramada Europe is very capital intensive (essentially all fixed assets represent the cost of hotels which are 100 percent owned by Ramada Europe).

EXHIBIT 1 *(continued)*

2. Ramada Europe has financed its hotels largely with foreign currency debt (most debt is 15- to 25-year mortgage debt).
3. Ramada's exposure to translation gains and losses under the current-noncurrent method is negligible.

Ramada's European exposure changes drastically under the translation methods proposed in the FASB Draft, as shown below: (Hereafter in this response, we will refer to the translation method proposed in the FASB Draft as the monetary-nonmonetary method.)

	Balance Sheet (at 2-28-75)	Exposure Unexposed	Exposure Exposed
Cash, receivables	$ 2,777		$ 2,777
Inventory, prepaids	301	$ 301	
Net fixed assets	35,434	35,434	
Deferred and other	1,490	1,490	
	$40,002	$37,225	$ 2,777
Short-term payables	$ 3,091		$ 3,091
Swedish kronor	5,875		
German DM	17,606		
French francs	3,121		
Belgian francs	5,375		
	$31,977		$ 31,977
Equity and dollar debt	$ 4,934	$ 4,934	
	$40,002	$ 4,934	$ 35,068
Net Exposure (short)			$(32,291)

To determine the effect which the monetary-nonmonetary translation method would have on Ramada's earnings, we have prepared balance sheets for Ramada Europe for each quarter beginning with the first quarter of 1973, and have computed translation gains or losses for each quarter using the monetary-nonmonetary method. The balance sheets and the basis for their preparation are shown and described in Attachment A. To summarize this attachment we present below the translation gains or losses which would have been reported for each quarter. Also, to illustrate the magnitude of these gains and losses, we have presented Ramada's reported Consolidated net income (for all domestic and foreign operations) for the same quarters.

EXHIBIT 1 (continued)

Quarter	Reported Consolidated Net Income	Translation Gain (loss)
1973:		
Second quarter	$4,047,000	$(1,647,000)
Third quarter	5,485,000	(1,284,000)
Fourth quarter	2,025,000	1,611,000
1974:		
First quarter	1,955,000	836,000
Second quarter	3,220,000	(1,631,000)
Third quarter	3,455,000	1,118,000
Fourth quarter	23,000	(1,800,000)
1975:		
First quarter	1,042,000	(2,714,000)
Second quarter		1,173,000 *
Total		$(4,338,000)†

* Through April 21, 1975.
† Gross losses are $9,076,000 and gross gains $4,738,000 for a net of $4,338,000.

The large gains and losses shown above illustrate the magnitude of profit fluctuations which Ramada can expect in the future if it must apply the monetary-nonmonetary translation method to its European operations.

In connection with the above comparison we would like to point out the following additional factors:

1. Ramada's primary business activity is the operation of its company owned hotels. In 1975 this activity will account for about 75 percent of consolidated sales and almost 100 percent of foreign sales. The cost of Ramada Europe's hotels represents slightly more than 10 percent of Consolidated fixed assets, and its foreign currency long-term debt also represents slightly more than 10 percent of Consolidated long-term debt.

2. In addition to the European exposure of approximately $32,000,000 (under the monetary-nonmonetary method) Ramada has a further exposure of about $13,000,000 in Canadian dollars. The Canadian currency has not been nearly as volatile as European currencies, but quarterly U.S./Canadian dollar fluctuations of 2 percent to 3 percent are not uncommon, and fluctuations of this magnitude would produce additional gains or losses of $260,000 to $390,000 per quarter.

3. The translation gains and losses might be reduced somewhat through the recording of deferred taxes. However, we presently believe that deferred taxes would apply to only about 50 percent of the gross translation gains or losses. (Hence, net translation gains and losses would be about 75 percent of the amounts shown above.)

II. Ramada's View of Its Exposure from European Operations:

We feel that the monetary-nonmonetary translation method is not appropriate for Ramada and that this translation method violates the accounting principle of matching revenue and expenses when applied to Ramada.

In our opinion the proper translation method for a company such as Ramada is the current rate method. Our reasoning for this opinion can first be illustrated by reference to the following flowchart, which describes our approach in building, financing, and operating a foreign hotel.

From the flowchart it is apparent to us that only our equity and U.S. dollar loans are exposed. These are exposed because foreign currency earnings and cash flow are used to pay dividends and repay U.S. dollar loans. Following this reasoning, the current rate method is the appropriate method for Ramada since under this method our translation gains and losses would be equal to our total dollar loans and equity, times the percent-

EXHIBIT 1 (continued)

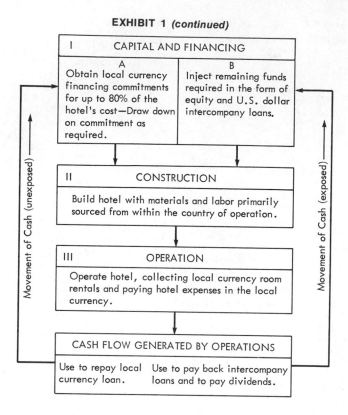

age by which the U.S. dollar changes in value, relative to the local currency in each country of operation.

Under the current rate method our net balance sheet exposure would be "long" by about $7,600,000. It should be noted that exposure under the current rate method is the opposite of monetary-nonmonetary exposure. For example under the current rate method we would realize a translation gain when the dollar devalued, whereas a loss would result under the monetary-nonmonetary method.

We have not adopted the current rate method because it is not permissible under present accounting rules. We therefore have adopted the current-noncurrent method which is permitted and which provides much more realistic results for Ramada than the monetary-nonmonetary method.

III. General Discussion

Our argument against the monetary-nonmonetary method is made on the basis of "Compatibility" or Objective E of the Exposure Draft. That is, we feel that the monetary-nonmonetary method when applied to Ramada, produces results which are not compatible with expected economic effects.

Objective E was rejected by the FASB. One reason given was "The proposed objective is impractical because foresight would be required to identify the future economic effects of a rate change at the time it occurs." We disagree that the objective is impractical because it is clear to us that a decline in the value of the dollar will increase Ramada's earnings and cash flow in terms of U.S. dollars, while an increase in the value of the U.S. dollar will decrease our earnings and cash flow in terms of U.S. dollars.

EXHIBIT 1 *(concluded)*

Other arguments against compatibility which were contained in the draft opinion related to areas such as imports and exports, commitments for purchases or sales in another foreign currency, and so on. These arguments do not apply to a company such as Ramada which is almost entirely dependent on the local economy.

The Exposure Draft also mentioned the opposing views that *(a)* historical costs should be measured in terms of dollars; versus *(b)* historical costs should be measured in terms of the foreign currency. The APB adopted view *(a)* and rejected view *(b)*. However, the APB's main reason for adoption of view *(a)* seemed to be that it is mathematically possible to determine the dollar equivalent of the cost of an asset on the date of acquisition. We agree that the use of dollar historical costs for fixed assets is mathematically possible, but we feel that it should not be the only acceptable method and in fact feel that it is not the proper method for us to use.

IV. Conclusions, Recommendation

The monetary-nonmonetary method as proposed in the Draft would essentially force us to finance all future foreign hotels with U.S. dollars in order to minimize translation losses. This would be unfortunate because *(a)* it would be against the U.S. public interest as it would cause an outflow of U.S. dollars; *(b)* it would hamper our expansion if the U.S. government should again impose controls such as the former OFDI regulations; and *(c)* financing in U.S. dollars runs counter to what we should do from an economic standpoint.

We could reduce or eliminate our present exposure under the monetary-nonmonetary method by entering into forward foreign exchange transactions. However, this is not an argument for the monetary-nonmonetary method because such transactions can be costly; and like U.S. dollar financing, they don't make sense from an economic standpoint.

In our opinion the monetary-nonmonetary translation method is not appropriate for Ramada or other capital intensive companies which have similar operations. We believe that the current rate method is clearly the most appropriate for Ramada, and that the FASB should permit the use of this method—at least for certain types of companies such as Ramada.

However if the FASB does not wish to permit the use of the current rate method at this time we recommend the following alternatives.

a. Use of the current-noncurrent method, or
b. Use of the monetary-nonmonetary method along with deferral of gains and losses that relate to long-term debt used to finance fixed assets.

We are anxious to meet with members of the Financial Accounting Standards Board to further discuss the figures, arguments, and comments in this response at any time, and in this connection ask that you contact the undersigned or Donald W. Hair, our director of international accounting.

EXHIBIT 2

RAMADA INNS, INC.
Ramada Europe Balance Sheets
Attachment A

	As Reported— Using Ramada's Current-Noncurrent Method	As Reported but Using Translation Method Proposed in FASB Draft and Exchange Rates on Dates Shown									
		4-21-75	2-28-75	11-30-74	8-31-74	5-31-74	2-28-74	11-30-73	8-31-73	5-31-73	2-28-73
Cash receivables	$ 2,777	$ 2,666	$ 2,777	$ 2,555	$ 2,388	$ 2,472	$ 2,333	$ 2,416	$ 2,555	$ 2,444	$ 2,305
Inventories, prepaids	317	301	301	301	301	301	301	301	301	301	301
Net fixed assets	35,434	35,434	35,434	35,434	35,434	35,434	35,434	35,434	35,434	35,434	35,434
Deferred and other	1,490	1,490	1,490	1,490	1,490	1,490	1,490	1,490	1,490	1,490	1,490
Total	$40,018	$39,891	$40,002	$39,780	$39,613	$39,697	$39,558	$39,641	$39,780	$39,669	$39,530
Short-term payables	$ 3,091	$ 2,967	$ 3,091	$ 2,844	$ 2,658	$ 2,751	$ 2,596	$ 2,689	$ 2,844	$ 2,702	$ 2,566
Long-term debt (in local currency)	29,332	30,817	31,977	29,288	27,507	28,616	27,001	27,827	29,422	28,169	26,519
Equity and debt (in U.S. dollars)	7,595	7,595	7,595	7,595	7,595	7,595	7,595	7,595	7,595	7,595	7,595
Translation gain (loss)		(1,488)	(2,661)	53	1,853	735	2,366	1,530	(81)	1,203	2,850
Total	$40,018	$39,891	$40,002	$39,780	$39,613	$39,697	$39,558	$39,641	$39,780	$39,669	$39,530
Translation Gain (loss) for quarter		$ 1,173	$ (2,714)	$ (1,800)	$ 1,118	$ (1,631)	$ 836	$ 1,611	$ (1,284)	$ (1,647)	

Ramada Inns, Inc., reports earnings on a calendar quarter basis, however, foreign earnings are cut off one month early. That is, Ramada earnings for the quarter ended March 31, 1975, include foreign earnings for the quarter ended February 28, 1975.

Notes to Attachment A

Foreign exchange markets have been very volatile since 1971, and all indications point to continued volatility for the foreseeable future. In this response we are attempting to demonstrate the effects of this volatility on Ramada, assuming use of the monetary-nonmonetary translation method.

We have done this by starting with actual Ramada Europe figures as of February 28, 1975, and then restating these figures as though the assets which existed at that time were in existence each quarter for the past two years. Actual foreign exchange rates were used for each quarter to restate local currency debt, current assets, and current liabilities.

Attachment A does not consider depreciation or repayment of long-term debt. However, this is not significant because (A) depreciation has no effect on translation gains or losses; and (B) repayment of long-term debt for the two-year period would be under $1,000,000 or 3 percent of total debt.

Figures used in the extreme left column are actual reported figures as of February 28, 1975, with one exception: on April 15, 1975, our Swedish subsidiary received SK 8 million (about U.S. $2 million), being the proceeds of a long-term mortgage. We attempted to draw down this commitment before February 28, but certain technical matters prevented this.

The February 28 balance sheet has been restated as though this commitment had been drawn down by February 28.

Chapter 24

DISCLOSURE BY DIVERSIFIED COMPANIES

During the last several decades, a number of companies have diversified into more than one industry, principally through acquisitions and mergers. This change in the business environment led to a new demand from investors that the stockholder reports of diversified companies disclose supplemental financial information related to the principal segments of their business. Previously, it had not been considered essential for fair disclosure that this data be published.

DIVERSIFICATION TREND

The modern diversification movement was characterized by the joining together of companies operating in unrelated or only slightly related industries. This type of expansion was in contrast to earlier corporate growth patterns which involved companies either integrating vertically to become distributors and suppliers of their products or horizontally to enter related businesses.

The principal corporate reasons for this diversification were:

1. To minimize economic instability resulting from cyclical market factors or overreliance on a single product line.
2. To acquire new products, technological know-how, and management skills more cheaply and with less risk through acquisition than by means of internal development.
3. To expand into nonrelated businesses so as to avoid the antitrust laws restricting horizontal and vertical growth.
4. To take advantage through mergers of the opportunity to boost earnings and sales through the "pooling of interest" and purchase treatments of acquisitions.

685

Investment Analysis

Concurrent with the diversification trend was a significant increase in the emphasis in the stock market on financial analysis and the role of the financial analyst. Increasingly, these analysts and astute, analytically inclined stockholders were frustrated in their evaluation of diversified companies because of their inability to relate the total revenues and operating results of these companies to their various segments.

The industry identification of the segments was essential in order to appraise properly for investment purposes the past performance and future risk and prospects of this type of company. For example, analysts noted, the fact that a company was losing money in one segment could be obscured from investors. These losses would be combined with the profits produced by other segments in the total company profit figure released to the public. Also, the relative importance of the diverse segments of the business changed over time. Without knowledge of the parts of the business, investors could not appraise how these changes affected the stability or risk associated with the total enterprise.

Issues and Response

The principal disclosure issues raised by this new business development were:

1. Are there any circumstances under which the issuers of financial data should report the results of operations on some basis other than total company figures?
2. If so, what, and how should they be reported?

In September 1967 the Accounting Principles Board issued a statement, "Disclosure of Supplemental Financial Information by Diversified Companies." The APB believed that there were:

. . . few practical problems involved in determining sales or revenues for segments of a diversified company. However, determining of profitability by segments in a form suitable for reporting to investors raises many complex problems.

Pending further study of these problems, the APB's recommendation was that diversified companies:

. . . review their own circumstances carefully and objectively with a view toward disclosing voluntarily supplemental financial information as to industry segments of the business.

Subsequently, in 1969, the Securities and Exchange Commission instituted a requirement that companies registering securities disclose the related contribution their major product lines and services make to sales and earnings. In 1974 the SEC expanded these requirements to include annual reports to stockholders. Next, in September 1975, the FASB issued an Exposure Draft of a statement dealing with the financial reporting for segments of a business. This Draft proposed that the financial statements of a business include information about the enterprise's operations in different industries, its foreign operations, its major customers, and its export sales.[1]

Others interested in business segment reports include the Federal Trade Commission, which in March 1974 approved an annual line-of-business report designed to collect information from about 500 large manufacturing companies, and Congress, which as early as 1973 introduced legislation that would have required energy companies to report segment information.

Management Reaction

Management was responsive to these requests and the APB and SEC recommendations. Increasingly more and more annual reports have contained data related to the parts of a business. Specific examples of disclosure found in 1975 statements by the FASB were:

a. Revenues by industry activity or type of customer.

b. Revenues and profits by separable industry segment.

c. Separate financial statements of segments of the business which

---

[1] At the time this book was being printed the FASB issued, in December 1976, *Statement No. 14*, "Financial Reporting for Segments of a Business Enterprise." The final *Statement* was similar to the Exposure Draft except for these major changes:

1. If it is impractical to present industry segment data by groupings on a worldwide basis, it is permissible to present foreign operations as an industry segment. (See page 689.)
2. Segment data need not be presented for interim periods, unless the statements are described as being in conformity with generally accepted accounting principles (See page 688.)
3. The disclosure of a profit or loss contribution figure is not required, but the *Statement* does not preclude its publication if an enterprise wishes to include it. (See page 690.)
4. Assets used jointly by two or more segments are to be allocated to the segments on a reasonable basis. (See page 691.)
5. Equity method investee data be limited as far as segment disclosure is required to the following: The net income and investment in investee companies whose operations are vertically integrated with the operations of a segment be disclosed on an industry and geographical basis. (See page 691.)
6. Identifiable assets by industry and geographical areas can be presented as a single amount. (See page 691.)
7. In the case of geographical presentations, some other measure of profitability may be presented on a geographical basis between operating profit and net income, since income tax rates can differ significantly between countries. (See page 691.)
8. The names of important customers need not be disclosed. (See page 692.)

operate autonomously and employ distinctly different types of capital structure, such as insurance or bank subsidiaries of merchandising or manufacturing companies.

d. Revenues by type of industry activity and type of customer, together with a general indication of the profitability of each category.

e. Information that the operations of a segment of the enterprise are resulting in a loss, with or without disclosure of the amount of such loss.

The response of companies to the FASB's Exposure Draft indicated that most managements support the basic concept of full and fair disclosure. However, many of them, in letters to the FASB, expressed a strong conviction that the content and format of segment disclosure should be on a voluntary basis and appropriate to the companies' interests. Forced disclosure of profits and revenues by business segments, they argued, might be:

1. Harmful, since it could be used against the company's interests by customers, competitors, labor unions, and governmental agencies.
2. Misleading, if it led to uniform rules for reporting the results of operations by segments that did not permit the reports to reflect the unique characteristics of a company.
3. Misinterpreted, due to the public's general lack of appreciation of the limitations of the somewhat arbitrary basis for most cost allocations.

The general response of management to the FTC proposal was negative. Management feared the data submitted would be used for antitrust purposes as well as prove costly to prepare.

FASB EXPOSURE DRAFT

The FASB believes that segment information permits statement users to appraise better a corporation's past performance and future prospects and risks than is possible using total enterprise data. The FASB's Exposure Draft would require that interim and annual financial statements which purport to be in accordance with generally accepted accounting principles include data related to the enterprise's operations in different industries on a worldwide basis as well as its foreign operations, major customers, and export sales: The auditors report would cover these disclosures. The required information may be presented in the body of the financial statements with appropriate explanations in the notes; entirely in the notes; or in a separate schedule included as an integral part of the financial statements.

Industry Segment

The Draft defines an "industry segment" as a "component of a business enterprise engaged in providing a product or service or a group of related products and services primarily to unaffiliated customers (i.e., customers outside of the enterprise) for a profit."

A "reportable segment" is "an industry segment or a group of two or more industry segments for which information is required" to be reported by the Draft.

The Draft suggests that in grouping products or services to form a reportable segment, the three-digit Standard Industrial Classification system (SIC)[2] and the Enterprise Standard Industrial Classification system (ESIC) may be helpful. However, the Draft recognizes that these classification schemes may not be suitable in all cases and that management judgment should be used to determine the appropriate segments. The Draft suggests that the following criteria should be considered in making the reportable segment decision:

a. *The nature of the product.* Related products or services normally have similar rates of profitability, similar degrees of risk, and similar opportunities for growth.

b. *The nature of the production process.* Similar degrees of labor intensiveness or similar degrees of capital intensiveness may indicate a relationship among products or services. Likewise, sharing of common production facilities or labor force, use of similar production facilities or labor skills, or use of the same or similar basic raw materials may suggest that products or services are related.

c. *Markets and marketing methods.* Similarity of geographic marketing areas, types of customers, or marketing methods may indicate a relationship among products or services. The sensitivity of the market to price changes and to changes in general economic conditions may also indicate whether products or services are related or unrelated.

Essentially, the test as to whether or not a segment is significant and reportable is whether or not it accounts for 10 percent of the enterprise's revenues, identifiable assets, or profits.[3] In addition, the total

---

[2] There are 421 three-digit industry groups. For example, the two-digit "machinery, except electrical" group includes the following three-digit groups:

1. Engines and turbines.
2. Farm and garden machinery and equipment.
3. Construction, mining, and materials handling machinery, and equipment.
4. Metalworking machinery and equipment.
5. Special industry machinery, except metalworking machinery.
6. General industry machinery and equipment.
7. Office, computing, and accounting machines.
8. Refrigeration and service industry machinery.
9. Miscellaneous machinery, except electrical.

[3] Thus, if over 90 percent of a company's revenues, profits, and assets relate to a single industry segment, industry segment disclosure is not required beyond the aggregate information presented in the financial statements.

reportable industry segment information presented must meet an overall test. At least 75 percent of the sales to unaffiliated customers of all industry segments must be represented by the defined reportable industry segments. If the aggregated defined reportable segments do not meet this test, then additional reportable segments should be identified until the 75 percent test is met. The Draft indicates that if defined reportable segments exceed ten in number and the test is still not satisfied, it may be appropriate to combine certain segments into broader industry categories in order to meet the 75 percent test while still maintaining a workable number of defined reportable segments.

For each reportable segment the following information is required: revenue, profit or loss contribution, operating profit or loss, and identifiable assets. Illustration 24–1 presents an example of the disclosure proposed by the Draft for each reportable segment. The note accompanying this disclosure would include a description of the segment, a definition of the accounts, a description of the methods used to derive the data, and comments that may be needed to make the data useful.

ILLUSTRATION 24–1

Information about the Company's Operations in Different Industries
Year Ended December 31, 1976

	Specialty Textiles	Glass Containers	Information Technology	Other	Eliminations	Consolidated
Sales to unaffiliated customers	$1,000	$2,000	$1,500	$ 200		$ 4,700
Intersegment sales	200		500		$(700)	
Total Revenue	$1,200	$2,000	$2,000	$ 200	$(700)	$ 4,700
Profit contribution	$ 500	$ 440	$ 800	$ 100	$ (40)	$ 1,800
Operating profit	$ 300	$ 290	$ 600	$ 50	$ (40)	$ 1,200
Expenses of central administrative office						(100)
Interest expense						(200)
Income from continuing operations before income taxes						$ 900
Identifiable assets at December 31,1976	$2,400	$4,050	$6,000	$1,000	$ (50)	$13,400
Assets employed at the company's central administrative office						1,600
Total Assets at December 31, 1976						$15,000

The information related to the company's sales to major customers may also be presented in this note.

Segment revenue is defined to include sales to unaffiliated customers and intersegment sales which are to be accounted for "at amounts that are consistent with the objective of determining as realistically as practicable the industry segments profit or loss contribution and operating profit and loss." As shown on Illustration 24–1, separate disclosure is required for intersegment sales and sales to unaffiliated customers. Intraindustry segment transactions should be eliminated.

The "profit or loss contribution" line on Illustration 24–1 is computed by subtracting from each industry segment's revenue the costs and expenses that can be directly related to that industry segment's revenue. These are costs and expenses that do not require to be allocated to the segment revenue.

The operating profit or loss figure shown on Illustration 24–1 is derived by subtracting from the profit or loss contribution figure those operating costs and expenses not directly traceable to the industry segment but which can be allocated to it on some reasonable basis.

The Draft specifically states that none of the following items is to be added or deducted in computing the operating profit or loss of an industry segment:

revenue earned and general and administrative expenses incurred at the enterprise's central administrative office; interest expense; domestic and foreign income taxes; gain or loss on discontinued operations; extraordinary items; minority interest; and the cumulative effect of a change in accounting principle. Income from investments in common stock accounted for by the equity method shall be included in computing operating profit or loss if included in computing profit or loss contribution.

"Identifiable assets" include those tangible and intangible assets that can be directly associated with or reasonably allocated to an industry segment.

Unconsolidated subsidiaries and investments in joint ventures should be accounted for by the equity method. Disclosure is required of the investee's products and services.

The Draft requires the industry segment revenue be reconciled to the consolidated revenue; the industry segment operating profit and loss be reconciled to consolidated pretax income; and the identifiable assets of the industry segments be reconciled to the total consolidated assets.

Foreign Operations

Business environments can vary significantly from country to country. Operations in different countries can entail differing types and degrees or risk, rates of profitability, and opportunities for growth. Because of these differences, the FASB in the Draft proposed that the financial statements of corporations should include information about their significant operations in different countries or groups of countries. Illustration 24–2 presents an example of the type of foreign operations information disclosure proposed by the Draft. The financial data and explanation notes are similar to those presented for the industry segments.

At a minimum, separate information should be presented for both the aggregate foreign and domestic operations. If the company has significant operations in individual countries or groups of countries whose business environments differ, the foreign operations should be further disaggregated by groups of countries or, if significant, individual countries. The Draft does not recommend any particular approach to group foreign operations. It simply suggests that the factors to be considered are geographical proximity, economic and political affinity, and the nature and degree of interrelationship of the enterprise's operations in various countries.

Major Customers and Export Sales

Irrespective of whether or not a company must report information about its operations in different industries or foreign countries, the Draft would require that when a company's total business or reportable segment significantly depends on a single customer or a few customers, the identity and relative importance of the customer(s) should be explained in the financial statements. In addition, disclosure should be made in the financial statements of significant revenue derived from export sales from the company's home country to unaffiliated foreign customers. If significant, this information should be reported by country or groups of countries to which the exports are made.

INVESTOR SURVEYS

Surveys of financial analysts and investment advisors conducted during the late 1960s and early 1970s as part of the research effort to determine what constitutes useful segment disclosure indicated that the dominent investment objective was a maximum return in the long run from a combination of dividends and capital appreciation. The most important company characteristics in achieving this goal were considered to be growth potential, managerial ability, and profits, in that order. The most useful measures of profitability were stated to be return on common stock equity, return on total assets, and net income

ILLUSTRATION 24–2

Information about the Company's Operations in Different Countries
Year Ended December 31, 1976

	United States	Western Europe	Latin America	Eliminations	Consolidated
Sales to unaffiliated customers	$3,000	$1,000	$ 700		$ 4,700
Intercountry sales within the company	1,000			$(1,000)	
Total Revenue	$4,000	$1,000	$ 700	$(1,000)	$ 4,700
Profit contribution	$1,100	$ 500	$ 200	$ (200)	$ 1,600
Operating profit	$ 900	$ 400	$ 100	$ (200)	$ 1,200
Expense of central administrative office					(100)
Interest expense					(200)
Income from continuing operations before income taxes					$ 900
Working capital at December 31, 1976	$2,400	$ 800	$ 500	$ (150)	$ 3,600
Property, plant, and equipment	$6,200	$3,800	$2,100		$12,100
Less: Accumulated depreciation	1,900	1,100	500		3,500
Net at December 31, 1976	$4,300	$2,700	$1,600		$ 8,600
Identifiable assets at December 31, 1976	$7,700	$3,400	$2,450	$ (150)	$13,400
Assets employed at the company's central administrative office					1,600
Total Assets at December 31, 1976					$15,000

as a percentage of sales. The preferred indicators of managerial ability were growth of the company, the return on common stock equity, and the personal reputation of key personnel. The growth potential of a company was best indicated, the analysts said, by the growth of its major markets, rate of growth in earnings per share, and research and development expenditures.

In the case of the diversified companies there was widespread agreement that it was necessary to appraise the major segments of the business on an industry by industry basis before they could be considered in combination, particularly where the sales and profits of different segments were affected differently by economic conditions. They felt it was not possible to do this adequately from data currently supplied in annual reports, although a large number of them tried to do it by estimation.

The information concerning business segments considered most useful by analysts was: contribution, net income and operating income, sales or gross revenues, and total or net assets devoted to the operations of the component. Most analysts apparently did not feel it was necessary for the independent auditor's opinion to cover this data. A large number of them did express a desire for a standard approach to defining reporting components on some product basis, such as the Standard Industrial Classification. Others, however, did not require uniform segment classification since intercompany comparisons of segment results was not considered to be significant in their work.

The minimum point at which it becomes necessary to report separately for a component was considered by most of the analysts to be when the component accounts for between 10 and 14 percent of whatever base was eventually selected. Some of the bases suggested were: sales, net income, assets employed, net income before allocation of common costs, and total expenses. Responses also indicated the maximum number of components reported upon should be 11 or less, in most cases.

CORPORATE SURVEYS

The surveys of corporate officers showed a lack of unanimity or even proposed unanimity on almost every important point covered by the surveys. This diversity of opinion was due principally to the great variety in business structure and practice.

Nevertheless, there were two areas of agreement: No serious opposition existed among executives surveyed to disclosing segment sales. In contrast, strong opposition existed among these same executives to disclosing segment profits. However, those companies that reported segment profits stated that the practice led to a better understanding of these companies without any objectionable reaction of consequence.

It was clear from the surveys that companies collected data for management purposes on the basis of organizational units. However, this was done in a variety of ways for a variety of management control purposes.

The sample companies split almost equally between those with a close relationship between organizational units and product lines and those with little relationship between units and product lines. More than half of the survey companies indicated they prepared fairly complete income statements by organizational units, whereas the remainder stated they prepared partial income statements of one sort or another for organizational units. Typically, the amount of information collected by product lines was significantly less than that available for organizational units.

An analysis of the survey results shows that a large number of corporations could not directly associate their assets with either organizational units or product lines. About 40 percent stated that they could identify less than 50 percent of their total assets with business segments. Slightly more than 40 percent indicated that they could associate 80 percent or more of their assets with either organizational units or product lines.

COMMON COSTS

A difficult problem in trying to determine the profits of business segments is how to handle common or joint costs. Common costs are those costs that are jointly shared by more than one business segment. For example, the headquarters accounting staff may keep the accounts for each of the company's components. The costs of this department are common to all of the company's operations. Typically, there is no clearly discernible way to associate these costs with the particular parts of a business. They must be allocated on some reasonable but nevertheless arbitrary basis if they are to be assigned to other parts of the business.

While most companies allocated all of their noninventoriable common costs to business segments, not all companies allocated all of their common costs to components of their business, principally because they considered that some costs could not be charged to segments on any reasonable basis.

Irrespective of the degree to which common costs were allocated, a variety of cost allocation bases are used. Some companies spread common costs on the basis of segment sales or profit before common noninventoriable cost allocations. Others use component asset or in-vestment as the basis. Some allocate noninventoriable common costs on the basis of specific segment expense items, whereas others do it through negotiations with the managers of the operation affected by the allocations. Another approach was to use a basis combining several of these methods. In addition, many companies use more than one method for allocating costs among the components of their company.

PROFIT CONTRIBUTION

One way to minimize the subjective element introduced into seg-ment reporting through the allocating of joint costs is to report the profitability of segments before joint cost allocations. This so-called profit contribution approach divides costs into two categories: those directly attributable to a single unit and those not directly relatable to a single unit. The profit contribution of the reporting segment is the difference between the revenues of the unit or product and costs di-rectly attributable to the reporting unit or product. This is the ap-proach that was adopted as part of the FASB proposal.

Profit contribution is the contribution a unit makes to covering the company's total common costs. If the total defined profit of all of the segments is greater than the total common costs, the company will be profitable. The relationship between segment defined profit and com-pany profit varies from industry to industry, depending on the mix of common and direct costs. For example, common costs such as advertis-ing represent a higher proportion of total costs for companies dealing with consumer products than they do for manufacturers of industrial goods, such as machine tool companies. Consequently, the profit con-tribution as a percentage of sales for these two business categories will differ.

A number of questions have been raised concerning the usefulness of profit contribution. Will readers understand the limitations of this figure? For example, will they recognize that the relationship between assets employed and profit contribution is in many cases meaning-less? Will readers try to make their own joint cost allocations, based on an inadequate appreciation of the situation? What are the dangers for management in publishing this figure? For example, the defined profit for a segment will be higher than its profits after joint cost allocations. Will customers use this defined profit as an argument for reduced prices? Will labor unions use it, rather than the total com-pany profit, as a basis for justifying wage increases?

Partly to avoid some of these possibilities, the FASB proposed that operating profit, which is profit contribution less certain allocated costs, be included in the segment disclosure.

TRANSFER PRICES

Transfer prices are those prices charged for goods and services transferred between units in the same company. The transfer price is revenue to the selling unit and a cost to the buying unit. These prices are not subjected to the pressures of arm's-length bargaining that exist in the marketplace, and hence lack the objectivity usually associated with sales to those outside the company. The costs and revenues created by these internal transfers are eliminated in the preparation of consolidated statements, since the transfers are offsetting and do not involve parties outside of the corporate entity. However, in the case of segment reports, these transfers would not be eliminated. Thus, the sales and costs of the individual segments may total more than those reported for the entire company on a consolidated basis.

A variety of transfer pricing practices exist in practice, often in the same company. Transfer prices range from the equivalent of market prices to direct costs. Some companies base their prices on established pricing formulas. Others leave the establishment of the price of internally transferred products or services to negotiations between the units involved.

A number of factors influence the setting of transfer prices. In some situations, the prices of goods moved into states that levy taxes on inventories are deliberately set at a low value in order to minimize taxes. Some companies use their transfer price system as a management control device. The pricing approach used will vary with the different motivational objectives top management hopes to achieve through its control system. Transfer prices between foreign and domestic operations are sometimes used as a device to repatriate cash from foreign operations, rather than through cash dividends which may be restricted by exchange controls.

REPORTING BASES

There are a number of different possible ways a diversified company could be divided for reporting purposes. These include:

1. Legal entities.
2. Organizational units.
3. Type of customer.
4. Geographical distribution of activities.
5. Product categories, or industry groupings.

In many cases, there will be a close relationship among some of these bases. For instance, a legal entity may be identical to an organizational unit or to a product line. The rest of this section examines the appropriateness of these segments for reporting to public investors. The issue raised is: Can one basis be applied effectively and fairly to all companies?

Some of the respondents to the surveys mentioned earlier suggested that legal entity be the basis for segment disclosure. This approach was rejected by the FASB. Typically, the *legal entities* through which a company operates often bear little relationship to the operating structure of the company. Some companies maintain separate corporate entities to hold property, to meet state legal requirements, to protect company names, or to lease property to other entities within the corporate structure. In such cases, corporate operations are often conducted without regard for these legal subdivisions. Also, unless required by law, financial statements are seldom prepared for these operationally insignificant entities. Many argue that to ask corporations to prepare statements for such entities would be an unreasonable requirement.

Since most companies maintain fairly detailed records by *organizational divisions,* it has been suggested this segment might be an appropriate basis for reporting purposes.

The FTC specially required this approach to segment disclosure while the FASB encourages it. Certainly, for most companies, organizational data is readily available and could be put in a form suitable for publication at little additional cost. However, there are considerations that may make this kind of data irrelevant for security investment decisions. For example, the organization of most diversified companies is constantly in a state of flux as new companies are added. This makes year-to-year comparisons difficult. Sometimes the activities of divisions are closely related to each other, as they are in vertically integrated companies. In these cases, it may be misleading to split their common activity into parts based on divisions. Other arguments against using divisional bases for reporting are: the divisional organization may reflect historical patterns of doing business, rather than the current realities. In some companies, the availability of talented executives may determine how the divisional units are structured. Then, there is always the question concerning the ability of uninformed investors to use data prepared for managers who have considerable knowledge about the industries involved, reasons for the divisional structure, and the limitations of the data.

The risk of diversified companies depends in large measure on the *type of customer* they serve. One important breakdown of a business for investment appraisal purposes is between government and civilian business. Another is between ultimate consumers; middlemen, such as wholesalers and jobbers; and those who add value to purchased items, such as manufacturers. Dealings with each of these customers typically have different risk and profit characteristics. For example, the margins on government business are often less than on civilian business. Also, generally, the risk of a sudden cutback in the level of expenditures is considered to be higher than for nongovernment sales. In addition, the things a company must do to be successful vary somewhat by the kinds of customers it serves. The FASB proposal recognizes that knowledge of key customers may be useful to statement users.

Companies seem to be able to generate reports of revenues by type of customer fairly readily. However, very few companies keep records of profitability by customer, and to require them to do so might impose a burden upon them.

Investors are often interested in the *geographical distribution* of a company's business, since this is a variable that may affect the risk and profit characteristics of a company. The economic fortunes of regions change, and the extent to which a company has facilities and markets in these regions will affect its future prospects. Most companies split their financial records between foreign and domestic operations. Thus, these figures can be made available to investors with little additional effort. However, few companies keep records by regions within the United States or the foreign countries in which they operate. Consequently, to give regional data to investors may require recasting the accounting systems of a great number of companies. Some argue that the cost of this change may not be worth the value of the data to investors.

The FASB apparently believes that the data is worth the cost since it has proposed a regional breakdown of consolidated results on a worldwide basis.

Product or industry categories seem to be the most often-suggested basis for segment reporting. This is the basic approach proposed by the FASB. Clearly, it is of interest to investors to know how much each of the broadly defined product categories of a company contributes to its success. For example, it makes a considerable difference to investors if the success of a diversified company with computer, typewriter, business machine, and office furniture products is due mainly to its computer or office furniture products, principally because a higher price-earnings multiplier may be applied to the earnings of computer-oriented companies than to those of office furniture companies.

There is little agreement on what constitutes a product line. Also, there are many practical problems to establishing an all-inclusive, well-defined list of product categories which could be uniformly used by all corporations. Some companies, particularly diversified companies, view their product lines very broadly. Others see their product lines in narrow terms. One company selling canned foods may simply view itself as being in the food business. Another company in the same business may regard its product lines as being canned fish, canned meats, and canned soups. It may go even further and break these categories down by different trademarks or container size.

The product lines of some companies tend to blend together. For example, it may be difficult for a company that makes soaps, detergents, window cleaners, waxes, and polish to draw a clear distinction between the cleaning compounds and polishing products, particularly as some products both clean and wax.

Two other problems are encountered in trying to define a set of product lines as a common basis for component reporting. First, some products are used in other products. For instance, one diversified company makes circuit boards which it and its customers use in computers, communications equipment, television sets, and satellites. In this case, it is not clear to what product category the circuit boards belong. Second, product innovation is widespread and frequent in our economy. This creates a problem in that any set of established product categories may well become obsolete in a relatively short period of time.

Reporting segments of a business by *industry groupings* is similar in approach to product line reporting, except the categories are broader. It also has many of the same problems: there is no common agreement as to what constitutes an industry; industries tend not to be discrete; and they are constantly changing as new products and markets are created and old ones disappear.

DIFFERENT VIEWS

No one basis appears to be universally acceptable for segment reporting. However, elements of all the possibilities discussed (with perhaps the exception of legal entities) can be appropriate in some cases. Also, the disadvantages of the Technical Committee's industrial and enterprise classification codes should not rule out the possibility of developing a similar system for segment disclosure, although the task may be a long, difficult, and frustrating one. In the meantime, it has been suggested that the best solution is a flexible one which leaves it up to each corporation to use the basis most appropriate to its specific case.

Those who doubt management's ability to be objective in such matters are dissatisfied with this latter approach. To make it operational, they suggest that at least concrete minimum reporting requirements using some uniform system applicable to all corporations should be defined. In addition, others believe that the authority for determining the number of reporting units and the kind of data disclosed should rest with the independent auditor rather than management. Also, any departure from the minimum guidelines would have to be justified by management and the company's independent auditors. However, even those who take this position agree that the bases for disclosure should be broadly defined. Also, they concede that the base selected should most probably be related to markets, products, or industry, which, when broadly defined, are all very similar in meaning.

There are others who, while agreeing that investors probably need segment data, are concerned that segment reporting will only increase the misuse of accounting statements by investors, unions, and government agencies. In addition, they argue, to pile the vagaries of segment reporting on top of the existing uncertainties of financial reporting will only make the corporate reporting system more chaotic and less useful.

Segment reporting is already an established corporate reporting requirement. The ultimate form it will take has not been determined. Even when some detailed concrete guidelines have been developed, the investor will have to be wary of how he uses such data. It can be very misleading unless the user has a firm grasp of the definition of the reporting base, the nature of joint allocation, the method used to price intercompany transfers, and the appropriateness of these three items to the company and its industry.

SUGGESTED FURTHER READING

BACKER, MORTON, and McFARLAND, WALTER. *External Reporting for Segments of a Business.* New York: National Association of Accountants, 1968.

FINANCIAL ACCOUNTING STANDARDS BOARD. "Financial Reporting for Segments of a Business Enterprise." *FASB Discussion Memorandum.* Stamford, 1974.

MAUTZ, R. K. *Financial Reporting by Diversified Companies.* New York: Financial Executives Research Foundation, 1967.

RAPPAPORT, ALFRED, and LERNER, EUGENE. *Segment Reporting for Managers and Investors.* New York: National Association of Accountants, 1972.

CASE

CASE 24–1. QUAKER OATS COMPANY
Segment Disclosure

As part of the annual review of the stocks held by the trust department, the director of equity research at the Collins Bank and Trust Company asked each analyst to describe how changing product mix and the business, industry, customer, and geographical diversification activities over the last five years of the companies they followed influenced the company's current and prospective risk characteristics, which he defined as the volatility of earnings per share, rates of profitability, opportunities for growth, and capital requirements. Peter Macey, the bank's food analyst, used the 1975 Quaker Oats Company's annual report data to make this analysis for Quaker Oats. Excerpts of this report are reproduced in Exhibit 1.

Questions

1. How helpful to Macey is the product line and foreign operations data presented in the 1975 annual report? What conclusions do you think he might reach based on these data? Prepare a draft of Macey's report.
2. How would the adoption of the FASB Exposure Draft "Financial Reporting for Segments of a Business Enterprise" change the information disclosed by Quaker Oats? As a member of the company's top management, would you be in favor of these changes? Why? Do you think Macey would find the additional data useful? In what ways?
3. Do you think the changes made to the exposure draft by the FASB when it adopted its final *Statement* will enhance Macey's evaluation?

EXHIBIT 1

Excerpts from Annual Report
For the Fiscal Period Ending June 30, 1975

To Our Shareholders and Employees:

Our 1975 fiscal year was disappointing. It was marked both by a continuation of the inflation that had adversely affected us in the prior year and by recession. While perfor-

EXHIBIT 1 (continued)

mance was excellent in a number of areas of the business, it was clearly unsatisfactory in others.

Fiscal 1975 earnings per share were $1.45 compared to $1.91 in the prior year. Consolidated operating income, including toy division charges described below, was down only 4 percent from fiscal 1974, despite an 86 percent decline in toys and recreational products. Our worldwide grocery products business continues to represent close to two thirds of our operating profit. After increased interest costs and a higher effective income tax rate, net income was off 22 percent from last year.

In the United States and Canada, operating income of our grocery businesses was up 4 percent. This profit performance improvement was achieved after increased marketing costs and the adverse impact of higher commodity prices.

Foods were well ahead of last year, and profit contribution was up significantly, illustrating once again our solid base in this business. Overall, we maintained market shares. Oatmeal—a low-cost, high-value food—was strong reflecting renewed consumer interest in basic foods. Corn products had a good year. Higher priced convenience foods were generally weak.

Pet food dollar sales increased, but volume was off as consumers resisted higher prices of canned pet foods—resulting in a significant decline in profitability. We did, however, improve market share in semimoist pet foods, where we have strong positions.

International grocery sales were up, but earnings were down from the record high of the prior year, which included $1.4 million from a tax-free land sale. European pet foods achieved substantial dollar sales growth. In July 1975, we increased ownership in our joint venture in France, and now hold a majority interest.

Results of our toy businesses were the principal negative influence on fiscal 1975 earnings. The disappointing Christmas toy season in the middle of our fiscal year was the major factor. In an effort to cut down inventories in an uncertain economy, the trade did not follow its normal pre Christmas reorder pattern. As a result, Fisher-Price full-year profitability was off about 50 percent, and Marx Toys had a substantial loss. These figures include the elimination of certain toy lines of limited potential and the consolidation of facilities in domestic and overseas toy operations which reduced consolidated earnings 19 cents a share.

In a difficult year, we should not overlook the fact that our strategy of balanced diversification strengthens our position over time. In fiscal 1975, for example, while the two toy companies had lower earnings, a different area of diversification—the Chemicals Division—helped offset the shortfall of the toy divisions through its increased contribution to corporate earnings.

Chemicals contributed almost $100 million in sales and accounted for 24 percent of our consolidated operating earnings in fiscal 1975—an essential development in view of the very high capital levels currently being invested in the future of this business. This division is becoming increasingly important to the company's total results as it expands production facilities to satisfy worldwide demand for agriculturally based furan chemicals used in the foundry, petroleum, plastics, rubber, and corrosion-resistant products industries.

Two newer businesses, though much more modest, also did well in fiscal 1975. The Needlecraft Division recovered very nicely from some problems it experienced a year ago, and our Magic Pan restaurants successfully continued their planned expansion. Both these businesses produced good increases in sales and earnings contribution, as did the Burry Division, which markets a specialty line of cookies and crackers. . . .

As we look ahead after a difficult year, we're confident that the tough corrective measures improved organization, and more effective internal controls that were initiated in fiscal 1975 have markedly strengthened the company. Though economic projections—rates of inflation, trends of commodity prices, and levels of unemployment—are far from clear as I write to you, we have planned our business both to recognize these uncertainties and to provide the flexibility to respond to them.

Sales trends are generally firm and margins improved as we start the new fiscal year. Even though we have not achieved our earnings goal—at least a 10 percent increase in per-share earnings averaged over any five-year period—in either of the last two fiscal

EXHIBIT 1 *(continued)*

years, we are encouraged about our future prospects. We have great confidence in our strengthened management team and in the unique dedication of 25.000 Quaker employees around the world.

Robert D. Stuart, Jr.
President and Chief Executive Officer
September 7, 1975

Consolidated Sales*

	Sales (millions of dollars)					Percentage of Total Sales				
	1971	1972	1973	1974	1975	1971	1972	1973	1974	1975
Toys and recreational products	81.9	116.8	224.7	270.1	243.5	11.7	14.7	22.7	22.0	17.5
Industrial and institutional products	83.4	87.6	104.1	131.3	185.9	11.9	11.0	10.5	10.7	13.4
International grocery products	87.0	106.7	133.9	197.0	224.6	12.4	13.4	13.5	16.1	16.2
U.S. and Canadian grocery products	449.6	484.1	528.1	628.9	735.0	64.0	60.9	53.3	51.2	52.9
Total	701.9	795.2	990.8	1227.3	1389.0	100.0	100.0	100.0	100.0	100.0

* These data were originally presented in graph form.

Grocery Products Area

	Sales (millions of dollars)					Percentage of Total Sales				
	1971	1972	1973	1974	1975	1971	1972	1973	1974	1975
Foods	215.7	234.6	262.6	322.2	399.8	40.2	39.7	39.7	39.0	41.7
Pet foods	148.1	159.2	174.1	202.1	217.4	27.6	26.9	26.3	24.5	22.6
Canada	43.8	46.8	47.2	59.8	68.9	8.2	7.9	7.1	7.2	7.2
International	87.0	106.7	133.9	197.0	224.6	16.2	18.1	20.2	23.9	23.4
Other	42.0	43.9	44.2	44.8	48.9	7.8	7.4	6.7	5.4	5.1
Total	536.6	590.8	662.0	825.9	959.6	100.0	100.0	100.0	100.0	100.0

Grocery Products Area

The United States and Canadian Grocery Products Group and the International Grocery Products Group were combined into a single Grocery Products Area, which includes foods and pet food products sold through grocery channels to consumers worldwide. Area sales and operating income are about two thirds of total consolidated results. . . .

In fiscal 1975, area sales increased 16 percent to $959.6 million, and operating income was about equal to last year, as margins on many products continued to be squeezed. U.S.. and Canadian operating income was up, but International was off. Throughout the Grocery Products Area, promotional expenditures were up considerably to support existing brand franchises as well as new products and market expansions.

Food Division

Almost all consumer foods marketed by Quaker in the United States are included in this division—hot and ready-to-eat cereals, pancake and baking mixes, corn products,

EXHIBIT 1 (continued)

frozen foods, and syrup. It is a large, basic business, built on the strengths of some of the best-known consumer brand names. Division sales in fiscal 1975 amounted to $399.8 million, 24 percent better than last year. Although there were substantial variations among product lines, overall profit contribution of the Foods Division improved significantly.

Food Sales

	Sales (millions of dollars)				
	1971	1972	1973	1974	1975
Hot cereals	65.3	64.8	62.9	69.4	94.9
Ready-to-eat cereals	58.9	60.3	77.6	102.6	116.1
Mixes, pancake, and					
syrup	75.1	78.0	81.5	100.5	134.3
Frozen foods	16.4	31.5	40.6	49.7	54.5
Total	215.7	234.6	262.6	322.2	399.8

Hot cereals, principally traditional Quaker Oats and Instant Quaker Oatmeal, achieved a 37 percent sales increase, improving on recent trends. Profitability was up on a volume increase. A new cinnamon and spice-flavored instant oatmeal performed well.

Although prices on competitive breakfast items such as meat and eggs declined during the year, Quaker oatmeal increased its longstanding attractiveness for families seeking wholesome breakfast food at reasonable cost. It continues to be true that more servings of Quaker Oats are consumed in the United States than any other cereal—hot or cold.

Ready-to-eat cereal performance varied widely among the different brands. Total ready-to-eat sales in fiscal 1975 were $116.1 million, up 13 percent, but volume was down and profitability declined largely because of lower margins on natural cereals.

Life cereal continued as an outstanding nutritional breakfast product and, despite heavy competitive advertising, established a new sales and volume record. A recently introduced fruit-flavored variety of Cap'n Crunch is expected to aid the established Cap'n Crunch product line, which encountered consumer price resistance during the year and experienced some volume decline. Quaker 100 percent Natural Cereal maintained market leadership and share in this category, which we pioneered in 1972. A newly introduced apple and cinnamon flavor was well accepted. The entire natural cereal market declined significantly, however, because of consumer resistance to higher prices necessitated by rising ingredient costs.

Mixes, syrup, and corn goods. These basic products continued to produce good sales and profit contribution, although physical volume remained about the same. Sales of Aunt Jemima Cornmeal and Grits, Pancake Mix, Syrup, and related products were $134.3 million.

Frozen food sales of $54.5 million improved 10 percent, but volume was off slightly from last year, largely because of a general softening in the entire convenience food market. Celeste Pizza products were affected somewhat by reduced consumer interest resulting from the recession and by aggressive competition from other brands entering the deluxe pizza category. Aunt Jemima Frozen Waffles and French Toast were also affected by the softening of the convenience food market. New Aunt Jemima Frozen Pancake Batter, introduced at year-end, received good initial trade orders.

A consolidation of production and distribution facilities at our Jackson, Tennessee, frozen foods plant is already reducing costs and should help improve margins, which are not yet satisfactory. Establishing adequate profitability is a principal goal in frozen foods.

EXHIBIT 1 *(continued)*

Pet Foods Division

Sales of our pet foods in the United States were $217.4 million, up 8 percent over last year, but volume was off. The division suffered a substantial decline in profitability, mainly because of volume weakness. Costs of raw materials and cans as well as high levels of promotional expense were also factors. Such costs have recently shown some improvement.

Pet Food Sales (millions of dollars)

	1971	1972	1973	1974	1975
Cat food	36.6	36.6	34.9	38.6	39.9
Dog food	115.5	122.6	139.2	163.5	177.5
Total	148.1	159.2	174.1	202.1	217.4

Because of the recession economy, many consumers shifted their purchasing from canned dog foods—where our Ken-L Ration products are very important—to the dry category, where we still have only a limited market position. Ken-L Ration canned dog food has maintained market share; with an improving economy, increased vitality in the canned market is expected.

In the important burger-type or semimoist segment of the market, the Ken-L Ration market share has increased to an all-time high, with Ken-L Ration Burger's Egg flavor as an important new product entry. The total burger market declined somewhat, however, reflecting economic conditions.

While our Puss'n Boots line of canned cat foods continued to decline in sales and market share, Puss'n Boots Moist Meals, a new semimoist variety, was introduced in several additional markets and is now available in 55 percent of the United States. Substantial marketing investments in this product have moved it to the point that, on a national basis, it is now the second largest brand in its category.

Other U.S. Sales (millions of dollars)

	1971	1972	1973	1974	1975
Other U.S. sales	42.0	43.9	44.2	44.8	48.9

The category of "Other U.S. Sales" includes the small but successful regional Wolf Brand canned chili business in the southwestern part of the United States. Substantial increases in sales and profitability were achieved by Wolf Brand in fiscal 1975.

Also included in this category are various industrial cereal products sales, government sales, and sales of miscellaneous grains and by-products of the milling process to nongrocery outlets.

Canada

The Quaker Oats Company of Canada Limited achieved sales of $68.9 million in fiscal 1975, an improvement of 15 percent over the prior year.

EXHIBIT 1 *(continued)*
Canadian Grocery Products Sales (millions of dollars)

	1971	1972	1973	1974	1975
Canadian grocery product sales	43.8	46.4	47.2	59.8	68.9

Profit contribution was up, despite the effect of a two-month strike at the Trenton, Ontario, pet foods plant. Margins were pressured by inflationary conditions and cost problems similar to those experienced in the United States. Overall, consumer foods were strong while pet foods did less well.

The Canadian company successfully introduced a number of new food and pet food products during the year, which contributed to its good performance.

International Grocery Products

Quaker grocery products are sold in 136 countries besides the U.S. and Canada. The five largest businesses are in the United Kingdom, the Benelux nations, Mexico, Scandinavia, and Brazil.

International Grocery Products sales were $224.6 million in fiscal 1975, up 14 percent from the prior year. Inflation was a major factor. Due to various economic and competitive conditions in the nations where we do business, operating income was below the record level set last year, when results in Brazil were exceptional and there was a $1.4 million gain from a tax-free land sale.

International Grocery Products (millions of dollars)

	1971	1972	1973	1974	1975
Europe	48.3	59.2	71.2	98.5	124.3
Latin America and Pacific	38.7	47.5	62.7	98.5	100.3
Total	87.0	106.7	133.9	197.0	224.6

Europe. Pet foods are the focus of the company's planned grocery expansion in Western Europe. Significant investments have been made in developing the semimoist dog food business in the United Kingdom, the Benelux and Scandinavian nations, and France. The company also operates well-established cereals businesses in these nations.

Sales in Europe were $124.3 million in fiscal 1975, up 26 percent over last year. Market share remained relatively constant in foods and in semimoist pet foods, with only a slight decline in canned pet foods. Profitability improved, reflecting the success of prior investments.

Quaker Oats Limited in the United Kingdom, which celebrated its 75th anniversary during the year, produced record results despite the difficult economic problems in that country.

In July 1975 we assumed a controlling interest in the French joint-venture pet foods business we formed in fiscal 1973. The reorganized operation should be better positioned to manage the business in France, which so far has involved high introductory and expansion costs.

EXHIBIT 1 *(continued)*

Latin America and the Pacific. Quaker's businesses in these areas of the world are more diverse—ranging from chocolate bar and beverage products in Mexico to canned sardines in Brazil and pet foods in Australia. Cereals, mixes, and grain-based beverages are basic to our subsidiaries in Latin America.

Sales in Latin America and the Pacific were $100.3 million—about the same as last year—with market shares generally remaining constant and profitability down on lower volume. In Mexico, the La Azteca chocolate business had a successful year. Toward the end of the period, price controls that had impaired profitability on rolled oats in Mexico finally became somewhat more reasonable. In Brazil the sardine business of Conservas Coqueiro, S. A., suffered in sales and profits from last year's record-high levels because of inflation and resulting erosion in consumer purchasing power. The entire canned fish market had a substantial overall volume decline, but we retained our share position.

Australia has been troubled with serious economic difficulties, which—combined with competitive pressures—had a very negative effect on our business there. Sales were off substantially, profitability was eroded, and market share remains below prior-year levels. We are watching political and economic conditions in Australia with concern.

Diversified Businesses Area

This area . . . consists of six operating divisions whose products move primarily through distribution channels other than retail grocery stores. . . .

During fiscal 1975, the Chemicals, Burry, Needlecraft, and Magic Pan divisions achieved very good growth in both sales and profit contribution. The profitability of our two toy divisions declined substantially, however; and there was a $6.1 million pretax charge against operating income to cover costs of eliminating certain toy lines of limited potential and consolidation of facilities. These actions were designed to improve future operating results at both Marx and Fisher-Price. . . .

Area sales increased 7 percent to $429.4 million.

Fisher-Price Toys Division

After a five-year period in which Fisher-Price sales grew from $32 million to $158.5 million, sales were $138.4 million in fiscal 1975, or 13 percent below the prior year. Earnings were off about 50 percent from last year's level.

Fisher-Price Fiscal Year Sales (millions of dollars)

	1971	1972	1973	1974	1975
Fisher-Price fiscal year sales	58.7	92.8	114.2	158.5	138.4

When comparing sales by calendar year, the toy industry's normal basis of comparison, Fisher-Price continued its growth, with an average annual sales increase of 37 percent for the last five calendar years.

Fisher-Price Calendar Year Sales (millions of dollars)

	1971	1972	1973	1974	1975
Fisher-Price calendar year sales	54.0	80.0	112.0	138.0	148.0

EXHIBIT 1 (continued)

Diversified Businesses Area

	Sales (millions of dollars)					Percentage of Total Sales				
	1971	1972	1973	1974	1975	1971	1972	1973	1974	1975
Fisher-Price	58.7	92.8	114.2	158.5	138.4	25.9	34.0	34.7	39.5	32.2
Marx	61.7*	68.2*	82.0	85.1	72.8	27.2	25.0	24.9	21.2	17.0
Needlecraft	23.2	24.0	28.5	26.5	32.3	10.2	8.8	8.7	6.6	7.5
Burry	43.3	39.8	42.3	49.4	66.2	19.1	14.6	12.9	12.3	15.4
Festaurants	1.4	2.9	5.6	11.2	22.5	0.6	1.1	1.7	2.8	5.3
Chemicals	38.7	44.9	56.2	70.7	97.2	17.0	16.5	17.1	17.6	22.6
Total	227.0	272.6	328.8	401.4	429.4	100.0	100.0	100.0	100.0	100.0

* Marx sales before acquisition.

EXHIBIT 1 *(continued)*

Two unusual six-month periods were principally responsible for the recent distortion between the fiscal and calendar years. In the first half of *calendar* 1974, retailers bought more heavily than usual because they anticipated price increases by Fisher-Price, reflecting escalating plastics and other costs. While this did not change *calendar* 1974 sales, it increased *fiscal* 1974 sales but decreased *fiscal* 1975 sales, the year covered in this report.

Another factor was the economic uncertainty that prevailed before Christmas, 1974—during the first half of Quaker's 1975 fiscal year. Facing this uncertainty, retailers did not reorder as they have done historically.

As a result, Fisher-Price, like many other toy companies, was left with unusually high inventories after the 1974 Christmas season. Therefore, production was curtailed sharply, and inventories have since been reduced to normal levels. In the process, division profits in the second half of the 1975 fiscal year (January–June 1975) were reduced because there was less absorption of fixed overhead into inventory.

Volume gains were made outside the U.S., and a direct selling operation was begun in Germany in 1974. Investments being made to broaden sales and distribution in Europe have precluded achieving an adequate return to date in that area.

Several new products with attractive potential were introduced in 1975. A set of uniquely designed, sturdy toy construction vehicles and a complete Play Family Sesame Street set are important additions to the product line. Also, Fisher-Price products were expanded somewhat beyond the preschool age with a new Adventure Series for older children.

Retailers have continued buying cautiously so far in 1975. Results for the full 12 months of the current *calendar* year will depend largely on consumer confidence and trade reordering for the Christmas season.

Marx Toys Division

Both sales and earnings at Marx suffered seriously during the 1975 fiscal year. Sales of $72.8 million were down 14 percent from last year, and the division operated at a substantial loss. Marx results were influenced by many of the same conditions already reported for Fisher-Price, but more drastically.

Marx Fiscal Year Sales (millions of dollars)

	1971	1972	1973	1974	1975
Marx fiscal year sales	61.7*	68.2*	82.0	85.1	72.8

As previously noted, fiscal-year toy sales volumes sometimes vary significantly from calendar-year results, with calendar results representing a more natural operating comparison. Marx sales had a modest calendar-year decline, as shown in the chart below.

Marx Calendar Year Sales (millions of dollars)

	1971	1972	1973	1974	1975
Marx calendar year sales	49.0*	59.5*	76.0	82.0	81.0

* Includes the following sales prior to acquisition.

1970	1971	1972
$40.0	$59.0	$14.7

EXHIBIT 1 *(continued)*

Major changes have been made in the product line, pricing strategy, marketing, research and development, and manufacturing operations. Marx continues to receive intensive review.

Needlecraft Division

Needlecraft Fiscal Year Sales (millions of dollars)

	1971	1972	1973	1974	1975
Needlecraft Division	23.2	24.0	28.5	26.5	32.3

A year ago, we reported that the Needlecraft Division had encountered a number of product mix and pricing problems that depressed sales and earnings. During fiscal 1975, the division addressed itself to solving these problems, and substantial progress was made. Sales of $32.3 million were up 22 percent, accompanied by a substantial improvement in earnings, as well as an impressive reduction in working capital needs.

The yarn and needlecraft kit business achieved significant improvements in manufacturing and operations, and greater trade acceptance of its line. The Herrschners mail-order business had particularly good gains.

Chemicals Division

The Chemicals Division had an excellent year in fiscal 1975, with sales of $97.2 million and operating income (income before interest and income taxes) of $22.1 million. Market demand exceeded supply throughout the year.

In the past two years particularly, and for several years prior to that, the company has committed substantially more than the division earned to improve its process technology and expand production facilities. From the commercial development of agriculturally based furfural in 1921, the company has pioneered research and development in furan chemistry. This has resulted in continued market growth for furfural and its derivatives, which has accelerated in recent years. Substantial new facilities have been needed. Expansions at Belle Glade, Florida, and Geel, Belgium, were completed this past year, and a major new plant at Bayport, Texas, is scheduled to start up in 1976.

Today the largest demand is for derivative products that have their own specialized uses. Furfuryl alcohol (FA) is the most important of these. Resins based on FA are widely used in foundries to bond sand for cores and molds, and demand for these resins is growing rapidly. The division provides extensive worldwide market and technical development programs for new applications in the foundry industry. Other furan chemicals are used in a broad range of industrial products and processes.

Chemical Sales (millions of dollars)

	1971	1972	1973	1974	1975
Chemical sales	38.7	44.9	56.2	70.7	97.2

In common with many other parts of the chemical industry, Quaker's specialty chemicals business is very capital-intensive. It is essential, then, to view investment in terms of current rather than historical costs. Significantly better operating income, such as that achieved in fiscal 1975, is necessary to support present investments and future commit-

EXHIBIT 1 *(continued)*

ments needed for expansion of capacity. The major expansions completed in 1975, plus the Bayport plant, and the continuing need to upgrade older plants to meet changed operating conditions and federal, state, and local requirements related to safety and environmental control, have required capital commitments of more than $54 million in the last two years.

The basic raw materials for furfural are agricultural wastes such as, corn cobs, oat hulls, sugar cane bagasse, and rice hulls. Experience in handling enormous quantities of these raw materials is a unique division strength. Both investment and operating costs associated with collecting and processing raw materials have increased sharply over the past two years, however; and our selling prices have had to reflect this.

Competitive products are derived from petroleum and also have been subject to upward cost pressures. In every important market served by the division's products, our success depends on competitive technological and economic superiority. With continued process and product development, we believe we will maintain a profitable growth and market leadership position.

Burry Division

The Burry Division markets its products to four different sectors: nationally, Quaker and Burry institutional products for the food service trade, cookies for sale by Girl Scouts, and wafers for ice cream sandwich producers; and, regionally, cookies and crackers for distribution primarily through grocery stores in the Northeast.

Burry Sales (millions of dollars)

	1971	1972	1973	1974	1975
Burry sales	43.3	29.8	42.3	49.4	66.2

Division sales of $66.2 million were 34 percent higher than the previous year. Significant price increases reflected rapidly rising commodity costs. Burry management exercised effective control over working capital during the year, and overall results were significantly improved.

Restaurants Division

Magic Pan, with restaurants in 28 locations at the end of the fiscal year, more than doubled its sales in fiscal 1975, reaching $22.5 million. Despite costs of opening 11 new units during the year, Magic Pan began making a positive contribution to corporate earnings.

Restaurant Sales (millions of dollars)

	1971	1972	1973	1974	1975
Restaurant sales	1.4	2.9	5.6	11.2	22.5

The division continues to give top priority to preparing outstanding and distinctive food served in a bright and attractive European setting by people who believe strongly in the unique Magic Pan concept. Even in a weak economy, units operating for a year or more showed gains in year-to-year comparisons of customers served. Magic Pan continues to concentrate on high-quality locations in projected expansion.

EXHIBIT 1 (continued)

Ten-Year Financial Summary
Year Ended June 30 (B), 1966–1975
(thousands of dollars)

	1975	1974	1973	1972	1971	1970	1969	1968	1967	1966
Net sales	$1,389,013	$1,227,345	$990,767	$795,240	$701,862	$612,845	$562,277	$554,199	$555,133	$498,358
Other income (expense)—net	(7,377)	2,412	1,815	1,702	1,152	2,741	2,745	966	881	432
	$1,381,636	$1,229,757	$992,585	$796,942	$703,014	$615,586	$565,022	$555,165	$556,014	$498,790
Cost of goods sold	1,029,355	914,979	692,723	545,783	482,312	411,796	382,065	387,921	403,010	358,178
Selling, general, and administrative expenses	256,834	215,293	201,461	172,409	153,148	142,663	130,344	122,777	114,397	103,048
Interest expense	28,154	23,007	12,853	8,194	6,749	4,546	2,119	2,354	2,417	1,950
	$1,314,343	$1,153,279	$907,036	$726,386	$642,209	$559,005	$514,528	$513,052	$519,824	$463,176
Income before income taxes and extraordinary item	67,293	76,478	85,549	70,556	60,805	56,581	50,494	42,113	36,190	35,614
Provision for income taxes	36,256	36,600	43,426	34,942	29,698	27,922	24,496	20,634	17,408	18,042
Income before extraordinary item	$ 31,037	$ 39,878	$ 42,123	$ 35,614	$ 31,107	$ 28,659	$ 25,998	$ 21,479	$ 18,782	$ 17,572
Extraordinary (charge) credit	—	—	—	—	(5,886)	—	(1,092)	—	898	—
Net income	$ 31,037	$ 39,878	$ 42,123	$ 35,614	$ 25,221	$ 28,659	$ 24,906	$ 21,479	$ 19,680	$ 17,572
Dividends:										
Preferred stock	426	429	452	484	490	490	495	507	528	568
Preference stock	677									
Common stock	16,550	15,523	14,711	13,006	12,636	11,737	10,704	9,710	8,868	8,864
Reinvested earnings	221,710	208,536	184,610	187,561	165,437	153,342	140,641	130,778	118,890	108,606
Current assets	357,671	406,278	313,810	247,708	199,906	185,808	149,761	149,314	137,461	134,190
Current liabilities	148,958	221,814	157,714	116,690	89,257	94,291	68,538	65,286	57,922	52,241
Net working capital	$ 208,713	$ 184,464	$156,096	$131,018	$110,649	$ 91,517	$ 81,223	$ 84,028	$ 79,539	$ 81,949
Net fixed assets	358,186	319,321	272,077	243,928	200,436	181,344	142,640	129,107	116,208	108,878
Long-term debt	158,283	171,427	125,321	131,521	96,421	68,845	18,882	21,399	22,892	25,179
Shareholders' equity	400,747	338,441	312,795	259,615	232,047	217,738	197,234	184,638	169,237	160,301
Return on common shareholders' equity	7.7%	11.8%	13.5%	13.7%	13.4% (C)	13.2%	13.2% (C)	11.6%	11.1% (C)	11.0%
Per common share: (A)										
Income before extraordinary item	$ 1.45	$ 1.31	$ 2.04	$ 1.78	$ 1.56	$ 1.45	$ 1.33	$ 1.11	$ 0.97	$ 0.91
Extraordinary (charge) credit	—	—	—	—	(0.30)	—	(0.06)	—	0.05	—
Net Income	$ 1.45	$ 1.31	$ 2.04	$ 1.78	$ 1.26	$ 1.45	$ 1.27	$ 1.11	$ 1.02	$ 0.91
Dividends declared	$ 0.80	$ 0.76	$ 0.72	$ 0.68	$ 0.67	$ 0.63	$ 0.58	$ 0.53	$ 0.49	$ 0.49

(A) Adjusted for stock splits.
(B) Results for 1972 through 1968 have been restated to reflect the July 1972 merger with Needlecraft Corporation of America Inc., recorded as a pooling of interests. Prior years have not been restated since effect is not material.
(C) Excludes extraordinary items.

EXHIBIT 1 *(continued)*

Management's Discussion and Analysis of Consolidated Statement of Income

In response to a new requirement of the U.S. Securities and Exchange Commission, we are adding this section to our Annual Report; much of it covers information reported in other sections.

Overview

Since fiscal 1973, unprecedented increases in the costs of commodities and packaging materials used in grocery products adversely affected the company's results. Also, sharply higher petrochemical prices resulted in increased costs of the plastics we use in toys. In fiscal 1974, price controls prevented full recovery of such cost increases, a situation that still prevails in some countries outside the United States. Since the removal of price controls in the United States in 1974, consumer resistance to higher prices and the recession have prevented the restoring of traditional margins while at the same time maintaining volume on toys, pet foods, and convenience foods, including some of our ready-to-eat cereals. A significant decline in the profitability of these product lines has resulted. Sales and earnings of hot cereals and corn products have been good.

The Chemicals Division continues to experience increasing sales and profitability, and demand for its products exceeds capacity. Two plant expansions were completed in 1975, and a major new plant is now under construction.

The Burry, Magic Pan, and Needlecraft Divisions all improved their results in fiscal 1975.

Fisher-Price profitability declined about 50 percent in fiscal 1975, after several years of rapid growth. Marx operated at a substantial loss. In the toy divisions, the elimination of certain product lines with limited potential and the consolidation of some operations resulted in an aftertax charge against net income of $4.0 million, or 19 cents per common share.

The six months ended June 30 has traditionally been a loss period for Marx Toys. In 1975 the loss in this half was substantially greater than in the prior year period, principally because of lower sales volume and lower production, which resulted in less absorption of overhead costs into inventory. This contributed significantly to the substantial losses incurred by Marx for the 12 months ended June 30, 1975. Major changes in product lines, manufacturing, and marketing were accomplished. Management is aggressively seeking to bring Marx to an acceptable level of profitability, and an intensive review to assess expectations for the future is in progress. If it is decided at a future date that acceptable profitability cannot be attained and that Quaker's investment in Marx may not be fully recoverable, a part of the carrying value may have to be reduced by a charge to income. At June 30, 1975, the investment was $47.8 million, of which $33.2 million was net working capital.

Comparison of Fiscal 1975 to Fiscal 1974

Sales increased from $1,227.3 million to $1,389.0 million, mainly as a result of price increases.

Cost of goods sold increased approximately 12.5 percent. Although the overall company gross profit margin remained constant with fiscal 1974, some ready-to-eat cereal products—principally Quaker 100 percent Natural Cereal experienced severe margin pressure because of the escalation in sugar and agricultural commodity costs. Life cereal, on the other hand, achieved very good increases in sales and profitability. Hot cereals and corn products improved their contribution to earnings, and chemicals margins improved significantly. Toy volume and margins declined substantially and pet food volume declined.

Selling, general, and administrative expenses increased $41.5 million, or 19.3 percent. Sixty-two percent of the increase, or $25.8 million, was in advertising and promotion expenses for domestic grocery products, to support established and new products in all major categories—particularly pet foods.

EXHIBIT 1 (continued)

Interest expense for 1975 was $28.2 million, an increase of 22.4 percent, required for increased debt necessary to finance working capital requirements and capital improvements and, to a lesser extent, higher interest rates in the early part of the year. All of the increased interest expense was incurred in the first half of the fiscal year. Interest expense for the second half was slightly lower than the same prior-year period due to lower inventory and receivable levels, lower interest rates and the effect of a preference stock offering.

The 1975 effective income tax rate is 53.9 percent compared to 47.9 percent in 1974. This increase was caused by: *(a)* the effect of the toy division charges associated with the elimination of certain product lines with limited potential and the consolidation of some operations (excluding these, the fiscal 1975 rate would have been 52.2 percent); *(b)* a change in the mix of earnings from foreign and domestic sources, including a reduction in tax-free profits from last year's record-high level in Conservas Coqueiro, S.A., our Brazilian sardine company; and *(c)* the fact that last year's rate was unusually low because pretax income included a $1.4 million gain from a tax-free disposition of land not required for future operations.

Net income for fiscal 1975 declined $8.8 million or 22.2 percent, compared with fiscal 1974. Included in fiscal 1975 results is an aftertax charge of approximately $4.0 million, or 19 cents per common share, representing costs related to the elimination of certain toy lines and the consolidation of facilities to improve toy operations.

Comparison of Fiscal 1974 to Fiscal 1973

Net sales increased $236.6 million, or 23.9 percent. There was improvement in all major product categories. About half of the 1974 increase was the result of higher prices. Sales of the toy divisions were particularly strong in the fourth quarter of fiscal 1974, because of customer anticipation of company price increases.

Cost of goods sold increased 32.1 percent because of exceptionally high cost increases in principal raw materials such as cereal grains, meat by-products, and plastics.

Sales and Operating Income by Groups
Year Ended June 30, 1971–1975
(millions of dollars)

Sales and Operating Income	*1975*	*1974*	*1973*	*1972*	*1971*
U.S. and Canadian Grocery					
Products Group	735.0*	628.9	528.1	484.1	449.6
	50.3†	48.3	51.1	43.5	43.2
International Grocery Products					
Group	224.6*	197.0	133.9	106.7	87.0
	11.5†	14.0	6.8	5.3	5.2
Toys and Recreational Products					
Group	243.5*	270.1	224.7	116.8	81.9
	3.5†	25.4	31.9	22.8	13.6
Industrial and Institutional					
Products Group‡	185.9*	131.3	104.1	87.6	83.4
	28.4†	9.9	6.7	5.6	4.3
Total sales	1,389.0*	1,227.3	990.8	795.2	701.9
Total operating income	93.7†	97.6	96.5	77.2	66.3
Less interest expense—net	26.4	21.1	11.0	6.6	5.5
Income before Income Taxes	67.3	76.5	85.5	70.6	60.8

* Sales figures.

† Operating income figures.

‡ Chemicals Division sales and operating income for the five years ended June 30, 1975, included in Industrial and Institutional Products are as follows:

1975	*1974*	*1973*	*1972*	*1971*
97.2	70.7	56.2	44.9	38.7
22.1	8.5	5.8	4.6	4.3

EXHIBIT 1 *(continued)*

The company was not able to fully recover these higher costs, mainly because of U.S. price controls and competitive factors in the grocery products and toy businesses.

The $10.2 million increase in interest expense was caused primarily by additional debt to finance working capital requirements—required by inflation, capital expenditures, and acquisitions and, to a lesser extent, higher interest rates.

The tax rate declined from 50.8 percent in fiscal 1973 to 47.9 percent in fiscal 1974 as a result of a more favorable mix of taxable income, due, in part, to the inclusion of the earnings of Conservas Coqueiro, S.A., acquired in July 1973, which were not subject to income taxes, and a tax-free disposition of land not required for future operations.

The 5.3 percent decline in fiscal 1974 net income compared with fiscal 1973 was due principally to the reduced gross profit margin and higher interest expense, as explained above. . . .

Selected Notes to Consolidated Financial Statements

Foreign Translation. Foreign currency items are translated into U.S. dollars at year-end exchange rates for assets and liabilities and average annual exchange rates for income items, except properties and intangibles and related depreciation and amortization, which are translated at rates in effect at time of acquisition.

Unrealized translation gains are credited to a reserve, except to the extent that they offset previously recorded losses; unrealized losses in excess of previously established reserves are charged to income.

Gains and losses on forward exchange contracts are recognized in income upon settlement.

Intangibles. Excess of cost over net assets of acquired businesses, including $27,915,000 related to acquisitions prior to November 1, 1970 (principally Fisher-Price Toys, Inc.), represents the amounts paid in excess of the fair values of the net assets of such businesses, less amortization. Such costs are considered to represent continuing values and are adjusted if reduction of the continuing values of underlying businesses is indicated. As required by current accounting rules, all such costs resulting from acquisitions after October 31, 1970, are amortized over periods not in excess of 40 years. Amortization for 1975 and 1974 was $808,000 and $618,000, respectively.

Costs incurred in acquiring patents, trademarks, and designs are amortized on a straight-line basis over their estimated useful lives. Amortization for 1975 and 1974 was $811,000 and $781,000, respectively.

Undistributed Foreign Earnings. Except for minor amounts, no federal income taxes have been provided on the undistributed net income of foreign subsidiaries since these amounts are expected to be permanently invested in those countries.

Foreign Operations. Summarized financial information for foreign operations are shown on the following page.

In 1975 the net exchange and translation loss amounted to $2,008,000 and was charged to income. The reserve for unrealized translation gains, included in other liabilities, increased by $12,000 during the year and at June 30, 1975, was $1,302,000.

In 1974 the net exchange and translation gain amounted to $613,000 and was credited to income. The reserve for unrealized translation gain decreased by $1,473,000 during the year and at June 30, 1974, was $1,290,000.

Acquisitions. In July 1973, Conservas Coqueiro S.A. (a Brazilian sardine processor) was purchased by the company for $14,503,000 in cash. The results of operations of this business, which are not subject to income taxes, are included in the consolidated earnings from the date of acquisition. The related excess of cost over the fair value of net assets amounted to $8,212,000 and is being amortized over 40 years.

EXHIBIT 1 *(continued)*

(thousands of dollars)

Assets	1975	1974
Current assets	$120,420	$128,237
Property, plant, and equipment (net)	60,894	54,337
Other assets	16,398	17,909
	$197,712	$200,483
Less:		
Current liabilities	$ 63,975	$ 73,537
Other liabilities	22,753	20,800
	$ 86,728	$ 94,337
Total Net Assets	$110,984	$106,146
Net assets:		
Canada	$ 21,366	$ 22,951
Europe	45,186	39,252
Latin America and Pacific	44,432	43,943
Total	$110,984	$106,146
Net sales:		
Canada	$ 83,939	$ 81,228
Europe	181,982	145,033
Latin America and Pacific	107,749	101,641
Total	$373,670	$327,902
Reinvested Earnings	$ 60,517	$ 52,397

EXHIBIT 1 *(concluded)*

Income Taxes. Provision for income taxes consisted of:

	(thousands of dollars)	
	1975	*1974*
Currently payable—		
Federal	$15,094	$18,635
State	2,337	2,746
Foreign	8,369	8,358
Deferred—(primarily federal taxes related to depreciation)	7,881	5,265
Deferred investment tax credit, net	2,575	1,596
	$36,256	$36,600

The provision for income taxes varied from the "expected" tax expense computed at 48 percent of income before income taxes, as follows:

	1975		*(thousands of dollars)* 1974	
	Amount	*Percent of Pretax Income*	*Amount*	*Percent of Pretax Income*
Computed "expected" tax expense	$32,301	48.0%	$36,709	48.0%
State and local income taxes, net of federal income tax benefit	1,497	2.2	1,615	2.1
Foreign tax rate differential	1,839	2.7	(1,777)	(2.3)
Miscellaneous items	619	1.0	53	.1
Actual tax expense	$36,256	53.9%	$36,600	47.9%

A more favorable mix of domestic and international earnings in 1974 (including a $1,400,000 tax-free disposition of land not required for future operations) resulted in a lower effective income tax rate compared to 1975.

Chapter 25

INTERIM STATEMENTS

Each quarter publicly traded companies publish for their stockholders and file with the SEC in Form 10-Q data related to their activities for the past quarter and the year to date. In September 1975 the SEC substantially increased both the content of quarterly reports filed with the agency and the amount of quarterly data disclosed in annual reports. Two years earlier, in 1973, the APB in *Opinion No. 28* set forth some suggested guidelines for preparing interim reports. Because the new SEC rules required greater responsibility by CPA's in the preparation and presentation of quarterly reports, in late 1975 the FASB added a project on interim reporting to its agenda. As a result, it is expected that eventually the FASB may modify the guideline included in the prior APB *Statement*.

To date, the only FASB *Statement* dealing with interim reports is *Statement No. 3*, "Reporting Accounting Changes in Interim Financial Statements."

Most of the issues involved in interim reporting are the same as those encountered in annual reporting. However, there are a number of reporting practices that are peculiar to interim reporting. This chapter concentrates on these latter issues.

Illustration 25–1 presents an example of an income statement presented in an interim report (page 720).

SEC REQUIREMENTS

The SEC requirements covered three topics: the content of the Form 10-Q; the disclosure of quarterly data in annual reports; and the relationship of the independent public accountant to the quarterly data.

Form 10-Q

The SEC 1975 amendments to Form 10-Q substantially increased the content of quarterly reports. Henceforth, these reports must in-

ILLUSTRATION 25–1

CONSOLIDATED STATEMENT OF EARNINGS

hoover ball and bearing company and subsidiaries

(Dollars and Shares in Thousands)

	NINE MONTHS ENDED APRIL 30		THREE MONTHS ENDED APRIL 30	
	1975(B)	1974(A)	1975(B)	1974(A)
Steel products............................	$ 86,249	$ 69,372	$ 26,520	$ 25,113
Plastic products and machinery..............	54,553	45,382	17,345	14,385
Aluminum, zinc and brass products.........	36,887	45,430	11,669	17,459
Miscellaneous products....................	27,406	26,779	10,105	9,520
Net Sales	$205,095	$186,963	$ 65,639	$ 66,477
Cost of products sold......................	$171,710	$155,736	$ 53,001	$ 55,764
Selling and administrative expenses..........	14,944	13,753	5,223	4,784
Interest expense..........................	2,103	2,197	594	762
Other deductions and credits—net...........	(185)	(598)	67	(308)
	$188,572	$171,088	$ 58,885	$ 61,002
Earnings before income taxes	$ 16,523	$ 15,875	$ 6,754	$ 5,475
Federal and state income taxes..............	8,350	7,300	3,400	2,500
Net Earnings	$ 8,173	$ 8,575	$ 3,354	$ 2,975
Depreciation and amortization..............	$ 6,024	$ 4,920	$ 1,910	$ 1,720
Average number of shares outstanding........	4,002	3,888	4,002	4,002
Earnings per share........................	$ 2.04	$ 2.21	$ 0.84	$ 0.74

(A) Earnings before income taxes, net earnings, and earnings per share have been restated from amounts previously reported to reflect the change to the "LIFO" method of valuing inventories during fiscal 1974.
(B) Subject to fiscal year-end audit.

clude a condensed income statement, balance sheet, and funds flow statement; a narrative analysis of the results of operations; the approval of any accounting change by the filing company's independent public accountant; and the signature of the company's chief financial or accounting officer. In addition, management is encouraged to make whatever additional financial disclosures it believes are appropriate. Also, a statement that the financial data has been reviewed by a CPA may be included if such a review has been made in accordance with the professional standards.

Annual Report Disclosure

The 1975 SEC rule requires disclosure in a note to the annual financial statements of certain registrants of net sales, gross profit (net sales less costs and expenses associated directly with or allocated to products sold or services rendered), income before extraordinary items and cumulative effect of a change in accounting, per-share data based upon such income, and net income for each quarter within the two most recent fiscal years and any subsequent fiscal period for which income statements are presented. Where this note is part of audited financial statements, it may be designated as "unaudited," but the release recognizes that auditors will be associated with the data.

Certain companies, such as those with limited trading interest in their stock, are exempt from the above Form 10-Q and annual report requirements.

Audit Review

The SEC quarterly reporting requirements encourage timely and retrospective auditor involvement in the quarterly reporting process. Also, the auditor must "be associated" with the "unaudited" disclosures in the annual report. Previously, a company's auditor took no responsibility for the interim data. As a result, the SEC and the Auditing Standards Executive Committee have had to work out new professional standards and procedures to guide the auditor in this new role.

INHERENT PROBLEM

The determination of the results of operations for periods of less than a full year presents inherent difficulties for the management trying to prepare a meaningful statement and the investor seeking to use the interim data.

The most common difficulty is that information for any period less than a full year may be of limited usefulness because of the shortness of the reporting period and the nature of a company's business. For example, the revenues of some businesses fluctuate widely among interim periods due to seasonal or random factors. In other businesses heavy fixed costs incurred in one interim period may benefit another period. In other situations costs and expenses related to a full year's activities may be incurred at infrequent intervals throughout the year. In this case, costs may be allocated to products in process or to other interim periods to avoid distorting the interim results.

Another reporting problem inherent in interim reporting is that in the limited time available it is impractical to develop the complete information needed to present the report. As a result, in interim reports many costs and expenses are estimated. For example, it may not be practical to perform extensive reviews of individual inventory items, costs on individual long-term contracts, and precise income tax calculations. As a result, the interim data are tentative, and subsequent refinement or corrections of these estimates may distort the results of operations of later interim periods. Similarly, the effects of disposal of a segment of a business and extraordinary, unusually or infrequently occurring events and transactions on the results of operations in an interim period will often be more pronounced than they will be on the results for the annual period.

FUNDAMENTAL ACCOUNTING ISSUE: INTERIM REPORTING OBJECTIVE

Interim reporting practices are very diverse because there is considerable controversy as to what the principal objective should be for interim financial reporting. *Opinion No. 28* settled on one of the two major contending objectives, but some of its recommendations seem to be more consistent with the rejected alternative than the one adopted.

The two principal alternative objectives proposed follow from their proposers' view of the nature of the interim period. Those holding to one objective believe that each interim period should be viewed as the basic accounting period. (This approach is called the "independent theory.") In contrast, the proposers of the alternative objective maintain that each interim period should be viewed as an integral part of the annual period (the so-called "dependent theory").

Basic Accounting Period

Those that hold the "basic accounting period" position tend to believe that an accounting period is a period irrespective of its length and that the events and transactions of each accounting period should be reported in that period. From this position they conclude that the results of operations for each interim period should be determined in essentially the same manner as if the interim period were an annual accounting period. Under this view, deferrals, accruals, and estimations at the end of each interim period would be determined by following essentially the same principles and judgments that the company applies to annual reports. For example, this means that if an expenditure was expensed in the annual statement, it should be expensed in any interim report, irrespective of the amount of the expenditure and its relationship to the annual amount or the revenues of other interim periods within this year.

Integral Part of Annual Period

The holders of the "integral part of an annual period" view believe that interim financial data are essential to provide investors with timely information as to the progress of the enterprise toward its annual results of operations. Therefore, the usefulness of interim data rests on the predictive relationship that it has to the annual period results. Thus, each interim period should be regarded as an integral part of the annual period rather than a discrete period standing on its own.

Under this view, deferrals, accruals, and estimations at the end of each interim period are affected by judgments made at the interim date as to the results of operations for the balance of the annual period. Thus, for example, a portion of an estimated annual expenditure that might be expensed for the entire annual period might be accrued or deferred at the end of an interim period as management allocates the estimated annual expense between interim periods on a basis that reflects time, sales volume, or production activity.

OPINION NO. 28 AND OTHER AUTHORITATIVE STATEMENTS

Opinion No. 28 adopted the "integral part" point of view. The *Opinion* recognized that, in general, each interim report should be based on the accounting policies used in the preparation of the latest annual statements, unless some accounting policies have been changed in the current year. However, it went on to conclude that certain modifications of these annual report practices may be required in interim reports so that the reported results may better relate to the results of operations for the annual period.

Interim Reporting Guidelines

Opinion No. 28 recommended a number of guidelines for the preparation of interim statements. The principal emphasis was on the matching of costs and revenues, the reporting of extraordinary items and the disposal of a business, and disclosure requirements. Here is a summary of the *Opinion's* recommendations.

Revenues

Revenues earned during an interim period should be recognized on the same basis as followed for the full year. For example, if the revenue from long term contracts is accounted for under the percentage-of-completion method in annual statements, the same approach should be used in interim reports. If future losses on such contracts become evident during an interim period, the projected losses should be recognized in full in the interim period, however.

Product Costs

Costs that are associated directly with or allocated to the products and services sold are called product costs. These costs for both annual and interim reporting purposes should be charged to the period in which the related revenue is recognized. Examples of product costs include: material costs, direct production wages and related fringe benefits, variable manufacturing overheads, warranty expenses, and other similar expenses whose total level tends to vary with or relate closely to business volume.

Most product costs are included in the income statement as an element of the cost of goods sold figure. This item in interim reports should be regarded as a very tentative expression of the expense, since the inventory valuation procedures used to measure it are typically based on perpetual inventory records, rather than physical counts, and estimates of future inventory replenishment cost experience. Inventory records are seldom accurate; and the future cost estimates of executives are seldom correct due to random factors, a desire to be conservative, a need to inflate current profits, or poor forecasting information and skills.

For interim reporting purposes companies should generally use the same inventory pricing methods as those followed to determine annual results. However, there are some exceptions that may be appropriate for interim reporting purposes. For example, some companies use estimated gross profit rates to determine the cost of goods sold during interim periods. Under this procedure management simply assumes a margin percentage, which is typically either the margin achieved in prior annual periods or budgeted for the current annual period, and applies it to the sales of the period to determine the period's dollar gross margin. This approach in times of inflation can produce misleading results if a company is not aware of its cost increases and is slow to raise prices.

Other companies that use the Lifo method may, at an interim date, encounter a temporary liquidation of the Lifo base period inventories which are expected to be replaced by the end of the annual period. If these base period costs are allowed to flow through to the income statement, profits would be inflated and not representative of the annual results.

In such cases the inventory at the interim reporting date should not give effect to the Lifo liquidation. The cost of sales for the interim reporting period should include the expected cost of replacement of the liquidated Lifo base. Again, in periods of inflation or commodity shortages, this estimate is difficult to make, since commodity prices are difficult to forecast.

Many companies use standard cost accounting systems for determining inventory and product costs. These companies should generally follow the same procedure in reporting purchase price, wage rate, usage, or efficiency variances from standard cost at the end of the interim period as followed at the end of the fiscal year. However, if the cost variances associated with an interim period are planned and are expected to be absorbed by the end of the annual period, they may be deferred and not recognized in the interim period. In contrast, unplanned variances should be recognized in the interim period in which they occur. The decision as to what is "planned" and "unplanned" rests with the reporting management.

The application for interim periods of the lower-of-cost-or-market rule for inventories also requires judgment on management's part as to whether or not to apply the rule. If a company has inventory losses from market price declines at an interim period date, the loss should be recognized in the interim period in which it occurs if management believes the loss is permanent. On the other hand, if a market decline at an interim date can reasonably be expected to be restored in the current fiscal year, the temporary decline need not be recognized at the interim date. Should management decide to recognize an inventory loss in one interim period and if the market price later recovers in the same fiscal year, the gain can be recognized in the later interim period in which it occurs.

Other Costs

All businesses have costs and expenses that are not allocated or associated directly with product and service revenues. These other costs include such items as advertising expenditures, vacation pay, maintenance costs, and property taxes. According to *Opinion No. 28* these other costs may be expensed as incurred *or* allocated among interim periods based on an estimate of time expired, benefit received, or other activity associated with the period. In line with its overall objective for interim statements the *Opinion* expressed a preference for allocating these other costs between periods, but it did not preclude the option to expense as incurred.

To guide management in their interim accounting for costs and expenses other than product costs, the APB set forth these standards:

1. Procedures adopted for assigning specific expense items to an interim period should be consistent with the bases followed by the company for that item in reporting results of operations at an annual reporting date.
2. When a specific cost item charged to expense for annual reporting purposes benefits more than one interim period, the item may be allocated as an expense between those interim periods that benefit from the expenditure.
3. Costs and expenditures incurred in an interim period that cannot be identified with the activities or benefits of other interim periods

should be charged to the interim period in which they are incurred.

4.   Arbitrary assignments of costs to an interim period should not be made.

5.   Gains and losses that arise in any interim period similar to those that would not be deferred at year end should not be deferred to later interim periods within the same year.

Opinion No. 28 presents a number of examples of the preferred accounting for costs other than product costs. Here are some of these examples:

Many companies schedule their major repair work during the annual plant vacation shutdown period, which is typically in the summer months. These repairs benefit the whole year's operations and relate to the use of the plant during the year. In these cases it is appropriate to estimate at the beginning of the year the cost of these repairs and to allocate the cost over the entire year for interim reporting purposes. This means that prior to the repair expenditure a portion of the expenditure may be charged to each interim period on an accrual basis. This is achieved through a debit to the repair expense account and a credit to a reserve for repair expenditure, which is a liability account. When the anticipated expenditure is made, the reserve is charged. Any excess expenditures above the reserve amount is deferred. Then, over the year's remaining interim periods the difference between the actual repair expenditure and the amount of the accumulated reserve (which is an asset called deferred repair expense) is amortized by a debit to expense and credit to the deferred asset account according to the allocation basis adopted at the beginning of the year.

Quantity discounts are often allowed customers based upon annual sales volume. In order to relate this discount to the sales of each interim period, an amount for anticipated year-end discounts should be charged to each interim period based on the relationship that the sales to customers during the interim period bear to the customer's estimated annual sales and discounts.

The accounting entry to record anticipated discounts at the time sales are made prior to the time the customer qualifies for discounts is:

Dr Discounts and Allowances
    Cr Reserve for Discounts and Allowances

Later, as discounts are earned by customers the reserve for allowances is eliminated and any discounts in excess of this reserve are charged to sales over the remaining portion of the annual period.

Property taxes, interest, and rents are usually payable as of a certain day. Typically, these costs are accrued or deferred at annual reporting dates so as to record a full year's charge.[1] Similar procedures should be adopted at each interim reporting date to provide for an appropriate cost in each period.

Advertising expenditures may benefit more than one interim period. If this is clearly the case, the advertising costs may be deferred and charged over the beneficial interim periods.

In some sales programs it is necessary to stock dealers with products prior to launching an advertising program. If a subsequent advertising program is clearly implicit in the sales arrangement, the anticipated advertising program costs may be accrued and assigned to interim periods in relation to sales recorded prior to the time the advertising service is rendered.

The amounts of certain costs and expenses are frequently subjected to year-end adjustments, even though they can be reasonably approximated at interim dates. Examples of such items include inventory shrinkage, allowance for quantity discounts, and discretionary year-end bonuses. To the extent possible year-end adjustments should be estimated at the beginning of the year and the estimated costs assigned to interim periods so that the interim periods bear a reasonable portion of the anticipated annual amount.

The accounting policies companies follow to report their nonproduct costs in interim statements vary considerably from company to company. For example, interim period accrual or deferral accounting for nonproduct costs usually requires management to estimate the annual expenditures for these costs in advance of their expenditures. This estimate may be influenced by the difficulty or ease that management encounters in reporting its desired level of interim profits. If management is having trouble reaching its interim period profit goal, it may be tempted to underestimate the annual expenditure and thus reduce the amount to be charged to the interim periods. The hope is that things will turn out better by year-end and the annual profits will be high enough to absorb the undercharge without anyone detecting what was done in the interim reports. Alternatively, if management is making more than its interim profits goal, the estimated annual expenditures may be overestimated so as to build up the interim period expenses. This will bring profits down to the desired amount and provide a profit cushion should business take a turn for the worse by year-end. Again, since the annual estimate is not disclosed, the statement user finds it very difficult to establish how management is using over- or underestimating to manage interim profits.

---

[1] Interim statements presume that the interim report user is familiar with the company's annual report accounting policies, which were disclosed in the latest annual report.

Income Tax Provisions

Opinion No. 28 recommends that the tax rate applied to each interim period's pretax income to determine the tax expense be the best estimate of the effective tax rate expected to be applied to the full fiscal year pretax profits. This requires that the interim period rate reflect anticipated investment tax credits, foreign tax rates, percentage depletion, capital gains rates, DISC tax deferrals, and other similar tax planning alternatives.

Some companies follow this recommendation. Others do not. They will report the actual tax rate applicable to the period by recording such tax savings as DISC tax deferrals and investment tax credits as received. Again, since a management estimate is required to implement the *Opinion*'s recommendation, the quality of the estimate may vary depending on the company's ability to reach its interim profit goals and management's willingness to use accounting to reach its interim profit goals.

Extraordinary and Unusual Items

Immaterial extraordinary items can be included as part of the income before extraordinary items calculation. In the case of interim reports, a question arises as to whether the interim period profit before extraordinary items or the estimated annual profit before extraordinary items should be the basis on which to measure materiality. *Opinion No. 28* recommends that the year-end profit estimate be used.[2] Thus an extraordinary item that is very material relative to the interim earnings results, but immaterial relative to the annual profit estimate, may be included in the interim period's income before extraordinary items. So that the statement reader may be made aware of the inclusion of such items in income, the *Opinion* recommends that all "unusual" events and items be disclosed.

The effects of disposals of a segment of a business should be reported separately in interim statements.

Other kinds of events that should be disclosed to provide the statement user with a proper understanding of interim financial reports include unusual seasonal results and business combinations treated for accounting purposes as poolings of interest and business acquisitions.

Extraordinary items, gains, or losses from a business segment disposal and unusual or infrequently occurring items should not be prorated over the balance of the fiscal year.

---

[2] The year-end profit estimate is the suggested test of materiality for all interim statement items.

Accounting Changes

In general if a company changes its interim or annual accounting practices, policies, or estimates in an interim period, the change should be reported according to the provisions of *Opinion No. 20*.[3]

In December 1974 the FASB modified this APB *Opinion* when it published *Statement No. 3*, "Reporting Accounting Changes in Interim Financial Statements." According to this FASB *Statement*, if a cumulative effect type accounting change is made, such as a switch from Fifo to Lifo inventory accounting, during the first interim period of an enterprise's fiscal year, the cumulative effect of the change on retained earnings at the beginning of that fiscal year should be included in net income of the first interim period (and in last-12-months-to-date financial reports that include that first interim period).

If a cumulative effect type accounting change is made in other than the first interim period of an enterprise's fiscal year, no cumulative effect of the change should be included in net income of the period of change. Instead, financial information for the prechange interim periods of the fiscal year in which the change is made should be restated by applying the newly adopted accounting principle to those prechange interim periods. The cumulative effect of the change on retained earnings at the beginning of that fiscal year should be included in restated net income of the first interim period of the fiscal year in which the change is made (and in any year to date or last-12-months-to-date financial reports that include the first interim period). Whenever financial information that includes those prechange interim periods is presented, it should be presented on the restated basis.

Translation Gains and Losses

FASB *Statement No. 8*, "Accounting for the Translation of Foreign Currency Transactions and Foreign Currency Financial Statements," requires that translation and forward exchange gains and losses that would not be deferred under this *Statement* for year-end reporting purposes "should not be deferred to later interim periods within the same fiscal year." Thus, in general, the effect of an exchange rate shift should be recorded in the interim accounting period when the rate change occurs.

Seasonal Business

The revenues of certain businesses are subjected to material seasonal variations. *Opinion No. 28* suggests that to avoid the possibility

---

[3] Discussed in Chapter 10.

that the interim reports of these companies be interpreted by statement users as being indicative of the annual results, the interim reports disclose the seasonal nature of the business. In addition, it recommends that seasonal businesses consider supplementing their interim reports with information for 12-month periods ending at the interim date on a comparative basis for the current and preceding year.

INTERIM REPORTS: TRADITIONAL ROLE AND LIMITATIONS

Often by the time a company's annual data are available, its stock price has already anticipated these data many months earlier. This discounting is in large measure influenced by the reports of the interim periods that precede the annual reporting date. As a result, there are many who believe that interim financial data is more important to the securities market than annual period data.

Fundamental investors use interim data in two ways: Some use it to predict the annual results. Others use it to check to see if the reporting company is on a track which will lead to the investor's prior prediction of its annual results.

While statement users use interim data in this fashion, they should not lose sight of three facts that will limit the usefulness of these disclosures. First, because of the shortness of the period, interim data are less reliable than annual data as a measure of corporate health. Second, despite the new SEC requirements, the interim disclosures are meager. Third, managements can—and do—create interim earnings through accounting judgments in order to meet statement users expectations.

Another problem that may limit the usefulness of the first two interim reports of each year is the interim reporting strategy many managements have typically followed in the past. Some managements like to understate their first- and second-quarter results so that (1) they can keep some profits in reserve should problems occur later in the year and (2) they can finish with a strong fourth quarter. If companies have followed this strategy in the past, then they may be able to top their prior year's first two-quarter results by simply not understating the current results as they may have done in prior years. In these cases any improvement over last year would not be real progress but just the result of a change in interim reporting strategy.

SUGGESTED FURTHER READING

EDWARDS, JAMES W; DOMINIAK, GERALDINE F.; and HEDGES, THOMAS V. *Interim Financial Reporting.* New York: National Association of Accountants, 1972.

CASE

CASE 25–1. LAMBERT INTERNATIONAL, INC.
Interim Financial Reporting Policy

Lambert International, Inc., was a conglomerate operating a number of diverse business operations on a worldwide basis. Its stock was traded in New York. Over the last 12 months it had become known as a "growth" stock. As a result, a number of the major mutual funds had acquired large holdings of the stock during the previous six months. This buying activity had been in large part responsible for a rapid rise in the company's stock price.

Typically, the company's interim statements presented the following on a comparative basis for the current quarter and year to date: the company's sales; income before taxes; provision for taxes; income before extraordinary items; extraordinary items (including related tax effects); and net income. Minimal balance sheet and funds flow data was provided. Also, unless a change had been made in accounting principles, no footnotes were included. The company's auditor did not express an opinion on the interim statements. In addition to the financial presentation, the interim reports included a brief letter from the president to the shareholders highlighting the important activities of the period covered and anticipated key events in the near future.

The following board of directors discussion of the first-quarter interim statements for Lambert International took place in early April. The statements were due to be released later in the month:

Lawrence (vice president, finance): The figures for the first quarter don't look good. However, I believe we have it in our power to push them over the same period results for last year, if we want to do so.

Franklin (outside director): What do you mean by that?

Lawrence: Let me explain. Last year we earned 0.52 cents per share for the first quarter, which was the best we had ever done to date for that period. This year we have only 0.47 cents per share, before any adjustments to my accounting decisions that you may wish to make.

Morris (president):   Frankly, I think it is imperative that we report a good first quarter. Last year our earnings were a record high and our fourth quarter was extremely strong. In fact, it was our best quarter ever. . . .

Powers (outside director):   Yes, I know. But didn't we pull a lot of income into the last quarter from this year to get those results? For example, we cut advertising, accelerated foreign dividend receipts, picked up DISC tax savings for the first time, deferred maintenance, accelerated equipment installation to get the investment tax credit, recognized income on advanced shipments. . . . It seems to me that what we did was to "rob Peter to pay Paul." Now we have to pay the price.

Morris: I admit we pushed a bit, but the fact is the stock market reacted favorably to our strong finish to last year and our stock price has really started to climb. In fact since mid-January our price-earnings ratio has gone from 21x to 24x this year's estimated earnings, which the market estimates will be higher than last year. I don't think we can afford to lose this stock price momentum.

Lawrence: I am convinced that if we report earnings for this quarter that are not substantially above last year's first-quarter results we will see our price-earnings ratio decline. This is a very "nervous" stock market we are in. The Dow is high, but it is subject to wide fluctuations on a daily basis.

Braun (vice president, marketing):   Why are the first-quarter earnings less than last year? What are the causes and dollar value? What options do we have? I for one want to keep the stock's price-earnings ratio up.

Lawrence: Here is an analysis of the differences between this year and last year: First, because we deferred maintenance on a worldwide basis from last year to this year, our first-quarter maintenance costs are up by 2 cents a share over last year. Also, since the first quarter is normally the heaviest maintenance month of the year, we have an extra 2 cents per share charge above what the average will be for the next three quarters, which have fairly equal maintenance expenditures.

I have charged the extra 4 cents maintenance to the first quarter.

Second, our DISC tax deferrals in this quarter ran at the rate of 3 cents per share. This is our peak export period. It is over one third of the year's projected DISC tax saving of 8 cents, which we can flow through to income.

Last year's fourth quarter was the first time we had material DISC tax savings. In that case we credited all of the savings to that quarter's income.

Now, I believe we should spread our DISC tax savings equally over the full year on a quarter by quarter basis. So, I picked up 2 cents for this quarter and deferred 1 cent. Actually the DISC tax impact on earnings is a "plus" from last year at this time.

Braun: Do we have to spread the benefit?

Lawrence: No. We can pick up the DISC earnings as earned. However, I felt "spreading" was the preferred approach.

Powers: It all depends on how you define "preferred."

Lawrence: Next, we have the costs of relocating the Southern Paper Sioux Springs plant and offices. These came to 3 cents a share. Actually, we had planned to do that last year but put it off because we didn't want to hurt last year's earnings. I included all of that cost in the first quarter.

Morris: I talked to Bill [Lawrence] about these charges which are depressing earnings and he tells me that it is good accounting to recognize costs and defer revenues. I suspect he is correct, but do we necessarily have to do this for interim reports?

Bill, you have some more items don't you?

Lawrence: Yes. This first quarter includes a dividend of 4 cents per share, we got from our Brazilian subsidiary in March. Since we account for this subsidiary on the cost basis, we only pick up income from it as it is received in dividends in the U.S.A.

Morris: Last February I felt we were having earnings problems, so I put extra pressure on Brazil to repatriate some dividends. As you know, they were held up by legal problems from getting these funds to us last year.

Cohen (vice president, personnel):   What do the dividends from overseas cost-basis investments look like this year?

Morris: Well I think we can get about 10 cents per share's worth in the last quarter, but between now and then I am not very hopeful. Incidently, 10 cents is all we budgeted for from foreign dividends this year.

Frankly, while domestic and exports sales and profits are on track from regular operations, our overseas operations are down. In fact, that is the principle reason for our problems. In particular the new Italian company, Grazini, which we picked up late last year and included in the consolidated results on a pooling of interest basis is a real "lemon."

I have to admit we were in a big hurry to acquire it. We wanted its full-year profits to be included in the full year's results. As you know its profits were up some 200 percent over the previous year.

Peter [Pike] why don't you explain the situation to us.

Pike (vice president, international):   Well, the company is still delivering operating profits, but its inventories and receivables turned out to be overstated. Once our internal auditors got in last January and examined what we had bought they found a lot of obsolete and damaged inventories. Also, the receivables had debt reserves were too low. In addition, some equipment was still carried on the books, but it couldn't be found. Then, some more equipment should be written off. It is junk.

All this amounts to a 6 cents per share write-off. . . .

Lawrence: I charged it to operating income.

Morris: Of course, we have a lawsuit in the Italian courts against the Grazini brothers to recover these amounts.

Braun: What do you think our chances are of collecting?

Morris: Very slim. However, I thought it was worth the effort. Maybe to protect their name they may settle out of court. They are not dishonest. They're just poor bookkeepers.

Outside of the Grazini problem, I expect our foreign operations will deliver their budgeted share of this year's earnings per share by December 31.

Braun: Bill [Lawrence], how did you charge the major advertising program we had in March?

Lawrence: I figured we spent about 2 cents a share above our average monthly budget. The principal cost was the "unusual" TV show and related radio and paper advertising. All of this was charged to March.

Braun: The benefits will come in April, May, and June won't they? In fact so far this month our sales are up just as we planned. It seems to me that—to quote you from an earlier meeting—"proper matching of costs and revenues" should require us to defer this "extra" 2 cents per share to the second quarter.

Morris: What about investment tax credit benefits?

Lawrence: Well, you'll recall we pushed the installation of qualified property from the first quarter of this year into the fourth quarter of last year. As a result, we only have a 1-cent-per-share benefit in the first quarter of this year which we flow through to earnings. Our projected credits for the year are worth 12 cents per share. This is fairly certain as most of the orders for the property have been placed and the delivery schedules call for the property to be installed by year-end.

Morris: Can we pull some of these into the first quarter? After all if we don't our effective tax rate will be different than for the year as a whole.

Lawrence: I'm not sure. If we did that we would have to take a second look at our DISC tax benefits accounting, also.

Morris: Are our projected DISC benefits as sure as our projected ITC benefits?

Lawrence: They're fairly sure, but not as certain as the ITC benefits.

There are two more items I wanted to mention. First, I have picked up in the first quarter one third of the third-quarter advertising costs related to this year's special fall campaign. I'll pick up another third in each of the next two quarters.

This special program, which is in addition to our normal advertising costs, is going to cost about 6 cents per share above our regular advertising costs, which are run fairly evenly throughout the year.

Second, due to the change in the dollar relative to many overseas currencies we had an exchange gain of 4 cents per share. I did not include this in the first-quarter results. In my opinion, by year-end we could end up with currency losses. So, I feel it is wise to defer this gain as a possible offset against future losses.

Morris: Thank you, Bill [Lawrence].

Well, here's our problem. The security analysts are predicting we will make nearly 60 cents for the first quarter. We don't have that kind of performance now. However, I feel that if we don't report 60 cents our price-earnings ratio will drop.

If this happens, I am fearful that our merger negotiations with Apex in Cleveland and Contrelli in Italy will collapse or not produce the earnings-per-share impact we expected. We need the earnings of both of these companies and at least one more merger to meet our forecasted profits for this year.

As I reported to the finance committee last month, these two mergers under negotiation will be for our stock and will be accounted for as a pooling of interest. . . . The Apex price-earnings ratio based on our offering price is 20x this year's projected earnings. . . . The Contrelli family are interested in us because they feel we are a growth stock. . . .

Well, gentlemen, what do you think we should do?

Questions

1. What do you think is Lambert's first-quarter earnings per share?
2. What first-quarter earnings-per-share figure should the management report to the public? Why?

Chapter 26

ACCOUNTING FOR CONTINGENCIES

The accounting for contingencies is covered by FASB *Statement No. 5* and *No. 11,* which were issued in March and December 1975. *Statement No. 5,* "Accounting for Contingencies," is the key *Statement. Statement No. 11* simply amended the manner in which the transition to *Statement No. 5* would be effected.

For the purposes of these *Statements* a contingency is defined as an existing condition, situation, or set of circumstances involving uncertainty as to the possible gain or loss to an enterprise that will ultimately be resolved when one or more future events occur or fail to occur. The resolution of the uncertainty may confirm the acquisition of an asset or the reduction of a liability or the loss or impairment of an asset or the incurrence of a liability.

The accounting process requires that estimates be made when accounting for many ongoing and recurring business activities. In most cases, the uncertainty inherent in these estimates does not necessarily give rise to a contingency as that term is used in *Statement No. 5.* For example, depreciation accounting requires that estimates be made to allocate the known cost of an asset over the period of use by the enterprise. The fact that an estimate is involved does not make depreciation a contingency, since the eventual expiration of the asset is not uncertain. Also, accrued amounts that represent estimates of amounts owed for service received but not yet billed are not contingencies, since there is nothing uncertain about the fact that an obligation has been incurred.

Statement No. 5 presents these examples of loss contingencies: collectibility of receivables; warranty obligations; risk of loss or damage of enterprise property by fire, explosion, or other hazards; threat of expropriation of assets; pending or threatening litigation; actual or possible claims and assessments; risk of loss from catastrophes assumed by property and casualty insurance companies; guarantees of indebtedness of others; obligation of commercial banks under standby letters of credit; and agreements to repurchase receivables (or to repurchase the related property) that have been sold. In these examples the likelihood that a future event or events will confirm the loss or impairment of an asset or incurrence of a liability can range from probable to remote.

Prior to the issuance of *Statement No. 5*, some companies accrued estimated losses for some types of contingencies by a charge to income prior to the occurrence of the event that was expected to resolve the uncertainty. The related credit entry led to the addition of a contingency reserve for a similar amount among the liability accounts. In these cases when the event occurred that confirmed the loss, the reserve was used to absorb the loss. For example, assume a company anticipated that it may have to pay $100,000 damages as the result of a claim brought against the company in the courts. In the period in which the management became aware of this possibility, it might have charged the anticipated $100,000 loss, less the related tax effect, to income and set up a $100,000 litigation reserves as a liability. Later, in another accounting period, when a court decision confirmed the loss and the successful litigant was paid, the loss would be charged to the balance sheet reserve and cash reduced by a similar amount. Under similar circumstances, other business recorded the losses only when the confirming event had occurred.

Statement No. 5 established new standards for financial accounting and disclosure for loss contingencies and reconfirmed the accounting for gain contingencies previously expressed in Accounting Research Bulletin (ARB) *Bulletin No. 50*, "Contingencies," issued by the Committee on Accounting Procedure in October 1958.

Before discussing the accounting for loss contingencies, it is important to note that the accrual for accounting purposes of a loss related to a contingency does not create or set aside funds which can be used to lessen the possible financial impact of the loss. The creation of a contingency reserve by a charge to income is simply an accounting provision. For example, an accrual for a possible asset expropriation or catastrophe loss does not protect the assets that may be lost or damaged. The accrual, in and of itself, provides no financial protection that is not available in the absence of the accrual.

STATEMENT NO. 5

Statement No. 5's key provisions are:

1. An estimated loss from a loss contingency shall be accrued by a charge to income only if *both* of the following conditions are met:

    a.   Information available prior to the issuance of the financial statements indicates that it is probable[1] that an asset had been impaired or a liability had been incurred at the end of the most recent accounting period for which statements are being presented. Implicit in this condition is the expectation that it is probable that one or more future events will occur that confirm the fact of the loss.

    b.   The amount of the loss can be reasonably estimated. If these two criteria are met, an accrual must be made.

2. Contingency gains usually are not recorded prior to realization, but may be disclosed in the notes prior to realization.

3. Reserves are not permitted for catastrophe losses, general or unspecified business risks and self-insurance, except for some self-insurance for employee compensation related costs which are excluded from the scope of *Statement No. 5.*

4. Disclosure sufficient to "not make the statements misleading" should be made of the nature and estimated loss for both accrued loss contingencies and loss contingencies that are not accrued, but represent at least a reasonable possibility for a loss.

5. Classification of a portion of retained earnings as "appropriated" for loss contingencies is permitted as long as it is shown within the stockholders' equity section of the balance sheet, but losses cannot be charged to an appropriation of retained earnings and no part of such appropriation can be transferred to income.

Statement No. 5 became effective for fiscal years beginning on or after July 1, 1975. In December 1975, *Statement No. 11,* "Accounting for Contingencies—Transition Method," specified that a change in accounting for loss contingencies to comply with the new *Statement* should be made on a retroactive basis. That is, the financial statements prior to the date of adoption should be restated to conform to the new rules. In addition, the effect of this restatement must be disclosed.

Loss Contingency Criteria

A loss contingency can only be accrued if the two specific conditions mentioned earlier are met. According to the FASB:

The purpose of those conditions is to require accrual of losses when they are reasonably estimable and relate to the current or a prior period. The require-

---

   [1] *Statement No. 5* defines the terms "probable," "reasonably possible," and "remote" as follows:

Probable.   The future event or events are likely to occur.

Reasonably possible.   The chance of the future event or events occurring is more than remote but less than likely.

Remote.   The chance of the future event or events occurring is slight.

ment that the loss be reasonably estimable is intended to prevent accrual in the financial statements of amounts so uncertain as to impair the integrity of those statements. The Board has concluded that disclosure is preferable to accrual when a reasonable estimate of loss cannot be made. Further, even losses that are reasonably estimable should not be accrued if it is not probable that an asset has been impaired or a liability has been incurred at the date of an enterprise's financial statements because those losses relate to a future period rather than the current or a prior period. Attribution of a loss to events or activities of the current or prior periods is an element of asset impairment or liability incurrence.

Loss Contingencies Subsequent to the Balance Sheet Date

Information concerning a loss contingency which becomes known subsequent to the date of the financial statements, but before their issuance, may satisfy the two accrual criteria. Whether or not this post financial statement date information requires accrual of a loss contingency as of the statement date depends on when the related asset was impaired or liability was incurred. If the post statement date information indicates that events leading to the loss occurred or were in process during the period preceding the financial statement date, then an accrual for a loss contingency should be made at the financial statement date. If the event giving rise to the contingency loss occurred after the financial statement date, no accrual at the balance sheet date should be made. However, disclosure of this post financial statement event is required if nondisclosure would make the financial statements misleading.

Accounts Receivables and Warranty Obligations

The FASB believed that the uncollectibility of receivables and product warranties constituted contingencies and as such were within the scope of *Statement No. 5*.

Accordingly, losses from uncollectible receivables must be accrued at the time of sale when both of the contingency loss accrual criteria have been met. These criteria may be considered in relationship to individual receivables or in relationship to groups of similar types of receivables. If the reasonable estimation criterion cannot be satisfied, it is doubtful if the sale or accrual method of income recognition is appropriate. Therefore, consideration should be given to using the installment method, the cost recovery method, or some other appropriate method for income recognition.

Similarly, if the two accrual criteria are met, losses from warranty obligations must be accrued at the time of sale. The criteria can be applied to either individual or groups of similar sales made with warranties. If accrual is precluded because the reasonable estimate criterion cannot be met, consideration should be given to delaying the recognition of the sale until the expiration of the warranty period or reasonable loss criteria can be satisfied.

Self-Insurance

Some businesses choose not to purchase insurance against the risk of loss that may result from injury to others, damages to the property of others, and business interruption. Exposure to future risks of this kind creates a contingency. However, the FASB concluded that mere exposure to risk of these types does not mean that an asset has been impaired or a liability has been incurred in the current or some prior period. As a result, the accrual of a loss contingency is not warranted.

Some companies do not carry insurance against the risk of future loss or damage to its property by fire, explosion, or other hazards. The occurrence of these events is random, and until they occur no asset has been impaired or a liability incurred. Therefore, it is inappropriate to accrue for this type of contingency loss prior to its occurrence.

Litigation, Claims, and Assessments

Statement No. 5 states that the following factors, among others, must be considered in determining whether accrual and/or disclosure is required with respect to pending or threatened litigation and actual or possible claims and assessments:

a. The period in which the underlying cause of the pending or threatened litigation or of the actual or possible claim or assessment occurred.
b. The degree of probability of an unfavorable outcome.
c. The ability to make a reasonable estimate of the amount of loss.

An accrual may be appropriate for litigation, claims, or assessments whose underlying cause occurred before the date of the financial statement and where an unfavorable outcome is probable and a reasonable estimate can be made of the loss. In the case of unasserted claims and assessments a judgment must first be made as to whether the assertion of a claim is probable. If such a claim is probable, an accrual can be made if an unfavorable outcome is probable and the amount of the loss can be reasonably estimated. If there are several aspects of litigation, each of which gives rise to a possible claim, then the accrual criteria should be applied to each possible claim to determine whether an accrual should be made for any part of the claim.

Threat of Expropriation

Statement No. 5 defines the threat of expropriation of assets as a contingency. Thus, the two accrual criterion must be met before an accrual for the loss can be made. The imminence of an expropriation may be indicated by a public or private declaration of intent by a government to expropriate assets of the enterprise or actual expropriation of assets of other enterprises.

Catastrophe Losses

At the time a property and casualty insurance company issues an insurance policy, covering the risk of property loss from catastrophes, a contingency arises. *Statement No. 5* prohibits property and casualty insurance companies from accruing estimated losses related to future catastrophes, since over the short run the actuarial predictions of the rate of occurrence and the amounts of loss "are subject to substantial deviations."

Items Not Affected

Statement No. 5 excludes from its scope the following items, which are covered by other decisions of the FASB and its predecessors: pension costs; deferred compensation contracts; capital stock issued to employees; other related employee costs, such as group insurance, vacation pay, workmen's compensation and disability benefits; net losses on long-term construction-type contracts; and write-down of carrying amount of operating assets because of questionable recovery of cost.

Contingency Gains

Examples of contingencies that may result in the acquisition of assets, or in gains, are claims against others for patent infringements, price redetermination upward, and claims for reimbursement under condemnation proceedings. Contingencies of this type which may result in gains should not be reflected in the accounts since to do so might be to recognize revenue prior to its realization. Adequate disclosure should be made of gain contingencies, however.

Objections

The FASB received a number of objections to its accounting for contingencies proposal. One objection was that it was a retreat from conservatism, which is one of the "characteristics and limitations of financial accounting" listed in APB *Statement No. 4*. The FASB did not agree that this was the case, since its proposal did not require virtual certainty before an accrual. In the absence of a probable occurrence of the contingency event and a reasonable estimate of the loss, the FASB believed accrual for unlikely events and uncertain amounts impaired the integrity of financial statements.

Another objection was that the matching concept required that estimated losses from certain types of contingencies that over a long period of time irregularly occur should be accrued in each accounting period. The FASB noted that the matching concept associated costs with revenues on a cause-and-effect basis and as such did not support the objection raised.

Other opponents claimed the new rules would lead to greater earnings volatility, which would lead to lower equity prices. The FASB felt that the use of accounting reserves to reduce inherent earnings volatility was misleading. In order to reduce earnings volatility, some critics of the FASB recommendations claimed, companies would be forced to purchase unnecessary insurance to cover contingencies.

The FASB recognized that insurance reduces or eliminates risks. In contrast accounting reserves do not reduce risks. Accordingly, the FASB rejected the contention that the use of accounting reserves was as an alternative to insurance against risk. The FASB could not sanction the use of an accounting procedure to create the illusion of protection from risk when, in fact, protection does not exist. Furthermore, the FASB believed that earnings fluctuations are inherent in risk retention and they should be reported as they occur.

SUGGESTED FURTHER READING

FINANCIAL ACCOUNTING STANDARDS BOARD. *Discussion Memorandum Accounting for Future Losses.* Stamford, March 13, 1974.

CASE

CASE 26–1. INTERNATIONAL INDUSTRIES, INC.
Accounting for Contingencies

This case presents selected excerpts from two meetings of the audit committee of International Industries, Inc.

The first meeting occurred in April 1975 when the audit committee of International Industries, a multinational conglomerate listed in the Fortune "500," met to discuss the implications for the company's accounting policies of the recently released *Statement No. 5*, "Accounting for Contingencies." International's 1976 fiscal year began on July 1, 1975, the date that *Statement No. 5* became effective.

The second meeting took place in August 1975 to discuss the implication for the 1975, and possibly 1976, fiscal year financial results of some events that had occurred subsequent to the close of the 1975 fiscal year, but before the financial statements for the year had been issued.

During the last decade the company earnings per share had grown at a 15 percent per year rate with little year-to-year variation from this trend. Management was proud of this record, particularly since it had been achieved during the mid-1970 inflation and recession period. Management wished to continue this growth rate and to satisfy what it perceived to be a preference of investors for a stable pattern of earnings, which management believed indicated less uncertainty or risk than fluctuating earnings. In turn, the management believed that a 15 percent growth rate with a low variability of the expected return would enhance the company's price-earnings ratio and minimize the amplitude of the swings in the company's stock price relative to changes in the market's average price as measured by such indices as the "S&P 425." In management's opinion, a stock with these characteristics was useful for convincing the owners of private companies to merge with International. During the last few years such acquisitions had been an important source of International's earnings growth. In addition, the company planned to issue subordinated convertible debentures as soon as security market conditions were favorable to such an issue. Management believed International's earnings characteristics would make this issue attractive to investors and at the same time allow the company to pay a low interest rate and set the conversion price well above the current price of the company's equity stock.

The audit committee consisted of three outside directors: Frank Noonan, the chairman; Louis Athos; and Harold Farrow. The audit committee had been appointed in late 1974. None of its members had financial backgrounds. Frank Noonan was a retired army general. Louis Athos owned an export-import firm. He was a close friend of the International president, Joseph Patterson. Harold Farrow was a substantial International stockholder. Two years earlier International had acquired his company. At that time Farrow had withdrawn from the management of his company.

One of the functions of International's audit committee was to report to the board of directors on the appropriateness of the company's financial reporting practices. As part of this responsibility the committee participated with management in setting the company's financial reporting policies.

International estimated 1975 net income was $150 million. The company's net assets were approximately $1.0 billion.

April Meeting

The following dialogue represents selected excerpts from the April 1975 audit committee meeting.

Noonan (chairman, audit committee): *Statement No. 5* of the APB has forced International to review all of its accounting practices related to contingency losses. The audit committee should participate in the process. Accordingly, I asked the financial office to prepare a list of the company's current practices. At this meeting I think we should discuss what changes the audit committee believes should be made in these practices. I have asked Joe [Patterson, the company president] and Peter [Kelly, the company's financial vice president] to sit in on this meeting. They can supply us with whatever additional data we need to form our conclusions.

The first item on my list is possible accounts receivables losses from bad debts. Currently we accrue for these losses based on our past experience, the experience of other companies in the same business and our appraisal of our customer's financial condition. So far, from the total company point of view, our actual write-off experience has been very close to the projection underlying our accruals. I do not think we need to change our policy on accounting for losses related to collectibility of receivables.

Athos (member of the audit committee): How has our experiences been for groups of similar receivables rather than for the company as a whole?

Noonan: As you might expect there are many variations. However, I couldn't locate any group of receivables where actual experience suggest that our loss reserves are not reasonable estimates.

Farrow (member of audit committee): What about those Plastic Division receivables we discussed last month? As I recall the division had some $50 million of outstanding receivables and some 50 percent of them are overdue, most of which are with smaller companies. In the past we seemed to have a good feel for the credit risks in this business, but I don't think that is true anymore. The oil crisis and inflation adversely changed the economics of our customer's business and the demand for their end products. The recession hit the smaller companies very hard. Let's be frank. We raised the bad debt reserve on these receivables from 2 to 4 percent of receivables but we don't really know if that is adequate. I heard that Tempo (the major competition of the Plastic Division) has a 7 percent reserve. Personally, I think that is a more realistic figure.

Kelly (financial vice president): You're right, but when I prepared the figures for Frank [Noonan], I included the Plastic Division receivables in with the total Chemical Group's receivables. When you consider that the Group's receivables are slightly over $150 million, the problems you raise with the Plastic Division receivables become immaterial.

Farrow: I guess from that perspective you are correct.

Patterson: While on the subject of the Plastic Division, you might be interested to know that at yesterday's executive committee meeting I got approval of my plan to increase our share of the plastic market by offering on a very aggressive basis more generous credit terms for our products. The small- to medium-sized companies need financial help. We will use our financial strength to tie them to us through long-term purchase contracts under which they will pay us the amount due for each shipment as follows: 25 percent 30 days after delivery, 25 percent 60 days after delivery, 25 percent 90 days after delivery, and the remainder within 120 days of delivery. The normal terms of credit are 1 percent 10 net 30 days.

We are prepared to invest $30 million in this effort. This is a large sum and there is no doubt that this approach to building market share carries some financial risk, but I think the gamble will pay off. However, just to be on the safe side I plan to establish a bad debt reserve equal to 5 percent of the receivables created by this marketing plan.

Noonan: That sounds prudent.

The next item on my list is losses related to warranty obligations. Currently, we have not been accruing for this contingency. The practice has been to charge warranty costs as incurred. The company has had a study underway since last January looking into the question of whether International should begin accruing for warranty obligations. Peter [Kelly], what is the status of that study?

Kelly: As you will recall the proposal to consider accruing warranty costs came from my office for several reasons. First, warranty costs were becoming very substantial. Second, they were beginning to vary considerably from our budgeted figures. This in turn made it harder to manage earnings. My proposed solution was to switch to the accrual approach. In this way we could smooth out the recognition of this cost item over the years.

The study group has not reached any conclusions yet. However, I know that the warranty costs for this fiscal year will be $2.5 million higher than budgeted. We don't seem to have a very good handle on this cost item.

Noonan: I think we should defer any discussion on this item until the study group's report is completed. Let's move on.

The next item is our self-insurance reserves for casualty losses to property and our two general reserves for unspecified business risks and foreign losses. The balances of these reserves are: self-insurance, $19 million; unspecified business risks $5 million; and foreign losses $25 million.

Statement No. 5 clearly states that losses related to these contingencies should not be accrued. So, we will have to eliminate these reserves. *Statement No. 5* requires that this be done by a one-time credit to income at the time *Statement No. 5*'s recommendations are adopted.[1]

Kelly: This requirement also applies to the catastrophe loss reserve of the Property Insurance Group, Inc. [a property and casualty insurance company in which International held a 40 percent equity interest].

Farrow: I think that the FASB decision on catastrophe reserves for insurance companies is a mistake. In my opinion catastrophes are certain to occur and as such are not contingencies. Also, on the basis of experience and the application of appropriate statistical techniques, catastrophe losses can be predicted over the long term with reasonable accuracy. Then, some portion of the premium is intended to cover losses that usually occur infrequently and at intervals longer than both the terms of the policies in force and the financial accounting and reporting period. As a result, it seems to me that proper matching of costs and revenues requires that catastrophe losses should be accrued when the revenue is recognized—or at least a portion of the premiums should be deferred beyond the terms of

---

[1] Subsequently, in December 1975 the FASB issued *Statement No. 11*. This *Statement* amended the accounting for the transition to *Statement No. 5*. *Statement No. 5* as originally issued required including the cumulative effect of prior years in current year's income. *Statement No. 11* requires retroactive restatement of as many consecutive periods immediately preceding the date of adoption as is practicable with any remaining retained earnings effect included as a cumulative effect adjustment in the earliest restated year.

An exception to retroactive restatement is provided for companies that adopted *Statement No. 5* prior to January 1, 1976. These companies are given the option of (1) adopting the revised transitional rules (retroactive restatement) provided that they do so the first time financial data is presented after January 1, 1976, or (2) continuing to report on the basis of the original transitional rules (cumulative effect in year of change). Even though the above exception to retroactive restatement is provided for companies previously complying with *Statement No. 5*, *Statement No. 11* strongly encourages retroactive restatement when financial statements, summaries, or other data are subsequently presented for the first time.

Statement No. 11 was effective retroactively for fiscal years beginning after June 30, 1975, the same effective date as *Statement No. 5*. *Statement No. 5* and *No. 11* both encourage earlier application.

the policies in force to periods in which the catastrophes occur—to match catastrophe losses with the related revenues.

Patterson: I agree with you, but the FASB didn't find those arguments persuasive. Now that the FASB decision on catastrophe reserves has been made, these are my concerns: First, irregularly occurring catastrophes will cause erratic variations in earnings. This runs counter to our whole earnings strategy. Second, Property Insurance is a prime insurer that does not buy very much reinsurance to protect itself against catastrophe losses. It uses the substantial catastrophe reserve that it built up during the 1950s to absorb these losses. The size of this reserve was one of the reasons we bought into the company. Now, to keep earnings stable the company will have to buy much more reinsurance than it did in the past. These premium will hurt the company's cash flow. However, it will be necessary to do this in order to make the risk characteristics of its earnings stream comparable to those of casualty companies that reinsure. Thus, the FASB accounting decision forces us to purchase reinsurance. This is wrong.

Kelly: One more small point. Reinsurance premiums reduce income before the catastrophe occurs. Thus, if you buy reinsurance or accrue for a catastrophe loss, the effect on income is the same—income is reduced prior to the catastrophe. I can't see why paying a premium makes a difference in the accounting that is allowed.

Noonan: Will the FASB decision mean that the insurance premiums paid by International for protection against the loss of its property by fire, explosion, or similar hazards will increase?

Patterson: Yes, we are planning to extend our insurance coverage to include all of those risks that formerly we self-insured against.

Farrow: The elimination in 1976 of our self-insurance reserves for casualty losses as well as general reserves for unspecified business risks and foreign losses will give earnings a big one time boost. This could distort our long-run trend line. It could also hurt our stock price when people realize that our 1977 earnings will not include this credit.

Patterson: Depending on the size of this 1976 reserve reversal, it is very possible that 1977 net income might end up being less than the 1976 figure.

Athos: Do I gather from that remark that you do not plan to adopt *Statement No. 5* retroactively for the fiscal year ending June 30, 1975?

Patterson: That's right. It would create earnings problems for us. The earnings plan for this year did not contemplate *Statement No. 5*, and it is too late now to change the earnings plan to accommodate this new development. Also, if we are one of the first companies to adopt *No. 5*, we will get a lot of publicity. This might raise questions about the way we have used reserves to smooth earnings in the past. This could hurt our stock market image.

Of course, the notes to the 1975 statements will indicate that *Statement No. 5* will apply to 1976. The note will also state that the short time since *No. 5*'s issuance and the close of our fiscal year, the effects of the *State-*

ment are unknown, but that management believes the effect will not be material.

Noonan: Let's move on to the litigation loss reserves. In the past we have accumulated a reserve for litigation losses. No additions were made to the reserve last year, but additions were made in every prior year for the last ten years.

Athos: Was the reserve set up with specific litigation in mind?

Kelly: No. You could think of it as a general-type reserve. In the past if earnings were good we charged litigation losses to income as incurred. If a big litigation loss was incurred and it hurt the earnings trend, we would use the reserve.

Athos: What have been our charges to the reserve in recent years?

Kelly: There have been no material charges over the last two years. Three years ago we made a $1.2 million charge to it to settle out of court a patent infringement claim. Today the balance of the reserve is $10 million.

Athos: What litigation are we involved in now, and what is its status?

Patterson: We have three major litigation problems at present. A number of female employees in one of our subsidiaries have joined together and are suing us on behalf of themselves and other women employees for $5 million. They claim the company's promotion practices have discriminated against women. They want to be paid the differences between the wages they believe they would have received if they had been promoted on the same basis as men and what they now get. The suit was filed in January of this year. At this time our legal counsel is unable to express an opinion that the outcome will be favorable to International. Should we lose, it is hard to determine what the ultimate settlement will be. This type of litigation is fairly new.

The second suit is a claim against us for failure to perform on a major glass division contract to install all of the windows in a new 50-story office tower. The project's completion was delayed for nearly a year due to our inability to solve some glass technology and installation engineering problems that arose when the windows kept blowing out. This suit was filed over a year ago. It is for $10 million in damages. The plaintiff is claiming for the cost of lost rentals, lost tenants, and damages done to surrounding property.

Our lawyers advised us to settle out of court as they believe the plaintiff will be successful. Also, the glass division's marketing department did not want to have a court trial. They thought it would be bad publicity. I agreed. So, I instructed our counsel to enter into negotiations. So far we have agreed to pay $1 million for lost rentals. The other claims are still being negotiated. It seems most likely that the lost tenants' claim will be settled for about $1 million, but we have no idea at this time what the figure will be for the damage to surrounding property. That is somewhat dependent on the outcome of suits by surrounding property owners for damages against the tower owners. We are not involved in those suits, but the tower owners feel that we are the cause of any losses that they may have.

The third suit is not in litigation. At the time of the patent infringement problem I mentioned earlier we discovered that our chemical division may inadvertently be violating some other patents held by others. These patent holders have not given any indication that they are aware of our possible infringement of their patent. If they should ever sue it would be for a large sum, which I estimate in the range of $15 million to $25 million. Of course, our chemical engineers have been busy trying to develop alternatives to these patents, but so far we have not been able to make a breakthrough. In the meantime, we have had to continue using these patented processes since they are critical to our chemical division's operations.

Farrow: What do you think are the chances that we might get sued?

Patterson: I have no idea. However, our patent lawyers tell me that if we get sued, our chances of a favorable outcome are not good. Based on their assessment of the possible claimants, similar cases, and our use of the patented process, they believe an out-of-court settlement in the order of $5 million to $10 million might be possible.

Farrow: Well, I think we ought to continue to have a litigation reserve. If these litigation losses occur, it would play havoc with our earnings stream.

Kelly: I agree with you, but under *Statement No. 5* I don't think that this will be so easy to do. . . .

August Meeting

In early August 1975 the audit committee met to review with International's senior management two events involving possible contingency losses that had occurred since the end of the company's fiscal year (June 30, 1975). Since the company's 1975 statements had not yet been published, there was a question as to whether or not the 1975 results should reflect these subsequent events.

Earlier, at the April board of directors meeting it had been decided that International would not adopt *Statement No. 5* retroactively for the fiscal year ending June 30, 1975.

The first event was the possible expropriation of the company's assets in a Latin American country. Sections of the audit committee discussion related to this agenda item are presented below:

Patterson: President Cruz has just announced that his government intends to nationalize the country's mining industry. Presumably this will include our mining subsidiary, International Mining S.A., and its related transportation subsidiary, International Transportation S.A. Ever since President Cruz took over power last March with the army's backing, we have been expecting such an announcement, since the nationalization of this country's raw material resources and communications network was a central part of his party's political platform. In early May, when the government took over the local telephone company, which was a subsidiary of a U.S. company, it became clear that Cruz meant what he said.

Noonan: Do you expect any losses?

Patterson: Yes. Cruz indicated that the government would issue government 30-year bonds bearing a 3 percent interest rate as compensation for the physical properties of the expropriated companies. Compensation would be based on the tangible asset's book value. The finance department estimates we would have a loss somewhere between $15 million and $17 million, after taking into account insurance coverage, the intangible assets that would have to be written off, and the real value of the bonds.

Athos: This turn of events should permit us to keep most of our foreign loss reserve on the books during 1976, since one of the contingency losses specified in the account description is expropriation. Then, in fiscal 1976 when the expropriation occurs we can write off our losses against this reserve.

Kelly: Well, there is another possibility. It might be argued that our assets were impaired when President Cruz took over the government and that his recent expropriation announcement was simply additional evidence with respect to conditions that existed before June 30, 1975. This interpretation might require a charge to the loss reserve for 1975 fiscal year.

I am meeting tomorrow with our auditors to discuss this matter . . .

The second event involving a potential contingency loss was the unexpected announcement in late July by one of the Plastic Division's largest customers that it was filing for bankruptcy. This customer owed International $3.4 million. Based on materials filed with the bankruptcy court, International's lawyers believed that the company would recover no more than 5 percent of the amount owed. Here are excerpts from the audit committee's meeting related to this event:

Noonan: How did we let this customer get so much credit from us?

Patterson: Well, our new marketing approach using trade credit was very effective. This particular customer was buying all of its plastic requirements from us.

Athos: Did you know they were in financial trouble when you offered them our new terms last April?

Patterson: No. However, since the bankruptcy announcement I have gone back and looked at the company's December 31, 1974, financial statements. They clearly indicated a bankruptcy was likely, since the company was in trouble with the senior lender's covenants and the days of trade credit used were way out of proportion to industry averages. I asked our credit people how they let this happen. They indicated that prior to our new credit terms program this customer bought very little from us, so no credit analysis had been made. Then, once the new program was offered to them they bought over $4.0 million of plastics from us in the period between April and June 30. This rapid build up of business caught the credit staff by surprise. Then, I suspect marketing was not anxious to push for a credit check, since the Plastic Division and Chemical Group were having trouble making their profit goal. This was profitable business. Our contribution margin was close to 50 percent.

As a result of my inquiries into how these sales were made, I will be making some personnel changes in the Chemical Group and Plastic Division.

Noonan: What was the status of the plastic customer receivables as of June 30?

Patterson: The balance was about $65 million of which $30 million were on the new marketing program terms.

Questions

1. How should International account for contingency losses in fiscal years 1975 and 1976?

2. How do you think equity investors will react to your proposals?

3. Do you agree with the comments related to contingency loss reserves expressed in the case?

PART X

Financial Accounting Policy: Review Cases

REVIEW CASES

REVIEW CASE 1. LIMITED EDITIONS, INC.

Establishing a Financial Reporting Strategy for a New Business

> "IF YOU HAVEN'T LEARNED TO LOVE IT BY 1979, WE'LL BUY IT BACK AT THE ORIGINAL PRICE."

The above statement appeared as the prominent headline in a Limited Editions, Inc., advertisement placed in a monthly magazine catering to a select, high-income readership. Its intent is to announce the company's new porcelain figurine, "Foxes in Spring," which would be offered in limited quantities at a price of $2,000. Limited Editions' idea is to offer literally "a beautiful investment opportunity" with capital gains potential to a wealthy investor. By guaranteeing that production would be limited, the figurines could immediately attain status similar to an antique.

The guarantee offered by Limited was quite simple:

> "SUBJECT TO BEING IN ITS ORIGINAL CONDITION, WE GUARANTEE TO REPURCHASE ANY OF OUR "FOXES IN SPRING" FIGURINES AT THE ORIGINAL PRICE OF $2,000 AT ANY TIME AFTER FIVE YEARS FROM THE DATE OF PURCHASE."[1]

The guarantee was not restricted to the original purchaser and hence was transferable from one party to another. The only other return provision allowed a purchaser to receive an 80 percent refund of the purchase price if the figurine was returned within three months from the date of purchase.

The figurines are offered for sale in only one extremely reputable store in each of ten large American cities. These stores were individually identified in the advertisement. Each of the ten was provided

---

[1] As printed in the advertisement.

with one "Foxes in Spring" figurine to be used for display. It was informally understood that Limited Editions would not ask for the return of the figurine. The stores otherwise have no inventory. When a customer signs a "subscription request," the store forwards it to Limited. The "subscription" was an indication of interest but carried no contractual obligation on the part of the buyer. Limited would fill the subscription by shipping directly to the customer. Upon notification of shipment, the retail store would then bill the customer. Upon collection, the store deducted its 10 percent commission and forwarded the net amount of $1,800 to Limited. If a figurine was returned in the first three months, Limited simply sent an 80 percent refund ($1,600) to the customer. Limited did not request a refund of the 10 percent sales commission from the retail store.

Production of "Foxes in Spring" was strictly limited to 500 pieces. The design of the figurine and the mold from which it would be produced were created by an artist for a fee of $50,000. This fee was paid in 1974. Production was contracted out to a reputable company which agreed to run batches of 100 pieces upon instructions from Limited. When a batch was produced, each figurine was then hand painted and finished by skilled workers. Due to the extremely high-quality standards demanded by Limited, producing, painting, and finishing the first batches expectedly required substantially more cost than the latter batches. Production cost data is summarized in Exhibit 2.

Limited Editions was incorporated as a separate legal entity in June 1974. The initial common stock was sold for $10,000. The corporation is 50 percent owned by a small, diversified, over-the-counter company engaged in a variety of businesses and 50 percent owned by a small number of self-proclaimed "venture capitalists" who play no active role in managing the company. The "venture capitalists" readily admit that their interest in Limited Editions, Inc., was in part nurtured by the widely publicized success stories of companies like The Franklin Mint[2] that have capitalized on the public's recent interest in "collector items" as an investment hedge against inflation. Both the management and owners of Limited Editions hope to build the company into a leader in this new, unexploited figurine market. Encouraged by the apparent success of the company's first figurine, management was already laying detailed plans for a number of future offerings.

---

[2] The Franklin Mint, traded on the New York Stock Exchange, is recognized as one of the leading producers of limited edition collectibles. Its issues include commemorative and art medals in silver and gold, sculptures in pewter and bronze, deluxe leather-bound books, and works of art in fine crystal.

Design and production began in July 1974; promotion in September; and sales in October. The bulk of 1974 sales appeared to be related to the year-end Christmas season. Of the 290 figurines shipped to customers in 1974, 100 were to shareholders (or members of their families), or to management employees (or members of their families). Since these sales were not made through a retail dealer, the full $2,000 purchase price was received in cash by Limited Editions. Of the 190 pieces shipped to nonrelated parties, cash had been received by year-end from the retailer for 140 pieces; 50 pieces were uncollected; none of the 190 pieces were returned in 1974 but 20 of them were returned in 1975, some after the three-month return period had expired. Each of the 20 customers promptly received a $1,600 cash refund.

Exhibit 1 summarizes the relevant unit data for 1974. Promotional and advertising costs of $20,000 were paid in 1974. Limited planned to do no further advertising of "Foxes in Spring" in 1975. General and administrative expenses for 1974 were $30,000, and all these expenses were paid in cash before year-end.

Questions:

1. Select in your opinion the best package of financial accounting policies for Limited Editions, Inc. You should not feel constrained by "GAAP" rules.
2. Defend your choices of financial accounting policies. The best way to defend your choices is (a) list what criteria are relevant in selecting an accounting alternative, (b) list the alternatives, and (c) analyze how well each alternative meets the various criteria.
3. Prepare Limited Editions, Inc., 1974 financial statements consistent with your choices in Question 1. (Assume that Limited will use *cash basis* accounting for federal income taxes and a 50 percent tax rate.)

EXHIBIT 1
Unit Data for 1974

	1974
Figurines produced.......................	400
Figurine subscriptions received	320
Figurines shipped	290
Figurines sent to retailers for display	10
Figurines returned	0
Figurines in inventory	100
Figurines for which cash was collected by December 31, 1974	240
Figurines for which cash was not collected by December 31, 1974	50

EXHIBIT 2

Batch Production Data

Batch	Date	Units	Cost
1	July 1974	100	$40,000
2	September 1974	100	30,000
3	October 1974	100	20,000
4	December 1974*	100	10,000
5	March 1975†	100	10,000

* Paid in January 1975.
† As of December 31, 1974, Limited Editions was not really sure what the last batch of 100 figurines would cost. The $10,000 ultimately paid would have been a reasonable estimate as of December 31, 1974.

REVIEW CASE 2. TEXAS LAND AND ROYALTY COMPANY
Evaluation of a Corporate Financial Reporting Policy

On June 1, 1976, Peter Small, a faculty member of an eastern business school, interviewed Phillip Lord, financial vice president of Texas Land and Royalty Company. During their interview, they discussed Texas Land and Royalty's policies regarding the recognition of income from the company's various activities.

Texas Land and Royalty Company

The Texas Land and Royalty Company was founded in 1888 to develop certain Texas real estate holdings. Over the years, this land and royalty company became involved, through a series of wholly owned subsidiary companies, in a number of activities related to agriculture, real estate, and oil (see Exhibit 1, page 766).

Initially, the company bred calves and range-fattened steers. Later, around 1903, the company created a water utility subsidiary to build an extensive irrigation system on the company's property. Subsequently, cotton was raised on this irrigated land by both the company and tenant farmers, who turned over part of their harvest to the company as rent. Both the company and the tenant farmers purchased their water from the company-owned water utility.

In 1938, oil was discovered on the Texas Land and Royalty properties. During World War II, the company leased its oil lands to a number of major oil companies who proceeded to develop the leases. In return, Texas Land and Royalty received a royalty on every barrel of oil extracted from its land. During the war and early postwar years, the company built up large cash reserves from these oil royalties. During 1975 oil royalties accounted for some 10 percent of the company's revenues.

Beginning in 1950, the company began to expand its operations. First, the company built a feed mill and acquired some feed lots in northeast Texas. The output of the feed mill was sold to the feed lots and used to fatten the company's beef cattle just prior to sale. In addition, the company contracted to fatten in its feed lots the cattle of other cattle companies.

Next, in 1958 Texas Land and Royalty acquired two manufacturing companies. The first company, Paxton Metal Products, sold small component parts to the capital goods industry. The second company, Specialty Installations, Inc., custom-built and installed large machinery installations, such as complete automobile body production lines. Both these companies were wholly owned subsidiaries. In 1975 they accounted for about 18 percent of the company's assets and 8 percent of its profits.

In 1974, Texas Land and Royalty expanded its oil activities by entering into several agreements with major oil companies to explore and develop oil concessions in Canada and South America. Recently, one of these ventures had discovered oil in commercial quantities in northern Canada. In all of these joint ventures, Texas Land and Royalty held less than a 50 percent interest. In June 1976 the company was considering the acquisition of a 60 percent interest in a proposed Canadian refining company to refine the newly discovered Canadian crude oil.

During 1974, Texas Land and Royalty became involved in the residential real estate business. The company purchased a 25 percent equity interest in a newly formed real estate development company, Dallas Apartments, Inc. (the remaining 75 percent of the equity was owned by two national real estate development companies). After making this investment, Texas Land and Royalty entered into a sale and option agreement with Dallas Apartments to sell to the development company certain parcels of land owned by Texas Land and Royalty in the Dallas area. The first parcel was transferred during 1975. In return, Texas Land and Royalty received a note for $4 million, collectible during a period extending to a maximum of ten years. These collections were contingent on Dallas Apartments selling the developed property to others.

More recently, Texas Land and Royalty Company had entered into a tentative agreement with another national development company to acquire land and build a $50 million industrial park in New Orleans, Louisiana.

Financial information related to Texas Land and Royalty Company is shown in Exhibits 2 and 3, pages 767 and 768. Exhibit 2 presents comparative balance sheet data for the years 1974 and 1975. Exhibit 3 presents profit and loss information during this same period.

Recognition of Income

The following are excerpts from Peter Small's interview with Phillip Lord:

Lord: As I understand it, you are interested in the policies Texas Land and Royalty follows with respect to the recognition of income from its various operations

Small: Well, why don't you tell me about your company's consolidation policy? This policy, I believe, is relevant to all the topics I plan to discuss.

Lord: Our policy is simple. We consolidate the operations of all companies in which we have at least a 50 percent equity interest.

Small: I have another general question: What do you think the stockholders of Texas Land and Royalty are primarily interested in? Current earnings or long-term capital appreciation?

Lord: Because we are the kind of company we are, asset values ought to be the most important consideration of our investors. Certainly our company policy is to develop future earning power. And, in an important respect, our assets represent the current value of these future earnings. Of course, this value is only significant when you produce the earnings. Nevertheless, the assets we hold currently determine to a large extent the future prospects for appreciation of our stockholders' investment.

We feel that by all odds the most significant factor determining the value of the company is the earnings that it produces. The assets derive their value essentially from their earning power. The assets otherwise are of value only as a matter of ultimate liquidation. Therefore, we feel, as management, our primary function is to generate further earning capacity from the assets which we now have.

The foregoing is not to say that it might not be desirable to give share owners a more accurate or better informed opinion concerning the value of the assets of the company as related to current market. There is serious distortion in our balance sheet when viewed in terms of present worth. I think it can very well be argued that share owners deserve to have further information concerning present worth of the assets of the company. This, however, should not be construed as meaning that the management considers this to be a significant factor in determining the market value of the stock.

Small: If you don't mind, I'd like now to talk about specific aspects of your operations. Why don't we begin with the manufacturing operations?

Lord: Fine. That's a fairly straightforward situation. We treat Paxton Metal products as a regular manufacturing company. We are essentially producing to orders, and we recognize income as of the date we invoice the customer. Most of the orders are small, and the production cycle is short. Few items are produced for inventory.

Small: Does Paxton Metals ever get involved in situations involving progress payments?

Lord: Occasionally Paxton gets into progress payment situations. They usually involve government contracts. However, because these progress payments contracts are so rare and involve small amounts of money, typically we expense the costs of these projects as incurred and treat the progress payments as income when received.

Small: You said "few items are produced for inventory." Does this mean some items are produced for inventory?

Lord: Yes. One of Paxton's biggest customers is the appliance industry. Each year Paxton supplies component parts to the appliance manufacturers. We build up large inventories of these items during our slow production months because we know we have *almost* assured sales. This practice smooths out our production cycle and helps us to avoid laying off our workers.

Small: When do you recognize the income from these sales to the appliance manufacturers?

Lord: When we ship and invoice the items. This is consistent with Paxton's general policy with respect to income recognition.

Small: I see, but what about Specialty Installations, Inc.?

Lord: That's a completely different kind of operation. Specialty Installations makes and installs a few large custom machine installations each year. These contracts typically involve progress payments, large sums of money, and take many, many months to complete.

In this case we pick up the profits as we accumulate the costs on each job. We take into revenue the percentage of the contract's total selling price to the contract's total expected costs times the accumulated costs. We follow this policy to avoid great distortions in income from year to year.

Small: Are there ever sales between Paxton Metals and Specialty Installations?

Lord: Sometimes, but these profits are washed out in consolidation.

Small: Could we now turn to your real estate operations?

Lord: Surely.

Small: As I understand it, most of the land Texas Land and Royalty Company owns was acquired before 1890. Also, this land is carried on the books at its original cost. Is this correct?

Lord: Yes. Our land is shown on the balance sheet at some $8 million.

Small: Do you think the stockholders would be more interested in knowing the appreciation in the value of this land, year by year, rather than just its historical cost?

Also, wouldn't the balance sheet be a more meaningful document if the land was shown at, say, its current market value and in current-value dollars? After all, the consumer price index has risen from, say, 100 in 1890 to something over 400 today.

Similarly, don't you think the annual increase or decrease in the value of the land should be recorded as some form of income?

Lord: Now you're putting me on the hot seat. Frankly, I have no idea of the value of our land, before or after federal taxes. There are parts of our holdings we could sell for $2,000 or more an acre. Whereas, there are other parcels we couldn't give away.

Also, there is another complication. We use our land primarily for cattle and farming operations. Now, if we began selling our land off in the fashion of a dealer in real estate, we would have to pay ordinary income taxes on the gain. We intend to remain in the farming and cattle business, so we are locked into holding our land. Under these conditions I am not sure it makes sense to talk about "market values. . . ."

In many respects, the balance sheet is one of the world's most misleading documents. Therefore, it is important for people to understand what its limitations are. Certainly, it doesn't show economic values. Yet, if we tried to portray current market values or price level adjusted values, I think we might well destroy the continuity of the balance sheet, which I believe is important.

I will readily agree that assets are seldom, if ever, worth in market terms the values shown on the balance sheet. But would these figures be any more meaningful if I inserted your estimate of the market value for the historic cost? Perhaps we could have a professional geologist estimate each year the value of our oil reserves. Yet, from experience, I know that professional geologists change their minds about the characteristics of a field and amount of recoverable oil.

I suspect I would be willing to accept discounted future market values if there was some systematic way of arriving at these values. To date, I can't convince myself that a systematic procedure has been proposed.

What I try to do is produce an honest income statement which gives a reasonable picture of earnings based on conservative accounting practices. . . .

Small: Recently, you sold some land to Dallas Apartments, Inc. How do you propose to handle the profit on that sale?

Lord: First of all, let me say that this was a nonrecurring sale of property no longer economically employed in our business. Therefore, it qualified for capital gains treatment.

Now, as to how we propose to recognize the profits. Basically, after applicable taxes are deducted, we will defer the $3,750,000 profit on this sale and take it into income as collections are made.

Incidentally, we have loaned Dallas Apartments some $2 million. We will recognize the interest on this loan as it accrues, because it will be interest income from a nonconsolidated associated company.

Small: Talking about investments, I notice you have some marketable securities listed as current assets. Why do you report these at original cost rather than current market value?

Lord: As you probably noticed, we do give the market values of these securities in the footnotes to our financial statements. However, to answer your question, we are not holding these securities for speculation. We are not a mutual fund. These securities are like our cash balances; they are simply liquid resources that we need to hold in order to efficiently operate our cattle and our farming business.

Small: You mentioned the farm operations—what policies do you follow here for the recognition of income?

Lord: In practice, this presents few problems. For instance, our policy is to recognize profit at the time the cotton crop is baled. We have a known market for the crop at that time.

Most of our farm income is derived from our share-rental agreements. That is, when our tenants pick their cotton crop, we get credit for one bale out of every four they press. The bales are not physically separated, they all go to market together. In fact, the cotton of the tenant farmers and the company is all sold through the same outlets. At year-end, about seven eights of the crop is harvested. For practical reasons, we don't try to accrue the income on the unharvested crop.

Small: Is cotton the only crop you raise?

Lord: No. Currently we are developing some citrus groves on one of our properties. We are deferring the costs of these groves until they bear commercial quantities of fruit. This should take about three years.

Also, we grow some barley, which we sell to the feed mill. This profit is washed out in consolidation.

Small: What is the policy with respect to your cattle operations?

Lord: Our cattle operations are decentralized. We have three breeding ranches, four stocker ranches, and a feed lot.

Small: What is the difference between these three types of operations?

Lord: At the breeding ranch, we breed and raise calves. The breeding herd can be regarded as a fixed asset. The calves are then moved to the stocker ranches and fed on range grass until the cattle obtain a weight of about 600 pounds. This takes about 15 months. Then the cattle are transferred to the feed lot. After about 120 days in the feed lot on a concentrated high protein diet, the cattle reach weights of 1,000 pounds or more and are ready for slaughter.

Each of these operations is managed as a separate unit with a profit and loss responsibility. A breeding ranch manager may sell to one of our stocker ranches or to buyers outside the company, depending on prices. The same company policy applies to the stocker ranches. In line with this policy, we transfer cattle from one inventory to another, say, stocker inventory to the feed lot inventory, at market price.

Small: I gather a known current market price exists for cattle at each stage of their development from breeding ranch to feed lot.

Lord: Yes. From the overall company point of view, our policy with respect to cattle is to recognize profits at the time of sale to persons outside the company. Thus, when a stocking manager moves his cattle to our feed lot, the profit we credit to the stocker is for internal management purposes only. This profit is eliminated in consolidation. However, should a stocking manager sell to an outsider, that profit is recognized for external reporting purposes.

Small: Why do you use the "outside sale" criterion as the basis for recognizing income from cattle operations?

Lord: I think it is prudent. Also, our various herds are so large—about 200,000 cattle in all—that it would be a tremendous problem to come up with a reliable income figure based on the herd's appreciation and depreciation in value based on changes in market prices.

Incidentally, you may be interested in our inventory pricing policies. Except for our breeding herd and company-produced farm products, inventories are stated at the lower of cost or market. The breeding herd is carried at cost less accumulated depreciation. The company-produced farm products are stated at their market value at the time of harvest or market at year-end, whichever is lower.

All inventories are costed on a first-in, first-out and specific identification basis.

Small: That's interesting. You said earlier you had a feed mill operation. . . .

Lord: Yes. This is truly an integrated operation. The feed lot uses the barley grown on our own land irrigated by our own water utility. Let me take you through the whole operation.

When the water utility sells water to the company, the utility recognizes the profit. It is required to do this for utility regulation purposes. We in turn recognize the full utility price as part of the cost of producing barley. Insofar as the profit of the utility is included in our barley costs, the profits from intracompany transfers of water are not eliminated. There is always a slight time lag, however, since the costs of the barley not harvested at the end of the year are deferred, not expensed. These amounts are not material. Therefore, we don't worry.

Now, the barley is transferred to the feed mill at market price. This profit gets washed out in consolidation. However, we do recognize and report as part of our annual profit the feed mill's profit from the sale of feed to our feed lots. We do this for two reasons. First, we regard our feed mill and feed yard as two distinct profit centers. Second, the feed cost is an important ingredient in the formula for determining what is owed to us by those outside the company for whom we fatten cattle.

Let me explain. We sell feed to those outsiders who place cattle in our feed lots under two types of arrangements. First, we might sell grain by the ton. Second, we might sell an increase of so many pounds weight on the animals.

Under both of these arrangements, we are prepared to finance the outsider's purchase of both cattle and grain. As security we hold the title to his cattle when they are placed in the lot. We also agree to handle the sale of the fattened cattle.

In return, we charge the outsider the cost of the feed plus an interest charge on our capital invested in his animals and feed. These interests costs are accrued.

For parent company financial reporting purposes, the milling profit is recognized when the feed is sold to the feed lot, irrespective of whether or not the feed is given to company- or outsider-owned cattle. The cost of feed is then incorporated in the deferred costs related to the cattle operation. These deferrals are expensed when the cattle are sold.

All of these sales of feed to the lots are made at market price.

Small: Can we now turn to your oil operations?

Lord: We have two types of oil operations: domestic and foreign. Domestically, our oil revenues are the royalties we receive from our leased oil lands. The lessees pay us a royalty based on the number of barrels of oil they extract. We recognize the income at the time the oil is extracted. Now, internationally, because we own less than 50 percent of the companies involved, we plan not to consolidate these operations. Rather, we will recognize the income from these operations when dividends are received in the United States.

Small: Why?

Lord: Primarily because of the risks involved. The political climate of the countries touched by our Latin American ventures is very unstable. In particular, the threat of nationalization is always present in the international oil business. Also, there are numerous currency exchange restrictions which make it difficult to repatriate all of your current earnings.

Small: Is this true of Canada? It is a fairly stable country, isn't it?

Lord: You have a point there. Because of the relatively stable political picture, I will have to recognize the Canadian refinery income as earned.

Small: If you go ahead with the New Orleans industrial park venture, how will you account for its income?

Lord: If we go into this deal, we will have a 50 percent equity. Like most real estate ventures, this will be heavily leveraged. I think we plan to use about 90 percent debt and 10 percent equity. We will use the equity method to account for this venture.

Question

Evaluate the corporate reporting policy of Texas Land and Royalty Company. Do you believe the company's financial statements "fairly" report the financial condition of the company and its results of operations?

EXHIBIT 1

Corporate Relationships

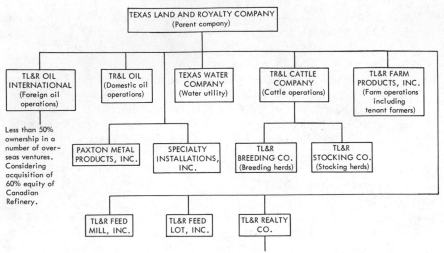

EXHIBIT 2

TEXAS LAND AND ROYALTY COMPANY
Consolidated Balance Sheet, December 31, 1974, and 1975
(in thousands)

Assets

	1975	1974
Current Assets:		
Cash	$ 2,402	$ 2,316
Marketable securities (Note 1)	14,100	12,600
Accounts receivable	11,000	10,012
Inventories (Note 2)	18,269	17,889
Other current assets	2,275	1,783
Total Current Assets	$48,046	$44,600
Investment and loans to associated companies	4,000	3,200
Property, Plant, and Equipment (Note 3):		
Land	$ 8,233	$ 8,483
Buildings	24,005	23,912
Machinery and equipment	21,293	20,665
Leaseholds	5,143	4,922
Land Improvement	9,201	8,436
	$67,875	$66,418
Less: Accumulated depreciation, depletion, and amortization	20,005	18,967
Net Property, Plant, and Equipment	$47,870	$47,451
Total Assets	$99,916	$95,251

Liabilities

	1975	1974
Current Liabilities:		
Federal and state income taxes	$ 4,601	$ 4,991
Accounts payable	3,500	3,406
Accrued property taxes	1,401	1,296
Other current liabilities	2,264	3,090
Total Current Liabilities	$11,766	$12,783
Long-term debt	2,600	6,600
Deferred profit (Note 4)	3,750	—
Capital stock (Note 5)	20,000	20,000
Retained earnings	61,800	55,868
Total Liabilities	$99,916	$95,251

The accompanying Notes to Financial Statements selected by the case writer are an integral part of these statements (see Exhibit 3).

EXHIBIT 3

TEXAS LAND AND ROYALTY COMPANY
Consolidated Income Statement, Years Ended December 31, 1974, and 1975
(in thousands)

	1975	1974
Revenues:		
Sales, royalties, and rent	$93,968	$92,111
Interest and other revenues	1,846	1,202
Total Revenue	$95,814	$93,313
Expenses:		
Costs and operating expenses	$71,426	$70,001
Oil and mineral exploration..............................	4,204	3,906
Selling, administrative, and general	7,016	6,847
Federal and state taxes	4,236	4,001
Total Expenses	$86,882	$84,755
Net income..	$ 8,932	$ 8,558
Less: Dividends	3,000	3,000
Amount Transferred to Retained Earnings	$ 5,932	$ 5,558

The accompanying Notes to Financial Statements selected by the case writer are an integral part of these statements:

Note 1: Marketable securities are stated at cost, adjusted for amortization of premium or discount. On December 31, the market value of these securities amounted to $15,120,000 in 1976 and $11,300,000 in 1974.

Note 2: Inventories as of December 31 were as follows:

	1975	1974
Manufacturing:		
Raw material and work in process	$ 3,211	$ 3,004
Finished goods	4,122	4,006
Cattle:		
Market herd	5,267	5,331
Breeding herd	3,621	3,100
Farm produce	1,233	1,640
Other inventories	815	808
Total	$18,269	$17,889

Note 3: All property, plant, and equipment is stated at cost. No discovery value has been assigned to the oil reserves related to the company's holdings in Texas. The cost of improvements to real property and of machinery and other equipment is being charged to operations in equal annual installments over their respective useful lives. For financial statement purposes, intangible drilling costs are capitalized and charged to operations on a unit-of-production basis. In determination of taxable income, these costs are deducted in the year incurred.

Note 4: In 1974, the company purchased an interest in the Dallas Apartments, Inc. At the same time, the company entered into a sale and option agreement with that company relating to some of Texas Land and Royalty's land in Dallas. During 1975, certain parcels of land were transferred under this agreement. In payment the company received a note for $4,000,000 collectible during a period extending to a maximum of ten years. The profit from this sale was deferred and is being taken into income, subject to applicable taxes, as collections are received.

Note 5: Under the company's incentive stock option plan, options at prices no less than 95 percent of market value at date of grant are held by ten key employees and officers. These options amount to less than 2 percent of the outstanding stock held by the Company's 6,052 shareholders.

Appendix: Present Value Tables

TABLE A: Present Value of $1

Table A shows the present value of one dollar received n years hence at i annual rate of return on the original investment. For example, to find the amount that would have to be invested today (the "present value") to receive one dollar ten years hence if the annual rate of return earned was 10 percent, follow these steps: First, go across the top of the table to the 10 percent column. Next, go down this column until the ten years line is reached. The factor 0.386 is found at this location in the table. This factor indicates that an investment of approximately 38 cents today at 10 percent annual interest will grow to $1 in ten years.

Years Hence	1%	2%	4%	6%	8%	10%	12%	14%	15%	16%	18%	20%	22%	24%	25%	26%	28%	30%	35%	40%	45%	50%
1	0.990	0.980	0.962	0.943	0.926	0.909	0.893	0.877	0.870	0.862	0.847	0.833	0.820	0.806	0.800	0.794	0.781	0.769	0.741	0.714	0.690	0.667
2	0.980	0.961	0.925	0.890	0.857	0.826	0.797	0.769	0.756	0.743	0.718	0.694	0.672	0.650	0.640	0.630	0.610	0.592	0.549	0.510	0.476	0.444
3	0.971	0.942	0.889	0.840	0.794	0.751	0.712	0.675	0.658	0.641	0.609	0.579	0.551	0.524	0.512	0.500	0.477	0.455	0.406	0.364	0.328	0.296
4	0.961	0.924	0.855	0.792	0.735	0.683	0.636	0.592	0.572	0.552	0.516	0.482	0.451	0.423	0.410	0.397	0.373	0.350	0.301	0.260	0.226	0.198
5	0.951	0.906	0.822	0.747	0.681	0.621	0.567	0.519	0.497	0.476	0.437	0.402	0.370	0.341	0.328	0.315	0.291	0.269	0.223	0.186	0.156	0.132
6	0.942	0.888	0.790	0.705	0.630	0.564	0.507	0.456	0.432	0.410	0.370	0.335	0.303	0.275	0.262	0.250	0.227	0.207	0.165	0.133	0.108	0.088
7	0.933	0.871	0.760	0.665	0.583	0.513	0.452	0.400	0.376	0.354	0.314	0.279	0.249	0.222	0.210	0.198	0.178	0.159	0.122	0.095	0.074	0.059
8	0.923	0.853	0.731	0.627	0.540	0.467	0.404	0.351	0.327	0.305	0.266	0.233	0.204	0.179	0.168	0.157	0.139	0.123	0.091	0.068	0.051	0.039
9	0.914	0.837	0.703	0.592	0.500	0.424	0.361	0.308	0.284	0.263	0.225	0.194	0.167	0.144	0.134	0.125	0.108	0.094	0.067	0.048	0.035	0.026
10	0.905	0.820	0.676	0.558	0.463	0.385	0.322	0.270	0.247	0.227	0.191	0.162	0.137	0.116	0.107	0.099	0.085	0.073	0.050	0.035	0.024	0.017
11	0.896	0.804	0.650	0.527	0.429	0.350	0.287	0.237	0.215	0.195	0.162	0.135	0.112	0.094	0.086	0.079	0.066	0.056	0.037	0.025	0.017	0.012
12	0.887	0.788	0.625	0.497	0.397	0.319	0.257	0.208	0.187	0.168	0.137	0.112	0.092	0.076	0.069	0.062	0.052	0.043	0.027	0.018	0.012	0.008
13	0.879	0.773	0.601	0.469	0.368	0.290	0.229	0.182	0.163	0.145	0.116	0.093	0.075	0.061	0.055	0.050	0.040	0.033	0.020	0.013	0.008	0.005
14	0.870	0.758	0.577	0.442	0.340	0.263	0.205	0.160	0.141	0.125	0.099	0.078	0.062	0.049	0.044	0.039	0.032	0.025	0.015	0.009	0.006	0.003
15	0.861	0.743	0.555	0.417	0.315	0.239	0.183	0.140	0.123	0.108	0.084	0.065	0.051	0.040	0.035	0.031	0.025	0.020	0.011	0.006	0.004	0.002
16	0.853	0.728	0.534	0.394	0.292	0.218	0.163	0.123	0.107	0.093	0.071	0.054	0.042	0.032	0.028	0.025	0.019	0.015	0.008	0.005	0.003	0.002
17	0.844	0.714	0.513	0.371	0.270	0.198	0.146	0.108	0.093	0.080	0.060	0.045	0.034	0.026	0.023	0.020	0.015	0.012	0.006	0.003	0.002	0.001
18	0.836	0.700	0.494	0.350	0.250	0.180	0.130	0.095	0.081	0.069	0.051	0.038	0.028	0.021	0.018	0.016	0.012	0.009	0.005	0.002	0.001	0.001
19	0.828	0.686	0.475	0.331	0.232	0.164	0.116	0.083	0.070	0.060	0.043	0.031	0.023	0.017	0.014	0.012	0.009	0.007	0.003	0.002	0.001	
20	0.820	0.673	0.456	0.312	0.215	0.149	0.104	0.073	0.061	0.051	0.037	0.026	0.019	0.014	0.012	0.010	0.007	0.005	0.002	0.001	0.001	
21	0.811	0.660	0.439	0.294	0.199	0.135	0.093	0.064	0.053	0.044	0.031	0.022	0.015	0.011	0.009	0.008	0.006	0.004	0.002	0.001		
22	0.803	0.647	0.422	0.278	0.184	0.123	0.083	0.056	0.046	0.038	0.026	0.018	0.013	0.009	0.007	0.006	0.004	0.003	0.001	0.001		
23	0.795	0.634	0.406	0.262	0.170	0.112	0.074	0.049	0.040	0.033	0.022	0.015	0.010	0.007	0.006	0.005	0.003	0.002	0.001			
24	0.788	0.622	0.390	0.247	0.158	0.102	0.066	0.043	0.035	0.028	0.019	0.013	0.008	0.006	0.005	0.004	0.003	0.002	0.001			
25	0.780	0.610	0.375	0.233	0.146	0.092	0.059	0.038	0.030	0.024	0.016	0.010	0.007	0.005	0.004	0.003	0.002	0.001	0.001			
26	0.772	0.598	0.361	0.220	0.135	0.084	0.053	0.033	0.026	0.021	0.014	0.009	0.006	0.004	0.003	0.002	0.002	0.001		0.001		
27	0.764	0.586	0.347	0.207	0.125	0.076	0.047	0.029	0.023	0.018	0.011	0.007	0.005	0.003	0.002	0.002	0.001	0.001		0.001		
28	0.757	0.574	0.333	0.196	0.116	0.069	0.042	0.026	0.020	0.016	0.010	0.006	0.004	0.002	0.002	0.002	0.001	0.001				
29	0.749	0.563	0.321	0.185	0.107	0.063	0.037	0.022	0.017	0.014	0.008	0.005	0.003	0.002	0.002	0.001	0.001					
30	0.742	0.552	0.308	0.174	0.099	0.057	0.033	0.020	0.015	0.012	0.007	0.004	0.003	0.002	0.001	0.001	0.001					
40	0.672	0.453	0.208	0.097	0.046	0.022	0.011	0.005	0.004	0.003	0.001	0.001										
50	0.608	0.372	0.141	0.054	0.021	0.009	0.003	0.001	0.001	0.001												

TABLE B: Present Value of $1 Received Annually for N Years Table B shows the present value of $1 received annually for each of the next *n* years if *i* annual rate of return is earned on the remaining balance of the original investment throughout this period. For example, to find the amount needed to be invested today to receive one dollar for each of the next 20 years if 10 percent can be earned on the investment, follow these steps: First, go across the top of the Table in the 10 percent column. Next, go down the column to the 20 years line. The factor 8.514 is shown at this spot. This factor tells us that a 10 percent investment of $8.51 today will return to the investor $1 for each of the next 20 years. At the end of that time the investor will have recovered all of his original investment plus a return of 10 percent. Therefore, the present value of $1 per year for 20 years discounted at 10 percent is $8.51.

Years (N)	1%	2%	4%	6%	8%	10%	12%	14%	15%	16%	18%	20%	22%	24%	25%	26%	28%	30%	35%	40%	45%	50%
1	0.990	0.980	0.962	0.943	0.926	0.909	0.893	0.877	0.870	0.862	0.847	0.833	0.820	0.806	0.800	0.794	0.781	0.769	0.741	0.714	0.690	0.667
2	1.970	1.942	1.896	1.833	1.783	1.736	1.690	1.647	1.626	1.605	1.566	1.528	1.492	1.457	1.440	1.424	1.392	1.361	1.289	1.224	1.165	1.111
3	2.941	2.884	2.775	2.673	2.577	2.487	2.402	2.322	2.283	2.246	2.174	2.106	2.042	1.981	1.952	1.923	1.868	1.816	1.696	1.589	1.493	1.407
4	3.902	3.808	3.630	3.465	3.312	3.170	3.037	2.914	2.855	2.798	2.690	2.589	2.494	2.404	2.362	2.320	2.241	2.166	1.997	1.849	1.720	1.605
5	4.853	4.713	4.452	4.212	3.993	3.791	3.605	3.433	3.352	3.274	3.127	2.991	2.864	2.745	2.689	2.635	2.532	2.436	2.220	2.035	1.876	1.737
6	5.795	5.601	5.242	4.917	4.623	4.355	4.111	3.889	3.784	3.685	3.498	3.326	3.167	3.020	2.951	2.885	2.759	2.643	2.385	2.168	1.983	1.824
7	6.728	6.472	6.002	5.582	5.206	4.868	4.564	4.288	4.160	4.039	3.812	3.605	3.416	3.242	3.161	3.083	2.937	2.802	2.508	2.263	2.057	1.883
8	7.652	7.325	6.733	6.210	5.747	5.335	4.968	4.639	4.487	4.344	4.078	3.837	3.619	3.421	3.329	3.241	3.076	2.925	2.598	2.331	2.108	1.922
9	8.566	8.162	7.435	6.802	6.247	5.759	5.328	4.946	4.772	4.607	4.303	4.031	3.786	3.566	3.463	3.366	3.184	3.019	2.665	2.379	2.144	1.948
10	9.471	8.983	8.111	7.360	6.710	6.145	5.650	5.216	5.019	4.833	4.494	4.192	3.923	3.682	3.571	3.465	3.269	3.092	2.715	2.414	2.168	1.965
11	10.368	9.787	8.760	7.887	7.139	6.495	5.937	5.453	5.234	5.029	4.656	4.327	4.035	3.776	3.656	3.544	3.335	3.147	2.757	2.438	2.185	1.977
12	11.255	10.575	9.385	8.384	7.536	6.814	6.194	5.660	5.421	5.197	4.793	4.439	4.127	3.851	3.725	3.606	3.387	3.190	2.779	2.456	2.196	1.985
13	12.134	11.343	9.986	8.853	7.904	7.103	6.424	5.842	5.583	5.342	4.910	4.533	4.203	3.912	3.780	3.656	3.427	3.223	2.799	2.468	2.204	1.990
14	13.004	12.106	10.563	9.295	8.244	7.367	6.628	6.002	5.724	5.468	5.008	4.611	4.265	3.962	3.824	3.695	3.459	3.249	2.814	2.477	2.210	1.993
15	13.865	12.849	11.118	9.712	8.559	7.606	6.811	6.142	5.847	5.575	5.092	4.675	4.315	4.001	3.859	3.726	3.483	3.268	2.825	2.484	2.214	1.995
16	14.718	13.578	11.652	10.106	8.851	7.824	6.974	6.265	5.954	5.669	5.162	4.730	4.357	4.033	3.887	3.751	3.503	3.283	2.834	2.489	2.216	1.997
17	15.562	14.292	12.166	10.477	9.122	8.022	7.120	6.373	6.047	5.749	5.222	4.775	4.391	4.059	3.910	3.771	3.518	3.295	2.840	2.492	2.218	1.998
18	16.398	14.992	12.659	10.828	9.372	8.201	7.250	6.467	6.128	5.818	5.273	4.812	4.419	4.080	3.928	3.786	3.529	3.304	2.844	2.494	2.219	1.999
19	17.226	15.678	13.134	11.158	9.604	8.365	7.366	6.550	6.198	5.877	5.316	4.844	4.442	4.097	3.942	3.799	3.539	3.311	2.848	2.496	2.220	1.999
20	18.046	16.351	13.590	11.470	9.818	8.514	7.469	6.623	6.259	5.929	5.353	4.870	4.460	4.110	3.954	3.808	3.546	3.316	2.850	2.497	2.221	1.999
21	18.857	17.011	14.029	11.764	10.017	8.649	7.562	6.687	6.312	5.973	5.384	4.891	4.476	4.121	3.963	3.816	3.551	3.320	2.852	2.498	2.221	2.000
22	19.660	17.658	14.451	12.042	10.201	8.772	7.645	6.743	6.359	6.011	5.410	4.909	4.488	4.130	3.970	3.822	3.556	3.323	2.853	2.498	2.222	2.000
23	20.456	18.292	14.857	12.303	10.371	8.883	7.718	6.792	6.399	6.044	5.432	4.925	4.499	4.137	3.976	3.827	3.559	3.325	2.854	2.499	2.222	2.000
24	21.243	18.914	15.247	12.550	10.529	8.985	7.784	6.835	6.434	6.073	5.451	4.937	4.507	4.143	3.981	3.831	3.562	3.327	2.855	2.499	2.222	2.000
25	22.023	19.523	15.622	12.783	10.675	9.077	7.843	6.873	6.464	6.097	5.467	4.948	4.514	4.147	3.985	3.834	3.564	3.329	2.856	2.499	2.222	2.000
26	22.795	20.121	15.983	13.003	10.810	9.161	7.896	6.906	6.491	6.118	5.480	4.956	4.520	4.151	3.988	3.837	3.566	3.330	2.856	2.500	2.222	2.000
27	23.560	20.707	16.330	13.211	10.935	9.237	7.943	6.935	6.514	6.136	5.492	4.964	4.524	4.154	3.990	3.839	3.567	3.331	2.856	2.500	2.222	2.000
28	24.316	21.281	16.663	13.406	11.051	9.307	7.984	6.961	6.534	6.152	5.502	4.970	4.528	4.157	3.992	3.840	3.568	3.331	2.857	2.500	2.222	2.000
29	25.066	21.844	16.984	13.591	11.158	9.370	8.022	6.983	6.551	6.166	5.510	4.975	4.531	4.159	3.994	3.841	3.569	3.332	2.857	2.500	2.222	2.000
30	25.808	22.396	17.292	13.765	11.258	9.427	8.055	7.003	6.566	6.177	5.517	4.979	4.534	4.160	3.995	3.842	3.569	3.332	2.857	2.500	2.222	2.000
40	32.835	27.355	19.793	15.046	11.925	9.779	8.244	7.105	6.642	6.234	5.548	4.997	4.544	4.166	3.999	3.846	3.571	3.333	2.857	2.500	2.222	2.000
50	39.196	31.424	21.482	15.762	12.234	9.915	8.304	7.133	6.661	6.246	5.554	4.999	4.545	4.167	4.000	3.846	3.571	3.333	2.857	2.500	2.222	2.000

Source: From tables computed by Jerome Bracken and Charles J. Christenson. Copyright © 1961 by the President and Fellows of Harvard College. Used by permission.

INDEXES

INDEX OF CASES

SUBJECT INDEX

A

Accelerated depreciation method, 76, 375–76, 394
Accounting, defined, 3
Accounting equation, 52, 54, 55, 71, 84
"Accounting for Certain Marketable Securities" *(FASB Statement No. 12)*, 523–24
"Accounting for Contingencies" *(APB Statement No. 5)*, 736–42
"Accounting for Convertible Debt and Debt Issued with Stock Purchase Warrants" *(Opinion No. 14)*, 561, 567
"Accounting for Cost of Pension Plans" *(Opinion No. 8)*, 624, 628–35, 638–639
"Accounting by Debtors and Creditors when Debt Is Restructured," 572
"Accounting for the Investment Credit" *(Opinion No. 2)*, 363
"Accounting for Lease Transactions by Manufacturer or Dealer Leases" *(Opinion No. 27)*, 576, 583, 589–92
"Accounting for Leases" *(APB Statement No. 13)*, 576–77n, 583
"Accounting for Leases in Financial Statement for Lessors" *(Opinion No. 7)*, 576, 583, 586–88, 592–93, 597
"Accounting for Research and Development Costs" *(FASB Statement No. 2)*, 258, 461, 463–64
"Accounting for Stock Issued to Employees" *(Opinion No. 25)*, 654–55
"Accounting for Translation of Foreign Currency Transactions and Foreign Currency Financial Statements" *(FASB Statement No. 8)*, 259, 663, 666, 672–73, 678–84, 729
Accounting mechanics, 94–100, 103
  accounts used, 94–95
  analyzing transactions, 97
  closing out accounts, 98

Accounting mechanics—*Cont.*
  debit-credit, 95–96
  ending balances, 98
  example of use of, 96–100
  journalizing original entries, 97–98
  posting journal entries, 98–100
  preparation of journal entries, 101–3
Accounting methods; *see also specific topics*
  accrual, 52
  cash, 52
  design of, purpose of, 54–55
  double entry, 55
  sources and uses of funds, 54
Accounting period convention, 48–49, 86
Accounting principles, 45–68
  accounting period, 48–49
  application of, 57
  authorities, 4–8; *see also specific authorities*
  "Basic Concept and Accounting Principles Underlying Financial Statements of Business Enterprises" *(APB Statement No. 1)*, 9, 84, 86, 213
  basic conventions, 45–57; *see also specific topics hereunder*
  behavioral implications, 14–18
  business entity, 46–47
  case-by-case approach, 10
  challenge in definition of, 22–23
  changes in, 251–64
  conceptual approach to, 10
  conservatism, 56–57
  consistency, 49
  consolidated financial statements, peculiar to, 108–10
  different approaches to, 10–11
  disclosure, 56
  dual aspect, 52–53
  economic versus, 59–62
  financial reporting problems, selection for, 20–22

777